MAX WEBER AND GERMAN POLITICS 1890–1920

MAX WEBER AND GERMAN POLITICS 1890–1920

WOLFGANG J. MOMMSEN

Translated by

MICHAEL S. STEINBERG

THE UNIVERSITY OF CHICAGO PRESS
Chicago and London

Wolfgang J. Mommsen is director of the German Historical Institute, London, and professor of modern and contemporary history at the University of Düsseldorf.

This translation is based on *Max Weber und die deutsche Politik, 1890–1920*, 2d edition, published in 1974 by J. C. B. Mohr (Paul Siebeck), Tübingen;

The University of Chicago Press gratefully acknowledges a subvention from Inter Nationes in partial support of the costs of translating this volume.

The University of Chicago Press, Chicago 60637
The University of Chicago Press, Ltd., London

Printed in the United States of America

91 90 89 88 87 86 85 84 5 4 3 2 1

Library of Congress Cataloging in Publication Data

Mommsen, Wolfgang J., 1930–
Max Weber and German politics, 1890–1920.

Rev. translation of: Max Weber und die deutsche Politik, 1890–1920. 2. überarbeitete und erw. Aufl. 1974.
Bibliography: p.
Includes index.
1. Weber, Max, 1864–1920. 2. Germany—Politics and government—1871–1918. I. Title.
H59.W4M613 1984 320.943 84-16274
ISBN 0-226-53397-2

Contents

Preface to the English Edition

When the original German edition of this book appeared almost twenty-five years ago, it received a rather stormy reception. The way in which Max Weber's views were presented challenged to some degree the interpretation then dominant of Weber as one of the (albeit very few) ancestors of German democracy, so successfully reestablished in the Federal Republic of Germany in the late 1940s and the 1950s. This book was written in a political climate of a rather specific kind, colored by the determination of a whole generation of Germans to make democracy work after all. Those historians who began their academic work in the 1950s were especially influenced by the West European and American examples; "reeducation" had left an intellectual mark on many of them. Many historians of this generation were familiar with the disastrous breakdown of Weimar Germany, partly because of the failure of German democrats to fight back against the challenge from the extreme right, attributed at the time not least to the alleged value neutrality of Weimar democracy. These historians tended to adopt a fundamentalist conception of democracy, which emphasized its base in the inalienable rights of natural law. From this point of view, they began critically to assess the recent history of Germany, and to rewrite it in a liberal-democratic manner, to help clear the way for the democratic idea in the Federal Republic and allow it to grow firm roots. The writing of this book was strongly influenced by this trend, and it undoubtedly owes some of its strengths, but possibly also some of its shortcomings, to the singular intellectual constellation that existed in the Federal Republic of Germany in the 1950s.

The first idea for this book was born while the author was reading Max Weber's most effective indictment of Wilhelmine Germany and, in particular, of the Kaiser's "personal rule." However, a closer analysis of Weber's political writings was to reveal, initially to the author's own irritation, that Max Weber had been not only a staunch liberal but at the same time a strong German nationalist, and, furthermore, that at least in his earlier years he had been a determined advocate of a German imperialist policy on a grand scale. In 1958, Fritz Fischer's monumental study *Germany's Drive to World Power* had not yet appeared, and against the backdrop of traditionalist interpretations of German history during the time of Bismarck and Wilhelm II, some of Weber's views indeed had to be judged extremist in nature. Weber's notion of "plebiscitary leadership democracy" and his plea for the rule of charismatic leaders appeared, at least in some points, to come dangerously close to the conception of fascist leadership, which was still vivid in everybody's mind. Hence it seemed worth taking an altogether fresh look at Weber's political views in the context of the historical events of his own time.

While this book is critical of some aspects of Weber's political views, and also of his notion of democratic rule, which he eventually defined as an "antiauthoritarian version of charismatic rule," it gives a fair assessment of his role in German politics at the time as well as of his political thought in general. It is based upon a thorough examination of all available sources—in particular the correspondence, which, due to particular circumstances, survived only in fragmentary form and was, furthermore, scattered between a great many archives and private collections. For the first time, newspaper reports on Weber's public speeches, which otherwise have not survived, were systematically collected. During the writing of this book, several previously unknown texts were discovered. Some have now been included in the editions of the *Gesammelte politische Schriften* that have appeared since 1978. The second edition of the present book, published in 1974, was thoroughly revised, and some new material incorporated. Little had to be changed in the description of the historical context of Weber's political activities, although substantial new research had been published by then, namely Fritz Fischer's monumental studies on German policies during the First World War. However, in view of the considerable controversy that this book aroused after its first appearance—a controversy that reached a second peak on the occasion of the *Sociologentag* in 1956 at Heidelberg in memory of Max Weber—an afterword was added in 1974, which is in part a reply to the book's critics and at the same time a survey of all the relevant literature published up to 1973 on Weber's political thought.

It was impossible for the English edition presented here to update this afterword to take account of research up to the present; given the upsurge of interest in Max Weber in the last decade, this would have been a monumental task. I hope that it will nonetheless be helpful for the reader, as it at least reflects the development of Weber studies over two decades. The same is true of the notes and bibliography. If all the recent literature on the subject were to be incorporated explicitly, the book would have to be rewritten. For the benefit of English-speaking readers, however, a selection of Weber's writings available in translation has been added to the bibliography.

It may be said that, on the whole, the book has withstood the test of time rather well. Most of the factual details regarding Weber's role in German politics at the time put forward here are undisputed, and the interpretation itself has been corroborated rather than challenged by material that has come to light since 1974. Of course, the evaluation and relative weight assigned to the liberal, nationalist, and elitist elements in Weber's political thought and in his sociological theory of domination will remain a matter of continued dispute. Seen against the backcloth of the time, Weber's views were almost always more sensible, more rational, more consistent, and, above all, more honest than those of his contemporaries; even so, they were radical, if not extremist.

The English edition follows the second German edition of 1974 throughout, except that a few factual errors have been rectified and several important new finds have been incorporated. In all practical respects, the book is a reliable presentation of Weber's political life work. However, citation of archival material and, in particular, of various private papers represents the state of affairs in 1974; only in some cases has reference been made to new archival material or to other finds that have since surfaced and that affect the interpretations given here. It was impossible to proceed otherwise, as any attempt to update the scholarly apparatus would have encountered insurmountable difficulties. Scholars who work with the original sources will find that in some cases material has been moved to other locations; sometimes the names of institutions that possess Weber materials have changed, as, for instance, the official archives of the GDR, which are no longer called Deutsches Zentralarchiv, but Zentralarchiv der Deutschen Demokratischen Republik. Apart from this, work on a new complete edition of Weber's works has been underway since 1977 under the auspices of the Bavarian Academy of Sciences; in fact, the present book provided a major impetus for the collecting of surviving Weber material to be edited according to stringent philological principles. The first volume of the *Max Weber Gesamtausgabe* is volume 15, *Zur Politik im Weltkrieg: Schriften und Reden 1914–1918*, edited by Wolfgang J. Mommsen in collaboration with Gangolf Hübinger, containing Weber's writings and speeches on political topics during the First World War. Two further volumes will appear in 1985: volume 16, *Zur Neuordnung Deutschlands: Schriften und Reden 1918–1920*, edited by Wolfgang J. Mommsen in collaboration with Wolfgang

Schwentker; and volume 9, *Zur Russischen Revolution von 1905: Schriften 1905–1909*, edited by Wolfgang J. Mommsen in collaboration with Dittmar Dahmann, containing Weber's essays on Russia. Together with the volumes still to come, they will provide a collection of primary evidence that complements, rather than contradicts, the story told here. Not least in view of the forthcoming complete edition of Weber's works, the appendixes to the 1974 edition, in which a number of recently discovered Weber texts were published for the first time, have not been included in this edition; in any case, they would be of only limited interest to English and American readers.

In addition, a complete edition of Weber's correspondence is being prepared by Wolfgang J. Mommsen and Rainer Lepsius in collaboration with Manfred Schoen, which will in due course publish all Weber's surviving letters. Beginning with the collection of Weber's letters that was made twenty-five years ago for the purpose of writing the present book, a substantial corpus of Weber's correspondence has now been collected; however, at this stage it has not been possible to make direct use of it in preparing this English edition, although we could draw upon it to correct obvious mistakes. In a few years time, scholars who wish to undertake further research on Max Weber based on the original correspondence will be able to do so with comparative ease; nonetheless, the letters quoted here according to the archival situation of 1974 will still serve as a reliable guide for all those who want to know more about the network of Max Weber's personal connections on a scholarly, political, and private level.

The translation of Weber texts poses almost insurmountable difficulties; and, as this book is full of direct quotations from Weber, its translation also presented a difficult task. It turned out to be impossible always to refer to the currently available English translations, which anyway differ widely as to how to render Weber's extremely difficult diction into English. Instead, the quotations are based throughout on the original German, although in a number of cases the relevant English translations were consulted. Unless otherwise indicated, secondary material has also been quoted according to the German versions, and not according to English editions available. In the context of my argument, modifications of the translations would obviously have been required anyway. To make up for this deficiency, a list of the English editions of all the relevant works by Weber has been added. Specific German terms such as *Verein für Sozialpolitik* have, as a rule, not been translated, as in many cases translation would have resulted in ambiguities and oddities. Wherever it seemed appropriate, English was added in parentheses.

At this point I should like to express my thanks to Michael S. Steinberg for translating the book, as well as to Gerd Schroeder for his help and advice in making this English edition possible. Thanks are also due to

Professor Edward Shils, who encouraged both publisher and author to go ahead with the English edition. At present we are witnessing a worldwide upsurge of interest in Max Weber. Although an English edition should have been published long ago, it is to be hoped that this book will be out in time to enliven the debate about Weber's achievements as a political thinker of unusual insight and as an eminent scholar. However much he sought to keep politics and scholarship apart, his sociological work was nonetheless strongly stimulated by his deep interest in the politics of his age. At the same time he was a "citizen" in the moral sense of the term, who was deeply devoted to his country and who considered it a duty to speak up whenever the political situation required it, even though throughout his life he remained on the sidelines of active politics. In his life story, an era of German, and of world, politics is reflected as if in a crystal, which concentrates light beams, thereby allowing them to achieve the utmost intensity. He lived through the decline and collapse of the old bourgeois order in Europe, and while his political views were partly conditioned by his age, the farsightedness of his analyses is still admirable. The intellectual honesty with which he confronted the fateful political events of his day will surely remain a model for future generations, however much their views may differ from his own.

WOLFGANG J. MOMMSEN

London, April 1984

Preface to the Second German Edition

Since the first appearance of this book almost a quarter of a century has passed. The circumstances and especially the political climate that occasioned this work have since radically altered. The book was written at a time when it was necessary for us to look critically at the catastrophic course of recent German history, especially the rise and rule of National Socialism, and to establish the spiritual and moral framework for a strong and stable German democracy. These two problems have by no means lost their significance, but they no longer dominate contemporary political consciousness. Democratic government appears to be secure in the German Federal Republic, and the problem of National Socialism is, justly or unjustly, more distant for us. Nevertheless, the issue of the legitimate basis of a democratic order is more urgent today than it has ever been; and it is precisely this issue that is central to Max Weber's political writings. This new edition, then, which should have been completed long ago, appears at a propitious moment.

I missed the opportunity to publish a second edition a few years after the first appeared. One reason for this was that intense attacks upon the book, author, and publisher at the time detracted from the pleasure of such an attempt. It therefore did not appear practicable to attempt a new edition without fundamental revisions and, even more important, without including newly discovered materials. Moreover, many other professional burdens, among them the creation of what was for all intents and purposes a new university in the humanities, persistently prevented the author from bringing the revisions to a conclusion. The task grew even weightier as the result of an overwhelming flood of literature and several significant monographic studies about Max Weber, the mountain of materials to master ever higher. It ultimately proved impossible to make detailed reference in the text itself to the most recent literature, insofar as this did not appear to be imperative. The reader will notice, however, that in all places where recent publications made changes necessary, appropriate modifications or additions have been incorporated.

It was never the author's intention to moderate the book's basic argument. When the book was first published, this argument was subjected to heated criticism—even to emotional and personal attacks. It also won widespread approbation. I saw no reason to revise my argument on any essential points. More recent works on the same subject offer differing interpretations; but none have suggested any significant misinterpretations in this author's interpretation of Weber's political tenets. Indeed, the opposite is true. Where they relate to Max Weber's political theories, the materials and texts which have appeared since the first edition completely support my interpretation. The author's position on the question of whether or not it makes sense to interpret Weber's work from the perspective of an abstract democratic system based on rational values and to criticize it on this basis will be reserved for the Afterword, where recent scholarship is discussed. It goes without saying that the author's position on this issue has not remained unchanged.

In this edition, an attempt has been made to draw on a great many new source materials the more precisely to portray Weber the politician. The literature that has appeared since the first edition, including works critical of it, has been carefully considered and, where appropriate and possible, incorporated. Finally, the notes have been keyed to the most recent edition of Weber's collected works, a tedious task undertaken to permit the reader to inform himself firsthand. It should be added that, thanks to Johannes Winckelmann's tireless efforts, a series of texts have been included in the third edition of the *Gesammelte politische Schriften* (Collected Political Writings) that until now were not generally known. I hope that even those readers who do not agree with my viewpoint will profit from my description of Weber's political thought and action set in the context of the events of his day. Much effort has been devoted to this end. I believe that this makes a convincing portrait of Weber possible, especially when his actual share in the events of that time is precisely ascertained and described. From Marianne Weber's *Lebensbild* (*Max Weber: A Biography*) to Karl Loewenstein's book *Max Webers staatspolitische Auffassungen* (*Max Weber's Political Ideas in the Perspective of Our Time*),[1] the literature is so riddled with errors in interpretation that a sober and critical description of Max Weber's political thought and action remains as necessary as ever.

1. The English translation of Marianne Weber's work was published in New York and London in 1975, that of Loewenstein's in Amherst, Mass., in 1966.

In spite of the strong criticism that has been leveled against my work, especially the criticism of the orthodox Weberians, the book has withstood the test of time quite well. It was, after all, written before Fritz Fischer's *Germany's Drive to World Power* inspired a flood of research into the history of Wilhelmine Germany. This new scholarship has provided us with a more precise view of that epoch and consequently of the political background of Max Weber's political thought and action. It is possible to say with no little satisfaction that few corrections have proved necessary as a result of this new research. However, in a few places I have added supplementary information and clarifications. Moreover, after years of sometimes tedious searches and often in connection with other projects, I have succeeded in discovering an entire series of new documents which round out the portrait of Weber the politician and in many places distinctively alter it. Letters and other documents, especially those I found in Friedrich Naumann's and Conrad Haussmann's papers, permitted me to describe certain aspects of Max Weber's political position more precisely than was previously possible. Drafts for a reform of the imperial constitution and of a proposal for the introduction of "the right of parliamentary inquiry" dating from 1908 were uncovered. The latter proposal found wide support after 1914; until my book appeared, Weber's original authorship of that proposal had not been documented conclusively. Similarly, the correspondence with the Foreign Office about the submarine memorandum of March 1916 has been found. This makes it possible to date the memo conclusively and above all to prove its actual purpose—the struggle against domestic political agitation.

In addition, in the light of new evidence, Max Weber appears much more distinctly than before as a convinced, albeit realistic, nationalist who did everything in his power to promote steadfastness in the war until the achievement of an "honorable peace." Weber supported Reich Chancellor Bethmann Hollweg's policies essentially from the perspective of raison d'etat. This appeared to be the sole means of preventing an internal collapse and bringing about a favorable conclusion to the war. In this regard, Max Weber's public support for the "German National Committee," which was very close to the imperial government, is especially noteworthy. A speech he made in Berlin on 16 January 1918, in which he stressed more emphatically than ever that parliamentarism was the only way out of Germany's chronic domestic and foreign plight, is perhaps of even greater significance. The background of the failure of Max Weber's candidacy for the National Assembly can now be further clarified as well.

In addition, the letters from Max Weber to Mina Tobler, which Professor Baumgarten considerately gave the author so that he could study those passages that were politically important makes it possible to describe Weber's political position during the war and the revolution more precisely in many areas than in the first edition. These private comments to a Swiss woman clearly reveal that Max Weber clung to a comparatively optimistic position during the war and gambled on the hope that there was still a chance for a negotiated peace that would secure the German Reich's predominance in central Europe and might even augment it. Both in private and in public, he always stressed the importance of "holding out to the end." Although he emphatically distanced himself from the hollow phrases of the pan-Germans and the "Fatherland party," he did not hesitate to use the strongest terms in attacking the allied powers or to describe the aims of German policy in rosy terms in order to strengthen the public's resolve. He believed that not only great power status but the future of German trade and industry, and therefore the life of every individual, hinged upon a favorable conclusion to the war. Accordingly, he thought it a self-evident national duty to work toward this end. On the other hand, the newly discovered documents make it clearer than ever that Max Weber viewed the achievement of parliamentary democracy in the German state as an absolute necessity. Without reform, Germany would lose the war and the subsequent peace.

Insofar as I have more strongly accented the chronological development of Max Weber's constitutional views, I have taken into account some of the recent scholarly interpretations of Weber's work. For example, the concept of plebiscitary-charismatic leadership was formulated in 1917. At first it was closely associated with his concept of a parliamentary constitutional system whose primary objective was to encourage the cultivation and rise of great political leaders. It was only in 1919, in the light of the failures of the postrevolutionary parliament, that he developed the antiparliamentary aspect of this theory fully in his concept of "plebiscitarian Führer democracy."

I have not greatly altered my portrayal of Max Weber's part in the history of the development of the Weimar constitution, as it has been accepted and adopted by other scholars with only minor qualifications. I have, however, modified those occasional passages in the first edition that gave excessive prominence to Max Weber's federalistic position in order to stress differences with the older school of Weber scholarship (Petzke, Mayer); i.e., the one-sidedly unitary interpretation that has since been carried even further by Karl Loewenstein. In the concluding chapter, "From a Liberal Constitutional State to Plebiscitary Leadership Democracy," which is an analysis of Weber's overall position, only minor alterations were made, although—and indeed because—this chapter has provoked serious opposition from many sources. I shall take a position on this matter, as well as on other recent scholarship, in the Afterword.

The bibliography has been significantly enlarged and updated. A new index fills an oft-mentioned lacuna.

It would be impossible to mention all of the people and scholarly institutions who helped to put useful materials at my disposal in my often unproductive, though not infrequently rewarding, researches. Among the many helpful institutions, I have space only to name the Deutsche Zentralarchiv I in Potsdam, the Bundesarchiv in Koblenz, the Politische Archiv of the Foreign Office in Bonn, the Zeitungsarchiv in Dortmund, the Max Weber Archiv in Munich, and Professor Eduard Baumgarten's Archiv Ebnet. Special thanks go to Walter Pehle for his editing assistance.

Wolfgang J. Mommsen

23 September 1973

Preface to the First German Edition

This study of Max Weber and German politics in the Wilhelmine epoch and the beginning of the Weimar Republic differs from previous works, which have generally sought to interpret Weber's political ideals and thought by reference to his theoretical writings. Taking the opposite approach, I attempt to trace Weber's development as a politician by means of a detailed assessment of his position on the day-to-day political issues. My aim is to achieve a firm basis for the analysis of the essential principles of Max Weber's political theory and to establish the historical context of his key political ideals. At the same time, this work is intended as a contribution to the history of German politics between 1890 and 1920.

Because of the special nature of this task, I have employed both monographic and biographical techniques. With the exception of the first, introductory chapter, I have attempted to interweave the narration of the various phases of Max Weber's political development with an analysis of those political ideals and causes which during these phases were central to this development. While the basic approach is chronological and biographical, the narrative also has a topical and problem-oriented organization. It was occasionally necessary, because of this procedure, to deal with some issues earlier or later in the narrative than would appear to be justified by strict chronology. For this reason, repetitions could not be entirely avoided. Yet I hope that the chronological development of Max Weber's political views will become sufficiently clear.

This study is based on the Weber papers as well as published sources and a few other scattered documents. It was begun in the expectation of finding an immense variety of source materials; but the results of the search were somewhat disappointing. Extraordinarily important documents, such as the memoranda that Weber delivered to Conrad Haussmann justifying his May 1917 proposals for constitutional reform and the second memorandum on the question of peace of 4 February 1918, could not be found anywhere.[1] However, we were able to uncover a rich vein of correspondence of which Marianne Weber made only partial use in her biography. The suspicion that it was necessary to study at first hand the originals of the letters cited by Marianne Weber proved only too well founded—in many instances, they had been misdated and questionably edited in that work. Unfortunately, such a review was not always possible since a significant portion of the original letters that she printed are not in the Weber papers. The author is very grateful to Marianne Weber for her efforts to bring Weber's widely scattered correspondence together. In many cases, letters that were destroyed or unavailable in their original form were accessible because Frau Weber had made copies. On the other hand, every future Weber scholar is handicapped by the fact that the original context of the letters has been completely destroyed and, further, that not one letter written by Weber's correspondents remains.[2] A search

1. The memoranda sent to Haussmann were not in the Haussmann papers; cf. below, chap. 6, note 88. Weber also informed Anschütz; however, a search for a copy in the Anschütz papers also proved fruitless. In the meantime, copies of the memoranda were found in the Holborn papers in the Yale University Library. For the peace memorandum, see below, chap. 7, note 323.

2. A short overview of the Weber papers is necessary here. The chief portion is located in the former Preussisches Geheimes Staatsarchiv, now the Deutsches Zentrales Archiv II, Merseburg, Rep. 92. Several items, almost exclusively letters, are in the possession of Professor Baumgarten, Mannheim. The rest, a significant portion, appear to be lost. The papers include:

a. A large portion of the manuscript of the biography with several scattered letters.
b. Weber's letters to his family and to a large number of fellow economists, for the most part in connection with editorial work for the *Archiv für Sozialwissenschaft*. On the whole these have little informative value (e.g., letters to Curtius, Gottl, Hellpach, Herkner, Kantorowicz, Lederer, Lotz, Rickert, Wilbrandt, Lukács).
c. An extensive typed manuscript with copies of some of Max Weber's letters, apparently prepared for Marianne Weber's edition of his letters but unfortunately including some questionable abridgments and even inaccurate dating. This collection includes the letters to his wife that were, for the most part, already quoted at length in the biography, and several letters to Oncken, Brentano, Eulenburg, and Michels. The original letters to his wife (the manuscript, too, breaks off in the middle of 1918) are partially in the possession of Professor Baumgarten, but the majority of them were not available to me.
d. A few fragments and individual pieces, that are in part cited below.
e. Notes about the conversation with Ludendorff, which do not relate much more than was previously reported in the biography.
f. Several manuscripts for lecture courses from the 1890s, in outline, that were filled in with information and judgments at the time of presentation and are therefore scarcely decipherable. They touch on the question of the working class, the politics of population movement, commercial policies, commercial politics, industrial politics, agricultural politics, and national economic issues.

for Max Weber's letters, similar to the one undertaken by this author, will face many obstacles. Supplementing the correspondence collected in the Weber papers would be a difficult task since, as a result of World War II and the confusion it entailed, numerous document collections have been destroyed or rendered inaccessible. Nevertheless, it did prove possible to reassemble an entire series of important Weber letters.[3]

The sources available for a more accurate analysis of Max Weber's political goals are meager. It must be borne in mind that Weber's political corpus is quantitatively small compared to that of other political commentators of his day. He set down his political proposals and ideals in a highly sublimated and compressed form in his articles in the *Frankfurter Zeitung*; we are somewhat in the dark about many of the concrete details. In particular, we have few documents from the World War I period. Since that period is a primary focus of this monograph, much had to be reassembled through the study of all of his correspondence and the use of careful comparative interpretations. To supplement this, I used newspaper reports of Max Weber's speeches. I have tried to reduce the errors that are possible as a result of the use of such secondary materials by bringing more than one report to bear if more than one exists. It would have been impossible to write this book without the use of such materials.

I shall have achieved my paramount goal if I have succeeded in clarifying the overall context that helped to mold Max Weber's political writings and principles. I have not limited myself to investigating the direct influence of Weber's age upon his political development. I sought to determine the impact of his political ideals and his proposals as well. On many basic political issues, Weber was a man of the Wilhelmine age, greatly influenced by the commanding figure of Bismarck. However, this work is far from a simplistic, relativistic interpretation of his political ideas. While Weber's political and theoretical views can be seen as a reaction against the political and social order of Wilhelmine Germany, I am convinced that significant aspects of his thought cannot be explained by the historical and political conditions of his day and that both philosophical concepts and moral convictions extrinsic to our central thesis played an important role. But I argue, in contrast to all "orthodox" Weber interpreters who have tried to apply Weberian analysis to contemporary situations without dealing with Weber's thought critically,[4] that it

3. The author hopes to continue his search for Max Weber's letters and to report on this search at a later date.

4. This applies to the various publications of J. F. Winckelmann on the problem of Max Weber's political sociology, about which more will be said below. With the premise that Max Weber's political sociology can be understood as a kind of timeless law book, Winckelmann was apparently prompted to assemble it as a mosaic from Weber's other writings, since Weber himself had not been in a position to complete the work. To succeed in this task he assumed it might be necessary only to eliminate all polemical writings, in order to put

is possible to come to terms with Weber's views on political and governmental sociology only when the historical circumstances in which these views were formed and the consequent limits of their application are taken into account. Misapplied efforts to turn his views into absolutes can only detract from Weber's crucial importance for contemporary political theory.

---

together what was supposed to be accepted as a "value-free" sociology of government. (*Wirtschaft und Gesellschaft* [*Economy and Society*], 4th edition [Tübingen, 1956], section 9, pp. 823 ff.) Cf. also Winckelmann's reaction to the critics of the fourth edition ("Max Webers grosse Soziologie," *Archiv für Rechts und Sozialphilosophie* 43 [1957] 117–24). We cannot of course know for sure whether this attempt should justly be viewed as scholarly or merely "didactic." From the didactic point of view this kind of compilation, apparently purified of "value judgments," is not a good thing since it skips over the problematical aspects of Weber's political theory altogether. The reader is offered sections from "Parliament and Government in a Reconstructed Germany" and "Politics as a Vocation," in an unsatisfying mixture that ignores the fact that between the two texts a major step in the development of Max Weber's political views took place, especially in his estimation of parliament. Above all, the effort conveys the erroneous impression that Weber's sociology of government, if he had been able to complete it, would for all intents and purposes have taken this form, when it is reasonably clear that a sociology of government completed by Weber himself would have formalized democratic-parliamentary "ideology" to a much greater degree and emphasized the plebiscitary element more strongly. We cannot understand what possible advantage for a serious study of Weber is gained by adding a very questionable ninth section to an already problematic edition of *Wirtschaft und Gesellschaft*, an edition that is questionable both in content and structure—and Winckelmann was not the first to create these problems. This brings us to the problem of the fourth edition of *Wirtschaft und Gesellschaft* itself. It is a considerable improvement over its predecessors and was therefore used extensively in this project. But it suffers as well from the tendency to perfectionism that we have encountered in the ninth section, a tendency that in the interest of Weber research would be better served by cautious reserve. We doubt that the numerous, difficult-to-control, at times intolerably pedantic and even misleading corrections to Weber's writing style—which was certainly not always good—are necessary to create readability (it is always essential to compare the text corrections in the index). On page 733, for example, the interpolation of a *nicht* confuses the meaning. Winckelmann has gone to much effort to improve the arrangement of the individual sections; at the same time, the arrangement of the whole remains a problem, and who knows what changes Marianne Weber had already incorporated in the first edition! Winckelmann makes many improvements in individual cases, but his attempt to create homogeneity is unsuccessful. Those parts written at different times, and at times with differing intentions, do not relate smoothly to each other. In the framework of a critical edition it would have been more worthwhile to extend Winckelmann's effort by introducing a clear division between individual sections, even at the cost of external unity. (Since this preface was first written, the manuscript of *Rechtssoziologie* has been rediscovered and Winckelmann has commendably published it separately [Max Weber, *Rechtssoziologie*, 2d edition, from the manuscript, ed. and introd. Johannes Winckelmann, Soziologische Texte 2, Neuwied, 1967]). In addition, the English edition of *Economy and Society*, edited by Guenther Roth, includes many improvements (compare also, W. J. Mommsen, "Neue Max-Weber-Literatur," *Historische Zeitschrift* 211: 616–30.) We may expect that the anticipated fifth edition of *Wirtschaft und Gesellschaft* at the least will incorporate several significant improvements in the text. (It eventually appeared in 1976.)

The author wishes to thank all of those who have contributed to the creation of this work. In the first place, I wish to thank Professor Theodor Schieder, who first encouraged this project, for his advice and support in every possible way. Thanks also go to Professor Eduard Baumgarten, who made the important Weber papers in his possession available to me; and to Robert Haussmann, who made the Conrad Haussmann papers available to me. I found much help and ready support in both divisions of the Deutsches Zentralarchiv in Merseburg and Potsdam as well as the Bundesarchiv in Koblenz. The author cannot possibly thank all of the libraries here that produced isolated and hard-to-obtain newspaper and journal materials for me. I would also like to thank my brother Hans Mommsen, of Tübingen, who typed most of the manuscript and also helped with countless references. Thanks also go to Professor Hans Kauffmann, in his capacity as rector of the University of Cologne, for a travel grant that made possible essential archival work that often dragged on for longer than originally planned because of Weber's almost indecipherable handwriting. The Arbeitsgemeinschaft für Forschung des Landes Nordrhein-Westfalen furnished a grant that made publication possible. Herr Siebeck generously took on the effort and risk of getting the book into print. Finally, I wish to thank the British Museum and the British Library of Political and Economic Science (London School of Economics and Political Science) for generous support in the concluding stages of the manuscript.

WOLFGANG J. MOMMSEN

Leeds, 7 February 1959

1
The Young Weber's Political Development

Max Weber was passionately engaged by the political issues of his day. Many of his contemporaries, and for a while he himself, expected that he would become a practical politician. All of his scholarly work, especially his unending struggle for intellectual honesty and scholarly objectivity, can in a sense be seen as an increasingly vigorous attempt to obtain distance and inner freedom from the political events of the day. In this light, politics, not just practical politics but politics in the larger sense, was central to his life and his life work. This is true even of the earliest stages of his life. Max Weber was born into politics; politics was the profession of his father, who was a high official in Berlin local government and an influential member of the National Liberal party in that city. City politics was his father's immediate concern, but his political activities extended well beyond that. For a time, the elder Max Weber was a member of the Reichstag. In the 1880s he even belonged to the central committee of the National Liberal party. More significant, of course, was his activity as a member of the National Liberal party delegation in the Prussian House of Deputies. To be sure, the elder Weber did not belong to the inner circle of the party's leadership, but he was extraordinarily influential as an organizer and coordinator of party business. As such, he had close relations to leading National Liberals. His large, hospitable house welcomed such visitors as Bennigsen, Miquel, Kapp, the one-time Prussian Finance Minister Hobrecht, and Aegidi, as well as distinguished scholars like von Sybel, von Treitschke, Dilthey, and Mommsen. In his childhood, Weber must have listened to frequent political discussions in his father's house; likewise he got to know the great figures of German liberalism through personal observation.[1] Weber listened no less curiously to his father's reports of day-to-day political work. The adult Weber's astonishingly precise knowlege of the history of German liberalism too may well have been acquired in these years.

It is scarcely surprising that Weber initially adopted the political views that he heard in his parents' house. His early political development was circumscribed by the moderate National Liberalism represented by his father. Later, Max Weber was to think of himself, in the first instance, as an heir of the *National* Liberals.[2] We do not know much about the political views of his father. The elder Max Weber, when a young man, had been close to the liberal conservative group, and for a while he even had edited the *Preussisches Wochenblatt*, the organ of the so-called Wochenblatt party of Moritz August von Bethmann Hollweg.[3] Even after the collapse of this group's expectations in the "New Era" under William I, the elder Weber remained loyal to his national conservative views. His first political position was the chairmanship of the central election committee of the so-called "Constitutional party," organized on 17 March 1862. Weber senior moved somewhat to the left as the result of liberalism's quarrel with Bismarck during the period of constitutional conflict. His close and lifelong friendship with his political colleague, the historian Hermann Baumgarten, dates from that period. After the foundation of the German Empire, Max Weber joined the National Liberal camp, a step in keeping with the pragmatic acceptance of compromise very much in accord with his earlier position. He associated with that large group of liberal politicians who, after the period of cooperation with Bismarck had ended, gave up their hopes for the liberal evolution of the imperial constitution and dedicated themselves to maintaining what had already been achieved. He counted himself a Bennigsen supporter and therefore criticized and rejected the secession of the anti-Bismarck group around Rickert; he tended to the left of the remaining rump.[4] Although he deeply

1. Cf. here and below, Marianne Weber, *Max Weber: Ein Lebensbild* (Tübingen, 1926) (hereafter cited as *Lebensbild*), especially p. 42; also Eduard Baumgarten, *Max Weber: Werk und Person* (Tübingen, 1964) (hereafter cited as *Werk und Person*); and Arthur Mitzman, *The Iron Cage: A Historical Interpretation of Max Weber* (New York, 1970), pp. 41 ff. Of fundamental importance is Max Weber, *Jugendbriefe* (Tübingen o.J., 1936), passim (hereafter cited as *Jugendbriefe*).

2. Cf., e.g., letter to Edmund Lesser of 16 June 1917, *Gesammelte Politische Schriften*, first edition, pp. 473 f., hereafter cited as *Pol. Schr. 1*. As a rule, the third edition (Tübingen, 1971) will be cited (as *Pol. Schr.*, without a number).

3. Cf. Ludolf Parisius, *Deutschlands politische Parteien und das Ministerium Bismarck* (Berlin, 1978), p. 56.

4. Cf. letter of Max Weber to Baumgarten of 14 July 1885, *Jugendbriefe*, p. 170; also Thomas Nipperdey, *Die Organisation der deutschen Parteien vor 1918* (Düsseldorf, 1961), p. 35, which reports that the elder Max Weber stood as a Reichstag candidate for the

regretted Bismarck's turn away from the National Liberals, he supported the most important lines of Bismarck's policies. He staunchly opposed the negative politics of the left-wing liberals. But he also lamented, as did many of his fellow liberals, the fact that "Bismarck sought to destroy all capable and independent forces surrounding him,"[5] a view that his son was to share. Like the majority of National Liberals, he absolutely opposed universal suffrage.

For all this, the elder Weber was not by temperament a natural politician. He was not instinctively combative, as his son would later be. There was a streak of self-satisfaction in his political conduct, and he was also easily appeased. Marianne Weber described him as "typically bourgeois, content with himself and the world."[6] Max Weber rebelled at an early age against this lifestyle, and decades later this rebellion led to passionate arguments with his father. Great political ideas did not underpin the political activities of Weber's father. Because, as a politician, his chief fields of experience were financial and administrative, he was much more preoccupied with practical, day-to-day questions than with major, long-term political issues. For many years he played a major role in the budget commission of the Prussian House of Deputies. Later, in 1894, in his capacity as representative of the National Liberals on the budget commission of the Reichstag, the elder Weber did get involved in a conflict with the chief of Prussian university affairs, Ministerial Director Althoff of the Prussian Ministry of Culture, who was notorious for the tactical politics of his personnel policy. Althoff had attempted to win National Liberal support for a new professorship in political economy in Berlin. Weber entered the fray for the sake of the academic future of his son, Max, who was already an instructor at the University of Berlin. He soon found himself impelled, perhaps at his son's urging, to resign as secretary of the committee.[7]

Secession in a Berlin electoral district in order to prevent the nomination of a more right-wing candidate, a tactic that the National Liberals then assented to nolens volens. These events indicate that the elder Max Weber was by no means on the right wing of the National Liberals.

5. Letter to his father of 23 February 1884, *Jugendbriefe*, p. 103: "If the author, in agreement with your often stated view, only somewhat more darkly shows the manner in which Bismarck strives to destroy all capable and independent forces around him." See, for a general view, Friedrich Sell, *Die Tragödie des deutschen Liberalismus* (Stuttgart, 1953), p. 227.

6. *Lebensbild*, p. 67.

7. This event measurably influenced Max Weber's later campaign against the "Althoff system." At the fourth German university teachers' convention in Dresden on 12 and 13 October 1911, Weber sharply attacked Althoff. He accused Althoff of starting from the premise, "in the treatment of personnel matters, that anyone involved is a scoundrel or at least a common opportunist." He referred in this context to the above-mentioned event that

Early in 1882, when Max Weber was just eighteen, he first left home for a prolonged period. He enrolled at the University of Heidelberg to study law, national economy, history, and philosophy. Although he thereby escaped the immediate influence of the political atmosphere surrounding him in Berlin, he continued to share his father's political views. For a while, of course, politics was a side interest. Max Weber enthusiastically applied himself to his diverse scholarly interests; he attended the lectures of Knies, a leading spokesman of the historical school of economics; Roman law with Bekker; and several other courses in law, among them Kuno Fischer's. He was very much absorbed by his work on historical themes in Erdmannsdörffer's seminar, where he concentrated on the sixteenth and seventeenth centuries.[8] His serious interest in theological questions was aroused in discussions with his older cousin Otto Baumgarten, with whom Weber studied during his first Heidelberg semester. Among other things, Weber read Ranke's *Geschichte der germanisch-romanischen Völker* (*History of the German and Latin Nations*) and his *Kritik neueren Geschichtsschreiber* (*Critique of Recent Historical Writers*).[9] In addition, he read Savigny, Jhering[10] and Schmoller and remarked that the latter was not as firm a state socialist as he had previously believed.[11] His studies in Heidelberg did not greatly influence his political views. Nor was he much affected by the beer party patriotism of his fraternity brothers in Alemannia of Heidelberg. Weber joined Alemannia in his second semester, a step he later regretted.[12]

An association with his father's former political compatriot, the historian Hermann Baumgarten, was much more important for Weber's political development. The Weber and Baumgarten families were related by marriage; Weber's father first met his wife in the Baumgarten house.

---

had led to his father's resignation from the budget commission. Cf. "Verhandlungen des 4. Deutschen Hochschullehrertages," report of the presiding committee, Leipzig, 1912, pp. 71, 73. A related item involved a dispute in the *Frankfurter Zeitung* about the "Althoff system," 24 October, 3d morning ed.; 27 October, evening ed.; 31 October, 1st morning edition, and 2 November, 1st morning edition. In a letter to the *Tägliche Rundschau* (497), supplement 2, 22 October 1911, Weber corrected the report and pointed out that his father had only dissociated himself from the report involved and had not left the committee. Cf. the reference by Mitzman, pp. 109 ff, as cited by Arnold Sachse, *Althoff und sein Werk* (Berlin, 1928). Mitzman confuses the elder Max Weber's membership on the budget commission with his professional position as city councillor, and constructs a bold thesis on the basis of this error, i.e., Weber's false presentation of the facts can be attributed to his guilt complex regarding his father. There was no "semiretirement of 1893."

8. Cf. especially the letter to his mother of 13 November 1882, *Jugendbriefe*, pp. 62 f.

9. Ibid.

10. Cf. letter of 15 December 1882, ibid., p. 65.

11. Cf. letter to his father of 3 September 1883, ibid., p. 75.

12. Cf. below, chap. 8, sec. 2.

During the Pentecost vacation of 1882, Otto Baumgarten took his cousin to Strassburg for the first time. This visit marked the start of close personal ties that became very important for Weber. The following year, he was frequently in Strassburg. He fulfilled his military obligations as a one-year volunteer there, and during that period he frequented the historian's house. Weber became the political confidant of the aging, solitary historian. The older Baumgarten poured out his heart to his nephew, especially his bitterness over the course of German politics in general as well as on specific issues.[13] Max Weber proved to be a worthy partner in discussion; he was surprisingly knowledgeable about day-to-day political events. His letters to his parents from Strassburg repeatedly report lively political debates with Baumgarten. When he began his studies in Berlin in the autumn of 1884, he remained in close contact with the Strassburg historian. Even as late as his years as a Berlin Privatdocent, Max Weber remained in regular if not always frequent contact with him. He continued to report his views on important political events in the late 1880s to Baumgarten from the perspective of Berlin.

Baumgarten had been a passionate forty-eighter who had abandoned his journalistic activities and become a historian only after the failure of the revolution and repeated conflicts with the official censors. Nonetheless, he continued to be deeply committed to politics. Although, until 1866, he had been a decided opponent of Bismarck's policies, he later became a Bismarck supporter; but, unlike the majority of the National Liberals of the Bismarck years, he did not forsake his faith in a liberal constitution. In his famous "self-criticism" of German liberalism, he sought to deflect liberals from the doctrinairism of the sixties, without altogether forsaking the politics of idealism.[14] He believed the creation of a German national state to be the paramount goal of German politics; "Unity, governmental power, national independence" were "the supreme political good, the basis and beginning of all earthly prosperity." Unlike many other liberals of his day, however, he was not prepared to be satisfied with what had been achieved in 1870–71, and his pride in the nation was tempered by a belief that unity must be followed by moral self-control and national purification.[15] Although he enthusiastically supported Bismarck in 1871, he became a keen opponent of the first chancellor when he observed German liberalism's defeat on decisive domestic

13. Cf. Weber's remark in a letter of 21 December 1883 to his father, *Jugendbriefe*, pp. 84 f. "It does Uncle a world of good . . . to speak his mind from time to time on fundamental issues." See also the letter to his father of 30 May 1884, ibid., pp. 115 ff.

14. *Preussische Jahrbücher* 18 (1866): 455 ff. and 575 ff. Cf. the biographical introduction by Erich Marcks to Baumgarten's *Historische und politische Aufsätze und Reden* (Strassburg, 1894), hereafter cited as Marcks.

15. Marcks, p. lxix. The citation comes from a "war sermon" by Baumgarten in 1870.

issues. Like Theodor Mommsen, he grew increasingly skeptical and bitter about the course of German politics after the end of the 1870s.[16]

Baumgarten criticized the great chancellor for "Caesarist demagoguery," for ruining independent forces and for radicalizing both Social Democrats and Ultramontanes.[17] In his view, Bismarck's Caesarism had led him to introduce universal suffrage in 1866. Bismarck himself was later to admit that he threw universal suffrage "in the pot" as a tactical move against Austria as the "strongest of the democratic arts."[18] Baumgarten feared that this act would have devastating consequences; universal suffrage threatened "not only the state" but "our entire culture" and would bring "the raw instincts of the masses to power in all matters."[19] Baumgarten also warmly criticized Bismarck's methods in the Kulturkampf. He objected to the fact that Bismarck was acting for reasons of political expediency and not from sincere Protestant feelings. For this reason, the form of the Kulturkampf was both deceptive and fruitless.[20] His opposition grew with his keen reaction against the government's political course that he observed at first hand in the Reichsland of Alsace and Lorraine.[21] He was discomfited by the rise of an uncritically submissive atmosphere in the country, which seemed to affect the younger generation especially. This atmosphere was accompanied by a dangerous decline in the capacity for political judgment. Baumgarten's bitter pronouncements about the German people's political immaturity, which he had begun to make in the 1860s, grew in sharpness and frequency.[22]

16. Marcks refers to the cloudy pessimism that the old historian had succumbed to (p. cvii). We are more likely to approve of Baumgarten's sharp criticism of the political developments in the eighties than Marcks did, since Marcks still lived at a time when the tradition of Bismarck's founding of the Reich was still very much alive. We are much less likely to attribute Baumgarten's attitudes to personal factors than Marcks did in his otherwise fine biography. Baumgarten's pessimism, which linked him to Theodor Mommsen, is of much greater significance.

17. Marcks, p. cxi, n. 1.

18. Bismarck, *Erinnerung und Gedanke*, in *Gesammelte Werke*, vol. 15, p. 287.

19. Marcks, p. cxviii. This corresponds to a widespread opinion held by liberals. See, for a general view, Walter Gagel, *Die Wahlrechtsfrage in der Geschichte der liberalen Parteien, 1848–1918* (Düsseldorf, 1958.)

20. Marcks, p. cxi. As he put it there: "Protestantism in Prussia must first become Protestantism again before it can successfully take the field against Rome."

21. Max Weber's later criticism of Prussian policy in the Reichland of Alsace-Lorraine directly echoed Baumgarten's.

22. For example, in 1861 he wrote: "We are a terribly stupid and, strictly speaking, a bad people politically. Nowhere can this be more clearly demonstrated than here, where you can find so much cultivation, such many-sided activities, so much ethical virtue, but in politics so much wretched ignorance, philistine tub-thumping, stupid inexperience, and cowardly lack of character. . . . Friedrich Wilhelm IV's twenty-year reign has wrought terrible devastation." Cited by Marcks, p. xlvii. The astounding similarity in direction, temperament, and critical focus with Weber's later comments about Bismarck, William II, and the political immaturity of the nation is remarkable.

In contrast to the one-sided emphasis on Prussia in the German historiography of the period, Baumgarten tried, although he himself had Prussian sympathies, not to neglect the South German tradition. His critique of the political situation was manifest in his fervent attack on Treitschke's *Deutsche Geschichte* (*German History*), the second volume of which appeared in 1883.[23] Treitschke's activities as a historian-politician personified the political tendencies that most alarmed Baumgarten.[24] He believed that Treitschke's work was characterized by narrow-minded Prussian chauvinism; Treitschke idolized the imperial status quo and had given up any more far-reaching constitutional ideals. Baumgarten argued that Treitschke lacked inner humility and that he gave free rein to arrogant and intolerant national feelings at the expense of other nations.[25] Baumgarten's uncharacteristically harsh tone in his quarrel with Treitschke estranged him from all of his friends, including, in the end, his old comrade, Heinrich von Sybel.[26]

Baumgarten strongly influenced the young Weber's political views. To be sure, Weber was in no way prepared to adopt Baumgarten's exaggerated opinions as his own; his own views developed in the constant confrontation with Baumgarten's gloomy and pessimistic outlook. But it was Baumgarten who helped him to free himself from the one-sided National Liberal point of view of his parents' home, and who opened his eyes to the internal weaknesses of the Bismarckian system. Even if Weber never accepted Baumgarten's sharp critique of the person and the policies of the great chancellor, he did accept the older man's judgments on important points. It is especially noteworthy that he came to share Baumgarten's opinion of the Caesaristic-demagogic character of Bismarck's policies. For example, Weber, at the time, condemned "the double-edged gift of Bismarckian Caesarism: universal suffrage, the purest death for the equality of all in the truest sense of the word," even if he could not bring himself to agree with the older man's pessimistic opinion that this measure would destroy not only the state but the nation's cultural life as well.[27] It was particularly significant for Weber's

23. Baumgarten's criticisms have been published together under the title, *Treitschkes Deutsche Geschichte* (Strassburg, 1883).

24. Cf. Marcks, pp. cxiii ff.

25. Cf. *Treitschkes Deutsche Geschichte*, pp. 41f.: "Every nation that after years of political weakness suddenly advances to power and prestige in the world has to resist several temptations. National arrogance, the inclination to idolize everything native and to disparage anything foreign, is the greatest of these. . . . We now have witnessed the recurrent appearance of a point of view in an important area of our intellectual life which was hitherto completely alien to us. We are beginning to boast in our scholarly work and to permit national pride and partisan passion to influence scholarly research."

26. Cf. the declaration of the *Historische Zeitschrift* 50 (1883): 556 ff.

27. Letter to Baumgarten of 8 November 1884, *Jugendbriefe*, p. 145. This opinion was certainly influenced by the liberal election defeat of 1884.

later political development that Baumgarten pointed out to him the effects of the Bismarckian regime on the nation's political judgment. Baumgarten's prediction that "this man will leave a great deal of trouble behind him" did, it is true, seem overpessimistic to Weber.[28] He could not believe that "a decline of the civil service and the spirit of our political beliefs would occur" in the long run, even if "the impact of the Caesarist regime could not be avoided in the immediate future," as he wrote to Baumgarten in 1888.[29] But Baumgarten's bitter comments to Weber about the uncritical submission of the younger generation sharpened Weber's sensitivity to his generation's lack of political maturity. He himself was able to avoid the naïve Bismarck-worship of his fellow Berlin students, much as he valued and respected the great statesman's genius.[30] He was saddened by the discovery that his fellow students, enchanted by Bismarck, collectively reproached him when he asked why Bismarck always forgot that it was "he himself who encouraged the partisan spirit and thereby destroyed the 'national spring of good feeling.' "[31]

Weber was distressed by his generation's lack of interest in political questions: "My admirable generation limits its regard for such matters either by making common cause with anti-Semitism . . . or, and this is the higher level, they think it meaningful to style themselves as 'Bismarck sans phrase.' "[32] He observed his politically immature fellow students release tension "in the frenetic jubilation . . . that broke out in Treitschke's classes when he said anything that smacked of anti-Semitism." He recognized the links between the Bismarck cult, anti-Semitic instincts, and naiveté. "The most unbelievable" part was "the fantastic ignorance of the history of this century" that characterized his generation.[33]

Treitschke's pernicious influence on a section of the educated German middle class led Weber to follow Baumgarten's example and take issue with the great historian. He was not inclined to join in Baumgarten's sweeping verdict,[34] but he was nonetheless of the opinion that Treitschke simply did not pay sufficient attention to standards of scholarly objectivity.[35] Yet Weber could not ignore the powerful impression that Treitschke made on his listeners, the magic that erupted from his volcanic nature. He recognized the genuine fervor and the seriousness of a great

28. Cited by Marcks, p. cxi, note 1.

29. Letter of 30 April 1888, *Jugendbriefe*, p. 300.

30. He once wrote very characteristically in a letter to his father of 15 March 1885, ibid., p. 153: "Yet what Bismarck says has a great deal of power."

31. Ibid.

32. Letter to Baumgarten of 14 July 1885, ibid., p. 173; cf. letter of 29 March 1885, ibid., pp. 154 ff.

33. Ibid., p. 174.

34. Cf. the letter ot 5 May 1883, ibid., p. 74; also those of 12 February 1883, p. 68, and 7 March 1883, p. 73.

35. Letter to Baumgarten of 14 July 1885, ibid., pp. 174 f.

personality behind Treitschke's one-sidedness. He read Treitschke's poems and sent them to Hermann Baumgarten because he found "the sincere idealism in them that this in many ways unfortunate man cannot lose even when he commits his greatest errors . . . If his notorious effect at the lectern is a misfortune," he wrote Baumgarten, it is "above all the audience's [fault] . . .

> It is the same case with Bismarck: had the nation known how to deal with him, to oppose him firmly at the time he needed it most, [had they] granted him their trust, when he deserved it—they should have understood this from the beginning, but now it is too late—then the effects of his personal policy, so often destructive, would not have taken on the dimension that they have. And if my generation did not already worship militarism and similar monstrosities, the culture of so-called "realism," if they did not already despise all those endeavors that aspire to their goals without appealing to the evil side of man, especially to man's rudeness, then a mass of one-sided opinions—often stridently so—the excitement of the battle against other opinions, and a predilection for what is now called Realpolitik that has arisen under the compelling impact of success would not be the only things they take with them from Treitschke's classes.[36]

Weber emphatically rejected the manner in which Treitschke fused politics and scholarship. This was the time when the seeds of his ardent campaign against every kind of professorial demagoguery and prophecy were sown. To be sure, he conceded that it was possible to recognize Treitschke's "great and enthusiastic campaign . . . for an ideal framework . . . in the extravagances of his partisan passion and one-sidedness"; but in practice this meant that "he neglected sincere conscientious efforts that were made without concern for the results and only in the interest of truth."[37]

Nevertheless, Treitschke's influence on Weber's political views should not be underestimated. Weber may have attended at least two of Treitschke's courses in Berlin, the one on "state and church" and the famous lectures on politics.[38] The ideal of power that Treitschke placed in the center of his discussions of the character of the state, the elevation of the

36. Letter of 25 April 1887, ibid., pp. 231 f.

37. Letter of 25 April 1887, ibid., p. 233. Moreover, Weber was also writing history that did not take the Treitschkean approach. Cf. the mention of disputes with Treitschke's students in a letter to Baumgarten of 30 September 1887, ibid., p. 273.

38. Cf. letter to Baumgarten of 8 November 1884, ibid., p. 145. In the autobiographical statement that accompanied his dissertation (now reprinted by Johannes Winckelmann, "Max Webers Dissertation [1889]," in *Max Weber zum Gedächtnis*, special issue 7 of *Kölner Zeitschrift für Soziologie und Sozialpsychologie*, 1963, p. 12), Weber did not mention Treitschke among his academic instructors.

national state to the norm of politics, and the degradation of life in small states were to reappear in Weber's own later political thought, in part even more harshly.[39] We suspect that Treitschke's energetic support of an ambitious policy of imperialist expansion overseas made an especially strong impression on Weber.[40] Weber's call, in his Freiburg inaugural address, for a German world power policy has quite rightly been linked to Treitschke's influence.[41] Nevertheless, as far as we can determine, Weber did not fully accept Treitschke's imperialistic goals then, and Weber never shared the characteristically anti-English bias of Treitschke's imperialism.[42]

We cannot determine to what extent other teachers may have influenced Max Weber's political development during the time he studied in Berlin. Weber himself singled out Gneist, Aegidi, and Adolf Wagner among others.[43] But their influence may not have been great; Weber's discomfort with all politicized scholarship made him unreceptive to such influences. In addition, while in Berlin, Weber soon began to avoid

39. See Treitschke, *Politik*: *Vorlesungen*, ed. Max Cornicelius, 2 vols. (Leipzig, 1897), especially vol. 1, pp. 32 f., 43. Also W. Bussmann, "Treitschke als Politiker," *Historische Zeitschrift* 174 (1954): 249 ff.

40. Cf. for example Treitschke, *Politik*, vol. 1, p. 42: "Germany has always been left out of the division of the non-European world by the European powers. But it is a matter of our existence as a great power for us to become a power overseas. Otherwise we face the frightening prospect that Russia and England will divide the world between themselves. And it is really not possible to say which would be more uncivilized and dreadful, the 'Russian knout' or the English money bag." Both of these opinions would recur in Weber's work: the idea of England and Russia dividing the world, and also the "Russian knout."

41. Bussmann, "Treitschke als Politiker," pp. 273 f.

42. It is difficult to offer a more precise estimate of Treitschke's influence upon the young Weber, since we have no information about Weber's position on foreign policy questions from this period. Later, all influences are so fused in Weber's works that it is difficult to give any direct proof of a connection. Individual points of similarity with Treitschke are numerous, but they cannot be precisely established. For example, Treitschke's judgment about Switzerland, including the comment that "neutralization" is really a "self-mutilation of the state" (*Politik*, vol. 2, p. 293), reminds us of later statements by Weber. Similarly, Treitschke's references to the American caucus system and the "spoils" method may have had some impact upon Weber (cf. *Politik*, vol. 2, pp. 274 ff.). An attempt to draw parallels between Treitschke and Weber on this point, as in J. H. Knoll's *Führungsauslese in Liberalismus und Demokratie* (Stuttgart, 1957), pp. 107 f., is misplaced. The references from Treitschke that he uses are of a very general nature. It was far from Weber's intention to compare German party relations to the Anglo-Saxon caucus system in the same way that Treitschke had attempted. Treitschke was essentially more conservative. But Treitschke's critique of the "false concept of freedom, which seeks freedom from the state rather than freedom in the state" (*Politik*, vol. 1, p. 157), is also reminiscent of Weber. Mitzman's thesis that Weber identified Treitschke with his father and that he fought the latter by passionately criticizing the former (*The Iron Cage*, pp. 36 f) fails to recognize that Weber was not so far away from the political position of his father at the time.

43. Cf. above, note 38.

attending lectures, preferring to remain at home reading through great piles of books. At that time his special interests led him most strongly to subjects that were far removed from politics, like his study of commercial law with Goldschmidt, which gave rise to his dissertation about the history of commercial guilds during the Middle Ages. His work in agricultural history with Meitzen was also in a completely unpolitical field. In addition to Brunner's and Beseler's lectures, Max Weber also attended Gierke's, but it can hardly be said that Gierke influenced his later political views in any significant way in comparison to his influence on Hugo Preuss. Max Weber rejected all "organic" legal and social theories even in their most moderate form, and he rejected Gierke's theory about associations with them, even though he recognized its significance as a great achievement in legal history.[44]

In Weber's letters of the time, Rudolf von Gneist was singled out just once for significant mention. Weber praised Gneist's classes on German constitutional law and Prussian administrative law as a "true masterpiece" in content and form and reported (not without disapproval) that the legal scholar occasionally commented on contemporary political issues and favored "rigid liberal views."[45] The liberal constitutional lawyer's enthusiastic support of the Kulturkampf may have had a strong impact on Weber. Gneist must also have alerted him to the characteristics of the patriarchal self-governing bodies in Prussia's eastern provinces so noticeably different from the circumstances prevailing in Germany's more urbanized western provinces.[46] In addition, Gneist's methodology of comparative law had some significance for Weber's later work on the sociology of law. But Weber scarcely approved of Gneist's thesis on the prior claims of self-government over parliamentary government, and later he formally adopted a contrary position. Weber saw an infinite distinction between mere administration locally or nationwide and a politics that sought the exercise of power. Good administration alone could never fulfill the global political tasks of a great nation.[47]

We must therefore conclude that the only meaningful and lasting influence on Weber during his student years was that of Hermann Baumgarten. And even Baumgarten did not greatly influence Weber's position on concrete political issues. In this area, Max Weber often differed

44. Cf. "Roscher und Knies und die logischen Probleme der historischen Nationalökonomie," *Gesammelte Aufsätze zur Wissenschaftslehre*, pp. 1–145, especially the special reference to Gierke in note 1 on p. 35; also *Wirtschaft und Gesellschaft*, pp. 446 ff.

45. Letter to Baumgarten of 8 November 1884, p. 145.

46. Cf. also Gneist, *Zur Verwaltungsreform und Verwaltungsrechtspflege in Preussen* (Leipzig, 1880), pp. 58 f.

47. Cf. *Pol. Schr.*, pp. 289 f. For Gneist, see Heffter, *Die deutsche Selbstverwaltungslehre im 19. Jahrhundert* (Stuttgart, 1950), especially, pp. 372 ff.

markedly from the views of his older, more pessimistic friend. Baumgarten taught Weber to view political events in the same way and with the same formal assumptions that characterized his own approach. This is especially clear in relation to their common views on the development of political leadership and the education of the nation in political judgment, which both saw as the underlying problem of all political phenomena. Both studied the interaction between the nature of a political system and the political maturity of the governed. For example, in his famous "self-criticism," Baumgarten attributed the collapse of German liberalism in the constitutional conflict of 1862–66, together with liberalism's unrealistic and doctrinaire policies to the lack of political education and the absence of gifted statesmen in the ranks of the German bourgeoisie. He pointed to the historical causes of this situation. Like Theodor Mommsen, he called for men "who had made politics their life work," and sought them in the ranks of the nobility, if these ranks were open at the bottom, because "the genuine political career is not characteristic of the bourgeois order."[48] Max Weber, as we shall see elsewhere, repeatedly returned to the problem of the political immaturity of most groups in the German social structure and attributed this above all to the effects of Bismarck's leadership.[49] He was to pay great attention to the problem of political leadership, and came to reject the merit principle of traditional liberalism, emphasizing instead the career politician as the bearer of political power in modern mass democracy.

The passionate debates with Baumgarten over Bismarck and the future of German liberalism, together with the many-faceted political discussions with his fellow Berlin students, helped Weber to view the National Liberal traditions of his parents' house with a critical eye and to arrive at an independent position on important political issues. Of course, even at an early stage his independent political judgment was extraordinary. Perhaps this is most clearly demonstrated by his position on the law against the Socialists, which his father as well as Baumgarten accepted as a necessary evil. Weber was skeptical about this measure as early as 1884:

48. Mommsen in 1865 in the weekly of the Nationalverein: the Prussian liberals must look around for other leaders, "who are not doctors, lawyers, or district judges on the side, but who give themselves exclusively to the higher profession of devoting themselves to the business of their party and the business of the country." Cited by A. Heuss, *Theodor Mommsen* (1956), pp. 174 f.

Baumgarten, *Treitschkes Deutsche Geschichte*, p. 173: "Politics is a profession like jurisprudence and medicine, and indeed it is the highest and most difficult profession that a man can enter. . . . It is one of the most pernicious errors to believe that every capable scholar, lawyer, businessman, or official who has interest in public matters and diligently reads a newspaper is capable of active involvement in politics. This is the product of our completely unpolitical nature and our lack of any significant political experience" (p. 472).

49. Cf. below, chap. 4, sec. 2.

"I would occasionally like to believe that equal rights for all take precedence over everything else, and it would therefore be preferable to muzzle everyone than to put some in chains."[50] His sense of justice was aroused by the clear attack against the liberal principle of equality before the law that the anti-Socialist law represented. At the time, he also claimed to observe a complete change in the positions and leadership of the Social Democratic party.[51] If this was not an accurate observation at that time, it still represented a moderate estimation of Social Democracy, free from bourgeois anxiety, an attitude that later was characteristic of Max Weber.

In other words, Weber also disapproved of departures from ideal principles or their abandonment in favor of practical Realpolitik. He unequivocally shared the liberal viewpoint during the Kulturkampf, but, like Baumgarten, he supported the struggle for its own sake and not as a means to achieve other goals. When in 1887 Bismarck again watered down the Kulturkampf laws, Max Weber protested that some National Liberals now accepted the fact that only "political" goals, the objective conditions of which no longer existed, had made the actions against Catholicism necessary: "This unceremonious 'peace' is depressing, and in any event it contains an admission of injustice, and even terrible injustice, if it is now said that political reasons alone prompted the struggle on our part. If in fact it was a matter not of conscience for us but merely of opportunism, then we have of course, as the Catholics maintained, ravaged their conscience for superficial reasons. . . . We have therefore acted unconscionably and we are also the moral losers; and that is the most difficult part of the defeat, since it prevents us from taking up the battle again in the way in which it must be taken up if it is to lead to victory."[52]

Max Weber generally followed his father's position on left-wing liberalism too. He condemned the Progressives' negative attitude toward all financial and military reform. In 1887 he argued that the Progressives had "unbelievably" compromised themselves with their absolutely inflexible opposition to all financial reform.[53] He also disapproved of the Progressives' opposition to the very modest colonial policy of the eighties.[54] He

50. Letter to Baumgarten of 8 November 1884, *Jugendbriefe*, p. 143.

51. Ibid.; Weber's father was not too happy that even the National Liberals voted with the Social Democrats (in the run-off elections), he notes on p. 145. Max Weber apparently did not agree!

52. Letter to Baumgarten of 25 April 1887, *Jugendbriefe*, p. 234.

53. "And what should be said to a political party which for years, whenever a request for funding was presented to the Reich, rejected it because the means to do it were not ascertained and, now that the means can be found, rejects it because the need has not been proved—quite a game!" Letter to Baumgarten of 29 June 1887, *Jugendbriefe*, p. 249.

54. Cf. letter to Baumgarten of 8 November 1884, ibid., p. 142.

wanted all questions that touched on the Reich's international position to be removed from partisan discussion. For that reason, he strongly disapproved of the confusion of budget proposals with domestic political quarrels that repeatedly absorbed the Progressives under Eugen Richter's leadership, and he deplored the recurring battles over the budget that resulted. These battles repeatedly gave Bismarck a pretext for dissolving the Reichstag under the cover of nationalistic rhetoric. He later blamed Bismarck more than anyone for making budgetary questions the focus of domestic political controversy. By "exploiting military questions as a weapon against uncomfortable opposition parties," Bismarckian policy had substantially contributed to transforming these questions, "very much to the damage of the army's interest from simple, straightforward budget questions to the focus of a recurrent domestic power struggle, much to Bismarck's advantage."[55]

Max Weber regarded the Progressive party's policies as pure and simple dogmatism. He believed the Progressives incapable of working positively.[56] He therefore saw little hope for future Progressive successes. He believed that the widespread liberal hope that Crown Prince Friedrich's government would move domestic policy onto a liberal track—Baumgarten and Weber's father shared this hope—was unfounded. The German party scene in no way offered the framework for a second "liberal era." Liberalism's divided and corrupted condition seemed in fact to rule out this possibility altogether.[57] Weber was contemptuous of the Progressives' "servile" speculation about the succession.[58] "The belief in any manner of positive political action in consort with these people," he wrote to Hermann Baumgarten, must "be wholly dismissed since this would mean perpetuating the liberal split and the comic operetta that has compromised [liberalism] with its stereotypically fanatical demagogues on one side and blind Bismarckians on the other. We must hope instead that with time some of the previously united elements on the left will find the way back to positive cooperation."[59]

55. Special supplement to the *Allgemeine Zeitung*, 1898, no. 46, pp. 4 f. Now in *Pol. Schr.*, p. 31.

56. Cf. letter of 14 July 1885, *Jugendbriefe*, p. 171. Later, too, Weber accused liberalism of ideological rigidity. The worst consequense was the political immobility that resulted: "The hereditary folly of not only . . . every radical party but every ideologically oriented policy is the capacity 'to miss opportunities.' " Max Weber discovered characteristic examples of this in the history of liberalism: Vincke's refusal to negotiate with the Ministry of the New Era, and the belated Progressive approval of the army budget in 1893. Both instances represented a fateful turning point for the cause of liberalism. See "Zur Lage der bürgerlichen Demokratie in Russland," *Archiv für Sozialwissenschaft und Sozialpolitik* 22 (1906), supplement, p. 115 (hereafter cited as "Zur Lage"). Partially printed in *Pol. Schr.*, pp. 33 ff.

57. Letter to Baumgarten of 30 April 1888, *Jugendbriefe*, p. 293.

58. Letter to Baumgarten of 29 June 1887, ibid., p. 249.

59. Letter to Baumgarten of 30 April 1888, ibid., p. 297.

As we have seen, Weber did not think much better of the National Liberals. At first, he defended them to Baumgarten, who in the 1880s leaned more and more toward the Progressives.[60] Gradually, however, Weber recognized that the National Liberal party had grown increasingly stagnant, especially after Bennigsen withdrew from politics, followed by many other great National Liberal leaders of the seventies. He disapproved of their growing rejection of the liberal tradition and the complacency and self-satisfaction that was turning them into mere defenders of the domestic political status quo. In 1887, on the occasion of the passage of the second law to terminate the Kulturkampf, Weber condemned the National Liberals' "excessive passive enjoyment . . . of that which 'we have,'" and criticized their unwillingness to entertain uncomfortable thoughts about the uncertain future.[61] As early as 1885, he noted that "it is doubtful whether the party can once again win popular trust. Human memory is short, and no one remembers what the party once achieved."[62] Nor did Weber believe that the National Liberals could be effective in the future without the cooperation of the Progressives; so the Progressives' decline hurt the National Liberals as well. By the late 1880s, Weber was extremely pessimistic about the future of German liberalism. He deplored the "general decadence" of the German party scene and feared that, in the long run, radical parties on the left and the right, alternately allying themselves with the Center party, would dominate the German political scene, a prediction that proved to be essentially accurate.[63]

It is not surprising that Weber eventually chose a position aloof from the liberal parties, both of which appeared destined to political ineffectiveness if not to absolute collapse, at least for the foreseeable future. In 1887 we first note that Weber had joined a circle of young political economists whose chief common bond was their "Manchester liberalism."[64] Through this group he came into close touch with the *Kathedersozialisten* ("socialists of the lectern," or academic socialists), who were attempting to counter the liberals' indifference to the social question. In contrast to the liberals, the Kathedersozialisten favored state action in economic life, especially in the field of labor. The assistance of the state, administered justly, would be the means of narrowing the dangerously wide class division between middle class proletariat.

Max Weber's attraction to the Kathedersozialisten signified a turning point in his development. This association was to have a major impact both on his future scholarly work and on his political activities and would

60. Cf., e.g., the letter to his father of 15 March 1885, ibid., pp. 151 f.
61. Letter to Baumgarten of 25 April 1887, ibid., p. 234.
62. Letter to Baumgarten of 14 July 1885, ibid., p. 170.
63. Letter to Baumgarten of 30 April 1888, ibid., p. 297.
64. Letter to Baumgarten of 30 September 1887, ibid., p. 273. Cf. *Lebensbild*, pp. 131 f.

carry him far beyond the principles of traditional liberalism that he had hitherto espoused. Well aware of this, Weber justified his stand, in detail, in a letter to Baumgarten. Among his contemporaries were many "jaded fellows who are anti-Semitic for form's sake and otherwise believe nothing, and many idealists who have been led into a kind of mystical, nationalistic fanaticism because of Treitschke; still others who are attracted by noble bravado and the so-called realism of the latest fashionable school." But there are also other elements among them, he was convinced, "the few who have their feet on the ground, who are genuinely full of energy, and who will take the lead in the future. . . . They have shaken off their anti-Semitism and similar current fashions and have distinctly moved away from the National Liberal positions of the seventies. But, like that generation of National Liberals, they have neither the desire for status nor high church tendencies, and are free of any trace of ambition or other vested interests. In short, their intellectual freedom is readily apparent to me. They too evaluate the period between 1867 and 1877 in a distinctly new light. Most of them are political economists and others interested in social policy. It is not at all surprising that they view state action on the so-called social questions to be more essential than action in other areas in the light of the present situation."[65]

To be sure, Weber felt uncomfortable from the start with the "strongly bureaucratic streak" of the Kathedersozialisten, just as he was later to become an outspoken opponent of Gustav Schmoller—the spokesman for and historian of the Prussian bureaucracy—and the bureaucratic group in the Verein für Sozialpolitik that surrounded Schmoller.[66] Yet he recognized a political farsightedness at work in the Verein as well as a commitment to praiseworthy tasks in the social sciences. He therefore resolved to join the Verein für Sozialpolitik and soon became one of its most active members.[67] His entrance into the Verein marked the decisive step in Weber's emancipation from old liberalism and hence from the views shared by Baumgarten and his own father. In the light of Germany's economic and social development into one of the leading industrial nations in Europe, Weber recognized liberalism's omissions in the field of social and economic policy and disapproved of its negative position on social legislation, which he blamed on outdated economic doctrines.

Scattered evidence suggests that Weber temporarily adopted conservative opinions at the time he joined the Kathedersozialisten. In Berlin he was frequently in the company of a circle of largely conserva-

65. Letter of 30 April 1888, ibid., pp. 298 f.
66. Ibid., p. 299.
67. Cf. *Lebensbild*, p. 135.

tive-minded contemporaries. In 1888, he noted that his views "always sharply contrasted with theirs."[68] But in the following years he seems to have moved closer to the conservative camp. Lotz, a year older than Weber and a fairly close friend at the time, reported that Weber was then "absolutely conservatively oriented."[69] He was regularly seen at weekly meetings for the "discussion of patriotic questions of the day and economic problems." This certainly refers to the "governmental science society" he once discussed with Baumgarten.[70] His friendly relations with Max Sering, the conservative political economist and agrarian, later Weber's opponent on questions of agrarian policy, point in the same direction.[71] Max Weber reported that the first time he voted, probably in 1890, he voted Conservative.[72] He later referred to this act emphatically and repeatedly.[73] But this statement should not be given too much weight, since it is possible that for the election in question no National Liberal candidate existed, although Weber asserted that he had put in a Conservative ballot and his father a National Liberal one.[74] A very sharp passage that was stricken from the published version of "Parlament und Regierung im neugeordneten Deutschland" ("Parliament and Govern-

68. Letter to Baumgarten of 30 April 1888, *Jugendbriefe*, p. 296.

69. Alfred Weber, of Heidelberg, confirmed this orally.

70. Cf. Lotz's letter to Marianne Weber of 12 December 1924, Weber papers; Lotz named F. Baumgarten and Dr. Ewert as participants. Also Weber's letter to Baumgarten of 3 January 1891 (*Jugendbriefe*, p. 327) and to Emmy Baumgarten of 14 December 1889 (ibid., p. 320). We cannot locate any closer source material about the conservative period in Weber's development. Marianne Weber does not report any more except for mentioning the fact that Weber voted for the Free Conservatives.

71. In 1896, Weber wrote very significantly to his mother: "I quarreled seriously in all friendship with Sering, who was here recently. It is time to counter the 'conservative rhetoric' that has now replaced the hitherto so maligned liberal rhetoric and which far surpasses it in offensiveness." Letter to Helene Weber of 2 May 1896 from a copy in the Weber papers. Apparently Weber had perceived the "offensiveness" of "liberal rhetoric" at the end of the eighties. Weber had already energetically argued against Sering in 1894. See "Die Verhandlungen der preussischen Agrarkonferenz," *Sozialpolitisches Zentralblatt*, 1894, pp. 533 ff.

72. On 21 April 1888, Weber could vote for the Prussian Landtag, a year later for the Reichstag; we are disregarding communal elections.

73. *Pol. Schr.*, pp. 157 and 309; cf. *Lebensbild*, p. 132.

74. If we ignore the improbable possibility that Weber's statement referred to the communal elections, then it probably referred to the Reichstag election of 20 February 1890. In Weber's electoral district, Electoral District I of the City of Berlin, in the main election of 20 February 1890 only the Conservatives, the Progressives, and the Social Democrats offered candidates. In the runoff election of 1 March 1890, the Progressive candidate defeated the Conservative (according to the *Statistisches Jahrbuch der Stadt Berlin*, Year 1, XVI–VII, 1889–90, p. 648). It was therefore not possible to vote either for a National Liberal or for a Free Conservative. Marianne Weber's version, that Weber voted Free Conservative, may be a retrospective correction.

ment in a Reconstructed Germany")—"Personally, I turned my back on these unclean hypocrites [the Conservatives] as a young man"—confirms Weber's temporary attraction to conservative views.[75] At the least, he preferred the Conservative party to the Progressives, who, in Weber's eyes, failed to understand the interests of a powerful national state and also subscribed to outdated economic principles. If Weber voted Conservative in 1890 because, as we suspect, he hoped the Right would represent the cause of the Reich's power without submitting to vested interests, as well as offering an energetic social policy, he must certainly have been speedily disappointed. As early as the beginning of 1891, he wrote to Baumgarten about "bureaucratically enlightened conservatism" that "unbeknownst to seven out of ten of my contemporaries has been infused with the support of the agricultural interests of large landed property."[76] Weber recognized that the kind of economic and social policy he deemed necessary for the expansion of the Reich aroused more selfish opposition from the Conservatives than from the National Liberals. For this reason, Weber's conservatism remained a mere episode. Because of his thoroughgoing bourgeois spirit, a long-lasting orientation to the right would have been no more likely than a leaning toward social democracy.[77] But none of the existing bourgeois parties comforted him. Neither the National Liberals with whom he was linked by heritage and by their forthright stand in support of the national state, nor the Progressives, with whom he shared loyalty to the liberal constitutional ideal, attracted him. Weber also did not seek a partisan link because he did not rate the liberals' chances highly in the existing political situation.

The young political economist recognized that Germany's rapid economic development and the accompanying transformation of its social structure had created problems that traditional liberal methods could not solve. In his opinion, the liberals had adopted a narrow ideological position, more distinctly so than was actually the case. He viewed this as their characteristic weakness. "As long as . . . economic and social issues remain the exclusive political focus, and interest groups remain dominant, liberalism's effectiveness will be limited, especially as long as liberalism itself is divided by quarreling interest groups," he wrote to Baumgarten in 1891.[78] Since Weber planned at the time to switch from his legal studies to political economy and political sociology, economic and

75. *Frankfurter Zeitung* of 27 May 1917: "The whole sad apparatus . . . rejected as 'cant.'" *Pol. Schr.*, p. 300. "Parliament and Government in a Reconstructed Germany" is the translation published in *Economy and Society* (Berkeley, Cal., 1978), pp. 1381–1469.

76. Letter to Baumgarten of 3 January 1891, *Jugendbriefe*, pp. 328 f.

77. "We bourgeois," he wrote in opposition to Naumann in 1894 in an article in *Christliche Welt*.

78. On 3 January 1891, *Jugendbriefe*, p. 329.

social problems were much on his mind, and it was precisely in these areas that liberalism had abdicated. The young Weber hoped to redress liberalism's weaknesses in this area.

Weber's newly awakened interest in social policy questions brought him into contact with the Christian Social movement that was then winning favor among educated Protestants. Weber was certainly not attracted by Stoecker's crude agitation—on the contrary. The little that Weber wrote about Stoecker in the letters that have survived from those years reveals that he decidedly rejected Stoecker's social conservatism, especially its demagogic side. In particular, Weber could never share Stoecker's anti-Semitism.[79] But Weber's own personal ties prompted his support of Christian Social efforts. Max Weber's mother was attracted to the Christlich-Sozialen because of her Christian conscience and her strong sense of social responsibility. In addition, Otto Baumgarten, his Heidelberg student friend and cousin, encouraged his interest. Max Weber therefore participated in the first Evangelisch-sozialer Kongress (Lutheran social congress) that Stoecker organized. The congress had the lively support of younger Protestant theologians and educated Protestant circles. It was a common meeting ground for older Christlich-Sozialen like Adolf Wagner, liberal theologians led by Adolf von Harnack, and the left-leaning Fronde of young Christlich-Sozialen under Friedrich Naumann's leadership who had emancipated themselves from Stoecker's conservatism. The congress was assembled for the purpose of discussing social policy in the framework of a Christian world view.

At the congress, Weber found comrades with similar views with whom he would make common political cause for years. The close friendship that bound Weber with Friedrich Naumann, which was to be of such importance for both men, dates from this occasion. At the time, Weber's friendship with Paul Göhre outweighed his relationship with Naumann. Göhre, who had recently achieved renown as a result of his book *Drei Monate als Fabrikarbeiter* (*Three Months as a Factory Worker*) urged Weber even more strongly to work in the field of social policy. Weber became a co-worker on Göhre's *Christliche Welt* (*Christian World*), a journal with a characteristic subtitle for that time: "Evangelical-Lutheran Community Newspaper for the Educated of All Classes." In 1892, after the Lutheran church's leadership had abandoned the era of social policy ordinances and entered a period dominated by the Saarland magnate, Karl Ferdinand von Stumm-Halberg, the hierarchy attacked Göhre sharply. Weber energetically supported his friend in the *Christliche Welt*. In an article "Zur Rechtfertigung Göhres" ("In Defense of Göhre") he

79. Cf. letter to Baumgarten of 30 April 1888, ibid., p. 294; also, p. 298 and especially p. 300: "The turn away from Stoecker has grown larger and larger in politically responsible circles."

attacked the reactionary position of the church leaders and called it an ignorant "superstition that dark and secret powers are at work in the laboring class."[80]

Weber also took on editorial work for the *Evangelisch-soziale Zeitfragen* (*Lutheran Social Questions of the Day*), a newspaper that his cousin Otto Baumgarten founded with the object of acquainting Lutheran theologians with social problems and gaining their support for Christian Social efforts. Weber greeted this effort as a counterweight to the Stoeckerist tendency. "There can be no doubt," he noted early in 1891, "that the needs of the time demand that energetic and idealistic young clerics do more than teach and preach on the burning social questions. If the Stoecker group remains the only one prepared to dedicate itself in this area, its victory is assured even in the sphere of dogma. It will undoubtedly occupy the terrain alone if others do not unite with it in those areas where cooperation is possible, and the present moment is uniquely propitious for this."[81]

During the following years, Weber continued to make common cause with Göhre and Naumann, and he greatly influenced his two friends' development. We should not forget, however, that Weber did not entirely share the Naumann group's motives. Because Weber was not a religious man, he did not share the underlying faith of the Naumann circle's Christian Social activism: the spirit of Christian charity. Nevertheless, Göhre was able to awaken Weber's conscience in this area. Yet social consciousness was certainly never a primary motive for Weber; the need for a politics of social reform was closely linked with his analysis of the structural changes taking place in modern industrial society, and ethical considerations were secondary. The ideal of a powerful nation state remained Weber's central incentive.

80. *Die Christliche Welt*, 1892, pp. 1104 ff.
81. Letter to Baumgarten of 3 January 1891, *Jugendbriefe*, p. 325.

2

Patriarchalism, Capitalism, and the Nation State

In the summer of 1888, during Max Weber's second stint of military training, he was a frequent guest in the house of Nollau, the district magistrate for Posen. Nollau interested Weber in the work of the Prussian settlement commission, which was carrying out the East Mark proposal of 1866 "to strengthen and increase the German population in the face of Polonizing efforts." Nollau invited Weber to join him on a tour of inspection of some of the estates on which "an attempt is being made to establish German peasant communities on noble estates purchased with state funds."[1]

At this time, Weber learned about the dramatic Polish inroads into eastern Germany since the 1870s and the practical results of Prussian settlement policy. The policy satisfied the nationalist demands of the National Liberals and was also an outlet for Bismarck's mistrust of the Polish nobility and clergy, which had been so evident during the Kulturkampf.[2] Weber did not turn immediately to a study of eastern Germany's agricultural problems, since he was then preoccupied with the final stages of his doctoral dissertation about the history of trading companies in the Middle Ages. His inaugural dissertation, under Meitzen's supervision, was his first venture into agricultural history. This work, which explored Roman agriculture in the light of state and private law, led him into a series of disputes with the venerable Theodor

1. Letters to his mother of 15 and 23 August 1888, *Jugendbriefe*, pp. 306, 308.

2. Cf. Hans Rothfels, *Bismarck und der Osten* (Leipzig, 1934), pp. 51 ff., also Martin Laubert, *Die preussische Polenpolitik von 1772–1914*, 3d ed. (Berlin, 1944,) pp. 144 ff., as well as Hans-Ulrich Wehler, "Die Polenpolitik im Deutschen Kaiserreich 1871–1918," in *Politische Ideologien und nationalstaatliche Ordnung: Festschrift für Theodor Schieder*, ed. Kurt Kluxen and Wolfgang J. Mommsen (Munich, 1968,) pp. 303 ff.

Mommsen, whose *Römisches Staatsrecht*, Weber was convinced, lacked a sociological analysis of the agrarian roots of Roman law.

Weber's interest in the Latifundia, which he viewed not only as the lever for the destruction of the republic's social base but also as the chief cause of the decline of ancient culture, must have led his versatile mind to the similar problem east of the Elbe, wary as he may have been of premature parallels. In his short essay on the decline of ancient culture ("Die sozialen Gründe des Untergangs der antiken Kultur"), which appeared in 1896, Weber engagingly described ancient cultural phenomena with East Elbian references in an aside: "Plinius's voice warns us from antiquity: 'Latifundia perdidere Italiam.' Thus—it may be said on the one hand—it was the Junkers who destroyed Rome. Yet—it can be said on the other hand—they did so only because they were ruined by foreign grain imports: if they had taken up Kanitz's proposal, the Caesars would still be sitting on their thrones today."[3] Weber's impression that the shortage of farm labor was the greatest threat to the survival of eastern Germany's large estates may well have influenced his assertion that lack of slave labor power undermined the ancient Latifundia.

Without a doubt, his studies in Roman agricultural history prompted his interest in the agricultural problems of eastern Germany. The decisive stimulus occurred around the beginning of 1890, when the Verein für Sozialpolitik commissioned his participation in an extensive survey of agricultural workers already in progress. It is scarcely surprising that Weber chose to investigate the most politically significant and controversial area: the treatment of Germany's East Elbian region.[4]

Weber embarked energetically upon the new task and speedily mastered the confusion and complexity of the statistical findings of the inquiry. Moreover, he masterfully grasped the intellectual and *political* significance of the raw data. His evaluation of the survey instantly established his reputation in the field of political economy. At the Verein für Sozialpolitik's meeting in 1893, Knapp confessed, the sentiment arose "that our expertise no longer exists and we must begin our study again."[5] In spite of Weber's objective and scholarly approach to the conditions of eastern land labor, the revolutionary implications were inescapable. Although he remained cautious about developing these implications and

3. *Gesammelte Aufsätze zur Sozial- und Wirtschaftsgeschichte*, p. 290. An English version of this essay is reprinted in J. E. T. Eldridge, *Max Weber: The Interpretation of Social Reality* (London, 1971).

4. "Die Verhältnisse der Landarbeiter im ostelbischen Deutschland," *Schriften des Vereins für Sozialpolitik* 55 (Leipzig, 1892) (hereafter cited as "Die Verhältnisse der Landarbeiter").

5. "Protokoll der Verhandlungen des Vereins für Socialpolitik 1893," *Schriften des Vereins für Sozialpolitik* 58:7.

temporarily desisted from suggesting any political measures, his study nevertheless turned him into a staunch opponent of the conservative magnate.

Painstakingly examining the agricultural situation east of the Elbe, Weber discovered a deep and far-reaching process of transformation. He concluded that the large estates in the east retained the vestiges of a well-defined patriarchal economic order, which he carefully reconstructed. He located its essence in the person of the *Instmann*, or attached laborer. The *Instmann* held a small plot for stock raising and farming and also farmed the estate with his family and a day laborer whom he paid himself. In turn, he was compensated with the produce of a definite section of the estate, which changed yearly with crop rotation. In addition, he shared a considerable portion of the threshing yield in the winter. For this reason, the *Instmann* was as interested in the yield of the estate as was the landlord. Both stood to gain from a rise in grain prices. While lacking total autonomy, the *Instmann* was relatively independent and economically secure. This was the basis of the characteristic community of interest between the landlord and his peasants.

Weber found this patriarchal form of cultivation in its pure form preserved only in a few places in Mecklemburg. The system was steadily collapsing everywhere. He pinpointed capitalism, the revolutionary power which undermined all traditional social structures, as the ultimate source of this decay. A capitalist-oriented economy forced the East Elbian landlords to manage their estates with capital-intensive methods. These pressures were increasing as international competition penetrated the domestic market; high grain tariffs provided only partial relief. The landlords' growing material requirements and the need to exact a greater monetary profit from their estates prompted them also to commercialize labor conditions. The threshing portion was partially or completely eliminated; and, in place of a share in the harvest and his stock-raising rights, the vassal now received a fixed allowance or cash salary. In this manner, the ancient community of interest between the landlord and his workers was dissolved, and the agricultural working class became a proletariat. This fact was often disguised since the land workers often became cottagers and small tenant farmers. Weber noted, however, that these small farmers were forced to seek salaried work under worse conditions and lived in far poorer circumstances than the landless laborers, whose freedom of movement was not bound by ties to miniature farms.

Weber observed that the land laborers were just as anxious to replace patriarchal ties with capitalist ones. The laborers preferred a sure, risk-free allowance or cash salary, although this increasingly worsened their economic situation. Their feelings were summed up in the maxim, "Release from the patriarchal household and economic community at any cost."[6] The deciding factor was not economic motives but the "powerful and purely psychological magic of 'freedom.' " From the workers' point of view, the central problem was that the traditional economic structure in the east offered them no possibility for winning an independent existence.[7]

Weber recognized that this was the chief reason that the land laborers, especially if they were well off, were emigrating in increasing numbers to western industrial regions and overseas. More and more, their place was taken by the so-called Saxon walkers (*Sachsengänger*), the Polish migrant laborers. The Poles were a far cheaper source of labor for the landlords. They were paid only in the summer, for now there was little work to be done in the winter because of the advancing sugar beet cultivation and, above all, because threshing was now done by machines. Moreover, because of their extremely low standard of living, the Poles were satisfied with meager wages and primitive accommodations. They therefore competed with the cheapest German workers and depressed the wages of the native laboring class as a whole. Later, Weber formulated his conclusions as a general principle: "In the countryside, production does not determine salary; rather, it is determined by the workers' minimum requirements according to their traditional standard of living."[8] The end result was the progressive deterioration of the East Elbian land laborers' nutritional level.

The current economic situation in the east, Weber argued, was marked by a conflict between the interests of the capitalistic estates and those of the national state principle. The patriarchal structure of the East Elbian manors, distorted by the transition from allowances to cash salaries, lacked the strength to tie the German agricultural workers to their home soil. The Poles, who arrived as migrant laborers, soon took the place of the German agricultural working class according to the principle of cheaper labor. This development served the economic interests of the large landlords, who were struggling with international agricultural competition. Weber deeply regretted "from the standpoint of the state's interest"[9] the progressive Polonization of eastern Germany.

At this stage, Weber was not yet ready to speak out explicitly on the radical political conclusions implicit in his findings. Scholarly objectivity checked the politician in him. The question of "what will happen and even what should happen" will "not be answered here."[10] However, the outcome was clear enough: "The patriarchal estates sustained the nutri-

6. "Die Verhältnisse der Landarbeiter," p. 797.
7. Ibid., pp. 797 f.
8. *Gesammelte Aufsätze zur Sozial- und Wirtschaftsgeschichte*, p. 487.
9. "Die Verhältnisse der Landarbeiter," p. 799.
10. Ibid., p. 796.

tional level of the agricultural working class and conserved its military fitness; today's capitalistic estates exist at the expense of the nutritional level, the nationality, and the military strength of the German east."[11] The traditional power of large land ownership in Germany's political life was undermined by economic changes which destroyed the community of interest between the landlord and his smallholders and transformed the former from an independent lord of the manor into an agricultural businessman.[12]

Weber only hinted at his political conclusions. "The agricultural labor question" constituted "a link in a chain of far-reaching transformations which would necessarily lead to a general displacement of the power of the imperial dynasty and government."[13] He expressly avoided stating whether or not internal colonization might provide a way out of the dilemma, although he cautiously suggested that the East Elbian nobility's days of political power were numbered. But he appended an explicit testimonial in which he tried to do justice to the "much-abused" Prussian "Junkers" and their past political role.[14] The *Kreuzzeitung* was able, with astounding shortsightedness, to quote these words in the agrarian cause and to claim Weber as a conservative. Weber was outraged at the *Kreuzzeitung*'s "impertinence."[15]

It was characteristic and not entirely "in the interest of objectivity" for Weber to record his respect for the Prussian nobility. He greatly admired their role as a political elite that had cultivated above all else an "instinct for power" and a "will to power," which Weber found lacking in the German middle class of his day: "It is eastern Germany's tragic fate that

11. Ibid., p. 795.

12. Ibid., pp. 795 f.

13. "Die Verhältnisse der Landarbeiter," p. 799.

14. "The large landed estates are considered—and rightly, in spite of the reservations that need to be asserted—the 'pillar of the monarchy.' It was possible and admissible to permit the much maligned 'Junker' to hold on to what remained of manorial rights because, to their credit, the Junkers disdained to become a class of revenue-consuming magnates. Instead, they acted as responsible employers and ventured into the hard battle of interests of business life. Also the labor structure was constituted in a way that in practice made the landlord, to a certain degree, the born representative of the interests of his people." Ibid., p. 796.

15. Cf. the letter to Lujo Brentano of 20 February 1893, *Jugendbriefe*, p. 365, corrected according to the original in the Brentano papers, Bundesarchiv, Koblenz: "I did not wish to attribute a *personal* merit to the eastern Junkers, only—as the result of circumstances—a relative merit in the character of social organization. If the large landholders had had greater capital resources, the peasants would doubtless have been completely impoverished. Perhaps I did go too far earlier. I did so because I deemed it necessary, in the interest of objectivity, to repress my native liberal antipathy for the eastern landlords. At the convention I shall make every effort to dispel any doubts about the conditional nature of my recognition [of the Junkers' value], in order to avoid any interpretation that favors the agrarians' interests such as in the impertinent interpretation by the *Kreuzzeitung*."

its formidable achievements for the nation dug the grave of its unique social organization. The east deserves the chief credit for the nation's political greatness. Prophetic foresight, not limited vision, prompted prominent Prussians and even their main representatives to struggle against absorption into the greater unity of the empire."[16] This retrospective judgment makes Weber's temporary conservative sympathies comprehensible. We shall have to bear in mind the "conservative" picture he sketched here. Weber's portrait of a "political elite" gifted with power instincts, self-awareness, and the qualities of political leadership foreshadowed significant elements of Weber's legal and political theory. It was to be joined with liberal and democratic conceptions, investing the latter with a characteristic patina. This description reappeared in a very different guise in the paradigm of the charismatic career politician as the unique bearer of the nation's political will, described by Weber in "Politik als Beruf" ("Politics as a Vocation") a year before his death.

Capitalism was the dynamic source of the economic changes that were destroying the social basis of the eastern Junkers' rule. Weber was clearly influenced by Marxian thought when he said that capitalism would free the agricultural laborers from their traditional bonds and mobilize them to "class struggle." It was at this time that capitalism became the young scholar's chief obsession. After this, the problem of the origins of the capitalist economic system and its impact on social structure and political organization assumed a central position in his social research and his political thought.

Weber, who regarded the patriarchal system as doomed, immediately recognized the political significance of his assessment. The glory and military greatness of Prussia and the Bismarckian empire had been based on patriarchal foundations. The underlying structural transformation now demanded the replacement of the old basis by new patterns of selection of the political elite. "It is . . . no accident," Weber stated in the summary of his investigation of agricultural policy, "that the rudder of empire lay in the hands of a powerful landowner for a generation. [Bismarck's] characteristic traits are incomprehensible apart from the soil which nurtured him. His personality united all of the brilliant qualities ripened by the hereditary art of rule over land and peasants, but also the dark shadows. The genuine hatred that millions of German workers and many sections of the middle class bore this man, though it was caricatured by the press, was a sincere and just response to the contempt for mankind that marked his every word and deed. His contempt also grew in the soil of the patriarchal system and was characteristic of the greatest and most energetic of his class. . . . But it is precisely in this regard that the nation is

16. "Die Verhältnisse der Landarbeiter," p. 803.

now more sensitive; in recent years we have repeatedly witnessed stormy protests at a mere hint of the patriarchal tone. The patriarchal system has no future in the hearts of the masses."[17] Weber's political conclusions were left unstated: assumption of power by the middle class; parliamentarization of the empire; abolition of the Prussian three-class suffrage, which propped up the Prussian nobility's political power. Instead, Weber temporarily concentrated on the implications of his work for agricultural policy.

Excited by the significance of his conclusions, Weber decided to supplement the Verein für Sozialpolitik's survey. With the aid of his friend Paul Göhre, he succeeded in persuading the Evangelisch-sozialer Kongress to conduct a further inquiry. Weber hoped that a more objective survey instrument would enrich his sources and add further support to his theories. The Verein's questionnaire had been circulated to employers only, which fundamentally limited the value of the testimony. The new questionnaire that Weber and Göhre prepared was addressed to rural parish ministers,[18] who Weber expected would take an independent stand regarding the class conflicts between the parties involved and would be in a position to give a more accurate picture of the land workers' conditions, since they had close contact with them. To be sure, only a few of the fifteen thousand ministers who were polled troubled to reply carefully, but Weber was satisfied with the results.[19] He was able to refer to them in an important lecture at the Verein conference in 1893.

On this occasion, Weber departed from his self-imposed political caution. He considered the question of the land laborers "exclusively from the point of view of reason of state" and added that he had no intention of debating the land laborers' plight and its amelioration, nor was he interested in how the landed magnates could otherwise procure workers.[20] He emphasized the ideal of the national state, and to this ideal he subordinated all social and economic considerations. He thereby arrived at the position which long afterward characterized his political thought.

Weber designated the progressive "Polonization" of eastern Germany as the quintessence of a process of social transformation. The dismemberment of long-established patriarchal economic relationships promoted the emigration of the native agricultural working class. The Polish

17. Ibid., p. 804.

18. Republished in *Werk und Person*, pp. 376 ff.

19. Compare Weber's report in *Christliche Welt*, pp. 535 ff.: The quality of the reports generally exceed expectations; the majority are superior to those of the landlords. The results of the second inquiry would first be published in 1899 under the title: *Die Landarbeiter in den evangelischen Gebieten Norddeutschlands* (Tübingen).

20. "Protokoll der Verhandlungen des Vereins für Sozialpolitik 1893," p. 74.

migrants who were replacing them endangered not only the survival of German nationality in the area but also the cultural level of the east because of the migrants' low living standards: "The ultimate decision about the countryside's nationality" would not be determined in the long run by the national allegiance of the propertied class "but by the nationality of the country proletariat."[21] To stem Polish inroads, he argued for the immediate closure of the eastern frontier to Polish migrant workers. He also abandoned his prior charitableness to the conservatives. The state had at one time depended upon the support of the estate owners, but there remained no present reason to accord them further "special obligations as a reward."[22] "The eastern agricultural interests" were today "the most dangerous enemy of our nationality," "our greatest Polonizer."[23] As a solution to this problem, Weber demanded an extensive governmental settlement policy, which went far beyond the previous activities and achievements of the existing Settlement Commission. Prompt governmental action was still possible even though it would have to overcome the opposition of the landowning interests as well as "the instincts of those groups who defend Manchesterism and free trade."[24] The establishment of many self-sustaining peasant farms, which could survive without foreign labor power, could solve the serious problem of agricultural labor supply and put a halt to "denationalization." Weber saw little value in the agrarian proposals to limit agricultural workers' mobility, although he would have been prepared "to accept even this as a last resort."[25] "Their fathers' sins avenge themselves on today's landed magnates," Weber was to write on a later occasion. "The peasant villages that have disappeared must be recreated through colonization."[26]

He formulated his program with resignation and not with positive political fervor.[27] This fact is essential for the understanding of his political personality. Weber did not view his proposal to create free peasant farms through state-sponsored colonization as an ideal solution but, rather, as the only practical alternative to the economically untenable

21. Ibid., p. 71.

22. Ibid., pp. 74 f and letter to Brentano of 20 February 1893, *Jugendbriefe*, 365.

23. "Protokoll der Verhandlungen des Vereins für Socialpolitik 1893," p. 72.

24. Ibid., p. 85.

25. He would, properly considered, "accept . . . an infringement of the supposedly general human right of free disposition over one's person . . . as a last resort." Ibid. p. 77.

26. "Die Erhebung des Vereins für Sozialpolitik über die Lage der Arbeiter," *Das Land* 1:129.

27. Weber himself said that he spoke under the pressure "of a certain resignation; . . . the proposals" that he sought to pose, "insofar as they were of a positive nature at all, . . . were equally the product of this resignation." "Protokoll der Verhandlungen des Vereins für Socialpolitik 1893," p. 84.

actions of the eastern landlords. His program offered the best possible end to an anachronistic situation already disrupted by the universal advance of capitalism, to the nation's injury. While he preferred small farms for reasons of population policy and military necessity, he recognized their economic drawbacks. Weber did not believe that small farming would serve the domestic market effectively.

"From the standpoint of business and industry, agriculture in the east has become a declining enterprise, incapable of standing up to competition; it is precisely the *decline* of competitive ability that creates a situation . . . where small farms are more capable of survival than large, market-oriented establishments."[28] The colonization of eastern Germany was "both necessary and fruitful because our international position has made east German soil worthless in the world market from the point of view of the interests of production."[29] Everything hinged upon the decisive question of how the future of agriculture was likely to develop; Weber was to write later on the question "whether, as von der Goltz argues, the future of the east lies in intensive farming for the market, . . . or whether the opposite point of view is taken for most of the east." In the latter event, the "colonizing activity must emphasize *peasant* colonization alone."[30]

The substitution of peasant settlements for large, market-oriented estates had other advantages. Farms producing for a limited local market were comparatively unaffected by the business cycles of the world market. However, Weber did not stress domestic agricultural productivity but the preservation and strengthening of the national character of eastern Germany. From the point of view of political economy, Weber's proposal to promote a peasant farming system which was static, largely self-sufficient, and therefore immune from economic crisis and the business cycle was greatly influenced by his acceptance of the apparent irreversible tendency for overseas grain production to dominate the German and international markets.[31]

28. Ibid., p. 81; cf. *Archiv für Sozialwissenschaft und Sozialpolitik* 23, supplement, p. 122, note 185. Weber here gives technical and economic precedence to large-scale farming over small farms.

29. "Verhandlungen des evangelisch-sozialen Kongresses 1894," p. 79.

30. Review by Baron Theodor von der Goltz, "Die ländliche Arbeiterklasse und der preussische Staat," *Jahrbücher für Nationalökonomie und Statistik* 6, no. 3 (1893).

31. Weber later emphasized this point of view much more strongly. Cf. "Verhandlungen des evangelisch-sozialen Kongresses 1897," pp. 111 f., as well as Max Weber's "Gutachten zur Frage der Einführung eines Heimstättenrechts," *Verhandlungen des 24. Deutschen Juristentages 1897*, vol. 2, pp. 18 f., 31 f., in which he asserted that emigration from the land could not be prevented with the help of legal obligations of landownership. He emphasized that in this light "unassailable" small farming units should be given preference over large ones: "The stability of the population rises with the decrease in average size of

Weber regarded England as the "natural" market outlet for eastern Germany's grain surplus.[32] This market had been lost because of English grain tariffs and cheaper overseas competition. Only small local markets were present in rural eastern Germany. Western Germany preferred to import grain from overseas by convenient water transport. Weber was convinced that east German grain production would increasingly be excluded from the market.[33] He may well have been overreacting to the crisis besetting German agriculture at that time. He therefore viewed the economic condition of the East Elbian estates as permanently catastrophic and regarded as hopeless all attempts to restore them to economic health.

He also opposed futile attempts to exclude overseas competition with higher tariffs in order to slow the inevitable decline of the East Elbian estate economy. Although prepared to support moderate grain tariffs,[34] he was a decisive critic of a highly protectionist agricultural policy, which would maintain the large landowners at the nation's expense; the social prominence of the East Elbian nobility was doomed in any event.[35] Some years later, he was prepared to tolerate grain tariffs as an "emergency measure" if it should prove persistently necessary and possible for Germany to fulfill its own grain needs. He had nothing but contempt for Kanitz's anti-industrial "proposal which smells of book-learning." He sharply rejected the "preservation of feudalism" with such methods.[36]

Weber had other reasons for viewing the transition to small agricultural units as a necessary evil. The small farmers who predominated in western Germany lacked the economic motivation that Weber held to be in the national interest.[37] According to Weber, they did not possess "the

---

agricultural units. Uncertainty increases in proportion as large agricultural units influence the economic situation. Large agriculture is entangled in the movements of the world market's trade cycle and is, by nature, a *seasonal* enterprise."

32. Cf. *Wirtschaft und Gesellschaft*, p. 522.

33. Cf. also Weber's lecture "Agrarschutz und positive Agrarpolitik," at the Freier Deutscher Hochstift, on 13 March 1896, reported in the *Frankfurter Volksbote* of 14 March and the *Frankfurter Zeitung* of 15 March 1896, 3d morning ed.

34. He distanced himself from Brentano's radical free-trade ideas in the agricultural area in 1893: "From the point of view of national policy, may one predict the exposing of agricultural production, too, to 'entanglement in the world economy' in the foreseeable future? I do not believe so. I even consider it to be a cultural danger as long as *the* natural conditions of production are no longer equal." Letter of 20 February 1893, with errors in *Jugendbriefe*, pp. 364 f (where *Stadtwirtschaft* is substituted for *Weltwirtschaft*), cited here according to the original in the Brentano papers.

35. "Verhandlungen des evangelisch-sozialen Kongresses 1894," pp. 77, 92.

36. Lecture to the Freier Deutscher Hochstift (see note 33 above).

37. We run into the specific idea of a vocation for rational and methodical economic activity based upon ethical motives here, which Weber later attributed to the spirit of Protestantism (cf. *Gesammelte Aufsätze zur Religionssoziologie*, vol. 1). For Weber, characteristically, this is an ultimate value!

concept of a duty to work" or the "characteristically Prussian concept of 'cursed duty and obligation.'" Weber could not charge the eastern landlords and their laborers with this lack. The commercial estates were spearheading the modernization of agriculture and were pacemakers of the modern dynamic economic mentality upon which Weber based the nation's welfare. Therefore, he did not view the complete destruction of the east's large estates as politically ideal.[38]

Weber offered his proposals with mixed emotions; they promised only accommodation to irresistible tendencies, not a positive national policy. He frankly confessed his deep concern at this state of affairs: "I do not know whether all of my generation perceives it to the degree that I do at this moment. It is the weighty curse of decadence that burdens this nation, from the masses to the highest circles. We cannot revive the verve and enthusiastic energy that inspired the generation before ours. . . . They built us a solid house, and we were invited to live in it and enjoy its blessings. We face different tasks. We cannot appeal to the common sentiment of the nation, as was done when the creation of national unity and a free constitution were the issues. We are a different breed of men. We are free from the countless illusions that formed our fathers' enthusiasm. Colossal illusions were necessary to create the German Reich, illusions that fled with the honeymoon of German unity and that we cannot recreate artificially or theoretically."[39] It was Weber's personal tragedy that he, "a doer to the core," had to wrestle his entire life with "action paralyzed by intellect."[40]

This same ambivalent and resigned position determined his stance at the Frankfurt conference of the Evangelisch-sozialer Kongress in 1894 when the investigation of agricultural labor was discussed. Göhre, who delivered the first lecture, candidly summarized the results of Weber's analysis. He went on to propose an extensive settlement policy that went well beyond the efforts of previous legislation. Göhre's characteristic ethical and social enthusiasm, which contrasted with Weber's rationally derived pessimism, colored his exposition. Göhre believed that wherever "the attempt was made to transform estate land into peasant land and manor into peasant village, it would succeed splendidly." The "only means" to this end was "a state initiative to create rental property, carried through by district according to a master plan. The large estates

38. "Protokoll der Verhandlungen des Vereins für Socialpolitik 1893," p. 65. His judgment that those regions of Germany that were characterized by an agricultural structure based on small peasant holdings were not granted "the achievement of that political organization and that form of political consciousness that would have contributed to the unity of the Reich" is a characteristic one. Ibid.

39. Ibid., pp. 84 f.

40. Cf. Erich Voegelin, "Max Weber," *Kölner Vierteljahreshefte für Soziologie* 9 (1930–31): 10.

would have to be totally supplanted. In as short a time as possible, the entire east should be populated with hundreds of thousands of German peasants. . . . This would mean an end to the predominance of large eastern estates and the elevation of thousands of Germans to a much higher economic, intellectual, and moral level."[41]

Weber's lecture, in contrast, was characterized by "heroic pessimism."[42] To be sure, he permitted no doubt that the days of the East Elbian landlords were numbered. "To preserve the Junker as Junker, as a status group with its traditional social and political character . . . would not be possible even with the economic means at our disposal. Can the state continue to base itself on a status group which itself requires state support?"[43] But at the same time he sharply dissociated himself from Göhre's optimism in the settlement question, although Göhre had merely assumed the consequences of Weber's own conclusions. Weber still shrank from the political ramifications of his own investigations as soon as they touched upon current political issues.

The worthy gentlemen attending the meeting of the Evangelisch-sozialer Kongress, an organization founded by Stoecker five years earlier, were dismayed by the "revolutionary" egg that Weber and Göhre had "smuggled" into their nest. They were anxious to prevent the Kongress from "joining the cavalry of a battle against the landed magnates."[44] Adolf Wagner answered Weber with the argument that it lay in everyone's interest "to preserve a status group with the virtues of the Prussian Junkers."[45] Conservatives sharply denounced the Kongress for conducting an agricultural survey "behind the landlords' backs." The agricultural debate at the conference had serious consequences for Stoecker's relations with the younger Christlich-Sozialen. Taking off from Weber's analysis, Schulze-Gävernitz posed the radical demand: "Give the land to the masses." Stoecker defensively replied: "The status of the large and small landholder is for me the highest and most honorable."[46] Ultimately, the conservatives precipitated the break that Naumann had repeatedly postponed. Naumann nevertheless wrote with self-assurance in *Die Hilfe*: "You have more power; we have more truth."[47]

Stoecker's resignation from the Evangelisch-sozialer Kongress the following year was ultimately caused by Göhre's and Weber's antiagrar-

41. "Verhandlungen des evangelisch-sozialen Kongresses 1894," pp. 57 f.

42. The term used by Werner Conze in "Friedrich Naumann Grundlagen und Ansatz seiner Politik in der nationalsozialen Zeit (1895–1903)," in *Schicksalswege deutscher Vergangenheit (Festschrift Kaehler)* (Düsseldorf, 1952), p. 358.

43. "Verhandlungen des evangelisch-sozialen Kongresses 1894," p. 92.

44. Ibid. p. 84.

45. Ibid., p. 89.

46. Cf. Walter Frank, *Stoecker*, 2d ed. (Hamburg, 1935), p. 248.

47. Quoted in ibid., p. 264.

ian behavior. The bitter arguments at the conference threatened the Kongress's existence for some time.[48] Years later, Naumann wrote to Rade when the Kongress was preparing to kick him out: "What is a congress worth which is so full of fear? . . . Let it be damned! It really isn't a *free* Lutheran concilium any longer."[49]

Weber soon forgot his reservations and exposed the particular interests which were behind the conservative agitation. The conservatives, fearing the loss of their social position and political influence, defended the economic interests upon which their position rested. "The economic interests of this class are incompatible with the interests of political power, let alone the social and political interests of the nation."[50] In his essay on developmental trends in the situation of the East Elbian agricultural workers ("Entwicklungstendenzen in der Lage der ostelbischen Landarbeiter"), published in the *Preussische Jahrbücher* and in the *Archiv für soziale Gesetzgebung*, Weber emphasized the role of the large East Elbian estates as "local centers of political power." "In accord with Prussian tradition [the estates] were designed to provide the material support for a stratum of the population which the state customarily entrusted with political domination and to which the state delegated military and political power."[51] With rising middle-class prosperity, these estates could no longer support the nobility in the required style. As a result, the nobles were pushed downward on "the political and social ladder."[52] The East Elbian landowners necessarily transformed themselves—and would have done so even without the infusion of new blood—into a class of agricultural entrepreneurs which in its social characteristics scarcely differed from the business class. The social situation no longer justified the large landowners' predominant position in society and government.

Taking another tack, Weber criticized the Prussian agrarian conference which convened in Berlin, from 28 May until 2 July 1894, for

48. Cf. Martin Wenck, *Die Geschichte der Nationalsozialen von 1895–1903* (Berlin, 1905), p. 20.

49. Quoted by Theodor Heuss, *Friedrich Naumann*, 2d ed. (Stuttgart/Tübingen, 1949), p. 155.

50. *Christliche Welt*, 1894, p. 670. At the time, Weber wrote to his wife combatively about his "rude article": "I am anxious to learn whether the pigs will find something new here to grunt about." Letter to Marianne Weber of 26 July 1894, Weber papers.

51. *Preussische Jahrbücher* 77 (1894): 437 ff. (hereafter cited as "Entwicklungstendenzen"). Now included in *Gesammelte Aufsätze zur Sozial- und Wirtschaftsgeschichte*. The quotation here is on 471. An earlier version, with only minor differences, appeared in *Archiv für soziale Gesetzgebung und Statistik* 7 (1894): 1 ff. The *Gesammelte Aufsätze zur Sozial- und Wirtschaftsgeschichte* erroneously designates this latter version as the one included.

52. "Entwicklungstendenzen," pp. 472 f.

ignoring the fact that landownership in Germany was still associated with a "specific social and political position in the life of the state and in society." This was the primary reason for the excessive price of land, and for the fact that the East Elbian estates were heavily mortgaged. The typical East Elbian estate could no longer support its owner's traditional political position. Nothing emphasized the need to redistribute eastern lands more than the Prussian Agrarian Conference's failure to come to a conclusion about a way to write off indebtedness. Weber proposed extensive, state-controlled colonization of large units instead of preserving the tenant settlement policy, which had created only miniature farms. The Settlement Commission should not immediately subdivide the purchased estates but should enrich the soil before settlers were brought in.[53]

A year later, in his inaugural address at the University of Freiburg, Max Weber emphasized his agrarian proposals, thereby giving his ideas a new significance. He put his program for reconstructing eastern agricultural policy into the context of a broad analysis of German political life notable for its incisiveness and for the radical nature of the proposals it contained. At the same time, the young political economist used agrarian policy as a taking-off point for his ideas about the relative nature of scientific truth.

53. "Die Verhandlungen der preussischen Agrarkonferenz," *Sozialpolitisches Zentralblatt 1894*, pp. 533 ff.; cf. also Weber's lecture to the Freier Deutscher Hochstift (note 33 above).

3
A Powerful Nation State as Weber's Political Ideal

1. The Freiburg Inaugural Address: The Nation as the Supreme Value of Economic Policy

Max Weber began life as a scholar with great inner reservations. For a time he considered accepting a legal position in Bremen after passing his initial legal exams. When he decided to seek the *Habilitation* in commercial law in Berlin, he did so ambivalently. He was in no way certain that he would find sufficient satisfaction in scholarly activity alone. "I am not at all . . . a genuine intellectual," he wrote to his childhood friend Emmy Baumgarten in 1892; he was more attached to the pedagogical side of an academic career.[1] His Berlin friends, too, expected him to pursue a political career in some guise "because his energetic personality is unlikely to be confined forever by the bonds of scholarly activity,"[2] especially after Miquel began to notice the young political economist. In this period, Max Weber undoubtedly entertained thoughts of political activity, and this was true even after he accepted an extraordinary professorship in commercial and German law in 1893. If he nevertheless made no attempt to win a secure political position, the reasons were primarily personal. Although his volcanic nature urged him on to active politics, he did not feel at home on the tactical field of daily political strategy. His capacity for critically analyzing political phenomena was too great for him to concentrate on the narrow area of the immediately practicable—a

1. Letter of 18 February 1892, *Jugendbriefe*, p. 339. Compare letter to Hermann Baumgarten of 31 December 1889, ibid., p. 323.

2. Hermann Schumacher, Weber article in *Deutsches Biographisches Jahrbuch* (Jena, 1917–20); see also Weber's later testimony: "Herr von Miquel und die Landarbeiterenquête des Vereins für Sozialpolitik," *Sozialpolitisches Zentralblatt* 8, (1898/99): 640 ff.

necessity for an active politician. Above all, the practical politician does not remain committed to one position but relativizes it just as he relativizes those of his opponents. Weber, as we have seen, deplored the loss of the "naïve enthusiasm" that had characterized the generation who founded the Reich. He lacked the necessary illusions to throw passion and energy into a struggle for specific political ideals at a time when goals could only be more limited. He was not enough of a fighter to let one goal exclude all others; his real vocation was to be an observer and describer of politics, not an active politician who had to view the most immediate issue as also the most important one.

No doubt Weber was not thinking along these lines at the time. His feet were not yet firmly on the ground; he felt crippled by liberal decadence and even the fight against the Conservatives in the East Elbian agricultural labor question appeared to him of secondary political importance. And so he left the door to politics half open and waited. For the time being he was content with his quasi-political activities within the framework of the Verein für Sozialpolitik and the Evangelisch-sozialer Kongress, both of which provided him with influential forums. When, in 1895, as the result of his outstanding analysis of the East Elbian agricultural labor question, he was offered the chair in political economy at Freiburg, he readily accepted it. Unlike his later appointments, the call to Freiburg did not mean a farewell to politics.[3] On the contrary, he believed he would be able to have an effective impact with a chair in political economy at a time when no party forum was available to him. In his inaugural academic address of May 1895, he stated this openly: "The science of economic policy is a *political* science. It is the servant of politics, not the transient politics of today's rulers and ruling classes, but the permanent political interests of the nation and its power."[4] The inaugural address was in no way an attempt to demonstrate scholarly qualifications: in it, Weber came close to developing his political program. The address should therefore be judged as the most significant documentation that we have of Max Weber's political philosophy until the war years. Arnold Bergstraesser has justly chosen to view this speech as the takeoff point of his critical analysis of the great sociologist's political and scholarly work.[5]

With unparalleled precision and ruthlessly consistent arguments, Weber outlined the political ideas he had developed in his studies of the East Elbian land laborers, and put them into the context of a universal

3. Weber also associated the acceptance of the Heidelberg and Vienna chairs with the intention of withdrawing from active political life. See below, chap. 5, sec. 3, and end of chap. 7.

4. *Pol. Schr.*, p. 14.

5. Arnold Bergstraesser, "Max Webers Antrittsvorlesung in zeitgeschichtlicher Perspektive," *Vierteljahrshefte für Zeitgeschichte* 5 (1957): 209 ff.

analysis of the historical situation of the German Reich, five years after the departure of the great "pilot" Bismarck. His political convictions could not be fully suppressed by the confines of an academic address. He offered his astonished and somewhat shocked listeners far more: a political confession, full of unorthodox views and radical theses that gave no quarter to the audience's preconceived notions or to generally accepted opinions. "With my inaugural lecture," he wrote to his brother Alfred, "I aroused general consternation about the brutality of my opinions. The Catholics were just about the happiest, since I dealt a firm blow to 'ethical culture.' "[6] In fact, it would not be amiss to ask whether the temperament of the political fighter did not push the scholar a little too far into the background.

This is especially surprising when we consider that Weber took issue with Treitschke precisely because of the historian's political effectiveness at the lectern, and that later Weber was to become a passionate proponent of a ban on political judgments in the lecture hall. "Of all the kinds of prophecy" he viewed "*professorial prophecy* as the only one that was completely inadmissible," he wrote later.[7] It appears paradoxical, though it is very characteristic of Weber, that in this inaugural lecture, saturated as it was with politics and value judgments, he also laid the foundations of the theory of objectivity and pure science that he was later to champion so heatedly. In his lecture Weber demonstrated that science could not develop the final value criteria for evaluating its subjects. These criteria could not be arrived at empirically but stemmed from a completely heterogeneous sphere of values. The sharpness with which Max Weber stressed the autonomy of values vis-à-vis science, and simultaneously disavowed any universally objective values, can be attributed above all to Nietzsche's influence. That influence, noticeable here for the first time, continued to mark Weber's thinking.[8]

Citing East Elbian agricultural conditions, Weber pointed out that the concept of "productivity" could not be an objective, value-free principle for judgment in matters of national economy. The productivity argument urged the retention of large agricultural units in the east; but the cause of German survival required a self-sufficient economic system that did not

6. Letter of 17 May 1895; original in Weber papers.

7. Max Weber, *Gesammelte Aufsätze zur Wissenschaftslehre* (Tübingen, 1922; 3d ed., ed. Johannes Winckelmann, Tübingen, 1968), (hereafter cited as *Wissenschaftslehre*), p. 492.

8. Cf. Robert Eden's Harvard dissertation (available to me in manuscript), "Political Leadership and Philosophic Praxis: A Study of Weber and Nietzsche." For the general relationship between Weber and Nietzsche, see my article "Universalgeschichtliches und politisches Denken bei Max Weber," *Historische Zeitschrift* 201 (1965), pp. 571 ff, as well as Eugène Fleischmann, "De Weber à Nietzsche," *Archives Européennes de Sociologie* 5 (1964).

produce for the market. The interests of productivity directly conflicted here with the national interest. At the same time, Weber opposed the application to political economy of unconsciously unclear value criteria that were in part eudaemonistic and in part moral. He wanted to ban eudaemonistic ideals from economics altogether. The hidden future of human history is inscribed above the gate through which we must seek the dream of peace and human prosperity: "Lasciate ogni speranza."[9] Weber also rejected the ethical approach of the older school of the Katheder-sozialisten, who, under the influence of the Hegelian philosophy of government, considered justice to be the highest guiding principle of all social policy. Weber wished to substitute the concept of *nation* as the only valid ultimate principle, transcending all such ideal values. "Economics as an explanatory and analytical science is *international*; but as soon as it involves *value judgments* it is linked to that expression of mankind that is peculiar to each nation. . . . The economic policy of a German state and the evaluative criteria of a German economic theorist can therefore only be German."[10]

Theodor Heuss believed Max Weber to be "an instinctive nationalist," and the tone at least of the Freiburg inaugural address seems to support this judgment.[11] Weber consciously styled himself in the address as an economic nationalist and passionately disputed the belief that "nationalistic" evaluative criteria as well as "national egoism" in economic policy should be consigned to the rubbish heap.[12] He continued to take this view without reservations even after he came to question the conclusions of his Freiburg inaugural address.[13] "Already in my Freiburg inaugural address," he wrote fifteen years later to some Freiburg professors, "immature as it may have been in many ways, I supported the sovereignty of national ideals in the realm of practical politics, including the so-called social policy . . . at a time when the great majority of my fellow scholars were taken in by the fraud of the so-called social monarchy. At the time I also stressed very deliberately that politics is not a profession with a moral foundation, nor can it ever be."[14]

The immediate pretext for Weber's blunt support of "national egoism" as the focal point of all economic policy was the Polish question. He wished to see the national state take energetic measures to protect itself

9. *Pol. Schr.*, p. 12. There is a Nietzsche-like spirit here too, characterized by a combination of pessimism and absolute freedom from illusions.

10. Ibid., p. 13.

11. Theodor Heuss, *Deutsche Gestalten* (Stuttgart, 1947), p. 382.

12. *Pol. Schr.*, p. 13.

13. Later, Weber described his inaugural address as an immature product of youth; cf. *Werk und Person*, p. 349; but the reference here cannot be traced.

14. *Lebensbild*, p. 416.

against the Polish wave in eastern Germany, regardless of the economic consequences to those affected. He again designated the closing of the eastern border to Polish immigrants as a necessary step. It is not accidental that he mentioned Bismarck here: "A 'class-conscious' large landowner at the head of Prussia excluded them in the interests of defending our nationality, and the despised enemy of the agrarians [Caprivi] let them in in the interest of the large landowners, who are the only beneficiaries of the migration."[15] Once again, he demanded a large-scale, systematic policy of internal colonization in the east. Weber anticipated that a systematic settlement policy would have a great impact upon German nationality. He favored a policy that included soil enrichment of all purchased land before German settlement. "A few villages, each with a dozen German homes, will eventually *Germanize* many square miles."[16]

For Max Weber, the issue of the East Elbian land laborers served primarily as a point of departure for a discussion of the international political situation overall. He described the denationalization process that he saw taking place in the east as an especially vivid example of the eternal battle of the nationalities for living space and self-determination. He viewed this battle as one of the fundamental sociopolitical laws of his time. The events in Germany east of the Elbe seemed to teach one thing above all: that the advance of capitalism, accompanied by the destruction of an older static social structure, necessarily sharpened tensions between nations just as it sharpened class conflict. The capitalist economic structure freed each individual and each nationality from their inherited bonds and aroused them to new struggles, especially in the field of formally free economic competition. In this manner, the struggle of nationalities stretched beyond the governmental and cultural sphere to the whole area of economic life. National self-preservation and economic growth were two sides of the same coin; the national economic community was only another form of the old competition between nations.

In Weber's opinion, this situation was intensified by the fact that the capitalist economic order, in contrast to earlier economic systems, did not necessarily favor physically and intellectually superior nations. The Polish migrant workers, precisely *because* of their lower standard of living, were in a position to drive out the German agricultural workers as a result of *capitalist* economic conditions. Weber emphasized that it was not always true that natural selection in the free competition of opposing powers favored the more highly developed or the indigenous nationality.[17] It was precisely this situation that gave economic policy makers a

15. *Pol. Schr.*, p. 10.

16. Ibid., p. 11 n.1. Compare also Delbrück's polemic against Weber's position on the Polish question in the *Preussische Jahrbücher* 81 (1895): 389n.

17. *Pol. Schr.*, pp. 9, 17.

far-reaching responsibility. Policy must not be oriented solely to supposedly objective, purely economic principles, but it must seek the preservation and advancement of nationality as the highest principle. Policy makers must develop appropriate measures that secure the nation even under unfavorable economic conditions. Ostensibly pure scientific value systems of whatever variety always appeared to stand in the way of such a consciously national economic policy. Therefore Weber strove to refute the very existence of scientifically valid normative categories. At the outset, his program for a value-free science rested largely on an effort to establish the ideal of the national state as the sole indisputable standard. Weber thereby opposed a framework based on eudaemonist precepts or principles of justice. He feared that the explosive situation he anticipated in the approaching struggle between nations for economic and political self-assertion made such an idealistic science not only utopian but dangerous. "There is no *peace* even in the economic *battle* for existence; only those who can accept the appearance of peace for reality can believe that the future promises peace and contentment for our descendants."[18]

2. The Relentlessness of the Power Struggle: The "Diabolical" Character of Power

If the Freiburg inaugural address "shocked" its listeners, it did so above all because Weber bluntly and unrestrainedly depicted the political sphere as a relentless power struggle. "We cannot lead our descendants to peace and contentment," he said unambiguously, "but only into the endless battle to maintain and expand our national culture and people."[19] It was this emphasis on the factor of power that first gave Weber's passionate appeal to national sentiments its cutting edge. All those who knew Weber personally were fascinated—and frequently repelled—by the extraordinary sharpness and defiance of compromise in his concept of power.[20] Weber emphasized the will and the instinct to power as the basic qualities of the politician. For Weber, the struggle for power was a basic element not only in the governmental organization of a people but in all cultural life. "You can change the means, the circumstances, even the basic course and those who are responsible for it, but you cannot put the struggle itself aside. . . . 'Peace' means the displacement of the form of struggle or of the enemy in battle, or of the circumstances of battle, or finally the chance of selection, and nothing else."[21] If struggle was in itself

18. Ibid., p. 12.
19. Ibid., p. 14.
20. Conversations with Else Jaffé, Alfred Weber, and Eduard Baumgarten always returned to this.
21. *Wissenschaftslehre*, p. 517.

the basis of all human association, capitalism, in particular, meant a relentless economic war under the principle of formally free competition. Capitalism made struggle even more unavoidable and inevitable in the sphere of the state, especially in international relations.

Weber did not hesitate to employ the Darwinist terminology of the "struggle for existence" and the "survival" of the fittest, in order to describe the inexorable character of this "struggle of man with man" for "elbow room," although he later rejected and fought all biological theories and concepts in the field of social science as unscientific.[22] In 1896, Weber accused the *Nationalsozialen* (National Socialists) of "miserabilism" because they practiced a politics of social empathy void of any sense of power and of the need for social selection; and he sharply attacked Naumann's daily *Die Zeit* for advising moderation in the Polish question. "Politics is a tough business, and those who take responsibility for seizing the spokes of the wheel of political development in the fatherland must have strong nerves and should not be too sentimental to practice secular politics. Those who wish to involve themselves in secular politics must above all be without illusions and . . . recognize the fundamental reality of an ineluctable eternal war on earth of men against men."[23]

Max Weber's concept of power is even reflected in his masterwork *Wirtschaft und Gesellschaft* (*Economy and Society*) in spite of its careful and concerted effort at scholarly objectivity.[24] In this work, Weber developed the typology of a specific "prestige of power" which, independent of all concrete culture, national, or other ideally or materially oriented political goals, strives for power and the exercise of power purely in and for itself and achieves a characteristic power ethos that becomes tranfigured as "the honor of power."[25] The following pages will demonstrate repeatedly the extent to which the "prestige of power" influenced Weber's own life and work. It is therefore not surprising that Weber *formally* defined all political institutions in terms of their potential for exercising effective power, and that he viewed the modern state's basic sphere as the monopoly of the legitimate exercise of power.[26]

22. See *Pol. Schr.*, p. 9, note 1; see also "Diskussionsreden auf dem 1. Deutschen Soziologentag," German sociologists' convention on Ploetz's lecture "Race and Society" and "Diskussionsreden auf dem 2. Soziologentag" on Oppenheimer's lecture "Racial Theory and Philosophy of History." Max Weber, *Gesammelte Aufsätze zur Soziologie und Sozialpolitik* (Tübingen, 1924), pp. 456 ff. and 488 ff. Also *Wirtschaft und Gesellschaft*, pp. 236 f.

23. Minutes of the representative assembly of all National Socials, Erfurt, 1896, p. 45. Also *Pol. Schr.*, pp. 28 f.

24. Cf. also the casuistry of the concepts "struggle" and "selection," *Wirtschaft und Gesellschaft*, pp. 20 f.

25. *Wirtschaft und Gesellschaft*, p. 520.

26. Ibid., p. 519; compare *Pol. Schr.*, pp. 505 f. Also see the critique of W. Hennis,

It is natural to attribute Max Weber's preoccupation with the concept of power to the historical development of German liberal thought. In 1848, the liberals' idealistic political goals could not be achieved because they lacked the physical power to implement them. They subsequently witnessed how Bismarck, who did not shy from a bloody internecine war with Austria, achieved the most important goal of the liberal movement with the power of the Prussian military state: a German national state. As a result, under the impact of Bismarck's victorious power politics, the German middle class significantly changed its attitude to power. Realpolitik replaced idealistic dreaming as the dominant ideal in a whole epoch of German bourgeois political thought. Indeed, the experience of Bismarck's statecraft should weigh heavily in any discussion of Max Weber's concept of power. It was precisely their instinct for political power that led Weber to admire, half against his will, the Prussian Junker "class" and especially its chief representative, the creator of the Reich.[27] When Weber repeatedly preached the "will to power" to the bourgeoisie, when he deplored the fact that the rising working class lacked the "great national power instinct" that was the precondition of any successful national policy, the experience of the traditional liberals' negative relation to power both past and in part in even greater measure in the present, was not far from his mind.[28] But this does not mean that Weber's concept of power should be traced directly to the "blood and iron pattern" of Bismarck's politics, as J. P. Mayer has tried to do.[29] Weber did not hold such a limited and unbalanced view of Bismarck's policies. The young Weber recognized the unfortunate side of naïve "Bismarckism": the uncritical admiration of mere power and purposeless Realpolitik. Weber recognized the negative impact that great and successful power politics could have on the popular consciousness, even when the people did not participate in these politics at a responsible level. He complained that German literati—whom he could not resist discussing with a certain contempt—idolized Bismarck "not because of the nobility of his commanding intellect, but exclusively because of the impact of the violence and artfulness in his methods as a statesman: his apparent or real ruthlessness."[30]

We would therefore be in error if we viewed Weber as a Realpolitiker in the negative sense who tied political action exclusively to reason of state and a narrow drive for success. His political theories were ultimately

Vierteljahrshefte für Zeitgeschichte 7, no. 1 (1959): 20 f; and Christian von Ferber, *Die Gewalt in der Politik* (Stuttgart, 1970,) especially, pp. 54 ff.

27. Even in the inaugural address, *Pol. Schr.*, pp. 19 f.
28. *Verhandlungen des evangelisch-sozialen Kongresses*, 1894, p. 81.
29. *Max Weber in German Politics*, 2d ed. (London, 1956), p. 119.
30. *Pol. Schr.*, p. 311.

rooted in ethical and cultural value judgments.[31] Weber certainly employed the concept of Realpolitik. He believed that constructive policy required power politics rather than politics based on ideological principles. But he always avoided the superficial use of the concept of power that he observed in his contemporaries.

Weber carefully avoided emphasizing "success" and distanced himself from all pragmatic arguments of this kind.[32] "On the whole, people have the inclination," he noted, "to adapt strongly to those things that promise success or temporary success—in itself easily understandable—not only in the means or the method by which they hope to achieve their final ideals, but even to the extent of giving up these very ideals. In Germany, people try to embellish such behavior with the slogan 'Realpolitik' "[33] "Adaptation" as a principle of life had a completely negative connotation in Weber's rigorous theories, since he always tended to say, "that's the way it is," without regard to temporary tactical aims.[34]

Nevertheless, Max Weber held it to be a comparable ethical duty to make a sober assessment of the necessary role of power politics in achieving political values. It was not sufficient to satisfy momentary ethical ideals without attention to concrete results and consequences. He expressed the old liberal alternatives of real and ideal politics in his dichotomy between an ethic of responsibility and an ethic of conscience.[35]

31. Mayer's presentation does this completely: "Weber was already thoroughly at home in the realm of German 'Realpolitik,' " he points out with the naïve equation of Realpolitik with Machiavellian lack of conscience that Weber strongly opposed; *Max Weber in German Politics*, p. 33.

32. Among the characteristic comments: letter to Baumgarten of 25 April 1887 and letter to Toennies of 9 May 1909, cited below, chap. 5, note 152. Weber was bitterly opposed to that "type of 'satisfied' German for whom it was impossible not to support whatever was 'presently successful' with a breast inflated by Realpolitik." See *Archiv für Sozialwissenschaft und Sozialpolitik* 22, supplement, p. 108. In 1906, he distanced himself from those Germans who had acquired the "systematic habit of 'thinking Realpolitikly.' " *Archiv für Sozialwissenschaft und Sozialpolitik* 23, supplement, p. 235. Also *Pol. Schr.*, p. 169: "Cultural tasks? The so-called modern German 'Realpolitiker' shrugs his shoulders about them. It is unique: Other nations carry on Realpolitik and do not chatter about it. But the German must turn Realpolitik into a slogan, which he then embraces with all the ardor of feminine emotion (I have to say this)." Ibid., p. 282: "today's ignorant philistines of 'Realpolitik.' " Weber's definition of Realpolitik, as well as the concept that he would have wished for it to have, *Wissenschaftslehre*, p. 515: "Application of extreme methods in a given situation" in contrast to "application from a choice of various possible final positions on the temporarily effective or apparent chance of realizing one of them (that kind of 'Realpolitik' that has brought our policy so many noteworthy successes in the past twenty-seven years)." (1913.)

33. *Wissenschaftslehre*, p. 513.

34. Compare the letter of 15 July 1909 to Frau Gnauck-Kühne: "My decisive inner requirement is 'intellectual honesty': I say, 'what is.' " Weber papers.

35. See Theodor Schieder, "Das Verhältnis von politischer und gesellschaftlicher Verfassung und die Krise des bürgerlichen Liberalismus," *Historische Zeitschrift* 177 (1954): 55.

The coolly realistic character of his theory of political power necessarily linked the ethic of responsibility with an assessment of the chances for success. In his view, this was clearly the politician's ethic.

Weber insisted that a politician ought to take full responsibility for the concrete results of his actions or of his failure to act. He ought also to give a rational accounting of his actions. Only then could he consider his responsibility with a clear conscience and properly give priority to ultimate ethical values in the light of the situation.[36] A concern for the real concrete situation forced a constant compromise in the sphere of values. The politician may not merely comfort his conscience with the knowledge of having been faithful to a "just" object and totally consistent with his principles, whether he succeeded or failed. Since he is responsible for the fate and the material existence of other men, he cannot avoid the "uncompromisable conflict" that is attached to setting ethical priorities. He cannot fall back upon the more comfortable ploy of leaving this task to a doctrine or even a "revealed" religion, although this would satisfy his conscience.[37]

Weber's intellectual honesty prevented him from concealing the tension between the requirements of political ethics firmly centered on the concept of power and those arising from normative ethics of duty, especially Christian ethics. He did not hesitate to point this out formally: "*Ethics* is perhaps not the only thing in the world that is [normatively] 'valid.' Other value spheres exist alongside in which values can be realized only by someone who takes ethical 'responsibility' upon himself. This is especially true of the sphere of political action. In my opinion, it would be cowardly to deny the tensions with ethics that exist in this sphere through recourse to a superficially universal Weltanschauung."[38] For Weber, the conflict between irrationally based fundamental value systems was as irreconcilable as the opposition between 'God' and 'Devil.'[39] In "Politics as a Vocation," he wrote: "He who meddles with politics, which means with power and violence," makes a pact with

36. Cf. Weber's statement to Brentano: "The ultimate determinants of policy arise from highly personal *values* that are weighed against each other, *not* from 'logic.' The latter engenders a logically oriented sect, which remains powerless." Letter of 16 September 1912, Brentano papers.

37. Weber to Robert Wilbrandt: "I believe that unsettled *conflict*, and therefore the necessity for constant *compromises*, dominates the sphere of values. No one knows *how* compromises should be made, unless a 'revealed' *religion* will forcibly decide." Letter of 2 April 1913, Weber papers.

38. From "Der Sinn der Wertfreiheit in den nationalökonomischen Wissenschaften" (1917), *Wissenschaftslehre*, p. 504. The bracketed places in the original manuscript: the assessment for the Verein für Sozialpolitik about the question of value judgments (1913). This has been published in *Werk und Person*, p. 117.

39. *Wissenschaftslehre*, p. 507; compare pp. 469 ff.

"diabolical powers." It is not true "that only good can come out of good and that only evil can come out of evil" in the politician's trade.[40]

Weber did not believe that any norms could be capable of providing a morally secure orientation in the unavoidable conflict of political value systems. "The relative weight of values caught in a conflict where none can be fully realized" cannot be determined according to formal rules. "A formal ethic is least capable of providing a basis for judgment when the realization of transethical values requires the breaking of ethical norms."[41] Weber was convinced that the politician who acts responsibly must come to terms with this conflict between political and ethical values and, in doing so, is thrown back upon the irrationality of his own personality. The charismatic-irrational core of his concept of politics as a vocation, in the Puritan sense of calling, is very apparent here.

Like Machiavelli, Max Weber assumed that power took primacy in the conflict of duties and idolized the model of those citizens who, in Machiavelli's words, "held the greatness of their native city to be of greater importance than the salvation of their souls." It was a contemptible weakness to recoil from the unavoidable use of power. Weber, who always tended to argue with the use of dichotomies (professionalization here, charismatic leadership there, extreme intellectual rationalism on the one side, division of the sphere of values from the area of rational knowledge on the other), emphasized these contradictions to the *n*th degree. He went so far as to designate the ethic of the Sermon on the Mount not only as incompatible with all political action but as an ethic that lacked dignity.[42]

Max Weber has been accused of teaching the German nation a "new Machiavellianism of the steel age" because of these views and because of his uncompromising support of the power state.[43] Yet, as much as his work is reminiscent of the great Florentine's, his ideas on power were even more firmly rooted in convictions of value of a transethical sort. Weber, unlike Machiavelli, was fully aware of the tragic nature of this conflict. It is characteristic of him that he continued to wrestle with the idea that political activity was dangerous for the "health of the soul." Machiavelli's residual Catholicism only led him to hint at this. There is no trace in Weber's work of the aesthetic glorification of great power politics that we find repeatedly in Machiavelli's writings. It was only because politics was "also a matter of belief," for Weber, because the choice of

40. *Pol Schr.*, p. 554.

41. Fragment about the possibility of a normative ethics, about 1912. Weber papers. Recently published in *Werk und Person*, pp. 399 f.

42. "Politik als Beruf," p. 550; cf. "Wissenschaft als Beruf," *Wissenschaftslehre*, pp. 604 ff.

43. Mayer, *Max Weber in German Politics*, pp. 109, 117 f.

served all political action could only arise out of the belief in ultimate values, that he was forced to face the conflict between the political and ethical spheres of values. It was the *conscientiously ethical* component of his theory of political power that led him to take such an extreme stand on power politics. It is therefore no accident that in great moments of political decision the "politician of conviction" aways won out over the sober Realpolitiker. The seeking and holding of power were only justified in defense of ultimate values. The duty to use power if necessary to implement these values was then inescapable. In Weber's view, to make power relations the sole measure of immediate political goals revealed a contemptible lack of character. He expressly warned of the ever-present danger for every politician—"enjoying power merely for its own sake without intrinsic aims." The mere "power politician," he wrote in "Politics as a Vocation," "the idol of a cult in our country, may get strong effects, but in practice his work leads nowhere and is devoid of meaning."[44]

We can conclude that Max Weber was far from the sterile ideology of mere power politics, an ideology that formed the faith of many educated Germans and especially the members of the Pan-German League until the First World War. It is to his credit that he recognized at an early stage that this variety of power politics was merely irresponsible swaggering, a special form of group hysteria, which was alien to any sincere will to action and the opposite of courage. He opposed such attitudes on the ground of power politics itself, and he recognized that they could only endanger the success of foreign policy.

Max Weber rejected, no less strenuously, all political ideologies based on the ethic of conviction. He did so by affirming the ethic of responsibility as the basis of political action and by an outspoken defense of the uses of power, linked with personal ethical rigor.[45] For Weber, the prototypical movement based on an ethic of conviction was anarchism, which committed revolutionary acts purely out of conviction about the basic injustice of the modern social structure, without concern for success or the immediate concrete effects. In Weber's eyes, an anarchist assassination served no concrete purpose but was merely a practical sign of belief in the truth of anarchist teaching.[46] For this reason he saw anarchism as the exact opposite of responsible politics. Weber opposed pacifist ideologies even more vigorously. When in 1916 Gertrud Bäumer publicly discussed with a Swiss pacifist the relations between "evangelical laws"

44. *Pol. Schr.*, p. 547.

45. It is also characteristic of this that in the caption draft of his lecture "Politics as a Vocation" (depicted in *Werk und Person*, picture 16), he first wrote "Power-" instead of "responsibility-policy" as the alternative to policy of conscience.

46. Cf. *Wissenschaftslehre*, p. 514.

and the "laws of the fatherland," Weber came to her aid with a very sharp position statement.[47] He derided the utopianism of philanthropic pacifism, which he accused of ignoring reality, and insisted that only two real alternatives existed: "Tolstoy's consistency" or the recognition of the unavoidable power struggle in the world. Whoever makes use of foreign labor takes advantage of the loveless, merciless economic war of existence, which is not in the least concealed by the bourgeois euphemism "peaceful cultural work."[48]

Max Weber affirmed struggle as a basic mode of human existence. He drew the consequences of this without intellectual compromise. Anyone with the courage to support his convictions fully and consistently, whatever these were, merited Weber's unlimited respect. For these reasons it was possible for him to have great respect for convinced pacifists when they had sufficient will to act on their consciences without compromise; indeed, he was even fascinated by them. At the second Lauenstein meeting at the beginning of October 1917, assembled at the invitation of the Jena publisher Eugen Diederichs to spread his ideals of spiritual aristocracy into the political arena, Weber encountered several left-leaning artists and intellectuals who stood for pacifist ideas.[49] In the winter of 1917/18, socialist and pacifist students, among them Klaus Uphoff and Ernst Toller, were frequently guests in Weber's house. Although he had no brief for their program, which called upon the people to lay down their arms in defiance of their governments, he nevertheless fought for the release of Toller, who had been arrested for planning a general strike.[50] He could not refuse to aid a convinced pacifist when he was genuinely prepared to follow "Tolstoy's road."

Jacob Burckhardt first coined the famous phrase that "power is evil in itself" and that it is an inordinate desire that is "*eo ipso* unrealizable" and therefore brings "unhappiness" to those who hold it as well as to others.[51] Weber also recognized the diabolical character of power, which necessarily sometimes places politicians in a state of "ethical" guilt. But Weber's concept of power was in some ways at the opposite pole from that of the great Swiss historian and thinker. Weber, to a much greater extent than Burckhardt, affirmed the state as the prerequisite to cultural

47. First printed in the monthly *Die Frau*; here in *Pol. Schr.*, pp. 142 ff.

48. Ibid., p. 144. Also compare the letter to Professor Goldstein of 13 November 1918, *Lebensbild*, pp. 614 f; also *Wirtschaft und Gesellschaft*, pp. 20 f.

49. Cf. also Knoll, *Führungsauslese in Liberalismus und Demokratie* (1957), pp. 190 f.

50. Weber also intervened for Toller later. I am grateful to Professor Hans Rothfels for telling me about a Berlin party meeting at which Toller spoke up in the discussion. When some of the participants tried to prevent him from speaking because of his radical ideas, Weber went up to the lectern, placed a protective hand on Toller's slight shoulder, and said: "Let him speak. He is a man to be taken seriously. He has something to say."

51. *Weltgeschichtliche Betrachtungen*, Kröner edition, 7th printing (1949), p. 97.

development, and unlike Burckhardt he viewed powcr as something positive. He considered it a natural tool that made all creative social acts possible. With a radicalism reminiscent of Hobbes and, especially, Nietzsche, he posited struggle as the fundamental principle of all cultural life.

His utterly pessimistic opinion of the political conditions of his age led Weber to believe that a growing intensity in international relations was inevitable. The idea of international understanding, which was suggested to Weber in 1910 as an alternative to a policy of armaments on all sides, was one he never seriously pursued.[52] There is scarcely another Wilhelmine figure who affirmed the "inexorable struggle of autonomous cultural institutions" with such a deep sense of responsibility, and who so relentlessly drew out its consequences.[53] Even in 1919, when national "power politics" appeared to lead only to crisis, and the League of Nations promised to bring about a new, more peaceful age, Weber expressly reaffirmed the ideal of power. Weber was a child of his times in his typical Wilhelmine overestimation of the role of practical political power in the political arena, even if he took this position only in the service of deeply held convictions.

3. The Concept of Nation in Weber's Thought

The nature of Max Weber's concept of the nation is central to his political value system; the national state's power was a fundamental value for him and all political goals were consequently subordinate to the nation's requirements. "I have viewed politics only in a national framework—not only foreign policy, but all politics," he could say with justice in 1916.[54] "*I would not fire one shot or agree to one penny in war loans* if this war were anything but a national one."[55] Weber remained true to this emphatic nationalist position all his life, and it would be a mistake to underestimate this side of his nature, which today seems so tied to his own time. At the time of the 1918 collapse, his national feelings were stirred precisely because so many had turned away from the national ideal. He ended his fervent speech in the stormy peoples' assemblies in December 1918 in this vein, "What is the future of German nationalism?" and answered the

52. Also compare below, chap. 6, sec. 1. Falk's criticism of Weber begins here: "Why is the principle of international understanding lacking in Weber's concept of Democracy?" In Falk's view,Weber thought a German democracy, supported by the bourgeoisie and the working class together, was only possible under the banner of German imperialism. In our view, Weber believed the reverse. See Falk, "Democracy and Capitalism in Max Weber's Sociology," *Sociological Review* 27 (London, 1935): 387.

53. Cf. Eckart Kehr, *Schlachtflottenbau und Parteipolitik* (Berlin, 1930), p. 403.

54. *Pol. Schr.*, p. 157.

55. Letter of 16 July 1917, *Pol. Schr.* 1, p. 469 (incorrectly dated here.)

question himself: "He, who in the threatened German irredenta is not prepared to employ revolutionary methods and to risk scaffold and prison, should not in future be called a *nationalist*."[56]

Max Weber shared his strong nationalist feelings with his entire epoch. He was deeply impressed as a young man with Heinrich von Treitschke's powerful national fervor as much as he was influenced by Baumgarten to distance himself from a one-sided glorification of the power ideal. In his writings, Weber augmented Treitschke's theory of the moral character of the national state, which itself had been a nationalist particularization of the Hegelian idea of the state. The national state took the same place here that Jehovah had taken in the history of the ancient Hebrews.[57] In fact, for Weber, who was an unbeliever in the Christian sense, national sentiment clearly took on, to some degree, the form of faith in Germany. It became what once, in his work on the methodology of the social sciences, he had called a "value concept."[58]

It is therefore essential to determine what Max Weber actually understood by a "nation state." The decisive factor for Weber's concept of the national state was the existing German state; the "normative character of the real" also molded his political conceptualization. He viewed Bismarck's founding of the Reich as the complete fulfillment of the national goals of the liberal movement for German unity.[59] Like the overwhelming majority of his contemporaries, he was inclined to interpret Bismarck's policies retroactively as the fulfillment of the nation's real goals. "In his deeds, not in his words, the presumptions of Bismarck's policies were guided by the ideal of the German national state," he remarked as late as 1915.[60]

Weber, who otherwise analyzed Bismarck's policies with extraordi-

56. According to the report of the *Vossische Zeitung* on 12 December 1918. Further evidence below, chap. 8, sec. 2.

57. Cf. Christoph Steding, "Politik und Wissenschaft bei Max Weber" (diss., Breslau, 1932), p. 34. Steding attempts to explain all of Weber's political and scholarly work by reducing it entirely to "the subjectivity of Max Weber's self-nourishing personality." This methodological position is in direct contradiction to Weber's expressed insistence that a personality in the scholarly realm is one that serves the "purity of the subject." This is apart from the numerous unbelievable generalizations (Weber is a positivist, p. 23, nominalist, p. 24; as well as the incomprehensible assertion borrowed from H. J. Grab that Weber identified formal-mechanical natural science with science in general and that its methods were for Weber the model of all sciences, p. 61; Weber indeed challenged this position). It appears to us that such an approach to the work and the personality of the great sociologist is entirely inadequate.

58. *Gesammelte Aufsätze zur Wissenschaftslehre*, p. 262. Cf. Dieter Henrich, *Die Einheit der Wissenschaftslehre Max Webers* (Tübingen, 1952), p. 95.

59. Cf. Weber's address at the Verein für Sozialpolitik convention in 1893, *Gesammelte Aufsätze zur Soziologie und Sozialpolitik*, p. 85; also *Pol. Schr.*, p. 21.

60. *Pol. Schr.*, p. 128.

nary foresight and objectivity, was confined here by the national enthusiasm characteristic of the Wilhelmine epoch. He failed to perceive Bismarck's actually very different concept of the state as the bearer of order in the conflict of social powers. When Weber once stated that the Austrian dynasty was "from Bismarck's point of view an institution that sacrificed the participation of ten million Germans in the Reich in order to neutralize thirty million non-Germans politically," he was projecting his own views onto Bismarck.[61] For Weber, the "little Germany" solution to the German problem was never in question; he completely rejected "a pure division of the Austro-Hungarian nationalities into independent, homogeneous national states. . . . A federation of nationalities under a supernational government alone was possible there."[62] To this extent he defended the politically possible even if he viewed the national state organization of nations as ideal.

If Weber did not hesitate to adapt to the national tradition of the *kleindeutsch* state, it is also obvious that his views, from the beginning, were far from those of the *völkisch* theorists. His strong stand against the Polonization of eastern Germany until the turn of the century prompts the conclusion that he tended toward an ethnologically and linguistically oriented concept of the nation, even though a belief in the differing cultural levels of nationalities played a considerable role in this view. But Max Weber increasingly distanced himself thereafter from emotional national feelings based upon linguistic and ethnic peculiarities.

Weber soon recognized, with the sharp eye of a sociologist, that national consciousness was in no way dependent upon objective ethnic or linguistic factors. The ethnic self-assessment of a group, he observed, was seldom based on true ethnic homogeneity but merely on the subjective belief in such homogeneity. Weber emphasized that this belief in an ethnic community sprang primarily from a common political fate, membership in the same political community, and not from any objective anthropological kinship.[63] Nevertheless, this belief was considered "one of the most loaded and emotionally charged of concepts: that of the 'Nation.' "[64]

It is therefore logical that Weber rejected Herder's definition of nation as a linguistic community. He repeatedly defended this view with reference to the Alsatians, who were German by speech and inheritance, yet felt tied to the French nation because of the common experience of the French Revolution. The Alsatians therefore perceived the French nation as the bearer of a specific culture and viewed the French language as "the

61. Ibid., p. 449.
62. Ibid., p. 175.
63. *Wirtschaft und Gesellschaft*, p. 237.
64. Ibid., p. 242.

true language of culture."[65] The example of Switzerland also demonstrated that a linguistic community was by no means a necessary precondition of national consciousness; the expression "Swiss nation" could even be found in official acts of the Swiss Bundesrat.[66] With the growing democratization of modern society, the importance of linguistic factors necessarily increased.[67] Now the pretention of calling oneself an independent nation was attached "frequently and routinely to the common cultural possession of the linguistic community."[68] Nationality was therefore not a sociologically distinct concept for Max Weber; it ought to be defined "not from the standpoint of common qualities that establish the national community, but solely from the standpoint of the goal, . . . of an independent state."[69]

This represents a fundamental departure from a concept of nation based on objective ethnic or linguistic characteristics and a far-reaching approach to the western European idea of the nation state that includes every citizen who subjectively acknowledges his relationship to the state without reference to his ancestry. Renan designated this subjective concept of community in the masterful formulation of a *plébiscite de tous les jours*. For Weber, too, the subjective consciousness of community—directed to the existence of an individual state—was the decisive factor in national consciousness. But Weber went much farther than Renan's internally self-sufficient democratic concept of the nation; Weber perceived the decisiveness and fatefulness of a political unit's power in relation to other units for the creation of a specific national consciousness. "Common political destinies, common political struggles for life and death" weld a group of people into a nation. The subjective conviction of ethnic, linguistic, confessional, or cultural homogeneity was of secondary significance. The decisive factor in the development of national consciousness was conscious participation in the process of deciding on the power status of one's own state.

It is the concept of power which—fused with the concept of nation—gives the concept of nation its characteristic properties in Weber's thought. In the Freiburg inaugural address, he linked the concept of nation closely to the ideal of power. "The *national state*," Weber began, "is not something indefinite that is placed at an ever higher level the more

65. Ibid., p.242 f., p. 529; "Diskussionsreden auf dem 2. Deutschen Soziologentag," *Gesammelte Aufsätze zur Soziologie und Sozialpolitik*, p. 484.

66. *Wirtschaft und Gesellschaft*, p. 528; cf. "Diskussionsreden," p. 485: "It is possible to maintain that there is a special Swiss national feeling in spite of the lack of linguistic unity" (corrected to linguistic diversity).

67. Ibid.

68. *Wirtschaft und Gesellschaft*, p. 528.

69. "Diskussionsreden," p. 487.

its nature is veiled in obscurity; it is the secular organization of the nation's power."[70] Note the unconscious association of the religious pair of opposites, secular—otherworldly. Thereafter, political power gained even more importance in Weber's concept of nation. Nation and national power state became two sides of the same coin. A section of *Economy and Society* written in 1913 provides a clear example of the fact that "power" in itself had become the dominant component of Weber's national idea. "Time and again," Weber noted, "we find that the concept 'nation' directs us to political power. Hence, the concept seems to refer—if it refers at all to a uniform phenomenon—to a specific kind of pathos which is linked to the idea of a powerful political community of people who share a common language, or religion, or common customs, or political memories; such a state may already exist or it may be desired. The more power is emphasized, the closer appears to be the link between nation and state."[71]

Weber tried here to define his epoch's concept of nation objectively. Nation had become increasingly associated with imperialism. Nations sought not only cultural and governmental independence but a powerful political position in the world. It is not difficult to show that he himself was in full agreement, indeed that the desire for the power of his own political unit dominated his own national consciousness in quite specific terms, at the expense of its ethnic, linguistic, and cultural components. It is not uncharacteristic that Weber was not prepared unreservedly to concede to the Swiss and the Belgians the quality of "nations"—not because of their multilingual population or ethnic heterogeneity, as might be expected, but because of their "conscious renunciation of 'power' [by] becoming 'neutral' political commonwealths." He was only able to grant them a specific national consciousness in an almost negative manner, and even here the power ideal played a decisive role. He stressed the conscious opposition of the Swiss both to "power" itself and to all militaristic power structures with their unavoidable internal consequences. Thus had the Swiss national ideal developed, and thus was it nourished.[72]

In another section of *Economy and Society*, Max Weber traced national consciousness to the specific feelings of prestige of social classes who were ideologically oriented to the ideal of imperialistic great power status. Such a prestige-consciousness, which evolves purely from the power of one's own political system, can "be associated with a specific belief in a responsibility to one's descendants for the way power and prestige are divided between your own and foreign political communities." This "ideal passion of power prestige"—a few pages later Weber

70. *Pol. Schr.*, p. 14.
71. *Economy and Society*, p. 398.
72. A very informative passage, ibid., p. 243.

used the phrase "naked power prestige"—is modified under the influence of the culture-bearing classes within the contemporary state into the "idea of the nation."[73]

As dispassionately as Max Weber points out the sociological background of nationalism here, insofar as nationalism is linked directly to the interests of the privileged and influential classes, especially the intellectuals, there is little doubt that he himself was close to a concept of nation saturated with the prestige of power.[74] He had moved far from the idea of the purely "cultural nation." He was only able to accept the national idea in association with a governmental system that pursues power politics on a grand scale. The model of the Bismarckian state is quite clear here, a model that incorporated the Prussian power-state far more than it did the national state dreamed of by the Frankfurt National Assembly. Even more than this, it corresponded to the modification of the concept of nation into that of the power-state at a time when Europe was an armed camp and it was widely held that national culture could be preserved only by imperialistic policies. Weber, with his extraordinary emphasis on the element of power in his concept of nation, was an exponent of Wilhelmine nationalism, a nationalism increasingly oriented to the elemental potency of the state's political power.[75] Weber championed the idea that the national state bore a heavy responsibility in its conduct at home and abroad, "to its descendants for the way in which power and prestige were distributed among the nations." To this extent, he partially subscribed to the imperialistic elements of the national idea.

Nevertheless, the more Max Weber concerned himself with the state and the fate of its political power in the international struggle, the more he was drawn to moderation on the question of ethnic minorities. Weber's basic reversal in his position on Poland is a prime example. Here his national ideal was tested by a concrete political problem; rational insight and the clarification of the nationalist impetus of the 1890s led him to an unusually realistic position. For this reason, the development of his position on the Polish question deserves extensive discussion here.

From 1893 until his illness in 1898, Max Weber approached the "denationalization process" of the east with such sharpness and brutality that

73. Ibid., pp. 527 f.

74. Weber spoke of the "partially material, partially hypothetical interests" of hypothetical privileged classes through the existence of a national power image. "This means above all those who feel themselves to be specific participants of a specific 'culture' that is common to those who participate in the political structure." Ibid., p. 528. Cf. the author's more extensive discussion in *The Age of Bureaucracy: Perspectives on the Political Sociology of Max Weber* (Oxford, 1974), pp. 32 ff.

75. Cf. Ludwig Dehio, "Gedanken über die deutsche Sendung, 1900–1918," *Historische Zeitschrift* 173 (1952): 479 ff.

the Left, with some justice, accused him of being a wild chauvinist and fanatical Pole hater. He himself later recalled that "I was known as an enemy of the Poles."[76] In 1894, defending himself against the frequent voices that saw "a prejudicial appeal to national sensitivities" in his Polish demands, he claimed that the problem in the east touched not only a national question but one of material culture. The inflow of the Sachsengänger was accompanied by a general sinking of the cultural milieu.[77] To this extent, his anti-Polish position rested not only on emotional prejudices but also on important arguments. The sharpness of his statements, however, overstepped all limits. When, in 1896, Weber accused the National Socials of "miserabilism," the Polish question was an important reason.[78] Heinrich von Gerlach attacked the firebrands on the Polish question and condemned excessive nationalism on this issue in the National Social organ *Die Zeit*. Weber was furious: "He deplores the repression of the Poles to second-class German citizens. But the contrary is true: we have turned the Poles into human beings." Any other opinion Weber viewed as sentimental disregard of the fact of the inevitable power struggle.[79] Gerlach protested energetically at the time that "I will never go along with the Nietzschean master morality in politics," and thereby earned the lively applause of the National-sozialer Kongress.[80]

The main reason Max Weber joined the Pan-German League in 1893 was his search for support on the Polish question.[81] At the time, Weber also generally sympathized with the league's efforts to promote an active imperialist foreign policy in the public mind. Nor was Weber then a distinct opponent of the league's outspokenly *völkisch*-oriented national-

76. *Pol Schr.*, p. 173.

77. Cf. Weber's response to an attack on Quark at the Verein für Sozialpolitik convention in: "Die Entwicklungstendenzen der Lage der ostelbischen Landarbeiter," original version, *Archiv für Soziale Gesetzgebung und Statistik* 7 (1894): 36, note 1: "I am of the view that a Pole or a Mongol who was the ruler of the East would not act any differently than a German would if he were presented with the task of maintaining the worker's cultural level. To be sure, this one demonstrable material reference does not exhaust the meaning for me of membership in a nationality. Sentimental cosmopolitanism . . . neglects the fact that it is highly questionable whether these peoples . . . will benefit from living here. Certainly the reverse is true. The great masses of workers . . . will be forced with mathematical certainty into the customary living conditions of these 'interesting' populations . . . if there is free international competition in the labor market."

78. See below, chap. 5, sec. 3, especially the letter from Weber to his wife cited there which offers this as the primary motive for his sharp rejection of the National Socials' treatment of the Polish question.

79. *Protokoll über die Vertreter-Versammlung aller National-Sozialen in Erfurt, 1896*, pp. 48 f. Also *Pol. Schr.*, p. 28.

80. *Protokoll . . . 1896*, p. 54.

81. Cf. Alfred Kruck, *Geschichte des Alldeutschen Verbandes 1890–1939* (Wiesbaden, 1954), pp. 17 f.

ism. Only later would the league develop the sterile and politically ignorant qualities characterized by Class's leadership that Weber came to attack so sharply. Weber lectured on the Polish question in many local Pan-German League groups.[82] His hope that the league would join in the demand that the borders be closed to Polish migrant laborers and that a concerted governmental policy of internal colonization be implemented was fulfilled. At the first convention of the Pan-German League in 1894, a special Polish program was agreed to that demanded the sealing of the eastern frontier to migrant laborers and generally supported an outspokenly radical Germanization program.[83]

The Polish problem remained a central focus of Pan-German League agitation. Hugenberg, who was at that time a league leader and who served the Posen settlement commission for many years, especially championed the East Elbian agrarian question. In any case he altered the emphasis. He stressed the agricultural labor shortage and urged social reforms to keep the German worker on the land, rather than peasant colonization and closure of the frontier.[84] Weber left the Pan-German League in April 1899 because of the tendency within the league to accommodate to the conservatives' agricultural interests. The league, respecting its agrarian members, consistently avoided an energetic demand for the closing of the eastern border to Polish migrant laborers. In his resignation statement, Weber said that these circumstances "did not prevent him from lively sympathy for the league's efforts," nor did it weaken his "high personal regard for the leaders."[85]

Thus we cannot see Weber's resignation from the Pan-German League as evidence that he had begun to look "critically" upon "the nationalist point of view as a normative one, a position he had hitherto accepted."[86] Weber withdrew from the Pan-German League because it betrayed its national demands for vested interests, because it was not "uncompromisingly" national on the Polish question. On the other hand, it is unlikely that Weber would have long remained associated with the league as it moved increasingly in the direction of pure dilettantism and irresponsible chauvinism.[87] Moreover, he was never totally in agreement with the radical Polish demands of the Pan-Germans. He never spoke of a

82. Cf. *Lebensbild*, pp. 214, 237.

83. Otto Bonhard, *Geschichte des Alldeutschen Verbandes* (Berlin, 1920,) pp. 77 ff.

84. Cf. Lothar Werner, *Geschichte des Alldeutschen Verbandes* (Berlin, 1935), pp. 96 ff.

85. Letter of 22 April 1899, *Lebensbild*, pp. 237 f.; cf. *Pol. Schr.*, pp. 173 f.

86. Bergstraesser, "Max Webers Antrittsvorlesung," p. 213, who remarks that in 1895, Weber was ready to take a critical position about the national impulse as it had been expressed until then by leaving the Pan-German League. The national idea remained a lifelong principle for Weber, though the specific conceptual approach changed.

87. Compare the letter to Brentano of 5 June 1908, Brentano papers. Weber distanced himself here from "rabid pan-German anti-Semitism."

repressive Germanization policy to maintain the German character of the east, and proposed only economic measures that would not directly affect the East Elbian Poles but would only bring about an economic restructuring in favor of the Germans.

Throughout his life, Max Weber viewed the Polish question as a decisive factor in German politics. Admittedly, his militance against the Poles lost its edge as international problems became more important for him. As his national consciousness became more moderate and more firmly oriented to the idea of the state, he grew less directly concerned with the inroads of alien ethnic groups. And the difference in cultural level between Poles and Germans that had been a major factor in Weber's radical position tended to narrow. As a result of the total collapse of the German settlement policy, which in any event had employed methods that he considered contrary to the idea of large-scale peasant colonization, Weber became increasingly resigned on the question of the Poles.[88] However, the problem of the national minorities never lost its importance for him.

The decisive impulse for Weber's complete reorientation on the question of nationalities came from outside and from a totally unexpected quarter: Zemstvo liberalism during the 1905 revolution in Russia. Weber initially welcomed the Russian revolution, which he hoped would effect the liberal transformation of the czarist empire. A closer study of events led him to see no immediate chance of victory for Russian liberalism, constrained as it was between reaction and the rising social revolutionary mood of the peasant masses. As a result, the most that could be hoped for was a pseudoconstitutionalism. But the Russian liberals had his complete sympathy, and he thought a gradual dismantling of the authoritarian czarist system was possible.[89] The revolutionary events in Russia made so great an impression on him that he learned Russian in the course of three months; and, with the assistance of a Russian liberal, Bogdan Kistiakow-

88. Cf. Max Weber's memorandum on social policy of 15 November 1912, recently published by Bernhard Schäfer in *Soziale Welt* 18 (1967): 265 f.

88. "Zur Lage." (Selections are published in *Pol. Schr.* but the original printing will be cited here.) Cf. the critical remarks by Richard Pipes, "Max Weber und Russland,"*Aussenpolitik* 6 (1955): 630 ff. The author has profited much from Pipes's treatment; nevertheless, it is not free from misunderstandings. Among others, Pipes commits the error of attributing a citation of Koellreutter's from Spengler's *Decline of the West* to Weber: "We late men of the West (in the original it says *Abendlandes*) have become skeptics. Ideological systems will no longer confuse our heads. Programs belong in the last century." Ibid., p. 629. Cf. in this regard, Otto Koellreutter, "Die staatspolitischen Anschauungen Max Webers und Oswald Spenglers," *Zeitschrift für Politik* 14 (1925): 482 f. For light on Kistiakowsky, see Vladimir Slarosolskij, "Bogdan K. und das russische soziologische Denken," *Abhandlungen des Ukrainischen Wissenschaftlichen Institutes in Berlin* 2 (1929): 117 ff.

sky, an active member of the "Emancipation League," he wrote two extensive articles about the Russian revolution.[90]

Max Weber gave special attention to the problem of Polish-Russian relations, which played an important role in the revolutionary events. He was surprised to observe that Russian Zemstvo liberalism conceded much in the area of Polish autonomy.[91] The Cadets, too, accepted far-reaching autonomy for the nationalities in their program. The "Union for Emancipation" went even farther. Comparing the Russian liberals' Polish policy with that of Prussia, Weber saw that the former clearly had a greater chance of success since it appeared to succeed in bringing the Poles, at least Dmowski's national Polish movement, into loyal cooperation with the Russian imperial union. Weber anticipated an extraordinary growth in power for the Russian empire if it succeeded in making the non-Russian nationalities, including the Poles, willing members of the empire by conceding cultural autonomy through this policy. For Weber, the immense attractiveness of such a system for Congress Poland as well as for Prussian Poland was obvious. Here he saw a model of a truly liberal, democratic nationality policy that had the further advantage of serving the power interests of the government itself much better than a violent policy of oppression. Weber was so impressed that he was prompted to make a careful study of the nationalities program of Russian liberalism in the revolutionary period with the explicit rationale that "sooner rather than later the search for a solution to intracountry nationality problems in many places [would] become a 'practical' [necessity]."[92] He was also deeply interested in all plans to transform Russia into a genuine federation of nationalities because of the important international ramifications, especially in relation to the Polish question.

Under Kistiakowsky's influence, Weber discovered the works of the Ukrainian federalist Dragomanov, who he believed had brilliantly solved the problem of nationalities.[93] It appeared possible to Weber, if Dragomanov's proposals were adopted, to bring the interests of the individual Russian nationalities under the same roof as an all-Russian great power

90. "Zur Lage"; and "Russlands Übergang zum Scheinkonstitutionalimus," *Archiv für Sozialwissenschaft und Sozialpolitik* 23, supplement, pp. 1 ff. (hereafter cited as "Scheinkonstitutionalismus"). (Selections from this are also published in *Pol. Schr.*, but the original printing will be cited.)

91. "Zur Lage," pp. 30 ff.; cf. Georg von Rauch, *Russland; Staatliche Einheit und nationale Vielfalt* (Munich, 1953), pp. 155 f., 158 f.

92. "Zur Lage," p. 30.

93. At the time, Kistiakowsky was an editor of the political writings of M. P. Dragomanov (*The Collected Works of M. P. Drahomanov*, 2 vols., Paris, 1905); cf. "Zur Lage," p. 21, note 1.

policy. As early as 1884, Dragomanov had demanded a sweeping federalist transformation of Russia into separate "regions" with full cultural autonomy on the basis of ethnic borders.[94] Dragomanov had evolved from a "socialist" to a "national democrat."[95] Weber was greatly influenced by Dragomanov's basic thesis: "the idea of national *cultural* independence."[96] He attributed the Cadet program for the political autonomy of nationalities to Dragomanov's ideas—whether consciously or unconsciously.[97] Weber would later refer to Dragomanov's writings as fundamental for any treatment of nationality problems.[98]

In 1906, Weber concluded that one of "the lasting political achievements of the Russian Zemstvo movement" had been to "unify . . . bourgeois liberalism" across the barriers of the conflict of nationalities.[99] He failed to recognize the extent to which the Russian liberal movement's tolerant attitude to the national minorities was merely tactical because the aid of these minorities was essential to the success of the constitution. After the convocation of the radical second Duma, the liberal position changed significantly, indeed the Octobrists deserted altogether.[100] Moreover, it is questionable whether the Polish drive for independence could have been contained in the long run by the concession of broader autonomy. Even at the time, the Left under Pilsudski's leadership energetically fought association with Russia, and Dmowski's National Democrats were not especially fond of the czarist empire. During World War I, Weber severely criticized the liberal program of autonomy, but his pen was certainly guided by the passion of the battle against "Russian imperialism." "The small group of ideologues in Dragomanov's school who strove for the transformation of Russia into a truly equal federation of nationalities" seemed at this date to have become either "deceived deceivers" or fully without influence; and Polish autonomy was important only as a means of extending Russian power westward.[101]

Nevertheless, the Russian liberals' program for the nationalities in 1904 and 1905 influenced Weber decisively, especially when his political

94. Cf. Rauch, *Russland*, pp. 131 ff. A short synopsis of the writings of Dragomanov in: "Mykhaylo Drahomanov: A Symposium and Selected Writings," ed. I.L. Rudnytsky, *Annals of the Ukrainian Academy of Arts and Sciences in the USA 2* no. 1 (New York, 1952).

95. "Zur Lage," p. 39.

96. Ibid.

97. Ibid., p. 21f.

98. "Diskussionsrede auf dem 2. Deutschen Soziologentag," *Gesammelte Aufsätze zur Soziologie und Sozialpolitik*, p. 487; cf. *Pol. Schr.*, pp. 128 f; also: Vladimir Levnskij, "Volk, Nation und Nationalität," in *Abhandlungen des Ukrainischen Wissenschaftlichen Institutes in Berlin*, p. 144.

99. "Zur Lage," p. 30.

100. Cf. Rauch, *Russland*, pp. 156 ff.

101. *Pol. Schr.*, pp. 200 f.

sympathies for the liberals were strong. He became convinced that the interests of national minorities could be harmonized with the interests of a national power through the concession of far-reaching cultural autonomy. This had an immediate impact on his position on the Polish question. He rejected Prussian language policy—especially Bülow's language law, which sharply restricted the use of Polish in political assemblies. "To enforce the use of a particular language," Weber wrote to Friedrich Naumann in 1908, was "morally and politically impossible and nonsensical."[102] He also opposed the law of expropriation passed by the Prussian Landtag in the winter of 1907–8, which gave the government the power to expropriate large Polish landholdings; this was a last attempt to salvage the threatening fiasco of the colonization policy with drastic measures. Weber saw the law as valuable only as a pawn against the Poles, and then only in a harsher form: "in order to offer them, with this weapon in reserve, a national compromise along with the recognition of their 'cultural independence' (a Russian expression from the Cadet program!)."[103]

During the war, Max Weber energetically championed the concession of cultural autonomy to the Prussian Poles and an honorable understanding with them.[104] He also suggested the possibility of the "demarcation of local settlement regions" for each nationality,[105] and a solution of the language problem through "the encouragement of voluntary relocation of German settlers from the kingdom of Poland to Germany and the reverse."[106] In Weber's view, the international interests of the German state demanded such a policy of fair compromise with the Poles on the basis of cultural autonomy. He pointed out that "a state [need] not necessarily be a 'nation state' in the sense that it [oriented] its interests exclusively in favor of a single, dominant nationality." The state could "serve the cultural interests of several nationalities in a way that was in full harmony with the interests of the dominant nationality."[107] Weber rejected a return to the "idea of the state," as we now would call it; it would be impossible, he thought, since all culture was unavoidably nationally tied, to put the "idea of the state" in the "place of na-

102. Letter of 26 April 1908, *Pol. Schr.* 1, p. 454. Weber could justly say of himself later: "I never shared in the pan-German, foolish, and ineffective language policy toward the Poles." *Pol. Schr.*, p. 174; further, pp. 123 and 180.

103. In the previously cited letter to Naumann.

104. E.g., *Pol. Schr.*, pp. 173 f., also 178 ff.: "Die Polen-Politik" (from the *Frankfurter Zeitung*, 25 February 1917).

105. *Pol. Schr.*, pp. 123 and 180. Of course, Weber saw the difficulties. Ibid., pp. 174 f. and also in "Diskussionsreden auf dem 2. Deutschen Soziologentag 1912," *Gesammelte Aufsätze zur Soziologie und Sozialpolitik*, p. 491.

106. *Pol. Schr.*, p. 180.

107. Ibid., p. 128.

tionality."[108] Much as Weber emphasized the state's identification with power, he was not prepared to give up the state's *national* definition.

Weber's observations and his consciousness of responsibility led him to change from a firebrand to a compromiser on the question of the Prussian Poles. But it should not be forgotten that his transformation was prompted primarily by the recognition that a moderate nationality policy was needed to counter the attraction of a potential Russian policy of autonomy. It was in this connection that he developed the conviction that only a sincerely liberal nationality policy could bring about a solution to the German-Polish problem. It was a short step to the idea that emerged in 1916, as will be shown later, of a sweeping annexation of an internally autonomous Poland to the Reich, the same thing that seemed to be developing in 1905 in Russia. It is historically fair to point out that, in 1916,[109] Weber was seeking for the central powers what in 1917 he labeled the crassest imperialism on the part of the Russian liberals, namely the peaceful acquisition of Poland by Russia.[110]

4. Nation, Power, and Culture: Problematics of Weber's Political Value System

Max Weber's most passionate scholarly polemics concern the objectivity of the sciences. From the time of the Freiburg inaugural address he repeatedly attacked the use of science to defend practical value judgments. All his life he emphatically opposed the idea that science was either entitled or qualified to produce value judgments. Science could only judge the worth of values with empirical descriptions and help to ease decisions between different sets of values by mapping the consequences. But science could never say anything, using its own methods, about the worth of values. Weber made his cooperation with the Soziologische Gesellschaft (the German Sociological Society), which he himself had initiated, conditional upon the acceptance of a constitutional paragraph that expressly ruled out discussion of any value judgments. In 1913 he provoked a heated discussion in the governing committee of the Verein für Sozialpolitik on the question of value judgments in which he ended up, of course, in the minority although his opinions were widely noted and admired. His search for a value-free description of social reality was one of the motives that led him to develop the ideal type, the fundamental theoretical concept of his great sociological work *Economy and Society*, which has of course come to us only as a splendid torso consisting of entirely heterogeneous sections.

108. Ibid.
109. Cf. chap. 7, sec. 1.
110. *Pol. Schr.*, p. 200.

Convinced that he could develop ideal types empirically, Weber believed to have found in them the methodological basis for a universal casuistry of the social relations of mankind through the centuries, which made all value judgments unnecessary and concerned itself with them only as the subject matter of empirical analysis. Today it is clear that this splendid undertaking could not fully succeed. Weber's major sociological work was in no way free of value judgments. It is thoroughly imbued with a universal-historical perspective anchored in Max Weber's liberal viewpoint, especially his concern that the free, individualistic society of the West was mortally threatened by bureaucratization. The radically individualistic point of departure of Max Weber's sociological method, which built upon Droysen in a one-sided manner that recognized only individual actions as atoms of social reality in analyzing social reality, can be understood only in the context of the European humanist tradition with its high esteem for the individual. A collectivist takeoff point would be formally just as conceivable. But even the construction of ideal types is meaningful only in relation to certain fundamental convictions of value.[111] Ideal types were constructed so that certain culturally significant aspects were accented in a manner that permitted corresponding phenomena to be accented in the presentation. Such concepts as charisma, dominance, struggle, competiton, asceticism, and professional man were, in their specific nexus, not, as appeared to Weber, merely the results of empirical analysis of reality, but rooted in the central axioms of his highly personal world view.[112]

All the same, Weber's extraordinary intellectual restraint in questions of value judgment is admirable. He actually succeeded in developing a universal sociological system based on a small number of general value assumptions; and he was able to construct it in an almost value-free manner or, at least, with values very much in the background. But this virtue of his sociology was also its decisive weakness. Weber constructed the lattice of his ideal types, which he spread like Kantian models over reality, consciously so that the essential problems of value were filtered out as much as possible. He did this because he was convinced, as we have seen, that scholarly methods could not assess the worth of values. They belonged rather to the sphere of the values of the personality that defied all *ratio*. Phenomenologists (Max Scheler and Nicolai Hartmann) tried to employ philosophical tools in an effort to penetrate the value realms that transcend the layers of empirical existence. Weber, confined by the

111. Cf. Löwith, "Max Weber und Karl Marx," *Archiv für Sozialwissenschaft und Sozialpolitik* 67 (1929): 76 ff. Now also in Karl Löwith, *Gesammelte Abhandlungen: Zur Kritik der geschichtlichen Existenz*, 2d ed. (Stuttgart/Cologne/Berlin/Mainz, 1969), pp. 3 ff.

112. For a systematic and theoretically more wide-reaching analysis, see my treatment in "Universalgeschichtliches und politisches Denken bei Max Weber," *Historische Zeitschrift* 201 (1965).

positivist tradition, rejected such attempts emphatically. Not only was it not the task of sociology or any other science to discuss the justification of appraising values; such a task was completely impossible. This occurred of course at a cost, since values with their constructive and destructive essence were thereby given freer scope to assert their power in irrationality: "All the old gods, deprived of their magic and now taking on the form of impersonal powers, ascend from their graves. They strive to gain power over our lives, and again they reserve their eternal struggle with one another."[113] The ultimate message of Max Weber's sociology was resignation; he offered no answer to the great ethical questions. The demagification of the world, the universal process of rationalization, which Weber described and fatefully affirmed, resulted ironically in the emergence of a new irrationalism.

We stand here at the limits of Weber's sociology, especially his political sociology. Because his sociology incorporated the principle of intellectual integrity as the only fixed point of his scientific value system, and attempted to avoid all value judgments, it lacked something vital.[114] It was only in a position to give functional answers to fundamental questions of political and cultural existence.[115] From the standpoint of his sociology, it is difficult to distinguish the charismatically qualified leader of a constitutional democracy from a charismatic fascist politician. Without a discussion of fundamental questions of value, such a political theory is incapable of setting goals. Weber, however, resisted, as in value questions generally, the critical analysis of his political system as long as its merit itself was in question. The "nation" as a "value concept" remained outside of the realm of scientific criticism for him. He was only prepared to subject the concept of nation to value-free sociological analysis as an empirical concept. He quite consciously did not question whether the national idea could fairly be judged as the highest guiding principle of political action.[116] The limits of Max Weber "the politician" lie here also. His fervent political conscience moved him to an intensive analysis of the political system of the Wilhelmine Reich and to an unprejudiced critique

113. *Wissenschaftslehre*, p. 605.

114. Cf. *Wissenschaftslehre*, p. 601.

115. Cf. Bergstraesser's related critique, "Max Webers Antrittsvorlesung," pp. 218 f.

116. Cf. Weber's commentary on the lecture by F. Schmid on the "right of nationalities" at the second German Sociologists' Convention in 1912: "Consider where it would have led if we had dragged the value of nationality or the value of national states into the discussion, as the first speaker nevertheless to a certain degree has done. We would have called forth the general chaos of opposing national recriminations, such as the Poles against the Germans and the reverse. This would have in no way promoted objective understanding. For the present, we have a constitutional paragraph that forbids this, and as long as it exists, we will stand on our right to demand that it is observed." *Gesammelte Aufsätze zur Soziologie und Sozialpolitik*, p. 488.

of traditional liberalism. But he could not move beyond the threshold of thinking in national categories. Here we encounter the ultimate cause of his own failure just at the time that "the German Reich in its ancient glory"[117] was collapsing.

It cannot be denied, however, that Weber's nationalist thought transcended the nationalism of his epoch. In spite of the vehemence of his national instincts, he possessed a great capacity for "judgment," which he praised as one of the three fundamental qualities of the politician. This divided him above all from the shallow emotional nationalism to which the majority of the German intelligentsia had succumbed in the Wilhelmine era. Objective enough to note the Alsatian attraction to the French nation, Weber did not succumb to a nationalistic approach to Alsace. In 1918 he "was willing to accept [the loss of Alsace] honorably as the final judgment in a long trial . . . since the old regime had *not* [succeeded] in fifty years . . . in winning over this land, which is German to the core."[118] Nevertheless, as private witnesses reported, he commented bitterly on the German withdrawal and was crestfallen by the loss.[119] Indeed, he had been able to study the errors of German Alsatian policy at first hand.[120] During the war he had also energetically opposed a policy of "national vanity" and had rejected the expansion of the German national state beyond its existing boundaries.[121]

The "nationalist" Max Weber—we use the term just as broadly as he used it about himself in the Freiburg inaugural address and later—knew how to respect the limits that constituted the ideal of the nation state itself. He avoided the hypertrophy of nationalist thought, which of necessity leads to self-contradiction. Bismarck had spoken of the "ethos of power that sets its own limits."[122] We find something similar in Weber's work: a concept of the nation state that remained conscious of its own limits. But this limitation of the national idea was double-sided, dialectical in nature. It was based not so much on respect for other nationalities and their right to existence as on insight into the preconditions of German great power politics. Germany must not fail in its real tasks by meddling

117. Cited from Weber's statement on the Arco case, 1920.

118. *Pol. Schr.*, p. 456.

119. To Mina Tobler, 4 December 1918, Archiv Ebnet II, 79: "Since then the 'dis-annexation' of Alsace has occurred with the *shameful* behavior of the French," and a few days before (Archiv Ebnet II, 78, undated): "Every day brings bad news first of all—the scenes of contempt with which we withdraw from Alsace (*what* feelings we have about this and what memories are attached to [Alsace]!)."

120. During his military days in Strassburg. The influence of Hermann Baumgarten is also important in this regard. See above, chap. 1.

121. An extensive discussion of these questions in connection with the war aims problem follows below, chap. 7, sec. 1.

122. Hans Rothfels, *Bismarck und der Osten* (Leipzig, 1934), p. 22.

with petty settlement policies in the East or elsewhere. To this extent, Max Weber's national thinking only changed emphasis. It came to concentrate on the global political future of the nation. The nation remained the norm of political action although it was now viewed in a broader framework.

Weber did not inquire about the theoretical limits of the national idea; in this respect he was a prisoner of his epoch. His entire political system of values depended upon it. It was the national idea as an ultimate norm that justified the exercise of power. If Weber, in his theory of a sphere of political values autonomous from other spheres of value, came close to Machiavelli's views and fatalistically accepted the unavoidable conflict between political action and ethical imperatives, then we can only admire the intellectual forthrightness with which he drew the ultimate ethical consequences from the idea of power. We share his conviction that political deeds—as, in the end, all creative and therefore destructive action—may make men morally guilty. But can we in good conscience follow Weber despite all possible consequences after we have lived through the fury of a regime that enjoyed similar power, that pushed aside all ethical restraint and bloodied its banners with mass murder? Should we consider ourselves bound by those supreme political values that Weber saw as obligatory for the possession of power, even in the event of conflicts with moral values? For us, the nation can no longer be such a value, even when we acknowledge that Weber saw not only the power and position of the German political state when he looked at the nation, but also the need to preserve the German people, its cultural uniqueness, and its distinctive governmental and social organization. Even if we affirm the national principle as the basis of the heterogeneity of European culture, we recognize that the cultural and libertarian aspects of the existence in independent states are unacceptably confined in an idea of nation that nurtured increasing enthusiasm for power and thereby became less and less capable of vindicating the view that the exercise of power involved the use of tools of "diabolical" origins.

Jacob Burckhardt, in his *Weltgeschichtliche Betrachtungen* (*Observations on Universal History*), formulated the problem of the national principle with prophetic foresight into the approaching national convulsions of the old Europe: "The nation seeks (in illusion or reality) power above all. Existence in small states is seen as a disgrace; forceful people are not content to work for small states. People wish to belong to something greater. They thereby clearly reveal that power is the highest goal and culture only a secondary one. Above all, they seek to impose their general will on others, in defiance of other nations."[123] These words can be applied to Max Weber.

123. Burckhardt, *Weltgeschichtliche Betrachtungen*, p. 97.

Max Weber abhorred life in small states. He viewed participation in great power politics as the great task and historical duty of the German nation; otherwise the foundation of the Reich would have been a "costly, vain luxury with culturally destructive effects."[124] Germany must be a "power state" in order "to have a voice about the future of the world," he said in 1916.[125] Weber saw it as a historical necessity that a great nation must seek "power above all." According to the "laws of this world . . . , [which include] the possibility and unavoidability of wars for power for the foreseeable future, the preservation of national culture is linked necessarily to power politics."[126]

The existence of small nations was possible only under the protective hegemony of great powers. Weber always recognized that the small nations were culturally more creative than those great nations that were called upon to organize as great powers.[127] For this reason, they are especially entrusted with the preservation of the cultural heritage. Jacob Burckhardt's theory about the character of power "as evil by definition" appeared to Weber to correctly reflect the perspective of a small-state mentality and therefore ought to be respected within certain limitations.[128] But Weber pledged himself, with historical arguments, to great and unsentimental power politics in defense of his own national culture.

Weber recognized the tragic association of culture and power, and since he did not hesitate to give the latter the necessary precedence, or else both would be lost, we must reserve our criticism and recognize the deep sense of responsibility that led him to such a position. Hence Burckhardt's notoriously harsh judgment that made modern nationalism Weber's primary goal and "culture at most a secondary goal" does not apply fully to Weber. Weber's theory of national power rested, in the final analysis, on a genuinely cultural ideal. To be sure, there was error in this, but Weber believed that in the foreseeable future all culture must be inexorably linked with the national principle, and that it was not possible to do away with autonomous national states.

We should not forget the conscious distance between his national theory and the hybrid justifications of national power politics, so often characteristic of the Wilhelmine era, that made power a goal in itself. In a conflict between the University of Freiburg and the *Frankfurter Zeitung* in 1911, Weber distanced himself explicitly from such "entirely empty and hollow sorts of purely zoological nationalism" that characterized German fraternity student journals.[129] That kind of nationalism led

124. *Pol. Schr.*, pp. 143, 175.
125. Ibid., p. 176.
126. Ibid., p. 145.
127. Ibid., pp. 142 ff., 175 ff.
128. Ibid., p. 142.
129. At a student celebration at the University of Freiburg, Lieutenant-General von Deimling made some extraordinarily pointed nationalistic and militaristic comments, e.g.,

"necessarily to a lack of conscience on all great cultural questions." These nationalists tried to compensate for "the total lack of any cultural ideal and the shameless narrowing of their spiritual horizons" by engaging in nationalistic demonstrations "of the most contemptible kind." Weber deplored the "cleft between the *emptiness* of the national sentiments of many of our students and the intensity of our national cultural needs."[130] He saw that the weakness in pre–World War I German national thinking, in spite of all of its noise and patriotism, was rooted in its departure from all genuine cultural ideals.

Max Weber never troubled to clarify the common threads that linked his national theory and his cultural ideal. It is nevertheless possible to reveal them in outline and to point out the bonds between his national theory and his social ideals. The ideal type of the professional who had his origins in the Protestant tradition and who had created, in modern capitalism, a world that conformed to his ideal values and at the same time has produced a hostile universe, demanded the preservation of a dynamic economic system and an open social structure. The alternative was a universal bureaucracy, "the iron cage of future serfdom," which would dictate tasks to individuals with inescapable repressive power. A world so constructed would render his specific sense of a profession as a spiritual form superfluous. To Weber, the development of such a static society seemed avoidable only, as we shall show, through a decisive imperialistic policy of power. Here we see a characteristic point of contact between Max Weber's national thinking and his cultural ideal. His cultural ideal, to be sure, involved transcendental questions; only in these could it reach its fulfillment. But this world was ruled by the power struggle of powerful national states that were bearers of autonomous cultures. Therefore, fatefully, national power policy took precedence over cultural development.

In a chapter in *Economy and Society* written between 1911 and 1913 but never completed, Max Weber was hoping, as a few manuscript notes point out, to pursue this question further. "Cultural prestige and power prestige are closely linked," Weber noted. "Every *victorious* war enhances cultural prestige [. . .]. Whether it furthers cultural development is another question, which cannot be solved in a 'value-neutral' way. Certainly it is not *obvious* (Germany after 1870!). *Not* with empirically

---

"Whereas once we 'stamped' in dragoon boots across the stage of the world theater, we now creep in felt breeches." The professors answered a critical article in the *Frankfurter Zeitung* of 31 October 1911 with a collective declaration (*Frankfurter Zeitung*, 10 November 1911). Weber hastened to aid the *Frankfurter Zeitung* at its request.

130. Letter of 15 November 1911 to his Freiburg colleagues, partially reprinted in *Lebensbild*, pp. 414 ff. A copy of the typed original is in the Weber papers. "Prof. F." is Professor Fabricius of Freiburg. "Herr Kollege M." is Friedrich Meinecke.

observable data! A pure and *characteristically* German art and literature did *not* develop in the political *center* of Germany."[131] In these few sentences, the fundamental conflict between national culture and national power theory surfaces again. In a remarkable parallel with Nietzsche's blunt statement about the "extirpation of the German spirit in favor of the German Reich,"[132] Weber explored the dialectical character of great power politics, which, by furthering a nation's "cultural prestige," might fatally destroy its cultural development. Were there unconscious reasons prompting Weber to give rein to such thoughts? Was it his recognition that the open chasm between national culture and power politics in the grand style could have undermined his basic convictions? We cannot tell. Weber shared the tragic overvaluation of the principles of power and their ideal fulfillment in the concept of the nation that was characteristic of the imperalist epoch—an overvaluation that was to lead the old Europe to catastrophe.

131. *Wirtschaft und Gesellschaft*, p. 530, note 1.

132. "Erste unzeitgemässe Betrachtung David Strauss," beginning. Cf. Theodor Schieder, "Das Reich unter der Führung Bismarcks," *Deutsche Geschichte im Überblick*, ed. Peter Rassow (Stuttgart, 1953), p. 565.

4

National Imperialism as the Future Task of German Policy

1. A World Policy as a Means of Defending Germany's International Standing

Max Weber's study of the structure of East Elbian agriculture led him to recognize that German food supplies would be dependent upon overseas world markets for the foreseeable future. This would be especially true when, for the sake of the nation, large market-oriented landholdings were replaced by self-sufficient small farms through an official settlement policy. Because a policy of agricultural autarky was both impossible and undesirable, Weber insisted that Germany's economic fate lay overseas in a major drive for exports and in the struggle for the world market in competition with other great industrial states.[1] If Germany were not to sink to the level of a secondary nation, it had to participate actively in the burgeoning of capitalism over the earth. Without a large-scale foreign trade, Germany could not match the economic development of other industrial powers and would therefore not be able to maintain its present position in the world. Weber viewed a concerted export policy in the grand style and active "world power politics" as two sides of the same coin; he was convinced that foreign trade would not be successful in the long run without powerful political backing from the national government. A powerful foreign policy, supported by strong armaments, that would expand German economic markets and investment possibilities throughout the world was the most pressing need of the hour.

Max Weber's conception of national power, by associating the nation's foreign political interests with international economic questions, de-

1. Cf. above, chap. 2.

veloped into a national imperialism of the most intense variety.[2] Whereas in 1893 he had still felt the "heavy curse of decadence" because the great task of national politics, the creation of a German nation state, had been fulfilled, he now saw the major task of future German policy as a concerted effort in world power politics. The preservation and expansion of a powerful nation state in a world of intense economic competition and imperialistic expansion now appeared to him the historically necessary consequence of the foundation of the Reich. In fact, it represented a continuation of the great national and liberal politics of the time of the Reich foundation under changed economic and international circumstances. In his Freiburg inaugural address he made this point frankly: "We must grasp that the unification of Germany was a youthful spree, indulged in by the nation in its old age; it would have been better if it had never taken place, since it would have been a costly extravagance, if it was the conclusion rather than the starting-point for German power politics on a global scale."[3] In the conditions of 1895, German involvement in world politics appeared to Weber to be a solemn duty, given her rulers' responsibility before history. . . . We cannot avoid the curse with which we live; as the heirs of a politically great era, we must therefore recognize how to become something other: the precursors of a greater one."[4]

The call for a German "world power policy," the appeal to direct the strong national feelings that arose with Bismarck's founding of the Reich to the new task of a great German "world policy" that Weber issued in his Freiburg inaugural address, provoked a tremendous response.[5] Most immediate and significant was the impact upon Friedrich Naumann. Naumann published a thorough account of the Freiburg inaugural address in *Die Hilfe* that concluded with the words, "It is not correct? Of

2. Cf. Ludwig Dehio, "Gedanken über die deutsche Sendung, 1900–1918," *Historische Zeitschrift* 174: 479.

3. *Pol. Schr.*, p. 23; cited from *Weber: Selections in Translation*, ed. W. G. Runciman, trans. Eric Matthews (Cambridge: Cambridge University Press, 1978), p. 266.

4. Ibid., p. 24.

5. To be sure the idea that Bismarck's policy would have its logical continuation in a German imperialistic policy of expansion was expressed frequently before this (see, e.g., Hans-Ulrich Wehler, *Bismarck und der Imperialismus* (Cologne, 1969), p. 339. But it was previously stated in passing and not with such force. Cf. also the 1896 invitation to join the Pan-German League in H. Grell, *Der Alldeutsche Verband: seine Geschichte, seine Bestrebungen und Erfolge* (Munich, 1898), p. 7: "We must intensify our national feelings and inform the mass of our people that German development did not come to an end in the years 1870/1871. We must not forget that millions of our national comrades live outside the black, white, and red boundary markers. The German people has as much right and duty as other cultural nations to participate as a master people in leading the fate of the entire world. We have only taken the first step, with the founding of the Reich, on the path to a world power position."

what use is the best social policy if the Cossacks come? He who wishes to carry out a policy must first secure the people, the fatherland, and the borders; he must strive for national power. . . . We . . . need a socialism with the capacity to govern. Capacity to govern means to carry out a better overall policy than heretofore. A socialism capable of governing must be German national."[6]

Max Weber introduced Friedrich Naumann to the idea of a state founded in national power. He decisively influenced Naumann's transformation from a Christian Social politician with socialist tendencies to a politician of national power and imperialism.[7] Weber's great influence on Naumann's development, especially through the inaugural address, was repeatedly evident in Naumann's writings. The description of the foundation of the Reich as the starting point, not the end point, of a development, that Weber had emphatically included in his presentation, greatly attracted Naumann. As early as 1896, he declared at the National-Social convention that 1870 was "not the end of German history." Now the concern is "the distribution of territory all over the world."[8] And he rephrased Weber's thoughts again in his widely circulated book *Demokratie und Kaisertum* (*Democracy and Empire*). "We are happy and content with the successful achievement of Reich unity and power; but we view it a simplistic sentimentality to pretend to act as if no waters have been troubled. Because we wanted to be a nation, we must now gladly accept and bear the consequences that arose from the fulfillment of our desires."[9] And he went on to try to prove, taking off from Weber's approach, that an imperialistic industrial and naval policy on a democratic basis was the natural course of action for Imperial Germany once Imperial Germany had been established. However, by placing the emperor—"the sovereign that makes world policy"[10]—rather than the nation state in the foreground, he departed decisively from Weber, who

6. *Die Hilfe* 1 (1895/96), 14 July 1895.

7. Cf. Martin Wenck, *Die Geschichte der Nationalsozialen* (Berlin, 1905), pp. 33 f. Also, in a limited way Theodor Heuss, *Friedrich Naumann* (Berlin, 1937; 2d ed., Stuttgart/Tübingen, 1949), pp. 102 ff.; alternatively, Werner Conze, "Friedrich Naumann: Grundlagen und Ansatz seiner Politik in der national-sozialen Zeit (1895–1903)," in *Schicksalswege deutscher Vergangenheit (Festschrift Kaehler)* (Düsseldorf, 1952), pp. 357 f. Also Richard Nürnberger, "Imperialismus, Sozialismus, und Christentum bei Friedrich Naumann," *Historische Zeitschrift* 170: 528 ff. The influence of Rudolf Sohms is also important. He was no less a supporter of imperialistic ideas. For example, in Sohm's address in Posen in 1895: "I would like to see a central power that is above all sufficiently strong for Germany's foreign policy, so that it will be possible to insert a powerful voice in the division of the globe." *Die Hilfe*, 17 November 1895. Cf. Conze, "Friedrich Naumann", p. 357.

8. *Minutes*, p. 39.

9. *Demokratie und Kaisertum*, 4th ed., p. 177; similarly in *Die politischen Parteien* (Berlin, 1910), p. 107.

10. *Demokratie und Kaisertum*, p. 187.

had long recognized the dangers of "personal rule" for a successful German foreign policy."[11] From then on, Friedrich Naumann increasingly championed the necessity of a German "world policy" from the standpoint of the national interest. From the end of the nineties, *Die Hilfe* was a pacesetting organ of liberal imperialism, a sounding board above all for Paul Rohrbach, who attempted to stir up the international emotions of the German bourgeoisie.

It was no less important for the development of German imperialistic thought that Hans Delbrück also picked up the ball from the Freiburg inaugural address.[12] Until 1895, the *Preussische Jahrbücher* had barely touched on world policy issues, Delbrück least of all. This now changed. Delbrück clearly stated his new views: "There is nothing so noble as a great power like Germany setting the preservation of peace as its goal. But the politics of a great nation must not stop here." And he asked, with reference to Weber: "Where is it, this German world power policy?"[13] "In actual fact, we have not yet entered the arena of the real contest for world power that can give satisfaction to a great people and may assure future generations a great future!"[14] After this, the *Preussische Jahrbücher*, under Delbrück's leadership, became a leading organ of German imperialist thought. On individual points, of course, the more conservative and government-minded Delbrück took a different course from the radical, democratic imperialism that Weber favored.

The Freiburg inaugural address was the impetus for the rise of liberal imperialism in Wilhelmine Germany. The liberal imperialists, as it was then said, first made imperialism "socially acceptable" in Germany.[15] With their help, a broad imperialist movement grew. The Pan-German League, on the other hand, had acquired only a limited following. Max Weber himself was on the left of this group; his imperialist ideas were far sharper and more radical than Delbrück's, Rohrbach's, or Naumann's. And he did not hesitate to carry the domestic implications of his politics to their logical conclusions. His imperialist arguments were couched in an almost brutal rhetoric that had earlier been encountered only in the works of such geopoliticians as Friedrich Ratzel and Ferdinand von

11. Cf. below, chap. 6, sec. 1.

12. Cf. H. A. Steger, "Deutsche Weltpolitik bei Hans Delbrück" (diss., Marburg, 1955), p. 36.

13. *Preussische Jahrbücher* 81 (1895): 388 ff., which includes the following: "The unification of Germany would be a youthful spree, Professor Weber said effectively in his previously cited address, if it were the conclusion and not the starting point of German global power politics."

14. Ibid., p. 390.

15. Dirk Oncken, "Das Problem des Lebensraumes in der deutschen Politik" (diss., Freiburg, 1948), p. 98.

Richthofen. It was Weber's outspoken idea of power that cast such an unusually radical hue on his call for a German imperialism.

For Max Weber, no basic distinction existed between pure economic expansion through conquest of markets and capital exports, and political imperialism, that is, the attempt to bring the still "free" regions of the globe under the political control of the nation and thus open them to the preferential exploitation of the nation's industrial and commercial interests. As we have seen, he viewed the "economic community" of nations as a struggle that differed from the political struggle only in means. This economic war of competition had as its real goal the advancement of the nation's economic potential at the expense of other nations. To this extent, Weber viewed an export-intensive economic policy as a national issue of the first rank. At the eighth meeting of the Evangelisch-sozialer Kongress of 1897, the political economist Karl Oldenberg attacked the Caprivi trade treaties for their one-sided export policy, because the treaties furthered Germany's dependence on overseas markets and therefore long-term economic risks and above all because they would lead to the development of indigenous industries in what we now call underdeveloped countries. He proposed a return to an economic policy of agricultural autarky instead. Max Weber passionately differed with Oldenberg and accused him of lacking a "positive ideal of the future." We know what he was referring to: German great-power status in the world.[16] An expansionist export policy that involved "interweaving with the international division of production" represented a "powerful risk" that "the nation's economy would have to bear on its shoulders." Weber was nevertheless of the opinion that "we cannot carry on a policy of national *comfort* but must seek one of national greatness and therefore [willy nilly] take this risk upon our shoulders, provided that we want a national existence different from that of Switzerland."[17]

Oldenberg rejected the idea of pursuing German greatness and world power along the "bombastic" English model, that is, the "ruthless destruction of foreign rights on all five continents," by the route of blatant power politics. He regarded greatness as not worth the striving if it brought "shame upon you."[18] It is characteristic of Weber's volcanic temperament that he seized upon Oldenberg's use of the word *shame* in association with national greatness and passionately protested. "It is not the alleged export policy but the *population increase* that will make the

16. *Verhandlungen des 8. evangelisch-sozialen Kongresses*, 1897, p. 105. Cf. above, chap. 4, sec. 1. The definition of great power policy in *Wirtschaft und Gesellschaft*, p. 521, is: Great powers seek "to add and to usurp an interest in the political and economic events of a large area, today usually one of the large expanses of the planet."

17. *Verhandlungen des 8. evangelisch-sozialen Kongresses*, 1897, pp. 107 f.

18. Ibid., pp. 55 f.

struggle for existence, the war of men against men, grow harder and more burdensome in the future. We are preaching the gospel of struggle as a national duty, as an economically unavoidable task for the whole as for the individual, and we are not 'ashamed' of this struggle, the only road to greatness."[19] A concern for the economic pressures of the population explosion that began in the early nineteenth century in association with the rapid progress in technological development was a major reason for Max Weber's conviction that the intensity of the international power struggle would increase for the foreseeable future. In his inaugural address, he noted that the overshadowing threat of the population problem was sufficient to preclude him from seeing "peace and contentment hidden in the womb of the future."[20] As far as we can determine, however, he did not join in the demand for additional colonizing space for German settlements in Europe or overseas that was often the result of this kind of thinking. For Weber, *economic* expansion and the enlargement of the nation's economic living space via a forceful export-oriented economic policy ought to be the nation's response to its growing population.

In connection with his discussion of Germany's economic position in the world, Max Weber also treated the question of stock exchange legislation, an important issue after the stock scandals at the beginning of the nineties. In 1892, the chancellor appointed a stock exchange investigation commission to work on proposals for a new stock exchange law. The lively controversy between the competing interests, the bank circles close to the exchanges on the one side and the agrarians on the other, hindered the commission's work. The quarrel was rooted in the political and economic opposition of the agrarian-minded conservatives toward the growing financial power of the bourgeoisie. The central point of the conservative agitation against the previous practices of the German exchanges was the trade in grain futures. Here, moral rejection of a purely speculative phenomenon was linked to mistrust of the determination of grain prices centrally at the exchange under the influence of the world market.

Max Weber observed the controversies surrounding the organization of exchanges attentively and soon was hard at work in a field that he had not previously known. The treatise on the stock exchange that he wrote for Friedrich Naumann's worker's library is a fruit of this work. In it, Weber tried to counter irrational, anticapitalist mistrust of the stock exchanges and to indicate the extraordinary importance of the stock exchanges for the functioning of the economy and above all for the

19. Ibid., p. 113.
20. *Pol. Schr.*, p. 12.

economic power and position of the nation in the economic nexus of nations. From the point of view of the "political and economic power interests" of the nation, he sharply rejected strict legal limitations on speculation, especially with respect to the trade in grain futures.[21] Legal restrictions upon speculative exchange trading would seriously weaken the Berlin stock exchange in comparison to foreign stock exchanges. "Carrying through demands that are *purely* theoretical and moral" should be "carefully limited, because as long as nations, however much they want to live in peace together, must carry on an inexorable and unavoidable struggle for existence and for economic power, it is not possible to disarm *unilaterally* in the economic sphere."[22] Therefore Weber favored certain revisions in the legal position of stockbrokers that would give them the right, in the manner of the capital-rich English "dealer," to trade for their own accounts.[23]

In 1895, when the proposals of the stock exchange inquiry commission were published, Max Weber attacked them sharply in the *Zeitschrift für das gesamte Handelsrecht* and in the *Handwörterbuch der Staatswissenschaften*.[24] In his view, the chief mistakes resided in the moral approach of the commission. There could be no " 'fundamental' solution of economic questions based upon economic or social 'justice' or, more generally, upon any 'ethical' point of view in one country as long as the state's power interests and those of the national community are themselves contested by other communities in the struggle for political and economic hegemony."[25] The "protection and expansion of the German market's international *position* and the *political* consequences associated with this" must "indisputably [be] the final and decisive point of reference" for any regulation. Weber opposed any kind of official limitation on the admission of foreign bank notes into this trade, since any restriction of issuing activity "would result in advantages for foreign nations in relation to the international prominence and power of their stock exchanges" and, in addition, because controls by the government upon foreign issues were better handled confidentially and not formally and officially. He also emphatically rejected limitation on futures trading, especially on agricultural products. A struggle against speculation by a

21. "Die Börse," in *Gesammelte Aufsätze zur Soziologie und Sozialpolitik*, p. 320.

22. Ibid., p. 321: "A strong stock exchange cannot be a club for 'ethical culture' and the capital holdings of the great banks are no more 'welfare institutions' than guns and cannons. There is only one thing to apply in an economic policy that aims at present goals: *the tools of power* in every economic struggle."

23. Ibid., pp. 280 ff.

24. "Die Ergebnisse der deutschen Börsenenquête," *Zeitschrift für das gesamte Handelsrecht* 43, 44, 45 (1895/96); *Handwörterbuch der Staatswissenschaften*, 1st edition; 1st supplement, vol. 1895, art. "Börsenwesen."

25. Art. "Börsenwesen."

precise, legal circumscription of the role of the brokers, which the commission favored, collided equally with the interests of the nation state.[26]

Max Weber's opposition to the general tenor of the findings of the stock exchange inquiry commission was also expressed in a sharp attack on agrarian interests, which apparently had influenced the commission's work a great deal. The "*real* objective of agrarian stock exchange criticism," he pointed out, was to "alter the balance of economic power also in favor of landed interests, especially the large estates, by *reducing* the commercial standing of the German stock exchanges." This was bound to be done, Weber did not hesitate to add, "at the expense of Germany's economic power position."[27]

In 1896, when the Reichstag nevertheless passed a stock exchange law in a form close to the one he had criticized, Weber intensified his attack. He labeled the law a severe "injury to Germany's commercial power." Above all, he disapproved of the prohibition of trade in grain futures, because they were a means "for a capital-requiring country like Germany," to protect "the independence of its market through the characteristically artificial market structure" that it produced. The effect of the law would be the "decline of Germany's economic position and power, increased dependence on foreign markets, and a decline in the significance of the German stock exchange."[28] The stock exchange law was "intrinsically one of the worst and most unsatisfactory products of agrarian legislative methods."[29] Within a few years it did, in fact, have to be revised.

There is no doubt that Max Weber both overestimated and very much exaggerated the impact of the stock exchange legislation upon Germany's international economic position.[30] But he wanted to avoid the smallest omission in all things that touched upon Germany's international standing. The stock exchange legislation was far more a qualitative than a quantitative question for him, a touchstone for the position of the Ger-

26. Cf. art. "Börsenwesen"; also "Die Ergebnisse der deutschen Börsenenquête," *Zeitschrift für das gesamte Handelsrecht* 43: 83 ff., 212 ff.

27. Art. "Börsenwesen."

28. "Die technische Funktion des Terminhandels," *Deutsche Juristenzeitung* 1: 249.

29. Art. "Börsengesetz." Cf. also "Die technische Funktion des Terminhandels," p. 250: "In judging stock exchange questions in a nation caught in an economic power struggle, questions of the 'morality' of speculative activities are not the issue. What is important is the technical question of the correct fixing of prices and the political question of strengthening the German markets at the expense of others."

30. Futures contracts constitute only a small percentage of the securities handled on the German exchanges. Cf. Werner Sombart, *Die deutsche Volkswirtschaft im 19. Jahrhundert*, 4th ed. (Berlin, 1919), p. 198, also p. 210. Sombart admitted that Hamburg maintained its position in the international coffee trade vis-à-vis Antwerp and Le Havre through futures contracts.

man parties in relation to a determined world power policy; this partly explains his unusually sharp attack.

In his encounter with the Polish issue Weber had already discovered that the agrarian interests were diametrically opposed to the interests of the national state. This dichotomy emerged even more distinctly in the stock exchange question. He was increasingly convinced that a foreign policy heeding the nation's real interests required an end to conservative predominance in Prussia and Germany. He soon had the opportunity to attack the representatives of conservative interests at close range. In the fall of 1896 he was invited, along with Wilhelm Lexis, to join the stock exchange committee that was to assist the Bundesrat's deliberations over the effects of the new law and was then entrusted with reporting the discussions to the Bundesrat.[31] As might be expected, he was elected to the grain trade commission and soon was involved in violent disputes with the agrarian representatives.[32] But Weber and Lexis were not reappointed to the stock exchange committee summoned in July 1897. Weber complained that agrarian attacks had led to the noticeable strengthening of the agrarian representation on the stock exchange committee while the academic experts had been eliminated.[33]

Hence Weber was denied an active influence upon stock exchange legislation. He made no public statements about the stock exchange bills of 1904 and 1906, which failed because of conservative opposition. He had barely recovered from his illness at the time and was concentrating on his scholarly work. The stock exchange law of 1908, which the liberals had made a precondition of their participation in Bülow's bloc politics, Weber welcomed as being in the national interest, since it largely lifted the restrictions that had been imposed in 1896 and appeared to better the opportunities for German stock exchange trading in the international money market.[34] He regarded the stock exchange question as a political issue of the first order because of its importance for German economic growth.

The bluntness with which Max Weber stressed Germany's international power even in his discussion of questions of economic policy is comprehensible only in the light of the deep pessimism with which he approached the future of international economic relations. Max Weber

31. *Lebensbild*, p. 210.

32. From Weber's humorous report about the meetings of the stock exchange committee in a letter to his wife of 20 November 1896, partially printed in *Lebensbild*, p. 210.

33. Art. "Börsengesetz."

34. Letter to Naumann from Florence (!) of 26 April 1908, *Pol. Schr.* 1, pp. 453 f: "You pressed the recognition that progress was *possible* in a liberal [direction] (the association law) and a *national* [direction] (the stock exchange law in the interest of our power position in the world—France today is the only investor, cf. the situation today in Turkey)."

did not believe that the economic competition of the industrial powers in overseas markets would remain peaceful forever. As capitalism's expansion throughout the world accelerated, and the last regions still "free" were rapidly disappearing, he feared that international trade would gradually decline or, rather, be restricted to trading within specific economic zones of interest. These economic interest zones would keep out all third party trade by high tariff walls, thereby permitting free access only to the commercial interests of the nation controlling a zone. Consequently, free international competition would be gradually replaced by a struggle of the great powers for economic outlets overseas. As early as the inaugural address, Weber had spoken about the "difficult struggles" of the future, for which the nation must adjust itself as long as there was still time to do so.[35] "Only complete political confusion and naïve optimism can prevent the recognition that the unavoidable efforts at trade expansion by all civilized bourgeois-controlled nations, after a transitional period of seemingly peaceful competition, are clearly approaching a point at which *power only* will decide each nation's share in the economic control of the earth and, hence, its people's sphere of economic activity and especially its workers' earning potentials," he pointed out in a December 1897 treatise on the first navy bill. Weber stressed the bill's "unexpected modesty in its demands" and the "wise objectivity of its advocacy."[36] He was blunter in a lecture in Mannheim on 13 December 1897 on the historical position of modern capitalism.

> With frightening rapidity, we are approaching the point at which the limits of the markets of half-civilized Asiatic peoples will have been reached. Then only power, naked power, will count in the international market. Only the petite bourgeoisie can doubt this. The German working class still has the choice to seek work at home or abroad. This will soon cease definitively, whether the worker wants it or not. The worker will then be limited for his sustenance exclusively to the area that the capital and power of his fatherland can make available to him. When this process will be completed is uncertain, but it is certain that it will happen; it is certain that there will be a bitter struggle for power in place of what appears on the surface to be peaceful progress. And in this mighty struggle, the strongest will be the victor.[37]

35. *Pol. Schr.*, p. 23.

36. "Die Ergebnisse der Flottenumfrage," *Münchener Allgemeine Zeitung*, 1898, no. 46, special supplement no. 3 of 13 January 1898, pp. 4 f., reprinted in *Pol. Schr.*, pp. 30–32; cf. Kehr, *Schlachtflottenbau und Parteipolitik, 1894–1901*, Historische Studien 197 (Berlin, 1930), where Weber's position is quoted in detail.

37. *Badische Landeszeitung*, no. 294, 2d ed. of 16 December 1897, p. 1 (Landesbibliothek Karlsruhe.)

The social position of the working class appeared to Max Weber to be tied directly to the success or failure of the imperialist expansion of the Reich. In 1896, Hans Delbrück gave a lecture at the seventh Evangelisch-sozialer Kongress on the problem of unemployment. He proposed the introduction of unemployment insurance and government employment agencies—modern ideas, it should be noted. Max Weber demurred. Behind the problem of unemployment was "the terrible gravity of the population problem," so that unemployment was far more than a purely technical problem associated with the regulation of supply and demand in the labor market. Only the imperialist expansion of the national economic territory could bring a real solution to the unemployment problem. "We need outlets overseas, a widening of job opportunites by the expansion of export markets. That means the outward expansion of Germany's economic sphere of power, and in the long run this is completely dependent upon the outward expansion of political power."[38]

Weber remained true to this unusually blunt argument for imperialist power politics—blunt even at a time when all nations were gripped by the fever to annex as much as possible of the still independent world to their spheres of power.[39] Even if he could not get around the fact that his predictions of the nineties had been too pessimistic, and that, in spite of great tensions, national conflicts had been settled, if only temporarily without recourse to war, and toll barriers had not hindered the revival of international trade, he still believed that this situation would not last. He was convinced that the steady increase in cooperative or state-guaranteed monopolistic forms of production and trade, which were especially apparent in Germany before the First World War, would drive capitalism increasingly on to an imperialist track. Monopolies and government involvement occurred above all with the imperialist expansion of the nature of the state. In a section of *Economy and Society* written in 1911 he noted: "Since the surest guarantee for monopolizing the prospects for profits in foreign regions for the sake of our political compatriots is now political occupation or the suppression of foreign political power in the form of a protectorate or similar action, the 'imperialist' interests of [economic] expansion are increasingly replacing the pacifistic interests that seek 'free trade.'" "The universal revival of 'imperialistic' capital-

38. *Verhandlungen des 7. evangelisch-sozialen Kongresses* 1896, pp. 122 f.

39. Cf. also *Wissenschaftslehre*, p. 167 (1904): "Now that the struggle is raging among nations all over the world in politics and trade policy . . . " Also letter to his brother Alfred of 30 January 1907: "In regard to Schulze-Gävernitz = 'imperialism,' I am of course in agreement with you. [His] exaggeration of views that I also support can only do harm to these views, outstanding as the book is" (Weber papers). Alfred Weber was considerably more moderate about the necessities of imperialistic policy than Max; cf. Gerhart von Schulze-Gävernitz, *Britischer Imperialismus und englischer Freihandel* (Leipzig, 1906.)

ism, which has always been the normal form of capitalist influence on politics, and with it the political pressure for expansion," is "no accidental occurrence," and "this tendency is likely to be maintained for the foreseeable future."[40]

Max Weber belonged to the circle of liberal imperialists who hoped to see the other great powers concede to Germany its fair share of the still free regions of the globe by means of a policy of increased armament. Perhaps sarcastically, Ludwig Dehio has referred to such a policy as a "cold war" strategy, which necessarily ran the risk of turning into a hot war at any moment.[41] Max Weber, at least, accepted the possibility of war. He was convinced that the nation might have to take decisive military action if the situation demanded it. The degree to which he considered the possibility of war can be seen in his remarks at the Congress of Arts and Sciences in St. Louis in 1904. Weber began: "Destiny, which has encumbered us with a history of thousands of years, which has placed us in a country with a dense population and an intensive culture, which has forced us to maintain the splendor of our ancient culture . . . in an armed camp in a milieu that is also armed." How different was the situation of the American people! They did not need to "wear the coat of mail like ourselves, who constantly keep in the drawer of our desk the march order in case of war."[42] In Weber's view, Germany had no choice; a decisive world policy, being an external and internal precondition for the nation's greatness, appeared to him to be Germany's inevitable duty in the face of history. This was the leitmotif of his political position until the tragic year of 1918. All domestic political measures, no less than foreign policy, had to be oriented toward this goal. In this sense Max Weber advocated the "primacy of foreign policy"; he wanted to see "all internal affairs arranged so as to contribute "to the goal" of carrying on "world politics."[43]

40. *Wirtschaft und Gesellschaft*, p. 526, also p. 205: "In antiquity and in the early modern period, the chief thrust of capitalist acquisition, in . . . relation to political power purely as such, lay in 'imperialistic' gains, and it is increasingly moving in this direction again."

41. Ludwig Dehio, "Gedanken über die deutsche Sendung," *Historische Zeitschrift* 174 (1952): 481 ff.

42. Lecture in St. Louis, published in *Congress of Arts and Science, Universal Exposition, St. Louis 1904*, ed. Howard J. Mayers, vol. 7 (Boston and New York: Houghton-Mifflin, 1906), p. 745, here cited according to *From Max Weber: Essays in Sociology* (New York: Oxford University Press, 1958), pp. 384–85.

43. Variation of the well-known Ranke phrase; cf. Leopold von Ranke, *Das politische Gespräch (Die grossen Mächte, Das politische Gespräch*, ed. Theodor Schieder [Göttingen, 1955], p. 60.) An expressed acknowledgment of the primacy of foreign policy as world power policy in Weber, *Pol. Schr.*, pp. 430, 443; also in the inaugural address, p. 23; cf. also "Diskussionsrede auf der Tagung des Vereins für Sozialpolitik," Vienna, 1909: "If one is to

Now that the colonialist period is over and the one-time colonial powers are burdened with the political problems that are the legacy of previously successful colonial policies, Max Weber's imperialist beliefs seem to us perhaps the most temporally confined aspect of his political thought. His ideal of a German Reich, a world power like England or Russia, proved to be utopian; and it was Hitler's subsequent drive for world power that pushed Germany back into the ranks of the smaller powers once and for all. Today we are more inclined to agree with Ernst Troeltsch, who in 1915, in the spiritual tradition of German idealism, fought bravely against German imperialism and pleaded for reconciliation among the world's great cultural nations. "The great cultural nations," Troeltsch argued, "are individual expressions of reason and must respect and fertilize each other. None of them needs world rule, either in power or in spirit, in order for a free people to take high-minded advantage of its characteristic cultural treasures."[44]

Weber's *understanding of imperialism* itself consisted of a unique mixture of political and economic elements. The basis for the rise of an imperialist drive for expansion, in his opinion, was the mutual rivalry of political power structures that first occurred only in military and political form but then engaged the economic sphere. In this sense, Weber expressly denied the primacy of the economic factor.[45] He emphasized that "neither the trade nor the banking policies of modern states . . . either in their genesis or in their content, can be understood apart from the unique political competition and 'balance of power' conditions of the world of the European states during the last half-millennium," as was "specifically recognized as early as Ranke's first monograph."[46] The sense of power prestige oriented toward the state that was an attribute of the classes who held political power was what Weber pointed to as the ideal core of the drive for imperialist expansion.[47] We have already discussed the close relationship between this sense of prestige and the national idea as Weber saw it.[48] To this extent, Weber's analysis of imperialism comes close to Schumpeter's later interpretation of imperialism as an irrational, object-

---

judge purely 'realpolitisch,' and, further, if the concern is ultimately the power ranking of the nations of the world—and many of us take the point of view that this is the final, ultimate value . . . " *Gesammelte Aufsätze zur Soziologie und Sozialpolitik*, p. 416, also p. 412.

44. "Imperialismus," in *Die Neue Rundschau* 26 (1915): 11. Ibid., p. 8, includes the comment, "The little word 'world' need not completely take precedence over all of our ideals and hopes."

45. *Wirtschaft und Gesellschaft*, pp. 521 f.

46. Ibid., p. 211. Compare on the question of imperialism and the world state system: Ludwig Dehio, "Ranke und der deutsche Imperialismus," *Historische Zeitschrift* 170 (1950): 307 ff.

47. Cf. *Wirtschaft und Gesellschaft*, pp. 520 f.

48. Cf. above, chap. 3, sec. 3.

less drive for expansion on the part of specific ruling classes.[49] In Weber's imperialist views, the prestige element, linked closely to national fervor, was much more dominent than he would have liked to admit.

In Weber's opinion, the ideal factor of power prestige and the real power interests of the modern national state corresponded totally. Together they were the driving factors of modern imperialism. In order to develop and strengthen economic power, the modern state willingly encouraged and aided capitalism domestically and was also prepared to support domestic entrepreneurial and commercial interests politically when these sought to expand economically beyond the country's borders. The state's power was essentially dependent on its economic capability. Therefore it was in the state's interest to open the way for its own entrepreneurs and capital to seek profit abroad, especially in economically underdeveloped countries, with political and military means. Imperialist capitalism, especially in the form of colonial plunder capitalism, had always offered "the greatest opportunities for profit, much more than export based on peaceful exchange with citizens of other political communities."[50] The expansion of the state's political power through the conquest of politically uncontrolled and economically unexploited regions brought the homeland's economy unexpectedly high possibilities for profit. In return, the resulting rise in the people's income permitted higher expenditures for governmental goals. The national power interests and private economic interests were therefore closely linked in this area.

Weber could concede great importance to the material factors that contributed to the imperialist expansion of the powers without forsaking the primacy of political factors. He emphasized that weighty material interests were in play here. For example, the banks that financed armaments and arranged war loans and major sections of heavy industry were "economically interested in warfare quand même," whether a war was won or lost.[51] In general, all commercial groups that were interested in the exploitation of governmental monopolies, or even in guarantees by governments for the exploitation of economic monopolies overseas, supported a policy of territorial expansion abroad because, as a rule, it opened up such profitable possibilities. So Weber considered it a given that the imperialist tendencies were bound to advance in line with the growth of the publicly controlled sector of the economy as well as of those commercial circles interested materially in the expansion of the governmental apparatus, which was likely to provide new opportunities for

49. "Zur Soziologie der Imperialismen," *Archiv für Sozialpolitik und Sozialwissenschaft* 40 (1918–19).

50. *Wirtschaft und Gesellschaft*, p. 525.

51. Ibid.

monopolistic gain. The advance of imperialist tendencies was furthered by the circumstance that, as the competitive struggle grew sharper, the desire of entrepreneurs to make their profits outside the free market through the exploitation of economic monopolies or preferential positions grew. Since such monopolies, railroad or canal construction, for example, were customarily granted in connection with imperialist expansionary policies, modern capitalism would be increasingly driven onto the imperialist path.[52]

Max Weber doubted that economic and industrial progress would last forever.[53] He expected individual national economic territories to become progressively saturated, competition within these territories to intensify, and chances for profit to decrease. Entrepreneurs would attempt more and more to stabilize their profits through cartelization. Eventually, monopolistic structures would replace competitive enterprises. The state would also take possession of an increasingly greater share of enterprise and carry it on on a cooperative basis. Dynamic capitalism would be replaced in the end by a stationary, bureaucratically consolidated economic order in which strict regulation would rob free, adventurous entrepreneurship of its freedom of economic movement. Imperialism seemed to Max Weber to be a transitional phase on the way to this final situation, in which nations' economic activities would be restricted to the territory that they controlled politically. It was essential, as long as "free territory," economically open regions, and free world markets existed, to win the greatest possible economic elbow room for the nation, for the nation would someday be irretrievably limited to the space it had acquired.[54]

52. Ibid., pp. 524 f.

53. *Christliche Welt*, 1893, p. 477; "Zur Lage . . . ," p. 119; also *Verhandlungen des evangelisch-sozialen Kongresses*, 1894, p. 80; 1897, p. 107.

54. Cf. the passages quoted above, text at notes 36–40. It appears that Max Weber's prediction that capitalism would eventually decline into a static economic order can be traced to John Stuart Mill. In his famous "Principles of Political Economy," Mill projected that capitalist economic development would inevitably end in a static situation that would be characterized by a reduction in the rate of profit below the necessary minimum and a weakening of competition (Ashley ed. [London, 1909,] p. 371): "When a country has long possessed a large production, and a large net income to make savings from, and when, therefore, the means have long existed of making a great annual addition to capital; (the country not having like America [1848], a large reserve of fertile land still unused); it is one of the characteristics of such a country, that the rate of profit is habitually within, as it were, a hand's breadth of the minimum, and the country therefore on the very verge of the stationary state." In Weber's view, this development had been retarded for a number of reasons including new discoveries and methods, the importation of cheaper raw materials and foodstuffs from the colonies but above all as a result of foreign and colonial investments (which even at that time were considerable in England.) In contrast to Weber, Mill saw this ultimate situation not as an evil but as a blessing for mankind (see pp. 731 ff. and especially, pp. 746 ff.).

This is turn would determine to what extent it would be materially possible, once the complete economic division of the world into separate national spheres for economic exploitation was complete, to hold off the growing trend toward bureaucratization of the economy and petrification of the social structure. As a result of this process, the future of individual liberty as it had developed in Europe would be at stake. Weber believed that individual liberties could survive in the long run only in a dynamic economic system, just as their development had been possible only as the result of a "unique, not-to-be-repeated constellation," namely the conjunction of "overseas expansion," the "economic and social structure of the 'early capitalist' era," and the "coming of age of the intellect" in modern science.[55] But Weber saw that the dynamic quality of the capitalist economic process (and here he was close to the Marxist interpretation of imperialism) depended on the existence of economically "not yet saturated" regions: overseas exhaust valves. Russia and America had "perhaps the 'last' chance to develop 'free' cultures 'from the ground up,'" because their spacious, thinly settled regions offered sufficient elbow room for dynamic economic development.[56]

History pointed in the direction of declining freedom. High capitalism in itself was no kin of "democracy" and "liberty"; the question could only be phrased in reverse: "How, under [high capitalism's] rule will all of these things remain 'possible'?"[57] Weber feared that capitalism's total takeover of modern life would finally lead to petrification in a completely rationalized, bureaucratic, and stationary economic and social order. "In American 'benevolent feudalism,' in the German so-called 'welfare institutions,' in the Russian factory constitution—everywhere the dwelling place of the new bondage is ready. It is only waiting for us to move in, following the deceleration of the tempo of technological-economic 'progress' and the victory of 'income' over 'profit' *in combination with the*

55. "Zur Lage," p. 120. Also on p. 121: "Today . . . , as long as the economic and intellectual 'revolution,' the much criticized 'anarchy' of production and the equally scorned 'subjectivism' remain unchecked, the self-assertive individual from the wide masses can expand the 'inalienable' sphere of personality and freedom. If the world is ever economically 'complete' and intellectually 'satiated,' such expansion might be impossible, at least as far as our weak eyes are able to see into the impenetrable fog of mankind's future."

56. "Zur Lage," p. 121; cf. Weber's lecture in St. Louis, p. 746. Gerth and Mills cite this on p. 385: "It was perhaps never before in history made so easy for any nation to become a great civilized power as for the American people. Yet, according to human calculation, it is also the last time, as long as the history of mankind shall last, that such conditions for a free and great development will be given; the areas of *free soil* are now vanishing everywhere in the world." Pipes ("Max Weber und Russland," *Aussenpolitik* 6 [1955]: 634) notes that Weber never said what his understanding was of this final opportunity. There are no further statements about this, and apparently the thought later receded.

57. "Zur Lage," p. 119.

exhaustion of still 'free' land and the still 'free' markets[58] that make the masses 'docile.'"[59]

Only from this universal-historical perspective can we understand why Max Weber viewed relentless power politics directed toward colonial accessions as an unconditional necessity. His universal-historical prognosis, when associated with the national ideal, gave his imperialistic beliefs their characteristic bluntness.[60] His diagnosis of the fate of capitalism allied itself with the conviction that future economic development would take place exclusively within individual national economies and their overseas extensions and would therefore become increasingly dependent on the relative power of the national state. Weber's prediction that national economies would become totally separated from one another has not been borne out. World trade has triumphed over imperialistic monopolistic trade. Even the irreconcilable blocs of the free West and communism maintain economic relations with each other. It has also proved true that capitalism is capable, by the unceasing creation of new needs, to create an increasingly receptive internal market. Weber's assertion—related to the Marxist interpretation of imperialism—that, with the penetration of the economically undeveloped regions, the dynamics of capitalism would slacken, has proved false.[61] At the same time it represented an important premise for his thesis that economic development would lead to an increasingly sharp economic and power struggle among the nations. Later, to be sure, he was to give up this position. He adopted a culturally based imperialism that emphasized the link between the nation's international power status and the standing of its culture.[62]

2. German World Policy and the Nation's Political Maturity

The fundamental reason for Germany's international failures before the First World War, in Ludwig Dehio's view, was the wide disparity be-

58. Author's emphasis.

59. "Zur Lage," p. 119.

60. Cf. the highly one-sided, but at the same time perceptive criticism by Lukács of Max Weber and liberal imperialism, in *Die Zerstörung der Vernunft* (Berlin, 1954), pp. 481 ff.

61. Here on it must be noted that Weber did not maintain to this degree the pessimistic prediction in regard to the development of capitalism to which I refer here. In *Wirtschaft und Gesellschaft* (pp. 191 ff.) this idea no longer appears in connection with imperialist conceptions. On p. 176, Weber refers to "times of stabilization of technical-economic development" (!) that will offer special opportunities for forms of political representation based on professional roles.

62. Cf. my book *The Age of Bureaucracy: Perspectives on the Political Sociology of Max Weber* (Oxford, 1974.)

tween its vital and its intellectual energies.[63] Max Weber posed the question more pointedly than other liberal imperialists: What were the intellectual preconditions of a German world policy? His analysis of German domestic politics proved that the disparity did exist, especially among the classes that capitalist development brought to the fore, mainly the bourgeoisie but also the working class.

Weber believed that, as a result of the historical evolution from a feudal, agricultural society to a capitalist industrial society, the hour of the bourgeoisie had belatedly arrived in Germany. Perhaps, it arrived *too late*, since a class-conscious working class was already knocking on the doors of the state, seeking to take it over. In Max Weber's eyes, the key question was whether or not the German bourgeoisie was willing and had the capacity to fulfill the political tasks set for it. Germany's future as a powerful state hinged on the answer. Anyone who did not believe in the future of the bourgeoisie must doubt Germany's future, Weber once remarked.[64] A passionate "however" was associated with this statement, since Weber viewed the German bourgeoisie with much skepticism and deplored "the petty carryings on of political second-stringers" in the German politics of his day.[65]

The decisive issue for Weber "in the economic victory of the bourgeoisie" over agricultural "feudalism" was whether what should happen, would happen: that "in [the bourgeoisie's] hands as in those of feudalism 'the power and greatness of the fatherland' was as safe as formerly in the hands of feudalism."[66] But "*economic power and the vocation of providing the nation's political leadership*" were not necessarily associated, as Weber repeatedly noted.[67] This appeared to him to be especially true of the German bourgeoisie. He believed that the bourgeoisie suffered both from a serious lack of political judgment and the absence of a positive will for power. These shortcomings were concealed in some circles by naïve Bismarck adulation and uncritical worship

63. Ludwig Dehio, "Gedanken über die deutsche Sendung, 1900–1918," *Historische Zeitschrift* 170 (1952): 501.

64. *Frankfurter Zeitung*, 15 March 1896, 3d morning ed. Report on Weber's lectures at the Freie Deutsche Hochstift. Cf. *Frankfurter Volksbote*, 14 March 1896.

65. Inaugural address, *Pol. Schr.*, p. 21.

66. *Frankfurter Volksbote*, 14 March 1896.

67. *Pol. Schr.*, p. 18. Compare letter to Michels of 7 November 1907 (copy in Weber papers.) Weber wrote to Michels, who sought to infer the political emancipation of the proletariat from its economic indispensability: "Necessity in the process of production means *nothing*, purely *nothing at all* for the power and opportunities of a class. At a time when no one who was a *Bürger* worked, the slaves were ten times, one thousand times, as necessary as the proletariat is today. What does this mean? The peasants of the Middle Ages, the Negroes of the American south, all of them were absolutely indispensable. What does this mean? This turn of phrase involves a dangerous illusion."

of so-called Realpolitik, and in others by blind hatred of Bismarck and rigid, dogmatic, oppositional politics.

Weber traced this situation, with a glance at England, to the German bourgeoisie's "unpolitical past" and to the fact that "the work of political education of a century cannot be accomplished in a decade and that the rule of a great man is not always a means of political education."[68] It was Bismarck who destroyed all independent forces around him and accustomed the nation to the fact that the fate of the Reich was in good hands and their active participation was unnecessary. To be sure, Weber placed considerable blame on the nation for its own abdication. Nowhere else in the world had "the unlimited admiration of a politician's personality required a proud nation to sacrifice its own objective convictions so completely."[69] A unique propensity for hierarchy, which many Germans shared as a result of Lutheran religiosity, contributed to this.[70] In 1892, Max Weber posed a question to the elder Baumgarten, who, embittered by the domestic political evolution of Germany, was inclined, like Virchow and Mommsen, to blame Bismarck alone for the decline of German liberalism: "Do we . . . ourselves not at least bear the same guilt as Bismarck?"[71] Similarly, Weber asserted in his inaugural address: "The powerful sun that stood at Germany's zenith and made the German name shine in the farthest corner of the earth appeared almost too big for us and burned out the bourgeoisie's slowly evolving capacity for political judgment."[72]

If this represented an important measure of bourgeois self-criticism, two years later Weber blamed the decline of the nation's political judgment entirely on Bismarck. "The type of regime we have known for the last twenty years, half 'Caesarist,' half 'patriarchal,' and most recently distorted by a narrow-minded fear of the red specter," has meant "*the opposite of political education for the nation*."[73] After this, Weber held religiously to this opinion. His great confrontation with Bismarck in the

68. *Pol. Schr.*, p. 22; cf. Weber's statement in his lecture at the Freier deutsche Hochstift, according to the report of the *Frankfurter Zeitung*, 15 March 1896, 3d morning ed.: "The German bourgeoisie lacks the great traditions of the English bourgeoisie."

69. *Pol. Schr.*, p. 311.

70. Cf. *Wirtschaft und Gesellschaft*, p. 660: "Viewed politically, the German was and is in fact the specific 'subject' in the deepest meaning of the word, and therefore Lutheranism was the adequate religiosity for him," similarly to Kayserling, 21 June 1911, Archiv Ebnet XI, I: "The mass of *Germans* have the *passive* religiosity of resignation particularly in 'vocation' and historical power."

71. Letter to Hermann Baumgarten of 18 April 1892, *Jugendbriefe*, p. 343.

72. *Pol. Schr.*, p. 21.

73. Cf. comment on the *Flottenumfrage* in the *Münchner neuesten Nachrichten*, published for the first time in the first German edition of the present book (Tübingen, 1959), pp. 421 ff. Now, with a few minor errors, in *Pol. Schr.*, pp. 30 f.

articles about German parliamentarianism written for the *Frankfurter Zeitung* during the war culminated in the same complaint: "What then was . . . Bismarck's *political legacy*? He left behind him a nation *without any kind of political education*, far below the level it had achieved twenty years earlier. And above all a nation *without any kind of political will*, accustomed to the idea that the great statesman at their head would take care of politics for them."[74]

In spite of its brilliance, no one can deny the one-sidedness of this critique. There is much that is true in it, but its overall thrust is a retrospective justification of liberalism. It was not the weakness of the liberal idea or the lack of liberal leadership personalities, but exclusively Bismarck's caesarist regime, which had survived "by *expediently covering itself with monarchical legitimacy*," that was the cause of the failure of the liberal movement.[75] In principle, this defense of liberalism approximated the views of many leading liberals of the older generation, but Max Weber endowed them with an entirely aggressive rather than a resigned tone: he aimed to free liberalism from the flaw of failure and prepare it internally for more resolute liberal policies in the future.

Max Weber was convinced that the political trauma the liberals had suffered with the failure of the bourgeois revolution of 1848, and Bismarck's brilliant founding of the Reich that followed, played a decisive role in the lack of energy and resolution of the German liberal bourgeoisie in the political arena and the concentration on economics instead of politics. "The German state was not created by the power of the bourgeoisie, and when it was created, a Caesarian figure not hewn from bourgeois wood stood at the nation's helm," Weber asserted in 1895 in the Freiburg inaugural address.[76] The rupture of the bourgeoisie's political self-confidence through the experience of the Bismarckian triumph on the question of the national state was exacerbated by an onset of follower mentality. Weber himself shared, as we have seen, the crippling feeling of being the descendant of a great era for whom there was nothing additional that was truly important to accomplish now that the German state had been founded. It appeared to him to be an urgent necessity to overcome this feeling and to awaken the German bourgeoisie to new political activity. It would be decisive for the nation's future if the bourgeoisie had the will to take political leadership resolutely in its

74. Ibid., p. 319.

75. Ibid., p. 347. Cf. Weber's letter to Professor Lesser of 16 June 1917, *Pol. Schr.* 1, pp. 473 f. Lesser argued that the Center party and the Social Democrats had managed to maintain themselves as independent forces in relation to Bismarck and that therefore the liberals were themselves to blame for their own decline. Weber strongly objected to this reasoning.

76. *Pol. Schr.*, pp. 20 f.

hands, as it was slipping away from the East Elbian nobility, which were irreversibly in economic decline.

Weber expected nothing from proletarian politics. He was much too much a "class-conscious bourgeois" to give full justice to German Social Democracy. He measured the political maturity of individual social classes on the basis of their readiness "to place the long-term economic, political and *power* interests of the nation above all other considerations."[77] On this count he had to judge the Social Democrats, who were at the least indifferent to his national and imperialist ideals, as unsuited for political rule. In his opinion, the German working class lacked "the great *power* instincts of a class called to political leadership. . . . No spark of the Catilinarian energy of *action*, and no breath of the powerful *national* fervor" that had once inspired the *conventions* of the French Revolution was present in the ranks of the German working class.[78]

It was politically necessary to win the proletariat, which had been estranged by the failure of Bismarck's patriarchal social policies, back to the support of the national state. "I cannot see how it is possible to conceive of the political future of the country without hoping for the rise of a politically mature workers' movement cooperating positively to achieve Germany's greatness," Weber said in 1894.[79] In England, which was a model for him as for most German liberals, Weber discovered that the workers had an entirely different attitude toward the state. He attributed this "to the *reverberation of a world power position*, which constantly faced the state with great tasks in power politics and involved the people in constant political education."[80] This was a judgment in which the facts mixed uniquely with Weber's political ideals.

It was the "reverberation" of German "world power policy" and "great tasks in power politics" together with "constant political education" that Weber hoped would heal the basic German political disease, the nation's political immaturity and lack of sound political judgment. He wished to cut the Gordian knot of the German political situation and overcome the spiritual shortcomings that prevented a world policy borne

77. Ibid., p. 18.

78. Ibid., p. 22; cf. the speech to the Evangelisch-sozialer Kongress in 1894, *Verhandlungen*, p. 81.

79. *Christliche Welt*, 1894, p. 671.

80. Inaugural address, pp. 23 f.; cf. also the *Verhandlungen des evangelisch-sozialen Kongresses*, 1894, p. 81: "No one has more interest in the power of the national state than the proletariat, if it looks past the next day. England's prosperous workers' groups would not be able to maintain their standard of life for one day—in spite of all unions—if the international power of their empire should decay. This also could be said to our proletariat."

by the entire nation through resolute imperialist action.[81] The German bourgeoisie would regain its political self-confidence by participation in this politics of power; the proletariat would be liberated from the rhetoric of internationalism and won over to positive support of the established political order. The fervor of a national faith enlarged by imperialsm should thereby provide a means for Germany's inner regeneration.

Today, of course, we question whether this was really a suitable way to educate the nation and create a mature political sensibility. Was not Weber putting the cart before the horse? Did the call for an active world policy not increase the German ruling classes' vanity and desire for prestige rather than their readiness for responsible cooperation on current political tasks? Certainly, only great political goals could awaken activity and passion. But were there not sufficient tasks on the domestic political front? Had they to be sought in overseas expansion? Germany's ruling classes were aroused by German failures overseas, not by internal grievances, and they lacked the power to alleviate these grievances even when, as the *Daily Telegraph* affair demonstrated, the domestic situation damaged the Reich's international position. Their eyes were deflected from German constitutional and social problems at home to questions of German world policy. They neglected the reordering of their own house for Zanzibar, Samoa, Tsingtau, and Morocco. This is why German policy would fail in the end and lead Germany into a world catastrophe. On these grounds we would argue that Weber's efforts to bring about an internal political transformation of Germany through outside involvement in great international projects was of dubious political value. He remained imprisoned by the National Liberal tradition. He held the victory of liberalism to be possible only in association with great *national* successes and therefore he never seriously questioned the primacy of national principles over liberal ideas.

Weber came to recognize that his hope of interesting the working class in the material successes of German imperialism and thereby winning them for the state was utopian. It became increasingly clear to the trained eyes of the sociologist that there were great difficulties in achieving this goal under the conditions of modern, industrial mass society. Although the working class certainly had an objective interest in German economic and political expansion abroad, successful imperialist policies subjectively and materially strengthened the power of the existing ruling

81. "Whether a great policy will again be capable of directing our attention to the significance of the great questions of power, will be decisive for our development also." Inaugural address, *Pol. Schr.*, p. 23. In this regard, see also Dirk Oncken, "Das Problem des Lebensraums in der deutschen Politik vor 1914," diss., Freiburg, 1948, p. 96.

classes.[82] Under the impact of Weber's imperialist theories, Friedrich Naumann had set out to win the workers for a German world policy. While Weber was initially optimistic about the prospects for this approach, he nevertheless opposed Naumann. For the foreseeable future, only a class-conscious bourgeois movement could further a German world policy.[83]

82. Summarized in *Wirtschaft und Gesellschaft*, pp. 526 f. After 1907, Weber believed that the possibility of cooperation with Social Democracy was completely impossible for the foreseeable future. See the letter to Michels of 1 February 1907, below, chap. 5, note 170.

83. Cf. below, chap. 5, sec. 3.

5

Weber and Germany's Internal Political Evolution before the First World War

1. The Great Alternative: Industrialism or Feudalism

Both national and imperialistic ideals led Max Weber to see the central problem of contemporary German internal politics in one question: Would Germany put all its strength into developing as one of the world's leading industrial states and decisively widen the nation's economic territory through "economic conquests everywhere in the world," or would the landed aristocracy of eastern Germany, in alliance with petit-bourgeois anticapitalist forces and—even worse—with sections of the grande bourgeoisie concerned with security and the preservation of the economic and social status quo, be in a position effectively to thwart this development? Or, to put it differently: How would the struggle between the two socially and economically divided sections of Germany, the agricultural east, dominated by large estates, and the business-oriented west, be decided?

Weber's own position was very clear; he was firmly opposed to the conservatives. He believed that German world policy could only be conducted successfully if the consequences of a "powerful bourgeois capitalist evolution were resolutely implemented, all the more so as this was the only possible long-term economic policy for Germany in the capitalist era, whether one loves it or hates it."[1] He dismissed an economic policy favoring agricultural autarky and supporting landed estates not only as utopian but as extremely dangerous if Germany wished "a national existence different in kind from that of Switzerland."[2]

1. "Stellungnahme zur Flottenumfrage," *Pol. Schr.*, p. 31.

2. *Verhandlungen des 8. evangelisch-sozialen Kongresses*, 1897, p. 108: Weber could only agree when Oldenberg preferred the future risk of an expansive export economy on a

For Max Weber, everything hinged upon the removal of the conservatives from their political offices, which they used to defend their economic position from the accelerating inroads of capitalist expansion. In his opinion, the conservatives, once a politically representative class, had long since sunk to the level of narrow representation of vested interests. This had been patently clear for a long time, not just since 1890. Max Weber believed that agrarian interests had always had a decisive impact upon German economic policies. As long as the agrarians could sell their products on the English market, they were as free-trading as the liberals. Protective tariffs appeared as soon as the agrarians needed them.[3] He remarked in 1896 that "the dominant feudal elite sees in the state's greatness only its own greatness."[4] The anti-industrial self-interested policies of the conservatives (Canal bill, Kanitz motion, stock exchange law) tended, in Weber's view, to endanger German world power and, consequently, the nation's future.

For the same reasons, Weber thought it essential to break the conservative's traditional prominence in the Prussian administration.[5] The Prussian civil service was not inclined to subordinate their private interests to their official duties. The famous ordinance of von Puttkamer, which Caprivi revived, that Prussian civil servants must support the government's policies, testified to this fact. Weber put the matter quite bluntly: whenever material interests were affected, the "district magistrates' electoral machine [worked] remorselessly even against the king."[6] Often the civil service quite unconsciously used its position in the agrarian interest.[7] In addition, the agrarian-bred conservative civil services' lack of understanding of the problems of modern industrial economic life prompted Weber to attack the conservative predominance in the Prussian administration. For purely psychological reasons, it was unwise to choose civil servants from a social group that looked upon "the broad

---

large scale to an economic policy of 'self-sufficiency': "We believe that those nations that do not seek to direct their economic future toward greatness will have no future at all." Ibid., p. 113.

3. Lecture at the Freie Deutsche Hochstift. Report of the *Frankfurter Zeitung* of 15 March and the *Frankfurter Volksbote* of 14 March 1896. See also his lecture in St. Louis in 1904, "Capitalism and Rural Society in Germany," in *From Max Weber: Essays in Sociology* (New York: Oxford University Press, 1958), p. 382.

4. Lecture at the Freie Deutsche Hochstift, report of the *Frankfurter Volksbote*.

5. Cf. Lysbeth Walker Muncy, *The Junker in the Prussian Administration under William II, 1888–1914*, Brown University Studies, vol. 9 (Providence, 1944).

6. *Pol. Schr.*, p. 300.

7. Weber saw a distinct example of this in the "credit and agrarian policy of the Prussian Landschaften," which operated "to encourage the amassment of property in the hands of landed gentry" and was thereby—completely unconsciously—to the disadvantage of the peasants (*Bankarchiv* 8 [1908]: 87–91).

levels of the modern bourgeois and working classes without knowledge or understanding and with nothing but a vague, agrarian-colored antipathy."[8] Weber was unable to see any objective justification for the traditional Prussian practice of giving precedence to government job seekers of noble background. Today no one can see the need, he said in 1904, for "a still greater emphasis upon privileged lack of talent in the Prussian administration." He viewed a contemporary proposal for a new entail law in Prussia as an attempt to create new sources of conservative recruitment for the state bureaucracy.[9]

While Weber, as far as we know, did not unconditionally oppose moderate protectionism, he disapproved of the "exorbitant" protectionism since 1879.[10] In his eyes, the protective tariff was the visible seal of an alliance of interest between industry and the conservative aristocracy that blocked both progressive constitutional development in Prussia and Germany and a determined social policy. It was no accident that Max Weber attributed this alliance to Bismarck's efforts to split the German bourgeoisie and achieve the "victory of feudalism."[11] He was all the more eager for an end to this pact between the German grande bourgeoisie and their conservative rivals. He went on to praise Caprivi's commercial treaty policy for its service in breaking this "reactionary alliance."[12] With Brentano and Schulze-Gävernitz, he demanded "the release of the now conscious bourgeoisie, who were now returning to the service of their own ideals, from this unnatural alliance, in the interest of a fruitful social development and of the country's political freedom."[13]

Max Weber's most significant scientific achievement was to recognize and explain the salience of intellectual and psychological motives in economic life. He showed how the special economic sentiment that gave birth to modern rational capitalism and the division of labor had sprung from the spirit of puritan religiosity.[14] For Max Weber, the spirit that originated with inward-looking asceticism and took on hard work for its own sake because it was man's central task on earth, not for mere utility's sake, was simply the norm of bourgeois existence. He once wrote to

8. "Agrarstatistische und sozialpolitische Betrachtungen zur Fideikommissvorlage" (1904), in *Gesammelte Aufsätze zur Soziologie und Sozialpolitik*, pp. 388 f.

9. Ibid. In more detail below.

10. In 1912 it came to a conflict with Brentano, because Brentano wanted to raise the free trade question in tandem with a public demonstration that Weber planned in favor of the continuation of social policy.

11. Lecture at the Freier Deutsche Hochstift; even more pointed in the "Stellungnahme zur Flottenumfrage" (position paper on the naval inquiry), *Pol. Schr.*, pp. 31 f.

12. Lecture at the Freier Deutsche Hochstift.

13. *Verhandlungen des 8. evangelisch-sozialen Kongresses*, p. 113.

14. In this connection it is not necessary for us to concern ourselves with the correctness of the Weber thesis.

Adolf von Harnack "that our nation has never in any way experienced the school of hard asceticism. . . . This is the source of all that I find contemptible in it (as in myself)."[15] For Max Weber it was both characteristic and suggestive of the puritan roots of his thought that he wished the German nation to be a puritan people, earnest and self-conscious about their economic goals, and gifted with that special economic motivation that grew from inward-looking asceticism.

German reality was far from this ideal. Weber believed that the German bourgeois had moved further away from bourgeois ideals and come to imitate the life styles of the conservative aristocracy.[16] This trend was nurtured in the army especially, in the Prussian administration, and at the courts of the German dynasties. It exercised a considerable attraction upon the upper strata of the bourgeoisie and especially the intelligentsia. Weber was disheartened by this milieu in which the ancient aristocracy still retained its privileged social position and the bourgeoisie began to develop pseudo-aristocratic social ideals. He saw the specifically bourgeois social-status principle of career success replaced by the "reserve officer" virtues and the aristocratic code of honor. Weber compared social selection in the West, especially in the United States, with these German phenomena. He argued that the American sects promoted a much more resilient system of social selection, based upon the principle of economic efficiency and strength of character, than anything that contemporary German society had been able to produce.

Although Weber reached the rank of captain during his military service, he scorned the reserve officers' cult that had become so common among educated Germans of his day. He disapproved of the fact that possession of a reserve officer's patent had become the basis of an entirely unbourgeois principle of social selection, and he despised bourgeois attempts to employ these means to participate in the social prestige enjoyed by the Prussian officers' corps derived from aristocratic tradition. The once loyal Heidelberg Alemanne turned likewise against the student fraternities. He did so not only because the fraternities fostered a narrow-minded academic class consciousness and frequently encouraged a "tasteless and grotesquely inflated appearance" which, whenever it revealed itself, produced "mockery everywhere outside the country."[17] He objected to the fraternities above all because their ideal was confused with the social life styles of the "circles in Prussia officially recognized as socially acceptable."[18] Weber sharply criticized "that feudal prestige . . .

15. Letter of 5 February 1906, Harnack papers.

16. Cf., in addition, Weber's address to the eighth Evangelisch-sozialer Kongress in 1897, *Verhandlungen* . . . , pp. 110 f.

17. "Denkschrift an die Handelshochschulen"; cf. also note 22; also "Capitalism and Rural Society in Germany," p. 373.

18. "Denkschrift an die Handelshochschulen."

that [is represented] among us in student life by the wearing of colors, dueling scars, the fraternity tradition generally, and the diversion from serious study for the sake of 'satisfaction' and the status of 'Reserve Officers.' "[19]

The spread of the fraternity system beyond the traditional educated professions to the commercial ones greatly disquieted Weber. He regretfully pointed out at the university professors' convention in Dresden in 1911 that the newly created business schools attracted a good portion of their students by dint of such "feudal pretensions," which were in turn associated with highly material opportunities for career advancement.[20] Although Weber expressed no doubts about the objective achievements of the business schools, his statements led to a major press campaign against him.[21] Both the Cologne and Berlin business schools felt obligated to defend their fraternity students.[22] Weber remained convinced nevertheless that the spread of pseudo-aristocratic life attitudes that he saw in the fraternities to bourgeois-commercial circles represented a danger for Germany's economic future. The office and the bank could not afford to replace a selective system based on purely economic and objective attributes with one of pseudo-aristocratic origin based on Corps membership or the possession of an officer's commission. Weber was also outraged by the increase of "diploma exam people," and he was convinced that the development of a special, academically educated stratum that felt itself socially superior to colleagues within the commercial realm had to lead to intolerable friction.[23] "Neither the possession of a color stripe nor an officer's commission" were "in themselves *in any sense* suitable as proof" that "their possessor was suited to hard and serious work" and "without the latter, our bourgeoisie would not be able to preserve Germany's world position."[24]

Weber opposed the "feudal pretensions" of the German bourgeoisie even more energetically when they played directly into the hands of the conservative landlords. At that time, bourgeois merchants and industrial-

19. "Die Handelshochschulen," *Berliner Tageblatt*, no. 548, 27 October 1911.

20. *Verhandlungen des 4. deutschen Hochschullehrertages*, report approved by the governing committee (Leipzig, 1912), pp. 66 ff.

21. Cf. ibid., p. 86: "I am able to discern that the German commercial colleges are doing an outstanding job, as far as I can judge. My point here is my concern that we have gone the route of special commercial universities and not the route of affiliation with the general universities. The reasons for this are those that I have pointed out . . . that men who want to be active in commerce are seeking to create a distinct qualification in the manner of our feudal German social order."

22. Weber's reply to the press attack: "Die Handelshochschulen"; memorandum to the Handelshochschulen (Cologne and Berlin), in the possession of Professor Baumgarten, partially quoted in *Lebensbild*, pp. 432 f; *Tägliche Rundschau*, no. 497, 22 October 1911.

23. Cf. *Pol. Schr.*, p. 276.

24. "Die Handelshochschulen."

ists in large numbers were taking advantage of the possibility of rising into the class of large, landholding Junkers through ownership of entailed knightly property and in this way also achieving titles of nobility. The family of Chancellor von Bethmann Hollweg had earned nobility and social status in this way. The grandfather, a member of a Rhenish merchant family, had been granted entail and a patent of nobility. Max Weber did not deny that political conditions strongly encouraged the bourgeoisie to do this. "The rank and file of the bourgeoisie are still excluded from participation in power by the feudal mentality that dominates the minds of ministers and industrialists alike, and are thereby forced to covet titles of nobility."[25] The institution of entailment and the practice of patent nobility, it seemed to Weber, revealed a blatant effort by the conservatives to strengthen their faltering social position by winning over to their own camp the highest levels of the upper bourgeoisie.

This was all the more reason for the "class-conscious bourgeois" Max Weber to fight these renegades of his own class tooth and nail. In contrast to them, he proudly identified with his descent "from Westphalian linen."[26] He hoped for a united front of the bourgeoisie against the conservatives and their reactionary predominence in the Prussian state. Only bourgeois divisiveness and lack of class consciousness permitted the conservatives to stay in the saddle. Weber's interpretation of the situation conformed entirely to the Marxist class analysis, with the characteristic variation that he considered the status group of the conservative landlords and their supporters a class in the modern sense of the word. In principle, he recognized clearly that the bourgeoisie were separated by class as much from the Junkers, the representatives of the feudal and patriarchal social order, as they were from the working class. He was resentful that the inevitable victory of the bourgeoisie over the aristocracy would be delayed by the desertion of sections of the bourgeois elite.

In 1904, when the Prussian government presented a bill for a new entailment law, Max Weber attacked it because he recognized it as a covert gamble on the feudal inclinations of the upper bourgeoisie. He categorically opposed the "romantic" belief that entailment had a state-preserving effect. In fact it preserved nothing but "agrarian and *Con-*

25. Lecture at the Freier Deutsche Hochstift; according to the report of the *Frankfurter Volksbote*, 14 March 1896. Compare also Robert Michels, *Zur Soziologie des Parteiwesens in der modernen Demokratie*, Kröner ed. (Stuttgart, 1957), p. 16; and Hugo Preuss's pamphlet: "Novae epistolae obscurorum virorum" in *Staat, Recht und Freiheit* (Tübingen, 1926), pp. 560 ff.

26. "I myself bear the name of Westphalian linen proudly, and do *not* betray my pride in this bourgeois ancestry in the manner of those circles of whom I spoke, who can do this all too readily" ("Die Handelshochschulen").

servative party rule within the local organizations and the civil service."[27] The bill's expressed goal was the conservation of existing large landholdings and the creation of new ones, although the agricultural and political situation in eastern Germany demanded peasant settlement to prevent the Polish advance. The bill was a national evil not only in the political sense; it was "completely devoid of moral responsibility in social policy" since experience proved that agricultural workers in regions dominated by entailed landholdings had by far the worst work conditions.[28] The decisive fact in Max Weber's argument was that the bill offered the bourgeoisie increased incentives to seek entailment. It offered up hundreds of thousands of German acres to "the contemptible ambition for noble symbols or a quasi-noble position." Weber noted sarcastically that "it is a part of the contemporary dominant wisdom of state in Prussia to reconcile bourgeois wealth with minimal bourgeois influence on politics in order to maintain a kind of 'second class court worthiness.' For those circles that benefited, nothing would be less popular than if the 'nobilization' of capital that was gained in trade, in industry, or on the stock exchange should face difficulties in the metamorphosis into noble landholding."[29] He also was aroused by the provision for a personal monarchical decision about entailment instead of a responsible decision by the minister, since this could only "excessively flatter the vanity of families permitted entailment." In this he saw the penetration of dynastic perceptions into domestic politics, something he fought wherever it appeared.[30]

For Weber, the entailment bill of 1904 was an ideal example of the conservative efforts to break up the united front of the bourgeoisie in opposition to the large landlords. The bourgeoisie's "tragic fear of the red specter" and their yen for social respectability through dynastic acts of favor were helpful enough to such attempts. Max Weber was deeply contemptuous of this. In 1917, when a new entailment bill was submitted in the Prussian Landtag, he argued even more forcefully against the "nobilization of war profits." A law that contemptibly played upon plutocratic vanity in order to reverse the decline in the social position of the conservative landlords was in fact a violation of the *Burgfrieden*.[31]

There were also purely economic and indeed imperialistic arguments that prompted Weber to fight all efforts that would make the winning of entailment privileges any easier. Weber argued that easier entailment

27. "Agrarstatistische und sozialpolitische Betrachtungen zur Fideikommissvorlage," *Gesammelte Aufsätze zur Soziologie und Sozialpolitik*, p. 381.
28. Ibid., p. 360.
29. Ibid., p. 379.
30. Ibid., pp. 362, 380.
31. *Pol. Schr.*, pp. 183 ff.

would accelerate the rise in eastern land prices, which, as a result of the social value placed upon noble landholdings, were already high. Above all he pointed out that productive capital would be withdrawn from economic life and put to the use of purely prestige-producing, economically unproductive land purchases. "The possibility of the establishment of *bourgeois* and patent noble entailment, since it flattered the most contemptible vanity, increasingly encouraged German bourgeois capital away from international economic conquests to the path of creating *rentier* life styles," Weber concluded.[32]

As the earning of pure interest replaced growth in capital investment, and the concomitant interest mentality replaced economic daring, Germany's economic position would be endangered. This trend appeared to Weber to have been boosted significantly by the protectionist economic policy introduced during Hohenlohe's chancellorship, which was based upon "all powerful *agrarian claptrap*."[33]

Weber preferred an economic policy that encouraged economic expansion and that did not favor the quiet risk-free earnings desired by people living on interest. He maintained that a puritan economic mentality aiming at profit and economic success for their own sakes without worrying about temporary utility ought to be both an ideal and a standard; certainly not the calm enjoyment of capital. He regarded it as frivolous when German "literati," as he always contemptuously labeled journalists who "saluted" whoever was in power, "called the German 'world spirit' the national congenital sickness" and dared to suggest "peace and contentment as a future ideal." This could only be the ideal "of a group that lived on trust funds and interest payments."[34] Those things that are so appealing about the romantic life style—safety from the exhaustion of career work, the opportunity for pure relaxation, the life ideal that is not associated with career "efficiency"—alienated Weber. He had no brief for the typical savings bank mentality of the French petite bourgeoisie and feared nothing more than an "Austrianization" of Germany.[35]

If Weber always decisively opposed the appearance of interest-income capitalism, whether in the guise of socially valued landholdings or social insurance, it was not only because he believed that this would damage the nation's industrial development, but also because of his universal-

32. *Gesammelte Aufsätze zur Soziologie und Sozialpolitik*, p. 391.

33. "Our entire economic policy encourages *pensioners*," ibid., p. 372, n. 1. "*Protection of pensions* is the signature of our economic policy," ibid., p. 391. Cf. speech at the eighth Evangelisch-socialer Kongress in 1897, *Verhandlungen*, pp. 110 ff. "Agrarische Phrase": "Stellungnahme zur Flottenumfrage," *Pol. Schr.*, p. 31.

34. *Pol. Schr.*, p. 249.

35. Ibid., pp. 252, 250, in association with pp. 137, 187.

historical perspective. If the static, security-conscious, economically conservative mentality characteristic of interest-income capitalism prevailed, bureaucratization would receive an additional impetus, which would eventually lead to the destruction of the liberal society of his time. Weber was convinced that only a dynamic form of capitalism could effectively prevent the bureaucratic glaciation of mankind that waited in the midst of a perhaps not very distant future.[36] Here, Weber focused the capitalist economic mentality that arose from the spirit of puritanism upon the screen of the philosophy of history. He might well be compared in this instance to Karl Marx. With justice, Karl Löwith pointed to Max Weber as the bourgeois antipode to the theorist of proletarian class struggle. No one had analyzed the spiritual bases of bourgeois existence more deeply and thoroughly. Scarcely anyone had championed bourgeois life ideals with such force as this descendant of French Huguenots.

Our consideration of Max Weber as a merciless critic of all feudal pretensions may be concluded with a glance at his quarrels with the Saarland industrialist Baron von Stumm. Stumm was an exponent of the socially repressive course that had circumscribed German domestic policy since Caprivi. He was not content to heap wild abuse upon Social Democracy. He also dismissed the Christian Social movement as mere Christian-tainted socialism and damned the efforts of Kathedersozialisten for a governmental solution to the social question as pseudoscientific comfort and aid to Social Democracy.[37] In response, a major press quarrel broke out; Naumann set the energetic tone in *Die Hilfe*. Adolf Wagner donned the gloves for the Kathedersozialisten. This press quarrel in which Stumm characterized his opponents as "megalomaniacs of gray theory" who indulged in real orgies that "had to open even the eyes of imbeciles to their nonsense," took bitter forms.[38] In the end, Stumm tried to withdraw from the affair by sending Adolf Wagner a challenge to duel. When the latter instead demanded a settlement in a court of honor, Stumm tried to take advantage of the demand in a public declaration in which he accused Wagner of cowardice.[39]

36. Löwith, "Max Weber und Karl Marx," in *Gesammelte Abhandlungen*, 2d ed. (Stuttgart, 1969), pp. 54 ff. Cf. Albert Salomon, "Max Weber," in *Die Gesellschaft* 3, no. 1 (1926): 131 ff. Salomon refers to Weber here as a "bourgeois Marx" (p. 144). For a systematic treatment of the relationship of Weber to Marx, see my treatment in "The Age of Bureaucracy," pp. 47 ff.

37. In his Reichstag speech of 9 January 1895.

38. Stumm's declaration in the *Post* of 15 February 1895, published in the *Neue Preussische Zeitung*, 26 February 1895.

39. "The vulgar attacks, in part based on falsifying my words by this society ('of deluded evangelical ministers or of arrogant professors'), that have slandered me in injudicious meetings, in the press, and in direct announcements, have not disturbed me since the combative gentlemen have refused to give personal satisfaction for their insults." Ibid.

At this point, Max Weber, who did not share the conservative Wagner's political views, could not resist attacking Stumm publicly. Of course, the *Kreuzzeitung* accepted the third, greatly softened version of his article about "the battle methods of Baron von Stumm," and they accepted it only when the Kaiser, under Stumm's influence, appeared to be turning against the conservatives.[40] Weber found it doubly contemptible that Stumm thought it proper in a political quarrel to fall back upon his "quality as an officer," for he saw at play not only Stumm's vain parvenu mentality but calculated tactics as well. Weber clearly recognized, in Stumm's attempt to transfer an objective quarrel to the field of personal honor, a plot to include William II himself. Stumm artfully speculated upon the Kaiser's sympathy for the aristocratic aspects of duels and hoped thereby to win the Kaiser's support against Adolf Wagner and the direction in social policy that he represented. Weber called the challenge to duel a "theatrical coup" in which Stumm had apparently assumed that it was possible to "make an impression on the monarch by the public and no less incorrect assertion that the Kathedersozialisten did not stand behind their statements with their persons." Eager for battle, Weber awaited a response from Stumm. He asked his brother "to observe the *Post*," so that if Stumm "opened his mouth," Weber "could quickly leap at his throat."[41]

For Weber, the Stumm affair had a paradigmatic significance. It was a thoroughly crass example of "truly loathsome public duel bravado" and the feudalizing ambitions of that part of the upper bourgeoisie who, dependent on the monarch and the conservative right, sought to prevent a progressive social policy and thereby a liberal domestic evolution. It was people of this ilk "who long for the moment when social policies can be shot down with cannons."[42]

40. Von Hammerstein rejected the first article with the comment that when it was necessary to attack an enemy, he would prefer to write it himself (compare Weber's letter to Clara Mommsen of 11 February 1895 and to Alfred Weber of 1 February 1895, Weber papers.). Thereafter, Weber softened his tone considerably. But Hammerstein refused the new version of the article because of an "insult to royalty" (letter to Alfred Weber of 24 February 1895, Weber papers.) Hammerstein threw the third version at Stumm's "head" (according to Weber) since it at least "avoided bringing the Kaiser in," and Stumm seemed to have set the monarch against the agrarians. The article appeared in the *Neue Preussische (Kreuz-) Zeitung* of 12 March 1895. The earlier versions are not extant.

41. Letter to Alfred Weber of 27 February 1895, Weber papers, partly in *Lebensbild*, pp. 231 f., with an incorrect date and characteristically weakened. Marianne Weber repeatedly removed the characteristic sharpness from Weber's letters and other statements. A second article by Weber against a reply not written by Stumm appeared in the *Neue Preussische (Kreuz-) Zeitung* of 12 March 1895.

42. Cf. Weber's statements about Stumm at the eighth Evangelisch-sozialer Kongress, 1897, *Verhandlungen*, p. 111: "We recently experienced the offensive appearance of the industrial patent noble with what even the supporters of duelling regard as truly loathsome

2. The Social Unification of the Nation

Max Weber considered a progressive social policy the necessary corollary of a successful world policy. As early as his Freiburg inaugural address, he pointed to "the *social unification* of the nation, which modern economic evolution had ruptured," as the most pressing task in German domestic politics in preparation "for the difficult struggles of the future."[43] It was essential to win the workers' positive cooperation with the government. For this reason all social policy ought to help protect the workers' free self-determination and educate them in self-responsibility. He certainly did not favor social policy out of a sense of social responsibility. His views were close to those of Nietzsche in this area; he held no brief for "pity." He also rejected eudaemonistic ideals. "We do not pursue a social policy in order to create human contentment," he declared at the Evangelisch-sozialer Kongress of 1894. "I believe that we must avoid seeking to produce positive feelings of contentment through social legislation. We wish and can only wish something else: that which is worthy in man, self-responsibility, aspiration for humanity's spiritual and moral legacy, this is what we wish to preserve and support."[44] He did not favor a leveling social policy but, rather, conscious support for the rise of the upper layers of the working class, on which (with a glance at England) he placed great hopes.[45]

Weber wanted a progressive social policy based upon self-determination and self-responsibility. The error of patriarchal social policy was that it coupled a well-meaning concern for the material interests of the workers with a wish to maintain or, if possible, increase their subordination and subjugation.[46] It paid absolutely no attention to the workers' efforts for independence and equality, which was of much greater significance than the efforts for mere material betterment. Max Weber expected little from such social policies in the long term. A modern social policy, for him, could have sense only if it placed the workers in an economic and social take-off position so that they could compete economically and socially with the corporate leadership. At the same time

---

public duel bragging: those involved are not the representatives of the old nobility, but of those swaggering parvenus who today make the Prussian minister of culture shudder."

43. *Pol. Schr.*, p. 23.

44. *Verhandlungen des evangelisch-sozialen Kongresses*, 1894, p. 80; cf. above, chap. 3, sec. 2.

45. Cf. Weber's heading in his lectures about the labor question (Weber papers): The English labor movement is aristocratic in origin: stress on quality, not solidarity of the subjugated (workers). This leads to the formation of a middle class from the workers.

46. Beyond the tendency of patriarchalism, to become a bearer of a "specific" social policy. Cf. *Wirtschaft und Gesellschaft*, p. 660.

this would permit them the necessary measure of positive social and political responsibility and would encourage them to support the existing government.

Max Weber therefore was sharply critical of Bismarck's social policy. It had failed because its only concern had been the workers' welfare and had ignored their efforts for independence. Moreover, Bismarck's policy had misguidedly counted on the "thanks of the content masses."[47] In his great polemic on "Bismarck's legacy" during the war in a series of articles in the *Frankfurter Zeitung*, Weber sharply attacked the demagogic one-sidedness of the chancellor's social legislation. Bismarck's social policy had denied "protective labor legislation, which was indispensable for the preservation of the nation's population resources, labeling it interference with the rights of the master." It had ignored "the health and strength" of the politically decisive group among the working class. Instead, Bismarck had "employed the police to destroy" the unions on the basis of the socialist laws and had thereby driven "the only possible bearers of the workers' objective interests" "into the most extreme and partisan radicalism."[48]

Max Weber was even less content with William II's early social policies, which had their roots in the Kaiser's own need for prestige and reflected the "fashionable" opinions of his advisers of the time. He wished to see social policy based on a *national* policy, not on an attempt at popularity. He later referred to the "fraud of the so-called social monarchy of those years."[49] It did not surprise him when the hectic enthusiasm of the "social policy ordinances" resulted in a revulsion to the opposite extreme. It distressed him to see the view gain ground that "in social policy as well there is only one ultima ratio: powder and lead."[50]

Max Weber agreed with Marxist theory insofar as he recognized "class struggle" as an "integral element" of the modern industrial social order.[51] But he deemed illusory the hope that a transformation of the social structure would end this fundamental antagonism between labor and capital and with it "the rule of men over men." He took socialist theories seriously only as ethical points of view. Characteristically, we find no systematic analysis of Karl Marx's key theories of economics or his

47. *Die Landarbeiter in den evangelischen Gebieten Norddeutschlands*, ed. Max Weber (Tübingen, 1899), p. 11; *Pol. Schr.*, pp. 19 f.; "Zur Rechtfertigung Göhres," *Christliche Welt*, 1892, p. 1107. The worker "accepts payments for sickness, accident, old age, and disability, because he regards it as his right. He would reject charity." Compare also, *Gesammelte Aufsätze zur Soziologie und Sozialpolitik*, pp. 394 ff.

48. *Pol. Schr.*, p. 318.

49. Letter to the Freiburg colleagues of 15 November 1911, cf. above, chap. 3, note 129.

50. Max Weber, ed., *Die Landarbeiter in den evangelischen Gebieten Norddeutschlands* (Tübingen, 1899), p. 11.

51. *Verhandlungen des evangelisch-sozialen Kongresses* 1894, p. 73.

philosophy of history in Weber's sociological works.[52] It could be argued, however, that Max Weber's grand attempt to identify the ideal components present in the rise of specific economic systems and social structures in his work on the sociology of religion was intended to refute the Marxist theory that intellectual life was the superstructure of economic conditions.[53] Weber, however, understood this theory in the vulgar Marxist sense. Indeed, Weber summarized the essential findings of these researches in 1918 under the title "Positive Critique of the Materialist Interpretation of History" in a lecture series in Vienna.[54]

Weber's argument about the religious bases of economic structures does not get to the core of Marxist theory. For Weber conceded readily that capitalism, once fully developed, could exist without any special economic work ethic as a "calling" inasmuch as competition as the motive force of the economic process made this special work ethic superfluous.[55] To this extent, the Marxist schema achieves full validity in the mature stage of capitalism. Capitalism, as a material system of production, becomes the great destroyer of the older social structures and undermines their specific cultural ideal. Through the competitive principle, capitalism imposes on man not a dynamic economic mentality that is rooted in religion but one that behaves as if it had religious roots. It rationalizes not only the social structure but the cultural ideal itself.[56] Max Weber masterfully described these consequences of capitalism.

Actually, Weber was closer to Marx's methodological position than he would have admitted. When he stated that "the so-called 'materialistic interpretation of history' as a *Weltanschauung* or as a formula for the causal explanation of historical reality is to be rejected most emphatically,"[57] he was thinking of the then current vulgar-Marxist interpretation of Marx rather than of Marx himself. His own sociological methods, which sought to depict the significant developmental trends in modern society ideal-typically in the light of a universal-historical back-

52. Max Weber planned to treat the problem of socialism systematically in a lecture series in the summer semester of 1920. His death prevented this before he appears to have begun. Compare Guenther Roth, "Das historische Verhältnis der Weberschen Soziologie zum Marxismus," *Kölner Zeitschrift für Soziologie und Sozialpsychologie* 20 (1968): 432 ff.

53. Cf. Löwith, "Max Weber und Karl Marx," p. 207, who writes of Weber's systematic "miscriticism." Weber is said to have concealed—to be sure in association with vulgar-Marxism—Marx's original point of reference, the human phenomenon of alienation, with anti-Marxist arguments.

54. Cf. *Lebensbild*, p. 617.

55. Nevertheless, he did not consistently maintain this view; rather he called for a dynamic economic conviction.

56. Cf. Joseph A. Schumpeter, *Kapitalismus, Sozialismus, und Demokratie* (Bern, 1946), p. 27: "All of Max Weber's facts and arguments conform completely to the Marxist system."

57. *Wissenschaftslehre*, pp. 166 f.

ground, were largely in accord with Marx's own brilliant outlines.[58] Weber of course maintained, in contrast to the Marxist theory of "superstructure," that "ideal" as well as "material interests" decisively determined men's social conduct.[59] Similarly, he disputed the position that class interest alone was a dependable gauge of the social behavior of members of a class.[60] Social status and the sociotypical behavior patterns that it determined were at least equally important to him.

He made no attempt to soften the image of capitalism in his ideal-typical description of the capitalist system in *Economy and Society*. Weber noted that the formally rational law of the bourgeois state corresponded to the interests of the property owners and in no way served the disappropriated proletariat. The maximum in "formal rationality" of the economic system could be achieved only when market-oriented exchange of goods was uninhibited and the "subordination" of the worker to the entrepreneur complete. He himself designated this fact as a "material irrationality" in the capitalist system, thereby anticipating much of the later critique of Herbert Marcuse.[61]

Weber could not conceive of any genuine alternative to the capitalist economic system, although he allowed for the possibility of socialist forms of society in theory in his considerations. He held the "future socialist revolution" to be a chimera. He responded to his student Robert Michels, who from a humanitarian and radical democratic position contended with the problems of liberal socialism, with the argument that the only alternative that existed was between a pure ethically-conscientious syndicalist socialism in the Tolstoyan sense and "cultural *affirmation* through adaptation to the social demands of technology, whether economic, political, or anything else." In the second instance, however, "all discussions of 'revolution' [were] farce; all theories that the rule of men over men could be overcome by any kind of socialist social system or by any other subtle forms of democracy were utopian."[62]

58. See Jürgen Kocka, "Max Weber und Karl Marx: Ein Methodologischer Vergleich," *Zeitschrift für die gesamte Staatswissenschaft* 122 (1966); now also in *Geschichte und Ökonomie*, ed. Hans-Ulrich Wehler, *Neue Wissenschaftliche Bibliothek* 58 (1973): 54 ff. See also my investigation, *The Age of Bureaucracy*, pp. 47 ff. The relationship between dynamic capitalism and bureaucratic socialism in Weber's political theory is discussed in detail there.

59. See *Religionssoziologie*, vol. 1, p. 252.

60. *Wirtschaft und Gesellschaft*, vol. 2, p. 533.

61. Cf. Herbert Marcuse, "Industrialisierung und Kapitalismus im Werk Max Webers," in *Kultur und Gesellschaft*, vol. 2 (Frankfurt, 1968), pp. 107 ff; and also my *Age of Bureaucracy*, pp. 67 f.

62. Letter of 4 August 1908, copy in Weber papers. In addition here: "A modern man who only wishes to live in *the* sense that he has his daily newspaper, railroads, electricity, etc. renounces your ideals for the future as soon as he relinquishes revolutionism for itself without any 'goal,' without even the *conceivability* of a goal. You are an honorable chap,

Weber's arguments against socialist ideology were similar to others of his time. He limited himself to drawing attention to Marx's theories of progressive deprivation and crisis and to noting the limited correctness of the theory of concentration.[63] He disputed the inevitability of an evolutionary trend toward socialism and anticipated the contrary: "an inevitable and prolonged capitalist era."[64] None of the theoretically conceivable forms of socialism appeared to him to be capable of realizing those ideals which he believed were championed by socialist theory. It was virtually impossible, in his view, to do anything about the expropriation of the *individual* worker by the means of production—the real cause of his reduction to a commodity and his alienation. He regarded the appropriation of the means of production by a syndicalist organization—a producers' cooperative, for instance—to be riddled with economic handicaps, above all because the rational accounting and management practices of entrepreneurial firms would not be feasible for that purpose.[65] Weber was convinced that the abolition of private ownership of the means of production in itself would in no way fulfill Marx's enthusiastic predictions about the emancipation from capital. "Any *rational*, unified socialist economy would retain the expropriation of the workers. It would only go one step further in the expropriation of private owners as well."[66] Weber argued that this would not in the least affect the workers' class position. Instead, the worker would be faced with an all-embracing state bureaucracy, incomparably more powerful than private entrepreneurs.[67]

Weber also warned that a socialistically organized economy that met human needs would not bring about a reduction in conflicts between interest groups. These conflicts would simply continue in new forms on a different plane.[68] He had no concrete notion of what form a socialist economic organization might take. He was certain that socialism's freedom from the irrationality of free competition, speculation, and recurring economic crisis would be bought at the greater cost of "a decrease in the formal, calculating rationality" characteristic of capitalist, free market economics.[69] Weber was convinced that "the maximum of formal ratio-

---

and on your own . . . you will go through the critical process that brought me to this point long ago and stamped me as a bourgeois politician—as long as the little that we can hope for is still possible."

63. Compare Weber's lecture "Der Sozialismus," *Gesammelte Aufsätze zur Soziologie und Sozialpolitik*, pp. 492 ff.

64. *Pol. Schr.*, p. 318.

65. *Wirtschaft und Gesellschaft*, pp. 50 f.

66. Ibid., p. 79.

67. *Pol. Schr.*, pp. 331 f.

68. *Wirtschaft und Gesellschaft*, p. 119.

69. Ibid., p. 60.

nality in capital accounting" was possible only through "subjugation of the worker to domination by entrepreneurs."[70] It was precisely this formal, rational calculation that provided the advantage to modern division-of-labor capitalism over all previous economic systems. A socialist economy oriented to the satisfaction of human needs (and Weber understood this to be an economy that seriously used the concept of "income" as a regulating factor, as well as "effective" market prices) would therefore be negatively encumbered.[71] In *Economy and Society*, Weber compared the variations of a market-oriented "trading economy" in ideal-typical form with all of the conceivable varieties of centrally controlled socialist "planned economies" in order to point out which system was in the best position to release the maximum social dynamism. From this vantage, the prize went to a production-oriented capitalist market economy with the highest degree of formally free competition. The conceivable forms of socialist economic organization, as well as those forms of capitalism that put the interests of bond investors ahead of the expansion-oriented interests of capital owners and managers, would lack this dynamism.[72]

The decisive factor, however, in Weber's rejection of the socialist ideal was his conviction that "any rational socialism" would appropriate the bureaucratic elements in capitalist society and increase them immeasurably. A socialist order needed to create "strict bureaucratic administration according to even firmer, formal *rules*" than a capitalist one.[73] At best, socialism could become a powerful bureaucratic consumer organization that would bring mankind markedly nearer to "the iron cage of the future."[74]

Max Weber thought it wrong to expect that the emancipation of the working class could only come through the destruction of the capitalist system. In his view, the advancement of the working class within the capitalist system was not only possible but even in the interest of capitalism. Socialist experiments were only likely to retard this development. Weber therefore necessarily rejected Social Democracy's revolutionary agitation and considered unrealistic its blind trust in a final victory for socialism. In the light of the situation, he had little hope that the working-class movement would be able to realize even a small part of its socialist ideals. "Political democratization is the only thing that is perhaps realizable in the short term, and that is no small achievement," he wrote in

70. Ibid., p. 78.

71. Weber viewed the border between socialism and social reform as measured by the extent to which "effective prices were maintained," ibid., p. 56. Cf. pp. 120 f.

72. Cf. *Wirtschaft und Gesellschaft*, pp. 59 f.

73. Ibid., p. 129.

74. *Pol. Schr.*, pp. 396 f.

1907 to Robert Michels, who, in contrast to Weber, passionately championed socialist views. "I cannot prevent you from believing in more; but do not press me to do likewise."[75] He hoped that the political emancipation of the working class in a democratized German state would split the "reactionary" alliance of industry with the conservatives that permitted the latter group to oppose a progressive social policy.[76]

Because Max Weber believed that the workers' movement had a future only *within* the capitalist system, he was relatively untroubled by the German Social Democrats' support of class struggle. He derided the German bourgeoisie's tragic fear of the red menace.[77] The German Social Democrats were "infinitely more harmless than they [appear] to themselves."[78] He was persuaded that a narrow-minded group ran the Social Democratic party, which was otherwise influenced by a clique of fanatical journalists. He did not miss the opportunity to attend the Social Democratic party's Mannheim convention in 1906 in order to win the best possible immediate impression about the party's character and its leading personalities. The convention went badly, and Weber felt fully confirmed in his views. He could not understand how the bourgeoisie could fear such a party; and he was of the opinion that the revolutionary Russian Social Democrats present on the platform must have clapped their hands over their heads to have witnessed such a sorry performance. Weber lacked the background to be just to the German Social Democrats' discussions at the convention. With his pronounced sensitivity to power, he had little taste for the tenor of the discussions centering on the general strike and its implementation. They seemed to make it clear that the party leaders lacked even an elementary instinct for power, the necessary quality for any able politician. Weber could easily understand the kind of radical, emotional politics that did not shrink from hopeless battles. He took the anarchists who were committed to social revolutionary action far more seriously than he did the Marxists, who took comfort from the belief that their eventual victory was a historical necessity. Weber recognized only two valid alternatives: radical anarchist politics based on emotional and ethical convictions and unconcerned about consequences—or revisionist politics focusing on the contemporary situation.

The contrast between revolutionary agitation and careful avoidance of all revolutionary action, coupled with simultaneous rejection of a meaningful revisionist strategy that he observed in Mannheim, greatly irritated Weber. He concluded that a feeling of total impotency lay behind all of the "revolutionary futuristic music." He reported to Robert

75. Letter of 6 November 1907; copy in Weber papers.
76. Cf. *Kapitalismus und Agrarverfassung*, p. 441.
77. *Die Landarbeiter in den evangelischen Gebieten Norddeutschlands*, p. 11.
78. *Pol. Schr.*, p. 22.

Michels that "Mannheim was very 'shoddy.' . . . I heard Bebel and Legien mention 'our weakness' at least ten times. In addition, I noticed an extreme petit-bourgeois manner, many plump innkeeper faces, a lack of imagination. They were incapable of deciding to move 'towards the right,' given the fact that the way to 'the left' is blocked or appears to be. These men no longer scare anyone."[79] It was the German Social Democrats' apparent powerlessness at Mannheim that made them seem so disappointing.

Weber had mixed views about the objective results of the Mannheim party convention. The trade union wing, unwilling to sacrifice union organization for uncertain experiments, had won a clear victory. This was in accord with Weber's own views. He believed that lost strikes would usually set back not only the unions themselves, but "every advance of the class movement as a whole for years, even decades."[80] Weber also realized that the party leadership could not openly take a revisionist course without seriously endangering party unity. He was caught in a contradiction when he concluded that since the party rejected revolutionary action, it had lost all "enthusiasm," while he complained at the same time that the party could not decide to work positively within the existing social fabric.[81]

Weber could no longer take Social Democracy's pretensions to be a class party with revolutionary goals seriously. Only sincere anarchists who were prepared to commit revolutionary acts without regard to their own safety found grace in his eyes. This was reflected in the picture of the party that Weber sketched in 1907 at the meeting of the Verein für Sozialpolitik. It was extremely negative: the party had lost the catilinarian energy of its faith. That energy had been replaced by "lame rhetorical grumbling and complaining, petty reasoning."[82] Robert Michels pro-

79. Letter of 8 October 1906; copy in Weber papers.

80. Compare the letter to Michels of 9 February 1908, copy in Weber papers, in which he also energetically rejected Michels's thesis that *every* strike works toward socialism and was therefore "correct." He referred to Michels's "measuring 'ethics' on 'success'": "Have you completely forgotten your Cohen? He could at least exorcise you in this regard. Finally, the *syndicalist* Michels! The syndicalist M. may (and must) perhaps say: The conviction that justifies the strike *is always* the 'correct' conviction; it is the militarist (class-militarist) conviction, it is *patriotic* (class-patriotic)—ergo, etc. But *what* weakness to cast furtive glances at success! And then to violate the clear facts!" Weber was able to accept socialistic and syndicalist theory only in their most extreme ethical guise (and therefore their most radical manifestation). He found the Socialists' rational and realistic wriggling between positive practical work (with the practical abandonment of all specific socialistic ideals of the future) and radical mass strike action to be philistinish. This was a natural reaction for someone who tended to think dialectically in extremes. But was such an estimate generally adequate?

81. Cf. the letter to Michels of 1 February 1907, below, note 95.

82. *Gesammelte Aufsätze zur Soziologie und Sozialpolitik*, p. 410.

tested against such a disparaging critique of German Social Democracy.[83] Weber replied in a characteristic way. Michel should regard "the speech that puzzled him simply as the speech of a 'class-conscious bourgeois' to the cowards of his own class."[84] Weber said it was an "insane idea" that "a class party with ostensible class ideals could ever become something other than a [party] 'machine' in the American sense of the word." He therefore had told his own class: "You numbskulls! Social Democracy, whether parliamentary or syndicalist, is and will become nothing 'more terrible' (from your vantage point) than an ordinary party machine."[85]

Max Weber observed the development of German Social Democracy for some time in this light with growing interest. He saw it as the first example of a new party type on the continent, the bureaucratically organized mass party that had already developed in America and to a certain degree in England as well. Weber was greatly influenced by Ostrogorski's treatise of 1893 about the organizational forms of parties in modern democracy. At the Verein für Sozialpolitik's convention in Mannheim in 1905, he pointed out that the Social Democrats were becoming an American-style patronage party that was "united by a few key slogans" but which otherwise was operated "entirely for the sake of furthering and defending its own interests and sinecures."[86] At the time, he tended to see this as a negative turn. But he believed that the trade unionists were acting as a counterweight to the supremacy of the "narrow-minded party men."

Weber's attitude toward party machines, however, soon began to develop and change. Taking off from Ostrogorski and Bryce's outstanding analysis of the American party system, he began to view the nonideological bureaucratically organized patronage party as the party type of the future. He came to recognize that a party's bureaucratic organization was bound to have a significant impact upon its political strategies and its mode of conduct. As early as March 1906, he pointed out the need for an investigation of the constitutional and organizational structure of the German Social Democratic Party to Robert Michels, who was working on his *Political Parties* at the time. This was important in Weber's opinion because German Social Democracy was the "*only* party pres-

83. Michels's letters, as all correspondences, are not in the Weber papers; compare Weber's next cited letter. Until now the author has been unable to get hold of the original correspondence.

84. Letter of 6 November 1907. Copy in Weber papers. Weber continued: "You know that my wife is now a part owner of a factory—in any case only in a modest dimension—but nevertheless!" Cf. also the earlier letter of 15 October 1907: "I have not 'reviewed' Social Democracy, but only made fun of those who fear it (and thereby indirectly of the German party itself), that is correct."

85. For Michels, "correspondingly ('nothing better than . . . ')."

86. *Gesammelte Aufsätze zur Soziologie und Sozialpolitik*, pp. 399, 405.

ently existing *outside* of the Anglo-Saxon countries that is *technically* fully developed and that is motivated by *absolutely* heterogeneous ideal principles [if only as a result of] its *class* character." German Social Democracy was of especial interest because "*unlike* those [Anglo-Saxon] parties [it represents] something like an 'ideology.' . . . [It is] not *just* a 'technical' machine" like the American parties.[87] In view of the developing structural changes in modern party systems, "the ideological character of parties *generally*, and its development," seemed much more important to him than the role of academics and revisionists in the party, which Michels emphasized.[88] Weber was convinced that parties that were ideologically oriented in principle had passed their prime and that the German Social Democratic exception could easily be explained by the reactionary domestic situation. He believed that the weight of the bureaucratic apparatus would prove more important for German Social Democracy too than any and all future ideologies. This corroborated the thesis that Weber had tried to assert in Magdeburg in 1907: that Social Democracy did not represent any danger for the existing bourgeois social order. In hindsight, however, this argument has lost some of its convincing power. While the growth of a bureaucratic apparatus made Social Democracy less revolutionary, a rigidly bureaucratized party can also be an outspoken ideological party. We need only mention the examples of the communist cadre parties and the fascist "parties of followers."

The contrasting positions taken by Weber and Michels on the bureaucratization of modern mass parties nevertheless remains interesting. At the outset, Weber deplored the loss of all idealism that went along with the development of American-style parties. Now he greeted this development as necessary to overcome a sterile political ideology. Later, he was convinced by the argument that "patronage parties" made it "far easier . . . for office seekers" of the American sort, i.e. "impressive personalities, to win the necessary following *ceteris paribus* . . . than for the petit-bourgeois organizations of notables of the German parties, especially the liberal ones with their inflexible 'programs' and 'ideologies.' "[89] For the convinced socialist, Michels, the situation was precisely reversed. The rise of a bureaucratic party machine with an almost unchangeable leadership corps was the central problem for him since it clashed with socialist and democratic ideals. Would such a de-

87. Letter of 26 March 1906, copy in Weber papers.

88. Ibid. We may well also attribute it to Weber's influence that Michels latter increasingly concentrated upon the position of the leadership committee vis-à-vis the party as a whole, and not alone on the role of the intellectuals within it.

89. *Wirtschaft und Gesellschaft*, p. 678.

velopment not inevitably cause a departure from the original ideals and eventually distort them into their opposites?[90]

Weber's prediction that the Social Democratic party might become nothing more dangerous than a party machine with sinecures for its functionaries, strengthened his opinion that the party should be drawn, wherever possible, into a responsible relationship with government and society. He made sport of the fears in dynastic and bourgeois circles that Social Democratic majorities would eventually appear in local governments. In local government, the Social Democrats could only carry out a "mercantilist" industrial promotion policy, not a socialistic one.[91] If socialists held positions in government, this could only endanger those elements within the party that still held revolutionary ideologies. In the long run it would demonstrate that Social Democracy would not conquer the cities or the central government but that, on the contrary, the state would conquer the party. Politically responsible cooperation would liberate Social Democracy from the net of politically fruitless ideologies that now damagingly confined the party.[92]

This unprejudiced assessment of the Social Democratic party appears obvious to us today. At the time, only a small section of the German bourgeoisie was prepared to accept it. Naumann's slogan of a few years later, "from Bassermann to Bebel!" faded away unnoticed. Of course, Weber argued that the labor movement could only blame itself for the fears that led the bourgeoisie to deny them equality. Social Democracy, by offering its supporters an "earthly paradise," created "a kind of smallpox vaccination for the interests of the existing order."[93] The

90. Cf. Michels, *Zur Soziologie des Parteiwesens in der modernen Demokratie* (Stuttgart, 1957) and also the exemplary postword by W. Conze in the new printing of the 2d edition.

91. "Diskussionsrede auf der Tagung des Vereins für Sozialpolitik in Magdeburg 1907," *Gesammelte Aufsätze zur Soziologie und Sozialpolitik*, p. 411; cf. the letter to Michels of 15 October 1907: He had "only determined" in Magdeburg "that, as for example Catania demonstrates, Social Democracy, in modern society when *in power*, does not carry out 'socialist' policy but only 'mercantilist' and at the same time—and always unsuccessfully—class policy and further 'to-the-victor-the-spoils' policy. Indeed it must do so." (Copy in Weber papers.)

92. *Gesammelte Aufsätze zur Soziologie und Sozialpolitik*, p. 409.

93. "Zur Lage," pp. 120 f. The complete quotation: "No shadow of reality defends the premise that economic 'socialization' as such must conceal either the development of inner 'free' personality or 'altruistic ideals' in its womb. Can we expect to find any trace of this, in your view, in those whom 'material developments' promise inevitable victory? 'Correct' Social Democracy drills the masses in marching tempo and points them not at an otherworldly paradise (which in Puritanism also proved very helpful for this-worldly 'freedom'), but at a this-worldly paradise. They thereby provide the masses with a kind of vaccination for the vested interests of the existing order. They accustom their followers to docility

intransigent hardening of Social Democracy in Marxist dogma, Weber noted, was a fundamental cause of the stagnation of Germany's political development.[94]

Weber was skeptical about the chances for fruitful cooperation with the Social Democrats on political, sociopolitical, and purely scientific issues.[95] Nevertheless, he strove for cooperation whenever it appeared realizable. He hoped to see the Social Democrats treated with equality, if only to reduce the pretexts for their sense of being pariahs. He made every effort to win the Social Democrats' participation in the *Archiv für Sozialwissenschaft und Sozialpolitik* (Archive for Social Science and Social Policy). He approached Eduard Bernstein repeatedly and successfully on this matter.[96] Aroused by the maltreatment that his student Robert Michels had received, Weber openly opposed the practice of German faculties of refusing to admit Social Democrats to their ranks. He did not hesitate, here as elsewhere, to put his hand in a hornet's nest. It was impossible either "in the interest of good taste or of truth to speak of 'freedom of scholarship and higher education' in Germany." This freedom was limited by "the margins of political and religious respectability."[97] He largely blamed Social Democracy for the situation,

toward dogma and party authorities, to fruitless mass strike spectacles, and to the idle enjoyment of the ennervated raging of their press (a press that is as harmless as it is ridiculous to their enemies). In other words [they are accustomed] to a 'hysterical enjoyment of affect' that replaces economic and political thinking and acting. Only spiritual obtuseness can grow in this sterile ground once the eschatological era of this movement has passed and generations have vainly clenched their fists in their pockets or grit their teeth at the sky."

94. Cf. also Weber's noteworthy argument at the Erfurt Congress of the National Socialists: "By opposing the bourgeoisie, the Social Democrats have cleared the way for reaction" (Minutes, p. 48).

95. Cf. the letter to Michels of 1 February 1907, copy in the Weber papers; Weber wrote here that he had "the feeling that every possibility of cooperation with the Social Democrats had *disappeared* for us" here. Although he was officially without a party, he was "in any event closer [to the bourgeois parties] than to contemporary [!] Social Democracy."

96. On the occasion of a lecture that brought Bernstein to Heidelberg, Weber warmly invited him to visit on 10 October 1904. He consulted with Bernstein about the question of the Quakers' interest in prohibition, in relation to Bernstein's *History of Socialism in the Seventeenth Century*. In addition, he asked whether the *Archiv für Sozialwissenschaft* could "count on Bernstein's participation" again "soon, perhaps in the summer." It is not known whether a personal meeting actually did take place. Cf. the letter of Max Weber to Bernstein in the International Archive for Social History, Bernstein papers, D817.

97. "Die sogenannte 'Lehrfreiheit' an den deutschen Universitäten," *Frankfurter Zeitung*, 20 September 1908, 3d morning ed. Cf. also "Die Lehrfreiheit der Universitäten," *Münchener Hochschulnachrichten* 19, no. 220 (1909); recently reprinted in *Süddeutscher Zeitung*, 3 November 1973. Also see the letter to Michels of 24 January 1906 (copy in Weber papers), where he says: "In my opinion, I need scarcely say that the circumstance in which a Social Democrat is excluded from *Habilitation* merely because he is one, or is otherwise confined, flies in the face of the alleged 'freedom of science' at our universities. It is obvious

since the Social Democrats, by their constant declarations of contempt for so-called "bourgeois scholarship," prompted such reactions.[98] He therefore also emphatically criticized the Social Democratic assertion that the silence of the German professors in this area was the result of "cowardice." "I doubt whether the 'Realpolitik' that is responsible for this silence and that, as I have clearly emphasized, I believe to be misguided and *contemptible* and which I will never associate with, can be blamed more on personally *despicable* motives in our own circles than on the obsequiousness of so *very* many of their comrades toward the party powers or the 'party interests.'"[99] Bourgeois anxiety complexes, linked to dynastic fears, were also a decisive element in this attitude. Both were, he was convinced, totally unfounded. At the third convention of German university professors in Leipzig in 1909 Weber heatedly attacked the groundless fears at German universities of the Social Democrats—without, of course, flattering the latter. "The nationalist press accuses me of wishing to raise the Social Democrats to the heights of professorial chairs. What I say is this: Let the Social Democrats try to win chairs at German universities and then we will see the disgrace that results. They do not have the resources to offer what German scholarship as a whole can offer."[100]

Max Weber also heatedly criticized the repression of the workers' movement unleashed by royal edicts after Caprivi's departure from office. When the subversion bill was first discussed, he wrote in the *Christliche Welt* that it was an ignorant illusion to believe that a cooperative and national workers' movement would develop if "the class con-

---

that I find this circumstance—when I compare it to the Italian, the French, and at the moment even the Russian situation—to be a blemish and a disgrace for a cultural nation. I am also sure that the majority of the best names in German scholarship would agree with me absolutely. . . . It is certain that the fault lies with what Prince Hohenlohe referred to a bit too politely in 1878 in reference to the Socialist law as the 'anxiety of the German bourgeoisie.'"

98. Letter to Michels of 2 January 1907; copy in Weber papers.

99. Michels brought the core of Weber's arguments about the barriers to the *Habilitation* of Social Democrats to the attention of the Social Democratic editor Max Quarck. Quarck expressed the doubt that Max Weber had the courage to publicly express his feelings on this issue. Weber reacted to this with a sharp phillipic, in which he reaffirmed that he regarded "the rejection (or even the impeding) of a Social Democrat's *Habilitation* merely because he was one, or publicly announced himself as one, as 'incompatible with the freedom of teaching,' as a 'mockery' of this and a 'disgrace for a land of culture.'" On the other hand, he resisted the publication of confidential details about the appointment proceedings and appointment prospects of Robert Michels. He did not have the "desire to shine as a model of 'courage' at *the expense of colleagues*." Letter to Max Quarck, 5 January 1907, Quarck papers, Archiv für die soziale Demokratie, Bonn–Bad Godesberg.

100. *Verhandlungen des 3. Deutschen Hochschullehrertages zu Leipzig am 12. und 13. Oktober 1909* (Report approved by the inner governing committee), Leipzig, 1910, pp. 16f.

sciousness of a rising social group is ignored or repressed or prevented from self-determination."[101] He planned to publish an article in the *Grenzboten* about the subversion bill. Instead of this, he joined a public declaration of protest.[102] Along with his Freiburg colleagues, however, he refused to sign a resolution sponsored by members of the Verein für Sozialpolitik written by Dr. Karl E. von Mangoldt, which appeared in the *Grenzboten* on 7 February 1895 with the signatures of numerous political economists. Weber did not care for this resolution's sharply moralizing tone, which reflected Schmoller's ethical Katheder socialism. The assertion that socialism was an "opponent" that had to be defused by "moral greatness that removed the grounds for complaint" thoroughly offended Max Weber's frank view that social conflicts were not susceptible to ethical or pseudo-ethical analysis. Weber therefore led his colleagues in a separate declaration in *Die Hilfe* that omitted the disputed passages.[103]

Weber rejected even more vociferously the "law for the protection of nonstrikers," which Count Posadowski proposed in the Reichstag in 1898. Thanks to the Kaiser's shrill speech in Oeynhausen, this bill had already publicly been labeled a "prison bill" and had been condemned to a quick death before parliamentary discussions began.[104] Perhaps for this reason, Max Weber did not go ahead with the publication of a "Declaration against the Coercive Law" that he had drafted for the *Frankfurter Zeitung*.[105] Because, like Brentano, Max Weber saw the unions' wage struggle as the natural means for carrying on the class struggle within the existing social order, he strenuously fought the *Zuchthausvorlage* (prison bill). The bill was designed to make strikes more difficult and would have established legal limitations on the workers that went far beyond those established by paragraph 153 of the Reich trade ordinance.

The dialectical character of Weber's thought is revealed in the fact that he did not wish for a *final* resolution to social antagonisms. "Struggle," for him, was not only an unavoidable element of social life but was desirable in principle, whether it took the form of open disputes, eco-

101. *Christliche Welt*, 1894, p. 671.

102. Printed in *Die Hilfe*, 3 March 1896.

103. A copy of the Mangoldt declaration with proposed changes in Lotz's and Weber's handwriting is in the Darmstädter Collection at the West German Library in Marburg, under Weber's signature. It bears this significant note: "*only in the above* version, and even in this one highly unappealing. Signed Max Weber." In addition to Weber's signature and those of his fellow Freiburg political economists, the declaration in *Die Hilfe* includes the signatures of numerous distinguished personalities including Lujo Brentano, Theodor Mommsen, Hermann Baumgarten, Paul Natorp, and Georg von Siemens of the Deutsche Bank.

104. Cf. Karl Erich Born, *Staat und Sozialpolitik seit Bismarcks Sturz* (Wiesbaden, 1957), pp. 126 f.

105. *Lebensbild*, p. 231. Marianne Weber places the prison bill in 1895, apparently confusing it with the revolution bill.

nomic competition, or biological or other "selection."[106] A wage struggle between social partners was an open form of class struggle and, therefore, a positive event. Weber started from the premise that when the worker at last achieved organizational and legal equality in the social struggle, the conflicting social interests would naturally achieve a climate of social justice.[107] He was therefore a radical proponent of liberal social reformism centered in the union idea. He was close to the position championed above all by the towering figure of Lujo Brentano.[108]

It was only consistent for Max Weber to show special sympathy to the trade unions. The unions' efforts in social policy and their work to improve the workers' social position within the capitalist economic system represented the single really positive side of the workers' movement for Weber. He grudgingly admitted that the unions could not be successful without the political support of the Social Democrats. He maintained that "the workers' associations were valuable in themselves, whether or not they achieved many or few tactical gains in open struggle." They were schools of responsible ambition where the workers learned responsibility and independence. He viewed them as the "only refuge of idealistic work and idealistic conscience within the Social Democratic Party" and thus hoped for the defeat of any proposal "that threatened their nature."[109]

Weber therefore opposed Lujo Brentano's proposal that a legal representative body be created for all employees in each economic branch to function as a party to a collective work agreement. These bodies were to include organized and unorganized workers, and the unions would have the right to send representatives in proportion to the strength of their membership. Brentano corresponded with Weber about this proposal, which seems so modern to us today. Collective agreements are now the rule, but the *united* union can act itself as the partner of management. Brentano went on to offer the proposal for discussion at the convention of the Verein für Sozialpolitik in Mannheim in 1905. The plan was "acceptable [to Weber] only as a check to be cashed in a pretty distant future." In the current situation, which was characterized by the existence of many competing union organizations, he expected that such a "mandatory organization" would result in the mediatization of the unions. Within the representative bodies legally established for

106. Cf. *Wirtschaft und Gesellschaft*, pp. 20 f.

107. But cf. below, last part of this section.

108. Cf. in this connection James J. Sheehan, *The Career of Lujo Brentano: A Study of Liberalism and Social Reform in Imperial Germany* (Chicago, 1966).

109. *Gesammelte Aufsätze zur Soziologie und Sozialpolitik*, pp. 398 f. Characteristically, in 1918 Weber referred to the creation of work associations between the unions and the employers' leagues with the "exclusion of the yellow class traitors" [!] as the "one worthwhile sociopolitical achievement of the revolutionary period." *Pol. Schr.*, p. 486; cf. also pp. 287, 305.

everyone, including non–union members, the unions would be reduced to "social parties." In his opinion, Brentano's trade union social reformism became irrational once it departed from the principle of free unions and forced the unions into the Procrustean bed of comprehensive, legally established, workers' agencies. From his aristocratic, elitist perspective, too, he disapproved of the leveling effect that had to result from governmental confinement of union activities. The benefits of Brentano's proposal had to be offset by the decisive fact "that if working conditions were set by a collective organization, the intelligent and highly developed sections of the working class would be outvoted by the masses beneath them. The majority would not be sympathetic to wage differentiation based upon the *quality* of achievement. The workers' elite would forfeit its natural leadership and the impulse to serve the common goals. At present, every wage increase they achieve, ultimately benefits everyone."[110] Since this point of view only applied, in a limited way, to the mining and foundry industries, Weber was inclined at first to support the implementation of the Brentano proposal if limited to the miners and foundry workers.

In his speech to the Verein für Sozialpolitik, Brentano took account of Weber's reservations but remained committed to his basic idea.[111] While Weber rejected legally created workers' representative bodies, he found himself in agreement with Brentano on all other points; or rather, Brentano was in agreement with him. Brentano even incorporated Weber's suggestions from their correspondence, at times word for word, in his address. This was especially true in reference to the form of the strike laws. Brentano, like Weber, viewed the law then in effect as highly biased in favor of employers. Like Brentano, Weber was especially opposed to the "exceptional law" of paragraph 153 of the Reich trade ordinance, according to which any attempt to move others to form a coalition or to prevent them from resigning by the use of "force, threat, injuries to honor, or a declaration of contempt" could be punished by imprisonment.[112] Weber bluntly and suggestively called this "a law for old

110. Letter to Brentano of 25 April 1905, Brentano papers. In Weber's view, Brentano's proposal "necessarily had wider implications—on the Millerand law: (1) *strike requirement* if the representatives so decided; (2) strike prohibition in the *absence* of such a decision—i.e., criminal arrest of the individual, legal representative of the association in such a case, since *without this* the proposal had *no chance* at all to become law within the foreseeable future; (3) *exclusion* of 'those willing to work' in the event of a correctly concluded strike decision." Cf. also Sheehan, *The Career of Lujo Brentano*, pp. 162 ff.

111. Brentano's address in "Protokoll der Verhandlungen der Generalversammlung des Vereins für Sozialpolitik zu Mannheim 1905," *Schriften des Vereins für Sozialpolitik*, vol. 116, pp. 135 ff.

112. Brentano spoke of "exceptional legislation."

women." It protects "lack of conscience and comradely honor."[113] He wished to see paragraph 153 either set aside in favor of the general penal law, or so narrowed that it would be put into effect "only in instances of an immediate threat of material damage."[114] In that case, the provisions of paragraph 153 that worked only to the disadvantage of workers should be extended to employers as well and should entail "legal prohibitions for employers too whose officers threaten workers (for example, with dismissal) about membership or nonmembership of organizations: protect also the right to association, not only as now the opposition to association."[115] The employers should not have the one-sided power to limit the workers' exercise of their right of association by threats of dismissal.

"Protect the right to association, not only . . . the opposition to association"—this sums up Weber's social policy program of the years before World War I.[116] Equal opportunities for the union-organized working class vis-à-vis employers; no bureaucratic weakening of class opposition by the creation of all-inclusive legal representative bodies or even government mediation organs, but, when necessary, open arbitration in the wage struggle. As early as 1898, Weber actively participated in a collection for striking Hamburg dock workers that had been organized by Friedrich Naumann and Otto Baumgarten.[117] In Mannheim, he heatedly defended the workers against the accusation of "breach of contract" during the great miners' strike of 1905. At the same time he castigated the regulation of work in German heavy industries, which openly expressed the total subjugation of workers. "These gentlemen [the industrialists] behave like policemen. The less the German citizen has a political voice in the German Reich, the more the government remains beyond his

113. "Diskussionsrede in Mannheim," *Gesammelte Aufsätze zur Soziologie und Sozialpolitik*, p. 397.

114. In the above-cited letter to Brentano, Weber called for putting it aside completely. Paragraph 153 was first repealed in July 1918!

115. Letter to Brentano, ibid.; Brentano incorporated the formulation cited word for word in the concluding section of his address (*Protokoll der Verhandlungen*, p. 145; compare the letter to Brentano of 16 August 1905 in which Weber wrote: "I am extremely pleased that you will also consider the idea of paragraph 153 GO as a parallel provision for the protection of coalition." To a certain extent paragraph 153 was already applicable against employer coalitions, but only when with each other.

116. Brentano accepted Weber's formulation in his headings (VI, 2), *Verhandlungen*, pp. 148 f. He entirely accepted Weber's view that "the 'recognition' of the professional associations *without* this protection . . . [could] mean their destruction."

117. Compare Otto Baumgarten, *Meine Lebensgeschichte* (Tübingen, 1929), pp. 219 f., as well as recently Dieter Düding, *Der Nationalsoziale Verein, 1896–1903* (Munich/Vienna, 1972), p. 110. Wenck reports on a similar collection of the National Socialists (*Geschichte der Nationalsozialen, 1898–1903*, pp. 72 f.); Weber was a member of the committee reported on by Baumgarten.

control and the more he is merely an object of statecraft, so much the more he tries to show in the places where he is a paterfamilias—and he is that in the giant firms—that he has a say, at least here, and others to boss around." Weber repeatedly pointed to the deleterious effect of such social conditions upon the nation's political consciousness.[118] Special social legislation was necessary for giant firms. "It should, in my view, have the same character as 'peasant emancipation' legislation—expedient 'welfare provisions' introduced by *mandatory* regulations in order to prevent their misapplication as a *means of control*."[119]

Weber was not comforted by the new Reich social policy adopted by Posadowski after the failure of his plans for repression. Although moderate, the new policy evaded decisive issues. Weber feared that increasing cartelization of private enterprises and the rapid expansion of state and communal enterprises would destroy any possibility for the implementation of his ideals in social policy. The new association law of 1908 had just codified the recognition of the right of association and a somewhat more independent position for the unions. At the same time, the social climate began to deteriorate as the result of an economic downturn. In this climate, the left-leaning circle in the Verein für Sozialpolitik that surrounded Weber and Brentano decided to stage a joint social policy demonstration by all the major figures in the field of political economy to bring about positive change. Social policy "is no longer in 'style' and *that* must change," Weber wrote to Brentano.[120]

The demonstration was originally planned in connection with the celebration of the fortieth anniversary of the founding of the Verein für Sozialpolitik; but Weber, having taken the lead in this matter, was well aware that the political split in the Verein would create almost insuperable difficulties for such an action.[121] Lujo Brentano, concerned by the direction of social policy during the previous decade, pressed for a "radical" demonstration by the committed, left-leaning social policy forces, and he also sought to link the social issues with the issue of free trade. Weber, although personally in agreement with this approach, tried to talk Brentano out of it, since it might render them ineffectual and few could be persuaded to participate. He was interested in having an impact on the public. He wished, therefore, to call a convention in Berlin, not in the name of the Verein but immediately following one of its executive

118. Discussion speech in Mannheim, *Gesammelte Aufsätze zur Soziologie und Sozialpolitik*, pp. 396 f.

119. Letter of 25 April 1905 to Brentano. Brentano took up this formulation: "We require a casuistry of welfare institutions with conclusive regulations that absolutely exclude any violations. Max Weber recalled the analogy of the regulations on the freeing of the peasants in this connection" (p. 145); also *Leitsätze* VI, 3, pp. 148 f.

120. Letter of 16 September 1912, Brentano papers.

121. Cf. also later in this chapter.

meetings, in order to allow all those "big name" members of the "discipline" of political economy to join a sociopolitical demonstration "with the slogan 'Progress in Social Policy,' with however loose a program—or even no program at all."[122]

After this, he hoped that a social policy association would be founded that would provide the basis for continuing propaganda for a progressive social policy encompassing the principle of unhampered labor action and personal freedom for workers even in an era of "rapid growth of the monopolistic-bureaucratic organization of capital."[123]

Even uniting the active social politicians on the left wing of the Verein für Sozialpolitik was a major problem. Some of the men who had to be included had the impression that Max Weber hoped to split the Verein für Sozialpolitik through this action. Significantly, Brentano wanted to include the free trade issue, which Max Weber strongly opposed, arguing that this would antagonize many of the more conservative social reformers. In a series of letters, Weber urged Brentano to reconsider and set aside the issue of free trade propaganda, if only temporarily, but was unable to convince him.[124] Others objected to Weber's wish to involve Friedrich Naumann.[125] The acceptance of Social Democrats into the new social policy association was also a matter for controversy. While Brentano insisted that the entire left be involved, Weber for tactical reasons wanted to include only bourgeois social reformers.[126]

122. Letter of 3 July 1912. The description is based on the numerous letters from Weber to Brentano in the Brentano papers. Cf. also Bernhard Schäfers, ed., "Rundschreiben Max Webers zur Sozialpolitik," *Soziale Welt*, 18 (1967): 261 ff.

123. From a draft by Brentano for the planned social-political demonstration, Brentano papers 67 BAK.

124. Cf. the letters to Brentano of 3 July, 5 September, and 11 September 1912 in the Brentano papers, 67 BAK. The letter of 5 September 1912 includes a decisive passage containing the core of Weber's arguments: "In the other matter once again: I will insist on absolute *clarity*: If you wish to found a *free trade*–social political sect (since a 'sect' it now remains; that we cannot conceal!)—fine! Then *expressis verbis*. In my view, the moment when free trade (which means *lowering* of tariffs in important areas, especially the grain tariff, of course) will have a chance has not yet arrived, given the existing constellation of power. I favor the *strict* exclusion of *all* things not closely related to the *specific* core points of *social* policy. Whether or not this 'works' theoretically is immaterial. For generations, the *free traders* were the enemies of social policy (even voluntary social policy). Many *still* are. It is not certain whether the high prices (which can be used less against the *grain* tariffs which support the large landholdings, than against the livestock barriers, thus partially against *peasant* interests!) will continue. It is impossible for *us* to orient a new association in this way, in any case an individual assembly. I consider any inclusion of *this* present constellation (also the exclusion of the Center Party) to be ruinous."

125. Johann Plenge. See Schäfers, "Rundschreiben Max Webers zur Sozialpolitik," pp. 263 f.

126. Vogelstein, too, implored Brentano not to refuse cooperation over this question: "Max and Alfred Weber, Lotz, Drill, Wilbrandt, and many of us younger ones are all

In October 1912 a preparatory gathering took place in Leipzig, and these differences were openly, and at times heatedly, discussed. Brentano, put off by the exclusion of tariff policies from the agenda, used the noninvolvement of the Social Democrats as a pretext for withdrawing from the planned social-policy demonstration.[127] Weber attempted to save the situation. In the middle of November he sent an exhaustive memorandum to the participants at the Leipzig meeting. The memorandum remains an important source for his views on social policy. He attempted to describe the common ground for a social policy based on liberal principles.

> There is no doubt a basic presumption for us in the area of the workers' question: We reject, partly in principle and partly as inadequate, the point of view of master rule or patriarchalism, the bonds of welfare institutions and those who would treat the worker as an object for bureaucratic regulation, and insurance legislation that merely creates dependency. We affirm the equal participation of the workers in the collective determination of working conditions, and to this end we also affirm the strengthening of their organizations, which spearhead this effort; we see the comradeliness and class dignity that develops in this way as a positive cultural value—whether or not solidarity expresses itself merely in pressure by the organization on the individual, which is somewhat the case within every social grouping based on honor and comradeship. We look upon the growing fruitlessness of orderly strikes as an evil caused by the increasing superiority of employers' organizations, legal and police chicanery, and the systematic creation of subsidized employer protection troops among the workers. We resist, without compromise, the conditions of capital hegemony, with government cooperation, according to the Pittsburgh pattern, in the Saar region and the heavy industry in Westphalia and Silesia, because we want to live in a land of citizens, not of subjects.[128]

This is a classic summary of Weber's social policy ideals: the strengthening of the workers' position in relation to the employers with the goal of

---

resolved to fight for the free development of the working class and to make sacrifices in this struggle. . . . If you and Max Weber march separately, it will cause great damage." Letter of 8 September 1912 to Brentano, Brentano papers, 67 BAK.

127. Brentano's accusation that Weber wished to exclude the Social Democrats for partisan rather than tactical reasons led to a serious quarrel between them that took time to bridge. Weber accused Brentano of breaking his word, while Brentano believed that his entire political line had been betrayed. Cf. also Sheehan, *The Career of Lujo Brentano*, pp. 175 f., and Schäfers, "Rundschreiben," pp. 261 f.

128. Memorandum of 15 November 1912: "To the participants in the Leipzig meeting." Newly published by Schäfers, "Rundschreiben," pp. 265 ff.

enabling the workers to protect their interests themselves. Only in this way could Weber conceive of the development of a working class that was broad-minded and capable of political judgment. But he began to have doubts whether his support of the unions, along with his affirmation of the development of private capital through cartelization and big industry and his rejection of all nationalization of industry and any extensive state intervention, was appropriate to changing circumstances.

Weber revealed that the chief reason for such a gathering was "uncertainty about the basic question of the direction that a future social policy should take in the labor area." In the field of social policy, a "new" situation had arisen, characterized by the fact

> that the trends towards governmentalization, communalization, and syndicalization pressed forward together, and that managerial positions in the syndicates attracted civil servants and influential state positions attracted industrial managers. For this and other reasons, the impact upon social policy would be the same whether the future was dominated by "nationalization" or state- "controlled" syndicalization, and regardless of the formal nature of the relationship between the governmental and community apparatus on the one hand and the syndicates on the other. In confrontation with such pervasive ruling institutions, the union policy developed in the past broke down along with all of those institutions that we associate with a resolute and liberal social policy.[129]

Weber admitted to perplexity at the time. He was disturbed by the recognition that liberal social reformism had entered a period of crisis because of recent economic developments, and that he would have to forsake his past opinions. Therefore, instead of the one-time demonstration that he had originally envisioned, he now sought periodic meetings of a nonbinding character. He was increasingly convinced that a single public assembly would achieve little. Only "the development of a collective position" could effectively counter "the drift of social policy issues out of fashion in Germany.[130] He hoped to create a kind of social policy shock troop based on liberal principles. The circle of fundamentally liberal-minded political economists could discuss the basic assumptions of a liberal social policy, taking account of the conditions of an economy that was largely determined by cartel and bureaucracy and arrive at a common position on the most important questions.[131] The final goal

129. Ibid., pp. 267, 269.

130. Ibid., p. 270.

131. Cf. letter to Brentano of the end of August 1912 (undated), Brentano papers: "It appears necessary to me to maintain what is indeed a fact: that as far as the progress of those controversial issues affecting social policy positions—'increase of state (and community)

would be the "working out of firm principles for the broadest possible 'lift' for social policy (which need not correspond indefinitely to the present political constellation)."[132]

Max Weber's hopes were not fulfilled. His efforts to create a kind of theoretical action group for the development of a liberal social policy failed in part because, in spite of all efforts to win him back, Lujo Brentano was no longer prepared for further cooperation. It is symptomatic of the fate of Max Weber the politician that, even in the narrow realm of social policy, he was unable to find a group of like-minded people who alone could supply support for his views and thereby practical effectiveness.

Weber's failure had unfortunate consequences. The domestic politics of Wilhelmine Germany remained unhealthy, and the Social Democrats remained isolated and tainted with the label "enemies of the Reich." The government's social policy certainly improved the workers' material situation, but it neglected their mental and psychological condition, especially the condition of the "healthy and strong." Its success was limited by its excessively patriarchal and hierarchical aspects. Above all, it could not free itself from the fear of the insurrectionary aims of the working class. It was a great tragedy for Weber, who was both socially concerned and a class-conscious bourgeois, that he was one of the very few who, in essential matters, correctly judged the character of the socialist workers' movement. He recognized that Germany's lack of a healthy domestic evolution was the result of a "bourgeois fear complex," which was the reverse side of the German bourgeoisie's "cowardly desire for powerlessness." As a young political economist, Weber had fiercely derided the German grande bourgeoisie, which, in part, "openly . . . [yearned] for the appearance of a new Caesar" who would "shield them against the rising masses from below as well as against the caprice that they suspect among the German dynasties on social policy issues."[133] At the same time, Weber hoped despondently for the German bourgeoisie

---

enterprises,' or not; increasing bureaucratization, or not; increasing compulsory associations (of workers), compulsory minimum wages, etc., or not—a unity of views does not exist over these and other questions of principle among us 'on the left.' This must first be achieved. . . . In my view that is the simple fact."

In addition, the following participants were considered: Max Weber, Geheimrat Bücher, Dr. Drill (preparatory commission), Lujo Brentano, Theodor Vogelstein, Friedrich Naumann, von Schulze-Gävernitz, von Zwiedenick, Toennies, Alfred Weber, Oppenheim, Jastrow, Cohn, Glesch, Lotz, Sinzheimer, Plenge, Levy, Salz, Radbruch, Calwer, Cohnstaedt, von Mangoldt, Professor Bauer, Leonhard, Eulenburg, Lederer, Potthoff, Rade, Heyde, Schücking, Heuss, Herkner, Gertrud Bäumer, Maubert. Cf. the memorandum of 19 December 1912 in the Weber papers, which includes this list of names.

132. Memorandum of 15 November 1912, in Schäfers, p. 269.

133. *Pol. Schr.*, p. 21.

to come to itself, detach itself with strengthened political consciousness from noble and dynastic social conservatism, and decisively go its own bourgeois way, while recognizing the equal partnership of the working class. Little, too little, was achieved here, as Max Weber had to concede. The catastrophe of the outbreak of the World War would mercilessly expose the weaknesses of the German social structure.

3. The Call for a National Party of Bourgeois Liberty

The domestic scene of the mid-1890s depressed Weber about the future. Liberalism was hopelessly split by ideological rigidity. Dogmatism and disunity characterized the left. The National Liberals, imprisoned by the spirit of security, made common cause with the Conservatives in Prussia under Miquel's protection. The Reichstag was dominated by the Center, a party that Max Weber had no use for because of his liberal background. He was never able to forsake totally the emotions of the *Kulturkampf*, which had been of such import for him as a young man.[134] Weber could see no party that was capable of supporting both his imperialistic and national ideals and his domestic goals. This was the reason that the young political economist avoided the jump into politics that would have been natural for him at the time.

His one connection with active political involvement was through Friedrich Naumann. Weber's friendship with Göhre had built the bridge that brought him close to the Christian Socials, but Friedrich Naumann was Weber's dominant influence after 1893. Max Weber was fascinated by Naumann's unusual ideas, as well as by his integrity and conscientious conduct, and this made possible the especially close relationship between the keenly analytical sociologist and the social idealist with the gift of communicating ideas to the people. While starting from different points

134. Compare the letter to Frau Gnauck-Kühne of 15 July 1909 (?): "If I consider the future possibilities, then in my view there are two powers: bureaucracy in the state and the virtuous machinery of the Catholic Church. [These powers], associated with the division of mankind into economic or other experts, have the best chance to dominate everything else. *In spite of* this, indeed *because* of it, I regard it as a demand on my humanity to fight these public powers, with the notation of course that the specific Catholic form of piety in all of its richness, is quite a different thing from what I have designated above as the 'machinery' of the church—in truth it is antagonistic to this machinery, and has only a meager chance for the future." Weber papers.

As late as World War I, at the time of the efforts in Salzburg to found a Catholic university, Max Weber criticized confessionally tied professors sharply and would have denied the planned Salzburg university equal rank with other universities since the planners wished to tie the appointment of five secular professors to the archbishop's consent. "Ein katholische Universität in Salzburg," *Frankfurter Zeitung*, 10 May 1917, 1st ed.

and championing different values, they met on the common ground of progressive social policy.

Weber supported Naumann's Christian Social politics, although a chasm divided him from Naumann's presumptions. He disapproved of Naumann's socialist leanings and rejected his efforts to improve the relationship between employers and employees through ethical growth in a Christian perspective. Weber believed this approach to be reactionary and outmoded. On 27 April 1892, Max Weber invited Naumann, in the name of the Evangelisch-soziale Vereinigung of Freiburg, to give a public evening lecture. Naumann was permitted to choose his own theme, but Weber attempted to dissuade him from making an ethical address in favor of taking a position against "economic patriarchalisms."[135] When, in 1894, Naumann published a collection of articles under the title "What Does Christian Social Mean?" Weber criticized them substantively in *Christliche Welt.* He touched on the basis of Naumann's then current ideals when he pointed out that "modern evolution" increasingly replaced the personal rule of the "large entrepreneur" "with the *impersonal* rule of the property-owning class; it replaced personal relations with business relations; personal subjugation with the obligation of tribute to an unknown, invisible, and inaccessible power." These changes prevented "the possibility [of] . . . explaining the relationship between the rulers and the ruled in religious [terms]."[136] Weber expressly styled himself a "bourgeois" in deliberate contrast to Naumann's admiration of the proletariat.[137]

Friedrich Naumann was not the kind of man who deferred to the judgment of a younger one; he went his own way and championed his own ideals. But he was unusually open to differing modes of reasoning and to alternative suggestions, which he then not infrequently made his own. Weber's arguments had some impact; Naumann assimilated them to his own value system, and eventually—after a time lag of about five or six years—he accepted Weber's position. On the other hand, Naumann's compelling preaching skills enabled him to win Weber's cooperation repeatedly in causes that Weber himself did not truly favor or regarded as hopeless.

135. Letter of 29 April 1892, Naumann papers, 119: "I ask you to make your decision about the theme. The wishes of the membership go in two directions: on the one hand, it is wished that you could place the 'duties of the educated to the lower classes' in the center; on the other side, the side of the majority and mine as well, is that you not narrow your discussions to *purely* ethical questions, and that you deal also with basic points of a programmatical character (e.g., generally to draw a sharp distinction with economic patriarchalisms. This would of course not exclude the heading 'duties of the educated, etc.' or a similar one.)"

136. *Christliche Welt*, 1894, pp. 472 ff.; cf. *Verhandlungen des 5. evangelisch-sozialen Kongresses 1894*, pp. 72 f.

137. Ibid., p. 477. There it says, "We bourgeois."

Weber participated in Naumann's workers' library and wrote a sparkling treatment of the stock exchange for it, which remains an unexcelled introduction to the problem of the nature of stock exchanges.[138] He also delivered lectures in Christian Social meetings about agricultural policy.[139] He supported the foundation of the Naumannist weekly, *Die Hilfe*, which quickly became the organ of a considerable section of the German educated class, both ideally and materially. His name was listed among the collaborators.[140] He helped with a large financial pledge. In these years, however, he did not contribute any articles to it; only much later, in 1917, did he begin to write for *Die Hilfe*.[141] Friedrich Naumann's great attempt to create a new political movement between the frozen fronts of the existing parties by founding the National Social Association would never have been undertaken without Max Weber.[142] It was Weber's intellectual influence that led Naumann to take the step from his Christian Social idealism with its primarily patriarchal character to national socialism, which attempted to link resolute domestic social reform with a strong national policy abroad. Naumann's notion that the workers could be won back to support of the national state and educated to uphold the national-imperial ideal, echoed the hopes Weber repeatedly returned to in the nineties for the rise of a workers' movement that would join in the effort for national greatness. Like Weber, Friedrich Naumann was convinced that Germany's future depended on such a combination. He therefore conceived of the bold plan of creating a crystallization point for a workers' movement in the new style, which rejected Social Democracy's internationalism and affirmed the national state.

Naumann enthusiastically embarked upon the attempt to realize his central goals. His "principled optimism" contrasted with Max Weber's "brave pessimism."[143] Weber, from the outset, energetically disputed Naumann's efforts because he believed they would fail. In spite of Weber's emphatic warnings, Naumann founded a daily newspaper with the title *Die Zeit* (Time)—"Organ for National Socialism with a Christian Basis"—in August 1896. It was to be the journalistic vehicle of the new movement. Weber's sober skepticism proved all too speedily justified. As

138. Printed in *Gesammelte Aufsätzen zur Soziologie und Sozialpolitik*, pp. 256–322.

139. The third morning edition of the *Frankfurter Zeitung* of 8 March 1896 included an apparently complete report of a speech on 7 March 1896 at the Christian Social Association in Frankfurt am Main about "Christian-Social agricultural policy" in the presence of Naumann.

140. *Die Hilfe*, proof ed. of 2 December 1894.

141. Cf. the complete description in *Lebensbild*, pp. 232 ff; also Heuss, *Naumann*, pp. 105 ff., Wenck, *Die Geschichte der National-Sozialen, 1895–1903* (Berlin, 1935), pp. 23 ff.

142. Cf. Düding, *Der National-Soziale Verein*, p. 110.

143. Cf. Conze, *Friedrich Naumann: Grundlagen und Ansatz seiner Politik in der national-sozialen Zeit (1895–1903)*, Schicksalswege deutscher Vergangenheit (Düsseldorf, 1952), pp. 358 f.

early as the following year, Naumann had to discontinue *Die Zeit* because of financial difficulties. Max Weber also sought to dissuade Naumann from formally founding a party that promised nothing in the contemporary political situation, but without success. In November 1896, Naumann summoned a representative assembly of all National Socials to Erfurt, where they decided to create not a party but an "association."[144] Naumann was extremely optimistic. He pointed out that "the Marxists, too" had started small.[145]

As a result, Max Weber entered into perhaps the most difficult situation of his political life. He was forced to take a critical position about an undertaking that was in many ways the fruit of his own intellect, although it flew in the face of his political intuition. He was personally close not only to Naumann but to the majority of the association's leaders, including Paul Göhre, Gerhart von Schulze-Gävernitz, his brother Alfred Weber, and his long-time friend Otto Baumgarten, and he respected their conscientious ethical idealism. His mother, Helene Weber, also took an active part in Naumann's efforts to find a new path between the social fronts.

It was at this same time that Max Weber's uncle, Adolf Hausrath, reported that Weber was being considered for a chair in Heidelberg in political economy, and advised Weber to distance himself from Naumann and the Christian Socials, who after William II's comment that "Christian-Social is nonsense!" were not exactly loved by the royal houses.

Weber's answer illuminates his political personality as well as his relationship to Naumann.

> I myself scarcely know whether I should wish an invitation to a chair. I am confronted with the following choice: to remain here and to continue my political activities as long as there is opportunity and stimulus, or to take an important position and with it the obligation to give up all other effectiveness. I would happily postpone [the chair] for several years. I would of course feel required to give up so much as a result of the greater obligations that would be demanded of me; and I know very well that offered the choice—*now* at the moment that politics, including the Naumannist project, offers a real field of action for me—I would choose the broader academic responsibilities. But I know not whether I might regret this in the future, and it would be too late. . . . But as to your advice

144. Compare Weber's letter to his wife at the end of November 1896: "Now, I have noticed in the newspapers that they have finally decided against the founding of a 'party' and have founded an association. We will see what will come of this. I believe little." *Lebensbild*, p. 234.

145. *Protokoll*, p. 39.

> for me to make a clean break with all "Christian Socialists," I could not follow it, as things now stand. I would have to act in conflict with my feelings. I am not a "Christian Socialist" in the least, but a pretty pure bourgeois, and my relationship with Naumann, whose character I so highly value, is limited to the fact that I am seeking to free him from his socialist illusions.[146]

Indeed, Max Weber saw little chance for political effectiveness in the situation existing in 1896. He did not think there was any possibility of working for his ideals or achieving even the slightest success. A year later, he turned down a Reichstag candidacy in Saarbrücken that had been offered him after a successful lecture tour. In the past, Naumann's vigorous efforts for a progressive social policy had appeared to him to offer the only possibility for politically meaningful activity. Naumann's idealistic enthusiasm attracted him. And he did succeed in winning Naumann's support for his ideals of nation, powerful state, and imperialism. But unbridgeable differences remained, and in the light of Naumann's high-flown national social plans, they now resurfaced. For Weber, a powerful national state was, above all and in spite of all of his national fervor, a means to gain domestic reform. For Weber, social policy was a tool in the struggle for national policy, and he looked upon all politics oriented purely to social concern with a distaste reminiscent of Nietzsche. He sharply distanced himself from Naumann's socialist tendencies. To be sure, Naumann's national socialism was purely rhetorical insofar as it was consciously limited to social reform "within the historically evolved economic order." Naumann's goal of eventually replacing social democracy was illusory enough. The "class-conscious" bourgeois, Max Weber, could never be persuaded to follow him on this questionable path.

Weber therefore looked upon Naumann's efforts with a mixture of sympathy and strong rejection. When, at the Erfurt congress in 1896, Weber criticized the founding of the new party somewhat unjustly, current political differences about problems of secondary importance played a greater role than was immediately apparent.[147] Weber was upset that Naumann had omitted the strong comments about large landholdings that had been included in the original program proposal, and felt that the Polish question should have been treated more to his liking.[148] In his

146. Letter of 15 October 1896, Weber papers. The letter closes with the characteristic sentence: "I wish that I had done nothing that would even distantly indicate an ambition for such an honorable position."

147. Cf. Weber's letter to his wife after the meeting, *Lebensbild*, p. 234. On this question, recently, Düding, *Der National-Soziale Verein*, pp. 53 ff.

148. Cf. in this regard above, chap. 3, sec. 3.

speech at the congress, Max Weber unmercifully unfolded the basic weaknesses that, in his view, would doom the national socials as a political movement.[149] Naumann had mentioned that the Nationalsozialer Verein (the National Social Association), as the crystallization point of a new party movement, must first win the "educated": "If the educated begin to lead the way in the social movement, a general transformation has to occur."[150] Weber feared this would turn out to be a dangerous politics of illusion. He could not believe that a socially and ideally unstable army of the so-called educated could become the core of a political movement. The assembly itself, which was made up almost exclusively of intellectuals, including a considerable number of theologians, hardly made a very encouraging impression.[151] Weber regarded it as rank utopianism to believe that the National Social Association could be a kind of intellectual general staff of the workers' movement, which, as Rudolf Sohm suggested, would simply replace the Social Democratic leadership. He knew it was necessary to descend into the proletariat's own social circle in order to work for their interests successfully.[152] He was tempted to view the foundation of a "national workers' party," which sought to win the upwardly mobile workers, as progress in itself; but in such a "class party" the educated, for whom Weber characteristically spoke, would of course have no place.

What Naumann now proposed, in contrast to his earlier views, was apolitical "miserabilism." A modern party could only develop on the basis of economic interests. From this reference point, the National Socials were "the party of the downtrodden, those whose shoes did not fit, all those who have no possessions and would like to have them." All rising classes, even the rising working class, would be the natural enemies

149. *Protokoll*, pp. 47 ff. Also *Pol. Schr.*, pp. 26 ff.

150. Ibid., p. 39.

151. Cf. the letter to his wife after the meeting, *Lebensbild*, p. 234. "The pastors, who composed two-thirds of the assembly, . . . complained about the masses."

152. Later, it appeared to him that the only way was to *join* the Social Democratic party; cf. the letter to Toennies of 9 May 1909, copy in Weber papers: "Your statement 'Politics must be "tactical" or not be at all' struck me most—that is, it surprised me coming from *you*. It seems to open every gate and door for 'Realpolitik,' and I know from our discussion about Naumann that this is not your opinion at all. I would not even reject your view that for *these* reasons entrance into the politically most fruitless party, Social Democracy, is *worthless*. But as things lie today, the acceptance of this party is practically for the same reason the *only* means of entering the proletarian cultural sphere, and to work for their interests (I do not mean the empirically existing efforts, but the *innermost* interests in the highest human sense.) Yes, even to be able to speak to them as man to men,—just as formal acceptance of the church is necessary for participation in contemporary society. I am only incapable of honorably accepting the S.D.'s credo and that prevents me—if I do not also continue to serve 'other Gods'—from entrance, although in the end it is just a lip-credo like the apostle's creed."

of the National Social movement. Weber was convinced that social sentiment and compassion could not provide the basis of a social program by themselves. Weber insisted that power struggle and dominance were intrinsic to politics. But social sentiment and compassion were the quintessence of the new party, and he therefore opposed it with a touch of the Nietzschean master morality. He insisted that the National Socials had to be identified with a clear position within a society fragmented into political interest groups. He saw no potential for a party whose orientation was purely ideological and whose sociological position placed it between all stools. Weber proposed that the new party adopt a consistently bourgeois emphasis—that it affirm industrial progress and the powerful national state. A *new* party foundation at this time had to face a crucial decision: would it support bourgeois progress or unconsciously prop up feudal reaction? The third choice, a politics on behalf of the "fourth estate," was impossible in this situation. Social democracy had, "by opposing the bourgeoisie, paved the way for reaction."

Weber believed that German politics at this time offered a clear alternative between feudal and bourgeois paths.[153] He was convinced that the most important contemporary task was to strengthen the bourgeoisie against the conservatives. A proletarian approach, whatever the form, weakened this effort and to this extent indirectly served the reactionary alliance of the conservatives with industry, since the latter saw this alliance as a means of preventing the rise of the working class. For this reason Weber emphasized that the entire "political point" had been omitted from the program item affecting the large landholders. In his view, the first order of business in social policy was the destruction of the Prussian noble landlords' rule. He hoped for the founding of a *bourgeois* party: "The new party must be a national party of bourgeois freedom, since this is precisely what we do not have; we lack a democratic organization that we can entrust with Germany's leadership through our votes, since we wish to have confidence that national and economic interests are protected in its hands."[154]

For the moment, these words had little impact. To be sure, Naumann immediately adopted Weber's demand for a concerted effort in favor of the development of large industry, and made possible its inclusion in the program.[155] But the necessary conceptual preparation was lacking. The

153. For the historical background and the impact of Weber's support for the industrial state, cf. Kenneth B. Barkin, *The Controversy over German Industrialization 1850–1902* (Chicago, 1970).

154. Winckelmann's interpolation: "*national*" *democracy* (*Pol. Schr.*, p. 28) on the basis of the *free* report by Wenck, *Die Geschichte der National-Sozialen*, pp. 63 f. appears unfounded to us.

155. *Protokoll*, p. 58.

National Social Association set off on its stony, thorn covered way through the thickets of the rigid German partisan scene. It adopted many of Weber's specific political demands: a strongly antifeudal orientation, the energetic propagation of German peasant settlement in the east. Weber, in spite of strong reservations, then joined the association and supported Naumann wherever he could.[156] We can assume that Weber's influence was significant when Naumann permitted a stronger rightward course and that he then finally engineered the rightward jump into the "Freisinnige Vereinigung" (Progressive Association) after his own association collapsed. It was during these years that Max Weber suffered from a severe nerve disorder. This forced him to give up all political activity. In the end, he had to give up his professorship in Heidelberg. He was not able to stand at a university lectern again until 1918. The contacts with Naumann continued. Naumann even visited him in Italy, where Weber sought to cure his severe attacks of depression and the almost ecstatic agitation that repeatedly beset him as the result of days of sleeplessness.

In 1903, when Weber's condition had improved but when he still avoided university teaching and the obligation of regular lectures, his supporters tried to persuade him to do what he seemed predestined for—publishing a political journal in association with Naumann and his brother Alfred Weber.[157] Weber energetically rejected this idea, especially after the collapse of the National Social Association: "To deal constantly with those political matters that stir me deeply is something that my body could at best manage for a few months. And what is even more important: If a political matter is not to be bungled, an absolutely cool head is required, and I simply cannot guarantee that now."[158]

He demanded that his circle work energetically for liberal causes, while he himself withdrew to scholarly pursuits.[159] In 1904, with Edgar Jaffé and Werner Sombart, he took over the publication of the *Archiv für Sozialwissenschaft und Sozialpolitik*, and barricaded himself—whether intentionally or not—with his great programmatic article "'Objektivität'

156. Cf. *Lebensbild*, p. 235.

157. A year earlier, Helene Weber had encouraged her son, who was in financial difficulties, to work on the *Preussische Jahrbücher*. Weber's answer, held by Marianne Weber (*Lebensbild*, pp. 269 f.) was: "The statement about Delbrück only proves that things are not well with the *Preussische Jahrbücher*; later it may be possible. But now my working strength is too uncertain and the political situation not tempting."(!)

158. Letter of 17 July 1903, *Max Weber: A Biography*, p. 277.

159. For example from Troeltsch: "Max Weber demands my active involvement in politics. I refused this with the argument that I am not liberal, in spite of all my sympathies for liberalism. I am not liberal, because of my Christianity and its impact upon political thought" (1904). Cited in Walther Köhler, *Ernst Troeltsch* (Tübingen, 1941), p. 292.

sozialwissenschaftlicher und sozialpolitischer Erkenntnis" ("'Objectivity' in Social Science and Social Policy")[160] from any effective political work in the framework of this journal. It is both tragic and certainly symbolic for the fatal condition of German liberalism at the beginning of the twentieth century that a man with such a superior capacity for politically penetrating analysis, a man who knew what was necessary in German politics, avoided active political involvement.[161] Certainly a very important factor in Weber's decision was his pessimistic view of the pettiness of the German politics of his day. He was repeatedly so disturbed by this that he saw no alternative to withdrawing totally from politics, so as not to "destroy [himself] physically."

On the other hand, Weber's will was too boundless. He greatly surpassed his politically active contemporaries both in his actions and in the sharpness of his critical judgment. He could not feel comfortable with the unavoidable daily petty struggles in politics, the constant compromises, and the tactical corner-cutting. His volcanic temperament could not long be contained by the tactical bonds of partisan and factional politics, which he himself described so perceptively. He was very conscious of this and was therefore ultimately repelled whenever the opportunity for active political involvement occurred. Karl Jaspers, who observed Weber closely, concluded that "he appeared prepared, but he was only prepared if *called* upon. He did not strive for power. He lacked the congenital will to power of the politician who wants to rule because that is his life."[162] Perhaps what Max Weber said of Marx is a fitting description of the kernel of his own will and aims: he wanted power over intellects, not dominion over the masses.[163]

At the time, Weber buried himself in questions about the theory of knowledge and began his great investigation, *The Protestant Ethic and the*

160. Now in *Wissenschaftslehre*, pp. 146 ff. An English translation appears in *Methodology of the Social Sciences*, ed. Edward Shils and Henry Finch (Glencoe, Ill., 1949), pp. 50–112.

161. Cf. Friedrich Sell's judgment: "The greatness and the shortcomings of turn-of-the-century intellectual liberalism in Germany manifest themselves in Max Weber's personality and fate, the depth of insight, the sincere effort for truth, and the incapacity to translate understanding into action." *Die Tragödie des deutschen Liberalismus* (Stuttgart, 1953), p. 10.

162. In *Max Weber: Deutsches Wesen im politischen Denken, Forschen und Philosophieren* (1932), p. 25 (2d ed. under the title *Max Weber: Politiker, Forscher, Philosoph* [Bremen, 1946]). Also in *Heidelberger Gedenkrede*, p. 18.

163. In an (almost unreadable) lecture manuscript consisting merely of notes on the "labor question" (Weber papers), he wrote of Marx: "Ruler by nature with unlimited personal ambition and without compassion. Belief in his mission for domination of minds. This, and not rule of the masses, was in fact his goal. *Contempt* for his associates and the masses."

Spirit of Capitalism. He kept an anxious eye, however, on political events and remained Naumann's advisor and helper. When, at the Mannheim convention of the Verein für Sozialpolitik in 1905, Gustav von Schmoller accused Naumann of demagoguery for an enthusiastic speech which, in any event, did not reflect the Verein's past views, Max Weber energetically defended his friend.[164] To be sure, he recognized that Schmoller's underlying aim was to distance the Verein from Naumann's radical opinions, and that Schmoller's stress on a defined, moderate position for the Verein also challenged the radical wing indirectly. In Weber's eyes, this represented an attempt to make the Verein a "Verein for a socially respectable social policy."[165]

Weber refused to be regarded as a "radical ornament" in an otherwise conservative association, and he objected to having his friends on the left in the Verein placed in such a position.[166] The Verein had to remain a "forum" open to every opinion.[167] Brentano had trouble preventing a public declaration by Weber against Schmoller in the *Frankfurter Zeitung*[168] that might have blown the Verein für Sozialpolitik apart.[169] Weber nevertheless observed that the majority of the Verein began to move strongly to the right and that if, as Schmoller wished, the Verein adopted a compromising line somewhere between social democracy and the social reactionary right, he and his left-leaning compatriots could no longer remain in the organization.

Weber was deeply disappointed by the results of the Reichstag elec-

164. Weber's declaration in *Gesammelte Aufsätze zur Soziologie und Sozialpolitik*, pp. 406 f.; cf. also the more or less official version by Franz Boese, *Geschichte des Vereins für Sozialpolitik, 1872–1932* (Berlin, 1939), pp. 108 ff. where Weber and Naumann are pointed to as constant disturbers of the Verein's peace. Recently also Dieter Lindenlaub, *Richtungskämpfe im Verein für Sozialpolitik: Wissenschaft und Sozialpolitik im Kaiserreich vornehmlich vom Beginn des "Neuen Kurses" bis zum Ausbruch des Ersten Weltkrieges (1890–1914)*, (Wiesbaden 1967), pp. 409 ff.

165. Letter to Brentano of 26 October 1905, Brentano papers; compare Schmoller's letter to Weber of 29 October 1905 in Boese, *Geschichte des Vereins für Sozialpolitik*, pp. 116 f.

166. Letter to Schmoller of 11 November 1905, Schmoller papers; compare the letter to Alfred Weber before 26 October 1905 (undated) in Weber papers. He keeps his distance, "in case the enemies take the position of treating us as 'decorations' and as swaggering radicals."

167. The term was used by Schmoller.

168. Thus Brentano, in a telegram to Weber of 24 October 1905, copy in the Brentano papers.

169. It is not possible here to go more deeply into the Weber-Schmoller quarrel, helpful as it might be for judging Weber's character. The extensive correspondence is in the Schmoller, Brentano, and Weber papers. Schmoller's letters are cited in Boese. Weber's judgment of Schmoller is corroborated by Schmoller's memorandum of 1906 in which he wrote that "those elements that seek, e.g., greater democratization of our constitution, our administration, and our economy, would be better off doing so outside of our association, as members of particular political parties." Partially reprinted in Boese, pp. 266 ff.

tion at the beginning of 1907, in which he had hoped for a general strengthening of the liberal parties at the expense of the Center. There appeared to be no possibility of a purely "bourgeois" coalition against the Conservatives, or an extension of this coalition to the left which Naumann was later to call for with the famous slogan "From Bassermann to Bebel!" In view of the Social Democrats' "rhetorical heroism" this was not an immediate prospect.[170] Although the bloc policy ran contrary to Weber's basic beliefs—he insisted on a *bourgeois* politics that *opposed* the Conservatives—he approved of the bloc at first. He approved most emphatically of Naumann's course of action. Unlike the leaders of the Progressive Association, who were close to his position, Naumann did not leave the Progressive People's Party because of the paragraphs relating to language in the association law.[171] In Weber's view, the achievement of a new stock exchange law was worth concessions on the association law question,[172] since this affected Germany's power in the world.[173] He was in no way content with the association law in the form in which it was finally passed, especially with the language paragraphs that were directed against the Poles and that severely restricted the use of foreign languages in public gatherings.[174]

Weber justified the liberals' willingness to compromise on this issue with the argument that a rejection of the association law "would achieve nothing, while the liberals would be split." For otherwise the road would have been clear for the Prussian Landtag to enact an incomparably worse law.[175] Weber's positive attitude about the "conservative-liberal diagonal" of the "Bülow bloc" rested in large part on the hope that William II

170. Cf. the letter to Brentano of 6 February 1907: "The one ray of hope: Naumann and the *possibility* that in future Social Democracy will lay aside rhetorical heroics and pursue practical politics. But whether?" (*Lebensbild*, p. 405.) A few days earlier he had written to Michels (letter of 1 February 1907, copy in Weber papers), that he had "the sense that every chance of cooperation with the Social Democrats had *disappeared*, since it is impossible to deal with political rigidity and 'poison and gall' are of course valuable substances, but are no surrogates for enthusiasm."

171. Letter to Naumann of 26 April 1908, *Pol. Schr.* 1, pp. 453 f.

172. In the bloc, the stock exchange law amendment was seen as compensation for the law of associations. Cf. Theodor Eschenburg, *Das Kaiserreich am Scheidewege* (Berlin, 1929,) p. 98.

173. Cf. above, chap. 4, sec. 1.

174. Cf. above, chap. 3, sec. 3.

175. Cf. Weber's letter to Brentano of 3 and 5 June 1908, Brentano papers. Brentano took Naumann's concessions in the question of the law of associations to task and accused him of betraying the liberal cause. Brentano saw in paragraph 12 especially a danger to the freedom of coalition. Weber energetically defended his friend: "Everything that you say has justification. But we cannot be 'through' with Naumann, for to do so would be to be 'through' with liberalism. And the Poles are not *alone* in Germany. I am in complete agreement with *your* view in this *language* situation although I disagree with you on other aspects of the Polish question." And on June 5: "I understand your deep disappointment. But the *situation* here was stronger than any politician."

and the conservatives would be prepared to concede electoral reform in Prussia.[176] He wished to see the liberals coordinate their policies in order to achieve this goal. In June 1908 he wrote to Brentano: "For me it will be decisive if [the liberals] succeed in trading concessions in the *financial* sphere in the Reich for *significant* suffrage concessions in Prussia. If this is *un*successful, *then* 'all *is for nought*.' And it *probably* will not succeed. But it *must* be given a try."[177]

In the fall of 1908, when the new elections to the Prussian House of Deputies had revealed that there was no real chance for a suffrage reform of any significance, bloc politics completely lost "their rationale" for Weber.[178] He now pressed Naumann, in direct contrast to his position during the earlier part of the year, to be "ready for a spring to *the left*," in opposition to the ever more rightward trend of the Progressive People's party.[179] He did not wish to see Naumann compromised in his role as representative of the liberal position by a fruitless policy of concessions to the Conservatives.[180] "It is impossible to be 'finished' with Naumann, unless we are 'finished' with liberalism altogether." He anticipated a "black" future—figuratively and literally—and saw no chance for progressive liberal politics to succeed for years. As early as 1907, he said to Michels that we should "be glad . . . to get through the generation of black reaction that lays before us with *that* amount of freedom that we now have, until better times arrive."[181] This pessimistic prediction was now definitely borne out. Liberalism appeared to him to have been pushed into the defensive for the foreseeable future.[182]

Max Weber took at least some satisfaction from the fact that Friedrich Naumann had adopted several of his own principal views and publicized them widely in order to achieve a "renewal of liberalism."[183] Naumann had already accepted Weber's advocacy of a concerted policy of industrialization as a basic theme of his programmatic book *Demokratie und Kaisertum* (*Democracy and Empire*), although in Weber's opinion it was

176. Eschenburg's formulation, *Das Kaiserreich am Scheidewege* (Berlin, 1929), p. 282.

177. Letter of 3 June 1908.

178. Compare the letter to Naumann of 5 November 1908, *Pol. Schr.* 1, pp. 454 f., abbreviated with some errors. It says, e.g., "Thereby the bloc policy has certainly also *lost* its rationale for you." Naumann papers, 120.

179. Ibid.

180. Cf. note 175.

181. Letter of 1 February 1907.

182. Cf. the letter to Naumann of 5 November 1908: "In four years, we shall have . . . a *clerical regime . . . everywhere*. . . . Then the difficult work will begin of preparing 'a road for freedom.'"

183. Theodor Barth and Friedrich Naumann, *Die Erneuerung des Liberalismus* (Berlin, 1906).

confused here with the illusionary concepts of "social imperialism."[184] Weber was definitely heartened when Naumann wrote that the German Reich must not be reduced to "a welfare agency for suffering agrarians" if it wished "to preserve its own spirit and historical character."[185] To be sure, it was more important that under Weber's influence Naumann gave up the effort to establish a progressive political movement on the inadequate basis of petit-bourgeois inertia and the political instability of the educated bourgeoisie.[186] This was the chief lesson of Weber's lecture at the Erfurt congress, and it was fully confirmed by developments. It finally persuaded Naumann, in 1904, to press for the open recognition of the class character of liberal politics, since only class-conscious liberalism had the firmness to hold its ground "in the general class struggle that will someday arise."[187] Max Weber repeatedly pointed to the divisions in Germany and worked for a closed phalanx of the bourgeoisie against the "large landowning conservative class." At Erfurt he pointed out that, above all, modern parties could thrive only on the basis of interests, and called for a party that fought consistently in the bourgeois interest.

It was even more significant that Naumann energetically adopted Weber's sociological analysis of political parties for the organization of the liberal party movement. By 1906, at the latest, Naumann accepted the view that the day of the old liberal honorific type of party was over and that the future belonged to the "party machine."[188] After 1906, Naumann repeatedly pressed for the creation of a liberal party organization that would be able to match the apparatus of the Center party and the Social Democrats, and yes, even the Peasants' League (Bund der Landwirte), the mass organization that cooperated closely with the

184. Cf. also my introduction to Friedrich Naumann, *Verfassungspolitische Schriften*, *Werke*, vol. 2 (Opladen, 1964), pp. xxxix ff.

185. *Demokratie und Kaisertum*, pp. 155 f.

186. Conze, *Friedrich Naumann*, p. 376.

187. *Die Hilfe* 10, no. 2 (1904): 2 f.: "Klassenpolitik des Liberalismus," now in Friedrich Naumann, *Werke*, vol. 4, *Schriften zum Parteiwesen und zum Mitteleuropaproblem*, ed. Thomas Nipperdey and Wolfgang Schieder, p. 257.

188. It is an error to attribute Naumann's departure from the liberalism of notables to Michels in the first instance as Joachim Knoll has done (*Führungsauslese in Liberalismus und Demokratie* [Stuttgart, 1957]). Weber directed Michels's attention to the phenomenon of the "machine" and encouraged Naumann to look at the problem of organization. It is probable that it was Weber who pointed out Michels's work to Naumann. All too often, Knoll's study falls into such premature generalizations. Its weakness lies, above all, in the fact that the fundamental concept of the elite remains unclear, and in the course of the narrative often wavers. All too often, the concept of the elite is linked with the monarchistic idea, to which it bears not the slightest relation.

Conservatives. The old liberalism had collapsed because it had been so poorly organized.[189]

Naumann's hope for the resurrection of a broad liberal movement nevertheless remained unfulfilled. Naumann's tragedy was the same as Max Weber's. Although he had an independent mind, was full of optimism, and was ready to adapt to new ideas, always trying to reach for the stars, he was also, in a sense, a mouthpiece for that "bourgeois Marx" who had himself retreated from politic's turbulant air into the cloister of pure scholarship.[190] Troeltsch was certainly correct in his obituary in 1920 when he said that Weber had "already had a historical impact on the German people through Naumann, who had adopted his ideas and molded them with his own."[191]

189. At first, as far as we can see, in "Liberalismus und Organisation," *Die Nation* 22, no. 30 (1905), in *Werke*, vol. 4, pp. 258 ff. Cf. "Die Lage des Liberalismus," in "Die Erneuerung des Liberalismus" (1906) *loc. cit.*, pp. 22 ff.; then: "Von wem werden wir regiert?" (1909), cited in Friedrich Naumann, *Freiheitskämpfe* (1911), p. 215 (*Werke*, vol. 3, pp. 390 ff.).

190. We cannot go any further here into Weber's influence upon Naumann. In the political terminology alone, this influence appears to us to have been great (for example, the concept of the state as a "large firm," "master nation" [see and cf. Conze, *Friedrich Naumann*, p. 368], industrialism." Also cf. above, chap. 4, sec. 1.

191. *Deutscher Geist und Westeuropa* (Berlin, 1925), p. 249.

6
Foreign Policy and the Constitutional System

1. Bismarck, William II, and the Failure of German Imperialism

Weber was convinced that it was not only Germany's task but its duty to maintain its position as a world power. He viewed this as a simple consequence of the foundation of the Reich. He regarded Bismarck's continental policy of eschewing all major overseas acquisitions and insisting that the Reich was "saturated" as a contradiction which he attributed to the chancellor's domestic antipathies. As early as that beacon of German imperialism, the Freiburg inaugural address, Weber, without mentioning the great statesman's name, spoke of the colonial policy of the eighties as overseas "power politics" carried on "timidly and half reluctantly," which did not really deserve the appelation.[1] Two years later he wrote in his statement on the Tirpitz naval bill, in which he championed naval construction, that an "ostensibly 'accommodating' policy, considerate of the status quo, and disinclined to all thoughts of overseas expansion," like the one begun "after 1871," had certainly "not promoted the awakening of interest in the fleet."[2]

During the war and under the influence of Italy's betrayal, Max Weber, as a convinced imperialist supporter, criticized Bismarck's foreign policy because it had offered the quadruple alliance powers, especially Italy, no opportunity for expansion. Weber saw the weakness of the Triple Alliance in "what from the standpoint of the preservation of peace was its primary aim: its purely defensive character." Therefore, it offered

1. *Pol. Schr.*, p. 21.
2. "Stellungnahme zur Flottenumfrage," *Pol. Schr.*, p. 30.

Italy "no chance to pursue its political need for expansion."[3] Weber's disenchantment with Bismarck's policy of preserving the status quo on the continent and consciously giving up almost all claim to overseas acquisitions could not be more clearly documented. Weber sought world equality for Germany and a respectable colonial empire. Purely defensive alliances would not help to achieve such goals.

Weber often agreed with Bismarck in his differences with the Pan-German annexationists. He recognized that Germany could not seek to overstep the limitations imposed by its geographical situation without penalties. But this only applied to the continent. He accepted the continental "saturation" of the Reich, however, only because this was the necessary precondition for an overseas world policy. Weber strongly criticized Bismarck's antipathy toward all overseas acquisitions that might engage Germany in international conflicts. He disagreed with Bismarck's efforts to exploit the colonial aspirations of the western powers by actions designed to enhance the Reich's hegemony in Europe and his unwillingness to enter into competition with them in the colonial sphere. Bismarck had not seized upon opportunities for an overseas colonial policy and had thereby placed the Reich in the fatal position at the end of the line of the world powers seeking colonies. Aside from the modest acquisitions of the eighties, Bismarck's lack of interest in colonial policy had accustomed the world to seeing "the events in overseas regions as things in which Germany required consultation merely because of her arrogance."[4]

Weber attributed Bismarck's rejection of an overseas policy primarily to domestic motives. Bismarck's foreign policy was "'conservative' in every sense . . . and it was in no sense a 'greater Germany' policy."[5] It was conservative in the first instance because Bismarck sought the protection and stabilization of the existing balance of power above all. It was not a dynamic policy seeking power expansion and colonial acquisition. It was also conservative out of domestic considerations. An imperialistic Reich policy could not be carried out with the traditional means of the Prussian-German state in which an agriculturally based Prussian nobility was predominant. Weber viewed the Prussian Conservatives as the primary enemies of a German world policy, and not without reason. It was natural for him to attribute Bismarck's rejection of an overseas policy to his conservative sentiments, even though he transcended these far more than the rest of his class. It is doubtless also correct that Bismarck, in spite of his own background, remained relatively removed from capitalist

3. Ibid., p. 113.
4. Ibid., p. 117.
5. Ibid., p. 113.

economic development and its result, bourgeois-capitalist imperialism, and therefore he lacked much understanding of it.[6] We must, however, continue to realize that Bismarck's abstinence on the world stage was primarily the result of his recognition of the Reich's exposed position in the middle of Europe. The *cauchemar des coalitions*, above all, prevented him from colonial engagements overseas.

Max Weber's concrete colonialist goals cannot be determined by reference to the few statements he made before World War I. He referred occasionally to this subject only after the war began. He desired "the establishment of colonial spheres of interest in the uncivilized regions like Africa in exchange for the scattered possessions" that uselessly involved Germany in conflicts of interest with every possible power.[7] "In place of our scattered possessions, we do not need world conquest but a rounded-out sphere of interest."[8] Weber never specifically detailed the means that German foreign policy would have to employ to facilitate significant participation in the division of the world.

Weber supported Tirpitz's naval policy—at least at first—with all his heart as a means to win weight overseas for the Reich. He warmly welcomed the first naval bill of 1898, although he regarded it as only a beginning.[9] To be sure, he spoke in 1918 of having fought the serious errors in "Tirpitz's upstart policy" which had led to the fact that "we now have to say the same thing about the widely discussed Anglo-Saxon world rule . . . that Thiers said in 1871 about German unity: 'Ah, c'est nous, qui l'avons faite.'" But at the same time he also said that Germany had achieved "a battle fleet of the size of the French fleet . . . for defensive purposes."[10] There is no doubt that he emphatically supported German naval policy.[11]

6. Cf. Hans-Ulrich Wehler, *Bismarck und der Imperialismus* (Cologne, 1969). Wehler's thesis that Bismarck hoped that he would thereby work to stabilize the German economy strikes me as a somewhat exaggerated interpretation. To be sure, after 1883, Bismarck temporarily pursued an active imperialist policy with the expectation that he would thereby split his internal opposition, and completely rupture the liberal camp; he gave this policy up quickly when it became clear that the domestic effect he expected did not materialize and at the same time, the Reich's direct overseas involvement was far greater than he had originally anticipated. The burden on foreign policy was thereby also greater.

7. Letter to Naumann of 8 May 1917, *Pol. Schr.* 1, p. 471.

8. *Pol. Schr.*, p. 166.

9. "Stellungnahme zur Flottenumfrage," ibid., p. 30.

10. *Pol. Schr.*, p. 496.

11. Compare the letter to Naumann, 12 November 1908, *Pol. Schr.* 1, p. 456: it is "a tragedy that we cannot act as the *Vorwärts* does daily in its beer boycott with 'Do not drink Ringbier.' If only in *every* issue of *every* independent paper we could print: 'The conservatives are opposed to any limitation of the personal regime—*therefore* it is impossible to pursue a 'world policy,' a naval policy, or any policy that Switzerland and Denmark cannot pursue."

In contrast to Naumann and most liberal imperialists of the day, Max Weber nevertheless favored a German world alliance with England. "Before the war [I] always . . . supported . . . a respectable understanding with England . . . for purely political as well as cultural reasons," Weber said late in 1918.[12] While this retrospective comment should be viewed somewhat skeptically, there is little doubt that he always favored cooperation with England in foreign policy.[13] Although he was later repeatedly to criticize "the *selfish* position of English policy," vis-à-vis the Reich on colonial matters, he thought that Germany's best chance for overseas acquisitions lay in association with England.[14]

Weber sought to defend this position in 1915, although it appeared to be contradicted by England's entrance into the war. He asserted that Germany's colonial acquisitions had not constituted a "reason for serious conflict" with England since they had "the value of a 'hostage' . . . for the ocean-dominating Albion."[15] He pointed to the threat of the German fleet as the decisive provocation for England. But he could still not quite admit the inconsistency of a world policy based on cooperation with Great Britain on the one hand and his support of Tirpitz's naval policy on the other. In his view, a timely naval policy, devoid of excessive and public demagoguery, would not have aroused English fears. Bismarck had been mistaken when he had rejected the fleet primarily because of domestic German political antipathies.[16] It was not the fleet itself, but fleet propaganda with its sharp polemics against England, that had engendered English enmity. Weber now complained that an agreement about German naval construction had not been sought in earnest because of pan-German agitation and imperial swaggering.[17]

Max Weber attributed the failure of international cooperation with

12. *Pol. Schr.*, p. 489.

13. Compare Weber's speech in Munich of 4 November 1918 at a meeting of the Progressive party: "Our compatriots did not die for an evil thing; they turned away the terrible danger of czarism. A result of our foolish policy was, however, that the war was also a war against England. It was the result of pan-German stupidity that the war effort was directed against England above all." According to the report of the *Münchner Allgemeine Zeitung*, no. 599, 5 November 1918.

14. *Pol. Schr.*, p. 496 et passim.

15. Ibid., p. 114.

16. Ibid., p. 116.

17. Ibid., p. 166; also p. 496. Compare "Bemerkungen zum Bericht der Kommission der Alliierten und Assoziierten Regierungen über die Verantwortlichkeit der Urheber des Krieges nebst einer Vorbemerkung zu den Anlagen der Denkschrift," *Das deutsche Weissbuch über die Schuld am Kriege. Mit der Denkschrift der deutschen Viererkommission zum Schuldbericht der alliierten und assoziierten Mächte*, 1st ed. (Berlin, 1919), p. 67 (hereafter cited as *Kriegsschulddenkschrift*) (now also *Pol. Schr.*, pp. 571 ff.): "We concede on our part that it was not the *fact* but the ultimate scope and the spirit of German naval construction in recent years that aroused England's mistrust."

England in overseas affairs primarily to shortcomings of German foreign policy caused by domestic factors, and not to the international situation. In his view, William II's foolish telegram to the president of the Boer Republic after the Jameson raid had done more than anything to cloud Anglo-German relations. "As a result, later attempts for accommodation, both before and after the Boer War, in Africa or generally, lacked the domestic support of the people of both nations whose honor had been engaged, although both sides would have gained from such an accommodation."[18]

In Weber's view, the real reason for the failure of German foreign policy during the Wilhelmine period was William II's interference and his unwise and aggressive statements on foreign policy issues. The clumsy, often ostentatious appearance of German diplomacy appeared to him to result from the Kaiser's "personal ambition"; he attributed the inconsistencies largely to William II's capricious character and a desire for prestige that led him to seek momentary successes. After Bismarck's retirement, dynastic vanity, not sober interest politics, seemed to determine German policy. Weber increasingly directed his attention and his critical scorn to William II's "personal rule."

At first he had hoped that William's independent rule would awaken the nation from its lethargy and blind Bismarck worship and force it, in the light of the conflict between the two "Caesars," to adopt a position independent of both.[19] But at an early stage he observed the fickleness of the Kaiser's policies with concern and the unfortunate influence of the Kaiser's quest for popularity.[20] As early as the middle of 1892, he became convinced that William II's "personal rule" increasingly threatened the Reich's internal and external existence: "What can we say in general about our situation and our prospects when both depend upon an absolutely unmeasurable factor, *the person of the Kaiser*? Unfavorable opinions of him continue to gain ground. He apparently treats policy from the limited standpoint of an eccentrically inventive lieutenant. No one will deny that he energetically fulfills his duty in the sense of 'service.' But his recurring confusion and uncomfortable relationship to power engenders such disorganization at the top that an effect upon the administration as a

18. *Pol. Schr.*, pp. 372 f.; cf. p. 160.

19. "From this reference point," Weber perceived it to be "a merit of the Kaiser" that he does not completely accept any particular tendency and until now has "temporarily offended one after the other." Letter to Baumgarten of 3 January 1891, *Jugendbriefe*, p. 328.

20. See Weber's very sharp-sighted statement to Baumgarten of 31 December 1889: "If only the young Kaiser would achieve consistency! These Boulangist-Bonapartist sorts of demonstrations are just what we do not want. It is like sitting in a railroad car traveling at a great velocity without being certain that the next switch has been put into position." Ibid., pp. 323 f. Weber made a similar comment in the letter of 3 January 1891, ibid., p. 330.

whole cannot be avoided. He demeaned Caprivi, who was such a worthy man, to a caricature, and it is currently impossible to speak about the authority of the Reich government. It is a wonder that we have been able to avoid serious diplomatic situations so far. But there is no doubt that the politics of Europe are no longer made in Berlin."[21]

Nor did Weber see a firm will or a unified course in the area of domestic policy. Social policy seemed to zigzag from extreme attempts at accommodation to the readiness to make "social policy with cannons." Weber also associated the growing feudalization of the bourgeois life style in Germany with William II's dynastic policies. He was enraged by the fact that right-wing politicians could influence the monarch because of their social position and consequent easier access than representatives of the bourgeoisie, let alone the proletariat. This had a powerful effect upon the course of German policy. In view of the courtly game of intrigue, and refined speculation about where the dynasty's sympathy lay in domestic politics, Max Weber carefully avoided the subject of "corruption in parliament and political parties." At the Verein für Sozialpolitik convention in 1905, when Schmoller attached parliamentarianism and parliamentary rhetoric, Weber opposed him sharply. What was "politically dubious" about parliamentarianism was not "parliamentary rhetoric" but parliamentary "patronage behind the scenes." This was an intrinsic characteristic of German "pseudo-constitutionalism. . . . We should not delude ourselves. We have no parliamentary state under the present organization of power. We do not have the benefits of parliamentarianism that other countries have, only the disadvantages. We have partisan rule here as much as they do elsewhere. Here, a party's domination is the result of a change in court fashions under the pressure of dynastic and all possible other interests. But partisan rule is as present here as anywhere else in the world."[22]

For Weber, the decisive problem was the impact of dynastic influence upon foreign policy, and there were indeed reasons for concern in this area. William II multiplied the danger to Germany's position in the most unfortunate way with the ominous Krüger dispatch, and he seriously weakened Germany's image in the Far East with the China addresses and the theatrical Waldersee excursion. The Kaiser's wish to maintain personal contact with the Czar also had an unfortunate impact. In 1898 he indiscreetly informed the Czar about Chamberlain's proposal for a wide-ranging alliance with the Reich. This action did not serve the Reich's interests in the light of Russo-German relations, and gave comfort to

21. Letter to Baumgarten of 18 April 1892, pp. 345 ff.

22. Discussion address at the convention of the Verein für Sozialpolitik in Mannheim 1905, *Gesammelte Aufsätze zur Soziologie und Sozialpolitik*, pp. 400 f. Cf. also Lindenlaub, pp. 396 f.

those in England opposed to alliance with Germany. The Treaty of Björkoe, which the Kaiser persuaded the Czar to sign in 1905 and which he viewed as a personal triumph, immediately proved a complete fiasco. Schuwalow and Bülow simply ignored it. Nothing proves so clearly that the age of dynastic foreign policy was over.

What worried Weber most about the Kaiser's personal interference with foreign policy was the emphasis on mere prestige that Bismarck had so emphatically warned against.[23] William II's characteristic quest for effect and popularity colored the whole conduct of German foreign policy. "Anyone that we have to reckon with in foreign affairs who considers the impact of our behavior upon foreign nations will readily recognize that our current policies give and must give the impression that displays of power seek to achieve not power itself but, above all, the appearance of power."[24] Weber saw a clear example of this in Germany's South African policy of 1896. He saw here a show of firmness purely for the sake of prestige. The moralistic promises in William II's telegram were not backed by the desire to defend the Boer Republic militarily. Weber viewed the Morocco policy of 1906 in the same way. Because Weber thought so much in terms of power politics, he was repelled by an insincere, trifling foreign policy that did not stake everything for the achievement of great national goals.

Weber's unhappiness with the course of German foreign policy, the influence of the monarch's emotions upon foreign policy, and the lack of a sober notion of power was clear again in his articles about the Russian revolution of 1905. The events in Russia appeared to him to be a kind of mirror in which the faults of the German political system could be observed as if enlarged, in a way that exposed their dangerous motivation. It was not so much, as Richard Pipes commented, that Weber was led to false conclusions by his preconceived historical and philosophical convictions. His conclusions stemmed from his inclination to read German political concerns and wishes into the Russian situation. To this extent, Pipes's accusation that Weber had described the Russian situation "ahistorically" and without reference to intrinsic preconditions has a certain truth to it.[25]

For Max Weber, the parallel between the necessity of replacing the

23. After his fall, Bismarck viewed a German move overseas as consonant "with the goals of German policy only if clear benefits, without proportionately great risks such as a conflict with a stronger and older naval power, could be expected. Nothing contradicts the German Reich's interests as much as involvement in adventurous enterprises as the result of a foreign policy based on the mere need of simply being there. Such involvements have no real basis in the nation's interests. They merely spring from the motives of flattering either the nation's vanity or the ambitions of the rulers." *Gesammelte Werke*, vol. 9, p. 401.

24. *Gesammelte Aufsätze zur Soziologie und Sozialpolitik*, p. 396.

25. Pipes, *Max Weber und Russland*, pp. 630, 635 f.

Czar's autocratic rule with a liberal regime and the necessity of overcoming "personal rule" in Germany were clear. He went so far as to link the Russian democrats' enmity toward Germany, which he also attributed to the German jailkeeper policy of repressing the Poles, and thereby aiding the Czar on the basis of common interests, with William II's "personal rule." The "reactionary character of German domestic politics," and the belief that a solidarity of dynastic interests existed through "the common desire for 'personal government' might destine the Kaiser, whose decisions gave an impression of unpredictability, to play the role of Nicholas I."[26] The distinct relationship between Weber's criticism of the German political situation and his judgments about Russian revolutionary events is illustrated by the following characteristic reference: "The consequences of the modern species of 'monarchism,' that in the worst case must reckon with a monarch that is a dangerous political dilettante and at best a one-sided military expert [the Czar], can be studied well through the events in Russia."[27] "A dangerous political dilettante": these words were doubtless directed at William II. In view of these disquieting observations, Weber could justifiably complain about the "present stylish discussion about the 'obsolescence of parliamentarianism,'" especially in the light of the achievements of Anglo-Saxon parliamentary politics.[28] "This discussion is presently misdirected since it promotes the critical comparison of the current achievements of the countries with parliamentary democracy and those with 'personal' rule and even in the one special region where the greater capacity of the latter should be clear—foreign policy—it comes out decisively the loser. A definite judgment on the achievement of German diplomacy is possible only through a study of the diplomatic files. But anyone can see that lasting successes and consistent direction are impossible if diplomacy is undercut by noisy intermezzi, speeches, telegrams, and unexpected royal decisions, so that the entire effort must be directed at retrieving the situation. The diplomats may even come to accept the idea of employing such theatrical methods themselves."[29]

Weber was as concerned about the impact of this behavior upon the political system as he was about the specific results of royal maneuvers for foreign policy. Here, too, Russia appeared to be a crude model of what could plainly be observed in Germany. Weber pointed out that dynastic ambition in both countries prevented genuine statesmen from rising to power. "Russia's circumstances, of course, 'scream' for a 'statesman'; —*but* dynastic ambition and 'personal government' leave little room

26. "Zur Lage," p. 7, note 2; compare *Pol. Schr.*, p. 125.
27. "Scheinkonstitutionalismus," p. 233, note 359.
28. "Zur Lage," p. 28, note 18.
29. Ibid.; also *Pol. Schr.*, p. 40, note 1.

for a great reformer, if one can be found. . . . Perhaps this is the case here too."[30]

Weber's recognition of the fatal consequences of "personal government" for Germany's international position appeared to be emphatically confirmed by German policy in Morocco. In 1906, this policy finally prompted Weber to forsake his reserve. He could still not quite bring himself to take public action. He sought to influence the Progressive People's party's position through Friedrich Naumann, especially in regard to the approaching elections. Late in 1906, Bülow dissolved the Reichstag because of the Center party's rejection of his colonial proposals. The Center had attacked the Colonial Office on personnel decisions. Bülow viewed this as an opportunity to break the Center's primacy in the Reichstag since 1890 with an appeal to national emotions. The campaign would be directed against the Center, which would be labeled an enemy of the Reich's power interests. Max Weber tried to convince Naumann to avoid the campaign slogan "For the *Kaiser*, against the 'power-hungry Center,'" for he believed that the Center's efforts to achieve some influence over appointments in the Reich administration were basically legitimate. It was necessary to campaign against the Center as the party of pseudo-constitutionalism that was using the issue of Reichstag control of the colonial administration to further its own desire for patronage. "But for God's sake," this should not be tied with a "vote of confidence" for the Kaiser and his political methods. On the contrary, the Kaiser's direct participation in foreign affairs had to be opposed energetically. "The degree of contempt that our nation increasingly encounters abroad (Italy, America, everywhere!)—and with justice—is the decisive issue. Our submission to *this* regime of *this* man is gradually becoming a power issue of 'world' importance for us. . . . We are becoming 'isolated' because this man rules us in this way *and because we tolerate it and make excuses for it.*"[31]

Weber believed that an end to personal government that was essential for the Reich's position in the world could come about only through the development of some form of parliamentary government. Success could be achieved only through effective and not just formal responsibility of the leading statesman to parliament. Weber tried to diffuse royalist reservations—and Naumann shared these—about such an infringement of royal power by pointing out that a parliamentary system did not necessarily imply the total exclusion of royal influence upon policy. "A purely parliamentary 'kingdom of influence' can, with conscious reserve

30. Also, p. 117; compare "Scheinkonstitutionalismus," p. 233: "The many outstanding individuals in the Russian . . . bureaucracy are not in the position to be 'statesmen' for great reforms under the existing system. Dynastic ambitions tend to that—there as here."

31. Letter to Naumann of 14 December 1906, *Pol. Schr.* 1, pp. 451 f.

on the monarch's part, achieve sufficient means to serve the country effectively in a way that is not possible for the 'kingdom of prerogative.' Dynastic vanity and egotism are easily aroused by the legally recognized existence of crown prerogatives. This can lead to personal ambitions that are very damaging to the modern life of state. A modern state cannot coexist with the dilettantism characteristic of Renaissance rules."[32] Weber idealized the English constitution here. He greatly overestimated the actual political influence of a monarch like Edward VII.[33] However, his principal aim was to encourage the conversion of convinced monarchists to the parliamentary system. He stressed that his criticism of personal government was not intended as an attack on monarchy itself: rather the reverse. It was essential to oppose the monarch's interference in government *from* the royalist standpoint, since in the long run this interference would endanger monarchical institutions.

Max Weber failed at the time to win Naumann over with his appeal for a struggle "against dynastic lust for power at home, and against a foreign policy of dynastic prestige and the grand gesture rather than a sober policy of self-interest." Naumann could not bring himself definitively to forsake his past confidence in a Kaiser who stood for the people, the navy, and industry.[34] The political situation in 1906 was not propitious for a drive against personal government. The common liberal and conservative struggle against the Catholic fortress took precedence.

The course of European affairs in 1907 could only increase Weber's disquiet about Germany's "policy of dynastic prestige." The Anglo-Russian agreement to delimit their respective spheres of influence in the Middle East and in Asia brought about a major shift in the balance of power. The antipathy between the English whale and the Russian bear, which Holstein had seen as an inalterable principle of European relations and which was a cornerstone of his policy, appeared buried. For the first time, the specter of an alliance of the two powers against the Triple Alliance darkened the political horizon. For Weber, Germany's worsened international position was the impetus for renewing his sharp attacks against the system of personal rule. "Nothing makes us so incapable of alliances . . . as the association of our social and political development with the growing influence of dynastic personalities in government. This is what has caused the failure of our policy in recent years, what has reduced the respect of the world for us as an international and cultural power step by step to such a degree that it is beginning to endanger our

32. "Scheinkonstitutionalismus," pp. 65 f.; cf. *Pol. Schr.*, pp. 203 f.

33. For Edward VII's actual political position, cf. R.C.K. Ensor, "England 1890–1914," *Oxford Modern History of England*, vol. 4 (Oxford, 1936), pp. 342 ff.

34. Naumann announced the slogan: "The future will be either 'The Center Party Kaiser' or 'Democracy and Kaiserdom.'" *Die Hilfe*, no. 52, 30 December 1906.

security."[35] Max Weber began a careful study of the possibilities of introducing a parliamentary system in a manner that would avoid upsetting the Reich's delicate constitutional structure, that is, as a federation of princely states balanced by the Reichstag's unifying power.[36]

Weber's speculations were unexpectedly overtaken by political reality. William II's *Daily Telegraph* interview in 1908 aroused the entire German public, and prompted calls from all sides for constitutional reform. The interview discussed the strains in German-English relations in an unfortunate manner and may have provoked the Japanese because it conjured up the yellow peril in the far east. Nevertheless, the immediate foreign reaction was greatly overestimated by the German public. But the interview occurred at the height of the Bosnian crisis at a time when the danger of a great European coalition against the Triple Alliance seemed imminent. General unrest over the failures of German foreign policy, especially the defeat at Algeciras and the Anglo-Russian rapprochement, found an outlet here. Even the Conservatives, previously so loyal, were deeply disturbed. Although the chancellor was formally and, in this case, also personally responsible, he left the monarch in the lurch. As a result, the German Reich suffered the severest internal crisis since its foundation. However, the movement to reform the constitutional system and introduce parliamentary responsibility for the chancellor got nowhere. The National Liberals were only in favor of a sort of impeachment for the chancellor in instances of serious violation of the constitution and therefore prevented the forging of a parliamentary majority in favor of concrete plans for constitutional reform. The single, meager result was a formal declaration by the Kaiser that he would exercise more reserve in the future. The incident also cost Bülow the chancellorship the following year. The nation's long-festering resentment over dynastic blunders and ambitions was wasted; no lasting political success was attained.

Max Weber was disturbed not only by the *Daily Telegraph* affair but by the course of the political debate surrounding it. After 1900, he had consciously avoided all active political involvement because of his weakened nerves. He now considered taking a public position on the issue of the monarch's place in a parliamentary monarchy.[37] For the time being, however, he contented himself with attempts to influence Friedrich Naumann.[38] He released the entire force of his volcanic temper in a

35. Discussion address at the convention of the Verein für Sozialpolitik in Magdeburg 1907, *Gesammelte Aufsätze zur Soziologie und Sozialpolitik*, p. 412.

36. Cf. below, chap. 6, sec. 3.

37. Cf. letter to Naumann of 12 November 1908, *Pol. Schr.* 1, p. 455.

38. Compare Heuss, *Friedrich Naumann: Der Mann, Das Werk, Die Zeit* (Berlin, 1937), p. 258. Naumann sought Weber out in Heidelberg. They had a heated argument.

passionate letter to Naumann in which he expressed his deep concern for the nation's future: "A dilettante holds the cords of policy in his hands. . . . The result is, as long as this lasts, that a 'world policy' is impossible. . . . The Hohenzollern dynasty knows nothing but the sergeant-in-arms form of power—command, obedience, standing at attention, boasting." Weber encouraged Naumann, who still shrank from fundamental constitutional reforms, to face the facts. "Nothing, *absolutely nothing*" had been achieved by the declaration that Bülow had forced the Kaiser to make. All had been caused by the faulty political structure of imperial Germany. "The King of England has ambition and power; the German Kaiser has vanity and contents himself with the *appearance* of power. This is a fault of the system, not of the person."[39] Naumann, however, who was influenced by Delbrück's arguments, hesitated to launch an energetic campaign for constitutional change.[40] Weber therefore repeated the thrust with a second letter: "Do not overestimate the importance of the quality of the *person*. It is the institutions . . . and your own lack of resolution that are guilty. This is the result of *Bismarckerei* and the political immaturity that it promoted."[41]

As a result of the crisis, Weber eventually succeeded in convincing Naumann in principle that constitutional reform was necessary. "I have to admit that you judged the Kaiser correctly," Naumann wrote him on 30 October 1908. "It is painful for me to concede this, but I believe that from now on our political considerations must emphasize the means to decrease the impact on German policy from this quarter."[42] Naumann now became a "conscious representative of the parliamentary principle."[43]

Weber watched the parliamentary debates on the *Daily Telegraph* affair closely and was extremely disturbed by the meager results of the debates of 10 and 11 November. These ended with Bülow's pale assurance that the Kaiser would exercise greater discretion in the future.[44]

39. Letter of 12 November 1908, *Pol. Schr.* 1, pp. 456 f.

40. Cf. Annelise Thimme, *Delbrück als Kritiker der Wilhelminischen Epoche*, pp. 18 ff. Also letter to Naumann of 18 November 1908, *Pol. Schr.* 1, pp. 457 ff. Delbrück asserted that "there, policy should be carried out in the German style." Weber's distinctly negative judgment about this is also reported here.

41. Letter of 18 November 1908, ibid.

42. Heuss, *Friedrich Naumann*, p. 258.

43. Ibid., p. 260.

44. Bülow, in his declaration of 10 November 1908, said: "The view that the publication of the conversations in England had not had the effect predicted by the Kaiser resulted in deep disappointment and painful regrets in our country. I have become convinced in these difficult days that the Kaiser must recognize the need to observe that reserve in both private and public conversations that is indispensable for a unitary policy and for the authority of the crown. If this does not materialize, neither I nor my successor can bear responsibility." *Verhandlungen des Deutschen Reichstags*, vol. 233, p. 5396. Cf. also Theodor Eschenburg, *Das Kaiserreich am Scheidewege*, pp. 146 ff.

"Nothing, *absolutely nothing* has improved: Bülow cannot promise anything because he does not have the power, and any Kaiser in this position will gratify his vanity in the same way."[45] Weber found the position of both liberal parties to be totally disgraceful. "A people that has never made up its mind to put the chair for its monarch outside the door, or at least seriously tried to limit his powers, condemns itself to political dependency," he pronounced.[46] For the first time in ten years he attended a public political meeting, a meeting of the National Liberal party on 30 November 1908 in Heidelberg, at which Georg Jellinek was to speak on "Kaiser and Reich Constitution." The significance of this issue, as well as the name Jellinek, prompted Weber to forsake the scholarly cloister in which his health had confined him.[47] Jellinek's speech approached the issue of constitutional reform in a remarkably cautious manner. He emphasized the need to give legal meaning to the responsibility of the chancellor according to article 17 of the Reich constitution, by making him responsible to the Reichstag and the Bundesrat. To be sure, he shrank from a purely parliamentary governing system.[48] Eberhard Gothein followed this up with a polemic against the introduction of parliamentarianism and partisan interest politics and declared, with references to Bismarck, who had stayed in power even when two-thirds of the Reichstag opposed him, for the retention of the existing system. Then Weber, who had originally planned to remain silent, spoke up passionately in opposition to Gothein. England and Belgium were "parliamentarily governed countries. This has brought them international respect and colonial possessions that dwarf ours. Moreover, the policies of these countries, known for their figurehead kings, show far more consistency and firmness than is perceptible in ours. In spite of all the gossip about the figureheads and their private lives that we so often object to, they have performed services for their countries that go beyond those of their predecessors. Why? These rulers practice Realpolitik, and that is more effective than a policy of 'prestige.'"[49] William II had been made to go to "Canossa" only by the defection of the other rulers of the German states.[50] Only the feeling of complete isolation had "forced [his] tractability." But he would not change his nature. The one probable result was

45. *Pol. Schr.* 1, p. 456.

46. *Lebensbild*, p. 408. Cf. also the cited letter to Rickert, as a reaction to an article of R. Sohms about the Daily Telegraph affair of 21 November 1908, published in *Lebensbild*, pp. 412 f. Original in Weber papers.

47. Cf. *Lebensbild*, pp. 411 f.

48. Jellinek had always energetically objected to the fact that "the responsible minister, who only acted defensively and thereby committed a sin of omission," remained in office. This suggested above all that the constitution ought to be revised.

49. According to the report in the *Heidelberger Tagblatt* of 2 December 1908, no. 282, p. 4.

50. To "Canossa"; cf. the letter to Rickert, see above, note 46.

that "in future, a little less would be *heard*" of dynastic influence. Weber opposed the meeting's complacence about what had been achieved: "The proud, self-confident Kaiser William II bowed his head and conceded what the people wanted."[51] He appealed to national feelings: "The honor of the nation is of prime importance—the welfare of the fatherland. Both recent and past experience proves that parliamentarianism, even in its crassest form, is an incomparably better guarantee of this than monarchical rule."[52]

Weber did not of course stop here. He did not follow up on Naumann's plan to take up the cudgel in *Die Hilfe* or the *Frankfurter Zeitung* against "personal rule."[53] He decided instead to write an article for the *Historische Zeitschrift* about authoritarian and parliamentary monarchy.[54] He planned to prove through the British example that the monarch was quite capable of exercising significant political influence in a parliamentary system, while his position among the people was much more secure than it could ever be in a semiconstitutional system with bureaucratic control.

Although Weber did not plunge into practical politics even during these agitated weeks, he tried to do as much as he could to assist those Progressive politicians close to him with expert advice. Georg Jellinek was working at the time on a draft of the law to amplify article 17 of the Reich constitution. This draft was designed as the basis for a suitable parry by the Progressive fraction in the Reichstag on the question of the chancellor's responsibility (it was possible that it was only Max Weber who initiated Jellinek's contacts with Friedrich Naumann and Ernst Müller-Meiningen, the spokesman for the Progressive party on constitutional issues). Weber discussed Jellinek's draft with him with special reference to the question of how the personal constitutional stipulation of the chancellor's responsibility could be harmonized with the Reich's federalist structure. In 1907, Jellinek had already flatly denied that this was achievable. Weber seems to have talked Jellinek out of the notion of making the Bundesrat a party to a possible vote of no confidence by

51. Professor Quenzer in his introductory address.

52. He closed with a completely characteristic reference to Russia: "If powerful Russia had had a democratic constitution, had it had parliamentarianism, we would really have experienced something; it would have been the most terrible power, a power that is contained today because parliament and constitution have little meaning in Russia." In another place Weber limited this by the remark that Russia would have to wait a generation to participate in an imperialist policy because of the necessity of carrying out basic internal reforms, especially agrarian reform. "But even the democrats will not do this." "Scheinkonstitutionalismus," p. 143.

53. Naumann to Weber, 7 April 1908, Naumann papers.

54. Weber to Naumann, 12 November 1908, *Pol. Schr.* 1, pp. 456 f. It is characteristic of Weber the politician, in spite of the fact that he was directly involved, to prefer a scholarly medium for his direct response to this question.

giving it the power to annul a vote of no confidence in the Reichstag through a simple resolution. "A draft that permits a two-thirds vote of the Reichstag to be overturned by a simple resolution of the Bundesrat runs the danger of becoming a farce," he argued.[55] Instead, he proposed to prescribe the mandatory dismissal of the chancellor when either two-thirds of the Reichstag members or three-fifths of the Bundesrat members demanded it. Further, he opposed the "disciplinary" character of Jellinek's scheme which would be applicable only when the chancellor "showed himself to be unworthy of the confidence his office demanded"[56] or "made that office unworthy."[57] Weber did not wish to see the purely political issue of responsibility confused by moralistic language that unnecessarily attacked the chancellor's honor although only "his political confidence" was at issue. Apparently, Jellinek largely accepted Weber's objections. In the final version of his draft, which appeared in the 1 December 1908 *Frankfurter Zeitung*, the gravamina that Weber criticized had been, for the most part, removed.[58]

Weber also sent, or so it would seem, his own draft to Naumann for referral to Ernst Müller-Meiningen; it included the Bundesrat in the no-confidence vote procedure in the manner described above, but avoided the weaknesses of the original Jellinek version (which has not survived). The chancellor was to be dismissed if 240 Reichstag members or twenty-four Bundesrat members withdrew their confidence. In addition, Weber wanted the Reichstag or Bundesrat to have the right of assembly "even without a special royal order" in order to retain the weapon of ministerial responsibility even when not in session.[59] On this

55. This is inferred from Weber's letter to Friedrich Naumann of the end of November 1908. Naumann papers 79, cf. below, note 59.

56. According to the published version of Jellinek's draft. Cf. below, note 58.

57. According to Weber's formulation.

58. Published in Georg Jellinek, *Ausgewählte Schriften und Reden*, vol. 2 (Berlin, 1911) pp. 436 f.

59. Letter to Friedrich Naumann, undated copy but in light of the contents after the end of November 1908, in any event after 18 November 1908; Naumann papers 79. The original letter is not in the papers. Unfortunately, the above-cited draft by Jellinek, which Weber draws on, has not been passed on. Therefore, we cannot specifically interpret Weber's position in all particulars; moreover several mistakes appear in the copy. The word "three" on line 7 of the letter must mean "thirty," i.e., 51 percent, although Weber's example notes 37 votes. Weber's letter including the draft about the chancellor's responsibility, the draft of an inquiry law for the Reichstag, and a proposal in response to the toleration bill of the Center party, is repeated here word for word because of its importance. It reads as follows:

"Dear friend! Jellinek's draft has since gone to Deputy Müller-Meiningen and is known to him. I can only repeat: a draft that permits a two-thirds vote of the Reichstag to be overturned by a Bundesrat resolution is in danger of becoming a farce. If for some reason something needs to be developed out of this then (1) unanimity by the Bundesrat is the least that should be demanded; (2) if at least three votes are required—thus a further concession—then in practice, the chancellor named by the Kaiser requires (a) a third of the Reichstag votes 133, (b) the confidence of Prussia, Bavaria, Saxony, Württemberg, Baden, and Hesse, in order to be secure from every attack. Any further concession would be ridiculous. (Jellinek favors 14 votes—only a juristic formalist could concoct this, a serious political party could not favor this.) The formulation also has a disciplinary character; for example, Jellinek admitted to me: 'if he were unworthy of confidence.' Therefore we have this necessity of attacking the chancellor slanderously; it suffices if he has lost political confidence, that this be expressed by a two-thirds vote of the Reichstag.

"If I were asked how the Bundesrat should be brought into the law, I would say:

"§ 1. The Reich chancellor is to be released from service and all his political functions without any possibility of reinstatement as a political official if three-fifths of the Reichstag or 240 votes demand it.

"§ 2. The Reich chancellor is also removed if three-fifths of the Bundesrat demand it (practically this means Prussia plus Waldeck plus Bavaria can always protect the Reich chancellor against the Bundesrat (17 plus 1 plus 6 equals 24 votes).

"§ 3. Reichstag and Bundesrat must also assemble without a royal order if one-quarter of the votes (equals 100 in the Reichstag and 15 in the Bundesrat) join in a notarized public demand that in the case of the Reichstag must be published in the official Reich gazette, in the case of the Bundesrat with a memorandum to the federal states. It cannot be terminated against the opposition of one-quarter of the votes (thus the Reichstag cannot be dissolved.) In the event of a proposal to remove the Reich chancellor, the Reichstag may not be dissolved if it has already been dissolved in the calendar year preceding the proposal.

"II. If the Reichstag's right of inquiry is not unconditionally established, then

"§ 1. The Reichstag is empowered to create commissions with the right to meet between sessions and to empower them to make inquiries about circumstances that relate to legislation or supervision of the country. This can be done by sworn (or if this is left to the judiciary) court sworn testimony by witnesses and experts before the commissions.

"§ 2. Selection of commissioners will be organized so that every forty members names one commissioner.

"§ 3. The commission must hear all witnesses and experts and pose all questions demanded by a minority of one-quarter of the members. N.B. The Prussian Landtag has this often fundamental right, article 82 of the Prussian constitution, but it is mangled: in contrast to the English parliament, it cannot itself examine the witnesses (cf. art. 81, para. III).

"III. Do you not wish to alter the Center party's toleration proposal with the following two amendments?

"1. No child may be forced against the will of his parents to attend a public school or a school that is qualified as equivalent to a public school (even one of his own confession: orthodox children with liberal teachers or visa versa). (The family principle! It corresponds to what even the Center theoretically understands as religious freedom.)

"2. No one can be compelled by a governmental authority of any kind to give any kind of information about his membership in a religious confession. (The situation in the Reich constitution of 1848 . . . it would not be accepted today; but it would cause great difficulties for the Center and takes the wind out of the sails of the very popular toleration proposal. If the Center rejects this provision, it will make it that much easier to reject the proposal.)

"I shall perhaps write an article about the right of inquiry for the *Frankfurter Zeitung*.

"In the next election, the liberals should not have the odium of not having attempted something serious.

"IV. The chancellor could only be charged with lack of loyalty before the courts (preferably the Reich Supreme Court). If it can be established that he can be charged with breaking the law including [ignoring: there is a break here in the manuscript—author] the prerogatives over the Reich of (1) the Reichstag *per majora*, (2) the Bundesrat *per majora*, then it would have more general application if the Reichstag might also dispute the legality of Bundesrat decisions. But such a provision has little chance, even though the right to bring

occasion, he also sent a draft of legislation granting the right of inquiry to the Reichstag along the lines of the English model. He viewed this as a constitutional means of strengthening parliamentary influence which would have a significant impact.[60]

After a faint-hearted attempt at unlimited parliamentary responsibility, the Progressives committed themselves merely to judicial responsibility. For Max Weber, this position made little political sense. He nevertheless believed that the achievement of such a constitutional provision was worth considering, if it would make it possible to contest Bundesrat decisions in the Reich court or the supreme court. But he urged, in any event, that it was better to take "a clear and objectively meaningful course," though it would be blocked by the Right or the Bundesrat, than to participate in the "farce of a fictitious bill. . . . I am certain that the Kaiser's extravagances will recur. Then the winds will blow against those who concocted the fictitious bills."

Weber's proposals greatly interested Friedrich Naumann and the constitutional spokesman for the Progressives, Müller-Meiningen, but they were not directly incorporated into the position of the Progressive fraction. The fraction's motion went as far as the formula of judicial responsibility permitted. Impeachment of the chancellor with the aim of bringing about his dismissal ought to be possible "for violations of the Reich constitution as well as serious danger to the Reich's security and welfare caused by actions contrary to duty or omissions."[61] Müller-Meiningen, in a major Reichstag address on 1 December 1908, strongly supported such a constitutional fixation of the chancellor's responsibility because it represented the first step in the direction of a parliamentary system like that in England. He declared, in complete accord with Weber's views, that "we have no great parties in the German parliament, because the parliament lacks the unifying element of power, because it lacks influence on the government. Give the parliament this influence, and it will strengthen the feeling of responsibility, and we shall have great parties in the Reichstag."[62]

---

charges by the Bundesrat would strengthen federalism. Even if the proposal is not opportune, it is better to follow a clear, objectively meaningful course, which can be rejected by the Right or the Bundesrat, than to participate in the farce of a pseudo-law. Then those who have fabricated the pseudo-law will have all of the winds against them. Certainly the bourgeois voters must first be enlightened, but their opinion could someday change radically."

60. Compare below, chap. 6, sec. 2.

61. Proposal by Ablass and others, no. 1063, *Verhandlungen des Reichstags*, vol. 250, p. 6024.

62. *Verhandlungen des Reichstags*, vol. 233, pp. 5904 ff. The citation is on p. 5909. Compare also Dieter Grosser, *Vom monarchischen Konstitutionalismus zur parlamentarischen Demokratie* (The Hague, 1970), pp. 61 f.

But in the face of the resistence of the right and the National Liberals to any changes in the constitution affecting the regulation of ministerial responsibility, this foray, and the more far-reaching one by the Social Democrats, got nowhere. In the circumstances, Max Weber was not surprised by this result. It only strengthened his concern about the shortcomings of the Wilhelmine constitutional system.

The failure of the attempt to save German interests in Morocco, which had already largely been given up by 1909, by dispatching the *Panther* to Agadir in July 1911 gave further impetus to Weber's criticisms. He was deeply disappointed with the "inglorious liquidation of our theatrical Moroccan policy."[63] We have reason to believe that Weber viewed the Reich's Moroccan interests as worth a war. At this time, he called for "stronger armament coupled with a sober and ruthlessly decisive foreign policy."[64] He wished to see the power of the Reich exercised unreservedly even at the risk of war. But the preconditions for such action would not exist until the monarch's constitutional position was fundamentally transformed: "I am of the view that even with the strongest armament, *we cannot in good conscience risk* a European war since we must anticipate, under present conditions, that a crowned dilettante will interfere in the leadership of the army and will botch up everything on the bloody field of honor as he has done in diplomacy."[65] Moreover, Weber was convinced that the monarch "notoriously" would always shrink back from war at the last second, in spite of all of his grand words. He would do so even when a war was necessary for reasons of "genuine Realpolitik."[66] Germany was therefore not in a position to tip the scales effectively with its military potential in the cold war of rivaling armament policies. The other powers had become accustomed to the fact that Germany, in spite of portentious moves in the world arena, always gave in when the going got rough. Therefore, Germany was denied any success in foreign policy. For this reason, Weber believed that the German monarch's constitutional position was incompatible "with the nation's world interests and those means necessary to protect these interests: war and diplomacy."[67] As long as

63. Letter of 11 November 1911 to Dr. Simon, copy in Weber papers; most of it is printed in *Lebensbild*, pp. 413 f. Cf. *Pol. Schr.*, pp. 374 f. Weber objected here (1917) to "giving up Morocco . . . *without any* adequate equivalent for us."

64. Letter of 11 November 1911 to Dr. Simon. In the letter cited above (chap. 3, note 130) to his Freiburg colleagues, Weber expressly insisted that his criticisms in the Deimling affair should not be taken as a rejection of strengthened armament. See also a second letter by Weber to Simon in *Lebensbild*, p. 417.

65. Letter of 11 November 1911 to Dr. Simon.

66. Compare *Pol. Schr.*, p. 377: this monarch "whose attitude has notoriously and repeatedly stressed the preservation of peace will have the decisive voice even if, in the light of pure Realpolitik, war would be the most effective course for us"(!).

67. This judgment appears in a totally unexpected place, namely, in Weber's statement

personal rule continued, Germany was fated to lose the diplomatic struggle that was taking place in advance of the hot war that lurked in the background of the gigantic arms competition among the great powers.

In summary, Weber concluded that, after Bismarck's fall, Germany had pursued not power politics but prestige politics, which spoke portentously but avoided danger. This judgment is accurate in a negative sense, although William II was less to blame than Weber liked to believe. But is it also accurate in a positive sense? It is a moot question whether a "relentlessly decisive" power policy that did not shrink from the use of force at critical moments would have spared Germany the catastrophe of 1914. A policy geared to an increase in power, combining armed pressure and diplomacy and thereby always entailing the possibility of a "hot war," would perhaps have temporarily encouraged the other great powers to show more regard for the Reich's international interests. But this would only have intensified the dangerous tensions among the European powers that culminated in the World War.

Max Weber was apparently himself aware of this dilemma. The fact that he temporarily supported the movement for international understanding and the goal of a general armaments limit spearheaded by Otfried Nippold and Walther Schücking did not fundamentally contradict his opinion that the German Reich should carry on a realistic and, if necessary, resolute power policy. In May 1910, under a public announcement for the founding of a "Union for International Understanding," the names of Georg Jellinek, Walther Schücking, Otfried Nippold, Friedrich Naumann, and Ernst Troeltsch appeared, to name a few well-known personalities—and also that of Max Weber.[68]

Apparently, however, Weber participated only half-heartedly. He did not take any part in the founding of the "Union for International Under-

---

about the question of value judgments for the Verein für Sozialpolitik of the year 1915 ("Äusserungen zur Werturteilsdiskussion im Ausschuss des Vereins für Sozialpolitik," printed as a manuscript). I thank Professor Hans Ulrich Wehler for the reference to Wilbrandt's copy here (Institut für Sozial- und Verwaltungswissenschaften at Cologne University, Sozialpolitische Abteilung). In 1917 it appeared in a modified version under the title "The meaning of objectivity in the sociological and economic sciences." Now in *Wissenschaftslehre*, pp. 483 ff (3d edition). The citation is on p. 492. He added: "It is not the worst patriots nor the enemies of the monarchy who today are (often) inclined to answer no to this question and to doubt the chance of lasting successes in *both* of these areas, unless thoroughgoing changes are introduced." ("Often" was in parentheses and "both" was underlined in 1917.)

Cf., ibid., p. 494: "But whether the modernistic cult of personality on the throne, in the office, or at the lectern endeavors to succeed—it outwardly appears effective, but its effect is actually quite small and in fact is generally counterproductive."

68. Text of the appeal in Jellinek papers, no. 6.

standing" on 11 June 1911.[69] In reality, he could scarcely associate with the utopian pacifism represented by Schücking and Nippold. A few weeks later, when the *Frankfurter Zeitung* was attacked by a group of Freiburg professors because of its public support for a group of pacifists, Heinrich Simon, one of the newspaper's editors, asked Weber for his opinion. Weber replied in a somewhat ambiguous manner. To be sure, he found hard words for the Freiburg university professors' declaration attacking the *Frankfurter Zeitung*'s support of the pacifists and mocked its "thoroughly parochial tone." At the same time, he distanced himself cautiously, but unmistakably, from the *Frankfurter Zeitung*'s positive attitude toward the peace movement. He also pleaded "more strongly than the *Frankfurter Zeitung* emphasized, for a strengthening of armaments together with a sober but at the same time ruthlessly resolute policy."[70]

Weber's connection to the peace movement remained but an episode. A cool analysis of the international situation led him to the conviction that in the present era it was necessary to reckon with an intensification rather than a decrease in imperialist conflicts among the powers. Therefore, pacifist proposals had no present chances for realization. He believed that there were, among other factors, compelling economic reasons for this, namely the "universal revival of 'imperialist capitalism . . . and with it the political pressure for expansion."[71] In such a world there was no alternative to an energetic imperialist policy that aimed at the expansion of Germany's territory and sphere of interest.

Weber was certainly not the sole supporter of a powerful *Weltpolitik* in 1911. He differed from his contemporaries only insofar as he pursued this goal with rigorous consistency. It prompted him to draw far-reaching domestic and constitutional conclusions. To this extent we have to respect his position. On the other hand, it is difficult to agree today with his inordinate stress on a consistent imperialist power policy, which he viewed as the central command of the hour for his nation. We can scarcely approve of the exclusive position he gave the exercise of military and economic power as the basis of German foreign policy. The European states' incapacity to compromise their competing interests peacefully cost Europe its leading position in the world. As a result of their

69. Cf. Roger Chickering, "A Voice of Moderation in Imperial Germany," *Journal of Contemporary History* 8, no. 1 (1973): 147 ff. Jellinek appears to have been the link to Weber. On 7 October 1910, Nippold asked Jellinek if Weber might not be invited to the representative assembly. But an invitation appears not to have been sent, and at least it can be concluded that Weber did not follow one up. Jellinek papers 6.

70. *Lebensbild*, p. 414. In this connection, Weber speaks disapprovingly of "a pair of pacifistic utopians" (p. 415).

71. *Wirtschaft und Gesellschaft*, p. 526. Weber also says here that "the 'imperialist' kind of expansion is again increasingly replacing peaceful, nonmonopolistic (at least not through political power) trade."

strife among themselves, this position fell to America and, in spite of the difficult times it was to face, to Russia.

Max Weber was not taken by surprise by the European catastrophe of August 1914, which plunged the Central Powers into a struggle for existence against all other European powers. He had always predicted major international conflicts. But he regarded it as a distortion of the unavoidable conflict of the great powers over the world's future that Germany had to go to war against such a militarily and economically superior coalition. He attributed this situation above all to William II's personal rule and the monarch's arrogant actions which had insulted one nation after another and awakened mistrust in the intentions of German policy. The break with Italy appeared to him to be the last confirmation of his pessimistic analysis of German foreign policy.[72] He now grew even more strongly inclined to seek the decisive causes for the failures of German policy in the Kaiser's behavior. He also blamed the Kaiser for the domestic crisis of leadership that broke out in March 1916 over the question of restricted submarine warfare, in which Bethmann Hollweg triumphed over Tirpitz only to give in five months later.[73]

Max Weber's bitter, decades-long resentment against William II's extravagances, which he had usually harbored in silence, burst forth in the series of articles he wrote for the *Frankfurter Zeitung* at the end of May 1917 under the title: "German Parliamentarianism in the Past and Future."[74] The article "Administrative Publicity and Political Responsibility" of 24 June 1917 included a strong settlement of accounts with "personal rule."[75]

The article is an unparalleled, thoroughgoing analysis and exposure of William II and his part in the failure of German foreign policy, notable for its power and rhetorical persuasiveness. Of course, Max Weber avoided a direct assault on the monarch himself. He thought it unwise to

72. Letter to Marianne Weber, late May 1915, *Lebensbild*, p. 562: "Yes, things are *bad*. All the statecraft of the last twenty-five years has collapsed, and there is not much satisfaction in having 'always said' it would happen."

73. Compare letter to Marianne Weber of 15 March 1916; *Lebensbild*, p. 574f.: "Like a hysterical collapse of this 'heroic Kaiser': it creates a means to make an end of it in a crisis; so a collapse in fear of war with America created a crisis . . . the repeated turning point. . . . It is miserable how we are ruled at a moment when our entire existence is at stake."

74. It appeared in much broader form and with some changes in 1918 under the title of "Parliament and Government in a Reconstructed Germany." *Pol. Schr.* pp. 306 ff. This version is generally based on the articles in the *Frankfurter Zeitung* of 26 April 1917 (now almost all in *Pol. Schr.*, p. 407, par. 3, to p. 413, par. 1), 27 May, 5 June, 6 June, 24 June, and 8 September 1917: The revision of article 9 of the Reich constitution (unsigned) printed in Appendix III of the first edition of this book, now in *Pol. Schr.*, pp. 222–25.

75. Now almost all in section 3, *Pol. Schr.*, pp. 357 ff. The original version was recently published in *Werk und Person*, pp. 224 ff., but not under the original title and with a few condensations.

attack the system of monarchy as such, since he was convinced of "the usefulness of monarchical institutions in large countries."[76] In 1908 he had said that the political structure was at fault; now he attacked the German political system itself, since it failed to prevent embarrassing public statements by the monarch and at times even forced him forward against his will. "This completely incomprehensible defect" had helped bring about the "unnatural world coalition" against Germany.[77]

The article had a great impact on the public and in government circles. The Kaiser's inclination to concede domestic reforms was considerably reduced by this attack. Bethmann Hollweg's circle was something less than joyous. Kurt Riezler, the chancellor's confidant on publicity matters, tried indirectly to influence Max Weber when he wrote to Conrad Haussmann: "Unfortunately the *Frankfurter Zeitung* has broken a carefully-tended cooking pot. We stand around it and deplore the spilled soup. Our enemies' joy is unrestrained."[78] Haussmann was not thrilled by Weber's attack either. He wrote him by return post that the feeling at the Reich Chancellory was that "the soup pot of the new orientation, or more correctly, the sentiment for it, had been broken in the highest circles, and the soup had spilled out."[79] While Weber's article may not have entirely fit the tactical situation of the moment, which was characterized by cautious negotiations between the government and the majority parties in the Reichstag on piecemeal reform measures, it did lend more weight to their efforts to force a change in the domestic and foreign course of the Reich. There was bound to be a reaction from above. On the direct initiative of the Supreme Command, the offending issue of the *Frankfurter Zeitung* was seized, but without public attention and only after it had been distributed.[80] For the time being, the *Frankfurter Zeitung* was placed under preventive censorship.

Weber protested in a long letter, which he sent to the *Frankfurter Zeitung* for wider distribution, sending a copy to Vice Chancellor Friedrich von Payer. The censorship action, he argued, was clearly "a purely

76. *Pol. Schr.*, p. 369.

77. Ibid., p. 377.

78. Riezler to Haussmann, 25 June 1917, Haussmann papers, 54.

79. Haussmann to Weber, 3 September 1917 (carbon in Haussmann papers): "Confidentially, I can report that your last article had a great impact, which you know from the preventive censorship of the *Frankfurter Zeitung*. After its appearance in the Office of the Reich Chancellory, the view spread that the soup pot of the new orientation . . . had overflowed. In any event, your article helped to create the atmosphere that led in July to stronger and every more unsatisfactory explosions."

80. Weber himself first discovered this some time later. Compare Weber's letter to G. Hohmann, undated, beginning of September 1917 (Weber papers): "The steps against me begin with the initiative of the *central authorities*. The court is said—as I have heard—to have *canceled* [the *Frankfurter Zeitung*] *immediately*; apparently, the Kaiser had previously read it daily."

partisan measure." For a year and a half, the censor in Berlin had permitted "agitation against the Reich government and [now it did so] against the Reichstag committee on constitutional reform and the loyal parties that were not conservative." It was therefore no wonder that "counterarguments would use strong language as well. . . . As long as the press in the pay of heavy industry is not muzzled, uncompromising support for the opposite point of view is a moral responsibility." He referred to the events in Vienna and Budapest a year earlier and pointed to the danger to the German-Austrian alliance caused by the German Kaiser's behavior. It had been demonstrated since then that "the troublesome scandal resulting from public reports of the Monarch's statements, which in private conversation may not be damaging or may even have positive effects, continues to exist even during the war, in spite of everything that has occurred."[81] He pointed out that the Conservative parties, although they agreed basically with the other parties on those points that touched on the "vital interests of our national policy," hid behind monarchistic phrases out of self-interest. He offered to prove this in court if it should become necessary.[82]

81. Letter to the *Frankfurter Zeitung* of 27 June 1917 with copies to Vice Chancellor von Payer and Hans Delbrück (Delbrück papers). He was asked by various Austrian politicians in 1916 "to inform the [Foreign Office] that Austria should be treated with the 'utmost care.' . . . At base it appears that the belief is widespread among many of the most influential Austrian circles that Austria has to suffer for the serious mistakes associated with the public actions of the Kaiser or from the publication of his statements and speeches. They are of the decided view that it is not possible to work closely with a governmental approach that offers its allies the risk of being drawn constantly into unexpected situations and developments. Of course, this view was never directly stated to Germans or official German offices. It is, however, the decisive point, and would have unavoidable consequences as soon as the conditions of Austrian policy would permit a free hand. The deep feeling shared by everyone from the dynasty to the last officer about the lack of consideration and bad upbringing of many representatives of Germany in the war, is relatively secondary and is more the popular expression of the same feeling. I was continually asked if in view of this it was not advisable to explain to the Foreign Office that 'guarantees' against the repetition of such occurrences in international policy will be introduced."

In late 1917, when Max Weber sought to republish his articles, the censorship office sought to get the Baden Ministry of Education to have Weber delete the controversial passages. Of course, Weber refused to do so; but the polemic lost some of its sharpness because Weber placed much more stress upon the failure of political leadership itself in the final version (cf. *Lebensbild*, pp. 602 f). In this situation, too, Weber pointed again to "these terrible injuries to our position": "Continuing discussions with important politicians, including former ministers in Vienna, have shown me what the opinion there is of the circumstances of a policy that is disturbed by unexpected incidents. 'Germany's reliability as an ally' is seriously endangered by their continuation." Letter to the Baden Ministry of Education of 8 August 1917, in part in *Lebensbild*, pp. 603 f. Copy in Weber papers.

82. Letter to the *Frankfurter Zeitung* of 27 June 1917 (copy in Weber papers): "*I only hope* that our opponents will issue a public protest against this situation as 'unpatriotic' or 'antimonarchical,' in order through drastic means to engender judicial proceedings, if in no

Max Weber also appealed to Conrad Haussmann to free him and the *Frankfurter Zeitung* from the difficult situation caused by the imposition of preventative censorship. He characteristically proposed that if the Censorship Office would not relent, it should place him personally, rather than the *Frankfurter Zeitung*, under preventive censorship. He would have no objection, since he had "enough else to do." Furthermore, he railed against the "rude clumsiness of these narrow-minded deputy commanding generals who are useless as soldiers . . . and therefore [are allowed] to dabble in politics." He urged Haussmann to encourage a Progressive party demand that the censorship be taken over by the political authorities. Censorship, at least as far as the newspapers were concerned, ought to be the chancellor's affair "once and for all."[83] The Progressive party now also pressed for the lifting of the censorship order against the *Frankfurter Zeitung*. In the plenum of the Reichstag the party inquired about the imposition of censorship which followed Weber's article, and in the budget committee it moved for the lifting of the preventive censorship against the *Frankfurter Zeitung*.[84] The party strongly protested that "a paper of the stature of the *Frankfurter Zeitung* should be confiscated and placed under preventive censorship by anyone, whether or not he has the capacity to judge such things, because of an article by a writer as distinguished as Professor Max Weber. It is against the spirit of the *Burgfrieden* to prevent scholarly analyses and seriously considered remonstrances and to censor serious criticism that touches on governmental organs and actions." Subsequently, War Minister von Stein declared the measure "temporarily lifted." Nevertheless, the *Frankfurter Zeitung* remained subject to the special wrath of the censorship authorities. At the end of August 1917, the measures of the censor against the *Frankfurter Zeitung* were renewed and intensified.[85]

The censor's interference only confirmed Weber's views. Under the impression of these events he wrote to Hans Delbrück: "Anyone who does not accept this formulation of the *political* problem—how can we *rid*

---

other way, against my person. [In this way] all of the *un*published statements of the pan-Germans and conservative leaders that I have heard from reliable sources about these grievances and *about the person* of the monarch will be made public with evidence. Then this game of concealment will come to an end, and it will be demonstrated that *there are no partisan differences in Germany about these things*, although some parties deem it advisable to conceal their views hypocritically."

83. Letter to Haussmann of 3 July 1917, Haussmann papers. "As far as newspapers are concerned, a *bill* would be correct that reserved *preventive* censorship to the Reich chancellor (or failing this, the minister of war)."

84. Minutes of the discussion of the chief committee of 4 July 1917. See also the *Frankfurter Zeitung*, 2d morning ed. of 30 August 1917.

85. Cf. the *Frankfurter Zeitung* of 31 August 1917.

policy of *this monarch*'s influence, at least in public?—seeks to cure the symptoms and closes his eyes to the real dangers. . . . If the nation accepts, under the influence of our publicists, the 'will to weakness' at home, then we ought not to speak about German foreign policy any longer."[86] After this, he redoubled his efforts to win a following for constitutional reforms that would facilitate eradication of this evil.

As early as May 1917, Weber had sent Conrad Haussmann, who as the most influential Progressive party member sat on the Reichstag's constitutional committee, drafts for amending the Reich constitution, accompanied by exhaustive memoranda, which he believed would be effective means of setting up constitutional limits on the Kaiser's influence.[87] He proposed "the creation of a criminal code against the publication of royal speeches and programs," and also pressed for the creation of a "Reich crown council" with the specific goal of "putting an end to any instance of royal speeches, telegrams, and other statements, such as those that had hitherto made any orderly German foreign policy, even for the most brilliant diplomacy, impossible."[88] In the article of 24 June that had greatly offended the throne and the Supreme Command, Weber further

86. "The only thing that failed completely during the war was the dynasty. . . . From this fact, we can draw the consequences, think whatever you will about 'parliamentarism.'" Purely *politically*!—corrupt parliamentary dealings cannot function any worse. There is no other way for me than to continue to say ruthlessly: 'what is!.' And that is: the destruction of our political future by the dynasty and those who praise it, whether out of interest or disinterest" (28 June 1917). Delbrück papers.

87. He did this with mixed feelings nevertheless, and tried internally to prepare himself for the event that it would once again lead to nothing. Cf. the letter to Mina Tobler, 7 May 1917, Archiv Ebnet II, 27, cited in *Werk und Person*, Archiv Ebnet, p. 500: constitutional opinion. "I worked breathlessly—(apparently without any success, but finally, what one can do is necessary)—early today it was finished—now I am returning to my much preferred private work." The last passage should be taken with a grain of salt.

88. Letter to Haussmann of 5 May 1917, Haussmann papers; Weber sent Haussmann drafts that touched upon the following points: (1) penalties for the publication of speeches and statements by the monarch without the permission of the Reich chancellor; (2) protection of the Reichstag's right of inquiry; (3) repeal of art. 9, 2, of the Reich constitution; (4) creation of a crown council in order better to serve the interests of the federal states, but above all as a means of controlling the "personal regime"; (5) fixing the relation of the Reich chancellor's office to the Prussian foreign ministry in the constitution. It should be expressly laid down that the Reich chancellor alone and under his own responsibility instructs the Prussian votes in the Bundesrat.

These proposals and memos, as far as we can tell, did not become the basis of the constitutional proposals of the Progressive People's party. They evidently existed in the Haussmann papers in 1920, but in spite of a search in the papers that are in the chief state archive in Stuttgart today they can no longer be located. Their contents are taken from the accompanying letters of 1 May and 5 May 1917, which we have. Cf. below, sec. 3. Recently, copies of these proposals have been discovered in the papers of Hajo Holborn, Yale University Library.

developed this proposal. In the event that a purely parliamentary committee would not be able to take on an advisory role in the publication of the Kaiser's political comments, Weber suggested that the Bundesrat Committee for Foreign Affairs be reactivated and expanded "by including the respective secretaries of state and elder statesmen," and be constituted as a "Reich crown council."[89] He also viewed this as a means of strengthening the south German states' influence upon Reich policy.

Weber knew that none of these measures would eradicate the defects but only minimize them. He was increasingly persuaded that the chancellor's responsibility for royal statements ought to be effective, not just formal. No political leaders should be permitted to "cover" royal statements after the fact, when they had not been consulted in advance. However, Weber did not go so far as to concede the Reichstag the right to force a chancellor's downfall by a vote of no confidence. In September 1917 he had not yet crossed the traditional line of German constitutional liberalism on this issue. "It *must* become an established principle that a chancellor who covers the Kaiser's statements when he has not previously approved them, should be declared *incapable of office* by a supreme court."[90] He also considered the possibility of impeachment by a parliamentary committee, but then dismissed this proposal as unrealistic.[91]

Beginning in late 1917, Max Weber kept close track of William II's statements and became even more convinced of their detrimental effect.[92] Even late in 1918, when a parliamentary government under Max von Baden had already been established, he declared the legal control of the publication of royal statements "by a strict procedure" and prior approval by the chancellor as "the most urgent reform measure" required in German public life.[93]

There is reason to believe that Max Weber considerably overestimated

89. *Pol. Schr.*, pp. 381 f., 437 f.

90. Letter to Haussmann of 7 September 1917, Haussmann papers.

91. *Pol. Schr.*, p. 380.

92. For example, in a letter to Oncken of 10 December 1917: "The greatest stupidity that has occurred here recently was the publication of the two speeches by the Kaiser in Kurtea de Arges (20 October) and on the Italian front. Czernin is rubbing his hands. We must hope that Hertling will put a stop to such disgusting behavior." Weber was especially aroused over the publication of the Kaiser's interviews regarding the Swedish reply to Wilson, which contributed a great deal to the collapse of the friendly Ministry in Sweden. This paralleled Goluchowski's fall for him. Letter to the *Frankfurter Zeitung* of 27 June 1917; also letter to the Baden Ministry of Culture on 8 August 1917, partially included in *Lebensbild*, pp. 603 f. (not the cited passages). The text contains two mistakes; it should read: "Bringing about change here is . . . far more important than any voting law or constitutional changes." The "or" as well as the introduction of *her-* instead of *aus* in the next sentence are, in one instance, interpolations by Marianne Weber that alter the meaning. Cf. also the above cited letter to Haussmann of 7 September 1917.

93. "The next task in domestic policy," *Pol. Schr.*, pp. 445 f.

the effect of William II's public statements on the failure of German foreign policy. Today we are scarcely inclined to blame William II for the developments that led to the fateful political isolation of the Dual Alliance. The leading German foreign policy statesmen, especially Holstein and Bülow, shared at least partially in the consistent prestige policy, whose most visible expression, but by no means the real cause, had been the swaggering and erratic behavior of the monarch. In reality, the Kaiser had not been responsible for the dangerous Morocco policy of 1906. Of course, Weber had not read the official files, nor had he been privy to internal governmental decision-making, and he judged only from outward appearances. The Kaiser's unfortunate behavior had indeed dominated public attention.[94] William II's weaknesses, however, as has been correctly stated before, were the nation's weaknesses.[95] At times, Max Weber recognized this too, as when he pointed to the "foolish emotional policy" in the Boer question, not as a failure of German diplomacy but as a symptom of the nation's political immaturity.[96] Nevertheless, he continued to concentrate his merciless criticism of Germany's political condition on the issue of "personal rule" right up to 1918. For Weber, who favored a sober, decisive policy without illusions, William II's policy of prestige represented the antithesis of a policy guided by an ethic of responsibility.

2. The Political Leadership Vacuum after Bismarck's Fall, and the Rule of Bureaucracy

Although William II's "personal rule" remained in the foreground of Max Weber's critique of the political conditions of his time, he also repeatedly reaffirmed that it was not the royal person alone but the political system as such that was the cause of the "cancerous damage" to German policy. No constitutional barriers existed to prevent the uncontrolled and emotional impact of the Kaiser on the course of German political affairs. But Max Weber recognized that these were causes of a secondary nature. The real reason that personal rule prevailed was the condition in which Bismarck had left the Reich, a complete absence of political leaders, and a lack of political institutions capable of creating leadership.

Weber therefore had concrete reasons for beginning his great series of articles in the *Frankfurter Zeitung* on the internal reorganization of Germany by settling accounts with Bismarck and forcefully summarizing

94. Weber himself later emphatically disapproved the intervention of the person of the monarch in German diplomacy in the case of the landing in Tangier. *Pol. Schr.*, p. 376.
95. Hans Herzfeld, *Die moderne Welt 1789–1945*, vol. 2, p. 14.
96. *Pol. Schr.*, pp. 159 f.

the complaints of a generation of German liberals who had been skipped over.[97] Weber had freed himself from Bismarck's powerful personality only after a mighty struggle. It therefore seemed all the more necessary for him to take on the Bismarck-worship of his generation and counter it with his most powerful weapons, since this worship endowed the Reich and its institutions with the luster of something ideal and inviolable and therefore prevented constitutional evolution.

Bismarck's policy was Caesarist in nature. To be sure, he found it expedient to hide this under the cover of "the monarch's legitimacy."[98] He had no patience with independent political forces. He therefore gave them no opportunity to develop and systematically prevented them from positive cooperation in government. "His entire policy," Weber wrote, "was based on the effort to prevent the consolidation of any strong and thereby independent constitutional party."[99] Bismarck's unscrupulous manner of exchanging parties in each new situation and of playing them against each other, his demagogic practice of transforming arguments over military appropriations from objective budgetary questions into elements of domestic power struggles, his attacks on the opposition for lack of responsibility or even for "enmity to the Reich" either split the parties internally or pushed them into extreme opposition. In Weber's view, this was especially true of the liberals, who, impressed by Bismarck's genius, were willing to cooperate with him on essential matters. But Bismarck forced them either to sacrifice their convictions or to withdraw into an opposition that was totally without influence. The great generation of leaders in all parties during the age of the Reich foundation, especially the National Liberals, was succeeded by a weak group, because no opportunities for winning power and responsibility were permitted them. Bismarck consciously limited the Reichstag to negative politics. Whenever Bismarck offered party leaders political offices, as he did Rudolf von Bennigsen in 1878, the price was always political uprooting. Political motives were also often in play, as in this case the hope for a resulting split in the National Liberal party. Bismarck "neither drew to himself nor tolerated . . . independent thinkers or [men] of strong character."[100] In the course of his reign, he eliminated all independent statesmen around him and replaced them with "conservative creature-bureaucrats" whom he exploited in unconditional bureaucratic dependence, and who lacked the will or capacity for independent political action. It was only natural that such men did not "grumble" about the fall, in 1890, of the great statesman who had raised them from nothing,

97. Cf. above, chap. 4, sec. 2.
98. *Pol. Schr.*, p. 347.
99. Ibid., p. 316.
100. Ibid., p. 319.

and that they readily adapted to the new order and accepted the new "sun." This dishonorable apostacy had "no parallel in the annals of any proud nation."[101]

Weber's depiction of the scene was devastating: conservative bureaucratic types, without political profile or any leadership qualities, used to acting under the chancellor's direction, directing the most important Reich and Prussian ministries. "No political tradition whatsoever" existed. No political personalities capable of national political leadership were brought in at this time. On the other hand, a "completely powerless parliament" was condemned to negative politics. Its intellectual level deteriorated, and it became incapable of producing the leaders that the situation demanded, or training them. Weber stressed that "statesmen" could thrive only in the soil of responsible parliamentary bodies. The development of leaders was dependent on a party's chances for power.[102] Weber offered Bismarck himself as a primary witness. After his departure from office, Bismarck "admitted that his chief mistake had been the repression of parliament."[103]

Max Weber once summed up the quintessence of Bismarck's legacy in one sentence: "What holds it all together—a statesman—is lacking. None exists, and no one can compensate for it."[104] The German diplomatic corps as such cannot be blamed for the failure of German diplomacy. On the whole, it was as good as that of other countries. "What is lacking is government leadership by a *politician*, not necessarily by a political genius; that can only be expected once in a century.[105] Not necessarily even by a man with significant political gifts, but simply by a politician."[106] Conservative bureaucratic types governed in Bismarck's place; they did not rule. For Weber, the most unfortunate fact was that they lacked the consciousness of responsibility that is linked with a passionate will to

101. Ibid., p. 312; "grumble" [*mucksen*]—original version in the *Frankfurter Zeitung*; compare *Wirtschaft und Gesellschaft*, p. 578: "After Bismarck, during his long rule, had subordinated his ministerial colleagues in unconditional bureaucratic dependence by eliminating all independent statesmen, he had to experience after his resignation, much to his surprise, the fact that these men continued untroubled and content in their offices. It was as if it had not been the gifted master and creator of these creatures that had been replaced but, rather, as if some individual figure in the bureaucratic mechanism had been replaced by another."

102. *Pol. Schr.*, p. 403.

103. Original version of section 3 of "Parliament and Government (Parlament und Regierung)," *Frankfurter Zeitung*, 24 June 1917.

104. Letter to Marianne Weber of 25 November 1915, *Lebensbild*, pp. 564 f. This was under the impact of the war situation, but corresponds completely to his earlier position. Compare the remarks cited above in the articles on Russia, in which he pointed out that the conduct of political affairs in Germany made the rise of a statesman impossible.

105. An allusion to Bismarck is apparent here.

106. *Pol. Schr.*, p. 336.

power. Weber believed that this will characterized the genuine politician. Bismarck's successors therefore proved themselves incapable of opposing William II's royal ambitions and keeping him within constitutional bounds.

Weber's despair over the failure of German foreign policy prompted his bitter criticism. At the same time, he did not mean to attack the German bureaucracy itself. He praised its high moral standards and objective ability. But in the field of policy, especially foreign policy, the bureaucracy had failed completely. The bureaucratic government in Germany suffered in comparison with political organizations in western democracies in all areas. "Democratically governed countries, even when their civil services are partially corrupt, have been far more successful overseas than our impeccably moral bureaucracy. If we judge the situation in the light of 'Realpolitik' and international positions of nations—and many of us agree that this ought to be the ultimate criterion—*then*, I ask: which system of organization . . . is the most 'efficient' *today*?"[107]

Max Weber exhaustively analyzed the character of bureaucratic rule and pointed to it as technically the most highly developed form of rule. Rational, consistent, bureaucratic rule based on a division of labor and strictly defined areas of responsibility was a more effective means of government than all historically successful forms of the exercise of power. Weber pointed to the expansion of bureaucratic rule in the economic realm, the consequence of modern rational capitalism and the division of labor, and the parallel growth of state and party bureaucracy as characteristic features of the mass age. The universal process of bureaucratization might contain the forces that some day in the distant future, to be sure, would destroy the free European peoples. For this reason, Weber's struggle against the pure rule of bureaucracy was raised to the level of universal history. Along with lifeless machine technology, bureaucratic organization was "at work creating the shell of that future iron cage, which a powerless mankind may someday be forced into, like the fellahin of ancient Egypt. This will occur when technical standards become ends in themselves, that is, when bureaucratic rule and bureaucratic self-perpetuation are the ultimate and sole principles."[108]

Weber believed that an economically static society and an entirely rigid social order would be the end of this development. The new bureaucratic society would be far more rational than the historical examples in Egypt, China, and the later Roman Empire. "A bureaucracy that

107. Discussion lecture at the convention of the Verein für Sozialpolitik in Vienna 1909, *Gesammelte Aufsätze zur Soziologie und Sozialpolitik*, p. 416.

108. *Pol. Schr.*, p. 332.

has reached this advanced state [is among] the most difficult social creations to destroy."[109] From this standpoint, Weber at the 1909 Verein für Sozialpolitik Convention in Vienna energetically opposed the view, defended by Schmoller and his group, that expanding the state bureaucracy's influence over industry would improve the workers' social condition. "This passion for bureaucratization . . . drives one to utter despair. . . . [We] must not further encourage and accelerate this trend but work against this machinery in order to protect a remnant of mankind from this parceling out of souls, from this omnipotence of the bureaucratic ideal of life."[110] He put the decisive question in this way in "Parliament and Government in a Reconstructed Germany": "How is it still *possible* to preserve *some* residue of *some* kind of individual freedom of action in view of the inevitable tendency toward bureaucratization?"[111]

Max Weber complained all the more bitterly of the Germans' hereditary inclination, the result of centuries of patriarchal rule by princes, to allow themselves to be impressed by office and administrative authority as institutional powers. He attributed the "common German [attitude] to [government] office and administrative authority, their excessive respect for it as a transcendent being," to orthodox Lutheranism.[112] Weber was at times very critical of Lutheranism, which had encouraged German liking for hierarchy and a "purely emotional metaphysics of the state."[113] This had laid the foundation for the uncontrolled reign of a civil service, cloaked by monarchical legitimacy, and had permitted it to grow and persist. "Luther towers above all others," Weber wrote to Adolf von Harnack in 1906. "Lutheranism, as a historical phenomenon, is the most terrible of terrors for me. I do not deny it. Even in the ideal form it takes in your own hopes for future progress, it is for me, for us Germans, a system whose powers for pervading life cannot be measured."[114] Weber much preferred Puritanism, with its dynamic economic spirit and its natural and rational inner attitude toward state and bureaucracy. Unlike the Germans, with their pseudoreligious adulation of office, the Puritans see government as nothing but a "business" like any other. They are

109. *Wirtschaft und Gesellschaft*, p. 577.

110. *Gesammelte Aufsätze zur Soziologie und Sozialpolitik*, p. 414.

111. *Pol. Schr.*, p. 333; Compare "Zur Lage," pp. 118 ff., and the related statement by Friedrich Naumann: "How shall we overcome the pressure of a centralized social order upon us?" *Die politischen Parteien* (Berlin, 1913), p. 109. Cf. Theodor Schieder, "Das Verhältnis von politischer und gesellschaftlicher Verfassung und die Krise des bürgerlichen Liberalismus", p. 74.

112. *Wirtschaft und Gesellschaft*, p. 683; cf. p. 660.

113. Ibid., pp. 683 f.; cf. also the speech at the first German sociological convention, 1910, *Gesammelte Aufsätze zur Soziologie und Sozialpolitik*, pp. 415 f.

114. Letter of 5 February 1906; cf. above, chap. 5, sec. 1.

therefore capable of organizing an administration of the state, sometimes with less "order" but far greater "efficiency."

Weber was very critical of the common faith in the omnipotence and high moral standards of the German civil service.[115] It was therefore all the more necessary for politicians to counterbalance its influences because bureaucracy is the "formally most *rational* form of exercising authority." Bureaucracy is characterized by "precision, stability, discipline, stringency, reliability . . . , calculability, its intensive and broad achievements, its formally universal suitability for all tasks, its purely *technical* perfection for the highest measure of accomplishment."[116] Bureaucracy must be the means in the hands of responsible statesmen, not an end in itself. Only politicians can set goals for administration by a civil service whose primary task is to implement these goals as efficiently and objectively as possible.

With dialectical keenness, Max Weber contrasted the bureaucrat with the politician. He did so far more radically—though this is not the place to discuss it—than appears justified to us. The bureaucrat should, he argued, administer in a nonpartisan sense, *sine ira et studio*. His special professional ethos centered upon his duty to carry out instructions to the letter as if they corresponded to his own convictions. The politician's element is constant struggle, passion, guided by exclusive self-responsibility for all that he does. He must, in *all* cases, reject any goal that appears wrong to him, whether it reflects a monarch's wish or springs from his own party or parliamentary majority. If necessary, he should resign; if not, he is a mere "hanger-on" (sticking to office for its own sake) Weber argued, using a phrase of Bismarck's.[117]

For this reason, Weber believed that it was impossible for leading political personalities ever to emerge from the ranks of the bureaucracy who would be capable of setting goals and limits for administration.[118] Candidates for higher positions in the bureaucratic hierarchy are selected for their expertise. This process of selection can produce excellent civil servants, but never great politicians gifted with an instinct for power, a consciousness of responsibility, and the capacity for leadership. Politicians emerge only in the struggle for influence and support in parliament and in the political conflict for support by the masses.

115. Cf. Weber's speech at the convention of the Verein für Sozialpolitik in Vienna, 1909, *Gesammelte Aufsätze zur Soziologie und Sozialpolitik*, pp. 415 f.

116. *Wirtschaft und Gesellschaft*, p. 128.

117. *Pol. Schr.*, pp. 337 ff., 524 f., et passim; compare also "Die Abänderung des Art. 9 der Reichsverfassung," *Pol. Schr.*, p. 224.

118. Cf. *Wirtschaft und Gesellschaft*, p. 671: "Precisely the pure type of bureaucracy, a hierarchy of *appointed* officials, requires some ultimate position that does not base its existence upon 'appointment' in the same sense."

Weber emphasized that bureaucratization was "the inescapable shadow of advanced mass democracy." Therefore, mass democracy must be the resolute enemy of bureaucratic "rule."[119] He pointed to the tendency of every bureaucracy tenaciously to defend its power against all rivals, whether parliaments or monarchs. Whenever possible, bureaucracies sought to expand their power. In Germany, the bureaucracy had even succeeded in opening the leading political offices to bureaucratic advancement.[120] The bureaucrats' special weapon against all competing institutions was "command of information," especially intimate and confidential "knowledge of office." For this reason, the concept of "official secrets" concealed more than was objectively necessary. It concealed the "bureaucracy's pure power interests." There was nothing, therefore, that bureaucrats "defended with such fanaticism as this . . . attitude."[121]

In order to undermine bureaucratic predominence and deprive it of its superior weapon of technical and official knowledge, Weber urged that the Reichstag be granted the right of inquiry. The Reichstag ought to be able to establish investigatory committees whenever necessary that could assemble information from time to time and to which civil servants would be obliged to give information and submit documents.[122] Because the Reichstag had hitherto lacked this power, Weber wrote in 1917, it had been "constitutionally relegated to dilettantish ignorance."[123] The Reichstag was therefore not in a position to control the civil service's implementation of political tasks effectively since it was hopelessly at a disadvantage relative to the bureaucracy with its superior information on all concrete issues.[124] In order to make the right of inquiry even more effective, Weber demanded that one-fifth of the representatives be empowered to force the establishment of an investigatory committee.

We can only fully appreciate Max Weber's stress on the Reichstag's right of inquiry if we recall his emphasis on bureaucratic tendencies in modern industrial society, especially the modern state, which he believed

119. *Wirtschaft und Gesellschaft*, pp. 130, 575, 580.

120. *Pol. Schr.*, p. 352.

121. *Wirtschaft und Gesellschaft*, p. 581.

122. The first instance we can prove is when Weber proposed the right of inquiry for the Reichstag to Naumann at the end of 1908 (cf. note 59 above); later, he adopted the right of inquiry in his constitutional reform proposals for Conrad Haussmann of May 1917.

123. *Pol. Schr.*, p. 352.

124. Compare also *Wirtschaft und Gesellschaft*, pp. 581 f. Noteworthy as well is the reference on p. 584 to Bismarck, who had argued the exact opposite in regard to the erection of a political economy council: "It is well known that Bismarck attempted to use the plan of a 'Volkswirtschaftsrat' [a representative body of economic interest groups] as an instrument of power against parliament and in doing so reproached the negative majority—to whom he would never concede a right of inquiry as in the English model—for trying in the interest of parliamentary power to protect the bureaucracy from becoming 'too smart.'"

was on its way to becoming a bureaucratic "enterprise." He viewed "parliament's decisive task" as control of the bureaucracy's exercise of its political functions.[125] Only a parliament that developed into a geniune counterweight to the administration would be in a position to carry out positive policy. Here Max Weber fell into the opposite extreme. He greatly exaggerated the importance of the parliamentary right of inquiry vis-à-vis the government and the administrative bureaucracy. This was partially the result of his conviction that the Damocles' sword of public disclosure was a sharply honed weapon with infallible impact in the political struggle. Weber's repeated proposals to expose political matters to the clear light of publicity through judicial complaints reflect this view. Much as I agree with the positive effect of the traditional liberal belief in open disclosure, I must state some reservations here. Weber is revealed here as an ethical man of conviction, who expected a great impact from public moral exposure of the enemy. His illusions are readily apparent in this instance.

Weber also passionately championed the right of inquiry because of his impression that when the most important German policy decisions were in the hands of the bureaucracy, decisions would be made for strictly bureaucratic reasons and the locus of responsibility would be concealed. His sharp opposition to the conservative bureaucracy in Prussia is also visible here.[126] The Prussian bureaucracy influenced the Kaiser in courtly society through personal contact. Weber focused his concern upon the need to remove the direction of German policy-making entirely from the uncontrollable sphere of technical bureaucratic decision-making and to transfer it to the bright light of public exposure. To be sure, this did not mean that all objective questions, even those of foreign policy, would be handled thus. Weber held secret diplomacy, within certain limits, to be unavoidable.[127] This did not matter very much to him—indeed not at all. He was concerned that authoritative personalities make the decisive

125. Original version (*Frankfurter Zeitung*, 24 June 1917): "the first fundamental task . . . ," *Pol. Schr.*, p. 352.

126. In this regard, Weber's judgment at the convention of the Verein für Sozialpolitik in Munich in 1905 is perhaps characteristic: "What kind of people occupy the [Prussian] ministerial chairs today? Completely honorable men in their way, but this way is: *matter-of-fact men, businessmen* [italic denotes English in original]. None of the gentlemen who occupy ministerial chairs today would claim to be a statesman. Today, none of them are like this anymore. They are *matter-of-fact men* who know how to, indeed must, conform to the existing situation controlled by dynastic wishes and other circumstances. It is characteristic enough that one of these gentlemen, and by no means the worst, after he had been appointed to the ministry, complained how unfortunate it was that he had spoken out so frequently in the past in public about pending questions." *Gesammelte Aufsätze zur Soziologie und Sozialpolitik*, pp. 402 f.

127. *Pol. Schr.*, p. 359; *Wirtschaft und Gesellschaft*, p. 581: "The business of diplomacy can only be publicly controlled in a very narrow sense and degree if it is to be successful."

political decisions in the *full* light of public exposure. Only in this way could politicians hold the specific responsibility that was necessary. The politician ought to provide direction for political action, and this direction should be based upon ethical values. He ought to take responsibility for the direction of policy before the nation and parliament and publicly defend the correctness and appropriateness of his measures and goals. He should not hide behind technical explanations and technical competence like a bureaucrat, and conceal the real responsibilities.

There is therefore an intrinsic link between Weber's desire for the Reichstag's right of inquiry as a means to withdraw the protective cover of bureaucratic expertise and inside information from the highest Reich officials and his call for political leaders of distinction, who were prepared to take on the global tasks that faced the nation in the imperialist age. "A nation that produces only good bureaucrats, honorable merchants, capable scholars and technicians, and loyal servants, and otherwise permits bureaucrats to rule with *no controls* under a cover of pseudo-monarchistic rhetoric, will *not* be a ruling nation. It would be better off returning to mundane business and forsaking its vain efforts to influence world destinies." With this sentence, Max Weber concluded his explosive *Frankfurter Zeitung* article of 24 June 1917.[128] His enthusiasm for a firm international policy endowed his critique of bureaucratic domination of Germany after Bismarck with a particular activity. Responding to the serious problems in German policy during the Wilhelmine period and his critical appraisal of pure "civil service rule," Weber's political reform program culminated in a call for great leaders. Other political thinkers of the day, like Hugo Preuss and Walther Rathenau, also regarded the striking absence of political leadership as the central problem in German politics.[129] Only Weber, however, so consistently and exclusively emphasized the leadership problem. This was the reason that he urged the parliamentarization of the German constitution in the great series of articles in the *Frankfurter Zeitung* after September 1917. In these articles he argued that Bismarck's mistake should be rectified. Parliament should be rescued from pure negativism and the inferior intellectual level that had been the consequence of its merely negative role in policy matters. It ought to be reconstructed into a source for the selection of political leaders. The rehabilitation of German political life would be possible only when parliament offered the chance for politicians with an inherited instinct for power to rise to real political power and

128. Now, *Pol. Schr.*, p. 442.

129. Cf. Hugo Preuss, *Staat, Recht und Freiheit* (Tübingen: 1926,) p. 551 (1909): "In our public life, there is perhaps only *one* point about which there is complete agreement; and that is the *amazing lack of political leaders in the grand style* in Germany." Further, Walther Rathenau, *Von kommenden Dingen* (Berlin, 1917), pp. 305 ff., 322 f., 329 ff.

responsibility. For Weber, in June 1917, one question about the future nature of the German government was paramount: "*How can we make parliament capable of power*?" All other questions were ancillary.[130]

3. Parliamentarization as a Means of Overcoming the Reich Leadership Crisis

Max Weber favored a parliamentary system in Germany for three major reasons. All started from the argument that the German nation had to alter its political structure in order to build the necessary basis for playing a role in the great powers' universal struggle for spheres of influence around the world. It must reform in order to take on "the great international policy tasks" that were its historical responsibility.[131]

1. Only a nation that had achieved the measure of political freedom that other nations had long possessed, only a *Herrenvolk*, a "master people,"[132] truly has the historical right to participate in decisions affecting the fate of other nations and in the struggle for the division of the earth. Only a free nation can permanently elicit sufficient respect and cultural regard abroad. This is the unconditional basis for a successful "world policy." In 1897, in reaction to the naval inquiry, Max Weber wrote that "only a regime whose internal policies make clear that it is *not afraid* to support and expand the fatherland's free institutions will command the indispensable trust that assures strength and courage in crucial moments. In the absence of these conditions, strong words notwithstanding, failure is inevitable."[133] Weber summed this up again in 1917 in more pointed and suggestive form: "*Only master peoples are called to turn the wheels of world development*. If nations that do not possess these qualities attempt to do so, they will not only be opposed by the sure instincts of other nations, but they will fail because of their lack of internal strength. . . . The 'will to impotence' at home, preached by the literati, cannot be reconciled with the 'will to power' abroad, although this contradiction has been so noisily trumpeted."[134] In other words, parliamentarization in Germany was a necessary corollary of an imperialistic policy abroad. It was a necessity both for cultural reasons and in order to achieve the unity and resolve of the nation as a whole.

130. *Pol. Schr.*, p. 363.

131. Ibid., p. 443.

132. The term *Herrenvolk* (master people) had primarily a domestic political meaning for Weber. It is thereby clearly distinct from Alfred Rosenberg's *Herrenvolk* ideology. But it is nevertheless linked with the concept of the exercise of political power abroad in a way that we justifiably view as questionable today. Cf. *Pol. Schr.*, p. 291: "Only a *master people* . . . can *and may* carry out a world policy." We find the same concept in Naumann's thought.

133. *Pol. Schr.*, pp. 31 f.

134. Ibid., p. 442.

2. An end to "personal government" and with it the "uncontrolled bureaucracy" that had made personal government possible would be effectively achieved only through a positive increase in the power of parliament. Weber asked whether the Reich's leading politicians, if they had held their offices through the confidence of a Reichstag majority, would have been in a position to cover for the monarch's past statements with the argument that they would otherwise be replaced. They would have been forced to oppose dynastic impulsiveness and ambition had they been effectively responsible to the Reichstag.

3. Parliamentarization was the best means for the selection of political leaders. Weber hoped that the struggle for supporters and followers in parliament and in the day-to-day work of its committees would produce leaders capable of furthering a successful German policy. It is not difficult to recognize Weber's most significant model for these views. England was the model for all German liberals, especially the liberal imperialists, for England had built an enormous empire and preserved it. Weber sharply criticized the disdain of the German "philistines" for the English parliament. They "ignored the fact that this was the body that produced those politicians" who had understood how "to subordinate a quarter of mankind under the rule of a tiny governmentwise minority."[135]

Max Weber did not deny the constitutional difficulties that the German Reich's complicated constitutional structure placed in the path of parliamentarization. Bismarck had hinged the entire federal system on the person of the chancellor, who presided over the sovereign Bundesrat and was only formally responsible to its unitarian counterweight, the Reichstag. The chancellor, by dint of his position at the head of the Prussian government, or at least by his control of the Prussian votes in the Bundesrat, guaranteed Prussian hegemony. Would not the parliamentarization of this ambiguous system destroy it altogether and increase Prussian hegemony intolerably, since many decisive aspects of policy were not covered by the Reich constitution? Weber had to consider such problems as he studied the implementation of parliamentary rule in imperial Germany in an evolutionary manner.

During the years that he taught in Freiburg and Heidelberg, Weber turned away from the national liberal tradition in which he had been raised and grew closer to South German federalist beliefs. He expressed his antagonism towards the Prussian Conservatives and their predominance in the Reich and Prussian administrations in an energetic struggle against Prussia's hegemonic position in the Reich. It was Prussia's position that opened the way for the Conservatives to influence the destinies of the other states. As long as the Prussian Conservatives held onto

135. "And to be sure—for the most part—a great part of them *voluntarily* accept this subjugation." *Pol. Schr.*, p. 355.

three-class suffrage in Prussia, Weber remained decidedly federalistic. There were other reasons as well for his attraction to federalism. "Treitschke's ideals are past history," he said in 1917.[136] For cultural reasons alone he wanted to maintain the south German dynasties.

Because of his adherence to federalist principles, Max Weber paid particular attention to the Bundesrat in his constitutional deliberations. In contrast to the restriction of the Reichstag to negative politics only, the Bundesrat was theoretically the body in which all decisive political decisions were taken. In the later years of his government, Bismarck himself had stressed the Reich's federal character. He had even considered arbitrarily changing the constitution in a way that would have limited the Reichstag's powers still further. In the Bundesrat, with the help of the votes of Prussia and the smaller states, the chancellor could get any resolution accepted, the Reichstag's will notwithstanding. If he did not like a resolution, he could always throw it out with a Prussian veto in the Bundesrat. In those rare cases in which the Bundesrat rejected a bill, Bismarck knew how to make the delegates pliable with threats of resignation. Max Weber's constitutional reform plans were in accord with Bismarck's conception of the Reich insofar as Weber viewed the Bundesrat rather than the Reichstag as the fulcrum of the Reich constitution.

Through the parliamentarization of the Bundesrat, Max Weber hoped to find a constitutional means of reconciling parliamentary institutions with the Reich's federal character. "Through the implementation of universal suffrage in the individual states and effective ministerial responsibility for instructions to the delegates to the Bundesrat, as for all governmental actions in the states, the Bundesrat will become a *representative body of the states* (rather than a representation of the *dynasties*, as at present)," he wrote his brother Alfred in 1907. "Only in this way [can] . . . the present situation, in which the Prussian three-class *Landtag* rules us all as vassals, be changed." Right now, "the twenty-three million [inhabitants of the non-Prussian federal states] count for nought in the Bundesrat and for the Berlin regime."[137] Weber called for parliamentarizing the federalist rather than the unitarian provisions of the Reich constitution, in order to avoid the Reich's compromising the federal states. In 1907, he viewed federalist reform as the best means to substitute the "'personal government' of a responsible minister, for the irresponsible meddling by the monarch."[138] The federal states would then be able to

136. Ibid., p. 438; cf. also p. 243.

137. Letter to Alfred Weber of 22 May 1907 after a copy in the Weber papers. A letter to Naumann of 18 November 1908 reads similarly, *Pol. Schr.* 1, p. 457: "*Parliamentarization of the Bundesrat* is the practical problem."

138. Letter to Alfred Weber of 22 May 1907. Observe the phraseology of the "'personal regime' of the responsible minister." This illuminates Weber's concept of the nature of the ministerial office.

name fraction leaders from the individual state parliaments or leading Reichstag politicians as Bundesrat deputies. The Bundesrat would consequently develop into a political body representing the political party constellation. This would enable party leaders to influence German policy directly. The Bundesrat would be transformed into the most important organ of control over the Reich leadership. Parliamentarization would have taken a course that did not undermine the Bundesrat's central position in the Reich constitutional system. This central position had been ingeniously established by Bismarck in order to pacify the royal houses and perhaps to hinder the transition to a parliamentary system as well.

Max Weber's proposals for constitutional reforms, detailed in the 1917 articles in the *Frankfurter Zeitung*, "Deutschlands Parlamentarismus in Vergangenheit und Zukunft" ("Germany's Parliamentarism in the Past and the Future") and published as a pamphlet in 1918, did not deviate all that much from his 1907 proposals. Of course, we have little information about the earlier proposals. In 1917, he phrased the German constitutional problem similarly: "How can the parliamentarization of Germany be reconciled with healthy, that is to say with active, federalism?"[139] But he now maintained that the stream of parliamentarization had "to be guided into the channel of the Reich." As before, he viewed the key to the parliamentarization of the Reich to be the parliamentarization of the Bundesrat.

Max Weber wished to develop the Bundesrat into a genuine representation of the federal states; but at the same time he wished to preserve and strengthen its function as the leading consultative body for Reich policy. The Reichstag ought to be incorporated in this system. In contrast to the proposals of 1907, he now suggested that politicians from the Reichstag parties have formal access to the Bundesrat. Weber emphasized that "the issue is to 'parliamentarize' the Bundesrat by permitting the party leaders from the Reichstag and from the major state parliaments to sit there as full delegates."[140] Weber therefore viewed the most pressing constitutional amendment to be the removal of article 9, paragraph 2, of the Reich constitution which proscribed simultaneous membership in the Reichstag and the Bundesrat.[141] Weber categorically rejected the idea that parliamentary delegates be taken into the government, appointed, as the rules made necessary, to the Bundesrat on condition that they gave up their Reichstag mandates and consequently

139. *Pol. Schr.*, p. 420; cf. p. 369: "The real problem of parliamentarization, and also of the Reich constitution in general, lies "not so much in the constitutional rights of the other federal states as in the relationship to the hegemonic state: Prussia."

140. *Pol. Schr.*, p. 437.

141. Weber sent a draft of a law along this line to Conrad Haussmann at the beginning of May 1917; cf. the letter of 1 May 1917 in the Haussmann papers.

their influence over their own parties. That would mean no more and no less than their "political decapitation." Like von Bennigsen, and Miquel, Center Deputy Spahn had lost all support of his party when he joined the Hertling cabinet.[142] It was entirely contrary to the meaning of parliamentarization to insist that members of the Reichstag resign their mandates in that body when they were called to high office and joined the Bundesrat. The elimination of this prohibition of dual membership would permit Reichstag politicians who entered the Bundesrat to be in a position to influence major political decisions, thanks to their parties' backing. At the same time, their parties would bear responsibility for their actions.

Weber believed it especially important to refute federalistic reservations about constitutional reform that were common at the time in Bavarian circles and were also expressed by Hertling himself.[143] Weber stressed, in harmony with his 1907 plans, that parliamentarization of the Bundesrat was possible even without the repeal of article 9, paragraph 2. Even under the existing constitution, the federal states were not prevented from naming state party leaders as Bundesrat delegates.[144] But if this happened, the Bundesrat would be parliamentarized in a particularist direction. Only the presence of the leaders of the Reichstag parties in the Bundesrat could turn the upper house into an organ in which the interests of the Reich could be satisfactorily reconciled with the interests of individual states. Only the Reichstag, and Bundesrat delegates who had their political roots in the Reichstag (including possible Prussian representatives), could form an effective counterweight to Prussian hegemony in the Bundesrat. There was also a danger that, with the retention of article 9, paragraph 2, the Reich state secretaries, who belonged to the Reichstag, could form a cabinet with the chancellor outside of the Bundesrat which would thereby forfeit all influence. This would mean that the political influence of the smaller states would be totally lost. A federalist resolution to constitutional reform was possible within the framework of the existing Reich structure only if the Reichstag members were permitted to enter the Bundesrat.

Weber developed this constitutional program convincingly in the 1917 *Frankfurter Zeitung* articles on German parliamentarianism. His approach met wide agreement and helped to prepare the ground for the left's constitutional reform efforts in the discussions that had begun early in May 1917 in the Reichstag's constitutional committee. Weber was in close touch with Conrad Haussmann, who sat as the Progressive repre-

142. *Pol. Schr.*, p. 238 and pp. 241 ff.

143. See section 6 of "Parlament und Regierung," *Pol. Schr.*, pp. 406 ff., and "Bayern und die Parlamentarisierung im Reich," ibid., pp. 233 ff., originally in the *Münchner Neueste Nachrichten*, 15 October 1917.

144. Compare Weber's letter to Haussmann of 7 September 1917.

sentative on the constitutional committee, where he worked energetically for the parliamentarization of the Reich constitution. Among other items, Weber sent Haussmann carefully argued proposals for the repeal of article 9, paragraph 2, of the Reich constitution and for the introduction of the right of inquiry in the Reichstag. Haussmann proposed the lifting of "'the incompatibility' provision of article 9" on behalf of the Fortschrittliche Volkspartei (the Progressives) to the constitutional committee, but withdrew it in the 5 May 1917 meeting because the "National Liberals were not yet in agreement."[145] Here we can see Max Weber's direct impact on political praxis. At the same time, his influence should not be overestimated. The constitutional committee's reform decisions went beyond the measures that Weber sought at the time; nor did they take the approach of parliamentarization of the Bundesrat. But at least Weber's efforts for constitutional reforms continued to have support in the press. The *Frankfurter Zeitung* called for the development of a parliamentary system in articles that were without doubt inspired by Weber's own deliberations in his May–June series of articles.[146] To be sure, Weber objected to the overcautiousness of the *Frankfurter Zeitung*, which had no chance anyway of avoiding criticism from circles unsympathetic to democracy.[147]

Weber continued to support Haussmann with advice and aid. On the constitutional committee, Haussmann encountered the objection shared by the conservative press that parliamentarization of the Bundesrat was impossible because of the stipulation that Bundesrat delegates had to vote according to the instructions of their governments, whereas Reichstag deputies had to vote from conviction. This situation could not be

145. Haussmann to Helfferich, 6 May 1917, Haussmann papers, 12.

146. In this regard, especially the article "Minister und Abgeordnete" of 14 August 1917. Also, it should not be overlooked that the *Frankfurter Zeitung* did not accept Weber's plan for parliamentarization through the transformation of the Bundesrat into a body in which political parties were represented. In this connection, the two articles "Das parlamentarische System im Bundesstaat" of 15 July 1917 and "Parlamentarismus und Parlamentarisierung" of 22 July 1917 cannot be traced to concepts of Max Weber as Winckelmann does in the foreword to the second edition of *Pol. Schr.*, p. xxxv, n. 2. These articles represent the exact opposite tendency, since they favored the unavoidable repression of the Bundesrat in a system of pure Reich parliamentarism. The articles call for a pure parliamentary system and the demand for the creation of responsible Reich ministries goes far beyond what Weber regarded as desirable and practicable in the existing situation. Only someone who has not understood the basic ideas in Weber's constitutional proposals could associate these articles with Weber. The only genuine impact of Weber's proposals can be found in Robert von Piloty's treatment. See Piloty's article about the nature of the parliamentary system in the *Frankfurter Zeitung* of 4 April 1918, evening edition, and especially the study completed by the end of July 1917: *Das parlamentarische System. Eine Untersuchung seines Wesens und Wertes*, 2d ed. (Berlin and Leipzig, 1917).

147. Letter to the *Frankfurter Zeitung* of 27 June 1917.

reconciled with the idea that Bundesrat representatives might act as representatives of their parties. Haussmann asked Weber's opinion on this question.[148] Weber answered immediately by letter and in an article on the amendment of article 9 of the Reich constitution.[149] The *Frankfurter Zeitung* published this as a lead on 8 September without mentioning Weber's name, thereby identifying itself with Weber's arguments.[150] Weber stressed that ending the incompatibility of membership in the Reichstag and the Bundesrat would permit "the Bundesrat and the Reichstag to [stop] treating each other like two opposing powers. . . . The removal of this basically absurd provision will of course not mean the introduction of the 'parliamentary system.' This would require that the chief minister also be the leader of the dominant party. The removal of this provision will merely *make this* [parliamentarization] *possible*."[151] Weber also refuted the conservative arguments against the representation of party leaders in the Bundesrat. If a leading Reich official who was also a member of the Reichstag received instructions in his capacity as a Bundesrat delegate "that contradicted his political *convictions* on decisive issues," he should "resign his office." If he did not resign, he could hardly be said to amount to more than a politically characterless "hanger-on." It was extremely desirable that "this duty to sacrifice office for conviction" be fostered among leading Reich politicians "through the possession of Reichstag mandates."[152] Weber's concept of the politician implied that actions must be based entirely upon independent decisions. Volition from other sources, whether from a politician's party, a parliamentary majority, the monarch, or the chancellor, as the instructor of

148. Letter to Weber of 3 September 1917, copy in Haussmann papers.

149. Letter of 7 September 1917, Haussmann papers. Weber informed Haussmann here of the appearance of his article "probably in code."

150. *Frankfurter Zeitung* of Saturday, 8 September 1917; reprinted in *Pol. Schr.*, pp. 222 ff. Later incorporated in "Parlament und Regierung." Compare *Pol. Schr.*, pp. 421, 344, note 1.

151. Weber would have been content if art. 9, 2, had been merely declared inapplicable in regard to the Reich chancellor and the state secretaries. He proposed the addition: "This stipulation is not applied to the Reich chancellor or the secretaries of state."

152. We are following Weber's letter to Haussmann here. The corresponding, extremely suggestive passage of the letter reads as follows: "There is *no* conflict of conscience inherent in the case of art. 9:

"a) it merely treats a Prussian plenipotentiary (since every Reich Chancellor and every Chief of a major Reich office *must* be a *Prussian* plenipotentiary to the Bundesrat.) A Reich Chancellor or a State Secretary who has received instructions that contradict his *political* convictions, *ought to resign his office*, or he is a politically characterless clinger to office ('Kleber') (as Bismarck once said. In one incident of this kind, he offered his resignation—whereupon the Bundesrat *changed* its vote.)

"b) It is only *hoped* that this duty to *sacrifice* one's office for the sake of convictions will be *enjoined* for leading Reich officials by the possession of a Reichstag mandate. They *should be politicians* and not 'officials.' "

the votes of the Prussian representatives, had to be secondary. For this reason, Weber perceived a political advantage in the legal contradiction between the vote by instruction and a free vote according to conviction. By no means was he calling for the repeal of the imperative mandate principle for the Bundesrat. He viewed that principle as a means to remind the Bundesrat representatives of their specific political responsibilities.

At the time, Weber went no further than this program of admitting the leading Reichstag politicians into the Bundesrat in order to open up the decisive institution of the Bismarckian constitution to parliamentary control. At this juncture it seemed sufficient to offer the leaders of the Reichstag parties the chance to win influence for themselves and their parties by filling major offices or acting as delegates of state governments in the Bundesrat. It was advisable for such party representatives to retain their political following by remaining in the Reichstag. In November 1917, when Friedrich von Payer was faced with the decision of accepting an appointment to the Bundesrat and giving up his Reichstag mandate, Weber would have "preferred it if von Payer had refused the Bundesrat seat and tried to establish the principle of a moderate and independent Reich government outside of the Bundesrat."[153] Yet Weber opposed the transition to a unitary parliamentary system since he feared a deflection of the balance of power in favor of the Reichstag and the central power at the expense of the federal state parliaments and governments. He fired back in the *Frankfurter Zeitung* when Erich Kaufmann, in a study of "Bismarck's legacy in the Reich constitution," bitterly opposed repeal of article 9, paragraph 2, because "Prussia would be overpowered by a bloc of parliamentary Bundesrat representatives from small states."[154] Weber was impressed by this opponent's objective arguments. But in the light of Prussia's supremacy in the Bundesrat, Weber argued that such a position could not be taken seriously and maintained that the danger of "the destruction of the middle-sized states [through] parliamentary centralization" could be avoided by means of his solution: "We wish to see the participation of Bavaria and the other middle-sized states [in the Reich's leadership] strengthened." Only the repeal of article 9, paragraph 2, would prevent the Bundesrat from "becoming a meaningless voting machine caught between the Reichstag and the Prussian parliament."

153. According to a letter by Anschütz to Haussmann of 18 November 1917, in the Haussmann papers 30. Anschütz had a differing position on this question, which he relayed to Haussman, before discussing it fully with Weber. It is significant that Haussmann and Anschütz considered republishing Weber's article "Die Abänderung des Artikels 9 der Reichsverfassung" at the time, but with "the polemics removed." Anschütz enclosed with his letter the relevant newspaper clipping with his proposals for deletions.

154. *Bismarcks Erbe in der Reichsverfassung* (Berlin, 1917). We are following Weber's formulation here.

Weber was anxious to prevent this.[155] Weber's defense of the rights of the federal states is very apparent here. Transition to a parliamentary system had to occur simultaneously on the Reich and state levels. The federalist constitutional structure of the Reich had to be retained and strengthened. It was of decisive importance that the Bundesrat be transformed into a council in which the Reich party leaders and the state leaders would share a commanding position.[156] In his view, effective reform of the existing federal constitutional system could take place only through the evolution of the Bundesrat into a parliamentary leadership council. Only in this way could the Prussian desire for hegemony be limited.

As late as 1918, when a parliamentary government led by Max von Baden took office, with the participation of the majority parties of the Reichstag, Weber still maintained that a "moderate" parliamentarization of the Bundesrat was the only sensible course given the existing constitutional structure. He complained that the new Reich government had been constituted outside of the Bundesrat.[157] He therefore urged the immediate repeal of article 9, paragraph 2, by the Bundesrat. He also demanded that the majority parties make "their responsible participation in the government dependent upon the *immediate* approval of the Bundesrat."[158] Only thus could a parliamentary government be formed in the Reich that would not result in a "greater Prussian" evolution at the expense of the influence of the large federal states.

We may well conclude that Max Weber's reform proposals were grounded in the conviction that the South German federal states had to be protected in times of political crisis. To this extent he judged the situation much more accurately than did Hugo Preuss and the north German liberals, who remained in the Treitschke tradition. Yet there were serious faults in his program, which placed the Bundesrat in the center of the constitutional structure and developed it into a representative body of Reich political groups. Weber wanted the political parties to exercise decisive influence over the government through the Bundesrat. It is difficult to imagine how the Bundesrat could successfully influence Reich policy from its ambivalent position as a house of states in which the Prussian votes were exercised by secretaries of state belonging to the Reichstag, and also as a broadened government council. This would be

155. Cf. the article of 28 October 1917 in the *Frankfurter Zeitung* recently discovered by Winckelmann: "Bismarcks Erbe in der Reichsverfassung," *Pol. Schr.*, pp. 241 ff; the citation is from p. 243.

156. Cf. also Weber's lecture in Berlin on 16 January 1918, "Aristokratie und Demokratisierung in Deutschland," in which he emphatically said that parliamentarization must include the Bundesrat. See below, chap. 7, n. 309.

157. *Pol. Schr.*, p. 444.

158. Ibid., p. 446.

the case even in the event that the states had fully adopted the parliamentary system—an adoption that Weber viewed as a precondition of the successful functioning of his scheme. The Bundesrat remained a unique, hybrid body of representatives of the current governing parties in the Reichstag and representatives of the states, lacking the right to force the chancellor to speak and reply to questions. Weber entertained the idea of making the chancellor responsible to the Reichstag, but he in no way urged responsibility in the sense that it was incorporated in the law of 28 October 1918.[159] In 1917, his sole concern was to find a constitutional means to bring about a government of political leaders who had the requisite backing of the parties in the Reichstag. Indeed, he rejected a formal obligation to appoint Reichstag politicians or those from state parliaments to the Bundesrat. On the contrary, he wished to leave the door open for capable leaders from outside parliament to take on Reich offices.[160]

A fundamental lacuna in his proposals was his failure to settle the question of the imperial chancellor's parliamentary responsibility. Nowhere in his *Frankfurter Zeitung* articles did he discuss the possibility of making the chancellor explicitly dependent on the confidence of the Reichstag, thereby making responsibility effective and not merely oratorical. Even in the revised and expanded treatise based upon his articles in January 1918, he did not go so far as to insist on an article on parliamentary responsibility in the constitution, similar to the article agreed upon by the Reichstag constitutional committee as early as May 1917. To this extent his parliamentary program lacked its fulcrum: the direct linking of the imperial chancellor's appointment and dismissal to a parliamentary vote.[161] This was true in spite of the fact that he clearly wanted the Kaiser to appoint the leaders of the current Reichstag majority to head the Reich government.

Certain major political reasons account for Weber's reluctance at this point. It was clear that the Kaiser was more prone to promote the leaders of the Reichstag parties to state secretaryships and as Prussian Bundesrat representatives than he was to formally accept the binding of a chancellor to a Reichstag vote in legalized form. In fact, things developed very much along these lines. The von Hertling cabinet included representatives of

159. Ibid., pp. 368 f.

160. Ibid., p. 425.

161. Compare ibid., p. 368, further p. 380. There Weber demanded 'effective' responsibility for the chancellor as a means of counteracting the "personal regime," but wants this to be achieved by the possibility of an appeal to the state supreme court [!] The concept 'effective' responsibility is therefore in no way distinctly applied in the sense of a link to an expressed confidence resolution by the Reichstag. Cf. also Carl Schmitt, *Verfassungslehre*, p. 335.

the Reichstag parties without any formal acknowledgment that this amounted to a transition to a parliamentary system. Moreover, Weber did not view the contemporary Reichstag as politically mature enough to be fully in charge itself. He only wished to create the "indispensable institutional preconditions" for a revitalization of the parliament.[162]

Nevertheless, this was not the decisive reason for the astounding fact that Max Weber pushed effective responsibility of the chancellor into the background. Because he sought to construct a parliamentary Bundesrat that would preserve the special privileges of Prussia, it was impossible to settle the chancellor's responsibility along the lines of English constitutional practice. This was because the chancellor was responsible to the Prussian house of deputies in his capacity as the bearer of the presidential vote in the Bundesrat, and to the Reichstag in his capacity as the leader of the Reich government.[163] Weber contended explicitly that the chancellor and Prussian prime minister must at least also serve as foreign minister; as such he would be responsible to the Prussian house of deputies.[164] It was conceivable that the Prussian house of deputies, if it could overthrow the Prussian minister by formally withdrawing its confidence, could command the instructional control of the Bundesrat representation, the presidential vote in the Bundesrat, and thereby the Reich government. In this event it would be necessary to clearly establish the fact that the chancellor was responsible to the *Reichstag*. But as long as such a conflict did not arise, Weber wanted to maintain the chancellor's dual responsibility or establish it more clearly by law. He hoped that Reich policy would continue to be a compromise between the Prussian Bundesrat representatives and the Reich government supported by the Reichstag.[165] He therefore wanted to center political decision-making in a parliamentarized Bundesrat rather than in the Reichstag or in a cabinet determined by the Reichstag alone. Such a parliamentarized Bundesrat would normally include the leaders of the Reichstag parties as *Prussian* Bundesrat representatives. Weber believed that in this way he could achieve his political goals without seriously altering the federalist constitutional system with its concomitant Prussian hegemonic position. The great question of the relationship between the Reich and Prussia, which hampered a harmonious solution to the constitutional problem in Germany between

162. *Pol. Schr.*, pp. 441 f. The sentence "One must of course not think that any such paragraph that would link the appointment and dismissal of the Reich chancellor to a parliamentary vote would suddenly conjure up 'leaders' who have been absent from parliament for decades because of its powerlessness"—is an insertion from the end of 1917!

163. Cf. also below, chap. 9, sec. 1.

164. Cf. the letter to Haussmann of 5 May 1917 and *Pol. Schr.*, pp. 410 ff. Contrary to Weber's view, the actual language in the Reich constitution did not necessitate the linking of the office of Reich chancellor with Prussian ministerial offices. Ibid., p. 410.

165. Cf. *Pol. Schr.*, pp. 430 ff.

1867 and 1933, also imbued Weber's constitutional plans with a certain imprecision.

In the end, we must rebuke Max Weber's basic political outlook for so conspicuously neglecting the effective responsibility of the imperial chancellor to the parliament. In contrast to the liberal tradition, Weber reversed the order of priority of the two central constitutional questions, the dependence of government upon the confidence of a majority in parliament and the chance for a party leader to attain governmental power. In principle, it was important to him only that the destiny of the Reich was in the hands of political leaders of stature rather than those of conservative bureaucrats. He believed that if his plans for a reformed constitutional system were adopted, capable politicians could be trained and could rise to power without the weapon of the confidence vote. The amount of direct parliamentary influence upon the choice of leading politicians and the direction of their policies, he regarded as secondary. He based his support of the introduction of a parliamentary system primarily on the argument that party rule was the only way to ensure strong leadership. Through the parties, "men will come to the fore . . . who possess the nation's trust, whom the parties will follow loyally as long as it is useful to them, that is, as long as the minister has the confidence of the people."[166] Party democracy means the principle of plebiscitary leadership, leadership that can demand the parties' unconditional obedience as long as the confidence of the masses is present.[167]

It is a fundamental principle of traditional liberalism to insist that the people's representatives, as the political elite of the nation, ought to prescribe the basic lines of government policy and supervise its details by parliamentary controls and, in a fully developed parliamentary system, by the confidence vote. Max Weber set this model on its head. He peeled away the last remnant of liberal opposition to government under a constitutional framework. With extraordinary consistency, he described the scheme for the creation of political will from *above* to *below*.[168] The parliament's rights of control serve only to continually remind the leading

166. *Aristokratie und Demokratisierung in Deutschland* (printed in Appendix V of the German edition of this book); cf. also below, chap. 7, text at note 309.

167. Here Weber's definition of the nature of political leadership, which he formulated with unparalleled precision and conceptual sharpness in his conversation with Ludendorff, is already anticipated.

168. Albertin's argument based on a citation from *Pol. Schr.*, p. 275 (see *Liberalismus und Demokratie am Anfang der Weimarer Republik* [Düsseldorf, 1972], p. 254, note 279), which challenges the interpretation of this author, appears to me to be inconclusive, in spite of the alliteration "of 'above' and of 'below'" In this passage, Weber is discussing responsible political leadership in which leading politicians must employ rational calculation and in which emotional factors from "below" in Weber's sense, are annoyances and cannot as such be viewed as unconscious or conscious influences upon the decision-making process (cf. below, note 187).

politicians of their responsibility, and to have them removed when they fail, not simply when their policy differs from that of the parliamentary majority. This sums up Weber's notion of parliamentary rule. In place of the "outmoded, negative kind of democracy that demands only freedom from the state," Weber wished to substitute a system of democratic rule which would make it possible for the tools of the state's power to be applied without restraint to achieve national goals.[169] This could take place only through "the self-reliant participation of parliamentary leaders in the exercise of this power."[170] The leading politician might then implement goals that he himself set, at least as long as he could maintain the masses' confidence in himself and his policies.[171]

After 1918, Max Weber developed this conception of parliamentary leadership in the light of the failure of postrevolutionary parliaments. His thought now took a distinctly antiparliamentary direction.[172] Now he wished to replace the traditional model of a "leaderless" parliamentary system with a "plebiscitary leader democracy" in which a great, charismatically gifted politician might pursue courageous policies. Weber stressed that in a "leader democracy" the politician is not a "mandatee" of his voters but is entirely responsible to himself. "Therefore, he will act according to his own judgment as long as he can successfully claim their confidence and will not [act] like an [elected] official, i.e., in conformity to the expressed or suspected will of the electors."[173]

169. *Pol. Schr.*, p. 269.

170. We are here taking into account Lothar Albertin's objection that in the presentation in the first edition of this book, the plebiscitary-charismatic conception of the political leader is presupposed for 1917–18 as completely developed and the role of the "working parliament" underestimated because of lack of attention to the chronological development (*Liberalismus und Demokratie*, pp. 251 ff.). Nevertheless, it was pointed out there that the contrast between parliamentary and plebiscitary leadership selection was already stated by Weber in 1917; if Weber at the time still held firmly to parliament as the existing place for the selection of political leaders, in contrast to 1919–1920, this does not mean that he conceded to parliament the function of independent political activity alongside of and in opposition to the elected leader. Also, the connection in which the concept "working parliament" arises (*Pol. Schr.*, pp. 355 f.) does not confirm Albertin's meaning. The accent here is distinctly upon the function of selection and instruction of politicians, which will be optimally achieved in working parliaments. The evidence of 16 January 1918 referred to above shows again that Weber permitted the leading politician a plebiscitary-charismatic precedence vis-à-vis his party as well as parliament, as early as 1917–18. This goes beyond the traditional concept of parliamentarism. Granted, the theory of "plebiscitary leadership democracy," with its distinctly antiparliamentary tendency, was first formulated by Weber in 1919 as a result of his deep disappointment about the renewed leadership of career politicians "without calling," and that this theory now had a distinctly antiparliamentary direction; but the origins of it are already there in 1917.

172. Cf. below, pp. 363 f, and, on individual points more complete, my article "Zum Begriff der 'plebiszitären Führerdemokratie' bei Max Weber," *Kölner Zeitschrift für Soziologie und Sozialpsychologie* 15 (1963): 308 ff.

173. *Wirtschaft und Gesellschaft*, p. 558.

No form of collective leadership could be reconciled with Max Weber's conception of "personally responsible leadership." As a result, he unhesitatingly shelved the old and "cherished liberal idea" of a collegial Reich ministry which would be subject to a greater measure of positive control.[174] Instead, Weber emphasized the central position of the cabinet chief since collegiality stood in the way of the specific responsibility he desired.[175] In addition, a collegial Reich ministry did not conform well to the Reich's federal constitutional structure that Weber wished to preserve through the integration of a parliamentarized Bundesrat into the parliamentary system. Preuss, in contrast, wished at the time to turn the Bundesrat into a pure house of states.[176]

Max Weber was among those thinkers who first recognized the political consequences that arose from industrialization and the transformation of the social system.[177] He saw clearly that the rise of modern mass democracy had seriously shaken the underpinnings of traditional liberal constitutional thought. He himself analyzed the process through which mass democratic party machines replaced liberal parties controlled by eminent leaders. Parliament had therefore lost its character as a political arena for independent personalities and became a place where partisan struggles worked themselves out before the bar of public opinion. Organized interest groups began to observe the political arena closely, and even the parties lost their character as free associations of independent personalities who joined together for common goals. Parties then began to take on the form of interest organizations with their armies of functionaries and members. The liberal demand that a political elite of independent personalities must take over the national state's leadership appeared to have been rendered obsolete by the way things had developed.[178]

Weber would not accept this development, however. He did not waiver from the belief that personalities who were both inwardly and outwardly independent should be called to political leadership. The policies of the national state ought always to be determined by political

174. *Pol. Schr.*, pp. 434 f.

175. Cf. *Wirtschaft und Gesellschaft*, p. 173, and especially pp. 163 f.: "It is not possible to direct a powerfully unified domestic or foreign policy in a mass state, *effectively*, with a collegial leadership."

176. Weber wished to retain the noncollegial structure of the Reich constitution completely; it was important to him that the Reich Chancellor *alone* instructed the Prussian deputies in the Bundesrat. Cf. note 88 above, and Preuss, "Vorschläge zur Abänderung der Reichsverfassung," July 1917, *Staat, Recht und Freiheit*, p. 305.

177. Cf. Theodor Schieder, "Der Liberalismus und die Strukturwandlungen der modernen Gesellschaft vom 19. zum 20. Jahrhundert," *Relazioni del X Congresso Internazionale di Scienze Storiche*, vol. 5, *Storia Contemporanea*, pp. 160 f.

178. Cf., in this connection, Gerhard Leibholz, *Der Strukturwandel der modernen Demokratie* (Karlsruhe, 1952), pp. 16 ff.

ideals and moral standards alone, not sectarian material interests of any kind.[179] The rule of a charismatic-plebiscitary politician was his solution for the dilemma brought about by the institutionalization of political objectives in organized movements and the supremacy of organized interests. He attempted to translate the liberal ideal of an independent political elite into the conditions of plebiscitary mass democracy. The goal was clear: independent political leaders should stand above the party machines as well as above a parliament controlled by those machines. This could be achieved by the political leader's consistent application of plebiscitary methods of mass rule. Weber transformed the liberal idea of the people's representatives as political elite of the nation into an extreme form. Only a small group of really gifted leaders would monopolize political action, and in the end, a great charismatic politician would hold the reins alone. "The broad mass of deputies would act *only* as the followers of one or a few 'leaders' who made up the cabinet and would obey them blindly *as long as* they were successful. *That is the way it should be*. 'The principle of small numbers' always rules in political action, i.e., the superior capacity for political maneuverability of *small* leadership groups."[180]

This also meant a change in the means through which a politician might rise to power and responsibility. Weber pointed out and insisted that under the conditions of active mass democratization "the political leader could no longer be proclaimed a candidate on the basis of the support of elite circles and then chosen as a leader because of his prominence in parliament. Rather, he must have won the trust and faith of the masses and therefore achieved power through instruments of mass demagoguery."[181] A great politician wins a "following" and mass "acclamation" through the emotional power of his speeches above all, through "demogoguery" in the true sense of the word. He does not attempt to convince people of the necessity of certain political measures in an objective way, but to awaken their faith in his "calling for leadership."[182]

Max Weber judged the "Caesarist transformation of leadership selection" to be unavoidable. He approved of it, even at the cost of rationality and objectivity in the formation of public opinion. He viewed it as the only way to bring about rule by independent and genuinely qualified leaders in an age of modern political "enterprise." He argued that "mass

179. Cf., especially, *Pol. Schr.*, p. 401.

180. Ibid., p. 348. This was inserted by Weber at the end of 1917 in order to intensify his position in the reediting of his article series in the *Frankfurter Zeitung*.

181. Ibid., p. 393. Cf. p. 401: "The politically passive 'masses' do not give birth to the leader, but the political leader recruits his 'following' and wins the masses through 'demagoguery.'"

182. Ibid., p. 393.

democracy" had "always bought its successes since Pericles' time with major concessions to the Caesarist principle of leadership selection, beginning at the time of Pericles."[183] We are now inclined to question the limits of such an irrational method of leadership selection, since we have witnessed the dangers of its transformation into a totalitarian state at first hand. Weber saw the problem from another angle: to what extent, in view of the bureaucratization of all political institutions, especially political parties, was the rise of leadership personalities still possible?

It was not only his insight into the conditions of modern mass democracy that led Max Weber to call for a great charismatic politician. He had in mind his hopes for his own nation as well, a national state whose policies had failed because of the lack of powerful statesmen. Paradoxically, he had the great model, Bismarck, in mind as well. Max Weber was a long-time stern critic of Bismarckian Caesarism; nevertheless, the figure of the chancellor permeated his political thinking. He once said of the National Liberals that they maintained the conviction that "if there were any chance that a new Bismarck would always appear to fill the top position, Caesarism, the governmental form of genuises, would be Germany's natural constitution."[184] It would hardly be an exaggeration to say this was his own opinion as well. After 1917, Weber preached precisely what he had condemned in Bismarck, the "'personal rule' of a responsible politician" on a Caesarist-plebiscitary basis.[185] The portrait that Weber drew of the model politician's character had clearly Bismarckian features in many details. The model politician ought not to follow the electorate's will; he ought to lead it. He should use his political skills and his charismatic abilities to seek recognition and supporters. He should use his demogogic genius to win a following for the achievement of his political goals. He should not be the advocate of the will of the majority but should use demagogic tools to win over the majority in parliament and among the masses. We are necessarily reminded of Bismarck's extraordinary capacity to fashion a parliamentary majority with both tactical and demagogic tools in order to realize his political projects.

Nevertheless, Max Weber wished to compensate for the weaknesses of plebiscitary-charismatic rule, which he had analyzed so thoroughly in the

183. Ibid., p. 395. Compare *Wirtschaft und Gesellschaft*, pp. 562 f.: "Technically considered, the capacity for success of 'Caesarism' as a system of rule, often arising from democracy, rests ultimately upon the position of the "Caesar" as a free, nontraditional individual holding the trust of the masses (the army or the citizenship). He is thereby unlimited master of a tribe of officers and officials that he has selected without regard to tradition and other considerations. This 'leadership of a personal genius' stands in contradiction to the formally 'democratic' principle of an entirely elected bureaucracy."

184. *Pol. Schr.*, p. 314.

185. Compare above, text at note 138.

case of Bismarck. The Achilles' heel of government by a great genius was the problem of succession—a problem demonstrated by the condition of German politics after the fall of the "Caesar" Bismarck. Therefore, Weber sought to prevent Bismarck's "error"—the downgrading of parliament to meaninglessness and the consequent destruction of its function as a source for the selection of political leaders. "In hereditary monarchies, parliamentary power must accompany 'Caesaristic' leadership. The reason for this is that there may be long periods in which there is no generally recognized person who enjoys the confidence of the masses."[186]

If the plebiscite were to became the chief means of forming public opinion in mass democracy, would parliamentarism still have much meaning? Weber conceded that there was a "conflict between the parliamentary and the plebiscitary selection of leaders," but he did not therefore conclude that parliament, the body for the training and selection of political leaders, should be cast on the rubbish heap. Parliament was also indispensable as a check on the dangers of Caesaristic rule. Because leaders would have to prove themselves within the conventions of parliamentary procedures, it "guarantees fairly well that these Caesaristic trustees of the masses respect the established constitutional arrangements and will not . . . be selected . . . merely on the basis of emotion."[187] Only parliament could protect bourgeois liberties from assaults by government and "assure a peaceful means to *remove* a Caesaristic dictator who [had] *lost* the confidence of the masses."[188] Weber expressly rejected a purely plebiscitary system such as the American presidential system. He viewed a parliament armed with the weapon of inquiry as the only effective counterweight to the administrative bureaucracy's acting as a law unto itself. The American democratic system, in which new officials were periodically appointed as a new president took office, was "coming to an end"; a career civil service was advancing inexorably there as it was everywhere else.[189]

His recollection of Bismarck's political genius, his passionate belief in national power, and his diagnosis of the Reich's chronic crisis in leadership after 1890 led Max Weber to a political model based upon a radical distinction between the character of the bureaucrat and that of the

186. *Pol. Schr.*, p. 401.

187. *Pol. Schr.*, p. 403. One asks oneself nevertheless whether this is the only guarantee of his respect for the legal order. Cf. in this regard Albertin, *Liberalismus und Demokratie*, p. 253.

188. *Pol. Schr.*, p. 395.

189. *Gesammelte Aufsätze zur Soziologie und Sozialpolitik*, p. 495. Cf. also my article "Die Vereinigten Staaten von Amerika im politischen Denken Max Webers," *Historische Zeitschrift* 213 (1971): pp. 378 f.

politician. As bureaucracy seemed to be pushing ahead everywhere, the dangers grew. Max Weber looked to democratic statesmen who, like Gladstone, had the gift of charismatic leadership and the confidence of the masses. Politicians of this sort might carry Bismarck's work forward and build the economic and political *Lebensraum* that Germany required to remain a great power. Parliament might then act as a counterbalancing power and a means to control the apparatus of bureaucratic government.

Weber repeatedly stressed that "the cause of the German nation and its future position" was far more important to him than were "questions of state organization."[190] Increasing German power took precedence over all specifically domestic considerations. He favored the democratization of the German state structure not in order to satisfy the "will of the people" but to unify all of the nation's political energies. Weber viewed arguments based upon the will of the people as pure fiction. He demanded a "Führer democracy" in contrast to a "leaderless democracy" characterized by the "effort to minimize the rule of man over man."[191] Weber noted that both liberalism and direct democracy[192] theoretically favored the reduction of state power through the "minimalization of rule" and egalitarian, responsible cooperation of all active citizens in the governmental system. He rejected all such ideals. Instead, he sought the highest possible increase in state power at home as abroad. Democratization was the means to assure the domestic support of the governed; parliamentarization, the way to unite all domestic forces for a national policy of power and especially to prepare capable politicians for leadership positions. His beliefs hinged on imperialism and power politics, and he pushed his former liberal ideals into the background. Foreign policy had become his primary concern.

190. E.g., *Pol. Schr.*, p. 439.
191. *Wirtschaft und Gesellschaft*, p. 157.
192. Ibid., pp. 169 f., 545 f.

7

The World War as Proving Ground for the German Reich as a Great Power

1. War Aims and Germany's International Future

Max Weber was not unprepared for the misfortune that befell Germany and Europe in August 1914.[1] He was nevertheless deeply disturbed that the Reich had to face a superior coalition in the battle to retain its position as a world power. He had viewed a war for German equality to be unavoidable, and he was in principle inclined to support such a war. The war turned out to be a struggle to preserve Germany's national existence. The catastrophic diplomatic situation that isolated Germany at the war's outset clouded Weber's prophetic eyes. "How can we think of a peace? And when? Hundreds of thousands are bleeding because of the embarrassing incapacity of our diplomacy. We cannot deny it. Therefore I do not expect a lasting and fruitful peace for us even in the event of a favorable outcome."[2] In the most favorable circumstances, he did not expect this war would permit Germany to enter the ranks of the world powers. For this reason the World War seemed to make little real sense. It was above all the bloody reckoning for a quarter of a century of a boasting and arrogant German foreign policy that had offended all the powers equally.

Max Weber did share the national enthusiasm of the late summer of 1914. He had frequently criticized the German people for quietism and apolitical attitudes. He was now deeply affected by the national élan and the willingness for sacrifice with which the entire nation took up the fight for national preservation. He was fascinated by the event itself, independent of the fearful question of what it would lead to: "*Whatever* the

1. Cf. chap. 6 above, text at note 72.
2. Letter to Toennies of 15 October 1914, *Pol. Schr.* 1, p. 458.

outcome, *this war is great and wonderful.*"[3] The nation's patriotic enthusiasm, its willingness to make sacrifices, its national unity—Weber sensed all this as of final and permanent value. To this extent he was able to find inner meaning in the bloody event, whatever the outcome might be. "We have proved we are a great cultural nation," Weber wrote to his mother in April 1915. "People who live in a civilized milieu and are nevertheless able to rise to the horrors of war (no achievement for a black man from Senegal!) and to return as honorably as most of our people do—that is real humanity. We cannot overlook this even in the light of much that is unpleasant. This experience will remain, no matter what happens in the end, and indeed it does not look good if Italy cannot be pacified."[4]

From the outset of the war, Max Weber viewed the chances for a German victory with skepticism. "I am more or less a defeatist," he once wrote his wife.[5] He foresaw the economic problems all too clearly. He recognized the incompetence of German diplomats "in dealing positively with the unfamiliar diplomacy of the 'democracies'" all too well to be optimistic about a negotiated peace favorable to Germany.[6] But because of his passionate patriotism he clung to the belief that in the end something could be achieved. In August 1915, when, as a result of the successful breakthrough near Gorlice in May 1915, the eastern front had been pushed far beyond Poland's historical boundaries, he wrote to his Swiss friend Mina Tobler:

> Will the wonderful successes and achievements in the east bring peace any closer? It does *not* yet appear to be so. It is nevertheless a joy—aside from my misery at not being there myself—to live through what none of us had believed possible. We can hope that it will continue this way. We must believe in the unbelievable.[7]

Later, he renewed his heroic optimism and fought against the tendency to skepticism in his personal circle as well as the public statements by others who raised the smallest doubts about the German people's resolve "to hold out until we achieve the peace that is required by our honor and our security."[8] In the middle of August 1915 he wrote to Mina Tobler, who had reported the view in the Swiss press that Germany was not holding firmly: "Now you see that my optimism has proved correct in the meantime. . . . No one can know how a war will end since there are many

3. Letter of 28 August 1914, *Lebensbild*, p. 530. Cf. also letter to Lili Schäfer, partially printed in *Lebensbild*, pp. 536 f.
4. Letter of 13 April 1915, *Pol. Schr.*1, pp. 458 f.
5. Letter of 11 March 1916, copy in Weber papers. Partially in *Lebensbild*, p. 574.
6. Letter to L. M. Hartmann of 20 April 1917 (?). Original in Weber papers.
7. Letter of 7 August 1915, Archiv Ebnet II, 7.
8. "Der Berliner Professoren-Aufruf," *Pol. Schr.*, p. 155.

accidents in war. But since I have never *over*estimated war victories, I can *not* now share the impressions of your pro-Entente Swiss press. The situation is excellent; but the war will last until our enemies recognize the fruitlessness of continuing it."[9]

Weber recognized the gravity of the situation when Romania's entrance into the war in 1916 brought the first sign of a change in the course of the war. At this time he claimed: "I believe now, as I always have, that we can come out of this with honor."[10] The ambivalence of this statement is obvious. The fact that an end to the war, which Weber could only conceive of as a negotiated peace, seemed to lie in the distant future, disturbed him deeply. He had no illusions about the long-term destructive effects of the war on German domestic conditions, especially on the economic situation. It took an enormous effort to escape constant depression.[11] In August 1917 he wrote characteristically: "I now look forward with optimism. . . . If we are reasonable and do not expect to rule the world, then we shall survive with honor, militarily and otherwise. But it will be good if the end comes, since it is truly the *best* who are being killed."[12] Weber increasingly felt it necessary to oppose the irrational and naïve desires for world domination that were gaining the upper hand both in public opinion and in government circles and especially in the camps of the military and the Pan-Germans.

Although Max Weber attributed the rise of a "world coalition" against Germany primarily to the failure of German foreign policy, he also rejected the view that Germany could have avoided the World War through a better and more modest foreign policy. "We have to be a world power, and in order to have a say in the future of the world we had to risk the war. . . . Responsibility before the bar of history" demanded that Germany resist the division of the world between the "Anglo-Saxon convention" and "Russian bureaucracy";[13] otherwise the foundation of the Reich would have been meaningless and Germany should have

9. Letter of the middle of August 1915 that cannot be exactly dated, Archiv Ebnet II, 21. Cf. also the letter of 16 August 1916, Archiv Ebnet II, 20; of 4 September 1916, Archiv Ebnet II, 24; and of 2 January 1917, Archiv Ebnet II; 26.

10. Letter to Helene Weber of 8 September 1916, partially in *Lebensbild*, p. 585.

11. At the end of 1917, he once put it this way: "I would be happy if I could again return to things that I have laid aside, which the present has carried off. Everything that is connected with it is somehow colored more gloomily and tugs at the iron ring that oppresses breast, head, and neck." To Mina Tobler, 23 November 1917, Archiv Ebnet II, 45.

12. Letter to Mina Tobler, 28 August 1917, Archiv Ebnet II, 39.

13. *Pol. Schr.*, p. 176. Cf. ibid., p. 143: "Future generations, our own descendants above all, will not hold the Danes, Swiss, Dutch, and Norwegians responsible if world power—and that means ultimately control over the nature of culture in the future—is divided without a battle between the regulations of Russian officials on the one hand and the conventions of Anglo-Saxon 'society' on the other, with perhaps a dash of Latin 'reason.' [They will blame] *us*."

remained divided into small states. In Weber's view, the World War represented the international battle over the building of a German Reich that had long been postponed by Bismarck's diplomacy and over the question of whether Germany would remain a factor in the world power struggle.

Weber was convinced that the only justifiable objective of the war was the preservation of the German Reich as a great power among the "European world powers." In view of the isolation of the central powers, he recognized that real *international* successes and acquisitions were completely impossible. He knew from the outset that not much more than the status quo could be achieved. At most, Germany could expect guarantees of military security in the West and modest expansion of the German sphere of influence in the east. Even so, he was not prepared to abandon his long-range imperialist ideals. On the contrary, he was especially concerned about the political situation that Germany would face *after* the peace. He believed that the international *world* struggle would only really begin then. He was therefore anxious to ensure that Germany came out of the war with sufficient strength to fight the future battle for world position under more favorable diplomatic conditions. As a result, he was worried that Germany might win the war and lose the peace. Germany was in a position to resist the foes' attack and to win the military struggle, but it would then be weakened at home and abroad, and diplomatically isolated. Primarily for financial reasons, Germany would be incapable of alliances and not in a position to take an active role in international events. The real task of German policy in the war, Weber therefore emphasized, was not to seek territorial acquisitions of any kind beyond its national boundaries but to create a favorable basis for a *future* German *world policy*.

He was especially concerned that the German course in the war might further narrow German diplomacy's already sharply curtailed maneuvering room for the foreseeable future. Weber therefore designated the "preservation of as much freedom of choice as possible for future alliances," together with military security in east and west, to be the overriding objectives of a German peace.[14] Excessive annexations on both fronts would merely multiply the Alsace-Lorraine problem, which had rendered France permanently hostile, and thereby condemn German diplomacy to eternal failure.

Weber also viewed a speedy conclusion of peace to be in the German interest because of the war's economic consequences. During the war, Germany had more financial strength than the western powers, but the

14. "Deutschlands weltpolitische Lage," draft of the Munich lecture of October 1916. Cf. the selective report of the *Münchener Neueste Nachrichten* of 28 October 1916, reprinted in *Pol. Schr*, pp. 563 f.

situation would be reversed after the war. Germany's economic exhaustion would long render it incapable of alliances and rob it of all strength for economic expansion. America's economic strength loomed in the background, and the fact that England and France would have to face it as well was scant consolation. In the light of Germany's future international position, a long war was a great danger, even if the Reich initially won substantial territorial or strategic benefits.

Weber also argued that a "dragged out" war would psychologically damage the German people's economic capabilities. He was convinced that a long war would cause the nation to forget how to work. Well-paid munitions workers now received their high wages for a minimum of effort. He feared that investments in fixed securities would push free venture capital out of the market more than anything else, because of the multiplying funds now going into war loans. This could only further a mentality that sought security through coupon clipping at the expense of a competitive enterprising spirit. This would damage Germany's capacity for economic expansion far more than all of the material losses caused by the war.[15] It was considerations of this sort that prompted Max Weber to oppose all annexationist war aim plans from the beginning of the war. His opposition to territorial annexations was not one of principle. He was motivated by his realistic appraisal of the position of German foreign policy during and after the war, not by any principled appreciation of other nations' right to existence. Weber feared that Germany's world position would be seriously undermined by substantial territorial acquisitions in Europe.

We do not know much about the details of Weber's position on war aims during the first years of the war. Weber had too much self-discipline to participate in the pseudo-war carried on by those memorandum writers during the first weeks of the war who could not fight themselves and therefore hoped to demonstrate their patriotic fervor through nationalist outpourings.[16] Weber's caution was in itself notable in the light of the war

15. Cf. *Pol. Schr.*, pp. 140 f.; further, the letter to Naumann of 2 November 1915 (the date is uncertain; it was added later to the original by Marianne Weber; it is possible that the letter was written earlier), Weber papers: "Today, the most important question is how it will ever be *possible* to agree to a 'peace'; since the dragging on of the war means: (1) the multiplication of those on pension: 40 to 50 million more in fixed pensions applied against German means; (2) a lack of capital for the use of areas that may be annexed; (3) the weaning of the nation from the adjustment to work; (4) passage of economic supremacy to America. And then: we should not be deluded. During the war, France and England have been at a relative financial disadvantage in relation to us. *After the peace*—the longer the war lasts the more that it will be true—we shall experience the opposite, the same surprise as after 1871."

16. For the German war aims from 1914 to 1918 and the flood of memoranda, especially during the first years of the war, see especially Fritz Fischer, *Griff nach der Weltmacht: Die*

aims ecstasy common among the German intelligentsia of the time. He maintained a clear view of the political situation and did not swim in the emotional waves of the first months of the war as did most of his colleagues. In spite of his own emotional commitments, he viewed the question of war aims with uncharacteristic sobriety and sought to see the whole issue in relation to the long-term future course of German policy.

Nor did Weber consider it his responsibility to discuss such problems in the press or in the form of the confidential memoranda made necessary by the "civil peace" (Burgfrieden) and the consequent prohibition of public discussion of war aims. He firmly believed that those at home ought not to set goals for the combat soldiers whose achievements and self-sacrifice would ultimately be decisive in these matters. He was personally distressed that he was incapable of joining the combat forces at the front. If the war "had occurred at the right time—twenty-five years ago," he complained, he could have been "there."[17] He confessed in August 1915 that it was misery "not to be there."[18] He felt emotionally tied to the war: "Of all your sons, I have the greatest natural 'warrior' instinct," he wrote his mother early in 1916. "It is wrong and uncomfortable for me to be useless now to the cause that is of prime importance today."[19] The atmosphere of the war helped him to overcome his nervous affliction, and he could at least volunteer for home service. He took on, together with one of his colleagues, the running of the reserve infirmary of the Heidelberg garrison district. It is a tragedy that a man like this was relegated to a subordinate role at a time when the very existence of the Reich was in danger. He was primarily entrusted with administrative duties and with disciplinary control over the wounded, many of whom were in serious condition. Weber dedicated himself to this task totally, from early morning until late at night, for over a year. He was content with this work, "although any minor official could have done the job."[20] He was at least satisfied that he had done his duty.

Max Weber's hospital work could not console him forever. Beginning

---

Kriegszielpolitik des Kaiserlichen Deutschlands, 1914–1918, 3d ed. (Düsseldorf 1964); Werner Basler, *Deutschlands Annexionspolitik in Polen und im Baltikum 1914–1918* (Berlin, 1962); Wolfgang Schieder, ed., *Erster Weltkrieg: Ursachen, Entstehung und Kriegsziele;* Neue Wissenschaftliche Bibliothek, vol. 32 (Cologne, 1969); as well as my article on specific aspects partially suggested by Max Weber's critique at the time: "Die Regierung Bethmann Hollweg und die öffentliche Meinung 1914–1917," *Vierteljahreshefte für Zeitgeschichte* 17 (1969).

17. Letter of 15 October 1914, *Pol. Schr.* 1, p. 458.

18. To Mina Tobler, 7 August 1915, Archiv Ebnet II, 7.

19. Letter to Helene Weber of 17 April 1916, *Lebensbild*, pp. 581 f. Cf. the letter to Frieda Gross of 25 June 1916: "I was in Berlin for a long time in order to help out there—but they have too many helpers. It is a sad thing, when one cannot be [fighting] in the field."

20. Letter to Helene Weber, ibid.

in May 1915, he sought political employment. He did so hesitatingly, since he still feared "constant" intellectual work. He was uncertain whether he was capable of it again. Political developments also offered him a pretext to abandon the reserve he had chosen and circumstances had demanded. The impulse to get involved resulted largely from others' encouragement and usually involved only isolated forays into politics without any clear continuity.

Max Weber was increasingly disquieted by the increase in war aims agitation during the first months of 1915. Since the beginning of the war, he had vigorously opposed any annexation of Belgian territory and had spoke out for a conciliatory policy toward Belgium.[21] He regretted "the preventive march through Belgium, which was painful for every German in spite of its compelling necessity," and demanded that Germany openly designate Belgium as a "pawn" for peace negotiations with the western powers.[22] At an early date, he adopted the view that the German government should declare clearly that it did not desire a long occupation and certainly not the annexation of Belgium. Weber was not aware at the time that the government of Bethmann Hollweg had abandoned its accommodating position toward Belgium entirely, and that under pressure from public opinion and the army and navy it planned to attach Belgium to the German Reich as a "vassal state." He was only aware of the overwhelming agitation for extreme annexationist goals that temporarily took the form of confidential forwarding of memoranda to numerous public personalities. The great memorandum assault upon the chancellor began in September 1914 with Matthias Erzberger's stridently annexationist memorial. It was fanned by the government itself. Early in 1915, the government asked several economic experts for memoranda about the possibility of levying war reparations (among others: Arthur Salomonsohn, Max Warburg, and Max von Schinkel).[23] The clandestine campaign reached its climax with the Six Economic Associations' memorandum of 20 May drawn up under the influence of the Pan-German League, and the Seeberg address, presented to the chancellor at the beginning of July, organized by Reinhold Seeberg, Dietrich Schäfer, and several other Berlin professors and signed by 1347 representatives of the cultural

21. Compare the letter to Michels of 20 June 1915, copy in Weber papers: "I have worked *against* the annexation of Belgian territory in every conceivable manner since the beginning of the war for reasons of world policy."

22. *Pol. Schr.*, pp. 120 f. (The statement was made in December 1915; we can assume that it was equally Weber's opinion in 1914.) Further, letter to Dr. Simon of 12 December 1915: "I demanded as early as September 1914 that the expression 'pawn' ought to be employed," *Pol. Schr.*1, p. 460.

23. Cf. the advice of Max von Schinckel of 31 March 1915 to the Reich Ministry of the Interior, in DZA II, Königliches Zivilkabinett, Rep. 89 H XXVI Militaria 11[c].

world, the majority of whom were professors and teachers.[24] The chairman of the Pan-German League, Heinrich Class, forwarded a memorandum of his own, which far exceeded the others in its lack of moderation. All these memoranda proposed limitless war aims for Germany. They demanded not only the complete annexation of Belgium but also of French Flanders as far as the Somme, Calais, the iron ore basin of Longwy-Briey, and Verdun and furthermore called for repressive measures with regard to the non-Germanic populations in these areas. Even more utopian plans were put forward for eastern Europe, culminating in the annexation of Poland including the Russian border regions and Courland, along with sometimes massive resettlement and expulsion plans for the non-German populations.[25]

At the time that the final signatures were solicited for the Seeberg address, an opposition began to form consisting of Bernhard Dernburg, the former Reich colonial secretary, Hans Delbrück, August Stein of *Frankfurter Zeitung*, Theodor Wolff of the *Berliner Tageblatt*, and Conrad Haussmann. This group sought not only to counter the extreme annexation fantasies of the Pan-Germans and their conservative and industrial associates, but also to come to the aid of the pressured government of Bethmann Hollweg. Theodor Wolff drafted a short declaration that described the memoranda as "political errors with grave consequences."[26] It was essential to reject the "incorporation or annexation of nations that were politically independent or that were accustomed to political independence."[27] This declaration, like the Seeberg address, was sent to many public personalities but had far fewer signatories. The signers were nevertheless a distinguished group. Delbrück was able to publish 141 names in the *Preussische Jahrbücher* including that of Max Weber.[28] With his signature on the Delbrück address, Weber for the first time publicly joined the war aims debate. We do not know the

24. For the background of the Seeberg address, see especially Klaus Schwabe, *Wissenschaft und Kriegsmoral: Die deutschen Hochschullehrer und die politischen Grundfragen des Ersten Weltkrieges* (Göttingen, 1969), pp. 70 f.; and Fischer, *Griff nach der Weltmacht*, pp. 198 ff.

25. This general description is based upon the numerous memoranda in the former Preussische Geheime Staatsarchiv, now DZA II, also in the former Reichsarchiv, now DZA I, RKA II, Kriegsakten 15 (2442–2247/2), 17 vols. The Class memorandum in the Beseler papers; also Fritz Fischer, *Griff nach der Weltmacht*, pp. 109 ff. (cf. note 16 above), along with Hans W. Gatzke, *Germany's Drive to the West* (Baltimore, 1950), pp. 40 ff. The literature that has appeared since on this question is extensive but does not necessitate a material change in the above text.

26. Not Bernhard of the *Vossische Zeitung*, as Fischer (*Griff nach der Weltmacht*, p. 201) incorrectly reports.

27. Text of the declaration in the *Preussische Jahrbücher* 169:306 f.; cf. Gatzke, *Germany's Drive to the West*, pp. 132 f.

28. *Preussische Jahrbücher* 162:165 f.

background for this action; Delbrück's efforts, however, since they were originally designed to support the government, were entirely in keeping with Weber's thinking. Weber regarded extensive annexations, at least in the west, as a great mistake. He viewed demagogic attacks on the government over this issue as very dangerous. He most certainly was anxious to ensure that the totally unrealistic demands announced by men like Reinhold Seeberg and Dietrich Schäfer did not appear to represent the opinions of the entire German scholarly community.

Max Weber's signature under the statement did not in itself mean that much. By no means were all of the signers consistently anti-annexationist. Wolff's statement was vague enough to permit various interpretations. In fact, the majority were in favor of the expansion of German power on the continent, but they wanted this to occur without compromising Germany's character as a national state.[29] They were united on only one point: opposition to the annexation of all of Belgium. Indeed, the high point of German military victories in the fall of 1915 had awakened expansionist hopes even in consistently left-wing liberal circles. Even Naumann, who was so close to Weber, opposed the restoration of the Belgian state. He favored transferring the Flemish regions to an enlarged Holland that would be economically tied to Germany and the division of the Walloon regions between Luxembourg and France in compensation for French territorial cessions to the Reich.[30] This probably explains the fact that Weber's attempt to invite a group of leading members of parliament to a "confidential conference" in Heidelberg early in July 1915 for the purpose of creating a political pressure troop "*against* the annexations" (especially Belgium) was apparently unsuccessful. It is unlikely that Naumann, Eduard David, and Wolfgang Heine, let alone Ernst Bassermann, would have accepted Weber's invitation at this time, although we only have clear information about Conrad Haussmann.[31] Bassermann was then very much an annexationist and was an unlikely candidate for participation in a revived bloc from "Bassermann to Bebel," or from "Bassermann to Scheidemann," so to speak, even if limited to the Belgian question. Max Weber probably underestimated the difficulties that stood in the way of the adoption of his views on war aims at that time. Nevertheless, his open-mindedness in including the Social Democrats in his plans was remarkable, although he preferred to

29. Cf. Delbrücks divergent interpretation, loc. cit.: "For me, the true goal of Germany has always been the freeing and annexation of the Baltic Sea provinces and a large central African colonial empire."

30. Memorandum of November 1915, RKA II, Kriegsakten 15, 2442/10. Since published in Naumann, *Werke*, vol. 4, pp. 446 ff.

31. Conrad Haussmann to Gothein, 24 June 1915, copy in Haussmann papers. The conference must have taken place on 3 and 4 July 1915.

approach only representatives of the party's more nationalist wing. In all probability the conference did not occur. We have no concrete evidence of it.

Max Weber narrowly escaped direct involvement in the machinations of German annexation policy shortly thereafter, in spite of the fact that he had attacked it in principle. Beginning in the early part of 1915, the German governor general of Belgium, General von Bissing, embarked on working for the future annexation of Belgium, though he was not authorized to do so by the imperial government. He assigned a "Political Section" of the Military Administration to this matter in February 1915, circumventing the civil administration of the General Government of Belgium that was responsible to the secretary of state of the Ministry of the Interior. The "Political Section" was charged with the working out of problems connected with annexation. An energetic protest from the secretary of state of the Ministry of the Interior led to the formal subordination of the "Political Section" to the ministry, but this had little effect. Bissing, with the assistance of the "Political Section," began to agitate for annexation. In a lengthy memorandum, which he personally delivered to William II, Bissing spelled out detailed plans for the "incorporation" of Belgium in the Reich. The memorandum noted that there was no such thing as a Belgian nationality; it was merely a myth created by intellectuals. Belgium should be subjected to an imperial governor and permitted limited self-government. For most purposes it should be treated as an integral part of the Reich. Specifically, Bissing proposed that Belgium be incorporated in the German tariff union and that German currency, German social legislation, and German law be extended there. The problems that would result from this union were also discussed, including the serious repercussions these measures would have for the Belgian economy.

The civil government was very much disquieted by Bissing's activities, especially because it feared that its freedom of action on the Belgian question might consequently be severely limited. However, no one dared to oppose Bissing rigorously. Meanwhile, Bissing appointed a brain trust in Brussels to study the problems attendant to the annexation and to prepare proposals to help solve them. Bissing also hoped thereby to propagandize for annexation, since the work of the brain trust could hardly escape public attention. Edgar Jaffé, Max Weber's coeditor on the *Archiv für Sozialwissenschaft und Sozialpolitik*, was involved in the Political Section in Brussels. Dr. Simon of the *Frankfurter Zeitung*, though formally head of an ostensibly neutral press bureau in Brussels, was also actively involved in these matters. Jaffé seems to have been responsible for a Political Section project that sought to "investigate the consequences . . . that the introduction of Reich social legislation would have on the competitive capacity of Belgian industry on the world market." This question would initially be discussed with interested parties in those branches of industry that were directly affected. Subsequently, a "summary report" would evaluate the results and interpret them. Max Weber was selected for the task.[32]

Weber responded lukewarmly to Edgar Jaffé's efforts to bring him to Brussels for this purpose. Although Weber was anxious for political employment, he was quite skeptical from the outset, especially because the project did not seem to be assured. Moreover, he did not wish to leave the Heidelberg infirmary without an official request. He was anxious to avoid any sign of opportunism. "If I receive orders to go to Belgium or am sent for with the consent of the military authorities, I am of course prepared for *everything* and *anything*, provided that I can be useful; but I am not 'applying for' anything."[33]

Nevertheless, in the second week of August 1915, Weber traveled to Brussels to find out on the spot whether he should assume the questionable task.[34] He reported that he was very disillusioned by the situation in

32. Cf. the "Summary of the memoranda submitted on behalf of the General Governor," DZA I, Reichsamt des Innern, no. 19523. Here the following projects among others were proposed:

"Investigation of the consequences for the competitive capacity of Belgian industry in the world market as the result of the introduction of the social legislation of the Reich.	Prof. Max Weber in Heidelberg as general reporter
What would be the anticipated effects for	
a) mining and foundary works	Poensgen
b) iron industry	Borsig, Hinnenthal
c) textile industry	according to Geheimrat Rinkel's proposal, Landshut
d) large chemical industry	Prof. Lepsius, Charlottenburg
e) stone and earth industry (with special attention to cement)	Geheimrat Schott, Herdecke
f) glass and ceramic industry; the financial relations of Belgium with the world market	Vopelius Jaffé, with the inclusion of the work already completed by Dr. H. Schacht, Berlin"

In addition, the written opinions of the "League of Farmers," the "War Committee of German Industry" and other economic interest associations were anticipated.

33. Letter of 9 May 1915 to Edgar Jaffé, *Lebensbild*, p. 543.

34. Cf. the letter to Mina Tobler, 10 August 1915, Archiv Ebnet II, 8: "I am traveling to Brussels tomorrow morning, initially just to see if I . . . *can* participate in a judicious fashion . . . in the work . . . that the government wishes: i.e., if I am enough of an 'expert' for the job. . . . In any case, it is not a long-lasting 'position,' but it involves the preparation of memoranda that then can be completed *here*."

Brussels and by the confusion there.[35] At the same time he was bitterly disappointed that the political position he so anxiously wished for did not seem to be in sight. Although he noticed considerable differences among the officials of the Political Section, the governor general, and the German civil administration in Belgium that must have alerted him to the problems involved, he nevertheless agreed to "complete the memorandum."[36] He did so with reservations, since the memorandum was based on the premise that Belgium would be annexed, an idea that he had rejected in principle.[37] He announced in Brussels that he was opposed to annexation, but found very little understanding for his position there. "All those with academic understanding of the situation speak against annexation. But such views are presently without influence. *Every victory brings us further away from peace, that is the essence of the situation.*"[38]

Fortunately, nothing came of Max Weber's willingness to put his expertise at the service of the archannexationist General von Bissing. The Reich government protested against von Bissing's activities and those of his subordinates. Berlin, unlike Bissing, was not disposed to annex Belgium directly. Instead, the government was looking for a formula that "would permit the economic penetration of Belgium and military use of the coast, fortifications and transportation system in the event of future wars, without assuming the burden of political administration."[39] Moreover, the Reich Chancellery was annoyed about von Bissing's efforts to employ leading business and academic personalities in the study of this question. They argued, quite correctly, that this would only contribute to the agitation against the government's allegedly timid Belgian policy.

35. Letter from Brussels (undated) to Mina Tobler, Archiv Ebnet II, 14: "At first my reflections about doing the job grew more serious for personal and objective reasons. But in spite of this, one listens and considers and arrives at a small—only a small! insight about it." Also Archiv Ebnet II, 15.

36. Cf. the letter of 23 August 1915 to Marianne Weber: "I was in Brussels for two days. . . . I have promised to try to complete this memorandum (have time!); this does not signify any kind of position, nor even the way to a position." Cf. further the letter to Marianne Weber of 24 August partially, and with an incorrect date, in *Lebensbild*, p. 544. At the end, he writes: "There is no position in Belgium for me. . . . There are hundreds who do nothing and devour their wages, and poor beasts of burden that cannot earn enough."

37. Cf. the letter to Marianne Weber of 30 August 1915 (copy in Weber papers) and the letter to his sister Lili Schäfer of 28 September 1915: "My Brussels matter is a dark story, actually more a pretext to go there again in order to see once again the ghostliness of this German rule over that beautiful city, French to the core."

38. Letter of 24 August 1915, somewhat misinterpreted and incorrectly dated in *Lebensbild*, p. 544.

39. Delbrück to von Bissing, 10 October 1915, Reichsamt des Innern, no. 19523, DZA I.

For this reason, the Reich Ministry of the Interior took over the direction of the Bissing project. The task originally assigned to Weber was transferred to the imperial statistical office.[40] Weber, quite innocently, had been first the object and then the victim of two opposing political strategies in the Belgian question. In any event, we can only suspect that, as soon as Weber's opinions had become clearer to him, Bissing would have removed him from the project notwithstanding the advantages accruing from the use of Weber's name. Nonetheless, it is noteworthy that even a man like Max Weber could temporarily be caught in the confusion in the Reich administration over war aims policy.

Weber was considerably irritated by the conversations he had had in Brussels. He wrote to Friedrich Naumann at the time, "I have the impression that the politicians currently in the ascendant lack *perspective* to a very irksome degree."[41] He was even more discomfited by the increasing distance of public opinion from political realities. Weber was in no way, as we have shown, a principled opponent of all annexations. He was rather sympathetic to the view current in Bethmann Hollweg's entourage, represented especially by Kurt Riezler, that Germany's power in central Europe could be secured through indirect rule over the smaller nations surrounding Germany. But he regarded as catastrophic the extreme passion of parties and groups on the right for annexations. In December 1915, he publicly expressed his exasperation over the right's war aims agitation and the countless memoranda coming from that quarter calling for a boundless annexation program. He did so in the two articles "Bismarck's Foreign Policy and the Present," which first appeared in the *Frankfurter Zeitung* and were written with the caution made necessary by the censor. Following Italy's entry into the war on the side of Germany's enemies in May 1915, Weber viewed such extreme programs of annexation as even less justified. In November or early December 1915, he detailed his opinions about Germany's war aims in an article that was probably intended to be published in the *Frankfurter Zeitung* but ended up in his desk drawer, presumably because the censorship restrictions prevented its publication. It was a full-scale exposure of the futility of the agitation for far-reaching war aims carried on in the form of a flood of semiconfidential memoranda.[42] In this article he

40. The president of the royal statistical office to the Reich ministry of the Interior, 7 March 1916, ibid.

41. Letter of 2 November 1915 (dating uncertain) to Friedrich Naumann. Cf. note 15 above.

42. *Pol. Schr.*, pp. 130 ff. The origin of this article, which Marianne Weber later printed as a "memorandum on the war aims controversy," must be related to the correspondence with the editors of the *Frankfurter Zeitung* at the end of 1915 over various war aims problems (letter of 25 December to Dr. Simon; and a no doubt later letter to the editors, *Pol. Schr.*1, pp. 459 f.) Unfortunately the letters were incompletely printed and a search in

attempted to demonstrate the wrongheadedness of German war aims in the west—war aims which, with some variations, were shared by government circles and wide sections of public opinion. He stressed here both the impossibility of inheriting Britain's political position and the lack of realism inherent in any extensive annexation policy in the west.

The article differs from countless others from this period because it predicts the serious long-term effects of annexation propaganda on public opinion. As soon as it became apparent that such unrealistic goals could never be achieved, disillusionment would become widespread and the fighting spirit would dissipate. Weber also pointed out that special social and political interests lay behind the agitation for radical war goals. This prompted him to protest the dominent interpretation of the *Burgfrieden* by the representative commanding generals and the censorship authorities. These groups had one-sidedly permitted free speech to pan-German dreamers and war suppliers.[43] He was all the more angered by the irresponsible annexationist agitation because it reflected not only emotional nationalism but massive self-interest. "The fear of peace" led to the unlimited multiplication of war goals, since these interests were threatened by the impact upon the social and political system of a peace that did not meet the expectations that had been created. A peace of compromise would result in constitutional concessions, especially on the issue of the Prussian three-class suffrage. The economic effects of the war would then force democratization of the political system. Therefore, the Right pressed for annexations. But no matter how extensive such annexations were, they could never compensate for the economic effects of the war. To demand such annexations served only to delay the end of the war and thus to increase incalculably the economic exhaustion that would follow the war.

Using Bismarck as a model, Max Weber demanded a German policy "with a clear view of the possible and of what was politically desirable in the long term." A peace "whose main result was that *Germany's boot stood on everyone's toes in Europe* . . . would mean the end of any constructive German foreign policy in Europe or overseas."[44] The German empire had to pursue a policy during the war that took account of the need for future alliances if the future was not to be lightly gambled away. The Triple Alliance could not be renewed after the war because of Italy's and Romania's behavior.[45] Only the alliance with Austria-Hungary

---

the *papers* for the original was unsuccessful. The article was certainly written before Weber's articles "Bismarcks Aussenpolitik und die Reichsverfassung," which were completed 25 December 1915.

43. *Pol. Schr.*, p. 139.

44. Ibid., p. 127.

45. Weber remarked on the entrance of Romania into the war: "It is not possible to know yet what the entrance of *Romania* means. The army's *quality* is unknown and

mained viable. Therefore, Germany had an unconditional interest in the survival of the dual monarchy.[46] Beyond this, any German diplomatic policy faced the alternative of seeking accommodation and mutuality of interests either in the east or in the west. An alliance with Russia, like the one that Bismarck had consistently worked for based upon the common repression of the Poles, was no longer possible. Russia had adopted a "vainglorious, naked policy of expansion," and could not be expected to agree to a compromise.[47] Russia was the only power that threatened Germany's existence as a national power.[48] Russia was likely to pursue an imperialist course for the foreseeable future, egged on by the land hunger of the Russian peasants, the inclination of the ruling classes to put off solutions to social problems through an expansionist foreign policy, and the imperialist fervor of the prestige-hungry Russian intelligentsia. German foreign policy must always take "Russian *popular imperialism*" into account.[49] It must therefore openly and decisively opt for an anti-Russian policy. Germany must seek "at least genuinely to merit" the Russian intelligentsia's "hatred."[50] West European annexations, especially the annexation, destruction, or even the limitation of the independence of Belgium, however, would turn France and England into mortal enemies of the Reich. In the present situation, the choice for Germany was clear: "*World policy* or a European and especially a west European expansionist policy. Russian enmity is unavoidable. An expansionist policy in the west would unite all of the western powers against us."[51]

Weber therefore viewed western annexations as unthinkable. At the same time, he was sympathetic to arguments that touched on national security. He recommended a solution to the Belgian question "that would not exclude eventual reconciliation with the Belgian people and that would merely assure us guarantees against surprise invasions, *without* [subjecting Belgium to] annexations or similar expropriations." For this reason, he believed a permanent military occupation (practically

untested. The situation is certainly serious, and frivolous talk by people like Schäfer, etc., should end once and for all. . . . Of course, the impact upon the future, as in the case of Italy, is not to be dismissed. We are becoming ever more isolated diplomatically and ever more limited in the choice of our alliances and friendships. This seems to me to have an important political consequence in addition to the uncertain military consequences, and very much narrows the framework of our 'world policy.'" Letter to Helene Weber of 8 September 1916, *Lebensbild*, p. 585. Here following the copy in the Weber papers. Also *Pol. Schr.*, p. 162.

46. *Lebensbild*, p. 585.
47. *Pol. Schr.*, p. 125.
48. Ibid., p. 169.
49. Ibid., p. 164.
50. Ibid., p. 126.
51. Ibid., p. 138.

indeed the annexation) of Luxembourg and of Namur and Lüttich for twenty years as a guarantee of *active* neutrality by the Belgian state toward France in future as well, to be desirable.[52] To be sure, he argued for "only what is *militarily* indispensable, but in no way 'annexations.'"[53] In any case, Weber demanded a peaceful solution to the Flemish question.[54] He was sorry that Bismarck had let the French retain Belfort, but he made no demands on the French now.[55] The problem of Alsace-Lorraine burdened French-German relations sufficiently. Even these objectives Max Weber viewed as "optimal."

Max Weber believed the main objectives of German policy during the war to be in the east. There, too, he rejected the annexation of non-German speaking regions. It was not possible to carry out a "German nationality policy" in the east. Any policy east of the German borders, if it was to be based upon Realpolitik, had to be "*West Slavic* and *not* a national German policy." A policy of Germanization would only serve to antagonize fifteen million Slavs and turn them into mortal enemies of Germany.[56] Weber strongly opposed plans for the resettlement of Courland and its incorporation in the Reich. This would only make Germany "politically" weaker.[57] He wished only to achieve autonomy for the Baltic Germans, according to the principle of individual national development, within the future political union that Courland would join. He did not wish German influence to be used there for any larger purpose.[58]

Instead, Weber favored an approach that would facilitate a complete reorganization of east central Europe in accordance with the nationality principle. Germany should liberate all the small nations from the yoke of greater Russian despotism. Weber hoped for the establishment of a Polish, a Lithuanian, a Latvian, and a Ukrainian national state, each with far-reaching autonomy but associated with the German Reich. The Reich should retain the right to maintain fortifications on the eastern borders of

52. Cf. ibid., p. 137, restoration of the situation prior to 1867 in Luxemburg.

53. Letter to Dr. Simon of 25 December 1915 and to the editors of the *Frankfurter Zeitung* at the end of 1915, *Pol. Schr.* 1, pp. 459 f.

54. *Pol. Schr.*, p. 167, also letter to Naumann of 8 May 1917, *Pol. Schr.* 1, p. 471.

55. *Pol. Schr.*, p. 117.

56. Ibid., p. 170.

57. Letter to Dr. Simon, *Pol. Schr.* 1, p. 460. Cf. letter to Marianne Weber, undated, beginning of February 1916: "This evening I am going to hear an address by Sering about the colonization of Courland [!]—fantasies, as if we were alone in the world." A later letter to the same party of 26 November 1915, *Lebensbild*, pp. 564 f. (misdated there): "Sering is colonizing Courland and Lithuania in his mind—where the people and the money will come from does not trouble him. He also does not ask what Germans should do in these forlorn outposts." Also the letter to Eulenburg of 2 January 1916 (copy in Weber papers): "For purely political-geographical reasons, I hold Sering's colonization plans for Courland to be foolish"; also *Pol. Schr.*, p. 170.

58. Letter to Dr. Simon, *Pol. Schr.* 1, p. 460.

Poland stretching northward from Warsaw. Austria-Hungary should be permitted to have similar privileges to the south. A right to maintain garrisons in Latvia and Lithuania and military railroads would complete the necessary defense measures against Russia. Domestically, Weber envisaged a tariff union with Lithuania, Latvia, and Poland that would tie these states economically to the Reich.[59]

This was scarcely a modest program. It was rather close to Kurt Riezler's concept of a German imperialism "with a European appearance" that sought to further a hegemonic position on the continent largely by indirect means, especially through the establishment of a middle-European tariff and economic union. But Weber's conception was distinct insofar as it emphasized a liberal approach and was oriented primarily to the east. Even with these reservations, it is clear that if the plan had been realized it would have secured a hegemonic position in east central Europe for the Central Powers. Garrison rights in Lithuania and Latvia, military railroads, a ring of fortifications on Poland's eastern borders—all would have subjected these nations to Germany military and diplomatic control and, secondarily to the control of Austria-Hungary. Incorporation in the German (or "Central European") tariff union would also have set narrow limits upon the freedom of these nations' internal policies.[60]

Max Weber later summed up these war aims proposals under the heading: "Search for Security in the West—Cultural Tasks in the East."[61] He was attracted by a kind of reversal of the autonomy proposals that had been supported by the Russian Zemstvo liberals of the 1905 revolution in order to facilitate the participation of the many non-Russian nationalities—especially the Poles—in a liberalized czarist empire. He expected that these plans would protect national autonomy and liberal constitutional bodies in Poland, Latvia, and Lithuania and he believed that these bodies could be persuaded to agree in all honor to joining an alliance against Russia.

Weber's east central European plans were basically similar to those of many liberal imperialists, like Hans Delbrück and Paul Rohrbach. During the war, since expansion of the German overseas empire seemed out of the question, these men focused their interests on the possibility of a policy of expansion in east central Europe.[62] They proposed that Germany become the liberator of the smaller nations in the east and create a new order in eastern Europe characterized by liberal and national state

59. Ibid. Cf. *Pol. Schr.*, p. 124.

60. Cf. below, sec. 2.

61. Outline of a lecture about Germany's world policy situation in Munich of 22 October 1916.

62. Cf. Dehio, "Gedanken über die deutsche Sendung," p. 496.

principles that would act as a buffer against the czarist empire. This would permit Germany to pursue a strong policy throughout the world after the war. At the same time, Germany would have expanded its economic *Lebensraum*. The east European states joining in Germany's new tariff union would offer ample opportunities for capital investment and a promising market for German commerce.[63]

Would this kind of freedom for these small nations have been more than a mere facade? It was doubtful that these states, especially Poland, would permanently put up with Germany's economic and military preponderance. In spite of the bestowal of domestic autonomy upon the east central European states, these policies would finally have led to a kind of east-central European satellite system confronting Russia. Moreover, Max Weber never faced the repercussions for Austria-Hungary if these plans were realized. The very existence of the dual monarchy would have been threatened if the national state principle had become the basis of the reorganization of the northern part of east central Europe. The Galician Poles would of course seek to withdraw from the dual monarchy and join the new Polish state. Weber's considerations never touched on this. His concern centered on the Prussian Poles who would also be attracted by an independent Poland. He had no intention of ceding those areas of Prussia heavily settled by Poles to a newly created Polish state. He hoped to alleviate irredentist longings among Prussian Poles by a long-lasting friendly alliance between Poland and the Reich.

The theses on the war goals question that Max Weber presented in a public meeting in Nuremberg called by the Deutscher National-Ausschuss (German National Committee) on 1 August 1916 took a similar approach.[64] Because this gathering had a quasi-official character and relatively extensive official publicity, Max Weber's statements here took on great importance. He used the occasion to attack Germany's war enemies. He also made it clear that direct annexations in Belgium as well as elsewhere would be detrimental to Germany's future foreign policy requirements. Belgium should be required to give military guarantees "as long as we are certain that Belgium will carry out a genuine policy of neutrality."[65] In the east, Weber pointed to the necessity of creating a free Poland, preferably with in the framework of an "indissoluble, permanent [central European] union of states with a common army, trade policy [and] tariffs."

Weber regarded these goals as an essential component of a peaceful order for all of Europe. The smaller nations of continental Europe would

63. Weber excluded Estonia. See below, note 327.

64. For the details, see below, text at note 178.

65. This and the following citation are from the report of the *Fränkischer Kurier*, 2 August 1916.

be arranged around the German empire as a central core of power. Their sovereignty would appear unquestioned but would practically be limited. Only with such an arrangement could Weber conceive of the preservation of the many national European cultures in an age of growing imperialist rivalry. In this respect, Weber's views about war aims rested upon a cultural and intellectual foundation. The *Fränkische Kurier* reported Weber's statement on this point as follows: "It would be shameful if we lacked the courage to ensure that neither Russian barbarism, English monotony, nor French grandiloquence rule the world. That is why this war is being fought."

Weber returned to this theme in his Munich lecture "Deutschland unter den europäischen Weltmächten" ("Germany's International Position").[66] By this time, Germany's plight in the war had worsened, and Romania's joining the war on the side of the Allied Powers temporarily made the situation look quite serious. Was Weber's program still sensible at a time when a separate peace with Russia seemed attainable, and England seemed as unwilling as ever to compromise? Weber admitted that at the moment a compromise with Russia was a greater possibility; but he continued to maintain that German policy should view Russia as the chief enemy. The "greatest present danger" was represented by England, but the "greatest future danger" was and would remain Russia. For this reason, an agreement with Russia was possible only with "very strong *permanent* guarantees made in the interest of national policy," while guarantees against England could be of a temporary nature, i.e., *only* until an agreement with England had been achieved.[67] Germany had no national interests in Belgium, aside from a peaceful solution to the Flemish question. It had only a "military" interest, namely "securing against a non-neutral policy like that of Greece."[68] Weber hoped to give up the Belgian pawn freely and speedily along with any strategic positions (the occupation of Namur and Lüttich) as soon as an honest and fair

66. At a meeting of the Fortschrittliche Volkspartei in Munich. Georg Hohmann, the leader of the Munich Fortschrittliche Volkspartei, had accomplished the impossible and persuaded Weber for the first time in almost two decades to give a public speech. The outline of this speech has survived. It is published in Appendix II of the German edition of this book. The speech was printed in *Die Hilfe* on 9 November 1916 with the deletion of the discussion about unlimited submarine warfare, now in *Pol. Schr.*, pp. 157 ff. Cf. the report of the *Münchener Neueste Nachrichten* of 28 October 1916, evening ed., printed below, note 170.

67. Following here the outline of the speech discussed, in which the decisive points were very much more sharply formulated; compare the objectively congruous exposition in "Deutschland unter den europäischen Weltmächten," *Pol. Schr.*, pp. 168 ff.

68. Outline. In the older edition of *Pol. Schr.*, we read: "Our interest is a purely political one: Belgium cannot be an attack gate for our enemies." In the third edition, p. 168, reflecting my suggestion at the time, this is now correctly interpreted as "military."

agreement was reached with the western powers, especially England. Of course, this was not an immediate prospect: "Peace remains in the distant future."[69]

Of course, even if Weber's western policy was guided purely by security considerations, especially on the Belgian question, we may well ask whether it still was not too presumptuous.[70] Even on this basis, peace negotiations would never have been possible. As soberly and skeptically as Weber was able to judge the German situation, he could not completely free himself from the idea that it was a mistake to give up positions of strength without real compensation. He did not want to give up the hope that the Belgian "pawn" could be used to exercise diplomatic pressure on the western powers and to pressure the Belgians to make concessions that would ensure the Reich's security. It was therefore possible for Weber to be satisfied with the chancellor's speech of 5 April 1916, which dodged a clear declaration about Belgium with the suggestion that "there existed *no* present prospect for serious peace negotiations."[71] Compared to the position taken by German diplomacy and the attitudes of the great majority of Germany's middle and upper classes, Weber's proposals were unusually clear-sighted. Yet, in spite of his sober appraisal of the Central Powers' overall situation, he too overestimated Germany's opportunities to some degree.

Weber's proposals for eastern Europe were scarcely reconcilable with a separate peace with Russia. Until the early part of 1917, he saw little advantage in pursuing the idea of a separate peace in the east.[72] He was

69. Outline. Weber excised this statement from the speech.

70. In any case, with the exception of Luxemburg.

71. Letter of 7 April 1916, *Lebensbild*, p. 577.

72. Cf. the letter from Berlin of 20 February 1916 to Marianne Weber (copy in Weber papers): "Politically, there is *little* here that awakens trust. . . . Repeatedly, one hears talk of the very doubtful hope of a separate peace with Russia." Weber showed the greatest interest in everything that he was able to discover about separate peace feelers to Russia. He succeeded in gaining partial knowledge of the negotiations that Hugo Stinnes carried on with Joseph von Koyschko in early June 1916 about the possibility of a German-Russian separate peace. Of course, he much overestimated the significance of these negotiations. On 18 August 1916, he wrote to his wife: "The peace negotiations with Russia have collapsed. There was agreement on the land exchanges (Poland to us, east Galicia to Russia.) But they still wanted money (very much!) and ultimately, they did not want to come to agreement *alone*. So the matter got no where." Actually, these negotiations were far less concrete than Weber assumed. (Cf. Stinnes to Zimmermann, 17 June 1916, in Schérer-Grunewald, no. 272, pp. 370 ff.) The Russians did not ask for money. Rather, the German government was prepared if necessary to offer money in unlimited amounts if this would make possible a separate peace. Moreover, the German side broke off contacts. For the peace feelers, see, for details, Fritz Fischer, *Griff nach der Weltmacht*, pp. 187 f.; Gerhard Ritter, *Staatskunst und Kriegshandwerk*, vol. 3, pp. 87 ff.; also Werner Conze, *Polnische Nation und deutsche Politik im Ersten Weltkrieg* (Cologne, Graz, 1958), pp. 78 f., 268 ff.

convinced that "Russian popular imperialism" would persist as long as Russia avoided drastic reforms.[73] For Austria-Hungary he still demanded the "emasculation of Serbia"; for Germany, "an acceptable solution to the Polish question, . . . [i.e.] the association of Poland as an allied but independent state" with a maximum of political autonomy but under the military protection of Germany.[74] Germany had to retain control of the "northeastern border" in its own hands. He did not now emphasize the idea of an eastern fortifications belt, however. Weber stressed that Germany was "in a position to go beyond the demands that Poland itself had made to Russia during the 1905 revolution. The [Polish] nation would have full self-government."[75] In the event of a close political association between Poland and the Reich, Weber was prepared to abandon the idea of a tariff union; a most-favored-nation treaty would suffice. Even without a formal tariff union, German influence over Poland would be sufficiently strong to bind Poland's economy to that of the Reich. He no longer pressed the idea of an independent Latvia and Lithuania attached to the German sphere of influence and the German economy. With the deteriorating war situation, his program for a political reorganization of east central Europe north of the Hapsburg borders concentrated on the proposal for an independent Poland, politically and economically oriented toward the West. Nevertheless, Weber remained faithful, in principle, to the idea that the smaller nations should be played off against Russia. Germany would become the "liberator of the small nations" in the east, "even *when*" they did not themselves wish it.[76]

On the other hand, Weber was prepared to accommodate Russia on important issues. He argued, in particular, that it was not Germany's mission to oppose the Russian drive to the sea. Indeed, the Russians might thereby become rivals of the British in sea power. Weber therefore wanted to assure the Russians free passage through the Dardanelles, as long as Turkey's territorial integrity was protected.[77] He also opposed the separation of Estonia from Russia, and he conceded Riga to the Russians as well because of its importance as an outlet to the sea.[78] He would not have been unhappy if Russian expansionism had been deflected to the southeast; however, he favored the delineation of Russian and Austro-Hungarian spheres of interest in the Balkans on the basis of the treaty of San Stefano, which had been forced upon the Russians.[79] His primary

73. Cf. *Pol. Schr.*, pp. 132, 164.

74. Outline; also *Pol. Schr.*, pp. 172 f.

75. *Pol. Schr.*, p. 173.

76. Ibid., p. 174.

77. Outline: "Dardanelles question (not insoluble)"; cf. letter to Naumann of 12 April 1917, *Pol. Schr.* 1, p. 469, as well as *Pol. Schr.*, pp. 132, 164.

78. See below, note 327; also *Pol. Schr.*, p. 302.

79. Letter to Naumann of 12 April 1917.

concern was to deflect Russian pressure from the Reich even if this meant problems for the Dual Monarchy. He shared Bismarck's opinion that the Balkans were not worth "the bones of a single Pommeranian grenadier."

Max Weber's war aims were both moderate and presumptuous. While his emotions led him to support the expansion of German power, he was able to resist the annexationist fever that had infected such a large part of the German people during the first years of the war. He recognized that an annexationist policy in Europe would make Germany's continental position so precarious that a foreign policy focused on the entire *world* order would become impossible. Germany would then have to limit itself to continuously stifling the glowing sparks of the European powder keg before major crises developed. Weber sought to construct a permanent foundation for the political expansion of the Reich. He wished to see Germany's position based not merely on military might but on a community of interests and neighborly relations. In the east he saw unusual opportunities to achieve this. He insisted that "the most burning question of the peace, the one that will appear increasingly more important, more than all the talk about the importance of Belgium, let alone the patriotic fantasies about the Baltic provinces, the one that makes almost all these questions disappear, the actual survival problem for us, is *Poland*."[80]

2. Poland and Central Europe: Attempts at Political Action

At the end of August 1915, when Weber learned indirectly that as a result of a reorganization of the war hospitals he was under consideration for a new position, he circuitously requested his release.[81] He decided to "'become a private person' for the time being and to wait quietly until something turned up."[82] But he could not bear to be on the sidelines for long, especially when his mental condition was better than it had been for fifteen years. He was anxious to find a position of influence, for his concern about events continued to grow. To be sure, he remained relatively optimistic. "*Who*, a year ago, would have thought that *such* a situation was possible? All of western Russia is occupied, along with Belgium, and the north of France! Bread is as expensive in England as it is here at home!"[83] But he watched with disquiet as Germany's political leadership and not only public opinion responded to military victories by immoderately expanding war aims. Weber viewed a speedy end to the

80. "Die wirtschaftliche Annäherung zwischen dem deutschen Reiche und seinen Verbündeten," ed. Heinrich Herkner for the Verein für Sozialpolitik, *Schriften des Vereins für Sozialpolitik*, vol. 155 (Munich, Leipzig, 1916,) part 3. Discussion in the meeting of the committee in Berlin on 6 April 1916, p. 28. (Hereafter cited as "Annäherung.")

81. Cf. *Lebensbild*, pp. 544 f.

82. Letter of 30 August 1915 to Marianne Weber.

83. Letter of 28 August 1915 to Marianne Weber (copy in Weber papers.)

war without European annexations as necessary in order to protect Germany's future position in the world.

In mid-November 1915, Weber went to Berlin to look for a political position. He hoped to find some job there that would permit him to involve himself in what he considered to be the most pressing issue of the day, the question of Poland. His first foray on the political scene had involved the Polish problem in the Prussian East Elbian provinces, and his interest in Poland had never flagged. Now was the time, it seemed, to apply the insights that he had won from his study of Poland during the Russian revolution to political use. Weber, the one-time "enemy of the Poles," now sought to contribute to effecting a compromise with them. He decided to learn Polish—"if my head is able to do it; I am not sure [it can]."[84] He energetically campaigned, wherever he could, for an honorable arrangement with the Poles. The Poles on their side had to be convinced that their national interests would best be served by cooperation with the Germans.

Weber clearly saw the difficulties that would have to be dealt with. It would not be easy to overcome the traditional dislike of the Poles for the Prussian state, a state that had approved and supported their national suppression for a century, as the foundation stone of a conservative alliance with the czarist empire. It would be equally difficult to dispel the mistrust that had been aroused by three decades of sharply anti-Polish policies in the eastern provinces of Prussia. In contrast to his position of the 1890s, Weber now favored a policy of tolerance and accommodation toward the Prussian Poles. Their cultural autonomy had to be guaranteed. Weber now distanced himself from Prussian settlement policy, which had failed in any case. At the time that he had favored active opposition to Polonization, he had based his position upon the sharply differing cultural levels of the two nationalities. This situation no longer existed.[85] Weber now proposed that the Poles be granted a considerable measure of self-government and that a Polish national representative body be created as soon as possible. As long as this did not occur, Weber hoped to see the *Prussian* Poles involved in the decisive political discussions that touched on the political future of Congress Poland.

In Weber's view, action was essential to remedy the serious economic handicaps that Polish industry and economy had suffered as a result of the loss of the Russian market and trade relationship. He hoped to be able to participate in this effort. But initially there seemed to be little opportunity for him to do so. Bethmann Hollweg's indecisive attitude on the Polish question meant that such matters were treated half-heartedly and

84. Letter to Marianne Weber of 26 November 1915, copy in Weber papers.

85. Cf. both articles in the *Frankfurter Zeitung* of late February 1916; "Deutschlands äussere und Preussens innere Politik," now *Pol. Schr.*, pp. 178 ff.

no one outside the government was invited to take part in them. For this reason, Weber's efforts to find an official position that would enable him to work for a compromise with Poland proved fruitless. In spite of Naumann's support, he found nothing worthy of his talents. To be sure, it was not in his nature "to constantly pester ministers."[86] Weber was disappointed that no one seemed ready to employ him. "One has to be either an ass or an opportunist to be acceptable to the authorities," he wrote to Felix Somary.[87] He contented himself with the study of Indian census reports in the Prussian state library. His study of the sociology of world religions, far removed from present concerns, helped him to overcome his bitterness at being relegated to the sidelines.

Sometime in the early part of December 1915, Weber heard the rumor that plans were afoot to associate Poland with the Austro-Hungarian monarchy as an independent kingdom. This information greatly alarmed him. An Austro-Polish solution to the Polish question was diametrically opposed to his own conception of an independent Poland, associated with the German Reich, as the core of an east central European ring of states opposed to Russia. Without Poland, these plans could not be fulfilled. The Right would demand the annexation of Courland as compensation. Moreover, Weber did not wish to see Austria-Hungary strengthened on the Reich's eastern border. He also feared that this solution would augment the opposition of the Prussian Poles, who would attempt to withdraw from Prussia when they witnessed the unification of Russian Poland and Galicia in an independent kingdom within the Habsburg empire. If a Polish state with close ties to Germany were created, an effective link would be established between the German and the Polish peoples, but an Austro-Polish solution would encourage irredentist tendencies among the Prussian Poles.

In fact, in the summer of 1915, the German government had toyed with the idea of giving in to Vienna's pleas and leaving Congress Poland to the Austrian sphere. To be sure, the German government was concerned that this solution would mean the further reduction of the status of the German element in the Danube monarchy and requested an explanation from the Austrian foreign minister, Count Stefan Burián, as to the Austrian conception of "the eventual union of Congress Poland with the monarchy."[88] In spite of serious reservations, especially on the part of the

86. Letter of 2 December 1915, after the copy in the Weber papers.

87. Letter to Somary (undated), partially in *Lebensbild*, p. 582 ("Would you like ultimately . . . "); copy in Weber papers.

88. Stefan Graf Burián, *Drei Jahre* (Berlin, 1923), p. 68. Following him, Walter Recke, *Die polnische Frage als Problem der europäischen Politik* (Berlin, 1927), pp. 248 f. Further, Conze, *Polnische Nation und deutsche Politik im Ersten Weltkriege*, pp. 80 f., also Ritter, *Staatskunst und Kriegshandwerk*, vol. 3, pp. 130 ff.

military, Bethmann Hollweg viewed the creation of a Polish state within the Danube monarchy comprising Congress Poland and Galicia as the "least unfavorable" solution in the circumstances of the time.[89] However, the Foreign Office pursued the Austro-Polish plans with little enthusiasm and tried to forestall any definitive decision in this matter. Yet the situation offered an opportunity to approach the goal of the creation of a central European union of states. In November 1915, discussions were held in Berlin about strengthening the relationship between the Central Powers, in particular the extension of the present alliance to the economic sphere in the form of a tariff union. The Polish question was not settled; but, seizing on Falekenhayn's initiative, the German representatives made it clear that if the alliance were extended in this way, German reservations about the Austro-Polish solution would lessen.[90] In a memorandum of 13 November 1915, the Austrian government was presented with a detailed program for a tariff union with the goal of "preparing the melding of the entire region in an economic union."[91] At the same time, the Austrians were asked how they planned to ensure the future predominance of the Germanic element within the dual monarchy, not so much as a precondition of a possible Austro-Polish solution, but in the light of the development of a closer alliance with the Reich.

Although the German government avoided taking a definite position on Poland's future and indicated only that Germany expected economic compensation from Austria-Hungary in the framework of the proposed tariff union in return for any claims on Russian Poland, the Austrian side assessed the German move as a trial balloon to find out what price Austria-Hungary was willing to pay for Poland. In Vienna, this appeared to mean that the German government agreed in principle to the attachment of Poland to the Danube monarchy. The German government's concern about German predominence within the Danube monarchy, which Bethmann Hollweg viewed as a precondition to an Austro-Polish solution, seemed to confirm the Austrian interpretation of the German position.[92] This misunderstanding arose from the confusion in the Ger-

89. Cf. Bethmann Hollweg to Falkenhayn, 11 September 1915, in André Schérer and Jacques Grunwald, eds., *L'Allemagne et les problèmes de la paix pendant la première guerre mondiale*, 2 vols. (Paris, 1962, 1966), vol. 1, no. 140, p. 173.

90. See Jagow's note of 14 November 1915 about discussions with Count Burián on 10 and 11 November, in Schérer-Grunwald, vol. 1, no. 167; also Conze, *Polnische Nation*, p. 143. For Falkenhayn, see Conze, *Polnische Nation*, pp. 139 f.

91. Deutsches Promemoria AS 5672, Berlin, of 13 November 1915, according to the note delivered personally by Ambassador Heinrich von Tschirschky on 18 November 1915. Geheim XLVII/ 3–10, Österreichisches Haus-, Hof-, und Staatsarchiv in Vienna, printed in Schérer-Grunwald, vol. 1, no. 165.

92. See the Austrian answer: Attachment to the instruction to Berlin, no. 5317 of 22 November 1915, as well as the accompanying note, ad 5317, of the same day. I owe knowledge of this document to the kind intervention of Professor Gerhard Ritter. He was

man position on the Polish question. Bethmann Hollweg was not prepared to make a final decision although he personally viewed the Austro-Polish solution as the most suitable answer. Moreover, the growing opposition to an Austrian Poland in German public opinion, as well as by the supreme command, prompted him to magnify the conditions for the cession of Poland to the Dual Monarchy.[93]

Max Weber received detailed information about the negotiations and the German memorandum of 16 November 1915 by dint of his relationship with the Austrian political economists consulted by the Austrian government on the economic issues involved in a tariff union. A letter Weber wrote to the Reichstag deputy Georg Gothein, who represented a Silesian district and was especially interested in the future of Poland, almost precisely reflected the Austrian interpretation of the German memorandum:

> *Minister-President* von Stürgkh *informed* two members of the Austrian professoriat (Professor von Philippovich and Wettstein), in an audience, that there is a note from the German government (Foreign Office)—if I am not wrong that of 19 November 1915—that touches on the attachment of Poland to Austria. He did not say that the note contained an "offer." Rather, they concluded from this and another report that it contained an inquiry: Under what economic and military-political conditions and guarantees would the Austro-Hungarian government be prepared to take over Congress Poland? I have heard that there was no answer for several months, but one was expected momentarily (I think within the past few days). (An *oral* answer through the ambassador was planned.) According to the reports I have, the section heads of several Austrian ministries, among them Herr Riedl, who was recently here, as well as *all* of the professors who took part in this meeting, appear assured of *this* highly *questionable* manner of "solving" the Polish question.[94]

Weber was a decided opponent of an Austro-Polish solution. He was therefore very alarmed by these reports. Because of the sources of his

---

able to use the relevent documents in the Haus-, Hof- und Staatsarchiv in Vienna. Details of contents in Gustav Gratz and Richard Schüller, *Die äussere Wirtschaftspolitik Österreich-Ungarns: Die mitteleuropäischen Pläne* (Vienna, 1925), pp. 12 ff. A later statement by von Tschirschky to the Austro-Hungarian Finance Minister Leon von Bilinski, in Recke, *Die polnische Frage*, p. 249, confirms in the Austrian reflection, in which it has come to us, how the Austrians interpreted the German memorandum. Differing on this point, Conze, *Polnische Nation*, p. 145.

93. Conze, *Polnische Nation*, pp. 139 ff.; see especially Bethmann's opinion expressed in Berlin on 13 November 1915, ibid., p. 144, note 24.

94. Gothein papers. Undated, from Charlottenburg, probably mid-April 1916, see below, note 96.

information, he took the German government's intentions to be more serious than they were, and believed that the German government had already decided to give up Poland.[95] He thought this solution "highly questionable" (although, in retrospect, it does not seem to have been the worst solution from the point of view of nationality policy) because he believed that German security required direct control over Poland in the face of the constant Russian threat. In private, he strongly condemned the plan to give Congress Poland to Austria-Hungary;[96] he was discreet in public, however, because of the confidential nature of his information. Weber's eventual position on this question was very characteristic. Although he opposed an Austro-Polish solution in principle, he accepted it on the assumption that it was a foregone conclusion. He would have regarded an attack on the government in this matter in the midst of the war as a terrible breach of national discipline.

It is illustrative of his own flexible approach to policy matters, and the secretive and isolated governing style of the late Wilhelmian Reich, that Weber now came to favor a close economic, military, and political association with Austria-Hungary in order to make the Austro-Polish solution bearable. He did so with the mistaken assumption that he was in agreement with official policy. Weber argued that a closer German-Austrian alliance in the sense of a "central European" policy was necessary as the minimum means of preserving direct German influence on the Polish situation. He also saw it as a long-term means to prevent any twists in Austrian policy with regard to Poland as well as other areas. But he viewed this policy as an uncomfortable response to circumstances only. His opposition to the German government's rumored plans in Poland is quite clear in his article "Bismarck's Foreign Policy and the Present," which appeared in the *Frankfurter Zeitung* on 25 December 1915: "Surely Bismarckian statecraft would have stressed . . . that it was politically and economically unacceptable to surround Silesia with a unified state, no

95. Compare the letter to Dr. Simon of 25 November 1915, *Pol. Schr.*, 1, pp. 459 f.: "The present situation is dangerously compromised" vis-à-vis Austria "if what I have certainly heard is true, that Poland has already been offered to Austria."

96. Something close to this to Joseph Redlich on the occasion of his trip to Vienna, according to Redlich's diary entry of 6 June 1916: "For Weber, the most weighty concern is Poland! He said that the offer that Bethmann made to Burián in November was unknown in Germany—in May [it must have been early April; on 9 April 1916 Weber discovered, apparently from Gothein, who had queried the Foreign Office, that the Austro-Polish plans had been abandoned] e.g., Deputy Gothein had first learned [of the plans] from him, had gone immediately to Zimmermann, who with embarrassment had half confirmed and half denied them. Weber said that if this were discovered in Prussia, Bethmann might be strung up: Silesia, West and East Prussia are bitter enemies of the enclosure of Prussia by an Austrian Greater Poland." *Das politische Tagebuch Joseph Redlichs*, vol. 2, 1915–1919, ed. Fritz Fellner (Graz/Cologne, 1954), pp. 120 f.

matter how friendly this state would be, without the creation of conditions that would permanently exclude any conflicts over economic or political policy."[97]

Hence, Weber became a reluctant spokesman for a central European policy. He did so because he saw it as the only way that Germany could find a solution to the Polish question that would satisfy its Austrian allies. He was opposed to a tariff union with Austria-Hungary for both economic and political reasons. He was impressed by Friedrich Naumann's *Mitteleuropa*, which was widely acclaimed after its publication in the fall of 1915.[98] Yet he did not share Naumann's optimistic, almost utopian enthusiasm for a central European economic union. In November, he wrote to his friend:

> I have read your book with the most intense interest . . . now when I am *beginning* to have a chance to read something. The book is unexcelled as a propaganda piece for the general *idea* precisely since it ignores certain problems. Of these, the most important is this: "Mitteleuropa" means that *we* shall have to pay for *every* stupidity with our blood—and you know it—that will be committed by the thick-headed policies of the Magyars and the Vienna court. The other side can also say: *every* stupidity of "his majesty," every "Krüger dispatch," all of German "world policy"; for these, we (the Austrians, etc.) are mercenaries that will have to fight these battles. This is the most difficult aspect of this problem. *Even* in this war for existence, *how* Vienna diplomacy has continued to err! And *what* a *senseless* policy we ourselves have carried on since 1895. Can we bind this all together so that each part has the feeling: I can live with these stupidities, since the other one is here suffering with me?[99]

It was only with much reluctance that Max Weber eventually agreed to participate in the "*Arbeitsausschuss* (Working committee) für Mitteleuropa" that Naumann formed at the end of 1915 in order to study the

97. *Pol. Schr.*, p. 124.

98. Cf. Henry Cord Meyer, *Mitteleuropa in German Thought and Action* (The Hague, 1955), pp. 197 ff.

99. Letter of November (?) 11, 1915; the letter continues: "Further: *any* tariff association demands: (1) a railroad union of a far-reaching kind (you have said); (2) a *tax* union of a far-reaching kind (i.e., similarity of *tax*-legislation); (3) unification of *social policy legislation*. None of this arises automatically. You know this as well as we do. This should perhaps have been emphasized more strongly." Cf. Weber's statement about Naumann's book in the debate of the committee of the Verein für Sozialpolitik, "Annäherung," p. 33: "Naumann's splendid book, written characteristically with the temperament of a politician, not with the skepticism of a specialist"; p. 34: "Naumann's book has succeeded in creating a store of ideas in ideological circles with which, along with other factors that come to mind, the politicians can work." Also *Pol. Schr.*, p. 171.

basis of a tariff and economic union between the Central Powers.[100] He agreed to do this primarily because of the "danger" of an Austrian Poland on Germany's eastern border.[101] He also hoped, like Friedrich Naumann, to be in a position to advise the Bethmann Hollweg government in its negotiations with Austria-Hungary.

In fact, the plans for the creation of an economically unified Mitteleuropa under German leadership were an important component of German war aims policy. The so-called "September program" of 8 September 1914 focused on the proposal for the creation of a central European tariff and economic union under German leadership—a project that was revived repeatedly if not always with total determination. Kurt Riezler strenuously pushed the plans for Mitteleuropa within the government as an alternative to a boundless annexation policy, the policy favored by parties and groups on the right and by the military establishment. At the beginning of 1915, Falkenhayn had also proposed the creation of a central European bloc in order to confront the allied blockade with something concrete. In 1916 and 1917, Mitteleuropa was the subject of intensive negotiations between the allies in association with plans for the future organization of the Balkans. However, Mitteleuropa plans never reached the stage of concrete policy. At least for Bethmann Hollweg, Mitteleuropa remained only a means to other goals. Government departments issued technical arguments against the realization of a tariff and economic association. Naumann and Weber therefore were on the wrong track when they thought that the German government had already entered into concrete negotiations with Austria-Hungary and that it would be grateful for political support as well as expert economic advice.[102] In truth, the government viewed the Mitteleuropa project positively, but under no circumstances was it then prepared to take any definitive steps to implement it. The government, in its efforts to avoid commitment and keep its hands free, neither supported the work of the Arbeitsausschuss

100. Cf. Meyer, *Mitteleuropa in German Thought and Action*, pp. 230 ff.

101. Cf. Weber's speech in the general debate of the Verein für Sozialpolitik, "Annäherung," p. 33: He joined Naumann's private "Committee for Mitteleuropa," "at first essentially out of political interest in the Polish problem," after he had heard "through the gravevine" of the possibility of an Austro-Polish solution.

102. This also corresponds to the definition of the statement produced by the working committee in its first meeting: "*The goal of the Arbeitsausschuss* is voluntary support for the negotiations of the German Reich goverment about the future political, military, and especially economic relations among the German Reich, Austria-Hungary, Bulgaria, and Turkey. The working committee does not intend to engage in promotional or propagandistic activities but will be a study association with practical goals. It is thereby already distinguished from other associations with similar tendencies." Minutes of the first meeting of the Arbeitsausschuss of 2 February 1916, in Baernreither papers, Österr. Haus-, Hof- und Staatsarchiv.

für Mitteleuropa nor did it hinder it.[103] Friedrich Naumann and Max Weber were angered by the government's duplicitous behavior in this matter. They grew suspicious of Bethmann Hollweg's methods, for the chancellor did not deal honestly with men who wished to serve the government loyally and who agreed with government policy.

In retrospect, Max Weber was justified in his caution toward the Mitteleuropa movement. But Friedrich Naumann's persuasiveness, coupled with Weber's wish to do something useful for the nation, encouraged his decision to put his doubts aside. "Naumann made me promise that I would help out here in a private bureau dealing with the Austrian question," he wrote discretely to his wife from Berlin at the beginning of December.[104] In spite of all his skepticism toward Naumann's plans, he offered aid in winning Franz Eulenburg's cooperation in the Arbeitsausschuss für Mitteleuropa, since Eulenburg knew more about the problems of a German-Austrian economic association than anyone else. Eulenburg had submitted the most worthwhile paper to a study of "the economic approaches between the German Reich and its allies," sponsored by the Verein für Sozialpolitik in the early part of 1915. He had ended up drawing negative conclusions about this prospect.[105] Weber shared Eulenburg's skepticism completely.[106] He tried characteristically

103. Cf. the highly informative letter from Naumann to Weber of 14 January 1916, in the Naumann papers: "It has been a long time since you received new information from the 'Arbeitsausschuss für Mitteleuropa.' The cause of the delay was that the approval of the governmental authorities was very slow in coming, and achieving it was somewhat painful for us. Since then it has now been determined that the Arbeitsausschuss für Mitteleuropa will be constituted to operate in a formally free way and at its own expense, but with continuous contact with the appropriate Reich ministries. Undersecretary of State Richter in the Reich Office of the Interior will assume the central tasks in the negotiations with Austria-Hungary. He wishes regular contact with us . . . " Nauman states here further that Weber should travel to Austria for the committee.

104. Letter of 3 December 1915; copy in Weber papers.

105. See Eulenburg's treatment, "Die Stellung der deutschen Industrie zum wirtschaftlichen Zweibund," in "Annäherung," pt. 2, pp. 3 ff.

106. Cf. Weber's letter to Eulenburg of 28 December 1915 (copy in Weber papers): "I have read your article (*Schriften des Vereins für Sozialpolitik*) with pleasure and agreement. It is by far the most useful thing that has yet been written against utopianism. *Either* complete *tariff* union with a tariff parliament *per procura* (which will not be done)—or that modest policy, which you have best justified until now. . . . I am in full agreement with you about this: that, next to *tariff rate*–union (and we ought to aim above all, in my opinion, for long-term stability of rates as a precondition for everything else, no matter how high the rates are), *administrative* preferences are important. [This means] common, equal participation in state and other concessions, common tariff jurisdiction, common merchandise lists and types of specialization, if possible: currency exchange determinations according to strict rules (in spite of the difficulty, the changing exchange notations must be a basis, or else the results will be disagreeable!). The same manner of expediting, a freight car cartel (*enduring*), railroad rate agreement, common patents, etc., and *then* the conditions for that

to enlist Eulenburg in this work because the expected association of Poland with the Danube monarchy made the economic association of the Central Powers necessary:

> At the present time, *Poland* is the central problem. It appears that the foreign office has *already offered* Congress Poland to the Austrians with the question: Under what conditions is Austria ready to accept it? This very dangerous political situation (Upper Silesia!) poses the question: . . . what are our relations with Austria-Hungary then to be? It is clear that for good or evil we cannot then avoid *very close and strong* economic ties and a customs union. . . . I believe it tactically prudent, despite my skepticism, to collaborate with Naumann, [Ernst] Jäckh, and [Felix] Somary with the belief that "something will come out of it"—perhaps something *completely* different and much more modest than what these men might wish—in order to prevent these very capable people from joining forces with the visionaries.[107]

Even in the event that Poland was not given up to Austria, but transformed into a joint "protectorate" of the Central Powers, Max Weber thought a far-reaching economic alliance between the Central Powers unavoidable. "It may become necesssary *quand même* to enter into some kind of close association (with Poland as a third party!) at the cost of all economic rationality, if Poland becomes a joint 'protectorate.'"[108] For Weber this was better than two other possible solutions to the Polish question. He viewed an annexation of Poland by either Austria or Prussia as an extreme misfortune.[109] A partition between the two states would be a great mistake. The political capital earned by freeing Poland from the Great Russians would thereby be completely forfeited. The division of Poland would "turn the Poles into mortal enemies of Germany because we would then become the Poles' only

---

preference of the highest degree will only be conceded in exchange for equal concessions by a third party. Also [tariff preference] will only be conceded [to others] when, by treaty in behalf of the international law of war, the present practice of confiscation is *eliminated* and forced 'inspection' of the enterprises of the enemy at home is entrusted to neutral officials (*directed* against England.) Personally, in spite of all of the highly justified considerations, which you have formulated better than anyone, I see the idea of propaganda for 'association' even in the form of 'preference' as attractive *at this time* and only at this time. It offers an effective opportunity to oppose the totally insane plan of achieving autarky in food supply by conquests in the northeast (the Baltic provinces). The reference to increasing the agricultural capacity of Hungary [offers an alternative]." Cf. also "Annäherung," p. 28.

107. Weber to Eulenburg, 28 December 1915, partially printed in *Lebensbild*, pp. 565 f.

108. Letter to Eulenburg of 2 January 1916 (according to the copy in the Weber papers).

109. Letter of 28 December: "If incorporation in Austria is not to be considered, and incorporation in Prussia even less so (free movement of those Jews across our borders!), then we ought to discuss the correct tariff policy toward Poland, should it become a 'protectorate' of both powers."

possible scapegoat."[110] Weber's goal was the precise opposite of this: to win the Poles as political, military, and economic allies of Germany by seeking their friendship. Austria's demands, however, seemed to block what he viewed as the best course.

Weber returned to Heidelberg at Christmas in 1915 without having found the political office he sought. He consoled himself with the thought that nothing positive could be achieved at the time, a view he shared with Naumann and Dernburg: "Dernburg has put it well: 'Where there is nothing to be done, we should not waste our energies!' And he is correct."[111] Weber remained in Heidelberg throughout January although Naumann had asked him to go to Austria for the Arbeitsausschuss to make contacts and look into the situation. Naumann was able to persuade him to return to Berlin in February to participate in the work of the Arbeitsausschuss, although, after four months of "Hinduism," questions of trade policy were not at the top of his mind.[112] He was only really interested in the political side of the Mitteleuropa question, and only insofar as it touched on the question of Poland.[113] He was still extremely skeptical about the practical results of the committee's work. "We will have to see if anything comes of this matter in spite of everything."[114]

Finally, Weber began to warm to the project. He took part in the second meeting of the Arbeitsausschuss für Mitteleuropa on 28 February 1916 in Berlin and urged an "investigation of the economic and financial situation in Poland," a theme that had not yet been studied by the Verein für Sozialpolitik. Weber dedicated himself to this problem with great energy and interest. He apparently tried at the time to win official support for an investigation of the problems that would accompany the inclusion of Poland in the German or the central European economic sphere, but this failed entirely.[115] The Arbeitsausschuss therefore appeared as a

110. Letter of 2 January 1916; cf. *Pol. Schr.*, p. 302.

111. Letter of 26 November (?), 1915 to Marianne Weber (according to the copy in the Weber papers.)

112. Letter of 17 February 1916 to Marianne Weber (according to the copy in the Weber papers); cf. the letter to Naumann of 7 February 1916, *Pol. Schr.*1, pp. 460 f.

113. Cf. the letter to Gothein, above, note 94. "My trip here and my interest in the tariff union is due above all to this information" (over the so-called German offer to Austria regarding Poland).

114. Letter from Charlottenburg, 17 February 1916, to Marianne Weber: "Yesterday morning, a meeting at Naumann's, after the conversation the day before yesterday. The matter is now in flux. Tuesday (23 February 1916) there is an 'organizing' assembly: the various big industries, the mayor, party members, etc. want to come; the Reich officials will be informed. If now . . ." Cf. letter of 20 February 1916: "Yesterday, at Naumann's again. Tuesday is the organizing meeting with the large industrialists, agrarians, shipping people. If afterwards anything ordinary [sic] comes of this, no one can know."

115. Compare the letter to Adolf von Harnack, undated, mid-February 1916 (Harnack papers, Deutsche Staatsbibliothek, Berlin): "I am in part involved with the Indian materials in your library here. There is surprisingly much here about German conditions—after the

substitute basis for this project. He planned to direct an investigation of the economic and financial relations of Congress Poland and of the entire Polish-speaking region.[116] In order to make association with Germany palatable for the Poles, it was necessary to discover those measures most likely to ameliorate the consequences of cutting Polish industry off from its Russian hinterland. To this end Weber attempted, with Somary's help, to make contacts with Polish economic circles.[117] Weber planned to send Eulenburg to Poland as a representative of the Arbeitsausschuss in order to collect information and to speak with industrial and economic leaders on the spot.[118] The Arbeitsausschuss was also still eager to cooperate with the government. Max Weber and Baron Albert von Rechenberg therefore made a direct approach to the Ministry of the Interior in March. The ministry proved especially interested in an investigation of the difficult monetary problems attendant to Poland's incorporation in the economic sphere of influence of the Central Powers. Nevertheless, the ministry was not prepared to support the project.[119] Weber knew that such an effort would be fruitless without official support. He therefore attempted to remove the danger of "latent official resistance—which would prove a great hindrance in an area under occupation!"[120] The respective negotiations with the government, however, failed completely.[121]

---

completion of military employment I would like to try, *if* it is possible, to involve myself in (private) preliminary work and reflections about the future of the relationship to Austria. The great mental confusion and the many highly careless measures and statements make the business a thankless one. Under the circumstances, I have given up seeking any *official* employment (in the east). Everything there is in safe hands. And the authorities have all too many 'advisers.' The path of thoughtful private preparatory work remains the only one."

116. Compare the minutes of the second meeting of the Arbeitsausschuss für Mitteleuropa on 28 February 1916 in the Baernreither papers; also Meyer, *Mitteleuropa in German Thought and Action*, p. 230. On the question of Weber's influence on Naumann on the Polish question, cf. Meyer, pp. 268 f. Nevertheless, Naumann went far beyond Weber's pessimistic program. See Naumann, *Was wird aus Polen?* (March 1917).

117. Cf. the undated letter to Marianne Weber in *Lebensbild*, p. 566, probably early March 1916.

118. Cf. Weber's speech in the general debate of the Verein für Sozialpolitik, "Annäherung," p. 34.

119. Cf. Rechenberg's report, Schiffer papers, 50, pp. 177–83.

120. Letter to Eulenburg of 4 March 1916 (copy in Weber papers).

121. Cf. the letter to Eulenburg of 9 March 1916, partially printed in *Lebensbild*, pp. 566 f., with a false date, errors (instead of "Polish" it refers to "political" matters), and distorted. The final sentence there: "This entire Berlin atmosphere . . ." belongs to another letter, probably to Marianne Weber—a striking example of the amalgamation of letters, unfortunately appearing so often in *Lebensbild*, without attention to dates. "Yesterday, I forced an interview with Undersecretary of State [Richter] on the question of whether someone would travel to Poland for the agreed-upon goal or even if it would be possible to get in touch with Polish industrialists. Failure is certain in this specific case if official circles directly obstruct us. Unfortunately, they are *doing* this, as was clear to me in the thoroughly

Weber believed that the primary reason for the official refusal to support his efforts was fear of competition.[122] He also suspected that the negotiations with Austria had in fact not settled the Polish question, and a private investigation of this problem might therefore be inopportune.[123] He had been informed that "the Foreign Office might have objections," even if this appeared to be a mere pretext. The real reasons for the failure of Weber's efforts were closely related. For some weeks, the German government had been under severe pressure from the General Staff about the Polish question; so they were totally uninterested in further pursuing the Mitteleuropa aspects of the Austro-Polish project. Indeed, the government had now adopted the notion of founding a Polish state closely tied to Germany.[124] The plan for an Austrian Poland was therefore discarded and replaced by the idea of a formally independent Polish state practically dependent on Germany.[125]

At the time, Weber and Naumann learned nothing of this.[126] The government permitted the Arbeitsausschuss to continue its work bliss-

---

annoying exchange, and to be sure this happened in spite of the helping hand I had from a Center deputy of influence and distinction: (1) any negotiations with Poland are unwanted; (2) they will be carried on by government officials; (3) we have no access to official materials. I was given a thousand reasons, *all* of which were pseudo-reasons. In truth, the gentlemen do not want these Polish matters looked into and are afraid of 'competition.' They only requested a technical investigation of Poland's monetary possibilities. I did not conceal the fact that under these circumstances I was doubtful whether I wished to proceed any further in this area. In any event, it unfortunately seems definite that we cannot give or obtain a commission for you regarding Poland."

122. Cf. Weber's letter to Eulenburg of 14 March 1916 (incorrectly dated [14 July instead of 14 March] copy in Weber papers): "In this instance absolutely *no one* is to blame for the sad course of the *Polish* matter outside of Privy Councillor von Schönebeck. . . . That chap is a blockhead and is scared of any competition from intelligent people." It was not possible to determine any more closely who was in question. They may have been, as Weber added, "insignificant" reporters from the Reich Office of the Interior in Poland, of whom he spoke in the letter of 4 April 1916.

123. Letter of 9 March 1916: "'The Foreign Office will raise objections.' If that is so and there is no pretense—then the matter will be rather difficult in the negotiations with Austria."

124. Cf. Ritter, *Staatskunst und Kriegshandwerk*, vol. 3, p. 138.

125. Cf. Conze, *Polnische Nation*, pp. 145 f.

126. If Weber and Naumann acted upon false premises, this was only typical of the domestic political situation in Germany of the time. He grounded his efforts to support *his* government on the basis of information he received from others. The government simply let efforts like those of Weber and Naumann run their course without making an attempt to direct them. In this case, there was no attempt either to inform them properly or to tell them their efforts were inopportune. Government policy and the activities of political and parliamentary circles proceeded in complete isolation. It is no wonder that Bethmann Hollweg soon lost control over the discussion of war aims instead of bending public opinion in favor of his policy. Cf. my "Die Regierung Bethmann Hollweg und die öffentliche Meinung," pp. 135 ff.

fully instead of informing them that the situation had changed. The third meeting of the committee, which Max Weber chaired, was still dedicated to the discussion of the Mitteleuropa aspects of an Austro-Polish solution, although by this point the chances for such a solution were as good as dead.[127] In the general debate of the Central Committee of the Verein für Sozialpolitik on the "economic association between the German Reich and its allies," at the meeting on 6 April 1916 in Berlin, Weber vigorously supported the continuation of the study of a German-Austrian tariff union. He did so because "compelling *political* circumstances"—namely the creation of an Austrian Poland—would make a tariff union necessary, although all economic arguments spoke against it. Even in the event that all that was planned was "some kind of allied community of interest in Poland, along with the greatest possible protection of Polish autonomy," especially "a permanent common influence over Polish trade and export policy—and otherwise as small a condominium as possible," a tariff and economic union between the two powers was necessary in order to ensure common action.[128] It would be greatly preferable in Weber's view, however, if "Poland were simply tied to the German tariff area" since this was "the most secure [route] and the best economic [course] for Poland [and Germany]."[129] This solution was in harmony with his overall plans for east central Europe. He had continued to champion his plan for a simple association of a domestically autonomous Polish state with the German Reich in opposition to Austrian aspirations. In his Munich speech of October 1916, he demanded that Austria-Hungary permit Poland to be treated in a way that would accord with "Germany's vital interests" as a test of Austria's loyalty to the alliance. Germany ought not to permit a "Serbia" at its gates as a result of the war, a Serbia which, because of its strategic importance, could manipulate the Dual Monarchy's relationship with Germany.[130]

Instead of a Mitteleuropa, Weber hoped to create a German economic and political sphere in east central Europe without burdening Germany with the problems of the multinational Hapsburg empire. Poland would be permitted far-reaching autonomy in domestic matters, while at the same time becoming the core of the German sphere of influence in the

127. Minutes of the third meeting of the Arbeitsausschuss für Mitteleuropa, in Schiffer papers. On 21 June 1916, Friedrich Naumann decided on a *démarche* with the Reich chancellor: It was "only expeditious to negotiate about the middle-European treaty situation" if the Polish question was still unsettled. Nevertheless, Bethmann Hollweg did not clarify the true situation for him even now. The chancellor's relevant memo for the files is characteristic: "I asked Naumann temporarily to treat the matter in a dilatory manner." Weltkrieg 180 geh. vol. 3, Politisches Archiv des Auswärtigen Amtes, Bonn.

128. "Annäherung," pp. 28 ff.

129. Ibid., p. 31.

130. *Pol. Schr.*, pp. 172 f.

east. It would be economically, internationally, and militarily dependent upon the Reich. This solution had much appeal from the political and strategic point of view. But was it realistic for Weber to hope, in the light of his own observations at the time of the 1905 revolution in Russia, for the voluntary cooperation of the Poles in this grandiose scheme?[131] Was the Poles' rejection of czarism and greater Russian oppression really strong enough to encourage them to accept German protection and extensive German military and economic privileges along with it? Weber's goals in this area bordered on the utopian, even if he was correct in his belief that only a liberal Polish policy could assure a peaceful solution to the situation in the east.

Immediately after the debate at the meeting of the Verein für Sozialpolitik, Weber no doubt received the news from Georg Gothein that "Poland would not be given up to Austria."[132] Weber had told Gothein about Bethmann's Austro-Polish views, and Gothein subsequently had made a call at the Foreign Office. This almost ended Weber's interest in Mitteleuropa. For secondary political reasons, he believed these plans ought to be pursued, in spite of his economic reservations, for the sake of achieving some indirect permanent influence over Austria. He wrote in this vein to Eulenburg: "We cannot openly state the real intentions: the 'pénétration pacifique' of Austria by German capital in order to prevent a connection with the English and French, who would otherwise try to enter."[133] Second, so that the Central Powers can have "the card of 'Central European tariff union'" ready before the coming peace negotiations, in order to play it there if necessary.[134]

Weber therefore continued to support Naumann's and Somary's efforts although he now withdrew from active work with the Arbeitsausschuss and returned to Heidelberg.[135] In May 1916, he traveled to Vienna and Budapest on behalf of the Arbeitsausschuss to make contact with

131. Of course, Weber said in the general debate, "Annäherung," p. 30: "It is difficult to arrive at a smooth solution to the Polish question that will satisfy all interests, above all security for Germany's eastern borders, and at the same time is acceptable to the Poles."

132. Letter to Marianne Weber of 9 April 1916: "Politically, there is nothing new, except that Poland will not be given to Austria (information from the Foreign Office), at least not those areas that we occupy. This lessens the necessity of a tariff union." After a copy in the Weber papers. Cf. above, note 96.

133. Letter to Eulenburg of 14 March 1916, copy in Weber papers.

134. "Annäherung," p. 33.

135. Cf. the letter to Somary, undated, probably mid-April 1916 (see above, note 87): "I am going to *Heidelberg* tomorrow and will remain there. I cannot refrain from saying how much pleasure it has given me to know you better. You were really the only happy thing here. Otherwise I would have been out of place, since I am only interested in the political aspects and I lack the necessary personal and industrial knowledge in the area of trade policy."

Austrian business representatives and political economists. He did not find much there to encourage future Mitteleuropa plans. Although Austrian military successes on the Italian front[136] led him to judge the situation in a somewhat more optimistic light, he could not avoid seeing Austria's difficult political and economic plight.[137] He did not delude himself now about the difficulties of realizing the Mitteleuropa project.[138] Both dynasties' ambitions seemed an almost insuperable barrier in themselves to any far-reaching association between the two empires. He also viewed Hungary as an "absolute barrier," especially as long as Count Tisza remained in power.[139] Weber viewed Naumann's hope for the expansion of the Central European tariff union beyond the narrow sphere of power of the Central Powers (Germany, Austria, Poland, and eventually the Balkan states), as totally illusory. "One middle-sized German city" could live, he argued, on all the "profits to be made" in Turkey.[140]

After April 1916, Bethmann Hollweg openly supported the principle of Polish autonomy, though in close association with the Reich. Max Weber's Austro-Polish fears were thereby laid to rest. However, he was not happy with the course of events. Weber's desire to conciliate the Poles was undermined by the Reich leadership's ambiguous treatment of the Polish problem due to caution in the face of public opinion, the wishes of the Austrians, and the military view held by the Supreme Command. Weber's goals were totally dashed by the hasty proclamation of the kingdom of Poland on 5 November 1916. This action was dictated by Ludendorff's demands for Polish divisions to relieve the German army's

136. Letter to Marianne Weber of 26 May 1916: The mood is splendid . . . "the Austrians will stick it out." Also the letter of 29 May and, still more optimistic, that of 5 June 1916. *Lebensbild*, pp. 582 f.

137. See also Joseph Redlichs, *Das politische Tagebuch*, vol. 2, *1915–1919*, p. 183: "On Sunday Max Weber from Heidelberg spent two hours with me: he is the first German politician to visit me who has realistic insight. He said to me: I see here and in Budapest that the war has not ameliorated Austria-Hungary's internal difficulties but, rather, multiplied them."

138. Letter to Naumann of 22 June 1916, Naumann papers 42/43: "I shall prepare a short memorandum for Zimmermann about my observations in Vienna and Budapest and shall send you a copy. I thought of it [i.e., the trip to Vienna and Budapest] as a private trip. . . . 'Mitteleuropa' will now not materialize—the source, Schiller [sic; he must mean Schüller], the negotiator. But a trade treaty of that nature, which is the apparent aim of Mitteleuropa, is (as the result of future development, Austria's finances, Poland's finances, etc.) finally—perhaps—unprofitable economically. The circumstances would afflict its creation."

139. Cf. letter to Schulze-Gävernitz of 21 October 1916, *Pol. Schr.*, 1, p. 465. Weber viewed Tisza as one of the sharpest opponents of the kind of Polish solution he hoped for. When, in 1918, Tisza spoke in a different vein, Weber was very pleased. Cf. letter to L. M. Hartmann, 28 June 1918 (?).

140. Letter to Eulenburg of 14 March 1916 (my emphasis.)

manpower reserves. Weber was probably too optimistic about the possibility that Germany could win Poland over through a guarantee of domestic autonomy and free constitutional instutions, and could ensure future cooperation between the two nations in a way that would serve Poland's own political interests. This possibility had now been undone by a policy that perpetuated the occupying regime behind the facade of a Polish kingdom existing by the grace of the Central Powers, without any real participation by the Polish people. Instead of gradually conceding control of their own affairs to the Poles, Germany had created a Polish state lacking the political institutions that would have made responsible political cooperation by the Poles possible. The Poles, to be sure, recognized that the Central Powers were primarily interested in Polish soldiers and had postponed the question of Polish autonomy to the distant future. The political capital that might have been earned by a policy of decisive advancement of Polish independence, within the limits permitted by military necessities, had now been lost.

"The generals botched up the Polish situation," Weber later wrote to Eulenburg.[141] As a result of the events in Poland, Weber decided to withdraw from participation in the Arbeitsausschuss für Mitteleuropa. After this, he was reserved about the idea of a closer link between the German Reich and Austria-Hungary. Yet even by the end of June 1917, he thought Germany had no other choice but "to continue to pursue the idea and to attempt to achieve what is necessary (military convention, trade treaty, legal uniformity) . . ., given the universal Russian hatred" of Germany. But as an economic union, "Mitteleuropa was finished."[142]

3. "U-Boat Demogoguery" and Bethmann Hollweg's Chancellorship

At the beginning of 1916, the danger of the United States entry into the war surfaced. The exchange of notes between Germany and the United States, provoked by the sinking of the Lusitania in May 1915, became increasingly heated. A break with the United States seemed an immediate possibility. Max Weber was very worried and wrote to Friedrich Naumann, early in February 1916, that the Wilhelmstrasse had "to settle the issue with America at *any cost—at any*," or else all would have been in

141. Letter of 23 June 1917, copy in Weber papers; cf. letter to H. Ehrenberg of 16 July 1917 at the time of Bethmann's fall, incompletely in *Pol. Schr.*, 1, pp. 469 f. Hindenburg and Ludendorff, "who are interfering with all policy although they understand *absolutely nothing* about it—brilliant army leaders that they are (note the total bungling of the Polish question, our real survival question, Ludendorff's fault alone)." Completed according to the original in the Weber papers.

142. Letter to Eulenburg of 23 June 1917, copy in Weber papers.

vain.[143] He clearly saw that the entrance of the United States into the war, if it did not bring defeat, would, at the least, prolong the war for two more years and cause Germany's complete economic ruin.

Max Weber urged that Germany give in completely without any attempt to salvage its prestige. But the opposite occurred. On 29 February 1916, because of Tirpitz's pressure, Germany delared a stepped-up, although not an unrestricted, U-boat warfare. Enemy trading ships would be spared only in exceptional cases, and all armed trading ships would be sunk without prior warning. It was hoped that this submarine war policy would not lead America to take more serious action, since U-boat commanders were strictly forbidden from attacking passenger ships without warning whether or not they were armed. Lansing himself had judged it "understandable," in his memorandum of 18 January 1916, that armed merchant ships should be viewed as auxiliary military craft and treated as such.[144]

Nevertheless, the Admiralty and the Naval Command called for more. They demanded unrestricted U-boat warfare even at the risk of an American entrance into the war. Weber followed developments with growing concern. He recognized clearly that the Naval Command would insist upon the ruthless use of submarines.[145] When, at the end of February, a decision about the future form of submarine warfare seemed to be in the offing, Max Weber used all his influential political contacts to warn about the results of a break with the United States. He had the feeling "of sitting on a volcano."[146] He did not then realize that the issue was not just the continuation of a "sharpened" submarine war, but the escalation into an "*unconditional*" U-boat war, the great card that the Admiralty staff and the Reichsmarineamt promised would destroy England within six months and that they now wanted to play.[147] Max Weber was only aware

143. Letter of 7 February 1916, *Pol. Schr.* 1, pp. 460 f.

144. Cf. Arno Spindler, *Der Handelskrieg mit U-Booten*, vol. 3; in: *Der Krieg zur See, 1914–18*, ed. Reichsmarinearchiv, 1934, pp. 86 ff., p. 132.

145. "If only the insane pan-Germans and the Reich naval people do not get us into trouble with America!" Weber wrote on 23 February from Berlin: "The result will be, first, that our half merchant fleet—a quarter in American, a quarter in Italian ports!—will be confiscated and employed against us, so that we will have an immediate multiplication of the number of English ships. Those asses do not take this into account. Second, we shall encounter five hundred thousand splendidly armed American sportsmen as volunteers against our tired troops—which those asses refuse to believe; third, 40 billion marks of ready money for the enemy; fourth, three more years of war and therefore certain ruin; fifth, Romania, Greece, etc., against us; and all of this so that Herr Tirpitz 'can prove what he can do.' Such imbecility has never before been devised." *Lebensbild*, p. 571. Here according to the copy in the Weber papers.

146. Letter to Marianne Weber of 11 March 1916, falsely dated 6 or 13 March, cited in *Lebensbild*, pp. 573 f. Copy in Weber papers.

147. Primarily on the basis of what consequently appeared to be an unbelievably superficial memorandum by the Banker Fuss of the Berlin Disconto-Bank, "Die englishche

of the Right's agitation aimed at pressuring the chancellor to permit the ruthless use of submarines. He was deeply disturbed when the government seemed to waver between the agitation of the supporters of unrestricted submarine warfare and pressure from the Reichsmarineamt on the one hand, and the pressing logic of the international consequences of unrestricted submarine warfare on the other.

Weber was especially worried by the sudden swing in opinion in high quarters on the submarine question, fueled by no new objective information but purely the result of psychological pressure aroused by "alarmist" agitation. He sensed that the U-boat war was seen as the final trump card, and if it did not achieve what it was supposed to, there would be no further cards to play. For Weber, the consequent domestic crisis would be far worse than the dangers brought about by unlimited submarine warfare. This judgment was indeed correct. Some of the navy's public supporters were steering in the direction of open catastrophe. They demanded an unrestricted submarine war because, they argued, it was "now fully clear" that Wilson and Lansing wanted to force America into the war anyway. The possibility of a break with America had to be faced; it would not really worsen Germany's situation.[148] Weber sharply attacked such views. He noted that "the few sensible people here *know* that the war will be lost if we go ahead [with unrestricted submarine warfare]. It will be lost financially because our war loans will no longer be underwritten. It will be lost economically because we still receive substantial amounts of raw materials from abroad, and they will no longer be available to us. . . . It is enough to drive one mad."[149] On one "exciting night,"[150] probably 8 or 9 March, and presumably with the assistance of Felix Somary, Weber composed a memorandum about the impact on the German situation of a stepped-up U-boat war.[151] The memorandum used

---

Wirtschaft und der U-Boot-Krieg, bearbeitet vom Admiralstab der Marine." See, in this connection, note 148 below; cf. also Hellferich, *Der Weltkrieg*, vol. 2, pp. 335 f. and Spindler, *Der Handelskrieg mit U-Booten*, vol. 3, pp. 71 f., 93.

148. Here I am citing Eduard Meyer's memorandum of 16 March 1916 on unrestricted submarine warfare, forwarded to the imperial chancellor. It was left to Meyer to make the Reich Chancellery aware that the strictly confidential memorandum of the Admiralty of 12 February 1916 that he cited had been circulating in Berlin academic circles. He attached an excerpt from the memorandum to his own memorandum. Documents of the RKA II, 2 Kriegsakten 51, 2410, DZA I. Excerpts from the Admiralty's memorandum are included even there.

149. Letter of 5 March 1916 to Marianne Weber, *Lebensbild*, p. 572.

150. Marianne Weber, *Lebenserinnerungen* (Bremen, 1948), p. 162.

151. The particulars arise from the following considerations: the memorandum is first mentioned in a letter of 11 March 1916, partially printed in *Lebensbild*, pp. 573 f. (with the false date of the 6th or the 13th): "Tomorrow, I am sending a memorandum about America to the party leaders [in *Lebensbild* slightly distorted]. The Foreign Office, to which I sent it previously, wrote circuitously (through a messenger) that I could send it on." Cf. in this connection the letter to Eulenburg (copy in Weber papers) of 14 March 1916: "Also, on this

economic arguments to demonstrate the hollowness of the expectations associated with this action. America's entrance into the war on the side of the allies would mean, in the event that England was not forced to capitulate quickly, the lengthening of the war by several years. England's early capitulation, however, was very unlikely for a variety of reasons. If America gave its complete economic support to the allies, the Germans would lose the war economically no matter how many military victories they won and whatever the conditions of the peace might be. Germany would then have "forfeited its future as a world power indefinitely." In view of the serious consequences of the expansion of submarine warfare, Weber demanded that those who called for this step be called to account.[152]

Weber sent this memorandum to the foreign secretary on 10 March, along with a respectful letter in which he explained that his occasionally critical tone toward the government was due to the goal of the memorandum. That goal was "purely and simply to counter the pressures of so-called 'public opinion' (i.e., the opinion of some of the members of parliament and other circles) since this had in some instances reached a hysterical pitch."[153] Undersecretary Zimmermann, who took charge of this matter, was very impressed and advised Weber to convey the memorandum "to as many of the firebrands as possible, and especially to Professor Eduard Meyer, who are trying to turn public opinion against our position!" Bethmann Hollweg and Count Maximilian Montgelas also read the memorandum attentively.[154] On 12 March Weber sent it on to the party leaders and a great number of other influential personalities. He assured them, characteristically, that the memorandum had been written without the Foreign Office's encouragement and that he was sending it "in complete sincerity . . . and without any interference by the Foreign

---

day I sent a memorandum to the party leaders and the Foreign Office about it." This evidence indicates that the memorandum was put together between 8 March and 10 March. A letter of 7 March (*Lebensbild*, p. 572) mentions nothing about it. Most probable is the night between March 9 and 10. The previous reference is carried over to the second edition of the book as an example of successful historical interpretation of sources, although since then it has been possible to discover Max Weber's letter to the Foreign Office, which accompanied this memorandum; it bears the date of 10 March 1916. Weltkrieg Nr. 18 geh., vol. 9, Politisches Archiv des Auswärtigen Amtes, Bonn. The dating of the memorandum on unrestricted submarine warfare given above is thereby proved once and for all.

152. Printed in *Pol. Schr.*, pp. 146 ff. There is an original copy with Max Weber's handwritten corrections, which he sent at the time to Professor Ignaz Jastrow in Berlin, in the British Library of Political and Economic Science (London School of Economics and Political Science). The corrections proposed at the time, on this basis, to the text published by Marianne Weber, are taken into account in the third edition of *Pol. Schr.*, pp. 146 ff.

153. Letter to the Foreign Officer, 10 March 1916, Weltkrieg Nr. 18 geh., vol. 9, Polit. Archiv d. AA, Bonn.

154. A marginal note of Jagow on Weber's letter with a paraph of 11 March, similar paraphs by Bethmann Hollweg and Montgelas of 13 and 14 March 1916 respectively, ibid.

Office whatsoever."[155] The memorandum had no immediate effect on any government decision, which had probably not been intended in the first place.[156] Already on 4 March, at a Royal Council meeting in Pless, to which Tirpitz was not invited, a decision had been made to abandon for the time being the plan for an unrestricted submarine war and even to deescalate present submarine activities somewhat. Helfferich and Bethmann Hollweg had prevailed over Tirpitz, who was replaced a few days later by Admiral Eduard von Capelle. Nonetheless, Weber's memorandum had considerable impact. Weber had anticipated that it would bring "the wrath of the firebrands upon his head" and win him a reputation as a "feeble coward."[157] The memorandum did help to strengthen the chancellor's hand against Tirpitz and the politicians and journalists on the Right who continued to press for restricted submarine warfare. Gustav Stresemann, at the time the political adjutant of National Liberal party leader Bassermann, replied to Weber's arguments against unrestricted submarine warfare in an exhaustive memorandum in which he did not hesitate to accuse Weber of "tragic demagoguery" and "hypocritical concern for the future of the dynasties."[158] Weber himself wrote to Eulenburg on 14 March: "Thank goodness the nonsense about an intensified submarine war has been put to rest and a break with America has become improbable."[159]

Apparently, Max Weber got to see the official memoranda on submarine warfare only after his own memorandum had been completed.[160] He had not seen the memorandum of the Admiralty although it had circulated in Berlin academic circles. He was only to find out about Tirpitz's actual plans somewhat later, and he attacked these severely. "Tirpitz had been playing an irresponsible game," he wrote. "He should have *known* that he could not possibly torpedo so many ships in a year that he could actually 'starve out' the British if they adopted our own standards of supplying the population and *our own* rationing measures. That is simply nonsense. But then he aimed even higher, like a desperate

155. Letter to Zimmermann, 11 March 1916; similar letter to Zimmermann of 13 March 1916, ibid.

156. Ibid., p. 574.

158. Printed in appendix III of the German edition of this book (1974).

159. After a copy in the Weber papers (falsely dated July). Compare the letter to Marianne Weber of 15 March 1916: "The danger of war, which between Friday and Saturday (11–12 March) was at its height, is now past." *Lebensbild*, p. 574.

160. Cf. letter to Schulze-Gävernitz of 2 October 1916, *Pol. Schr.* 1, pp. 464 f.: "The plans were *not* made, when I saw the memoranda, which were all *equally* bad—including Helfferich's—early in the year." In this matter, the letter to Marianne Weber of 14 March 1916, *Lebensbild*, p. 574: "We ostensibly have ten new submarines. And we would blockade England with them! And colleague L[evy] as Pythia of the Admiral staff! He who so *fundamentally* miscalculated on the grain provision question. . . . *That* sends shivers up my spine. Can't those people even calculate reliably?"

gambler, and declared that he could 'guarantee' success only if all ships that approach the English coast, including Dutch, Scandinavian, Spanish, and so on, were torpedoed [without prior warning]. *This* was the gist of his reasoning."[161] This analysis is not quite accurate, since Tirpitz had worked energetically for the introduction of unrestricted submarine warfare as early as the end of 1915.[162]

Weber was nevertheless distressed by Tirpitz's dismissal. He was concerned about the impression this step would make in Germany and abroad, an impression as serious as "a lost battle."[163] At the time, he was unaware of the political background of the admiral's departure.[164] The controversy about submarine warfare was not the sole reason for the dismissal. Bethmann was irritated that Tirpitz had supported, or at least tolerated, the press campaign against the chancellor over the submarine question. Tirpitz was deeply offended at his exclusion from the meeting in which crucial decisions were taken; he therefore felt it necessary to submit a request to be released from his post.[165]

Weber continued to see the American issue as a sword of Damocles hanging over Germany. He was close to despair when the torpedoing of the *Sussex* caused a new crisis in Germany's relations with the United States. "A peaceful compromise seems highly unlikely and will only postpone the inevitable."[166] When the conflict was nevertheless settled at the cost of a total return to classical cruiser warfare, and the submarine war was almost halted for nearly six months because of the obstruction of the Naval Command, Weber was very relieved. At the same time he disapproved of the German proviso that unrestricted submarine warfare might be resumed, if necessary in the near future. "Everyone knows that the longer it is postponed, the more *impossible* it will be to risk this war [with the United States.]"[167] He again demanded capitulation without any attempt to "save face." The consequences of a break with the United States were too severe. He believed it necessary to make every possible concession.[168]

161. Letter of 15 March 1916.

162. Compare Spindler, *Der Handelskrieg mit U-Booten*, vol. 3, pp. 73 ff.

163. Letter of 17 March 1916 to Marianne Weber, *Lebensbild*, pp. 575 f.

164. Later, he publically stigmatized Tirpitz's press demagoguery. *Pol. Schr.*, p. 296 (1918).

165. Compare Spindler, *Der Handelskrieg mit U-Booten* vol. 3, pp. 103 f.; von Tirpitz, *Erinnerungen*, pp. 365 ff.; *Politische Dokumente*, vol. 2 (Berlin 1926), pp. 485 f. Here, von Tirpitz attempts to shift the blame for the failure of the censorship and the press agitation away from himself.

166. Letter to Helene Weber of 17 April 1916, *Lebensbild*, p. 581.

167. Letter to Marianne Weber of 7 May 1916, *Lebensbild*, p. 578.

168. Cf. the letters to Marianne Weber of 5 April, 2 May, and 10 May 1916, ibid., pp. 577 ff.

Weber therefore opposed the renewed agitation for unconditional submarine warfare that now stretched into the ranks of the Center party. This agitation could only encourage the English to prepare for the difficulties they would face and provision themselves in advance.[169] Weber reasoned that it was not mere national feelings that lay behind the submarine agitation, founded on ignorance of the situation and failure to understand the consequences. It was a sense of weakness, clamoring in desperation for unrestricted submarine warfare as the one means that could not fail. "People with courage and strong nerves are not the ones that scurried behind the submarine warfare demagoguery, but hysterically weak people who were no longer able to bear the burden of the war. If this [agitation] is tolerated much longer, the result will be hysterical demoralization. But the war will have to be carried on for several years."[170] The real causes of submarine agitation, in his view, lay at least

169. Compare the letter to Naumann of 18 September 1916; also the letter to Schulze-Gävernitz of 2 October 1916 (*Pol. Schr.* 1, pp. 463 f.): "the *submarine hysteria* of people that are not able to persevere."

170. Lecture in Munich on "Germany's world policy situation," October 1916. Weber's sharp polemic against the submarine agitation is left out in the version "Deutschland unter den europäischen Weltmächten," in *Pol. Schr.*, pp. 157 ff. cf. *Die Hilfe*, 9 November 1916. Letter of Weber to Herkner of 11 November 1916 (Weber papers), which proposed the printing of the lecture in a special number of *Die Hilfe*: "The lecture must be somewhat modified in form (by the omission of the *very* sharp comments that appeared in garbled form in the *M[ünchener N[eueste] Nachr[ichten]).* The relevant passages in the report of the *Münchener Neueste Nachrichten* of 28 October 1916, evening ed., read:

"For many years we have been hearing of the blessings of the monarchical government, of its power and decisiveness. But in no country governed by a parliament have we heard of the unconscionable permitting of agitation about the conduct of military affairs at a time when the foremost German soldier stands at the head of our troops on sea and on land. Would it not be a crime to alert the enemy with noisy agitation so that he can prepare against the danger of sharpened submarine warfare?

"The agitation began in the Reichstag Commission after the admiralty made known the pertinent figures in the presence of 200 deputies. Soon, thousands knew about it, and a few weeks later the enemy might have known it. Such an occurrence is scandalous. The party leaders had already been told the same thing in a confidential meeting. In spite of this, we had to endure this event. *What effect will it have upon our people on the front when they are told in memoranda, in the press, through letters, and in all other possible ways that there is a means to end the war in a few months?* How do they think that our people will be able long to sustain this psychological burden? It seems incomprehensible that the Berlin censor will permit this agitation against the Reich chancellor. This would not be possible in a country governed by a parliament. People with strong spirits and powerful nerves were not behind the demagogues of submarine warfare; rather, they were hysterically weak spirits, that could no longer carry the burden of war. If this is tolerated any further, the only result can be hysterical demoralization. But the war must still be carried on, perhaps for years. The real reasons for the submarine agitation lie in part in the area of domestic politics." This passage has since been incorporated in the third edition of *Pol. Schr.*, pp. 563 f. Compare also the letter of 1 April 1916, *Lebensbild*, p. 576.

in part in domestic political speculation. He acidly remarked that the grenade manufacturers and the agrarians were working for unconditional submarine warfare because every extension of the war meant higher earnings for them.[171] He also pointed out that many supporters of the submarine agitation had the same motivations as those who supported annexations. They shared "a fear of peace," that is, a peace that failed to achieve those goals that had been so widely trumpeted and therefore would have to be paid for with domestic political concessions.[172]

Weber was incensed at the Right's orchestrated campaign against Chancellor von Bethmann Hollweg, the man of the "Burgfrieden" at home and relatively moderate aims abroad. He sensed the chancellor's precarious situation. Bethmann Hollweg had to fear continuing charges of weakness from the forces of the Right, for these forces greatly influenced the Kaiser and the Supreme Command, on whom his political position depended. This was all the more necessary because Bethmann could not depend on a firm Reichstag majority. Weber could therefore point out with justice that the situation would not have been possible in a parliamentary system. In Weber's view, Bethmann Hollweg's Reichstag address on 5 April 1916, with its substantial concessions to the pan-German demands, was paradigmatic of this regrettable state of affairs. "The chancellor had to show that he was the 'strong man,' just as 'strong' as Tirpitz, otherwise he would have been lost because of the Fronde of the Conservatives. And the policy of the Conservatives and industrial magnates is quite simple: the *longer* the war lasts, the *more* social Democrats swing to the 'left,' the better for us, the pillars of the throne and of the altar. No compromise peace, for then concessions would have to be made in the question of suffrage."[173] Weber was annoyed by the fact that Bethmann Hollweg was incapable of using the powers at his disposal to put an end to this right-wing demagoguery. He complained that the chancellor had not found the strength to hold his own against "the *internal* enemies, people totally without scruples."[174]

By the end of 1915, Weber was resigned to the fact "that we do not have a powerful 'statesman' around and that the Kaiser is not good for anything."[175] What he regretted most about Bethmann Hollweg was his "inability to make a decision." Skeptical as he was about the chancellor, however, he still considered it his responsibility to support him against the Conservative Fronde. Weber was convinced that the success of the moderate view rose and fell with Bethmann Hollweg, since he would be

171. Letter to Marianne Weber of 7 March 1916, ibid., p. 572.
172. Cf. above, text at note 43.
173. Letter to Marianne Weber of 7 April 1916, *Max Weber: A Biography*, p. 567.
174. Letter to Marianne Weber of 7 May 1916, ibid., p. 578.
175. Letter of 25 November 1915 to Marianne Weber; copy in Weber papers.

replaced by someone far worse. He no longer expected the Reichstag majority to act sensibly, especially after the Center party followed the Supreme Command's lead in the submarine question. Weber sympathized with Bethmann Hollweg and supported him because the chancellor was the target of the Conservative Fronde, who were determined to torpedo all internal reforms and especially the reform of the three-class suffrage in Prussia. Weber came close to overstressing the link between a victorious peace and the preservation of the domestic political status quo. He stood on the chancellor's side in part because the pan-German victory agitators viewed Bethmann Hollweg as the chief block to their goals on the domestic front. Weber was also well aware that Bethmann Hollweg was a convinced opponent of unrestricted submarine warfare.[176]

When a group of Berlin professors objected to the chancellor's weak support of a victorious war, Weber declared his support of Bethmann Hollweg in a public statement issued in July 1916. "Next to the military leadership, the *current chancellor deserves* credit in every trench. Everyone knows that this war is not being fought for rash goals but only because (and only as long as) it is necessary for our survival."[177]

For similar reasons, Max Weber decided to lend his assistance to the "Deutsche National-Ausschuss," an ostensibly independent propaganda organization that in fact had close ties with the government. The committee's goal was to mobilize support for a comparatively moderate line in war aims policy and thereby to create a political basis in public opinion for a German peace offensive. Erzberger had earlier suggested the founding of a propaganda organization with supporters throughout the country in order to win wide support for the government's policies. Its task would be "to organize a bodyguard for the government in the war aims discussions." It would target not only "as much of the press as possible" but prominent people in public life "who, in turn, were in a position to influence certain corporations, associations, faculties, professional organizations, etc., and would be able to issue public resolutions or employ other means of voicing their opinions in public."[178] The outward form of a

176. Cf. also *Lebensbild*, p. 634. A letter from a childhood friend calls it Weber's "warm intercession for Bethmann."

177. In the form of a letter that appeared in the *Frankfurter Zeitung* of 27 July 1916 and for tactical reasons did not name the author (printed in *Pol. Schr.*, pp. 155 f.) In the letter, the appeal by professors von Gierke, Kahl, Eduard Meyer, Dietrich Schäfer, Adolf Wagner, and von Wilamowitz-Möllendorff of 26 July 1916 (appearing in the 2d morning ed. of 27 July 1916) was characterized as not representative and only inadvertently published. For this reason it was denied any political weight.

178. For the "Deutsche National-Ausschuss," see Dirk Stegmann, *Die Erben Bismarcks* (Cologne, 1970), which erroneously characterizes it as a continuation of the "Free Patriotic Association [Freie Vaterländische Vereinigung]" (p. 472) as well as Klaus Schwabe, *Wissenschaft und Kriegsmoral: Die deutschen Hochschullehrer und die politischen*

private committee was chosen in order not to discredit the undertaking in advance as a mere instrument of the government. The Reich chancellor's staff, especially Undersecretaries Arnold von Wahnschaffe, Kurt Riezler, and Ulrich Rauscher, helped in approaching a large circle of leading personalities from political and social quarters, soliciting their cooperation. Major industrialists were among those approached. The official opening ceremony took place on 7 June 1916 under the chairmanship of Prince Carl Wedel. A massive public demonstration with assemblies in fifty of Germany's larger towns was planned for 1 August 1916.[179] A large number of speakers were recruited for these gatherings, primarily from the academic community, including Adolf von Harnack, Gerhart von Schulze-Gävernitz, Lujo Brentano, and Hermann Oncken; Max Weber was asked to speak in Nuremberg.[180]

We do not know how Weber was chosen for this task. But his name appears in the first memorandum on the founding of the National Committee, which was probably written by Rauscher, in which he was already listed as a possible speaker. Although Weber had not made public speeches for more than fifteen years, he was prepared to do all that he could in order to help win support for a policy of reason in the area of war aims, and the National Committee appeared to have this same goal. But the actual conditions attached to his appearance as part of the National Committee's speaker campaign must have considerably tempered his pleasure. Instead of relaxing the prohibition of the discussion of war aims for the 1 August event, as Ulrich Rauscher, the guiding spirit of the National Committee had suggested, the government decided to restrict the discussion within a narrow framework.[181] At Wahnschaffe's instigation, the speakers were urged to address the war aims question only in very general terms. "A circular to the speakers," which must also have gone to Max Weber, set general guidelines for the speeches. It stressed that the most important goal of the war was the preservation of national unity, and that this would put the whole discussion of peace in a healthier

---

Grundfragen des Ersten Weltkrieges (Göttingen, 1969), pp. 117 ff. See also my commentary to the article by Raymond Aron in *Max Weber und die Soziologie heute* (Tübingen, 1965), pp. 133 f., as well as the material in Rk 2448, DZA I, Potsdam. The memorandum by Erzberger of 11 April 1916, with concurring paraphs of Bethmann, Jagow, and Zimmermann, ibid.

179. It is wrong to include Weber among the members of the "Deutsche National-Ausschuss," as Stegmann does, *Die Erben Bismarcks*, p. 472.

180. Compare Rauscher's memorandum of June 1916 in Rk 2448, pp. 8 ff. Kurt Riezler, who knew of Weber's political position through Conrad Haussmann, may have proposed this.

181. Letter of the German National Committee to Bethmann Hollweg of 14 July 1916, and Bethmann Hollweg's answer of 18 July 1916, in which "special permission for the discussion of peace aims for this day" was denied.

framework and strengthen the defense of the fatherland against a powerful and superior foe. The Reich leadership's goal was a peace formula that guaranteed "the Reich's security and was free from megalomania."[182] The National Committee was expected to go with this negatively defined program to the public, along with some vague positive points, and propagandize for the government without undermining the prohibition of the public discussion of war aims. This made Weber uncomfortable, and he was assuredly even more disconcerted when, a few days before the event, he and the other speakers were told that "under no circumstances were they to deliver peace speeches."[183] A few hours before his Nuremberg speech, he wrote to Mina Tobler of his inner conflict: "If I felt better about the entire event, I would say something good. But we are not supposed to offend other views and not be too precise—and that is not my way of doing things."[184]

Max Weber was convinced that the situation required him to stand behind the chancellor and protect him from the attacks of the extreme annexationist forces. But he was offended by the manipulation of the speakers, who, according to the announcement of the German National Committee's formation, were "completely independent, patriotic men of all political persuasions."[185] This is probably why, at the outset of his lecture on 1 August at the Industrial and Cultural Association in Nuremberg, he stressed that he did not belong to the German National Committee and planned to freely air his opinions as an independent person.[186] With sleight of hand, he also dismissed the well-founded suspicion that the meeting was merely a government contrivance: "I do not know the chancellor directly or indirectly. I do not know any secretaries of state or anyone else in the Foreign Office. I have received no money from the Treasury, nor am I a party politician. I do not speak for anyone, nor under anyone's directives, but only according to my own convictions."[187] This blunt disclaimer, in view of the framework of the gathering, was scarcely to the liking of the German National Committee.

Weber stessed a policy that would bring about a negotiated peace in his

182. Undated, but late July 1916, Rk 2448.

183. A telegram from Wahnschaffe, the undersecretary in the Reich Chancellory, of 25 July 1916, to the "Deutsche National-Ausschuss" states: "The Reich chancellor wishes that peace speeches not be delivered under any circumstances." Rk 2448.

184. Letter to Mina Tobler from Nuremberg, probably 1 August 1916, Archiv Ebnet II, 17.

185. The founding proclamation in Rk 2448, pp. 69–71.

186. According to the report of the *Fränkischer Kurier* of 2 August 1916, evening edition, under the title "An der Schwelle des dritten Kriegsjahres." Cf. also the report of the *Nürnberger Zeitung* as well as the *Fränkischer Tagespost* of 2 August 1916, and finally the official report of Weber's speech in the archives of the Reich Chancellory, Rk 2448.

187. Verbatim citation in the *Nürnberger Zeitung* of 2 August 1916.

speech. He warned, however, against undue optimism in this respect. "Peace is still far off, for the leaders of the states allied against us are fighting with a rope around their necks."[188] They are not able to achieve the peace that they would like to, since they would thereby lose their support in their own countries. In contrast, the German government is in a position to achieve a peace "that protects our honor and threatens no one." For the rest, Weber focused on Germany's internal development. He dissociated himself firmly from the "ideas of 1914." No one knew what those ideas were really about. He emphasized that the problem was not to produce ideas that would justify the war but to do what duty and responsibility demanded. He defended Bethmann Hollweg in this respect. "I am not in total agreement with everything he has said, but the men in the trenches see him as the man who offers them the guarantee that the war will not go on an hour longer than our continued existence absolutely demands." From this vantage point, Weber severely criticized the campaign for unrestricted submarine warfare.

Weber wanted to see three primary lessons drawn from the war. First, it was demonstrable that economic interests had not played a major role in causing the war, but that the war had produced new economic interests, which pressed for its continued prosecution. Weber discussed these economic interests in the allied countries in some detail, surely with the aim of alluding indirectly to those material interests that stood behind the agitation for extreme annexationist war aims in Germany. Such factors, he pointed out emphatically, must not play a role in Germany. "Our war aim is German survival, not profit." Because of the character of the meeting, Weber did not feel that he should say more. The war's second great lesson had been the indispensability of industry and business for the war effort. For this reason, attacks on capital and the bourgeoisie should end once and for all. The third lesson of the war touched on the role of the state. "When it is said that the state is the highest and ultimate principle in the world, this is entirely correct, provided that it is correctly understood. The state is the highest organization of power in the world; it has power over life and death. . . . The antithesis and the error is that such discussions turn exclusively around the state and do not take the nation into account." Using Austria-Hungary as an example, Weber explained "that a correct relationship between state and nation, in which the latter is defined by language and culture," is of great importance for the state's power status. It was therefore unwise to annex great peoples with strong national cultures. We see a modification of Weber's under-

188. This and the following passages, unless otherwise designated, are cited from the report in the *Fränkischer Kurier* of 2 August 1916.

standing of the character of a nation here, in which the element of a common culture is stressed more than the special emotions associated with the historically evolved, institutionalized power system of a nation.

Weber emphasized that Germany had to carry on the war in order to win recognition as a great power in the middle of Europe. "A people of seventy million has a responsibility before the bar of history to protect its honor for its descendants [and] shake off the chains of political serfdom and vassalage." This too would be a guarantee for the survival of the smaller nations in central Europe. No citizen could be indifferent about the German Reich's position, since everyone's welfare was bound up with Germany's strength. "It is Germany's power that will decide the fate of our trade and our industry." Everything depends upon whether or not Germany is victorious in this war. "Our descendants, millennia from now, will speak about what Germany suffered in this terrible war for survival, what it struggled for, and what it achieved."[189]

The immediate effect of Weber's speech, with its special stress on the strenghtening of the will to persevere, must have been great, even though his views were by no by any means shared by all his listeners.[190] Weber himself was far from satisfied.[191] He reported: "It is not easy to be inspired about this 'National Committee.' It is crippled, and everything has to be approached with subterfuge. I did not conceal the fact that I consider my enemies to be *asses*, and that angered the radical Social Democrats and some of the pan-Germans as well."[192] In spite of the German National Committee's publicity about it, Weber's lecture did not have a broad

189. According to the official report in the records of the Reich Chancellory, Rk 2448. The *Fränkischer Kurier* transmitted the passage as follows: "Our descendants will speak for millennia of our achievements in this war, the like of which the world has hitherto not seen." Similarly, the *Fränkischer Tagespost*: "Millennia from now, they will talk about what Germany suffered and struggled for to maintain its existence and its future."

190. Compare the report of the *Fränkischer Tagespost* of 2 August 1916: "Professor Max Weber from Heidelberg is certainly a very determined and consistent personality. This is immediately demonstrated by the manner of his rhetoric, the structure of his lecture, the sharp wording and the presentation of [his] views and hopes. A strong temperament and a very refined intellect are united in this personality, who stands behind his words with seriousness and force. The sonorous, ringing voice effortlessly dominated the room, and the self-confident oratorical demeanor witnessed to a practiced and experienced instructor. The overall design of the lecture as well as many individual parts prove its clarity for the professors. The intense countenance of the large, imposing man, wearied from so much contemplative work, strikingly reflected the pressure of the subjects he discussed, and his hands underscored especially impressive places with weighty and carefully expressive gestures. The personal impression of the speaker was certainly stronger than the objective impression of the speech."

191. To Mina Tobler, letter of 3 August 1916, A.E. II, 50: "Overall: Preparation miserable; attendance—*moderate* or less; *essential* satisfaction of those present slight."

192. Ibid.

impact.[193] This was also true of the German National Committee's activities as a whole. Because of its limited room for maneuver, the diversity of its membership, and, above all, its official-bureaucratic character, the committee was unable to win any significant influence over public opinion. Instead of helping the government gain a dominent voice in the public discussion of the war aims question, the committee spurred the extreme Right to intensify its polemics against the government and to found a countervailing organization, the "Independent Committee for a German Peace."[194]

Max Weber watched these developments with some concern. In Nuremberg, he had avoided serious criticism of the pan-Germans. In that speech he had accepted the German National Committee's strategy of bringing together all "reasonable men" who were outside of the partisan groups and of avoiding sharp polemics against both left and right as long as the "Burgfrieden" continued in force. Weber did not want to make this mistake again. It now seemed essential to counter the extreme Right's irresponsible agitation decisively. In mid-August 1916, he sent the *Frankfurter Zeitung* an article in which he criticized the conservative and pan-German agitation so severely that even that newspaper could not bring itself to print it.[195]

At the time, Max Weber was essentially in Bethmann Hollweg's political camp. His opinion of him deteriorated, however, as the chancellor increasingly lost control of the public debate over war aims. Weber was also concerned about Bethmann Hollweg's diplomatic failures. As early as the end of August 1916, he wrote, "it is widely held that Bethmann should not be retained, since he has suffered setbacks in the peace negotiations with Russia and in the talks with Austria on the Polish question, and he is incapable of *making decisions*.[196] This would appear to be the case. He is also no 'statesman,' poor chap(!), any more than Moltke the younger was a strategist. But if he goes, then only Hinden-

193. The report of the lecture was circulated among others by the Wolff Telegraph Bureau, which was close to the government. Nevertheless, we did not succeed in obtaining a text.

194. Cf. Stegmann, *Die Erben Bismarcks*, p. 465.

195. Cf. letter to the editors of the *Frankfurter Zeitung*, 20 August 1916, *Pol. Schr.* 1, p. 463. The article was not preserved. A lively argument with the editor, Dr. Simon, preceded it. A role was played by the fact that the *Frankfurter Zeitung* was not as unreservedly for Bethmann Hollweg as Weber appeared to be in the article. Cf. the letters to Marianne Weber of 18 and 22 August 1916 (copies in the Weber papers): "I met an editor of the *Frankfurter Zeitung* in the evening, to whom I had sent an anti–pan-German article, which they do not wish to accept. Well, that's up to them."

196. Cf. above, note 72.

burg can hold the nation together. I know no other leader that can achieve peace. And he is no 'statesman' either."[197]

Weber did not see a way out of the Reich's fatal crisis of leadership. In the fall of 1916, when the submarine agitation reasserted itself in even stronger guise and now was clearly directed at the chancellor, who did not seem capable of stifling it, Weber wrote to Naumann: "I do not understand the chancellor any more. It seems that he *cannot* accomplish what he believes is correct. If this is so, then he should go."[198] Not long after this, he told Dr. Heinrich Simon, one of the editors of the *Frankfurter Zeitung*, whose political beliefs were close to his own, "Bethmann is a heavy burden for us! This has always been my view. It is only because of this submarine hysteria—and they are hysterical—that I am forced to support him out of sheer necessity. And where is his successor?"[199] For these reasons he continued to support Bethmann Hollweg in public when he could. He participated in a public declaration by Heidelberg citizens in the *Heidelberger Tageblatt* on 25 November 1916 protesting the "objectively unstiflable and often personally insulting ill will" that is again "directed against the responsible head of German policy. . . . The chancellor's public announcements give us the impression that he is acting conscientiously and steadfastly. We therefore hope that the chancellor will continue to guide our people's destiny with a firm hand, free of irresolution and free of impetuousness too, but deeply imbued with the duties of his office. We expect him to assure a peace for us that will meet the nation's wishes and be worthy of the sacrifices of this war."[200]

197. Letter to Marianne Weber of 22 August 1916, after a copy in the Weber papers; cf. *Lebensbild*, p. 584. Also a letter to Mina Tobler, late August 1916, A.E. II, 23: "*Hindenburg*: I greet his appointment above all for political reasons: a peace, that *he* participates in, will be accepted by everyone in Germany, no matter what its contents. And that is important." Cf. also the letter previously quoted to the editors of the *Frankfurter Zeitung*.

198. Letter of 18 September 1916, *Pol. Schr.* 1, p. 465. Likewise, a little later (2 October 1916) to Schulze-Gävernitz: "Either Bethmann enforces his prohibition of all and every direct or indirect discussion of military matters, or—he goes." Ibid. Cf. also Weber's lecture in Munich (above, note 170); also, the draft "Deutschlands weltpolitische Lage" (Germany's world policy situation); finally, the letter to Schulze-Gävernitz of 21 October 1916: "*Ceterum censeo*: They must take steps against the submarine demagoguery with a *cudgel* from above—otherwise I do not know why we are called a 'monarchy.'" *Pol. Schr.* 1, p. 465.

199. He continues: "*Jagow* [the secretary of state for foreign affairs], this stupid cipher, is our misfortune. *He* has to go." Letter of 27 October 1916, Weber papers; cf. letter to Schulze-Gävernitz of 21 October 1916, *Pol. Schr.*, 1, p. 465.

200. Nothing more is known about the circumstances behind this declaration signed by 190 distinguished citizens of the city of Heidelberg, including von Anschütz, Gothein, and Oncken; the text as such probably was not originated by Max Weber but could very well have been influenced by him. We reproduce it here in full:

"We, the undersigned citizens of Heidelberg, supporters of all political parties, protest

Weber was already far more critical of Bethmann Hollweg than this somewhat ambiguous statement indicated. Yet the situation seemed to demand the support of the chancellor. Any change in the chancellorship would be problematical. Weber opposed Bülow's return.[201] The only alternative was quasi-plebiscitary rule by Hindenburg. For a time, Weber carefully considered this possibility. It conformed to his own political theories: a peace concluded by Hindenburg would be acceptable to the entire nation.[202] But Weber soon realized that Hindenburg was himself in the annexationist camp and was therefore certainly not the man to bridge the deep chasm between the proponents of a victorious peace and the nonannexationist Left, especially the workers. The alternative, as Weber saw it, was to continue to support the chancellor and to strengthen him against the Right. After Romania's entry into the war and speedy defeat, Weber still hoped for a negotiated peace, and he blamed the allies for the fact that negotiations had not yet begun. He took the failure of the German peace offer of 12 December 1916 calmly: "The . . . Entente note," he wrote on 2 January 1917, was "what we had expected. . . . We cannot anticipate a peace *before* autumn. Others will wish to try it again and hope for American help. But I believe that we should remain strong, wise, and calm. Then nothing can befall us."[203]

Yet fateful decisions needed to be made precisely at this time. Since there seemed to be no way out of the military stalemate on the western

---

publicly against the objectively unjustified, often personally insulting ill will that the responsible leaders of German policy have recently repeatedly been exposed to at such a grave time.

"We do not doubt that many of those who are participating in these attacks are convinced that they are acting patriotically. We are also not of the opinion that it is a civic duty to remain silent when we may hope to help the Fatherland with a free word.

But we have to deplore and condemn it when the right of criticism is misused and confidence in the Reich leadership is destroyed by constant repetition of unfounded assertions and the spreading of baseless suspicions. This seriously endangers the unity that is especially necessary today.

"The public statements of the Reich chancellor have given us the impression that he directs Reich policy conscientiously and surely. We therefore hope that the Kaiser will henceforth guide the destiny of our people with a firm hand, free from anxious faltering but also free from ill-considered daring, and deeply conscious of the duties of his very responsible office. We expect him to secure us a peace that will reflect the nation's wishes and the sacrifices of this war." Copy in Max Weber Archiv, Munich.

201. Letter to Schulze-Gävernitz, *Pol. Schr.* 1, p. 465.

202. Letter to the editors of the *Frankfurter Zeitung* of 20 August 1916, ibid., p. 463; cf. letter to Helene Weber of 8 September 1916, partially in *Lebensbild*, p. 585: "That Hindenberg is finally brought forward now, when the dynasty is in trouble, is deplorable. But the peace that *he* concludes will be accepted by the nation, as he would also have it. That is the *sense* of the thing."

203. To Mina Tobler, 2 January 1917, AE II, 26.

front, and the government's own political initiative had failed, the government of Bethmann Hollweg could no longer resist the pressure of the Admiralty for the unrestricted use of the submarine weapon, which was widely held to be the route to peace. Hindenburg and Ludendorff had now joined the submarine supporters. On 9 January, even before the completion of the crucial negotiations associated with Wilson's peace initiative, the opening of unrestricted submarine warfare was set for 1 February 1917. Weber was now ready to bow to the inevitable. However, he objected to the form of the German note announcing unrestricted submarine warfare. In his view, it was a great error to omit a passage that promised to cease this action as soon as negotiations between the combatants on the basis of equality were agreed to by both sides.[204]

Now that the break with America could not be prevented, Max Weber "forced" himself to take a more optimistic position on the situation. He was hopeful about the strength of the pacifist forces in the United States. In a letter to one of his students, who like Weber had linked American entry into the war with certain defeat, he mixed pessimism with a continued will to carry on. "We will still be grateful for being German and not *anything* else, even *if* things go badly—and this is still unlikely. The worst part is the *prolongation* of the war which will probably be the result. But we must endure it, both abroad and, consequently, at home."[205]

Max Weber remained a supporter of Bethmann Hollweg. He fiercely disapproved of the right-wing efforts led by Stresemann to supplant Bethmann Hollweg—efforts that became all too public in the so-called "Bring Bethmann down conference" in the Hotel Adlon in Berlin on 25 February 1917.[206] Weber's continued hope that Bethmann Hollweg would succeed in bringing about the reform of the Prussian three-class suffrage despite the resistance was sufficient reason for Weber to continue his support of the chancellor in spite of all of his reservations. Moreover, he was convinced, as many other reasonable people in Germany were, that if the parties and associations on the right succeeded in overthrowing Bethmann Hollweg, there would no longer be even the slightest chance for a negotiated peace settlement.

Weber was enraged by the events that led to Bethmann Hollweg's fall

204. Letter to Naumann of 3 February 1917, *Pol. Schr.* 1, p. 466; similarly, Dernburg insisted at the time, in a petition to the Reich chancellor, that he should at least declare that the unrestricted submarine warfare "would cease the moment the grievances" against which it was directed ceased on "their part." DZA I, Reichskanzleramt II, Kriegsakten 1, vol. 11, (2398/10), pp. 58 ff.

205. To K. Löwenstein, 10 February 1917, *Pol. Schr.* 1, pp. 466 ff.

206. Cf. Max Weber's hint in his article "Ein Wahlrechtsnotgesetz des Reiches," *Frankfurter Zeitung*, 28 March 1917: "The events in Hotel Adlon . . . " now in *Pol. Schr.*, p. 194; also Haussmann, *Schlaglichter* (Frankfurt, 1924), p. 87.

in July 1917. He was especially incensed at the ambivalent role of the parties and the direct intervention of Hindenburg and Ludendorff, who had blackmailed the Kaiser with their own resignations.[207] "I would not shoot a single bullet and give not even one penny for a war loan if this were not a national war but a war about the form of our government fought to preserve this incapable dynasty and an unpolitical bureaucracy." He saw "no way out now but thorough parliamentarization after all in order to 'remove' these people."[208] The way in which Bethmann Hollweg was overthrown (by Ludendorff) and the fact that the Kaiser did not restrain the Supreme Command or remind them of the constitutional limits of their responsibility strengthened Weber's conviction that "the present manner of governmental decision-making and political operating" was bound to "condemn to faillure *any* German policy, no matter what its goals."[209]

4. The Need for Constitutional Reforms to Strengthen the Domestic Front

Max Weber was increasingly convinced of the need for constitutional reforms as it became clearer to him that the irresponsible annexationist war aims agitation was largely caused by considerations of domestic politics. Furthermore, the supporters of a *Siegfrieden* (victorious peace) succeeded in exercising their influence in extraparliamentary ways, namely, working through the emperor's entourage and especially through the Supreme Command. The cleavage between Left and Right, which had been bridged in the national enthusiasm of August 1914, he now saw reappear. The radical Left was least responsible for this situation. Weber blamed, rather, the Prussian Conservatives, who, oblivious to the feelings of the masses who bore the brunt of the war's burden, were seeking to enhance their own privileged position and to secure it. Weber viewed the introduction of a new bill on entailment as the final blow to the Burgfrieden. He viewed the bill as an attempt to secure the crumbling social position of the East Elbian landlords at the cost of the multitude of free farmers. This was clearly not in the nation's interest.[210]

207. For the details of the complicated events, see my "Die deutsche öffentliche Meinung und der Zusammenbruch des Regierungssystems Bethmann Hollweg im Juli 1917" in: *Geschichte in Wissenschaft und Unterricht* 19 (1968): 656 ff.

208. Letter to H. Ehrenberg of 16 July 1917, *Pol. Schr.* 1, pp. 470 f. The date given there is incorrect, as Meinecke has already pointed out.

209. *Pol. Schr.*, p. 309.

210. See Weber's article, "Die Nobilitierung der Kriegsgewinne," *Frankfurter Zeitung*, 1 March 1917, *Pol. Schr.*, pp. 183 ff.; also letter to Naumann, 3 February 1917, *Pol. Schr.*, pp. 407 ff.

Weber abandoned all moderation at this point in his campaign against the Conservatives. He now spoke up in stronger terms against the Prussian three-class suffrage that assured the Conservatives a predominent position in the Prussian political arena. Weber viewed the three-class suffrage as incompatable with Prussian hegemony in the Reich. He therefore argued that it was an issue that transcended the competence of the Prussian House of Deputies. Weber pointed out that "The Prussian suffrage was a 'Prussian' affair only if Prussia renounced the privileges it enjoyed under articles 5 and 37 of the Reich constitution as well as the military conventions."[211] Prussian ministers exercised major functions in the Reich government. Leading Reich officials guided the Reich's fate in their capacity as Prussian representatives in the Bundesrat. As such, they were directly or indirectly responsible not only to the Reichstag but to the Prussian House of Deputies as well. The composition of the Prussian House of Deputies was therefore not a matter of indifference for the Reichstag. Weber believed the Reichstag entirely justified in concerning itself with the Prussian suffrage, and so he thought it expedient to circumvent the Prussian parliament body's stubborn resistance. The Reich could lead the way in breeching the three-class suffrage without attacking it formally or interfering in the individual states' constitutional rights. This appeared possible to him in the form of a "Reich emergency suffrage law," which would permanently grant the vote to every combat soldier in the best class of his federal state.[212] The law would have the effect of undermining the three-class suffrage from within. This measure would have had the same effect as a wholesale nomination of new peers and would have led in the end to the repeal of the three-class suffrage by the Prussian House of Deputies.

Max Weber argued that Reich interference of this nature was "a national necessity" and an obligation to the soldiers in the field. Because the Prussian Conservatives could not be expected to bring about this kind of reform, there remained no other way. It would be completely irresponsible to postpone reform until after the war. It would be "impossible" to end the Prussian three-class suffrage after the war, even though many others were suggesting postponement until then. He projected a dim picture of the probable composition of a postwar Prussian House of Deputies elected on the basis of the plutocratic three-class suffrage. The first and second classes would be controlled by "those who had benefited financially from the war (both legitimately and through war profiteering)," those who had received large dividends from the war, and those

211. Letter to Oncken of 20 April 1917, according to copy in Weber papers. Cf. the explanation in *Pol. Schr.*, pp. 407 ff.

212. *Frankfurter Zeitung*, 28 March 1917, 1st morning ed. Now in *Pol. Schr.*, pp. 192 ff.

who had remained at home and had therefore improved their economic situations. The overwhelming majority of the returning soldiers who would vote in the third class would be condemned to political powerlessness.[213]

At this time Weber also discussed Prussian suffrage reform in more detail in an article in the *Europäische Staats- und Wirtschafts-Zeitung*. In it, he discussed the various alternative proposals which stopped short of granting equal and direct suffrage, and pointed out that none of them was suitable under modern conditions. Given the fact that the war was likely to continue for a considerable length of time, there was no alternative to introducing suffrage for the Reichstag elections in Prussia as well. The British could alter their suffrage in the middle of the war; surely the Germans should be capable of doing the same. Apart from that, the internal struggle about the issue of suffrage had to be brought to an end at all costs. "If the present opportunity is missed, and all the energy of the nation thereby directed toward the suffrage struggles, then in my opinion Germany will have forfeited its role as a [great] power, regardless of the outcome of the war."[213a]

At Bethmann Hollweg's urging, and in the light of growing public impatience, William II finally promised a reform of the three-class suffrage in his Easter Message of 7 April 1917. However, he avoided mentioning *equal* suffrage, and this led to disputes about the meaning of the imperial message. The Conservatives tried to interpret the message as a move to moderate reform but not as abandonment of the pluralistic character of the suffrage. It was soon evident that the Prussian Conservatives could not be moved to give up their traditional position and that a considerable part of the middle classes also feared the consequences of equal suffrage. Max Weber was disappointed by the delay on the suffrage issue. He blamed it mainly on the Prussian House of Deputies, although the enemies of reform in the Prussian State Ministry, above all Minister of the Interior von Loebell, still had the upper hand. Weber wrote Oncken that if the Prussian House of Deputies did not cease its obstruction of suffrage reform, "we [are no longer] willing to remain vassals of the Prussian privileged classes."[214]

In an article in the *Frankfurter Zeitung* on 26 April 1917, Weber once again joined the debate about the reform of the Prussian three-class suffrage.[215] He attacked the suffrage because he believed that the growing bitterness of the masses against the Conservative fronde and their grand-

213. Ibid., pp. 193, 247.

213a. "Das preussische Wahlrecht," *Europäische Staats- und Wirtschafts-Zeitung* 2, no. 2 (21 April 1916), p. 401.

214. Letter to Oncken, 20 April 1917; copy in Weber papers.

215. Article of 26 April 1917; largely reprinted in *Pol. Schr.*, pp. 406 ff.

bourgeois accomplices was very dangerous. He argued that the creation of a uniform, equal suffrage for all political bodies in the Reich was a fundamental precondition for the internal unification of the nation in its difficult struggle for existence. The Prussian nobility's hidden hegemony, protected by their predominence in the Prussian three-class Landtag, had to cease once and for all. Weber hoped to eliminate the influence of the Conservative circles close to the court over German policy. It was "absolutely necessary to put an end to a situation in which steps were taken, even in the most important government policies, that revealed the influence of a *Prussian caste*'s suffrage privilege and their special interests. The effect is *indecisiveness, lack of resolve, and unclarity*. This has been clear in the superficiality of many of the government's most important actions both before the war and *during it*."[216] Weber bluntly pointed both to the selfish reasons that led the Conservatives to oppose equal suffrage in Prussia, and to "the pitiful cowardice in the face of democracy" that led many in the middle class to support the Conservative position. Behind this cowardice lay a "fear that the legitimacy of property could be threatened as well as the existing social structure."[217] But anyone who wanted Germany to play a great power role in the future had to accept the unavoidable democratic consequences. If the democratization of Germany's constitution were thwarted now, it would occur "at the expense of Germany's future."[218]

Max Weber was in no way one of those dogmatic supporters of universal suffrage who base their thinking on natural law or some such global principle. As a student, like Baumgarten and the elder Max Weber, he had viewed universal suffrage in Germany as a "Greek gift of Bismarckian Caesarism," which in turn had had the questionable result of the law against the Socialists.[219] He was certain throughout his life that Bismarck had introduced general suffrage in 1867 because of his confidence in the intrinsic conservativism of the masses.[220] As late as 1917, Weber raised the question of whether a restricted or graduated suffrage might not have better fitted the nation's political maturity in 1867.[221] As he saw it, the tragedy of Russian Zemstvo liberalism in 1915 had been that it became impossible in good conscience to support a graduated suffrage even though this would have suited the Russian people's political matur-

216. Ibid. This passage is not included in *Pol. Schr.* It is part of the original article and was eliminated in the publication as a separate treatise. It stood at the end of the first paragraph on p. 413.

217. This citation stems first of course from December 1917. *Pol. Schr.*, p. 252.

218. *Pol. Schr.*, pp. 291, 295.

219. Cf. above, chap. 1, text at notes 28–29.

220. Perhaps *Pol. Schr.*, p. 394.

221. Ibid., pp. 245, 313.

ity at that time, and would have temporarily assured the power of the bourgeoisie to implement the essential reforms. He attributed this to the fundamental changes in the social structure resulting from the development of "capitalism with its power to form classes." "Economic conflict of interest and the proletariat's class character always stab specifically bourgeois reforms in the back. That is the fate of their activity, here as everywhere."[222] Modern mass society no longer offers the basis for a restricted or pluralistic suffrage or the means to maintain it.

During the war, Weber always took the view that only universal, equal, and direct suffrage could put an end to the "poisoned debate about suffrage."[223] He specifically excluded any attempts to replace Prussian three-class suffrage with a general, direct, but pluralistically graduated suffrage. He argued that the Easter Message apparently excluded such an interpretation since, although it did not mention the word *equal*, it followed "the precise wording of the Reich constitution" and referred to the existing Reichstag suffrage. Today, no one could interpret the phrase *universal suffrage* in any sense but that of the Reichstag suffrage law.[224] Weber ridiculed all cleverly contrived plural suffrage systems discussed at the time. "Privileges attached to children? The proletariat, and the Poles, have the most children! The privilege of examination? The literati are the most politically immature of all classes. Privileges for the middle class? This will serve the Center party and the most reactionary plebeians (look at Austria)."[225] Weber was especially opposed to any preference for particular population groups. In his opinion, such a preference would extend political influence to those social strata who possessed a rentier's mentality and who therefore favored a static economy. Weber feared that this would damage Germany's economic future for many years.[226]

Weber criticized those "good people and bad musicians" who favored a suffrage based upon occupational groupings in order to represent all of the people's interests "organically." In his view, such "childish literary soap bubbles" took no account of the fact that in the constantly changing conditions of modern industrial society, a clear division according to vocational lines was more impossible than ever.[227] A vocational suffrage

222. "Zur Lage," pp. 22 ff., 25 f.

223. Letter to Oncken, 20 April 1917; article in the *Frankfurter Zeitung*, 26 April 1917 (included, not in the later version, in *Pol. Schr.*, p. 412): "The Reichstag suffrage alone" will bring about "the politically unconditionally necessary *conclusion* to the suffrage battle."

224. *Frankfurter Zeitung*, 26 April 1917; cf. the letter to Oncken quoted above: "The 'Easter Message' literally reflects article 20 of the Reich constitution, article 2 of which means the *Reichstag* suffrage, although it avoids the word 'equal.'"

225. Letter to Oncken of 20 April 1917; similarly in more moderate form in an article of December 1917, now *Pol. Schr.*, pp. 247 f.

226. Ibid., pp. 248 ff.; cf. above, pp. 105 ff, regarding the imperialistic aspects, which played a role here.

227. *Pol. Schr.*, pp. 252, 255 f.

system would also put too much power into the hands of economic interest groups and at the same time remove the exercise of power further from the control of public opinion. Moreover, it would serve to accelerate the process of bureaucratization, which in Weber's view was increasingly solidifying all social relations in modern society. It was also a mistake to believe that this system of representation would lessen the partisan struggle. Either the parties and the economic associations would continue their activities behind the facade of a representative system based on occupational groups, or the political process itself would be petrified.[228] In Weber's eyes, this would pave the way to future subjugation, which was precisely why he regarded it as extremely dangerous to replace voluntarism in politics and in economic competition with governmentally mandated corporate bodies such as state-franchised syndicates. He predicted that in times of economic stagnation accompanied by a hardening of the social order, a vocational representative system could prove attractive, but for him this was all the more reason to fight the idea passionately.[229]

Max Weber's ideal of political life emphasized a *voluntarist* organization of the body politic, unconfined by material interests. This would make it possible for a charismatic personality to exercise creative initiative and set moral ideals for society as a whole. Weber was diametrically opposed to any type of social order that was reminiscent of traditional liturgical practices and medieval guild rule. He was convinced that the power of the economic pressure groups could then only be checked by the political organization of consumer interests. Democracy was only conceivable in modern capitalist society if universal suffrage assured the consumer interests a high degree of political influence.[230]

Max Weber also considered the repeal of the three-class suffrage in Prussia necessary for a very specific reason. Only with this change "would the basis for the desired annexation of Alsace to Prussia be established. Otherwise, that would be impossible."[231] Weber had long pressed for a solution to the Alsace-Lorraine question that would be satisfactory on both domestic and international grounds. It was clear to him that Alsace-Lorraine prevented an understanding between France and Germany. It was therefore absolutely necessary to give the Reichsland a status that would accord it full and final participation in the Reich and therefore end all doubts on this issue in England and in America, whose president promised a permanent peace to the world based upon the nationality

228. Ibid., pp. 256 f., 267 f.

229. *Wirtschaft und Gesellschaft*, p. 176: "The possibilities for 'professional' representation are not inconsiderable. At a time of stabilization of the technical-economic development, they will be *quite* large. Then 'party-life' will suffer a thoroughgoing collapse."

230. *Pol. Schr.*, p. 268.

231. Letter to Oncken of 20 April 1917: "One cannot say that publicly."

principle. In the Central Powers, too, support was growing for a compromise on the Alsace-Lorraine question in view of the fact that it would otherwise prove impossible to get peace negotiations underway. Weber had always rejected this view categorically. In his opinion, Alsace-Lorraine's association with the Reich was not negotiable.[232] He stated this decisively in Nuremberg: "As to the Alsace-Lorraine question—any Reich chancellor who attended a conference where this 'question' was a subject for discussion would not come back alive."[233] He angrily rejected Robert Michels's suggestion of a plebiscite on this bone of contention between France and Germany.[234] He was incensed by Philipp Scheidemann's declaration in April 1917 that the annexation of Alsace-Lorraine had been a "mistake."[235] It was urgent all the same to repair the sins and omissions of the imperial administration in Alsace-Lorraine once and for all.

Many years before, when in Strassburg, Weber had been able to observe the mistakes of German policy in the Reichsland directly. The imperial bureaucracy, which administered the Reichsland rather autocratically without any feeling for the Alsatians' democratic mentality, together with the unnecessarily crude conduct of the military, had nourished the pro-French attitudes of the populace. The Alsatians had been denied full equality in the Reich for decades, and the territory still had a special political status even after the granting of a constitution in 1911. It was still to be governed by an imperial governor, in the name of the Kaiser, who could make use of wide-reaching special powers when necessary. The parliamentary institutions in Alsace-Lorraine had no influence over the Reichsland's votes in the Bundesrat. Now that the reconquest of Alsace-Lorraine had become a declared war aim of the allies, Weber believed that a final healing of this "wound" was essential.[236] Above all, he wished to see the anomaly of the imperial governorship, the visible symbol of the autocratic rule of the Reichsland, eliminated. Beyond this, he hoped to see the Reichsland developed economically with generous financial aid from the Reich. The territory appeared to him to be too small to stand on its own feet economically; he

232. Cf. Weber's letter to Oncken of 10 December 1917 (copy in Weber papers): "Even Friedjung in greater German-Austrian circles asked me if in reality no arrangement about Lorraine had been proposed; I thought it appropriate to deny this categorically."

233. *Fränkischer Kurier*, 2 August 1916; cf. above, text at note 188.

234. Letter to Michels of 20 June 1915, according to a copy in the Weber papers: "Such 'kitsch' from the political nursery as a plebiscite in Alsace-Lorraine should in my view be kept secret. An uninfluenced plebiscite in Rome would have resulted in papal rule; an uninfluenced plebiscite in Sicily would have supported the Piedmontese. In any case, I promise to stage one with the necessary measures."

235. Cf. letter to Naumann of 12 April 1917, *Pol. Schr.*, 1, p. 468.

236. *Pol. Schr.*, p. 492.

therefore pleaded for the annexation of the Reichsland to Prussia, which would assure the necessary economic support. He rejected its annexation to Bavaria, an idea supported by Bavarian circles at the time. Even more, he disapproved of the plans to divide the territory among the various contenders.[237]

As long as Prussia was ruled by a Landtag elected through a plutocratic suffrage, however, annexation to Prussia was out of the question. Weber therefore changed his position and after 1917 suggested that Alsace-Lorraine become an independent federal state. At the same time, he rejected the suggestion that the Alsatians, influenced as they were by French republicanism, should have a dynasty foisted upon them. "The Alsatian Landtag should be permitted to choose a *governor for life* from among the German princes," Weber proposed in a letter to Conrad Haussmann. "If they want a hereditary governor (the title was held by the House of Orange in Holland for 200 years), that is fine. If they should decide later to give him the title of 'Grand Duke,' that is fine too." But for the moment, it could suffice if the governor were elected instead of being appointed by the Kaiser and that his ministers should be responsible to the Landtag of Alsace-Lorraine and legislate with it. "In this way, Alsace-Lorraine will become a 'federal state,' and we would have a 'republic *with* a grand duke' on the basis of the 'self-determination' of the Alsatian people—and this is useful politically (as well as for peace negotiations.)"[238] Since the composition of the Prussian three-class Landtag made annexation to Prussia impossible, Weber saw this as the best approach to bring about a satisfactory solution to the Alsace-Lorraine problem that would be acceptable both at home and abroad.[239] We shall return to this conception of an "elected" monarch when we discuss the problem of the Reich presidency. It is far removed from the concept of monarchical legitimacy. Precisely for this reason, the consent of the

237. Ibid., pp. 165, 234. For a thorough treatment of the contemporary background, see Karl-Heinz Janssen, *Macht und Verblendung: Kriegszielpolitik der deutschen Bundesstaaten 1914–1918* (Göttingen, 1963), pp. 21 ff., 130 ff., 156 ff.

238. Letter to Haussmann, 29 July 1917, prompted by the attack of the majority parties against Michaelis on the Alsace-Lorraine question (Haussmann papers); originally, Weber wished to send Haussmann a "position paper on the question of Alsace-Lorraine." Instead, he made his suggestions in a letter. Weber wanted the following specific changes: "(1) in future, the Statthalter should be elected instead of *appointed* by the Kaiser; (2) he should have the immunity and the *rank* of a federal prince; (3) in accordance with the responsibility of his minister to the *Alsace-Lorraine* Landtag, he should instruct the Alsace-Lorraine votes in the Bundesrat (as currently); (4) *he* should make *laws* with the Landtag (state laws) (instead of the Kaiser)."

239. Cf. *Pol. Schr.*, p. 234 (October 1917); Weber preferred the federal state solution to incorporation in Prussia, even "if equal suffrage should remove the chief hinderance [in Prussia]."

German dynasties would have been scarcely possible to attain in 1917, in spite of its simplicity.[240]

As the war continued, the parties of the Left increasingly viewed a reform of the Prussian three-class suffrage as a test case for the good will of the conservative Right. Max Weber was very skeptical about the prospects for reform and believed that at best a pseudo-reform "behind the backs of the fighting army" might be possible.[241] He was disquieted by the fact that the Conservatives' obstinacy on this issue, in combination with the pan-Germans' completely irresponsible agitation, increasingly deepened the cleft between the workers and the radical Right. He bitterly suspected that the Right was speculating on the radicalization of the working class. "The agrarians know that bread must be bought even if we are defeated. Industry and the merchant marine would be ruined; that is to say, *these* contenders for power would be removed. The demoralization and revolutionary despair of the working class would ensure that the large landowners would retain power. The monarch would then be in their hands. And therefore they say 'va banque.'"[242]

But the dangers present in the radicalization of the working class could not be so easily removed. Weber feared, with good reason, that the German working class might be driven to revolutionary steps along the lines of the February revolution in Russia. The armament workers' strike in April 1917 was an unhappy portent. Although the immediate pretext was the catastrophic food supply situation, political demands surfaced. Socialist premises were not mentioned, either now or later, but the Leipzig workers demanded a negotiated peace and universal, equal, direct, and secret suffrage in all federal states. Although Weber could not condemn these strikes, he was very disturbed. He wrote to Hermann Oncken at the time: "I fear that the Berlin events—the product of real deprivation—and the actions of [Baron Clemens] Schorlemer-Lieser and other Prussian ministers are only a prelude to future unpleasantness, and we will again see that the bus is always missed as we did with the peace offer, the Easter Message, and, it seems, everything else."[243] Much as he disapproved of the workers' position from the national point of view, he thoroughly understood their plight, and he observed repeatedly that the

240. Weber himself added in defense of his proposal that it was the simplest solution because it necessitated no adjustment of existing rights of military leadership and no military convention—a somewhat peripheral argument. In the letter to Haussmann, 29 July 1917.

241. Cf. "Ein Wahlrechtsnotgesetz des Reichs," *Frankfurter Zeitung*, 28 March 1917, *Pol. Schr.*, p. 194.

242. Letter to Marianne Weber of 5 March 1916, mildly distorted in *Lebensbild*, p. 572. Here, following the copy in the Weber papers.

243. Letter of 20 April 1917, following the copy in the Weber papers.

large industrialists contributed substantial financial aid to the irresponsible propaganda for a victorious peace.[244] It is hence not altogether surprising that we find sharp attacks against big business that might be expected from a Social Democrat but not from a bourgeois politician like Weber in his wartime articles.

Weber reacted ambivalently to the attempt by the parties of the second Socialist International to explore ways to peace at an international conference of all Socialist parties in combatant countries, now that the governments were clearly unable to bring an end to the war.[245] On the one hand, he could only welcome an initiative that sought to bring peace closer; on the other hand, he was not certain of the effect that the participation of the German Social Democrats in Stockholm would have upon the German military and political situation. To be sure, he did not doubt the national loyalty of the Social Democratic delegation, and especially Philipp Scheidemann, but he wished to strengthen their backbones indirectly. It seemed to him to be essential that the Social Democrats adopt a firm position in advance in order not to arouse hopes abroad, especially among the Russians, that Germany was close to collapse. Weber considered this issue so important that he was prepared to help finance the assignment of a Russian emigré to Scheidemann as contact man and translator. This acquaintance of Weber shared his views about the German Reich's national requirements. Weber asked Friedrich Naumann to approach Scheidemann with this suggestion:

> Dear friend, in the event that Reichstag Delegate Scheidemann requires a *Russian* on his trip to Copenhagen (or Stockholm) for that conference who (1) speaks both German and Russian perfectly, (2) is a Russian Social Democrat, (3) is dependably pro-German (and pacifistic)—you rarely find pro-Germans among Russians of any party—then I shall attempt to persuade Herr Dr. Gutmann, who is here now (a Russian Jew), who has been in Germany for years, was interned at Rappenau and who was released here to edit the papers of a late colleague, to accompany him. . . . He can be of use: as an interpreter and *informant* for the Russians who will be there as well. They will judge him "trustworthy." He can inform them about our *military* strength and our will to persevere and also of the fact that if the German *Social* Democrats conclude a *bad* peace, we will face the reaction from the pan-Germans after the war and they will lose every influence. He knows this very well. He moves in our circles. He can sufficiently brief

244. Cf. perhaps *Pol. Schr.*, p. 343.

245. Cf. in this regard Hilde Marie Meynell, "The Stockholm Conference of 1917," *International Review of Social History* 5 (1960): 2 ff.

> Tscheidse (or whoever comes). His "pacifism" will not be disturbing there.[246]

To be sure, nothing came of this somewhat devious proposal. It nevertheless documents Weber's passionate interest in the outcome of the Stockholm conference as well as his fears that the German position would be weakened if the German delegation permitted any doubts about the German people's will to persevere.

Max Weber's article in *Die Hilfe* of 26 April 1917 about "Russia's transition to pseudo-democracy"[247] was also dictated by his concern that "German Social Democracy might be tempted to participate in the swindle of Russian Duma plutocracy and morally attack . . . the German army in the rear."[248] To this extent, Weber's analysis of the Russian February revolution was an outspokenly tendentious tract. It is necessary to realize this in order to do it justice.[249] It was addressed above all to the Social Democrats to warn them against taking radical steps along the lines of the presumptive Russian model.

Max Weber tried to prove that there was no chance of reaching a peace settlement with the new rulers in Moscow.[250] He tried to interpret the uprising not as a "revolution" but as a "simple 'removal' of an incapable ruler," while nothing essential had changed. The Russian ruling classes' hatred of Germany and their imperialistic bent had not weakened by one iota. The present rulers needed the war to keep the great mass of peasants far from home and thereby hinder them from actually achieving their radical political objectives. A Socialist victory over the bourgeoisie could not be anticipated since the regime's credit needs did not permit the

246. Letter to Friedrich Naumann, 14 April 1917, copy in Naumann papers 44. He says further: "I will vouch for his return; he has pressing reasons to be here. *Absolute* secrecy can be guaranteed (because of the Foreign Office). *I* will pay the costs of Herr G[utmann]'s trip up to a maximum of 1000 marks. (He is not totally without means anyway.) Everything, *if* Herr Scheidemann finds the participation of this completely reliable man to be possible, or if he regards such a thing as desirable and necessary—which I cannot know. It is so important that the Russians who come have the correct *impression*, that we do not have to *beg* for peace. Pan-German influence is rising here."

247. Now excerpted in *Pol. Schr.*, pp. 197–215.

248. Ibid., p. 215.

249. Pipes neglects this, *Max Weber und Russland*, pp. 636 ff., in his brilliant, if devastating, critique of Max Weber's articles on Russia, to which I am much indebted in my treatment of this subject.

250. In retrospect, he judged the matter, significantly, in a quite different way. In October 1918 he stated: "We tempted fate when we rejected Kerensky's [peace] move. Kerensky appears to have had the ambition and the good will to have contributed to world peace. The circumstances are still unclear, but it appears that the German effort to annex the so-called protective layer—a strip of land on the Prussian-Polish border—made the negotiations impossible from the outset." Lecture at the end of October 1918, cf. below, note 313.

exclusion from power "of the bourgeois circles who alone were credit-worthy."

Weber greatly overestimated the bourgeoisie's actual role in the revolutionary events because he was convinced of its absolute indispensability, an opinion we shall encounter again. He believed that experience had proved "that today a long-lived revolution could not be carried out *either* by the bourgeoisie and the bourgeois intelligentsia alone, *or* by the proletarian masses and the proletarian intelligentsia alone."[251] Weber ignored the fact that the Russian bourgeoisie had initially stood on the sidelines during the revolutionary events and only involved itself later, and that their influence had decreased in the face of the advance of the working class and the peasants. In order to clarify for the German workers why Russian socialists could sit in a leading position in the government and still permit an imperialist course, Max Weber latched onto the theory that because of the radical opposition between the peasants and the working classes, the well-paid workers in war industries agreed to the prolongation of the war in order to keep the peasants in the trenches. Under the circumstances, the Russian Social Democratic leaders had no choice but to play along with this "pitiful game," or else they would lose all influence or find themselves overrun by the socially, economically, and politically reactionary Russian peasant masses. The extension of the "revolution" was impossible and the development of a "military dictatorship" inevitable.

However much the questionable points in this diagnosis must be ascribed to the fact that it was consciously designed as polemic, it is also necessary to point out the many mistaken judgments. Max Weber's excessive overestimation of the "personal regime" of William II contributed to the errors in his analysis of the February revolution. He overstressed the role of the czar's personal rule. In hindsight, it appears almost grotesque that Weber could describe the February revolution exclusively as the removal of an incapable ruler. Of course, he did not avoid referring to the German situation. When Weber pointed to the "swindle of Russian Duma plutocracy," it was primarily a polemical argument; for if he had been objective about it, he would not have categorically rejected a plutocratic suffrage for Russia. Weber was consciously painting a black and white picture and thereby affirming his view that the use of demagogic techniques in politics was legitimate. He was also attacking the Prussian three-class suffrage indirectly. The future of German-Russian relations was also very much in his mind. He did not wish to depart from the axiom of a "Russian popular imperialism," which was at the heart of his war aims program in regard to Russia. In spite of

251. *Pol. Schr.*, pp. 198 f.; cf. ibid., p. 204.

the transformation of Russia, he clung consistently to his plan for the indirect extension of German control in east central Europe and especially the creation of an independent Polish state closely tied to imperial Germany. Indeed, he stridently emphasized that the Polish eastern border should be fixed in accordance with the Poles' wishes.[252] Such demands were certainly incompatible with the conclusion of a separate peace with Russia, a development very much in the German interest.[253]

While Max Weber was unconvinced of the Kerensky regime's willingness to enter into a separate peace without annexation, he was very much afraid of the attractions of the Russian example and the impact of Russian propaganda upon the Left. Because of the mood in Austria-Hungary and the attitude of the German workers, he insisted to Naumann that Germany had to make an unequivocal peace offer to Russia and also to the western powers on the basis of "no annexations, no reparations."[254] It is clear in hindsight that Weber's own program still exceeded what was realizable. For example, he still supported the "protection of Flemish rights" and international guarantees against a future sea blockade of Germany, as well as "the delineation of colonial spheres of interest in the uncivilized regions of Africa." He was willing to grant the Russians free transit through the Dardanelles.[255] He continued to insist upon the resurrection of a "free Poland" but was prepared to be content with guarantees of its neutrality, in place of his earlier call for a line of fortifications on the northeastern Polish frontier. In any event, Weber believed the international impact of such a declaration was only a secondary consideration. He did not believe in the possibility of peace negotiations. The important point was that this attempt would counter the right's irresponsible agitation. The workers' growing anger about the ambiguity of German peace

252. *Pol. Schr.*, p. 212.

253. Although the influence of bourgeois forces increasingly declined in Russia, Weber continued to maintain his completely one-sided interpretation of the February revolution. Cf. the letter of 18 May 1917 to Hartmann (copy in Weber papers), in which he opposed the way the Social-Democratic Vienna *Arbeiterzeitung* treated the Russian question: "What insanity is abroad in the *Arbeiterzeitung*? There is a maximum of political stupidity that is tolerable. Even V. Adler knows the significance of Russian 'freedom,' the Duma, Messrs. Gortschkow, Radjenko . . . [an illegible name], Miljukow, the most provocative warmongers and imperialists. This agitation against Germany is foolish and dangerous." And at the end of July, Weber wrote again to Hartmann: "I have been quite correct in regard to the Russians. This literati-democracy is much too dependent on English money to maintain its power domestically to make peace, and it is *opposed* to the return of the peasants from the trenches as long as its power is not secured." Letter of 24 July 1917, original in Weber papers. Weber still said the same things in February 1918 (again for tactical considerations); see *Pol. Schr.*, p. 293.

254. Letter of 8 May 1917; cf. the previous letter of 12 April 1917, *Pol. Schr.* 1, pp. 468 ff.

255. Cf. also above, end of sec. 1.

intentions would be calmed. Weber realistically accessed the probable outcome: "If next year, we are still in the same diplomatic situation as today, and if the food and coal situation worsens, we will plainly lose the war, because (1) it would no longer be possible to maintain the *home* front; and (2) financial bankruptcy would be unavoidable. The latter would mean that even with the most favorable peace conditions we would be unable to pursue any sort of world and colonial policies for generations and we would become financially incapable of alliances."[256]

Weber clearly saw the danger that the domestic political situation would be overstrained as the result of the right's war aims agitation and the conduct of the Supreme Command. He therefore began to urge not only the repeal of the three-class suffrage during the war, but the immediate parliamentarization of the German state.[257] He also hoped, almost against his best instincts, that a basis for negotiations between the combatants would soon appear. But he could not escape the fact that the war seemed likely to continue until both sides were completely exhausted. The furies of war had escaped the reins of political leadership and raged uncontrolled. The war seemed to have lost its meaning completely and to have been transformed into a totally destructive phenomenon. "If we only could see an end to this now senseless war! It is horrible and ghastly when a war becomes 'the everyday' both outside and within us."[258]

For these reasons, we might assume that Max Weber could only have welcomed Center Deputy Erzberger's initiative in the Reichstag Budget Committee for a common peace resolution of the Social Democratic, Progressive, and Center Reichstag majority. The peace resolution was in almost complete accord with the positions that Weber took in his letter to Naumann of April and May 1917. He later proudly pointed out that his own article in the *Frankfurter Zeitung* had not been without influence on the course of the July crisis.[259] Erzberger's views on the situation in Austria, which had led him to this step, were in complete accord with Weber's own views.[260] Nevertheless, Max Weber's reaction to the Reichstag majority's move, which ended in a fiasco although it was an important step in the direction of parliamentarism, was completely negative. He

256. Letter to Naumann of 8 May 1917.

257. Weber's activity in this area is explained above in chapter 6 in context.

258. Letter to Eulenburg (copy in Weber papers), 23 June 1917; cf. the letter to E. Lesser of 16 June 1917, *Pol. Schr.* 1, p. 474: "It is unbelievable that no one knows *how* to bring an end to a war that long ago came to the end of its life[!]. Nevertheless, if nothing unexpected occurs, human judgment can see the way out."

259. Letter to Hohmann, undated, early September 1917, Weber papers: "As Conrad Haussmann wrote to me, this article also had a significant impact upon the crisis in July and August." Cf. above, chap. 6, note 79.

260. Cf. the letter to the *Frankfurter Zeitung* of 27 June 1917; see above, chap. 6, note 81.

wrote to Georg Hohmann, rather impetuously, that "Erzberger is an ass."[261]

We can see here a certain "irrationality" in Max Weber's political position attributable in part to the fact that he himself was prevented from active political involvement. Party politicians who had to operate in the light of the immediate political situation found such sudden turnabouts incomprehensible and uncomfortable.[262] During the decisive weeks, Weber was in Oerlinghausen, the Westphalian home town of his wife, aloof from all politics. He had not expected the events in the Reichstag. He was incensed: "The *manner* in which Reichstag Deputy Erzberger has proceeded is criminal. First this sensation in the Reichstag, then the slogan, 'parliamentarism will bring peace!'—completely scandalous, for who can be sure of that?"[263] The parties' behavior in the Reichstag was completely impossible. "The manner in which the Reichstag discussions were carried on, first this mindless 'panic,' then this confusion, was . . . extremely unpleasant . . . above all for the impression that it made."[264] The manner in which the party leaders' aimlessness and indecisiveness contributed to the fall of Bethmann Hollweg, without achieving the slightest influence upon the choice of his successor, was deplorable. Moreover, Weber disapproved of the majority parties' strategy on the issue of the peace resolution: "I also do not care for the *manner* in which this peace resolution was put together; above all the *nature* of this party constellation."[265]

One thing in particular led Weber to reject Erzberger's initiative so firmly: the impact upon the allies. "Abroad, they suspect weakness to be the reason for the democratic confessions of faith and they hope for more: revolution. This will extend the war."[266] Because of his pessimism,

261. Letter to Hohmann; Weber wrote to Haussmann on 7 September 1917: "This *Erzberger* is an ass. The *approach* of this '*peace*' propaganda is completely useless and damages democracy. Democratization must be demanded and carried through. But this cause is injured when it is confused with 'peace.' If peace than does *not* come *in spite of* [democratization], then democracy will be *blamed*."

262. Normal partisan politicians often found Max Weber's political position to be "unfathomable." Examples are his sudden support for Tirpitz or later for Ludendorff, and for the officers in opposition to the possibility of Jewish members of a people's court. I am grateful for the reference to this in a lecture manuscript kindly made available by Professor Baumgarten.

263. Letter to Marianne Weber of 13 July 1917, according to a copy in the Weber papers. The second sentence is inserted in another letter that is incorrectly dated 21 July; 19 July is correct. The letter has also been altered in other ways.

264. To Mina Tobler, 18 July 1917, Archiv Ebnet II, 33.

265. Ibid.

266. Letter of 19 July 1917 after a copy in the Weber papers, distorted and incorrectly dated 21 July as in *Lebensbild*; cf. the letter of 13 July 1917: "The world outside is getting the impression that we are at the end of our strength." Similarly also to Mina Tobler, 18 July

Weber wanted the enemy to have no doubts about the nation's willingness to carry on this battle for existence until it should achieve an honorable peace. His nationalist ideas made it impossible for him to accept Erzberger's attempt to gain advantage from the uncertainties in Germany. He wished as much as possible to preserve the illusion abroad of the nation's unified battle will and of the strength of the Central Powers' military position. Germany must not lose face abroad. Its prestige as a major nation with its own political system had to be defended. The importance Weber assigned the prestige factor in the international power game is remarkable; indeed, he probably overestimated it. Domestically, Weber favored democratization in order to strengthen the home front. But when a Reichstag majority united in a decisive declaration for peace, he judged it to be a sign of weakness to those outside of Germany. As a result, Weber ended up in self-contradiction.

Weber also sharply rejected the peace resolution because it associated democratization with peace hopes. Weber believed this to be very questionable because of the effect that this would have on the nation's attitude toward a parliamentary governmental system: "In the future they will say at home that 'the outside world forced democracy upon us.' That is a miserable heritage."[267] Weber was anxious to avoid this danger, especially because if an honorable peace did not prove possible, the democratic ideal might be compromised. "We must act to prevent the danger that we will have to face the accusation from the reactionaries for decades that we helped *foreign countries impose a constitution on the nation* that suited them [these foreign countries]," he wrote. "We cannot predict the effect that this will have on the electorate in peacetime. And if *in spite* of democratization, peace does *not* come, and for the time being I regard this as possible, then the disappointment may also accrue to the benefit of our enemies here."[268]

This critique forecast the situation the Weimar Republic faced when it had to defend itself against the accusation that it was merely a creature of the will of the victorious powers. Had Wilson not in fact forced the abolition of the monarchy? Was the parliamentary system not a shameful result of the defeat? We may nonetheless question whether it was really possible, as Weber would have wished it, for the Reichstag majority to separate the struggle for parliamentarization from the struggle for peace in their battle against the Supreme Command and the traditional forces. Did not Erzberger have to summon all political resources including the

1917, Archiv Ebnet II, 33: "The world outside is hoping for 'revolution,' and that is a great hinderance to peace."

267. Letter of 13 July 1917 to Marianne Weber, copy in Weber papers.

268. Letter to Labor Secretary Thomas, 17 July 1917, Weber papers.

longing for peace in order to appeal to the masses and thus defeat the opposition? In reality, he did not do this in full measure; that remained for a Lenin to do. Erzberger, always the practical politician, had to think of the moment in order to achieve victory. Weber, to be sure, was more far-sighted, but this did not change the fact that the supporters of a victorious peace still retained the upper hand.

Weber, himself, was unable to find a way out of the dilemma caused by the confusion of the peace issue with the constitutional issue. Edgar Jaffé and Georg Hohmann persuaded him to speak, at the beginning of August, at a public meeting in Munich along with the Social Democratic deputy, Wolfgang Heine, on the subject, "For a peace of negotiation and against an enforced peace." Under the influence of the events in Berlin, Weber refused, arguing that "we should not *call* for peace in this way as long as the Russian offensive continues. That looks like fear."[269] Here, the conflict in Weber's position was clearly visible. On the one hand, he pressed for democratization and a negotiated peace. On the other hand, he feared the repercussions of public support for this goal abroad, because in his view the western powers hoped that democratization would weaken Germany.[270] All steps in this direction should therefore be taken guardedly and especially outside of public sessions of the Reichstag in order not to strengthen the allies' will to victory. Moderate as his war program was, he still felt that it was necessary to act with reserve and he demanded that the Reich appear strong and self-confident. Weber was still not prepared to give up the hope that Germany's enemies would ultimately be prepared to give in when faced with the unconquerable German will to fight on.

Weber's ambivalence was also apparent in the article requested by the *Frankfurter Zeitung* on the chancellorship crisis.[271] Because he feared the impression of weakness which, in his view, the peace resolution had created, he thought it necessary to state the opposite, i.e., that no one, in

269. Letter of 17 or 18 July 1917 to Marianne Weber, copy in Weber papers; similarly to Mina Tobler, 13 July 1917, Archiv Ebnet II, 32: "I should speak in Munich next week (*peace*), but I will not do it: at the earliest after the first of August. The events in Berlin are not gratifying, because they are so nervous and panicky." Also telegram of 16 July 1917 to Munich: "Advise against a peace assembly before the fall"; and letter to Labor Secretary Thomas of 17 July 1917: "*Properly considered*, it is certainly desirable to activate peace propaganda then in full strength if the current Russian offensive is to be repulsed or brought to a halt, or the matter could easily be viewed as a consequence of fear."

270. Ibid.

271. It is not surprising that Weber agonized about the article. Compare the letter to Marianne Weber of 1 August 1917 (copy in Weber papers): "I am doing quite well; only my spirits are low. I think of nothing. Not even that the article promised to the *Frankfurter Zeitung* about the *crisis* will be completed, in spite of telegrams that press me urgently: it will not go." The article appeared on 7 September 1917 in the *Frankfurter Zeitung*, now in *Pol. Schr.*, pp. 216 ff.

view of the current "outstandingly good (!)" military situation, regarded it as a symptom of weakness. Moreover, he sharply criticized the manner in which the crisis took place. Parliament had panicked with a kind of "slave uprising" because of the lack of capable political leadership.[272] Admittedly, the majority parties' peace action was actually an aimless undertaking inasmuch as it sought neither to prevent the fall of Bethmann Hollweg nor to install a new chancellor who would have their confidence. Instead, they permitted the Supreme Command to impose Michaelis, a completely unknown quantity, as chancellor. On other occasions, Weber also publicly and strongly protested the association between democratization and the hopes for a peace of negotiation. "No party that abandons Germany's interests and honor will be able to retain power for a moment."[273]

While Weber was critically disposed to the peace resolution, once it was an accomplished fact he defended it against the attacks from the Right, which had now created a new propaganda organization, the "Vaterlandspartei" (Fatherland party).[274] He joined the Volksbund für Freiheit und Vaterland (Popular Alliance for Freedom and Fatherland) and attempted, insofar as his powers permitted, to counter the pan-German war aims proposals.[275] He also continued to consider it absolutely essential to do what he could to strengthen the will of the masses to persevere and to neutralize any rising symptoms of defeatism. The allies ought not to be given any reason to believe that Germany's or Austria-Hungary's battle will was flagging, nor should false hopes be aroused at home for a quick end to the war. Such hopes—if, as was likely, they were not fulfilled—would lead in the end to despair and depression. These goals were manifest in Weber's articles in the fall of 1917 in the *Frankfurter Zeitung*, "Die Lehren der Kanzlerkrisis," "Vaterland und Vaterlandspartei" ("The Lessons of the Chancellor Crisis," "Fatherland and Fatherland Party") and "Die siebente deutsche Kriegsanleihe" ("The Seventh German War Bond Issue").

272. Cf. also the letter to Marianne Weber of 17 or 18 July: "All these events in Berlin tend to arouse panic and are therefore painful and encourage the enemy"; also letter to Hartmann (Weber papers) of 24 July 1917: "In recent days, our own parliament has not been an advertisement for democracy. May heaven improve it!"

273. Declaration in the *Heidelberger Tageblatt* of 12 December 1917, also printed in the *Frankfurter Zeitung*, 1st morning ed. of 13 December 1917. The declaration adds: "Make an effort to ensure that it cannot be said: that 'which you achieved with the sword, you permitted to be ruined by letting it be dragged in the machinery and onto the slippery ice of domestic partisan struggles.' An officer that ventures into an area he does not control jeopardizes his authority with his troops as well as with the nation, when they are at his service unconditionally." Partially printed in *Lebensbild*, p. 630; cf. *Pol. Schr.*, p. 217.

274. Cf. the article "Vaterland und Vaterlandspartei," ibid., pp. 229 ff.

275. Cf. *Lebensbild*, p. 629.

The last article, especially, should be read in the light of Weber's tactical efforts to shore up wavering home front resolve under all circumstances. In this article, referring directly to the Supreme Command, he maintained that "Germany could not be militarily overpowered . . . and that final victory was only a question of time if the enemy was not prepared to cooperate with Germany's peace initiative." At the same time, he pointed out that the Reichstag's peace resolution, "the position of the government . . . , the army in the field, and the German people guaranteed" that "the war would *not last a day longer* than was necessary to secure the national existence . . . and the free economic development of Germany."[276] Even on the basis of the information Weber had at the time, this was a very questionable assertion; neither Michaelis nor Hertling had formally accepted the peace resolution, and the resolution itself could be given an annexationist interpretation. The German secretary of state for foreign affairs, von Kühlmann, continued his predecessor's policy of "pawns." Even in his reply to the pope's message, he had avoided an unambiguous declaration about Belgium. Weber had pointed out on other occasions that that was absolutely necessary before serious negotiations between the powers could take place. In fact, Weber had painted everything in a good light purely out of carefully weighed reason of state, and discussed conjectures as if they were realities. When he wrote that "a German government *supported by the Reichstag* will be strong enough at home to achieve a reasonable peace at any time in association with our allies,"[277] We must read the passage skeptically. Weber also attempted to support the majority parties' reform efforts and to pacify the domestic unrest about the government's course in the war aims question, a contradictory task.

It was these tactical calculations that led Weber to blame the failure to enter peace negotiations exclusively upon the allied statesmen in demagogic language that was almost unique in his career. "*Sheer scoundrels and adventurers*" stand "at the helm of some of the powers that oppose us. . . . This is clear if you contrast the tone of their official statements with those made in Germany. . . . They slander us dishonorably, accuse us of malicious plans that no people with *feelings of honor* could be capable of discussing, discuss the war with phrases suited to prize fighters, and above all repress their own peoples' longings for peace and the longings of their allies and those whom they have subjugated. The *only reason* that they act this way is that they have made unfulfillable promises

276. *Pol. Schr.*, p. 226.

277. Ibid., pp. 227 f. This declaration was in distinct contrast to the position of the Reich government at the time; the government never was prepared at any time during the First World War to enter into peace negotiations on the basis of the renunciation of significant annexations.

about the war's outcome (in contrast to the German government). They will face a *personal* day of reckoning after the war. They are therefore postponing the end with the delusion that the German people's will to preserve itself may still collapse."[278] Given a situation in which Weber deemed it improper to discuss concrete, positive goals, a polemic against the allies and their war aims appeared to him to be a permissible approach, and he did not shrink from attacking the enemy as the devil. He argued that the opposing army was made up primarily of barbarians: "On the western front, we face African and Asian savages and all the robbers and devils of the world," he said. "They are ready to devastate German territory the first moment that we cease to supply our army with sufficient arms to carry out the war." We may well deplore this descent into the swamps of contemporary war propaganda. But it was clear to Weber, in the fall of 1917 when the military situation looked more

278. *Frankfurter Zeitung*, 18 September 1917. This and the following passages were omitted from *Pol. Schr.* with the justification that they do not contribute "anything to the issue" (p. 227). One asks: *which* issue? We can deplore the fact that Max Weber ever could have penned such sentences and even viewed it as scarcely possible. But is it right, especially in a scholarly edition, to hide one's head in the sand? It is impossible to avoid the fact that it is part of the picture of Max Weber as a "heroic nationalist" that in extreme situations he did not hesitate to seize upon extreme means or extreme phraseology. We therefore offer the relevant passage here verbatim: "But then *sheer scoundrels and adventurers* are at the head of some of the enemy powers—as is proved by the tone of their official statements, in contrast to those of the Germans. They are incapable of speaking about us except in the form of unworthy and at the same time clever insults, charge us with malicious imputations that *no people with a sense of honor* could bring themselves to utter. They speak of the war with the phrases of a prize fighter, and above all they forcefully repress the yearnings for peace of their own people, those of their allies, and those whom they subjugate. They do all this exclusively because they have to fear *their own* personal days of reckoning after the peace in view of the totally unrealizable fruits of war they have promised (in contrast to the German government). They therefore postpone the peace in the illusion that the German people's will for survival can yet collapse. As long as they maintain this illusion, *there will be no peace*. The German people alone know what fate would be prepared for them. The enemy armies are composed *increasingly of barbarians*. On the western frontier, the flotsam of African and Asiatic savages and all of the robbers and rabble of the world are fighting *with* them. They are ready to devastate the German countryside the moment our army is no longer adequately supplied with the means of war. The bestial abomination that the undisciplined Russian hordes committed during their temporary advance in a region inhabited in part by their own *racial comrades*, recalls the medieval Mongol period. A part of the dominant classes of the enemy countries seem to have become completely *insane with hate*. An educated large landlord who was previously war minister of the Russian revolutionary government openly recommended the use of the knout against unarmed prisoners. In France, students have joined in the practice of spitting at unarmed foes that elsewhere has been characteristic only of prostitutes. No one can therefore doubt what would await the German people if there is any decline in war preparedness, all the more so because the enemies openly discuss, without dispute, plans for the systematic looting and permanent enslavement of Germany."

promising than it had for some eighteen months in view of Russia's approaching withdrawal from the war, that everything depended upon the strengthening of the people's fighting will with any means available.

For the same reason, Weber referred to allied "plans for systematic plunder and the permanent enslavement of Germany's labor in the event of an [allied] victory." He offered a highly exaggerated interpretation of the decisions of the Inter-allied Economic Conference in Paris in June 1916. Weber had no brief for the pan-Germans' hybrid nationalism, but he brooked no rivals in his consistent efforts on behalf of his nation's struggle for survival. He did not mince words about Germany's enemies. His disparagement of the allies should not be interpreted as agitational propaganda alone. It was also an expression of his personal disappointment that the allies made no effort at all in the direction of a policy leading to a negotiated peace settlement.[279] As a result, there was a clear danger that the hopeful beginnings of democratization in Germany, apparent in the peace resolution of July 1917 and the entry of parliamentary representatives into the government, would be burdened from the outset with the odium of failure in foreign affairs and that it was very possible that at the first opportunity Germany would be overwhelmed by a new wave of reactionary pan-Germanism.

Weber therefore regarded the annexationist Right's counteroffensive and the foundation of the "German Fatherland party" on 3 September 1917 as extremely dangerous. In the *Frankfurter Zeitung* he pointedly warned about the conservative and pan-German circles who, as he expressed it, did not shrink from "using the name of the fatherland for their demagogic party business and thereby demean it."[280] Even worse, it seemed likely to him that as a result of these events the "rhetoric about the peace" would be fanned anew.[281] Unlike the great majority of the politicians, even in the Reichstag majority parties—including Stresemann—he feared that the policy that had begun with the peace resolution would peter out and that peace negotiations could not soon be expected: "I do not believe," he wrote on 7 October 1917 to Ludo Moritz Hartmann, "that peace will come early next year. . . . Wilson won't and Kerensky *can't*; he never could, as it would have meant the withdrawal of credit and thereby collapse. . . . All this peace talk *is* a misfortune, and discredits democracy since it is also demoralizing."[282] In Weber's view it

279. Cf. letter to Mina Tobler, 8 September 1917, Archiv Ebnet II, 41: "But the situation has not been as favorable for us for the past year and a half as at this moment, and this twaddle of the enemy about the conditions that *we* must fulfill in order to gain peace is simply stupid! Let alone the criminality of permitting the slaughter of hundreds of thousands for the sake of retaining their ministries."

280. *Pol. Schr.*, p. 232.

281. Ibid., p. 231.

282. To Ludo Moritz Hartmann, 7 October 1917, copy in Max Weber archive, Munich.

was necessary to carry on to the end and do one's duty and to pursue the "new orientation" of domestic affairs in Germany not as a means to peace but as an essential precondition for ensuring a more effective conduct of the war and for achieving a maximum of national unity.

Weber viewed Austria-Hungary as the weak link in the Central Powers. The internal situation worsened there because of acute deprivation and mounting tension between nationalities. It therefore appeared doubtful whether the Dual Monarchy would be able to continue the war for several more years. For some time Weber had observed with concern the growth of defeatist attitudes in Austria-Hungary. As early as July 1917, he complained to Hartmann about the tone of the *Wiener Arbeiter-zeitung* and especially about an article that referred to "this war as a brutal war of conquest for Germany." He implicitly threatened to break his personal relationship with Hartmann when he urged that the Austrian Social Democratic party leadership officially dissociate itself from the views expressed in that article.[283] He repeatedly objected to the attitudes taken by the Austrian press.[284]

In October 1917, Weber had an unexpected opportunity to hear about the Austrian situation at first hand. He went to Vienna for several weeks though for private rather than political reasons.[285] At the suggestion of the Austrian historian Ludo Moritz Hartmann, whom Weber had befriended during his 1916 visit, Weber was invited to fill the chair in political economy at the University of Vienna. When this opportunity arose, Max Weber had not stood at the lectern for two decades. At first he could scarcely believe his fortune: "It would be wonderful, but a utopia."[286] He was especially attracted by the chance to regain a proper academic position after all his attempts to win a responsible post in the political arena had failed. Moreover, as a result of the July crisis, his yen for political and journalistic life had flagged considerably. Besides, there might be the chance in Vienna to work for the steadfastness of the Central

283. To Ludo Moritz Hartmann, 5 July 1917, copy in Max Weber archive, Munich. He also says: "Until now no cleric has been moved to write openly, like the *Arbeiter-Zeitung*: 'This war is a *brutal war of conquest* by Germany,' for the sake of a sloppy need for peace. The effect of this in Russia is well known to me: It has cost us possibly many months more of war and thousands of lives. From such occurrences, since you will not oppose them, I must also draw lasting conclusions. So far, I have not seen that that statement by the apparent party organ has been disavowed."

284. E.g., in the letters to Hartmann of 7 October 1917 and 25 February 1918, after copies in the Max Weber archive, Munich.

285. The time of departure is established from the letter to Hartmann of 10 October 1917 in which the trip was announced and lodging discussed. Original in Weber papers.

286. Letter to Hartmann of 24 July 1917: "As to what you have written about the position in Vienna—I do not believe that the faculty or certainly the government would consider me. There are very able Austrians there (Schumpeter), and Herkner in Germany is also an Austrian, if somewhat undynamic. So . . . "

Powers (if only from the sidelines) since he viewed the Austrian position as a severe future danger point.[287] However, he remained uncertain about whether his health could withstand the pressures of regular academic teaching obligations; but he finally decided to make the attempt at least for the 1918 summer semester.

Weber was very distressed by the political impressions that he gathered while in Vienna in his many meetings with Austrian politicians. "Things are very bad in Austria. This is primarily because of the personalities of the new emperor and of Czernin. The situation surrounding the Austrian railroad minister's confidential declaration that he could no longer guarantee a regulated food supply after April, given the rapid and now irreparable overuse of railroad materials, is perhaps no longer so threatening, since railroad cars are now available from the Russian front. But the mood is unfortunately very tense. . . . As far as future policy is concerned, the decisive fact is that our allies all know that they will be dependent upon America's financial help after the war, since *we* shall not be able to give them anything."[288]

Although, as an outsider, Weber learned little about actual political events, he instinctively judged the situation quite correctly. His mistrust of Czernin was excessive, but his views on Emperor Karl and the court party were entirely justified. The emperor had already sent a peace offer to the western powers through Sixtus of Parma, behind the back of his foreign minister, that included the return of Alsace-Lorraine to France. To be sure, Weber overestimated the influence of pacifistic currents at the imperial court. It was the catastrophic economic and political situation that prompted the emperor to enter into his duplicitous policy of appeasement. Max Weber was aware that Austria's withdrawal from the war was very possible. It would have been unrealistic to expect that the economically and politically exhausted Danube monarchy would be willing to fight on much longer for the interests of imperial Germany in east and west, now that its real enemy, Russia, had been defeated. Weber felt it necessary to warn: "I believe it necessary to state publicly that the alliance is more in danger than commonly held if these idiots give the impression that they will gain influence."[289]

287. Letter to Mina Tobler, 30 October 1917, Archiv Ebnet II, 43: "I consider it *politically* not a matter of indifference to be there."

288. Letter to Oncken of 10 December 1917, after a copy in the Weber papers.

289. Letter to Oncken, 2 February 1917, after a copy in the Weber papers. He says further: "The situation in Vienna, as a result of the influences Kaiser Karl [is exposed to;] (among others, Lammasch, F. W. Förster, etc.), is essentially unfavorable, as is often assumed. I told the gentlemen in Vienna that they did not need to seek out as 'susceptible' a politician as Erzberger to explain the situation to them and the background of the peace resolution."

5. From Brest-Litovsk to Catastrophe

Max Weber's experiences in Vienna led him to revise his opinions about the peace resolution. He was now prepared to admit that it had been correct in July for the Reichstag to publicly press for the speedy achievement of a "negotiated peace" since Austria-Hungary would not be able to pursue the war beyond the fall. During his stay in Vienna, he apparently found out about Count Czernin's memorandum, which had prompted Erzberger to make his dramatic step in the budget commission of the Reichstag on 6 July 1917. The majority parties' initiative in the Reichstag, which Weber had viewed as a mere product of general panic in July, now seemed to him to have been justified for reasons of foreign policy: "Concern for the allies was one of the chief motivating factors for the Reichstag resolution of 19 July. Now this can be said openly. The enemies of a negotiated peace settlement were aware that the Reichstag majority had to conceal this decisive motive. Their attacks were therefore all the more despicable."[290] Of course, the Central Powers' situation had improved dramatically, at least temporarily, because of the triumph of the Bolshevik revolution. So one of his reservations against the policy of the July resolution was eliminated, namely, that an open call for peace would have raised hopes among the allies for a speedy German collapse.

Under these circumstances, Weber now gave his approval to the mass meeting that had been planned in July 1917 in Munich in favor of a "negotiated peace." The departure of the eastern enemy from the fray now opened up the possibility of a favorable peace at least if this opportunity was not lost through nationalistic megalomania. On the other hand, the Russian October revolution had had some impact upon the internal German situation and contributed considerably to unrest among the working masses over the German government's unyielding position on domestic reforms. It was more important than ever to uphold the German nation's political unity both through an energetic struggle against the pan-Germans' rhetorical heroism and through accelerated introduction of constitutional reforms. In the given critical situation, when for the first time there seemed to be concrete possibilities for a negotiated peace, Weber considered it to be absolutely necessary to speed up democratization in order to lay the domestic groundwork for the successful defense of Germany's interests as a major world power.

The mass meeting "for a peace of negotiation and against the pan-German danger"[291] took place on 5 November 1917 in Munich, with Max

290. In Weber's speech of 5 November 1917 in Munich, see the following note.

291. The speech was reported in the *Münchener Neueste Nachrichten* of 6 November 1917.

Weber and the Social Democratic deputy Wolfgang Heine as the chief speakers.[292] The meeting had been called by an independent committee consisting of members of several parties. Originally, Lujo Brentano was supposed to be the first speaker. Instead, introductory comments were made by a Munich bank director named Böhm. It is of some significance that Weber shared a platform here with several Social Democrats to speak out against the "Fatherland party's" agitation. It was indicative of Weber's political tolerance and also helped him to win his later popular reputation. His speech sharply settled accounts with the pan-Germans and their inclination to carry on a "big-mouth policy." Their noisy agitation had damaged pre-1914 German policy, and they held a great responsibility for its failure. The pan-Germans were above all responsible for the fact that an understanding with England had not been achieved before the war. Weber devastatingly exposed the domestic motives that

292. Two days later, on 7 November, Weber delivered his famous lecture "Science as a Vocation" in Munich in the framework of a lecture series of the Bavarian Land Association of the Free Student Union (Freistudentischer Bund). Hausenstein and Kerschensteiner were also to have spoken on "art as a profession" and "education as a profession" respectively. The brief report of the *Münchener Neueste Nachrichten* of 9 November 1917, morning ed., gives a brief summary of the most important points. (For the exact date of the lecture "Science as a Vocation," see Guenther Roth and Wolfgang Schluchter, *Max Weber's Vision of History: Ethic and Methods* [Berkeley, 1979], pp. 113 f.) Because of the special significance of the lecture in Weber's works, the 9 November newspaper report is reproduced here:

"*Mental work as a Vocation*. It must be admitted that the discussion of this theme is of value at a time in which physical achievement receives exceptional emphasis. The Bavarian Land Association of the Free Student Union plans to expound the association of mental work with professional life in four lectures.

"University Professor Max *Weber* (Heidelberg) opened the lecture series in the Steinicke Kunstsaal with a commentary on the theme 'Science as a Vocation.' It was an uncommonly lively, profound seminar, arresting from beginning to end. It would have been a shame to miss it. It began with a discussion of how scholarship is constituted as a vocation in the external sense; this permitted him the opportunity to bring in some memories from the American university scene. The area of consideration widened, as the lecturer proceeded to discuss the internal vocation of scholarship. Here he gave far more than the announcement had promised; he expounded upon his philosophy of life. He pointed out that the able achievement today is the specialized achievement. Passion, unconditional 'dedication to the object' is the presupposition of scholarly achievement. The artist and the scholar have one thing in common, the brainstorm, the fantasy; but *Wissenschaft* serves progress, its inclination is to be surpassed. A basic concept proposed was 'absolute *Wissenschaft*.' Scientific work is enveloped in the fulfillment of progress. Intellectualization signifies the knowledge of life conditions; it signifies the belief that man wishes to know something, and can know; it signifies the demystification of the world. What does *Wissenschaft* achieve for life? It offers information, methods of thinking, clarity. If science is a vocation today, that is the result of historically developing, inescapable logic. On the question, What should we do? science gives no answer. The large audience expressed particular gratitude to the lecturer."

were involved: "The hatred of England was above all a hatred of the English constitution. 'For God's sake, no alliance with England. That would lead us to parliamentarization!' " Above all, he openly stigmatized the fatal effects of their prophecies about unrestricted submarine warfare. This had undermined the mood at home far more than the peace resolution could ever do. He underscored the blindness of right-wing circles: "The pan-Germans behave as if they can carry on a policy of annexation in this war of alliances without reference to our allies." He denied the pan-Germans any right to speak for the masses either at home or on the front. Even the name "Fatherland party" was "a shameless scandal."

Weber greeted the appointment of Count Hertling as Reich chancellor above all because Hertling had committed himself to a German answer to the pope's peace message for a negotiated peace. He also noted that he expected that Hertling would henceforth consult closely with parliament in order to "avoid tactical mistakes made in connection with the 19 July resolution." In addition, he pointed out that progress toward democratization was a precondition of successful negotiations at a future peace conference. "Democracy will never enter into a shameful peace. Our descendants would never forgive us," he declared in order to pull the ground away from the widely held thesis that democratization would weaken an effective defense of Germany's national interest. On the contrary, he anticipated that a democratic government would be a necessary precondition for a powerful world policy: "We wish to pursue a world policy, but this is possible only for a master nation, not a master nation in the sense of the pan-German parvenu rhetoric, but quite simply a nation that holds control of its government firmly in hand. The pan-German movement will only lead to the depoliticization of the people. As a free, mature people we shall be able to enter into the circle of the master nations of the earth."

At the same time, Weber once again spoke out in the press for constitutional reforms. In an article entitled "Bayern und die Parlamentarisierung im Reich" ("Bavaria and Parliamentarization in the Reich"), which appeared at the time in the *Münchner Neueste Nachrichten*, he attempted to allay the Bavarian fear that the parliamentarization of the Reich would come at the expense of the power of the individual states.[293] In December 1917, the major essay *Wahlrecht und Demokratie in Deutschland* (*Suffrage and Democracy in Germany*) appeared, one of the classical constitutional treatises of those years. In this work, Weber again demanded a reform of the Prussian three-class suffrage as the

293. *Pol. Schr.*, pp. 233 ff.

decisive step on the road to the transformation of the political system in a liberal-democratic direction.[294]

Weber was very much distressed that the military authorities increasingly made common cause with the reactionary forces and that the Fatherland party could more or less depend upon the support of the Supreme Command. He believed it a self-evident national duty to give complete support to the military leadership during a war in all military matters. The military's partisan support for the parties of the Right seemed all the more dangerous since this would have a retarding effect upon a policy that sought to achieve moderate democratic reforms at home and a negotiated peace abroad. Weber therefore sharply attacked the "irresponsible cogovernment" of the military.[295] He also opposed the "politicization" of the army through patriotic educational programs by well-meaning officers who were in fact playing the game of the pan-Germans.[296] He warned that the officers were skating on the "slippery ice of politics" although they did not know how to maneuver on it and were thereby endangering their troops' confidence in their qualities of *military* leadership. In an assembly of the Heidelberg Fortschriftliche Volkspartei in December 1917, he heatedly insisted that the military should remain outside of the party political struggle so that it would not later be said of them, "What they achieved with the sword was later spoiled by their pen."[297] This sentence was reported in mutilated form in the press and served as the pretext of a protest telegram to the Reichstag against Weber's alleged slander of the *military* leadership. This was of course far from Weber's intention, much as he opposed the incursion of the military into the political arena. He of course readily seized this occasion to renew openly his vigorous attacks on "the politicization of the army in general and the introduction of the Supreme Command into the party struggle."[298]

At the time, of course, all eyes were fastened on Brest-Litowsk to see if a separate peace with Russia would be achieved after, as was expected, the allies rejected the Russian proposal to enter immediately into general peace negotiations.[299] The deep differences between the political and the

294. Ibid., pp. 245 ff.

295. Speech in Munich on 5 November 1917.

296. *Pol. Schr.*, pp. 231, 301, 450 f.

297. Not the Volksbund, as Marrianne Weber wrote on p. 630. Compare *Heidelberger Tageblatt*, 10 December 1917 as well as in the *Frankfurter Zeitung*, 1st morning ed., 13 December 1917.

298. Cf. Lebensbild, p. 630; Weber's explanation in the *Heidelberger Tageblatt* of 10 December 1917, cited there, also appeared in the *Frankfurter Zeitung*, 1st morning ed., 13 December 1917.

299. Nevertheless, Weber retained some hope that the western allies were generally open to the idea of negotiations. He so interpreted Lloyd George's speech of 5 December

military leadership over the strategy of peace negotiations promised little good, although of course the public knew very little about what was actually taking place in Brest-Litovsk. At the high point of the first phase of the negotiations, which were resumed after a ten-day pause on 8 January 1918, Max Weber visited Berlin. On January 12, he delivered a lecture in the Prussian House of Deputies to six hundred listeners about "the western bourgeoisie." Although claiming to treat the theme "purely scientifically," Weber sketched it against a universal historical background that justified the end of the primacy of the aristocratic elite and their replacement by the bourgeoisie.[300] The course of the negotiations in Brest-Litovsk in no way conformed with Weber's wishes.[301] He hoped for the creation of a permanent peaceful order on the basis of honorable negotiations with the smaller east central European nations and rejected direct annexations entirely. Germany's security interests, he believed, ought to be safeguarded in indirect ways. Great Russian interests should, if possible, not be questioned. In this sense, Weber favored the honorable acceptance of the Russian call for a peace without annexations or contributions. He was somewhat annoyed by Kühlmann's "quite unnecessarily blunt declaration"[302] of 11 January 1918, which announced that the peripheral states would no longer belong to the Russian empire as a result of the desires of the representative bodies set up there by the Central Powers. (These bodies, drawn from a narrow upper class that in Courland and Lithuania was primarily German, were mere puppets.) It seemed to Weber that the possibility of a liberal solution on the basis of the principle of national self-determination had been fundamentally thwarted. Weber's discomfort grew to patent disillusion in the light of the so-called "fisticuff speech" by General Hoffmann, the representative of the Supreme Command, at the peace negotiations of 12 January 1918.[303]

1917: "Lloyd George's speech indicates to me that they are becoming somewhat 'milder' and are anxious, but also that peace is still far off. The French have the key and the dawn is coming there very slowly and hesitantly. I hope that the political situation in Italy is as bad as possible." Letter to Mina Tobler, 9 January 1918, Archiv Ebnet, II, 52.

300. Announcement in the *Berliner Tageblatt*, 10 January 1918. Cf. letter to Mina Tobler, 13 January 1918, from Berlin, Archiv Ebnet II, 48 (the letter can be dated on the basis of the internal criteria).

301. Cf. Wolfgang Steglich, *Die Friedenspolitik der Mittelmächte*, 1917–18, vol. 1 (Wiesbaden, 1964), pp. 330 ff.; Fritz Fischer, *Griff nach der Weltmacht*, pp. 621 ff.; Gerhard Ritter, *Staatskunst und Kriegshandwerk*, vol. 4, pp. 109 ff.; and Winfried Baumgart, *Deutsche Ostpolitik 1918* (Munich, 1966), pp. 13 ff.

302. Letter to Mina Tobler, 13 November 1918, Archiv Ebnet II, 48. Cf. also letter to Hermann Oncken, 7 February 1918, partially printed in *Lebensbild*, p. 631.

303. Fritz Fischer confused this aggressive speech with Hoffmann's declaration of 18 November 1918, *Griff nach der Weltmacht*, p. 684.

Here, for the first time, the massive German demands were put directly and openly on the table. Hoffmann made his declaration in accord with Kühlmann, but in Germany, as in Austria-Hungary, this was viewed as the result of a direct interference by the Supreme Command in the peace negotiations, since it was well known that the Supreme Command supported extreme war goals. Max Weber, like much of German public opinion, was very irritated: "The Hoffmann incident was a scandal. It could cost us the alliance."[304] Weber feared that the postponement of the conclusion of peace would have fateful consequences in Austria-Hungary and predicted that the Danube monarchy would not be prepared to fight on indefinitely in order to achieve German war goals and thereby risk its existence as a state. He therefore demanded that Germany acquiesce in the Russian program and, beyond this, declare once and for all that the German Reich did not plan to enserf Belgium.[305]

Weber knew nothing at all about the serious conflict going on during these weeks between the political leadership and the Supreme Command.[306] He was inclined, also in accord with much of German public opinion, to blame the Supreme Command alone for the fact that the line of negotiations based on a liberal right to self-determination had been definitely replaced by a solution based on brute force. Actually, the political leadership was just as little prepared to forsake extensive annexations in the east at that time. Kühlmann's own plans were not that different from those of the Supreme Command in regard to the details of implementation. The German secretary of state for foreign affairs ignored the practical benefits of self-determination in east central Europe. However, Weber's diagnosis was correct to the extent that the Hertling-Kühlmann government was incapable of achieving a moderate solution in the face of the massive campaign carried on by the united forces of the Right in association with the Supreme Command, especially since the Kaiser had something to say about the direction of the peace talks.

Weber was deeply disturbed by the almost boundless agitation of the Right against a moderate peace: "The storm against von Kühlmann is unprecedented and all for domestic political reasons."[307] The situation

304. Letter to Hermann Oncken, 7 February 1918, partially printed in *Lebensbild*, p. 631.

305. Cf. the letter to Hermann Oncken of 7 February 1918.

306. Cf. in this regard Ritter, especially, *Staatskunst und Kriegshandwerk*, pp. 122 ff. and Baumgart, *Deutsche Ostpolitik*, pp. 18 ff. Fritz Fischer correctly points out that the political leadership's goals were extraordinarily far-reaching. But his point that the political and military representatives in the Reich leadership [were] in agreement, that "not for a minute . . . did disharmony" arise, is purely his interpretation, and an exaggeration that is in no way supportable.

307. Letter to Mina Tobler, 9 January 1918, Archiv Ebnet II, 52.

appeared entirely black to him. Berlin was the equivalent of a "political insane asylum. . . . It is difficult to believe this is all possible, and the worst part is the alliance between the military and heavy industry in this absolutely infamous movement. This band catches Ludendorff repeatedly in its net."[308] In this situation, the cooperation among the Conservatives, pan-Germans, Fatherland party and the Supreme Command seemed to him to be a complete scandal. He did not hesitate now to say openly that only parliamentarization could save Germany from the abyss. In a lecture on "aristocracy and democratization in Germany" on 16 January 1918 for the Association of Berlin Merchants and Industrialists, he demanded once again the repeal of the three-class suffrage with unusual pointedness. This would be tantamount to the transfer of political responsibility from the aristocracy to the bourgeois classes. He saw it only as the first step on the way to the introduction of the parliamentary system.

> The parliamentarization of Germany is *the only way to avoid another war* under difficult circumstances similar to those of the war now being waged. Parliamentarization is also the only way to save the dynasty and the monarch, for the current regime is heading for catastrophe both at home and abroad. Parliamentarization means the rule of political parties, and this has to be so. At the present time, the parties, like the administration, have become increasingly bureaucratized. This means control of the parties by small groups. This is caused by the present constitutional system. If the parties have access to power, the road will be open to the rise of political talent. Men will then rise to the top who have the confidence of the nation, and they will have the support of the parties as long as this is useful to them, that is, as long as the ministers retain the confidence of the people.[309]

It became quite clear in this presentation that Weber did not believe that the existing half-bureaucratic regime had the capability of bringing the war to an end, either in the east or elsewhere. Moreover, the government permitted insufferable agitation and tolerated the "department struggles to be fought out in the press. . . . The current insane demagoguery should not be conceivable," he asserted. He singled out the convergence of pan-German agitation with the political activities of the Supreme Command. He condemned the fact that "respectable officers have been caught in the net of the pan-German demagogues out of guilelessness and

308. Letter to Mina Tobler, 16 January 1918, Archiv Ebnet II, 53; cf. the letter to Marianne Weber, 13 January 1918, copy in Weber papers.

309. A shorter version of his speech prepared by Weber himself and appearing in the *Berliner Tageblatt*, 17 January 1918, morning ed.

are innocent of the vulnerability of the cause they are serving." Weber closed with a summary of his own platform.

> To choke off the present wicked demagoguery, we must have party rule: parliamentarization and democratization. The most important step to this end is the removal of the three-class parliament in Prussia. Its influence on the Reich government, through the Bundesrat, which also must be parliamentarized, has already been a burden. After the conclusion of a peace, it will be totally unbearable. Germany will not permit itself to be subjected to a parliament of profiteers, and [those are the people that] will become the dominant voice in the three-class House of Deputies under present conditions.

Under these circumstances, Max Weber was very pessimistic about the chances for peace in the east. He complained that "sensible people are powerless," and pointed out that no one knew "what will happen in the east, nor do they know how long Kühlmann and even Hertling can hold out against the intrigues of the large industrialists and the pan-Germans, who always have access to the army leadership. Ludendorff is completely blind in all nonmilitary matters."[310]

The Russian negotiators asked for a ten-day recess on 18 January 1918 in order to consult with the government, with the result that they subsequently broke off the negotiations with Trotsky's famous declaration that the war was proclaimed at an end but they would not sign this dictated peace. Weber saw clearly even before this occurred that the German government had missed the opportunity to achieve a peaceful solution and that the negotiations were about to collapse: "In any event, if a 'peace settlement' now does come about [it was not without reason that Weber put the words 'peace settlement' in quotation marks], much will be messed up anyway. And whether it will come, no one can say since the Russians have no need for it, while we, because of insufficient means of transport, cannot advance any further."[311] Clearly, Weber underestimated the Supreme Command's resolve for gigantic annexations without regard to the homeland's difficult supply situation.

In retrospect, Max Weber viewed it as a "challenge of destiny" that Germany had not entered into serious peace negotiations with Kerensky because it did not wish to give up the chance for territorial annexations. Above all, after the Russian October revolution, "a rational sense of the achievable had been lost," and at the Brest-Litovsk negotiations a "dictatorship of the Supreme Command from afar" had been permitted. "It is our misfortune," he wrote "that in Brest, we adopted neither of the

310. Letter to Marianne Weber, 13 January 1918, copy in Weber papers.
311. Letter to Mina Tobler, 16 January 1918, Archiv Ebnet II, 53.

courses of action that were associated with a negotiated peace. We might have based our policy upon the nationality principle[312] and created a union of free nations associated with the German culture and economy. Or we might have neutralized Courland and Poland by putting them on the same footing as Luxemburg toward us, while Russia would have adopted a similar solution for Estonia and Courland."[313] Of course the question arises whether even such a severely reduced program was practicable in 1918 if it still involved the hegemony of the German Reich in east central Europe. But Weber was also under the spell of the imperialistic illusions that continued to exaggerate Germany's opportunities even at the second high point of German power in the early part of 1918. Nevertheless, this kind of program would have been a far better taking-off point for the creation of a general system for a peaceful European order than the dictated peace of Brest-Litovsk, which was not unjustly pointed to as a concrete manifestation of Germany's drive for world power.

While the negotiations in Brest-Litovsk were proceeding, the Supreme Command was preparing a new great offensive in the west that was expected to bring the great decision there just before the American troops were brought to the front. Max Weber had some knowledge of the preparations: "They have decided on the great offensive against the west. *Our losses* alone are *calculated* at 600,000 casualties (!)"[314] "All hopes are placed upon the outcome. But is this justified?"[315]

At the time, Friedrich Naumann and Alfred Weber petitioned Ludendorff with a call for a political offensive in advance of the military offensive, for reasons of both domestic and foreign policy. They advised a wide-ranging peace offer to the allies that detailed war aims, because of the effect that this would have upon the mood at home and abroad. We do not know why Max Weber was not involved in this effort since it must have accorded with his own political views. Probably, he believed that a

312. In the manuscript, no doubt erroneously: "nationality policy."

313. Lecture in Frankfurt at the end of October 1918, after the record by Professor Ernst Fraenkel, who heard this lecture as a student, and was deeply affected by it. I am indebted to Professor Fraenkel for giving me a copy of his notes made in the form of a letter to a relative. Attempts to find a report about this lecture in the press have until now been unsuccessful.

314. Letter to Marianne Weber (undated, probably from 13 January 1918) after a copy in the Weber papers. Cf. the letter to E. Trummler of 17 January 1918, *Pol. Schr.* 1, pp. 474 f., and the letter cited below.

315. Letter to Eulenburg of 17 January 1918: "On the 'peace question': the offensive in the West has been decided upon (the calculated losses are fantastic and horrible!) The results . . . "; after a copy in the Weber papers, partially in *Lebensbild*, p. 631. He wrote similarly to Mina Tobler, 16 January 1918, Archiv Ebnet II, 53: "The future offensive in the West, the General Staff calculates, will bring 600,000 deaths—and if it fails, or half fails?"

renewed German initiative for negotiation made little sense or would have been a tactical error. To be sure, outside circumstances kept him from actively taking part in politics at the time. The beginning of the semester in Vienna demanded all of his time and strength.[316]

Even after the great turning point in the east, Max Weber was not convinced that the Central Powers had the strength to force a decision with their own resources. He became increasingly concerned that Germany could not hold out in this endless struggle, either organizationally, financially, or, above all, internally. He was extremely disquieted by the suspicion that government circles continued to reckon upon a war that would "continue for *years*."[317] He himself hoped for peace in the fall. He angrily rejected Rathenau's prediction that the war would last three more years: "This has to be insanity. This cannot happen without a revolution." He expected, in any case, new domestic explosions. "If the suffrage bill fails and a general strike results, then serious repercussions are possible," he asserted eleven days before the outbreak of the great armament workers' strike in Berlin.[318]

Weber was therefore scarcely surprised that mass strikes broke out in Vienna at the end of January and a few days later in Berlin and other large cities as the result of the failure of the Brest-Litovsk negotiations. "Hoffman's speech spoiled everything in Vienna and, consequently, in Berlin as well. No one on the Left expects equal suffrage to be granted (not even Neumann), and it is crystal clear that, as a result, the Social Democrats *can* no longer hold back the workers. (They have always maintained this and pointed to the consequences.) They are not in an easy position, since, as the result of recent impressions, *everybody* is moving to the left, to the Independents."[319] Weber approved of the fact that the Social Democrats had declared solidarity with the striking workers. This seemed necessary for the Social Democratic leaders simply for reasons of honor. Under the circumstances, this presented the only possibility of separating the strike movement from a politically dangerous leadership and holding it back with peaceful means. Therefore, he viewed it as a serious error when the authorities refused to receive a delegation of striking workers and forcibly strangled the strike by militarizing the affected factories. Weber was

316. Cf. the letter to Mina Tobler, 11 April 1918 (?), Archiv Ebnet II, 57: "I shall get through the summer, in spite of everything. Above all, I shall look neither right nor left."

317. Letter to Marianne Weber of 13 January 1918: "At all events, they are speaking about a war that will go on for years. However, I do not believe this, but at least until *after* the fall! Then a reaction will occur."

318. Letter to Eulenburg of 17 January 1918: "I wager 2 to 1 that there will be peace in the fall, but I do not wager confidently, since our military is insane."

319. To Oncken, 1 February 1918, *Lebensbild*, p. 632. Compare the letter of 7 February 1918 to the same party: "That the strike would come in *these* Berlin conditions and that it would be morally *impossible* for the party and the unions to oppose it, was very clear."

incapable of "anger" over the strike. "The cowardice and outcry of the bourgeoisie, . . . which loses all perspective over any strike that in other lands would be a common occurrence," he considered "appalling."[320]

Weber blamed these events above all—along with the behavior of the German representatives at the peace negotiations in Brest-Litovsk—on the agitation of the Fatherland party, which abetted the actions in Brest with the help of the "unscrupulous activities of the war press office and its clandestine partisan and political supporters."[321] The absence of a satisfactory settlement of the Prussian suffrage issue was a serious additional factor. Weber now demanded that this be rectified immediately. "It is the fruit of *trust*, thanks to which . . . a 'democratic' state . . . proves stronger in the decisive points of foreign affairs."[322] He wrote a new memorandum, which has not survived, on the question of peace at the time; we do not know whether it was submitted to the Foreign Office or to other Reich authorities.[323]

Although Weber assessed the armament workers' strike moderately and impartially, he still feared that it might have grave consequences. In three articles in the *Frankfurter Zeitung* at the beginning of February he sought to encourage the Left's prudence.[324] He attacked Trotsky's peace propaganda because its appeal to the Left considerably concerned him. He asserted bluntly that the Bolshevik government really did not want peace. In reality, it was "an *unalloyed military dictatorship*, though a dictatorship not of generals but of *corporals*." Everything else was "objectively a swindle." "Bolshevik soldier imperialism" now had taken the place of "Russian popular imperialism." The effects for Germany were the same whether the imperialist drive for expansion bore a czarist, a Cadet, or a Bolshevik label.[325]

Objectively, this was quite misleading, and Weber admitted as much to Oncken: "I have only given *one* side of the picture in describing the Bolsheviks (which I addressed to the Social Democrats!). The other, pacifistic current is *also* there."[326] Weber understood quite well that the

320. Ibid.

321. Ibid.: "If this continues, we can expect very nasty things."

322. *Pol. Schr.*, p. 300.

323. Introduced in *Lebensbild*, p. 718 as "Second memorandum on the question of concluding peace" occasioned by the armament workers' strike, dated 4 February 1918 (unpublished). Apparently the memorandum was not available to Marianne Weber when she composed *Lebensbild*; nor could it be located in the Weber papers (or in DZA II or with Professor Baumgarten). The author's search in the papers of the RKA and the RAdI as well as in the Haussmann and Naumann papers was fruitless. It is possible, though improbable, that Marianne Weber gave it to an unknown third party.

324. The first part was sent on 31 January to the *Frankfurter Zeitung*.

325. *Pol. Schr.*, pp. 292 ff.

326. Letter to Oncken of 7 February 1918.

chief reason Trotsky refused to sign the peace was the unlimited demands of the German negotiators along with the illusion that the slogan "neither war nor peace" would mobilize the workers of Europe to action against their governments.[327] At the same time, Weber thought it was necessary for tactical reasons to defend the German position in the negotiations at Brest-Litovsk. He only took exception to the "tone" of General Hoffmann's speech.[328]

Weber's position on the Brest negotiations was also influenced by the supposition that the Bolshevik rule would not last for long. He believed that it would take three months at most before the reactionaries returned to power. This prediction was influenced by the views of Otto Bauer, the Austrian Social Democrat, who gave "the revolution only until the spring before a bourgeois coup d'etat would occur."[329] Weber's description of the Russian events was to some extent erroneous. He did not have adequate conceptual tools to interpret the Russian revolution of 1917. Weber did not believe in spontaneous mass movements, but only in political movements whose goals and direction were set by great personalities who controlled them with the assistance of a well-organized administrative apparatus. In his view, as we have seen, a lasting revolutionary transformation, regardless of its form and location, was unthinkable without bourgeois cooperation.[330] The complete destruction of the old state machinery, which Lenin consciously sought to achieve, went beyond what in Weber's political and sociological theory was thought to be possible in modern times.[331] Weber believed in the permanence of the bureaucratic apparatus. In *Economy and Society* he had maintained that in the contemporary world, revolutions in the old style were no longer possible and that coups d'état, changes in the leadership group that controlled the state apparatus, had become the rule.[332] He could only

327. It continues in ibid.: "But *no* Russian, without absolute force, can deliver Riga to Germany. Any peace on this basis would be an absolute pseudo-peace that would only last as long as Russia cannot disturb it. Trotsky has *no* pressing interest in peace, we have to say, since we do not have the possibility of occupying significant parts of the country (and garrisoning it)."

328. *Pol. Schr.*, p. 296: "General Hoffmann's statements at the negotiations also proved to be true, and also did not contradict, in their contents, the statements that were made in the name of the political leadership." On both points, Weber was of an entirely opposite opinion; in spite of this, he believed it necessary to state the contrary for tactical reasons.

329. Letter to Oncken, 10 December 1917, copy in Weber papers; cf. *Pol. Schr.*, p. 292.

330. Cf. above, pp. 275 f.

331. Cf. the splendid critique by Pipes, *Max Weber und Russland*, pp. 634 ff., which nevertheless makes the serious error of overlooking the *tactical* limitations of Weber's comments on the Russian revolution, which leads him in part to false conclusions.

332. *Wirtschaft und Gesellschaft*, p. 579; also the part written in 1919, ibid., p. 155: "The overthrow of rulers through the initiative of the administrative staff has occurred in the past

explain Trotsky's and Lenin's success with the assertion that their authority rested on a military dictatorship, and that they used the military apparatus to maintain themselves in power.[333] But even the military organization appeared to be included in the general process of disintegration Weber believed present in Russia. Nor, in Weber's view, did military organization present a firm basis for lasting rule. This could only be guaranteed under modern conditions by a bureaucratic administrative staff. For all of these reasons, Weber predicted the collapse of Bolshevik rule. He expected the speedy return of a reactionary regime, a new "Miliukov government." In this perspective, he justified keeping the occupied regions in German hands until the end of the war.[334]

Weber's tactical justification of the German negotiators' position at Brest-Litovsk (put forward against his better judgment) was also apparent in a lecture "Der Sozialismus" ("Socialism") that he delivered to Austro-Hungarian officers in June 1918. Here he was less concerned about the domestic position of the Left than he was about the dangerous impact that the conduct of the German delegation in Brest-Litowsk had had upon the Austro-Hungarian alliance. "The German side negotiated in Brest-Litovsk in the most loyal[!] fashion . . . and with complete sincerity," Weber felt compelled to maintain, "in the hope that we would be able to arrive at a genuine peace settlement with these people." Their failure was Trotsky's responsibility alone: "It is impossible to conclude a peace with ideological fanaticism. It is only possible to neutralize it and that was the intention of the ultimatum and the dictated Brest-Litovsk peace settlement. Every socialist ought to perceive this, and I do not

under a wide variety of circumstances . . . The precondition was always a socialization of the members of the staff, which, according to circumstances, could take on the character of a partial conspiracy or even more of a general fraternal bonding and socialization. Under the conditions of existence of modern officials, this has been made much more difficult, if also, as Russian conditions demonstrate, not entirely *impossible* [my italics]. As a rule, they do not have the impact that workers hope to and can achieve through (normal) strikes." Weber's planned theories of revolution would presumably have been very "conservative"!

333. Compare Weber's letter to Naumann, cited by Heuss, *Friedrich Naumann*, 2d ed. (Stuttgart/Tübingen, 1949), p. 415 (here without a date; the letter, in contrast to other Naumann letters, could not be found in the papers): "The militarist, Trotsky. . . . He is a soldier Caesar, not a Napoleon of generals, but a praetorian leader of corporals and privates—and today, his single goal has to be to maintain groups of mutineers as a revolutionary instrument, even if the rest of the people have to be neglected." Also *Wirtschaft und Gesellschaft*, p. 163: "The 'dictatorship of the proletariat' for the sake of socialization requires, above all, a '*dictator*' suported by the confidence of the masses. . . . In Russia alone this has happened through *military* power supported by the interest in solidarity of the newly appropriative peasants." An interpretation that departs somewhat from actual developments.

334. *Pol. Schr.*, p. 303.

know anyone—no matter what his position—who does not acknowledge it, at least inwardly."[335]

It is clear that Weber was attempting here to efface the unpleasant impression that the Germans' unyielding position in Brest-Litowsk had made, because of his concern that it might serve as a pretext not only for Austrian attempts to seek a separate peace but also for revolutionary action by the workers. In Austria, especially, the danger of a general strike by the working masses was imminent in any case. It was only for this reason that Max Weber also passionately attacked the syndicalist movement, and the "romanticism of the general strike and the revolutionary expectations as such." No forces for directing production in peace-time could grow out of this. He again described the Russian experiment in very negative terms. He argued that he had observed the partial reemployment of the bourgeoisie by the Bolsheviks, but maintained that "in the long run, the state machinery and the economy cannot be run in this manner." It was surprising that this organization was able to perpetuate itself for such a long time, but this was entirely due to the existence of a military dictatorship.[336] In his description of events, Weber completely failed to recognize the political élan of the Bolsheviks under Lenin's powerful leadership. For political reasons of a transitory nature, Weber the sociologist avoided an objective analysis of the true character of the Russian events.[337]

Beginning in February 1918, Weber withdrew entirely from political activities. He expected little from the discussions of a negotiated peace, as he was convinced that there was no chance for peace negotiations in the near future.[338] Now, arms must decide. To have called for peace negotiations during the offensive on the western front would have appeared "cowardly" to him. Perhaps it was motives like this that prevented him from associating with the peace efforts of Naumann and Alfred Weber with the Supreme Command, while Legien, Bosch, and other personalities of note were involved.

In April, Weber took up the chair of political economy at the Univer-

335. *Gesammelte Aufsätze zur Soziologie und Sozialpolitik*, p. 515; cf. p. 517: "It is clear and acknowledged that Trotsky did *not* want peace. No Socialist that I know disputes this any more." Weber's real views appear, e.g., in an (undated) letter to Herkner of June 1918 (Weber papers): "The few [relations to Russian circles] that I had were ruptured by the peace of Brest-Litowsk and the insane hatred that has arisen since them among all Russian circles against everything German."

336. Ibid., p. 514; Cf. also "Politics as a Vocation," *Pol. Schr.*, p. 529; also Weber's statement in a speech in Munich on 4 November 1918, according to the report in the *Munchener Neueste Nachrichten*, 5 November 1918: "Bolshevism is a military dictatorship like any other and will collapse like all the others."

337. Cf. Pipes, *Max Weber und Russland*, p. 639.

338. Cf. also the letter to Frau Edinger of 18 March 1918, *Pol. Schr.*, 1, pp. 475 f.

sity of Vienna for the summer semester as a trial run. He was fully absorbed in the new task. He put politics completely aside for the time being, although he continued to observe events with concern: "I am aloof from politics. It is not possible *to do* otherwise here. And that is good and spiritually relaxing since everything seems bad and gloomy. If I were home, I would have to leap into the fray."[339] He lectured on his studies of the sociology of world religions, on the theme "positive critique of the materialist conception of history," and he delivered a series of new lectures on "the sociology of the state," a theme that concerned him deeply.[340] He gave of himself totally in the crowded lectures, and it was no wonder that the old feeling soon returned that he was not up to the pressures of regular academic lecturing. We must bear in mind that this man was not content merely to transmit known knowledge but attempted to bring something original to every lecture.

Once again, Vienna exercised its magical powers upon Weber. He enjoyed the beauty and the cultural activity of the imperial metropolis and was delighted by the hospitality and the modest and helpful willingness to oblige that he found everywhere, even in the highest government circles. His time in Vienna was perhaps the happiest of his life. The letters that have survived from that time have no equals among his correspondence in beauty and harmony. Even his political worries seemed to dissipate somewhat: "When one thinks what we have been preserved from, one realizes it is almost a miracle, and one throws off all 'pessimism.' "[341]

However, all the attempts of the Viennese authorities and the pleas of his friends could not persuade Weber to stay on. Beautiful as Vienna was, he did not feel at home there, and the slow old Viennese "ways" offended his puritanical nature. The decisive factor was that Weber did not feel up to the strains of permanently teaching and living in a large city. Moreover, he no longer wished to abstain from all political activities. "For me, settling in Vienna meant leaving political activity altogether," Weber wrote to the Royal Ministry of Education. "But under the present circumstances it is difficult to withdraw from one's duty to play even a small political role in Germany." This would, however, be incompatible with the acceptance of "a secure and apparently well-paid position in the neighboring empire with which we are allied."[342] So, once again, Weber

339. Letter to Mina Tobler, 1 June 1918, Archiv Ebnet II, 62.

340. Cf. *Lebensbild*, pp. 615 ff.

341. Letter of 22 April 1918, *Lebensbild*, p. 623.

342. Letter of 5 June 1918, carbon in Weber papers; he writes: "I did not expect at the time that, after about January of this year, both in German domestic policy as in certain points in foreign policy, several tendencies would come to the fore politically that in my view are opposed to German interests. In the future perhaps these would also have an

gave up an academic position in spite of great success at it; he yearned for involvement in politics and journalism. It was, of course, a "painful confession" to say to himself, "No. I was born for the pen and for the speaker's platform, not for the lectern."[343]

At the end of July 1918, Max Weber returned to Heidelberg. Nothing came of the political activities he had in mind. His nerves exhausted by the Viennese "exertions," he avoided all politics.[344] Moreover, he was distressed about political developments, and this silenced him. At home, nothing had improved. Germany was moving inexorably toward military defeat. Bulgaria's collapse in September 1918 was the prelude to catastrophe. Weber was deeply depressed.[345] His political ideals were collapsing. Germany's future as a world power had been gambled away.

---

unfavorable effect upon the purpose and the strength of our alliance although at least outwardly it is not seriously threatened for the foreseeable future.

343. *Lebensbild*, p. 625. How difficult it was for Weber to recognize that he was not in a position to work as an academic *teacher*, is seen in the fact that he wished to resign again from his office as second chairman of the Verein für Sozialpolitik, since the "precondition" under which he had accepted the office—that he would "become an Ordinarius in Vienna"—was no longer operative. Letter to Herkner, early July 1918, from Vienna; Weber papers.

344. Cf. Marianne Weber's remark to Helene Weber: "He does not like to talk about war and politics—it does no good." *Lebensbild*, p. 627.

345. Cf. ibid., p. 628.

8
Collapse and a New Beginning

1. Defeat and Revolution: Weber's Work for the German Democratic Party

On 29 September 1918, Ludendorff and Hindenburg called for the immediate formation of a parliamentary government that should issue to the allied powers an immediate request for an armistice on the basis of Wilson's fourteen points. The new government of Prince Max von Baden, installed accordingly, pleaded for a few days' delay so that the request for an armistice might to some degree be prepared diplomatically. In vain. Fearing that any day could bring the total collapse of the western front, Ludendorff rejected the plea. On the night of 3–4 October, the German request for the immediate cessation of military operations was sent to Wilson. Germany's defeat had become reality.

Max Weber's constitutional reform program was thus fulfilled almost overnight and in a more extensive form than he had expected for the near term. But at what price and under what circumstances! The Supreme Command ordained parliamentarization at the hour of catastrophe although they had opposed it with such force in the past, and they thereby burdened the new democratic government with the terrible odium of defeat. The great dream of a powerful German Reich that would take its place in the world alongside Great Britain, Russia, and the United States was now a thing of the past. The nation had to face extreme humiliation and abasement.

At first, Max Weber could not fully accept the extent of the catastrophe. He did not want to believe in Ludendorff's declaration that the "military situation is absolutely hopeless." In fact, the fears of the Supreme Command that the western front might fall apart any day as a result of a new allied assault had been much too pessimistic, largely, however, because Foch had a great respect for the German army's fighting spirit and overestimated its remaining defensive capacity. But although Max Weber was dubious about the correctness of Ludendorff's step, he accepted reality: "What remains to be done? The new government—completely untrained—must take the terrible odium upon itself even if in fact Ludendorff has lost his nerve and—as *I believe*—the situation is not quite so bad. This does not change the fact that we have to withdraw and reassemble (at our frontier) before a new man (Gallwitz?) can take over. The outlook for the peace settlement under such circumstances will be very bad indeed."[1] Weber viewed the overhasty request for an armistice as the result of sheer panic, similar to the panic that in his view had led to the Reichstag peace resolution in July 1917. He believed it necessary to give warning, in a letter to Naumann, about decisions being made on the basis of "an unstoppable loss of nerve" that seemed prevalent in Berlin. "This can prove terribly costly for the nation. I hope that I am wrong about it. Now that calamity has arrived, I am absolutely cool. I hope that you are too."[2] Nonetheless, he was depressed by the hopelessness of the situation. He decided, since he lacked sufficient information, to stay put for the time being in relation to the precipitous events.

One thing, however, he considered an absolute necessity: to fix the responsibilities for the decisions that had led to the appeal for an armistice. First, he still could not quite believe that Ludendorff's extremely pessimistic judgment of the military situation had been correct. Later, because he had no further doubts about this, he angrily condemned Ludendorff's "reckless gambling."[3] Above all, Weber wished to forestall the danger that the new democratic government would be made responsible for the defeat. He clearly saw what a terrible burden the government faced in liquidating the lost war. Therefore, he suggested to Naumann that an immediate documentation of the course of events that had preceded the decisive step on the night of 3–4 October should be arranged. Naumann had of course already attempted to bring this about.[4]

Weber was convinced of the need to remain cool, not to give vent to hysterical panic, and to conduct oneself with dignity. It seemed to him that national self-condemnation at the moment of defeat was a cheap way

1. Letter to a relative who cannot be identified more closely, 10 October 1918, original in Weber papers; "military situation . . . (as a letter from Berlin by a fully versed parliamentary member reports)."

2. Letter of 11 October 1918, *Pol. Schr.* 1, p. 476.

3. Letter to Crusius of 24 November 1918, *Pol. Schr.* 1, p. 482.

4. Letter of 11 October 1918; cf. Naumann's detailed answer in Heuss, *Friedrich Naumann*, 2d ed., pp. 430 f.; Naumann rejected Weber's diagnosis of the Berlin events in this letter.

out for weak personalities and did not accord with the dignity of a great people. Weber's speech in Frankfurt early in October 1918 is an impressive example of his mood at the time. "We have to face the fact that we have lost a war to the Anglo-Saxons both in terms of world politics and, even worse, militarily. To lose it with dignity is our next task."[5] He emphasized that Germany had "had to" fight this war—whatever the outcome (and the full extent of the German defeat was not yet apparent). It had to fight the war against czarism in particular, and "we have won that war." Three times during the war, Germany had tempted destiny: with unrestricted submarine warfare, by the refusal to enter into sincere peace negotiations with the Kerensky regime, forfeiting all annexation demands, and above all else by concluding the peace of Brest-Litowsk. It was not the war that was at fault, even if it had been entered with "a mistaken international strategy," but the political manner and means that were employed. In this regard, the most serious blunder had been that much too little attention had been paid to Austria-Hungary: "A state that watched its children starve, that was torn by national divisions, had, in the short or long run, to seek a separate peace." Weber touched a nerve here. As it happened, the collapse of Austria-Hungary on 28 October 1918 rendered illusory the remaining hope that the worst could be avoided through a final mobilization of all national resources and that a peace settlement with tolerable conditions was still possible to achieve.[6]

At this moment, Weber still believed that Germany need not conclude an immediate armistice at any cost. Later, he repeatedly stressed that only the revolution had made this unavoidable. He still believed at the time that the German side could set certain conditions, for example, the occupation of Belgium by Belgian forces only and not allied ones, Wilson's arbitration on the future of Alsace-Lorraine, and a moderate war contribution. The economic conditions seemed more important to him than the territorial ones since he feared that if Germany was overburdened financially, its economy would never get back on its feet. "It is better to abandon a scrap of land that can later be regained than to become a slave to debt. We cannot concede forty billion to them. . . . That would strengthen the belief that the enemy fought for money, which would put us in a better moral position to resist. But the payment would destroy us as a nation." Weber was not yet prepared to give up all hope of overcoming the "crisis." His national fervor led him to attempt the utmost. Temporarily, he believed it still possible to continue the fight. The Social Democratic leaders had the task of explaining the real

5. According to Ernst Fraenkel's report. Cf. above, chap. 7, n. 313.

6. Weber apparently expected Austria-Hungary to seek peace without conditions, which would make the situation hopeless: "Austria's withdrawal would close us off from sources of petroleum and render the submarine war impossible."

situation to the people and the troops and encouraging them to hold out. Behind this lay his possible efforts to save what still could be saved. However, it was clear to Weber, and became even clearer with the compelling events of each day, that Germany's role as a great power was a thing of the past, and a period of humiliation lay ahead. Pessimistic as Weber had been since the beginning of the war, he had always hoped that Germany would come out "of it all with honor" and at least preserve its territorial integrity. Now it was necessary to accept destiny and retain inner strength.[7]

Before the full extent of the defeat was publicly known, he wrote from Heidelberg: "We shall now have peace next year, and our lives will be reoriented. It will be a peace that none of us had contemplated, including myself even in all my sobriety and skepticism. . . . We must begin once again to reconstruct Germany from the bottom up, and we will do it. Even so, it will be worth it to be a German."[8] He was bitter, however, that he could only offer half strength to this task because his health would not permit more.[9] He also believed that, because of the defeat, his own personal existence had become problematic.

> People like *myself* are now outwardly as well as inwardly "luxuries.". . . The kind of work I can do pays absolutely nothing—and with justice. The nation will now have to struggle for its bread, and there will not be much left for academics. But enough of this. Somehow we will, outwardly—adjust, even if—and I think it just—75 percent of pure *pension* income like our own (at least for the childless)—will simply be confiscated.[10] "Inwardly" it will be more difficult. My inward "calling" is scholarly work and scholarly teaching. And the nation does not need that now. So I shall have to try to reorient myself. But how? To what? I still do not know. I do not know if I shall be successful either. But in spite of all this, life is important and will again find beauty.[11]

7. Cf. the letter to Mina Tobler, 29 September 1918, Archiv Ebnet II, 76: "Our future has never looked *so* grave. But now, after what we have feared has begun, there is a sense of relief after those agonizing long weeks and the grief about the blindness of so many others. At least then when the conclusion is here and it is possible to perceive its consequences. Of course it has *not yet* gone that far."

8. Letter of 10 October 1918.

9. Cf. the letter to Marianne Weber, November 1918, *Lebensbild*, p. 644.

10. This corresponded essentially to his views about how to raise the costs of the war, and their liquidation after the conclusion of peace, as he stated in a letter to Herkner of 11 November 1916 (Weber papers): "I am completely incompetent about *financial questions* at this time; I do not know the situation and the important data—*emotionally*, I am for the 'greatest' measures: confiscation of wealth up to 50 percent, if necessary."

11. Letter of 10 October 1918.

Of course, all did not yet seem lost. Max Weber grasped wholeheartedly onto Rathenau's idea of a levée en masse, an appeal to the masses for a struggle for national defense with all of the resources and means available. A people's war, like the great model of 1813, would have been in complete accord with his basic political convictions. But he was sober about the terrible difficulties. Not only were great numbers of the German people weary and apathetic, longing for peace at any price, but, in the event of a national "war of despair," the unity of the Reich would be lost.[12] Weber visited Munich at the time and observed that almost everyone wanted peace there even at the price of dissolving the Reich. He wrote in almost identical phrases to Delbrück and Oncken at the time: "In the event of a call for 'national defense,' the loss of Bavaria from the Reich will follow automatically. *No* one here and *no* party has a contrary opinion. The king has no other choice if he wishes to retain his throne."[13]

As Weber watched the growing separatist and radical pacifist tendencies in Bavaria at close hand, his concern and bitterness grew. In the event of a final despairing struggle of national defense, and he was sympathetic to this idea if the armistice conditions proved unacceptable, he feared the worst in Munich. On 4 November, three days before Eisner seized power in Munich, the revolution broke out in Kiel and from there spread quickly throughout Germany. In the hope that better peace conditions could be achieved by fulfilling the Wilsonian demands, Weber took a sharp position in a public gathering of the Fortschrittliche Volkspartei against secessionist sentiments in Bavaria: "The call, away from Prussia, is criminal folly," he told the party meeting.[14] Opposing the widespread pacifist and radical socialist current of the day, he defended the idea of power as the essence of political action. The pacifistic slogan "peace at any price" was politically irresponsible.[15] He flung the words of the Left back at them: "Playing with revolution means that in the need to make a rhetorical impression, to make *words*, a pleasure trip is taken at

12. Cf. also the postscript to the letter to Naumann of 18 October 1918, *Pol. Schr.* 1, p. 480.

13. Letter to Oncken of 6 October 1918, partially in *Lebensbild*, pp. 636 f.; compare letter to Delbrück on the same day (Delbrück papers): "In the event of a summons to 'national defense'" etc.

14. *Lebensbild*, p. 638.

15. Compare the report of the *Münchener Neueste Nachrichten*, 5 November 1918: "There are two paths *to peace*. [The first] is that of the politician, which the speaker has always sought. The minimum requirement of a lasting peace is that all participating nations can sincerely accept it. The second path is the sermon on the mount, based on the principle of peace at any price, on any condition. It is possible to have great respect for the supporters of this view, if they also live according to the sermon on the mount in their private lives."

the expense of the proletariat."[16] For "what will be the results of the revolution? To have the enemy in our country and then a reaction worse than anything that we have lived through. And then the proletariat will have to pay the cost."[17] The *front soldiers* had to decide whether or not to take up a defensive war in the face of unbearable armistice conditions. Those who "remained at home" would have to keep their mouth shut. Weber's words fell on deaf ears in the mostly radical-minded audience. It was as if two worlds were meeting: the heroic national belief in power of the great age of the German Reich that felt justified in preserving the national state won with so much difficulty, and the internationalism of the left-wing socialist movement, which rejected the social structure of the old state and its one-sided nationalist direction and hoped for a peace of the peoples against their governments.[18]

Weber was even more disturbed about the attitude of wide sections of the middle classes who hoped for more favorable peace conditions and even financial advantages through the separation of Bavaria from the Reich and possibly a union with German Austria. Immediately after his return to Heidelberg, he wrote resignedly to Oncken that "loyalty to the Reich" had become an impotent idea in Bavaria, especially among the bourgeoisie: "Only the left is 'loyal to the Reich,' but the Social Democrats attach the proviso that William II has to go, otherwise they believe in nothing. Apart from this, the mood even among the best men is so radically in favor of peace at *any* price that it was enough to make one despair. Every attempt to organize resistance [Weber had apparently thought of this] would lead to immediate anarchy."[19] The following day, the revolutionary flood in Munich made Weber's hopes and fears superfluous.

As early as the beginning of October 1918, Weber pressed for William II's immediate abdication. In his view, this would be the honorable thing to do; after the monarch had led his people to a catastrophic defeat, he could not simply remain on the throne as if nothing had happened. In addition, Weber recognized that in view of Wilson's hedged but unmistakable declarations that the allied powers would not negotiate with the old imperial authorities and especially William II's government, the Kaiser's abdication had become unavoidable. At the same time, Weber clung to the hope that through the immediate abdication of the Kaiser, the desperate situation of the Reich might be improved and Wilson

16. "Playing . . ." later report by Weber in an undated letter to Oncken, probably from 11 or 12 November 1918, copy in Weber papers.

17. Report of the *Münchener Neueste Nachrichten*; similarly, Weber to Oncken in the previously mentioned letter.

18. Cf. *Lebensbild*, p. 639.

19. Letter to Oncken, 6 November 1918, *Lebensbild*, p. 637; "The Deputy H," mentioned there, is of course Held.

moved to greater concessions: "It has been indicated via Switzerland that his resignation would change everything [!]"[20] In December, Weber declared in the *Frankfurter Zeitung* that the Kaiser would "bear the odium forever, whether or not it is just," because he did not take the one honorable path of abdication at the right hour. "The enemies' conditions," were thereby made harder for Germany.[21]

Max Weber was by no means an enemy of the monarchy as such.[22] He still maintained that he was "a supporter of monarchical institutions that were subjected to parliamentary control."[23] But his views did not reflect royalist sentiments. His support for the monarchist system was the result of technical considerations about the best form of government and had nothing to do with emotional loyalties. He believed that a "strong parliamentary monarchy" was technically the most adaptable and in *this* sense fundamentally the strongest form of government.[24] Its superiority to all republican systems of government was based on the important formal advantage "that the highest position in the state was permanently occupied" and therefore healthy limits were put on the drive for power of personally ambitious politicians.[25] It was also the only institutional form of government capable of neutralizing the constant desire of the military to expand its power from the military into the political realm.

As early as the St. Louis Congress of 1905, Max Weber had defended German monarchical institutions in Germany with these same arguments:

> If, in old civilized countries such as Germany, the necessity of a strong army arises in order to maintain independence, this means, for political institutions, the support of an hereditary dynasty.
>
> The resolute follower of democratic institutions—as I am—cannot wish to remove the dynasty where it has been preserved. For in military states, if it is not the only historically endorsed form in which the Caesarian domination of military

20. Letter to Oncken, 6 October 1918; the passage cited here is according to the copy in the Weber papers; cf. *Lebensbild*, pp. 636 f.; cf. the letter to Delbrück of 11 October 1918 (Delbrück papers): "In relation to the interest of the dynasty as such, the fact that his remaining makes the conclusion of peace more difficult and perhaps will cost us severe conditions of peace is a secondary consideration; at the same time it is a weighty one." Similarly in a letter to Schulze-Gävernitz of 11 October 1918, *Pol. Schr.* 1, p. 477.

21. *Pol. Schr.*, p. 450.

22. Cf. also above, chap. 6, text at note 33.

23. Letter to Delbrück of 10 October 1918; cf. letter to Schulze-Gävernitz, 11 October 1918.

24. *Pol. Schr.*, p. 449; Weber argued this point similarly in the election speeches for the National Assembly.

25. *Wirtschaft und Gesellschaft*, p. 689.

> parvenus can be averted, it is still the best. France is continually menaced by such domination; dynasties are personally interested in the preservation of rights and of a legal government. Hereditary monarchy—one may judge about it theoretically as one wishes—warrants to a state, which is forced to be a military state, the greatest freedom of the citizens—as great as it can be in a monarchy—and so long as the dynasty does not become degenerated, it will have the political support of the majority of the nation.[26]

The decisive reason for Max Weber's positive attitude toward monarchy was its function as a source of legitimacy that was in a position to awaken a belief in the legitimacy of the existing governmental and social conditions. Even in its "objectified" and institutionalized hereditary version, charisma was still a source of legitimacy that could not lightly be replaced by something else in the modern mass state. For this reason. "a parliamentary king [was frequently] retained in spite of his powerlessness, above all because through his very existence and because of the fact that power was exercised 'in his name,' the *legitimacy* of the existing social and property order was guaranteed by the strength of his charisma. Everyone who had an interest in this order necessarily feared the undermining of the belief in its legitimacy that would follow [the king's] removal."[27]

Max Weber nevertheless did not concede the kind of genuine charismatic power to the modern monarchy that he associated with the formative monarchies based upon the power of princely war leaders. Weber sarcastically criticized the dynastic system of his own age and contrasted this system with its "comfortable pretensions" of contemporary "grace of Godhood—with its justification in the 'unfathomable' decree of God 'to whom alone the monarchy is responsible,'" with a genuine charismatic monarchy bound by constant "justification" in the eyes of the retinue, which thereby sets goals and limits.[28] But modern

26. "Capitalism and Rural Society in Germany," in *From Max Weber: Essays in Sociology*, ed. H. H. Gerth and C. Wright Mills (New York), p. 370.

27. *Wirtschaft und Gesellschaft*, p. 689; cf. p. 148: "Namely, the retention of the hereditary monarchy—along with the certainly not insignificant ideology of loyalty—is very strongly affected by one consideration: all inherited and legitimately earned property will be shaken, if inward subjection to the sacred heredity of the throne ceases. Hence, it is not by accident that [hereditary monarchy] is more adapted to the propertied classes than it is perhaps to the proletariat."

28. Ibid., p. 664; see the comparison between the English *kingdom of influence* and the constitutional monarchy on p. 689, which is quite unfavorable for the continental monarchies (Prussia, Russia, Austria-Hungary): "The 'parliamentary' kingdom in England signifies selectivity in admission to power in favor of a monarch who is qualified as a statesman. . . . For this reason it is very much more genuinely charismatic in form than the official kingdom of the continental variety which equally endows the simpleton and the political genius with sovereign pretensions merely on the basis of hereditary rights."

mass society, which was becoming increasingly "legalistic" and value-neutral as a result of bureaucratization, should retain a monarchy as the surviving link to the source of charismatic legitimacy. Weber argued in this way because he believed that the legitimization of domination based upon a belief in legality was much weaker than one based upon charismatic or traditional forms of legitimacy, even though he viewed them both to be formally equivalent. Fundamentally, he held only the charismatic form to be a source of genuine legitimacy. In his opinion, only a great personality who could establish values, rather than abstract regulations, is capable of arousing inner support for a governmental system of whatever nature. This thoroughly aristocratic notion departs from the rationalistic structure of Weber's overall approach to political problems.

Even at the moment of imperial Germany's collapse, Max Weber wished to see the dynasty preserved. Nothing appeared to him to be less desirable at this very moment than a radical break with monarchic traditions. Like many others, he could not quite conceive of a strong republican Germany. There is a conservative strain here in his political thought that surfaces again in his plans for constitutional reform. To be sure, he correctly sensed that a new democratic state that departed from monarchical institutions without good reason would earn the hatred of the Right and would thereby render its legitimacy suspect from the outset. He therefore actively opposed the republican currents in Munich right up to the revolutionary outbreak, although even in October he became aware that his support for the monarchy provoked general head-shaking. However, he had the well-founded hope that even the Social Democrats would not oppose the preservation of a monarchy that was strictly subjected to parliamentary institutions.[29] He considered it out of the question to retain the reigning monarch, who by his swaggering was responsible for much of Germany's misfortune. As early as 1917, Weber had confided to Delbrück that "the dynasty was the one thing that had completely forsaken its duties during the war."[30] William II had completely failed in fulfilling the single function of the Prussian-German monarchy on behalf of which Weber had defended it in republican America. The emperor had not "prevented plain military rule."[31] Instead, by the end of 1917 at the latest, Germany had lived under a half-plebiscitarian, half-authoritarian dictatorship of the Supreme Command.

29. *Pol. Schr.*, p. 336; cf. Scheidemann, *Memoiren eines Sozialdemokraten* (Dresden, 1928), vol. 2, p. 262: "In all candor, a 'father of the country' with speech and telegraph censorship in political matters, bound to cut-and-thrust provisions of a democratic constitution—can a man believe that a revolution would break out in Germany to remove such a 'ruler'?"

30. Letter of 28 June 1917, see above, chap. 6, note 86.

31. *Pol. Schr.*, p. 450.

Max Weber recognized, at a remarkably early state, that the future of the monarchical system would ultimately depend upon the willingness of the Kaiser to yield to the thinly veiled demand by Wilson that he give up his throne immediately. If he refused to do so, the antimonarchical currents in Germany would grow stronger. Weber was therefore incensed when he heard that the Kaiser had moved his headquarters to Spa in order to avoid discussions about his abdication. Weber wrote bitterly to Delbrück on 6 October 1918 that the fact that William II "could *desert* his post in *Berlin* in order to try to avoid it all is terrible, and this can only bring misfortune upon the future of the dynasty. . . . It is and will remain dishonorable for him to cling to his throne after having been forced to bow to an American professor."[32] A few days later, he insisted, in similarly worded letters to Naumann, Delbrück, and von Schulze-Gävernitz that "the present Kaiser must resign in the interests of the Reich and the dynasty."[33] "I would be lying if I feigned sympathy with him. For the sake of the nation and the interests of Kaiser*dom*, I cannot wish for a *dishonorable* conclusion to the Kaiser's rule, which can be anticipated if he retains the trappings of his role in a smaller Germany or one otherwise stunted, in which he will be, so to speak, a 'Kaiser in penury.'"[34] In Weber's opinion, the honor and prestige of the monarchy demanded the Kaiser's immediate abdication through his own free decision, before he was pressured into it either from abroad or at home, in view of the humiliations that he had experienced and that he still had to reckon with. Otherwise, the survival of a monarchy rooted in the people, which could fulfill its primary function as the source of legitimacy of the existing governmental and social structure, would become impossible because of the domestic situation. Even inherited charisma has to justify itself; when it fails, when it fails as completely as it had in this case, it becomes powerless and loses its intrinsic meaning.

Max Weber attempted, through Delbrück and Naumann, to encourage a conservative and monarchistic-minded man to inform the Kaiser about his dishonorable and hopeless situation.[35] Who took on this task was irrelevant. It could be Hindenburg or another high officer, Prince Max von Baden, or someone else. The attempt proved fruitless. Later Weber accused the prince of having been "imprisoned by dynastic sen-

32. Letter from Munich (Delbrück papers); cf. the letter to Oncken of the same date, *Lebensbild*, pp. 636 f.

33. Letter to Delbrück of 10 October, Delbrück papers; to Schulze-Gävernitz of 11 October and to Naumann of 12 October 1918, the latter in *Pol. Schr.* 1, pp. 477 f.: also Naumann's answer of 16 October 1918, which discusses the possibility of influencing the monarch, in Heuss, *loc. cit.*, p. 575.

34. Letter to Delbrück of 10 October 1918.

35. Cf., besides the already cited letters, those to Naumann of 17 and 18 October 1918, *Pol. Schr.* 1, pp. 478 ff.

timentality which blinded him to the realities of the situation and permitted costly days and weeks to expire."[36] Max Weber viewed it as a "life-and-death situation for the nation" to preserve the monarchy "at the expense of its present impossible representative." He saw it all gambled away by a monarch who clung to his throne dishonorably. Weber continued to castigate the ruler after he had fled to Holland. William II had "just about provoked the revolution" by his "desertion of the capital and by playing with [the idea of a] coup d'etat."[37] He thought William II's declaration of 22 November 1918, in which the Kaiser released the army and the bureaucracy from their loyalty oaths, was "dreadful . . . , cowardly and deceitful, dishonorable right to the end."[38]

Even after the revolution had finally triumphed in Berlin and enforced the Kaiser's abdication, Weber believed it was still possible to insist that the "fundamental issues of the constitution, including the dynastic question," must be decided "not by the acts of a minority, but through a free plebiscite. . . . Since I wish to see the dynasty preserved and because I am not doubtful about the results of a—free—vote, I would join in such an effort. But from the point of view of strict legitimacy, it would be scarcely acceptable. The latter, however, would not be binding for me."[39] Even in May 1919, after Weber had already for six months been declaring his support for the republic because the Hohenzollern dynasty "in all its branches [had] been ruined,"[40] he wrote to Delbrück that he "remained a supporter of—a strictly *parliamentary* democratic monarchy."[41] To be sure, the wheel of history could not be reversed.

Weber refused to speak in public about the reasons and causes for the

36. Prince Max von Baden, *Erinnerungen und Dokumente*, 1926, p. 511.

37. *Pol. Schr.*, p. 450.

38. Letter to Mina Tobler, 4 December 1918, A.E. II, 79. At the urging of the people's representatives the declaration was replaced by a formal declaration of the same tendency.

39. This statement relates to a possible open declaration of the Senate of the University of Heidelberg(?) against the rule of the "Rat der Volksbeauftragten." Weber advised against it. "Now that the revolution is here," he opposed "*playing* with counterrevolution, and in my view this would amount to a mere paper protest by the Senate that is not based on any power, nor could be. Perhaps it would have a different impact if the university, the entire faculty, declared that 'it expected that the basic questions of the constitution . . . were going to be decided by a—free!—plebiscite.' . . . I believe that mere discrediting of the only organized power that can prevent plunder and has stopped the shameless treatment of officers, only in order to make a 'gesture,' is politically senseless and moreover without internal value. The wheel that began to roll because of the Kaiser's dishonorable hesitation, and ultimately his desertion in headquarters, will soon roll back again—perhaps only too far." Letter to Oncken, undated, perhaps 11–12 November 1918, copy in Weber papers. Cf. also below, text at note 78.

40. Cf. *Karlsruher Tageblatt*, 1st issue of 5 January 1919. The question of the dynasty received a remarkable emphasis in Weber's election speeches. He confessed himself to be a republican out of reason, since the dynasties had all failed. Cf. below, note 83.

41. Letter of 15 May 1919, Delbrück papers.

German catastrophe or even to seek to apportion blame. He found the general "enthusiastic burrowing in feelings of 'guilt' " to be unhealthy and weak. "The God of battle is with the larger battalions": the result of the war proved nothing about the moral justification of past German policies.[42] "A lost war is not a divine judgment."[43] Weber passionately opposed the idea that German policy over the previous decade could be criticized on an ethical basis. "The policies of the last two decades were frivolous because they were *superficial* and confused. Our policy before the war was stupid, not ethically objectionable. The latter charge is completely wrong. I stick to this."[44] Weber maintained that Germany had lost the game because it had gambled for excessively high stakes. Germany had twice tempted destiny—with unrestricted submarine warfare and with its policy in Brest-Litowsk, which had destroyed the possibility of a general peace settlement. And these mistakes had returned to haunt Germany.[45] It was cowardly and dishonorable to complain about this in retrospect. It was necessary to bear the consequences manfully and *silently*. "We lost the match, you won it"; Weber wished to go no further.[46] He refused to turn his back completely upon the policies of the past and to condemn them in principle. He could not do so because of his sense of national honor. He believed it shameful when the German press slandered Ludendorff in October 1918, and he therefore decided to end the silence that he had initially imposed upon himself. He sent an article to the *Frankfurter Zeitung* in which he *defended* Ludendorff, the "reckless gambler. . . . A warlord must gamble. A warlord must believe in his star." The *Frankfurter Zeitung* understandably refused to publish it.[47] Even in the frenzy of the November revolution, Weber stood by Ludendorff and Hindenburg: "He who insults our commanders in chief in the hour of defeat is a cur."[48] For Weber, this was a characteristic expression

42. *Pol. Schr.*, p. 488.

43. Letter to Löwenstein of 21 October 1918, *Pol. Schr.* 1, p. 480: "The war can no longer be won [!]; that is the truth. But Prometheus' word carries weight here: 'Do you think,' . . . etc. I at least do not despair, the way others do."

44. Letter to Prof. Goldstein, 13 November 1918, *Lebensbild*, pp. 614 f.

45. Report of the *Wiesbadener Tagblatt*, 6 December 1918, and the *Heidelberger Tagblatt*, 3 January 1919. On the newspaper reports, see below, note 83.

46. Letter to Oncken of 29 February 1919, copy in Weber papers; erroneously "your sake is" in *Lebensbild*, p. 658.

47. The article was not preserved. Letter of the editors to Weber on 29 October 1918: "We return this article about Ludendorff, as you wish, with our most sincere thanks." For the presumed contents, cf. *Lebensbild*, pp. 662 f. and the following note. Marianne Weber's report, ibid., that Weber discontinued the article before completing it is incorrect.

48. Weber as a discussion speaker in a Mannheim meeting in November 1918. Report by Professor Baumgarten, who was himself there. I was able to take this from a Weber lecture that Professor Baumgarten kindly made available. Compare the *Heidelberger Tagblatt*'s report, 3 March 1919, on an election speech made by Weber the previous day on

of the ethics of conviction. He felt obliged to stand by those who were the objects of public scorn since honor and justice demanded it. He regarded the defense of the nation's honor at the moment of its deepest humiliation to be more important than all questions of material survival. Germany's hope for regeneration depended on this.

He nevertheless detested hollow emotions that served to conceal realities. He sadly related his feelings on the occasion of the reception of the front soldiers in Frankfurt: "The arrival of the troops here was a frightful event—flags, wreaths, roaring cheers that lasted for hours, and at the same time those exhausted bodies with steel helmets—a parade of ghosts and a carnival at the same time: horrifying. . . . And then the officers' corps, bursting within from scorn, i.e., some are irretrievably frivolous. . . . they are also rabble, worse than the dregs that call the tune in Berlin. I never saw 'Germany' like this, nor could I ever have foreseen it. For all this, we must get to work. In spite of everything, our capability remains, only deeply hidden and buried."[49]

Max Weber had foreseen the revolution for some time. It was clear to him that the ruling elites had done nothing to check the working masses' growing radicalization. The "eternal 'whipping up' of the 'atmosphere' by promises" had to have its revenge one day.[50] The final straw, as Weber correctly saw, was William II's hesitation to renounce his throne at the right moment. Weber had attempted to oppose the revolutionary currents in Munich in the days before Eisner's seizure of power, but had to face the fact that his arguments had lost the power to convince. He was personally acquainted with Ernst Toller and many other revolutionary-minded socialists; but he had not been able to convince them, for all his persuasive powers. They responded that he was out of step with the times and that he remained committed to ideals that had been superseded.[51]

Weber was thereby prepared for the revolution. He was nevertheless

---

the theme "Germany's reconstruction": "Hindenburg towers above all of it; he has proved himself not only the greatest field commander on earth, but now as just as great a German too. The accusations that have been made against the chief headquarters are aimed not at him but at *Ludendorff*. But we also must openly recognize him as well as one of the greatest field commanders of our time, and a great field commander has the belief in his own star." Cf. further the report of the *Heidelberger Neueste Nachrichten*, no. 2, of 3 January 1919, which appears to confirm that statement exactly. Weber spoke similarly in Wiesbaden. See the *Wiesbadener Tagblatt* of 6 December 1918. A little later, however, he had radically altered his opinion. On 14 January 1919 he declared in Fürth: "Ludendorff, the bloody dictator, has carried on a criminal game with our nation. He and all of his accomplices belong behind bars." According to the report of the *Fürther Zeitung*, 15 January 1919.

49. Letter to Mina Tobler, 4 December 1918, Archiv Ebnet II, 79.

50. Compare the letter to Helene Weber of 18 November 1918, *Pol. Schr.* 1, p. 481.

51. Compare the letter from G. W. Klein to Weber of 6 or 7 November 1918, *Lebensbild*, p. 640.

bitter when the revolution broke out at the moment of the triumph of the enemy, and his *political conviction* led him to take a very strong and outspoken position against it, in spite of his recognition of its inevitability. He did admit that the leaders of the Majority Social Democrats did not deserve the blame for what had occurred. Yet he no longer was able to keep his "absolutely calm temper," and his passionate nationalist feelings burst forth uncontrolled. He raged against this "bloody carnival that does not deserve the honorable name of a revolution."[52] To be sure, he was prepared to admit—at least when he was able to contemplate coolly after his excitement of the first weeks—that sufficient grounds for a revolution "*after* the war" were present, but "during the war" he regarded it as a "terrible misfortune" whose catastrophic impact upon foreign policy could not yet be completely foreseen.

Weber had retained the desperate hope that Wilson, the law professor become president, would soon come to realize that his position as mediator between the powers was dependent upon the preservation of German military power. If Germany were disarmed and lay defenseless on the ground, the French would no longer need American aid for the possible continuation of the war and could therefore dispense with Wilson's moderating influence.[53] Weber therefore wished to keep open the possibility of a final, desperate national uprising as a card in the game of negotiations. The revolution had ended this possibility, for it had led to the immediate dissolution of the German army and had made the resumption of military operations impossible by its call for peace at any price. Weber publicly declared in Wiesbaden and Berlin that the revolution had knocked the weapons out of Germany's hands and thus destroyed Wilson's position as the arbiter of world peace. To this extent, the revolution was responsible for selling Germany out to alien rule.[54] In retrospect it is clear that Weber came quite close to a thesis that later, in the much cruder form of the stab-in-the-back legend, was to disrupt the domestic politics of the Weimar Republic.[55] But Weber avoided blaming

52. *Lebensbild*, p. 642; cf. *Pol. Schr.* 1, p. 484, n. 1.

53. "Waffenstillstand und Frieden," *Frankfurter Zeitung*, 27 October 1918, *Pol. Schr.*, p. 447.

54. Report of the *Wiesbadener Tagblatt*, no. 570, evening ed., and the *Weisbadener Zeitung*, no. 621, evening ed. of 6 December 1918. Also report of the *Vossische Zeitung* no. 653 of 22 December 1918. In Frankfurt, Weber was not as precise. See the special report of the *Frankfurter Zeitung* in a Sunday extra of 1 December 1918, now *Pol. Schr.*, p. 484. The note by Winckelmann there is misleading; it draws from a much shorter report by the *Frankfurter Zeitung* about the same speech in its Monday edition. See *Frankfurter Zeitung*, 2 December 1918. On the newspaper reports compare below, note 83.

55. That did not take its first departure from the *Süddeutsche Monatschefte*. Cf. an article in the *Fränkischer Kurier* of 2 January 1919 with the title "The Innocent Social Democrats": "We should never let it be forgotten that it was a tendency nurtured by the Social Democrats which, with the approval of many Majority Socialists, stabbed the

the Social Democrats for the revolution. His judgment about Wilson's influence upon the form of the peace negotiations was correct, but it failed to recognize the extent of the military defeat and the purely military impossibility of resuming the war.[56]

Weber was no less disturbed about the domestic impact of the revolution. He strongly disapproved of the local seizure of power by workers' and soldiers' councils, who cooperated with the regular, career civil servants' administration in a kind of love-hate relationship. He expected chaos to result and the wasting of what remained of Germany's economic potential. He changed this opinion to an extent when he himself was elected to the Heidelberg workers' and soldiers' council and realized that it was made up not merely of revolutionary literati, but, in general, of people of sincere conviction who were interested in getting things done in a proper manner.[57] At the same time, he publicly deplored the terrible mismanagement by revolutionary bodies that were incapable of proper administration. "Things are not going well and nothing can be done about the excessive stupidity [in high quarters]," he pointed out once at the end of November 1918. "The Berlin government—let alone the simply base and dishonorable one in Munich—is carrying out a policy of hatred, or has to do so since it must defer to the demagogues and has no troops that it can depend upon. You can work with the people as individuals, but as a mass they are stupid, as always."[58]

None of this prevented Max Weber from moving closer to the Social Democrats. In a meeting in Frankfurt on 1 December 1918, he admitted that he "was very close to the views of many Social Democratic party leaders who had received some training in economics."[59] Also, he repeatedly used the argument that some constitutional measures, for example a powerful Reich presidency, a unitary constitution, or similar institutions, were indispensable if there were to be a socialist order. A superficial observer might have thought that Weber had actually adopted a

German people in the back in its hour of fate and delivered Germany up in complete impotence to the mercy and pitilessness of its revengeful enemies so that it can now not even defend itself from the Poles and the Czechs."

56. Naumann had already pointed out in October that it was not possible to see things in a purely military way. Cf. Heuss, *Friedrich Naumann*, pp. 430 f.

57. Cf. also the letter to Mina Tobler, end of November 1918, Archiv Ebnet II, 78: "*Only* the really modest people, *including* the revolutionaries who are labor leaders or similar men who really *work*, as the very uncomplex people here do, are truly and (relatively) refreshing. I always have unconditional respect for them."

58. Letter to Mina Tobler, Frankfurt, 29 November 1918, Archiv Ebnet II, 30, published with an incorrect date in *Werk und Person*, p. 501.

59. *Pol. Schr.*, p. 484. Weber said the same in Wiesbaden: In view of the current mismanagement by the current Socialist system, especially in Berlin and Munich, he could not *join* the Social Democrats. According to the cited report in the *Wiesbadener Zeitung*.

moderate socialist position and that he really believed in a new social order founded on socialist principles, although he thought that the pace of transition ought to be comparatively slow. How else was it possible to understand the thesis with which Weber fought the politics of the people's representatives: that their actions would discredit the idea of socialism for a hundred years? For example, when Weber declared in the Frankfurt assembly that "we wish to secure the achievements of the revolution which have been generally negative to date, without any reservations or ambiguity, and help to build in the direction of planned socialization,"[60] this was only said *rebus sic stantibus* and not *pour jamais*.[61] He only chose such arguments to make an impression on the moderate Left. He wished thereby to gain the necessary attention to prove that socialization under the present circumstances was insane and that the reconstruction of the economy without bourgeois entrepreneurs was unthinkable.

In truth, Weber did not in any way believe in the socialization of the economy either in the near or the distant future, even when he seemed enchanted by the demagogic weapon of defeating the socialism of the future by the socialism of the present.[62] To be sure, he believed that, as a result of the present economic emergency, centralist direction of the economy was necessary for the foreseeable future; he saw, with a certain fatalism, that the future would bring a further expansion of bureaucracy and therefore a more strongly "socialized" economy in which entrepreneural initiative would be more severely confined than in the past. By no means did he see even the glimmer of an ideal in this state of affairs. He remained as loyal as ever to the principle of a *voluntarist* organization of the economic system as far as this was possible.[63] In no way did he share the "belief" in the future of socialism as a new and better social order that was then common among wide sections of the intelligentsia including,

60. Ibid., p. 484.

61. Cf. letter to Crusius of 24 November 1918, *Pol. Schr.* 1, p. 484. In any case this tactic arroused resentment in bourgeois circles and cost Weber not inconsiderable sympathy, at the expense of his political activities of the time.

62. Weber averred in Munich on 4 November 1918: "Bourgeois society is tenacious. It should not be thought that it can be carried over to a future state based on socialist principles." Report of the *Münchener Neueste Nachrichten*, 5 November 1918.

63. Cf. Weber's statement in response to Redlich of 4 June 1916, *Das politische Tagebuch*, pp. 120 f.: "Weber discussed finance and economics after the war as an incomprehensible problem: he said that the worst would be governmentally administered monopolies. It was necessary to conserve the powerful factor of industrially independent enterprises and their managers as the chief bearers of the German economy. The German civil service required an enlivening counterpart in private entrepreneurs, engineers, and managers. This dualism of 'governmental' and 'free' in relation to the social order has been characteristic of all of German history." Further, letter to Neurath, commissar for socialization of the Bavarian Council Republic, of 4 October 1919, *Pol. Schr.* 1, p. 488.

among others, Weber's own "students" Schumpeter and Lukács.[64] If he associated himself with the idea of "socialism" in concrete form, it was with an economic order dominated by governmentally controlled syndicates and cooperative enterprises, in which free economic competition was increasingly replaced by governmental controls. Weber did not believe for a minute that the irrationality of the capitalist economic system could thus be done away with; it would merely be transferred to another plane. Such a socialistic state-directed economy might have certain political or social advantages (Weber assumed that for the foreseeable future Germany would have to make use of state socialist and management methods in order to revive from the catastrophic economic situation after the war); but in the long run it would lead to economic stagnation and an increasing petrification of all social relations. This would be the beginning of the future bondage that Weber so greatly feared. It was only his fatalistic view that in the long run such a development was inevitable that prompted Weber not to dismiss all socialist opinions wholesale.

His tactical approach to the Left, expressed in pseudosocialist turns of phrase, did not last. After temporarily exercising some restraint, from the beginning of December 1918 Weber began to direct his attacks, with increasing intensity, not only against the revolutionary fervor of the Sparticists and the Independent Social Democratic party but also against the Rat der Volksbeauftragten. The latter had permitted the complete disbandment of the army and, rather than decisively opposing the "Liebknecht gang," had permitted the shameful treatment of the officers. They had allowed the economy to fall apart and had promised "socialization against their own convictions," although they knew well enough that "this was impossible in the moment of the most extreme need for credits from abroad." Like William II, they failed to appreciate personalities of character such as Solf (who had irreconcilably fallen out with Haase as a result of the Russian revolutionary money). Above all, they were irresponsible in their lack of "any foreign policy whatsoever"; nor were they in a position to put one into effect.[65] "The revolutionary

64. Compare the letter to Frau Else Jaffé-Richthofen, mid-November 1918, ibid., pp. 480 f. Also Theodor Heuss, "Max Weber in seiner Gegenwart," *Pol. Schr.*, pp. xxviii f.

65. This citation is taken from a letter to Ludo Moritz Hartmann, the envoy of the Austrian Republic in Berlin, of 3 January 1919. The contents were intended for Otto Bauer, the Austrian secretary of state for foreign affairs. Hartmann passed the letter on to Bauer (letter of 7 January 1919, Gesandtschaftsakten Berlin Staatsarchiv Wien, NPA 140); Weber's letter is also there, along with a correct copy. I am grateful to Dr. Stump for informing me of this source.) In this letter, Weber's arguments against the policies of the Rat der Volksbeauftragten is summarized with concentrated force. It is repeated here verbatim:

"Dear friend, we accuse the Council Government of this:

"1. That it is decidedly minority rule and is supported merely by *force*, just like any other military dictatorship.

"2. That it does *not* guarantee free elections. In most cases, the automobile is demanded

government employs propaganda in no way different from that conducted by Ludendorff during the war. In the end, they will thoroughly discredit socialism," the *Vossische Zeitung* reported in summing up the relevant passages in Max Weber's Berlin speech of 20 December 1918.[66] In his later speeches, too, Max Weber permitted no doubts about his position. He had, to be sure, occasionally remarked that a certain degree of socialization was "necessary" because of circumstances, but at the same time he warned against any thoroughgoing attempts at expropriation, of the mines for example, if only because this would place "excellent pawns" into the enemies' hands. It was decisive for him, of course, that only a bourgeois-capitalist system, at least in view of the great dependence of the German economy on overseas markets, could return Germany to economic strength.[67]

---

by the Council and used by it in agitation, thus an 'official influence on the election' which makes the vote *invalid* according to our principles (and those of the old Social Democracy).

"3. that they have acquiesced in and, ultimately, sanctioned the replacement of *officers* by reserve officers, who cringe before them and the soldiers, leading to shameless lack of discipline, pillage, and inability to maintain order and, e.g., oppose the Poles on purely German national lands.

"4. that they are too cowardly, in the face of their own conviction, to enter into an open coalition with bourgeois parties and instead have tolerated unsavory elements (Haase, Barth) all too long in their midst.

"5. that they endure people with character (Solf) as little as did William II.

"6. that they have permitted and are permitting the dissolution of our economy and are promising 'socialization' in the face of their own convictions, although they know that it is impossible now at the moment of greatest need for foreign *credits*.

"7. that they have absolutely *no* foreign policy, nor could they conduct one.

"8. that they are aiding reaction by indulging such fools as Adolf Hoffmann and pathological personalities like Liebknecht and are hopelessly discrediting not only socialism but even democracy for a long period.

"9. that, all in all, they do not recognize, nor will they, the *currently* inevitable need for bourgeois help, or at least they only lay a claim to it in a form that makes it *impossible* for an honest man to put himself in their service.

"They will *not* be able to avoid civil war but—like Kerensky—will grasp at it too late, and they will deliver us to alien political and economic rule, which would not have been necessary to this degree.

"In the question of the Reich constitution, they understand theoretically the necessity of a strong administration, thus a unitary, plebiscitary apex, for *any* socialization, but they lack the courage to draw the consequences. Instead, they commit the oldest mistake of old-bourgeois, philistine democrats, and only out of resentment again an 'elected monarch.' They will bungle this question out of sheer dogmatism, and will thereby forfeit the Reich's future and the socialization of the economy."

66. No. 653 of 22 December 1918. Cf. the report by the *Wiesbadener Tagblatt* on Weber's speech of 5 December, which probably missed the emphasis somewhat (belief in socialism), evening ed. of 6 December 1918: "The current propaganda, which is certainly as bad as that of the old regime, will collapse and with it, the belief in Social Democracy."

67. Cf. inter alia the report of the *Heidelberger Tageblatt* of 18 January 1919 on Weber's speech.

Probably Max Weber's unreserved criticism of the Council of the People's Representatives fatally damaged his chances of gaining a position in high quarters. Initially, Friedrich Ebert had considered appointing Max Weber and not Hugo Preuss to the post of secretary of state of the interior. This plan was soon abandoned for reasons that we do not know.[68] It would have been difficult anyway to find a position for a man that had called the revolution an irresponsible "carnival" in a government that was officially composed of Majority Social Democrats and Independent Socialists. Weber's combative temperament would soon have led him into quarrels with the independents. Hugo Preuss, who was given the task of preparing a draft for the new Reich constitution, did draw Weber into the constitutional discussions in the Reich Office of the Interior; but a position inside the government, which Weber might have wished for, was not forthcoming. Even before the revolution, Conrad Haussmann in a cabinet meeting had suggested Weber as a suitable candidate for the ambassadorship at Vienna.[69] The chances of obtaining such a position under the revolutionary government, slight as they were,[70] were utterly destroyed by Weber's public statements.[71] Admittedly Weber also regarded it as senseless to cooperate with the Rat der Volksbeauftragten. "Participation in *this* government, or even working for it, would be well-nigh impossible. *These* people—i.e., Herr Haase and his comrades, in contrast to the trade union officials and to Ebert—*only*

68. Minutes of the meetings of the Council of People's Representatives, Internationales Institut für Sozialgeschichte Amsterdam (former SPD-Archiv), cabinet meeting of 15 November 1918, 10:30 a.m.: "2. Filling the post of the state secretaryship of the interior. [The cabinet] considered whether Professor Max Weber, Heidelberg, should be in question along with Preuss. The cabinet agreed that Ebert should carry on the unbinding negotiations with Preuss." On the same day it was decided that Preuss should be named. Appointment and delaration of the Council of People's Representatives in DZA I, RKA 2^2, State Secretaries, vol. 2, no. 1609. Now published in *Die Regierung der Volksbeauftragten 1918/1919*, first part, ed. Susanne Miller with the assistance of Heinrich Potthoff, *Quellen zur Geschichte des Parlamentarismus und der Politischen Parteien*, vol. 6/1 (Düsseldorf, 1969), p. 41. Probably, Max Weber himself never learned of this greatest political opportunity of his life.

69. Haussmann to Weber, 24 November 1918 (after a copy in the Haussmann papers): "Three weeks ago I told the cabinet members in Berlin that Max Weber would be the best representative for Germany in Vienna." Cf. Weber's letter to Marianne Weber of 25 November, *Lebensbild*, p. 646: "Haussmann writes that he has proposed me as envoy to *Vienna. Nothing* will come of this, that is clear. These people only want to be deceived, in a pacifist sense."

70. Apparently Weber viewed it as possible and overlooked the fact that a *new* government had since come into office.

71. Relevant is Weber's remark in the letter to Crusius of 12 December 1918, *Pol. Schr.* 1, pp. 484 f.: the fact that he had called the revolution a "bloody carnival" "cost me employment in an important position on the part of the present government—which to me was only justified (that please between us!)." After the original in the Weber papers.

require lackeys, just as the monarchy did. This set of literati (Eisner, etc.) is irredeemable too."[72] But it was not at all easy for Weber to draw such a conclusion. He noted with considerable bitterness that "politically I won't get anywhere. *This* amateurish government has no use for me."[73] He therefore completely abandoned the idea of active political activity in an official position, although it remained attractive to him.

Like Hugo Preuss, Max Weber publicly and emphatically insisted, from the November days onward, that stabilization and the preservation of the results of the revolution were not possible without the bourgeoisie's cooperation. Socialization at this time would result in complete economic exhaustion and would subordinate Germany forever to America's economic supremacy; German workers and businessmen would then be reduced to wage slaves and agents of American capital. Only with the cooperation of the economically knowledgeable entrepreneurial class could Germany be restored economically. Only bourgeois business people could assure that the necessary credits for construction would be forthcoming from the purely bourgeois governments abroad. Weber therefore demanded clearly and openly that the bourgeoisie receive "*equal participation in political power and appropriate economic responsibility*."[74] His estimate of the hopes of the Left was sober and realistic, mixed, to be sure, with a proper dose of wishful thinking: "With free elections there will be no Social Democratic majority."[75]

These arguments reflected Weber's view, which we touched on earlier, that a revolution would not be successful without the cooperation of the bourgeoisie and that without that cooperation an even stronger reaction from the Right would be the result. Early in January 1919, Weber accused the Rat der Beauftragten of knowing this but not daring to act accordingly. They were "too *cowardly* in the face of their own convictions . . . to enter into an open coalition with bourgeois parties." They have "instead [tolerated] . . . unclean elements (Haase, Barth) all too long in their midst."[76] Another practical argument that Weber used in order to demand a bourgeois share in governing the country was that the western powers would only be willing to conclude peace with a *bourgeois* government, or at least a government with bourgeois participation. To carry the revolution further would lead to a civil war and then to the shame of an enemy occupation. And inevitably this would eventually bring about a

72. Letter to Lili Schäfer, undated, around 4 December 1918, Weber papers; cf. the letter to Marianne Weber of 29 November 1918, *Lebensbild*, p. 646: "This government will never need me; I will never serve it."

73. Letter to Mina Tobler, 2 December 1918, Archiv Ebnet II, 80.

74. In an article series in the *Frankfurter Zeitung*, now in *Pol. Schr.*, p. 486.

75. Ibid., p. 453.

76. Letter of 3 March 1919 to Hartmann; cf. above, note 65.

wild reaction that would last for decades. He therefore demanded the immediate convening of a constitutional assembly, a political goal whose realization still seemed completely uncertain in November 1918.

At the same time, Max Weber directed a passionate appeal to the bourgeoisie to throw off once and for all "the spirit of 'security': the security of the protection of authorities, the fear of any bold innovation; in short—the cowardly will to impotence," and to rally together in self-conscious and responsible action. He was prepared to greet the end of dynastic legitimacy inasmuch as it "finally put" the bourgeoisie "on its *own feet*."[77] Without the bourgeoisie, Germany's reconstruction could not succeed; so the bourgeoisie must find the courage to decide in favor of loyal cooperation with Social Democracy. Only with the help of the bourgeoisie could the "disastrous amateur economy" of the soldiers' and workers' councils be overcome; only the loyal cooperation of the governmental administration supported by the bourgeois intelligentsia could produce a way out of the chaos of the revolution. The radical bourgeoisie and socialist democracy devoted to peaceful policies could travel together frankly and honorably for the decades to come, "shoulder to shoulder," before they might eventually come to a parting of the ways.[78]

In the middle of November 1918, a group of men around Alfred Weber, Theodor Wolff, and Friedrich Naumann met in Berlin in order to create an organizational basis for the political activities of the democratic-minded bourgeoisie by founding a new German Democratic party. Max Weber appeared predestined to participate in this. But for reasons of political conviction, he at first refused to join in. He declined to sign the founding proclamation since it declared itself in favor of a republican form of government. He still privately and openly favored the retention of the monarchy and did not feel ready to make such a political turnabout even though the political situation seemed to dictate it. It also appears that he wished to keep the question of governmental form open and to postpone any final decision until a referendum.[79] It seems, moreover, that he favored the creation of a larger party, which would encompass the National Liberal Right, represented by Gustav Stresemann; he therefore considered the foundation to be somewhat premature. He finally did however decide to take his stand with the German Democratic party. He

77. *Pol. Schr.*, pp. 453 f.

78. Ibid., p. 487.

79. Weber's declaration in the *Frankfurter Zeitung* (*Pol. Schr.*, pp. 454 f.): Weber's initially expressed position on the question of monarchy was two-sided. We will submit "loyally to every majority decision by constituent assembly and plebiscite, but remain on our part on the ground of the republic" without reservation or ambiguity. The "without reservation and ambiguity" is to be read, as often in such connections, precisely *with* reservation; compare also *Pol. Schr.*, p. 451.

temporarily moved to Frankfurt in order to be in immediate contact with the editorial staff of the *Frankfurter Zeitung*, for which he now quickly produced a series of articles about "Germany's future form of government."[80] The goal of the series was to stimulate the political mobilization of the democratic bourgeoisie. "*Without the bourgeoisie's cooperation, the government will not achieve peace, and occupation will occur sooner or later*," Weber emphasized in a warning intended for the Rat der Beauftragten. At the same time, he appealed emphatically to the bourgeois classes "to stand at last *on their own political feet*."[81] Through the efforts of the *Frankfurter Zeitung*'s editors, Weber was put into direct contact with the leaders of the Deutsche Demokratische Partei (German Democratic party) in Frankfurt, including Erich Dombrowski and Hermann Luppe, and he even counted on participating in the formulation of the party program.[82]

He now placed himself actively in the cause of the political agitation for the new and decisively democratic bourgeois party. From the end of November, he delivered speeches in its behalf in Wiesbaden, Frankfurt, Berlin, Heidelberg, Fürth, and Karlsruhe, with extraordinary success.[83]

80. Letter to Mina Tobler, Frankfurt, 17 November 1918, Archiv Ebnet II, 77: "I have happily stopped here for a while and am enjoying work, writing articles . . . and attending editorial conferences with really *very* intelligent and respectable journalists—a tribe that I have always enjoyed, if they are able and objective."

81. *Pol. Schr.*, p. 454.

82. Cf. Ludwig Luckemeyer, "Die Deutsche Demokratische Partei bis zur Nationalversammlung, 1918–1919," (diss., Giessen, 1972, machine printed), pp. 301 ff. Also the letter to Mina Tobler, 4 December 1918, A.E. II, 79: "There is not much to relate from here—writing articles, conferences. In the evening occasional gatherings with a pair of editors. Early on Sunday, I am going to Hanau; tomorrow evening, I shall speak in Wiesbaden—on the whole, much to keep me busy. I do not know whether much will come out of it, but the people believe so. Here, we have since been working on the organization of the 'Democratic party'; in Heidelberg I will probably participate in the formulation of the party program."

83. Not in Hanau, as Marianne Weber reported in *Lebensbild*, p. 653. The planned assembly did not take place, as Weber had to go to Berlin to attend the Prussian constitutional committee. *Frankfurt*: 1 December 1918, special report of the *Frankfurter Zeitung* in a Sunday extra, now *Pol. Schr.*, pp. 484 ff.; cf. also the report of the *Frankfurter Zeitung* of 2 December 1918; cf. also Weber to Mina Tobler, 2 December 1918, A.E. II, 80: "Yesterday evening roaring applause (7000 people) *and* opposition, but the latter was merely shy." *Wiesbaden*: 5 December 1918, Reports of the *Wiesbadener Tagblatt* no. 570, evening ed., and the *Wiesbadener Zeitung*, no. 621, evening ed. of 6 December 1918; cf. also Weber's commentary in a letter to Mina Tobler, 6 December 1918, A.E. II, 85: "Yesterday, a speech in Wiesbaden, mild success, since it was *purely* bourgeois"; *Berlin*: 20 December 1918, report of the *Vossische Zeitung*, no. 653, of 22 December 1918, and the *Karlsruher Tagblatt* of 22 December 1918; *Heidelberg*: 2 January 1919 on "Germany's reconstruction" (*Heidelberger Neueste Nachrichten*, no. 2, and *Heidelberger Tagblatt*, 3 January 1919); *Karlsruhe*: 4 January 1919, on "Germany's past and future" as a "last appeal" the day before the election for the Baden National Assembly (*Badische Landeszeitung*, no. 7,

In these talks, a radical break with the past political system was accompanied by very sharp criticism of the existing situation. Weber turned special fire upon the indecisiveness and weakness of the People's Representatives, who set no limits on the specter of Sparticist activities. "Liebknecht belongs in the madhouse and Rosa Luxemburg in the zoo." Today, we can only see "dirt, dung, manure, disorder, and nothing else."[84] But none of this could destroy his vision of Germany's revival. Germany had once proved itself to be one of the leading cultural nations under foreign domination. This time too, from deprivation and ruin a rebirth would come.

Max Weber appeared destined to be a leading representative of the German Democratic party at the National Assembly. Conrad Haussmann proposed him for the party's chairmanship.[85] He was in fact elected to the Central Committee only in the following year.[86] Max Weber himself, however, did not seek a mandate for the National Assembly. It would not have been difficult to obtain one. His closest political friends, like Friedrich Naumann and Conrad Haussmann, would have used their considerable political influence in the new party for his benefit. But Weber hesitated to attempt a candidacy for the National Assembly, although he had played with this idea since the beginning of December. He wondered whether he would be able to win the necessary local support anywhere.[87] In addition, he doubted if it were not too early to take such a step into active politics, since he reckoned with the likelihood of an allied occupation that would make all these efforts illusory. Even more, he believed that a reactionary counterattack would follow upon the

---

midday ed. of 6 January 1919; *Karlsruher Tagblatt*, first ed. of 5 January 1919, *Badische Presse*, no. 7, midday ed. of 6 January 1918). *Fürth*: 14 January 1919, report of the *Fürther Zeitung* of 15 January 1919, and the *Nordbayrische Zeitung* of the same day, the latter under the title "Spartacus in the Park Hotel"; *Heidelberg*: 17 January 1918 "The people's state and the parties" (*Heidelberger Zeitung* of 18 January 1918). Weber also seems to have made an election trip to Thuringia, but nothing more is known about it.

84. Speech in Karlsruhe, according to similar reports in all three newspapers. Max Weber of course strongly condemned the murder of Liebknecht and Rosa Luxemburg, which occurred several days later; characteristically his sense of justice broke through. "The dictator of the street has found his end, which I did not wish him." *Lebensbild*, p. 653. Nevertheless, Weber considered this outcome of events necessary in view of Liebknecht's political battle methods: "Liebknecht, who was no doubt an honorable man, *summoned the battle in the street*. The street killed him." *Heidelberger Zeitung*, 18 January 1919. Compare also Wilbrandt, "Max Weber, ein deutsches Vermächtnis," *Die neue Rundschau*, vol. 1 (1928), no. 1, p. 154.

85. Haussmann to Weber, 24 November 1918 (copy in Haussmann papers): "Yesterday I telegraphed our entry into the 'Democratic Party': *Max Weber* should be designated as its *Chair*."

86. Report of the *Frankfurter Zeitung* of 4 August 1919.

87. Letter to Mina Tobler, 6 December 1918, Archiv Ebnet II, 85.

amateurish revolutionary policy of the Council of the People's Representatives and that the reaction would quickly destroy the efforts for a democratic reorganization of Germany. Under these conditions, it was perhaps better not to make such a great effort prematurely: "I would prefer to sit quietly at home and believe that nothing will come of the excitement. Later I shall be needed."[88]

However, Weber was immediately ready to offer his services when the impetus came from *outside*. In a crowded and turbulent members' meeting of the Frankfurt German Democratic party, Weber was nominated as a candidate of the Reichstag electoral district of Hesse-Nassau, along with other candidates, namely, Frankfurt Mayor Luppe, Weber's friend Maria Baum (the factory inspector), and Walther Schücking. This decision was subject to the final determination of the list of candidates by the delegates' convention of the province of Hesse-Nassau, set for 29 December 1918. The assembly ignored, with one exception, the roster proposed by the local party leadership and consciously chose well-known personalities who had no immediate connections with Frankfurt. With only two opposing votes, they put Max Weber at the top of their list of nominees. In Weber's eyes, this event appeared to be a spontaneous choice of leadership by several hundred participants, and only for that reason did he accept the nomination.[89]

It is, however, almost incomprehensible that Weber considered his candidacy at the top of the list in the nineteenth Reichstag electoral district to be an accomplished fact. He himself had penetratingly pointed out the power of the party bureaucracy in the modern mass parties. He should have recognized that the provisional Frankfurt nomination in no way assured a promising position on the candidate list of the German Democratic party for Hesse-Nassau, Wetzlar, and Waldeck. He could easily have won the necessary backup in the party with the help of his political friends. But what did he do? He did not trouble himself about his candidacy, sought no contacts with leaders of the Hesse-Nassau party organization, and did not even consider preparing election speeches in his electoral district, as might have been expected. He was already confident that he would "almost surely" be elected.[90]

The delegate convention in Wetzlar was not ready to agree to the

88. Ibid. Cf. letter to Mina Tobler, 4 December 1918, Archiv Ebnet II, 79: "I have the impression about the whole business [i.e., the efforts to create the Deutsche Demokratische Partei] that it will come to nothing, since the Putsch and the reaction will nevertheless come. The people in Berlin will not create anything since they have no power behind them. Cf. also letter to Hartmann, 3 January 1919, above, note 65.

89. Report of the *Frankfurter Zeitung* of 20 December 1918, 2d morning ed. Cf. also Luckemeyer, *Die Deutsche Demokratische Partei*, pp. 301 ff.

90. Cf. letter to Preuss of 25 December 1918: "It appears that I will almost surely be elected in Frankfurt." See below, chap. 9, sec. 4.

plebiscitary acclamation of Max Weber as the first candidate by the Frankfurt party assembly, for the party delegates from Kassel and Marburg claimed appropriate representation for themselves. In addition, Max Weber, who was supported by the Frankfurt delegates without great inner enthusiasm but out of duty, was now burdened with the fact that he allegedly had agitated for socialism in Berlin, although he had done so for tactical reasons and with many reservations. In other words, he appeared to be too left-wing for the honorable delegates from Kassel and Marburg.[91] Weber's tactical finesse and the abrupt changes of position in his political agitation completely confused them and led them to grossly misunderstand his political position. Moreover, Weber was regarded as self-willed and "excessively pedantic."[92] He had two rivals, Mayor Luppe of Frankfurt and Mayor Erich Koch of Kassel, who knew their way about the party stalls, and possessed a solid power base. Weber's candidacy therefore came to nought. He was only considered for the candidate list by a hair. When he then found out that the Wetzlar conference of delegates had put him in a hopeless position on the list of candidates of the Reichstag electoral district of Hesse-Nassau, he angrily withdrew.[93] It did not help that a Heidelberg party assembly on 3 January 1919, at which

91. Cf. August Weber, *Erinnerungen*, August Weber papers, BAK, p. 367: "Professor Max Weber, on the few occasions that we conferred together about a new liberal party, was unrestrained in his pedantic attitude and was as little receptive to counterarguments as Theodor Wolff. It does not detract from his greatness as a scholar when I say: the field of politics was alien to him. He had been too far removed from party life to recognize those personalities who should be considered in the creation of a party that would unite all liberals." Cf. Luckemeyer, *Die Deutsche Demokratische Partei*, p. 81, note 42. See also Lothar Albertin, *Liberalismus und Demokratie am Anfang der Weimarer Republik* (Düsseldorf, 1972), p. 252.

92. Cf. Luppe's report in his unpublished memoirs, Luppe papers, 9, BAK, pp. 308 ff. (here after Luckemeyer, p. 303, n. 156): "It was clear that Hesse-Nassau was an electoral district where I would run, while for Kassel, Mayor Koch came into question. The *Frankfurter Zeitung*, however, had its own candidate, Professor Max Weber, without doubt a towering man, who immediately joined the editorial staff and began to publish his views about Germany's reconstruction. The selection of candidates took place in an overflowing membership meeting, in which a normal vote or anything similar would have been impossible. Therefore, the chairman permitted negative votes. About twenty-five of those present voted against Weber, who was unknown to the majority, sixty voted against me, and over a hundred against Schücken [sic]. At the end of December, the final candidate selection took place in Wetzlar. It happened that the Kassel and Marburg representatives decisively rejected Weber. In an assembly in Cirkus Schumann, he had spoken out so broadly for socialization, that agitation in the country for the Democrats had been made much more difficult. At the same time, he had spoken against the Yellow Labor Associations with insulting sharpness. After negotiations that lasted for hours, in which we Frankfurt delegates, as per our instructions, had to stand firm first with Weber, then with myself, then Schücking, Weber's candidacy collapsed. I was at the head of the list, after me came Koch, Schücking, Anna Schulte. The *Frankfurter Zeitung* after that opposed me more than they supported me."

93. Cf. *Lebensbild*, p. 655f.

Weber had spoken with great success about "Germany's restoration," wanted to put him on the Baden state list at the last minute, and that on the same evening a delegation was sent to Karlsruhe for that purpose.[94] It was too late; the list was already complete. Weber himself, with extraordinary brusqueness, torpedoed any further attempts to place him on another list or on the party's Reich list. He did not want to enter the National Assembly as a "patronized mandate hunter" but as a leader elected in a free vote.[95]

Were Max Weber's "gifts as a political statesman" not employed merely because of the petit-bourgeois style of practical politics?[96] On reflection, this is debatable. He did not seek this candidacy himself but accepted it with considerable hesitation. He did not grasp for power. When the candidacy was endangered, he refused to fight for it. He waited for "a call" and did nothing "to bring it about."[97] If he had wished to make the step out of intellectual life into active politics enthusiastically and energetically, the way would have been open. Basically, however, he did not wish to. He recognized that he neither could nor wanted to become a part of the often petty rules of the game of party life. For party politicians, Weber's wavering between realistic adjustment and the most extreme ethical rigor was uncomfortable and unfathomable. He could not fight for a prescribed party line. All his life he remained a "political 'loner,'" as he once called himself.[98] Moreover, his ultimate political ideals, his continued stress upon the power of the German national state in the world, did not fit the situation of 1919. He therefore tried to adjust to the situation in a spirit of Realpolitik, as in his tactical approach to Social Democracy (a maneuver that paradoxically hurt his standing with the delegates); and he admitted that everything that was said openly at the time only reflected the current situation and had no long-term significance.

Accordingly, Max Weber's political attitude was not without contradictions. In April 1920, the German Democratic party wished to send him as their representative to the so-called first socialization commission. Max Weber was beside himself. He appeared predestined for this post and not only because of his outstanding professional qualifications. He

94. Cf. *Heidelberger Neueste Nachrichten*, no. 2, 3 March 1919.

95. *Lebensbild*, p. 656. A declaration by Weber in the *Frankfurter Zeitung* is printed there (5 January 1919) in which he forbade "the continued public discussion" about the collapse of his candidacy "in the interest of discipline." He disdained to "make any concessions" to the party notables.

96. Marianne Weber in *Lebensbild*, p. 656.

97. Wilbrandt, *Max Weber*, p. 155. Further: "Is it a born politician, a statesman, who speaks this way? Must not one who is called to look after his nation strive for influence, if he only lacks the appropriate position in order to lead them?"

98. Letter to Haussmann of 1 May 1917.

had rejected all immediate plans for socialization, but had never spoken against socialization in principle. On the contrary, he had previously offered loyal cooperation with the left "in the direction of planned socialization."[99] Weber felt caught in a corner. This was clear in the different reasons that he gave others for his refusal. When Kautsky asked him if "he were prepared for Stinnes and his cronies to decide Germany's future?" Weber answered courteously that he himself could not join the commission because of his health.[100] He justified his refusal to his wife with the argument that he had always claimed to "be indispensable" in Munich and had therefore to remain "consistent," a remark that clearly demonstrated his inner indecisiveness.[101] He wrote his sister far more frankly: "Since the Democratic party . . . has dared me to concern myself with 'socialization' and I believe that this is insanity at this time, I have to withdraw. Politicians *have to* compromise—a scholar cannot justify this.[102] Weber, who had committed himself too much by positive statements about future socialist plans, hesitated between Realpolitik and principle. Finally, the latter proved victorious, although he was not without severe misgivings. Since he believed that the party could justly demand his cooperation, he drew the consequences and resigned from the party committee.[103] He then withdrew from the German Democratic party itself.[104]

Weber defended this fateful step with much the same argument in a personal letter to the chairman of the DDP, Senator Carl Petersen. He made it clear at the same time that this action meant his retreat from active politics altogether:

99. Cf. above, p. 320; now also, he did not distance himself distinctly and completely from socialistic conditions in the future; cf. letter to Dr. Neurath of 4 October 1919: "I . . . consider the 'planned economy' plans to be amateurish and, *objectively speaking, absolutely irresponsible rashness*, which can discredit 'socialism' for a hundred years and will throw all that could *now* perhaps succeed into the abyss of stupid reaction." *Pol. Schr.* 1, p. 488; also letter to Georg (still at that time) von Lukács (undated, March 1920, after a copy in the Weber papers): "Distinguished friend, of course our political views diverge; I am absolutely convinced that these experiments can and will only lead to the discrediting of Socialism for 100 years."

100. In consequence of Weber's letter to Lederer of 12 May 1920, Weber papers; also he justified his refusal to Lederer on the basis of health. The author looked in vain for the correspondence with Kautsky in the papers of the first Socialization Commission (DZA I); they were also not in the Kautsky papers.

101. Letter of 15 April 1920, in the possession of Professor Baumgarten.

102. *Lebensbild*, pp. 702 f., here corrected according to the original manuscript. The insert reads: "Senator Petersen, a splendid fellow."

103. Ibid.

104. Letter to Clara Mommsen of 4 May(?) 1920, after a copy in the Weber papers: "'Socialization Commission.' I have *declined* to participate and have left the party, which otherwise could justifiably require my participation."

> I cannot become a "Majority Socialist" since this party *must* make *the same* compromises (against the convictions of their more learned members). I certainly cannot join the "Burschen" like Herr Stresemann, who should have been "dead" politically after he recommended the Mexico dispatch in the Reichstag in 1917. I will *always* vote Democratic, and *always* stress that I see it as a terrible sacrifice to govern today. You can be completely certain of my loyalty. . . . But since your offer extending a responsibility to a party comrade is fully justified, as long as I remain a member, and I *cannot* and *may not* accept it, then I must depart with heartfelt respect and my best wishes for the party.[105]

105. Letter of 14 April 1920, Petersen papers, 53, in the private possession of Dr. Edgar Petersen, Hamburg, published for the first time, with numerous misreadings that distort the meaning, by Bruce B. Frye, "A Letter From Max Weber," *Journal of Modern History* 39 (1967): 122–24, and reprinted, with all the errors, by Ilse Dronberger, *The Political Thought of Max Weber*, p. 247. We print the letter here with the correct wording according to the original:

"Munich, 14 April 1920.

"Dear Herr Senator, I am now leaving the party committee and must also reject (*definitively*) your offer, which *highly honors me*.

"I am *not* in a 'quarrel' with the party. But, in every assembly, *everywhere*, I have privately and publicly declared 'socialization' in the now commonly understood sense to be '*folly*.' We need the *entrepreneur* (Herr Stinnes or one like him). I have said about the business council law: 'Ecrasez l'infâme.' *From the point of view of the potential future of socialism*: the politician should and *must* make compromises. But I am a *scholar* by profession. The party has *helped* to induce the fact that I have remained one, in a manner deserving of thanks, by keeping me from parliament at the time. I had no compulsion to be there; to sit there *today* is neither an honor nor a joy, but perhaps I would have belonged there while the constitution was discussed. The scholar does not need to make compromises *or to cover* folly. I reject this certainly. Those who have other views, like Professor Lederer and Dr. Vogelstein, abdicate their responsibilities. I would act as an offender toward my profession.

"I am also *not* in agreement with the *selection* and the *conduct* of the committee of inquiry: gentlemen who are pacifists (and are *considered* to be 'Jews,' in some cases quite wrongly) should *not* be appointed. Almost my entire circle is Jewish, a cousin of my mother's was Felix Mendelssohn's wife; I think that I am unsuspected of being an 'anti-Semite.' *Here, I* am also considered to be a 'Jew' (letters from officers to me!)

"I am *not* in accord with the position of the party here—whose leader I value highly—which should not be concealing reactionary machinations. But that is perhaps *vis major*.

"I cannot become a 'Majority Socialist' because that party *must* make *the same* compromises (against the conviction of its *scientifically* trained members.) I can of course not go over to the Burschen, like Herr *Stresemann*, who should have been 'dead' after his recommendation of the Mexico Dispatch in the 1917 Reichstag. I will *always vote* democratic, always emphasizing that I view it to be a terrible *sacrifice* to 'govern' today—you can be completely certain of my loyalty in this. And of my unlimited respect for you personally, since the constitutional commission, where I came to know and honor you: the party has *one* lucky thing in this; in the election of *this* leader.

"But since your offer—pressing a *duty* on a party comrade!—is fully justified, as long as I

Weber thereby finally burned the bridges that still bound him to active politics, and returned completely to his scholarly work. Rigorous research was his self-chosen therapy. As early as January 1920, he admitted that his own "contemplative existence" was "once again" his "form of life. . . . I am now further from politics than ever. There is nothing left for me to do there for the rest of my life and so 'basta.'"[106] But this did not happen without a severe inner struggle. For politics had been and remained, as he had once said early in 1919, his "old 'secret love.'"[107]

2. The Treaty of Versailles and Germany's Future in the World

Max Weber looked upon the German negotiations in Versailles as unworthy of a great nation. He believed that the German side had had to indulge in self-humiliation, in the hope of winning better conditions from the enemy, and he rebelled against that. He attacked "this incapable peace commission."[108] He demanded "'more honor' on the German side."[109] His national feelings were aroused by the allies' monstrous peace conditions. He was inclined to see the worst. In December 1918, he believed that the deepest point of German humiliation had not yet been reached. He anticipated a civil war at home and the occupation of the country by allied troops. If this occurred, "*then* the sooner the better. . . . We must unfortunately let the cup run out to the dregs and then build totally anew."[110] He toyed with the idea that it was almost

---

am a member, and I *can* and *may* not obey it,—then I leave with heartfelt respect and with the best wishes for the party.

"This letter is—from *your side—not* 'confidential.' I therefore refer to it in my resignation statement.

"I do not understand how the party can pass over Professor *Alfred* Weber, who *understands* socialization and finances ten times better than I do, who can control Helfferich, and who is (in moderation!) for socialization. I have no 'advice' to give. But I can nevertheless say this, *since* my brother and I defend very different views. Of course, he must not be told about this, or else he would abruptly decline. With greatest respect, yours very Professor Max Weber."

106. Letter to Mina Tobler, 3 January 1920, A.E. II, 117.

107. Letter to Mina Tobler, udated, probably 17 January 1919, A.E. II, 86. "And of course the political as well. It is my old 'secret love' and these men spoil everything that was once dear. Aside from the total darkness of the future, politically, also personally and materially, which one faces. But also, when a rope lies around the neck and someone slowly, slowly twists it, for three years, ever tighter, ever tighter, then one cannot say and write what is, no matter how one feels."

108. Letter to Marianne Weber of 25 November 1918, *Lebensbild*, p. 646.

109. Letter to the editors of the *Frankfurter Zeitung* of 9 February 1919, *Pol. Schr.* 1, p. 486, which includes the phrase: "Entente personalities, who recently in the interest of 'reconstruction' implore 'more honor' on the German side."

110. Letter to Lili Schäfer, perhaps 4 December 1918, Weber papers.

desirable to suffer the terrible shame of a foreign occupation because he hoped that this would kindle a passionate national resistance among the German people of all classes and defeat cowardly pacifism.

He contemplated national resistance with revolutionary means. "If the Poles should invade Danzig and Thorn, or the Czechs move into Reichenberg, the first task is to establish a German irredenta. I cannot do it myself, because I do not have the physical strength. But every nationalist must do it, especially the students. Irredenta means: nationalism with revolutionary instruments of force."[111] Weber called for this openly. His speeches during the revolutionary period climaxed, without exception, in the exhortation to use revolutionary force—we would say partisan war today—in order to oppose the loss of German land. In an assembly in Heidelberg, he called this the national task of the younger generation. "You know," he said, "what it means to stand up to an invading enemy who can no longer be offered military resistance . . . to give everything for the future, and abandon your personal hopes. The lot of the living is only imprisonment and summary trial. [We must quietly make certain that] the first Polish official that dares enter Danzig will be met by a bullet."[112]

Weber directed his appeal above all to students. "Only a scoundrel could still go around in his student colors at a time when Poles rule German cities in the east. Put your caps and bands away and give up this *feudal* nonsense, which does not fit these times and is of no use to anyone," Weber said in his speeches in Heidelberg during the campaign for the National Assembly and again in Berlin, in Karlsruhe, and elsewhere.[113] "Once and for all, the end has come for sentimental Burschenherrlichkeit and beery stupidity.[114] He who is not willing to

111. Letter to Professor Goldstein of 13 November 1919, printed in *Lebensbild*, p. 615; the words "to war" are an interpolation of Marianne Weber's.

112. According to a report of a participant, *Lebensbild*, p. 643.

113. Report of the *Heidelberger Tageblatt*; the *Heidelberger Neueste Nachrichten*'s report is not quite so clear; cf. *Lebensbild*, p. 644.

114. By 17 October 1918, Weber had conclusively resigned from his old fraternity. He wrote at the time to Fritz Keller, the chairman of the alumni commission of Allemania (12th war report of Burschenschaft Allemania of Heidelberg, Heidelberg, February 1919) (after the copy in the Max Weber archive, Munich):

"I ask you to strike me from the list of the alumni of Allemania.

"I think with thanks of what the fraternity color meant to me as a young man and am pleased to know that your members—as expected—held their own. But I am of the view that after the war the day of fraternity color life, if it has not already actually passed, then should pass. Conditions are not appropriate for the old 'joviality' of the fraternity student, and the cultivation of manliness, which doubtless the fraternities did much to nurture, must seek other means and ways. I do not believe in a 'reform' of the existing fraternities; that is hindered by the ownership of houses, which I always rejected as inappropriate for students, and the resulting dependency upon the money bag and thereby on the 'traditions' of the *Alte*

employ revolutionary methods in the regions where a German irredenta will emerge, and to risk scaffold and prison, will not deserve the name of nationalist in the future."[115]

Max Weber hoped that the allies would be so alarmed by discussion about the inevitable rise of a massive German irredentist movement that they would make far-reaching concessions in the east. In his articles in the *Frankfurter Zeitung*, he deliberately threatened the rise of a German nationalism that would employ revolutionary means in order to serve national self-determination. If the unification of all Germans (Austria!) was prevented, if Germany were forced to give up Alsace and more in the west or even(!) eastern territories, if it were burdened with reparations to compensate Belgium, then "after an epoch of pacifism born of exhaustion, even the last worker who perceives this will become a chauvinist!"[116] Recourse to the use of force by German irredentism was at once *program* and prediction: It was to become reality in a different and much more horrible way than Weber had dreamed.

Weber demanded resistance by any means and at any price, especially in the east. The Free Corps movement, which arose shortly afterward, corresponded precisely to his wishes. He chastised the Rat der Volks-

---

Herren. I especially do not believe that the spiritual inbreeding that became ever narrower over the years and was accompanied by the narrowing of personal relationships will disappear. I do not view exclusivity as entirely an evil in itself, rather the manner in which it manifests itself in the fraternities, in the face of Germany's future tasks.

"These views put me so much in opposition to those who represent the color, that they themselves will regard it as correct that I untie the band in friendship and with the best wishes.

"With the very best wishes to you personally,

Max Weber."

115. Report of the *Vossische Zeitung*; cf. the other cited newspaper reports about Weber's election speeches, above, note 83.

116. *Pol. Schr.*, pp. 456, 490; cf. the report of the *Vossische Zeitung*: "What will become . . . of German nationalism? If the dictated peace that threatens us comes, we will all be chauvinists in ten years." Weber also advised in the case of a political or merely an economic annexation of the *Saar region* to France "the revolutionary accomplishment of the right of self-determination against foreign power and tribute rule. If German brothers in the east or the west are politically assaulted, then the world will witness the rise of a German irredenta movement, that will differ only in its revolutionary means from the Italian, Serbian, or Irish only insofar as the will of 70 million will stand behind it and—I presume it will be so, I say openly, I expect—the academic youth. Nothing else would be possible. Even a private man forgets injuries to his interest, but not injuries to his honor. A nation more so." Speech by Weber at a protest assembly of the faculty and students of the Ruprecht-Karls University of Heidelberg on 11 March 1919: "Gegen Frankreichs Anspruch auf Pfalz und Rheinbecken, 1919," p. 36. Weber declared earlier that economic questions should not play a decisive role in the question of the ownership of the Saar region since "in this question, the nation's honor is affected," p. 30. For an abbreviated version of this speech, in which some of the most pointed of Weber's declarations are omitted, cf. *Pol. Schr.*, pp. 565 ff.

beauftragten for having tolerated "the replacement of *officers* by reserve officers who cringed before their predecessors and the soldiers. They had thereby sanctioned a shameless lack of discipline and looting and made it impossible . . . to oppose the Poles even in regions inhabited only by Germans."[117] Because of the revolution, it was now impossible "to send even one division against the Poles."[118] In May 1919, Weber insisted that "the east can and should take up its weapons and refuse obedience to the Reich government, no matter what form the peace takes: 'force us [to obey] if you can.' "[119] Today, we can reasonably doubt whether this was a realistic strategy to retain the German territories in the east. Such a desperate explosion of national heroism, even if it reached the level of Weber's heroic fantasy, would certainly have made an impression on the allies; but whether this forceful expression of the right of self-determination would have ameliorated the peace conditions is uncertain. Probably it would only have led to even greater reprisals against the Reich. Weber expected that a German national partisan war would have real political impact. In reality, it would have been merely a heroic, emotional, political confession of nationalist sentiment that did not shrink from the worst and did not fear the most severe punishment—a nationalist counterpart to syndicalist ideas. This line of reasoning was praiseworthy for its intellectual consistency. But was it capable of becoming a guiding principle to lead a weary and exhausted people out of the inner and outer collapse of the year 1918?

Max Weber was very bitter that the Independent Social Democrats agreed with the allies' argument that Germany bore sole guilt for the war. When the allies attempted a moral justification of the "dictated peace of Versailles" with the thesis of German war guilt, Weber reacted at the beginning of January in an article in the *Frankfurter Zeitung*. In accordance with his previous views, he tried to demonstrate that the sole guilt for the war belonged to "czarism as a system," in spite of the many objective errors in the policies of the Central Powers as well as those of the western powers.[120] In order to create a broader basis for the public battle against the war guilt thesis, at the instigation of Prince Max von Baden, a "Heidelberger Vereinigung für eine Politik des Rechts" (Heidelberg Association for a Policy of Justice) was founded at the beginning of February 1919 in the Ziegelhäuser Landstrasse house of Max Weber.[121] The association set itself the goal of rallying as many

117. Letter of 3 January 1919 to Hartmann; see above, note 65.

118. On 4 January 1919 in Karlsruhe; concurring report of the *Karlsruher Tagblatt* and the *Badische Landeszeitung*.

119. Letter to Clara Mommsen of 13 May 1919, Weber papers.

120. *Pol. Schr.*, pp. 488 ff.

121. Cf. here Albertin, *Liberalismus und Demokratie*, pp. 212 ff.

well-known people as possible from public life who were not compromised by their support of annexationist war aims (although Weber himself thought little of this requirement!) in order to protest, with a voice that could not be overheard, the crushing peace conditions and the distortion of truth represented by the war guilt propaganda of the western powers before world public opinion. Weber himself would have liked to give the association a more offensive character, that is, he wanted it to do "more than" just counteract "the enemies' 'horror' propaganda, which is now more prevalent than ever" by "objective, *non*chauvinistic, but convincing utilization of our own evidence of horrors." In addition, he would have liked it to propagandize for the "reconstruction of the army . . . on a *democratic* basis."[122]

A respectable number of prominent people soon declared themselves ready to cooperate within the framework of the association. They included, in addition to the Weber brothers, Hans Delbrück, Hermann Oncken, Lujo Brentano, Walther Schücking, Conrad Haussmann, Count Maximilian Montgelas, and Albrecht Mendelssohn-Bartholdy. In its first public announcement on February 7, 1919 in the *Frankfurter Zeitung*, the Heidelberg Association demanded the establishment of a nonpartisan, neutral commission of investigation to clarify the question of war guilt objectively. At the same time, the statement noted the existence of "*a common guilt* of all the great powers of Europe involved in the war." It passionately protested the western powers' attempt to achieve "imperialistic war goals" under the pretence of their claim to judge Germany and to punish Germany, although they had "ceremoniously committed" themselves to abandoning such goals.[123]

But paper protests had little impact on the western powers' intransigent position, while Wilson was less and less in a position to exercise a moderating influence. The Heidelberg Association had to look on powerlessly with the rest of the German public while a peace treaty was negotiated in Versailles designed to subdue Germany forever. Little came of its activities. The only tangible success that the Heidelberg Association had arose from an appeal that Max Weber wrote at the instigation of Prince Max von Baden for the publication of German records and at the same time for a hearing for the prominent personalities involved by an independent, completely nonpartisan investigatory committee.[124]

122. Letter to the *Frankfurter Zeitung* of 9 February 1919, *Pol. Schr.* 1, pp. 486 f.

123. *Frankfurter Zeitung*, 1st morning ed. of 13 February 1919.

124. Letter to the *Frankfurter Zeitung* of 20 March 1919, now *Pol. Schr.*, pp. 503 f. It was suggested by Prince Max von Baden and Count Montgelas, but for tactical reasons came from Max Weber. Compare letter to Oncken of 21 March 1919, copy in Weber papers. We can therefore attribute the declaration to Weber in a *limited* way *only*.

Max Weber actually was not unconditionally in favor of publishing the German records, as long as Germany, and not the western powers, was the only country to do so. Privately he said: "I dread *our records* somewhat. Of course, I dread the multiplication of these 'memoirs' à la Ludendorff, Tirpitz, and others even more."[125] If he now supported the publication of German records, he did so to forestall an appeal from eight German deputies in Bern concerning the publication of war records that would treat Germany's guilt as *res judicata*, especially since the British government had rejected the German offer to establish a neutral commission to investigate the war guilt question.[126] The German Foreign Office was informed in advance, and it appeared to welcome Weber's initiative.[127] Weber's additional call for an investigatory commission to question the leading figures in the German government before and during the war was founded on his rigorous ethic of responsibility. He sought to fix responsibilities. His suggestion was, of course, realized later in a form that provoked his strongest protests.[128]

The Heidelberg Association's activities reflected the position of the leading negotiators in the German peace delegation in Versailles, and it was welcomed there as well as in the Foreign Office. As a result, Max Weber, Count Maximilian Montgelas, Hans Delbrück, and Albrecht Mendelssohn-Bartholdy were brought into the Committee for the Peace Negotiations' deliberations in the middle of March 1919. This was a commission of experts that had been involved with preparations for the peace treaty since November 1918 under Count Bernstorff's chairmanship and that had also been selected to accompany the peace delegation to Paris. They were asked to formulate a detailed German reply to the allied memorandum about the German Reich's war guilt—a memorandum that at this stage had not been officially delivered to the German delegation but had been brought to its attention indirectly.

Weber at first strongly resisted participating in any way in the creation of this "treaty of shame" and was inclined to reject the government's request.[129] But eventually he overcame his reservations and promised his cooperation. This was not merely a result of the preparatory deliberations of the "committee" in which he had participated since the end of

125. Letter to Delbrück of 8 October 1919.

126. With the argument that became famous: "This point needs no answer, because it is long since established that the German government is responsible for the outbreak of the war."

127. Cf. letter to Oncken of 21 March 1919, copy in Weber papers.

128. Cf. below, text at note 158.

129. Cf. letter to Count Bernstorff, undated, 20–24 March 1919, in which Weber first of all refused participation. *Lebensbild*, pp. 660 f. Cf. also letter to Oncken, 25 March 1919, copy in Weber papers.

March; he felt that the most important general matters were neglected in favor of questions of technical and economic detail. For this reason, he protested the composition of the committee in which representatives of industry, trade, and agriculture predominated.[130] Finally, he saw almost no possibility to influence the negotiations positively, and it took some effort to persuade him to continue to participate.[131] He eventually agreed to go to Paris with the hope that he could later "be heard as an expert" in the National Assembly on the decisive question "accept or reject,"[132] only after a second attempt to withdraw.[133]

Basically, Weber viewed the German negotiating position as hopeless from the outset and expected nothing from the negotiations and opposing arguments in Versailles. His advance judgment was firm: "This entire situation is much more terrible than could have been believed, the more we study the treaty. *Such* a thing has never occurred before. . . . Everybody argues for *not* signing. The Ostmark will take to the arms it possesses and refuse obedience to the Reich government if the treaty is signed. This is the only effective response for the east—but otherwise? I see no way out."[134]

In Paris, together with Delbrück and Mendelssohn-Bartholdy, Weber was supposed to work on the German notes about the war guilt question with which the Reich government hoped to upset the treaty's justification. He had reservations here as well: "In any event, I will not participate in the *guilt* notes if any dishonorable conduct is contemplated or will be sanctioned."[135] Finally, he was assigned the writing of the "introduction"[135a] to the memorandum about war guilt that was then delivered to the allies along with the German note on 28 May and was

130. Letter to Mina Tobler, undated, end of March or beginning of April 1919, Archiv Ebnet II, 90a. Cf. also Albertin, *Liberalismus und Demokratie*, pp. 313 f.

131. Compare Weber's letters to his wife of 30 March and 2 April 1919, *Lebensbild*, pp. 661 f.

132. Ibid.: "Today, I was at Count Bernstorff's. . . . From what he said, we could perceive that we were viewed as the group which was to be listened to authoritatively on the decisive questions before the National Assembly: 'Accept or reject.' The whole thing will now claim only one to two weeks in Paris. Under these conditions, I agreed." Probably Bernstorff at the time did not expect serious negotiations and started with the view that the issue was to work for the rejection of the treaty and to create the necessary diplomatic basis for this.

133. Cf. letter to Clara Mommsen of 13 May 1919, Weber papers, partially printed in *Lebensbild*, p. 663, cited below, note 162.

134. Letter to Mina Tobler, between 12 and 14 May 1919, Archiv Ebnet II, 93.

135. *Lebensbild*, p. 666.

135a. It is not clear what exactly is meant by "introduction." It could refer to the "Bemerkungen zum Bericht der Verantwortlichkeiten der Urheber des Krieges" as a whole. But it is likely that it refers to the last section, "VI. Rückblickende Betrachtungen," which presumably were originally intended to serve as an introduction.

later published as the German White Book about guilt for the war. Weber viewed this as an outrageous demand. He had "not been questioned about anything, that is, authoritatively questioned."[136] Apparently, from the beginning he had vigorously opposed the investigation of the war guilt question on the level of diplomatic negotiations and evasions, on which later an entire library of war guilt literature was written that was not capable of solving the question. He did not prevail on this point of procedure, however, because the primary objective was a precise refutation of the allied memorandum about Germany's responsibility for the war. His political and demagogic temperament rebelled against the kind of academic argumentation suggested by the experts of the Foreign Office. Nonetheless, his protest against such an approach must at least have contributed to the fact that Delbrück's original draft, which defended William II and justified the Austrian position on the Serbian question, was abandoned.[137] It was probably not until then that Weber was assigned the final formulation of the "Retrospective Observations."[137a]

Weber decided to do it in such a way that he could be confident that "they will not accept it."[138] "In the light of [the allies'] unbelievable imputations," he did not regard a counterpresentation as making much sense and was inclined to throw out the whole thing. After another revision by the commission, the final draft was eventually found satisfactory. It appears to have been polished and softened somewhat by the other members of the commission.[139] In contrast to Delbrück's version, any defense of Austrian policy in the Serbian question was abandoned. There had doubtless been errors in German policy also, but there was no question of moral guilt in any sense. "The ideas of the leading German

136. Ibid., pp. 667 f.

137. Delbrück's draft in Delbrück papers, 27.

137a. Cf. note 135a above.

138. Lebensbild, p. 668.

139. The so-called war guilt memorandum, "Bemerkungen zum Bericht der Kommission der Alliierten und Assoziierten Regierungen über die Verantwortlichkeit der Urheber des Krieges," was eventually presented to the allied and associated governments, against the advice of the Reich cabinet, which had objected to Brockdorff-Rantzau's strategy of squarely attacking the war guilt issue. It appears that Weber and his three colleagues had been but pawns in a diplomatic maneuver. The memorandum was published in *Das Deutsche Weissbuch über die Schuld am Kriege*, 1st ed., 1919, pp. 56–68; 2d ed., 19 [?], pp. 63–67. The first edition is cited), printed in *Pol. Schr.*, pp. 571 ff. It is in any case incorrect to attribute the "Bemerkungen" so exclusively to Weber as Winckelmann does. It must not be forgotten that the memorandum was based on a draft put forward by the Foreign Office and that the other members had a substantial share in the redrafting. Although Weber was in some ways the dominant figure, he was quite unable to get his own intentions fully accepted. Only for the "retrospective considerations" can Weber's authorship be safely assumed. Ibid., pp. 63 ff; *Pol. Schr.*, pp. 580 ff.

statesmen were far removed from plans of conquest."[140] The question of guilt could be answered by looking not at the blunders of the diplomats but at the general political strategies of the powers; it had to be approached with an eye to the question of "which governments had pursued political and economic goals that could only have been realized through a war."[141]

Weber had no doubts about what the answer had to be. He was convinced that there was but one power that could have achieved its objectives only through a war of aggression: the czarist system associated with the imperialist attitudes of Russia's *ruling* classes. The real responsibility for the war lay with czarism, while the Central Powers had not been able to avoid "a military conflict . . . in any honorable way. . . . Czarism . . . constituted the most terrible system for the enslavement of men and nations that had ever been devised—until the peace treaty that has been presented here." The German people had "taken up the battle unitedly and resolutely" in 1914, "*only* as a defensive war against czarism."[142] There is no point in quarreling here with the characteristic one-sidedness of this judgment. It was closely in line with Weber's previously discussed attitudes.

Weber's experience in Paris strengthened his view that the peace treaty must be rejected "whatever the risks."[143] His national feelings passionately resisted any such "peace of shame," and here he was in agreement with the opinions of the German public as a whole. He suggested that Trotsky's model should be followed and treaty ratification refused. Then the allies would have to take the next move. He also considered the alternative possibility of dissolving the government and transferring sovereignty to the League of Nations—"some action of this kind, which would have made *war* measures impossible." A foreign occupation would lead, he hoped, to "the awakening of the national inner resistance."[144] But he seriously doubted whether such a heroic step

140. "Kriegsschulddenkschrift," p. 63.

141. Ibid., p. 64.

142. Ibid., p. 68.

143. Letter to Oncken of 25 March 1919: "In regard to peace, the mood in Berlin is apparently for *rejection* whatever the danger. That is also my view."

144. Letter to Marianne Weber of 1 July 1919. Looking back, Weber wrote: "Yes, you say that I am writing nothing about this 'peace.' Oh, at the time in Wolfratshausen, I was so tired and 'indifferent' that I *understood* the nation's exhaustion [!]. Of course, 'rejection' could not have been a rejection, but actually the dissolution of the government and the transfer of sovereignty to the 'League of Nations'. . . . That at least would have been possible. When I of course reflect upon the mood here, then I naturally ask in hindsight [!] whether there was any chance that anything good would have come of it: awakening of national (internal) resistence." Somewhat altered in *Lebensbild*, pp. 669 f. Cf. ibid., p. 668. Weber disapproved of the fact that the government had no clear conception of what ought to have occurred in the event of a rejection.

would be palatable in Berlin: "For all this, I believe—fear!—that there *will be* negotiations [on the basis of the treaty] and it *will be* signed. The situation is so hopeless and the people involved are not up to it," he argued shortly after returning from Paris.[145] But he also soberly predicted the consequences of a treaty rejection. "If they send troops in—fine! However, at most, they will take Baden and the Westphalian industrial region. They will put the rest under blockade. And then—the Haase-Barth government will plead—for peace! Bavaria will secede. What will then have been won? Well, we shall have to wait and see, but it is easier to *say* 'reject it,' and I of course say this too, than to see how we can then survive with honor and save the existence of the Reich."[146] Weber had to face a difficult inner conflict between rejection at any price on national grounds and the sober evaluation of the consequences of such a step, which had to lead to renewed radicalization and the destruction of the Reich's unity. In view of the situation, he could no longer defend a rejection in June, although he still personally favored one. He admitted to being "politically, completely at a loss," especially because he feared that even if parliament and the government rejected the peace treaty, a plebiscite would nevertheless lead to acceptance. "This would be even worse, since it would tie us morally [to the treaty]."[147] At the same time, he disapproved of the German Democratic party's position on the question of the peace treaty, since the party did not hold consistently to the decision to refuse support to the signing of the treaty after all.[148] But once the treaty was accepted, he viewed it as senseless to quarrel about it: "Now—it has occurred, and we must turn to a positive policy." Of course, he viewed the future with pessimism; with *this* peace "misery had only just begun." He correctly predicted that France would use the reprisals in the treaty to "make things worse" for Germany, "to torment it" and possibly to attempt to detach the Rhineland from the Reich.[149]

Max Weber opened his lectures in Munich, where the storm of the

145. To Mina Tobler, 1 June 1919, Archiv Ebnet II, 94. Weber reported movingly about the departure from Paris: "Champs Elysees, Boulevards, Madelaine, Opera, etc., all viewed for the last time in my life in brilliant light! Unforgettable."

146. Letter to Clara Mommsen of 13 May 1919, Weber papers.

147. Letter to Marianne Weber of 20 June 1919, *Lebensbild*, p. 668.

148. Letter to Marianne Weber of 28 June 1919, after a copy in the Weber papers: "The position of the Democratic party was *not* faultless. Ultimately they also gave full power to sign albeit through a back door, and that should not have occurred if they really took the position which they gave the appearance of." This passage is omitted in *Lebensbild*, p. 669.

149. Ibid.; the text in *Lebensbild* is somewhat misleading: instead of "*the* partial occupation," it should read "a." Also: "I have come to the conclusion that refusing to sign would have brought about secession [of Bavaria] within a short time through a revolution by the USP *and* the clericals. And I understand *this* argument. Otherwise, I do not yet see the situation clearly. The peace delegation *and* all experts, also all from here, were *unanimously* against acceptance."

Soviet Republic had now passed, with a declaration about the political situation. These were probably his first and last words about politics in the lecture hall, since such words belonged in a place where the free air of criticism was possible. The national emergency following the acceptance of the Treaty of Versailles seemed to justify this uncharacteristic step. He spoke with passionate national urgency: "We can only have . . . a common goal: to turn this peace treaty into a scrap of paper." The right of revolution against foreign domination could never be denied.[150]

Weber's political value system was in no way shaken by the collapse of the imperial Reich. On the contrary, his national emotions quickened in the hour of defeat, at a time when he observed a general retreat from national thinking, to passionate nationalism. He stood by his principles and could still see no errors in the principles of political power that had guided German policy in the past (or that he would have liked to see guide it). In 1918 and 1919, at a time when there was a general retreat from the belief in power characteristic of the Wilhelmine epoch, he expressly advocated power as the means and presupposition of all policy, and sharply attacked pacifism.[151] The kernel of his political hopes and goals at the moment of defeat was contained in his announcement in January 1920 to the Munich students who approved of Count Arco's assassination of Eisner and applauded his release: "I would ally myself with *any* power on earth and even with the devil incarnate to restore Germany to its old splendor, if I still participated in politics. But not with the power of stupidity."[152] The nation and its power in the world remained

150. *Lebensbild*, p. 673.

151. Among other places, in his lecture "Politics as a Vocation" to the Freistudentisches Bund in Munich, which according to Eduard Baumgarten's researches, was held on 28 January 1919, while the lecture "*Wissenschaft* as a Profession" preceded it on 16 January 1919 ("Reihenfolge und Datierung der Vorträge 'Politik als Beruf' und 'Wissenschaft als Beruf,'" Max Weber archive, Munich. Compare also Wolfgang Schluchter, *Wertfreiheit und Verantwortungsethik. Zum Verhältnis von Wissenschaft und Politik bei Max Weber* (Tübingen, 1971), p. 8, note 2. Weber had earlier delivered the lecture "Science as a Vocation" in 1917 before the same association, the Freistudentischer Bund (cf. above, chap. 7, p. 268, note 292). At first, Weber had only promised one talk, "Science as a Vocation." (Cf. Immanuel Birnbaum, "Erinnerungen an Max Weber," in "Max Weber zum Gedächtnis," *Kölner Zeitschrift für Soziologie und Sozialpsychologie*, supplement 7, 1963, pp. 19 f.) Apparently he stepped in for Friedrich Naumann, who for health reasons had been unable to give the talk. See Guenther Roth and Wolfgang Schluchter, *Max Weber's Vision of History*, pp. 114 f.

152. After the original draft in Weber's handwriting in the Weber papers: "*Pertinent* (allegedly 'political') remarks on 19 January" (published in Appendix VII of the German edition of the present book). According to the notes prepared by a listener, Weber then said something like: "I can say this, gentlemen; if it meant restoring Germany to its old honor and grandeur, I would immediately ally with the Devil, but *never* with stupidity." The report in *Lebensbild*, pp. 684 f. is a compilation of both texts. Compare also Weber's report to Mina Tobler, 19 January 1919, Archiv Ebnet II, 119: "The subject was a moderately strong

the ultimate political value for him. He argued that all cooperative action ought to orient itself around this principle. He retained the unshatterable belief that Germany would once again arise from its condition of complete degradation. The German nation would not remain a "pariah people."

In November 1918, Weber reflected on Woodrow Wilson's program in the *Frankfurter Zeitung*. He maintained that the future goal of German foreign policy ought to be "clear rejection of imperialist dreams and a purely autonomist ideal of nationality."[153] Had Max Weber thus given up the hope that Germany would play a future role as a power among the great powers of the world? Everything we know about Weber at this time speaks against such an assumption. Nothing was changed in the *goal*. It was only necessary to begin anew:

> We are once again starting from the beginning, as we did after 1648 and 1807. That is the simple nature of the matter. Only today we must live more quickly, work more quickly, and act with more initiative. It is not *we* but the next generation that will see the beginning of reconstruction. Of course, the self-discipline of truthfulness prompts us to say that Germany's world policy role is at an end. Anglo-Saxon world domination—'ah, c'est nous qui l'avons faite' as Thiers said to Bismarck about our own unification—is a fact. This is very unpleasant. But we have turned back *far* worse: the Russian knout. This glory remains ours. America's world domination was as inescapable as that of ancient Rome after the Punic

one: Politics (Bismarck). Now a terribly *bad* area. I literally read newspapers only once a week and miss nothing. On the contrary, a gray misery seizes hold of me when I look at them, although I still have complete inner certainty, things will once again improve. At the same time, we still experience all kinds of stupidities close by. For example, the student demonstrations for clemency for Count Arco. Of course, I would have him shot in spite of and *because of* his *impeccable* behavior. That would be better than to permit him to become a coffee house curiosity (since he would not become any *more* at this time) *and* : let Eisner live on. Since it would *only* have been settled *with* him (hypothetically). Now, he lives on! But, be that as it may—the stupidity of these demonstrations along with a 'conspiracy' (publicly discussed) with the Reichstag, insults to those who think differently which the presiding Rector does not reprimand, my designation of the insulters as low scoundrels, *thereupon*: withdrawal of the insults, finally (allegedly) prospective demonstrations in my lecture hall—all of this is so silly and childish in view of the threatened unity of the Reich and the demands for deliveries that face us, that it can excite loathing. The hooligans have learned *nothing*. This evening, nevertheless, I will drill them once again in how one begins to treat opponents *respectfully*. Since the 'assassins' only withdraw their insults under pressure—the others threatened not to cooperate with them as long as they carried *my* designation—then I will naturally do the same. You can see, *what* level of 'gentlemen' we deal with here."

153. *Lebensbild*, p. 443.

> War. We can hope that it will not be shared with Russia. *This* is for me the goal of our future world policy, since the Russian danger has been averted only for now, not forever. At the moment, of course, the hysterical, nauseous hatred of the French is the principal danger.[154]

Weber was still speaking of German *world* policy. The chief thrust of that policy was directed as strongly as ever against Russia as the future great power that Weber regarded as Germany's natural enemy. "The resurrection of the . . . imperialist danger from Russia has . . . not been eliminated once and for all," he argued. The most urgent task was to put Germany in a position to be able to defend itself against this danger.[155]

Of course, the first task for Germany was to overcome the consequences of defeat at home and abroad. This meant, first, restoring Germany's "face," which Weber viewed as destroyed through humiliation, revolution, and dishonorable conduct vis-à-vis the enemy. No people in a similar situation had seen this happen in such a painful way. For the moral regeneration of the nation, according to Weber, went along with the restoration of respectability and "honesty" as the basis of bourgeois economic life. He recommended that Germany employ puritan methods: "the means: the American 'club' and associations of every kind based on *selective* choice of members, starting with childhood and youth, no matter what the [association's] goal—beginnings can be observed with the 'Freideutsche Jugend.'"[156] He had long before recognized the lack of bourgeois forms of social selection as a cause of the weakness of bourgeois self-consciousness in Germany, and he wanted to see this remedied conclusively.[157]

At the time, it seemed urgent to Max Weber to create the intellectual basis for German regeneration in the face of what he viewed as the dishonorable actions of the pacifists and of the extreme Left. Above all, the nation's honor had to be restored in the face of the "enemies"; the national consciousness that Weber sought could not grow in abasement and German self-accusations. Even in defeat, national prestige had to be

154. Letter to Crusius of 24 November 1918, *Pol. Schr.* 1, pp. 482 ff.

155. *Pol. Schr.*, p. 456; Weber also said the same thing in his speeches, for example in Heidelberg (according to the report of the *Heidelberger Tageblatt*): "The internal element for the construction of Germany is the necessity of restoring German honor. The war was unavoidable; it had to be fought because German honor demanded it. And one day, history will praise Germany for freeing the world from czarism. Germany won *that* war. The fact that we finally lost the war proves nothing about our good cause. . . . I cannot possibly harbor doubts about Germany's future."

156. Letter to Crusius, here after the original in the Weber papers. The relevant passage is incorrect in *Pol. Schr.* 1, p. 483.

157. Cf. above, chap. 5, sec. 1; also Wilbrandt, *Max Weber*, pp. 454 f.

maintained. When, at the beginning of May, the western powers demanded that Germany deliver all military leaders and politicians who had broken international laws of warfare to be prosecuted before an allied tribunal and announced that William II would be indicted "for serious injury to international morals and the sanctity of treaties," Weber's volcanic temper exploded. He demanded that the leading military people and politicians, especially Ludendorff, who practically had exercised responsibility for German policy alone after 1917, voluntarily and immediately present themselves to the enemy. In such a way, he hoped to make the allied demands look absurd. Above all, he expected that a wave of sympathy would awaken among the German people and they would lose any suspicion that they had risked life and limb for the interests of the dynasties and the generals and that they now had to suffer for them as well. "The decisive thing is the *domestic* impact," Max Weber wrote to Naumann. "The *leaders must* 'offer their heads.' Only this will have an impact on the masses (in the *future*, and this is the only thing I am thinking about)."[158]

He wrote with similar words to Delbrück: "Only in this way can the officers' corps and the general staff return to the hearts of the nation. *Only* then can the phrase 'we are paying' for the leaders, who were not prepared themselves to 'offer their heads,' be completely destroyed." Above all, Ludendorff, as the man most responsible, should immediately give himself up to American imprisonment "with the declaration to the enemy that '*he* had advised the Kaiser that *he* was responsible, that they might proceed against him in a manner for which they could take responsibility, provided that they would promise protection against the curiosity and insults of the mob.'"[159] Bethmann Hollweg should give himself up as well: "Surely he will be able to stand there in complete innocence. This will be all the better for us. As an old lawyer, I would 'defend' him before the 'court' of the enemy with great pleasure. Only in this way is domestic

158. Letter of 10 May 1919, partially printed in Heuss, *Friedrich Naumann*, 2d edition, p. 488; he says further: "Should the general staff and the officers' corp ever revive, this step would be absolutely necessary and its omission a heavy, never again reparable infamy. Otherwise it will always be said: 'we are atoning for them.'"

159. Letter of 15 May 1919, Delbrück papers. He says further: "We can*not* protect them, thus honor commands the step. I do not promise myself (at the moment) very much from this with our *enemies—but at home*. And that is most important. . . . For Ludendorff per procura, the 'Supreme Court' is purest farce. Of course he will be exonerated—this is so a priori—but of what use is this for him and the Officers' Corps? The Left and the masses say: 'because of nationalistic motives,' 'the great thief . . . ,' etc., and nothing can be done about it." Weber said similar things to Mina Tobler: "If our officers would have had as much dignity as the Chinese and Japanese. Instead of writing 'war memoirs,' had they drawn the consequences that an honest man draws when life condemns him to *lose* a crucial game, the impression would be different!" Letter of 22 April 1920, A.E. II, 91.

restoration possible, not through 'memoirs.' "[160] It was extremely difficult for Friedrich Naumann to fulfill Weber's request that he relay this suggestion to the first war chancellor. Even he was unable to share his friend's heroic idealism, which refused to compromise with the hate-filled reality of the domestic and international struggle.[161]

At the same time, Weber addressed to Ludendorff the suggestion that the leaders give themselves up voluntarily to the enemy. Ludendorff would thus offer one last great service to the nation and at the same time create the domestic preconditions for the reawakening of a militant mood among the German people who would remember their pride in the officers corps's bravery even in defeat.[162] Weber, of course, completely misread Ludendorff's personality when he endowed him with his own idealistic heroism. Ludendorff rejected any such step as a useless self-sacrifice. After his return from Versailles, Max Weber personally sought out the quartermaster general to try once again to convince him. The gist of this noteworthy conversation of two such opposing personalities is known to us from Weber's later reports. It developed into a passionate confrontation about all of German policy in the war and ended with a completely negative response to the matter at hand. Weber was deeply disappointed. He realized retrospectively that Ludendorff was not worthy of Weber's defense in the face of public opinion. "I now understand why the world resists when men like him try to place their heels upon the necks of others."[163]

Max Weber's heroic demand, that the leaders ought to "offer up their heads" voluntarily, was a genuine product of a rigoristic ethic of responsibility. It was necessary to accept the consequences of one's acts. He included the person of the Kaiser in this demand. The latter would do

160. Letter to Naumann, 10 May 1919 (cf. note 158 above). In the letter to Delbrück, Bethmann Hollweg was also named.

161. Naumann forwarded a copy of Weber's letter to Hohenfinow, with the explicit comment that he himself did not share this view. "The nation's flexibility has become weak! Only so can I explain Professor Weber's letter. He himself is true and brave, but he, like me, sees only dimly into the future." Naumann understood the essential meaning of Weber's request as little as everyone else. Naumann's letter of May 18, 1919, in Heuss, *Friedrich Naumann*, pp. 488 f.

162. Weber's letter, which may have been written on 12 or 13 May, as well as the short negative answer by the general, was not passed on to us. Compare the letter to Clara Mommsen of 13 May 1919: "I am just now going to Versailles, on pressing request—to what purpose? I do not know. It promises nothing for me or the matter. But one does his bit. Earlier, I sent Ludendorff advice in a letter: He, Tirpitz, Capelle, Bethmann, etc. *must know* what they now have to do *immediately*—in view of the enemies' demand for their delivery. The Officers' Corps can only rise again proudly one day, if *they* voluntarily 'offer up their heads' to the enemies. We shall have to wait and see!" After the original in the Weber papers; cf. *Lebensbild*, p. 663.

163. *Lebensbild*, pp. 664 f.

better to risk "an 'Elba' or even a 'St. Helena' rather than to accept the unholy end of a fugitive fleeing 'punishment.'"[164] Weber pressed this point not merely on moral grounds and in order to save the nation's honor but also from the conviction that it would be a "powerfully unburdening and rehabilitating step" for Germany.[165] At the same time, he believed it essential to create the internal preconditions for the reconstruction of a German army and a stronger German state and eventually for the restoration of the monarch in the consciousness of the mass of the people.

For related reasons, Max Weber wrote an extensive memorandum objecting to the fact that more than a third of the politicians on the parliamentary investigatory committee appointed by the National Assembly on 20 August 1919 to investigate the omissions and mistakes that had contributed to the outbreak of the war, its extension, and finally to the defeat, were of *Jewish* origin.[166] Weber was not moved to this criticism out of anti-Semitism, rather the contrary, although his Jewish friends, especially, did not understand that. He was anxious that antimilitarist resentment on the part of the Jewish committee members should not be allowed to influence the questioning of German officers (since Jews in the Wilhelmine Reich were normally not permitted to become officers). He wished thereby to forestall a depreciation of the image of the German officers' corps, which he believed might otherwise occur. He also feared that such a depreciation would contribute indirectly to anti-Semitism.[167]

In November 1918, Weber pointedly declared in the *Frankfurter Zeitung* that the "military epoch of German history" was at an end and proposed the introduction of a "militia system" on a democratic basis.[168] *Rebus sic stantibus*, not *pour jamais*. As early as the fall of 1919, one of his chief worries was the question of how the honorable German officers' corps might arise again "in the heart of the nation" and how the general staff could be recreated by circumventing the provisions of the Treaty of Versailles designed to prevent it. In October 1919 he wrote to Delbrück: "I hope to seek you out this winter to bring you a plan that requires your advice and that is designed with the long view in mind: the preservation *of the traditions of our military science instruction in spite of* the ban of the *peace treaty*. Everything must be reconstructed from the ground up. I can

164. Letter to Delbrück of 15 May 1919.

165. Ibid.

166. Cf. Ziegler, *Die deutsche Nationalversammlung 1919/20 und ihr Verfassungswerk* (Berlin, 1932), pp. 205 f.

167. Cf. *Lebensbild*, p. 660, also letter to Petersen, 14 April 1920, above, note 105. I am grateful for further information from Professor Baumgarten. The memorandum, the last political memorandum, was destroyed later by Marianne Weber.

168. *Pol. Schr.*, p. 456.

only discuss this very confidential circumstance orally."[169] And when asked by one of his students in his Munich sociological seminar in the early part of 1920 "about his political plans" he replied: "I have no political plans except to concentrate all my intellectual strength on the one problem how to get once more for Germany a great General Staff."[170]

These were the last political projects that Max Weber championed after he had withdrawn from active politics because, and as long as, "from the left to the right—insanity [is able] to dominate politics."[171] The ideal of the powerful national state remained the norm of his political desires and efforts. He remained a national power politician of the Wilhelmine type, as he had always been, even under the conditions of the Weimar state. But although he stood close to the national Right in his foreign policy objectives, in moderation and judgment he was a world apart from them. Much as his national sensitivities were aroused at the time of defeat, he nevertheless emphatically distanced himself from all merely emotional nationalism. When the national agitation increasingly began to direct itself against the democratic forces as well as the far Left, he sharply opposed them. As early as November 1918, he had rejected "*playing* with counterrevolution."[172] He continued to reject this emphatically. He had accused the Sparticists and the Independent Social Democrats of engendering a wild reaction with their politics. This prediction was borne out by the events in Munich. After the fall of the soviet republic in Munich, the public was engulfed in an extremely right-wing atmosphere. Even in academic circles a completely reactionary mood prevailed. Max Weber publicly and emphatically opposed the right-wing radical currents that he saw as increasingly gaining the upper hand. He thereby encountered some difficulties. Because of his decidedly democratic views, he suffered a certain isolation in university circles; it was symptomatic of this that many of the members of the Munich Academy, especially the natural scientists, vigorously opposed his election to membership. They did not wish to sit with the "spiritual father of the soviet republic," the "demagogic loudmouth," the author of the "shame report" (i.e., the war guilt memorandum).[173]

The right-wing extremist and strongly anti-Semitic student body in Munich also opposed Weber forcefully. From his viewpoint, there was no

169. Letter to Delbrück of 8 October 1919, Delbrück papers; the word "this" is my interpolation.

170. Gustav Stolper, *This Age of Fable* (New York, 1942), p. 318n. He was a participant in Max Weber's seminar at the time.

171. Declaration on the Arco case, according to the version published in *Lebensbild*, pp. 684 f.

172. Cf. above, note 39.

173. Weber to Delbrück, 8 October 1919.

reason to defend a literary intellectual like Eisner, who was "a prisoner of his own demagogic success."[174] Yet Weber strongly disapproved of the pardoning of Eisner's murderer and the nationalist agitation among the students that was associated with it.[175] Nor did he hesitate to announce this publicly in the bluntest form, which led to the disruption of his classes by right-wing student groups.[176] The same thing resulted in demonstrations by student fraternities in front of Weber's house.[177]

Max Weber was distressed by the Kapp Putsch for national reasons: "This Kapp business is such spine-chilling stupidity that I am in total despair. To play thus into the hands of the French!"[178] At the time, he wrote bitterly and informatively to his wife: "This ridiculous political situation makes me completely *sick*, if I think about it or remember it."[179] He feared that the right-wing extremist experiments would lead to the same thing that could result from left-wing extremism—the disintegration of the Reich. This was reason enough for attacking the Deutschnationale Partei (German National party) with passion and without reserve: "If the Reich falls apart, then it will have been these dogs that have done it (Kapp, Lüttwitz, I am sorry to have to say Ludendorff as well). I am afraid that the rabble will not be shot or put in prison like any worker in a similar situation, although the worker does *not* have their 'education.'"[180] He expected a rightward swing of the pendulum, which

174. *Wirtschaft und Gesellschaft*, p. 140.

175. Declaration on the Arco case. See note 153 above.

176. Cf. also the reports of Friedrich J. Berber and Max Rehm, in "Max Weber zum Gedächtnis," pp. 23 f., 25 ff.

177. Compare Weber's letter to Hofrat von Lukács (father of Georg Lukács) of 9 January 1920, Weber papers: "The reaction here to the communist regime of spring 1919 is still so strong that even I am exposed to student demonstrations. The academic mood has become extremely reactionary and also radically anti-Semitic." (Weber therefore saw himself as not in a position to advise Georg Lukács to seek a *Habilitation* in Munich, although he himself would have welcomed one.) Also letter of 17 February 1920 to Eulenburg, whose call to Munich had been engineered by Weber. But Weber feared that it would eventually be torpedoed because of the reigning anti-Semitism (Eulenburg was of Jewish anscestry). Weber writes of the "often insane anti-Semitism of the fraternities here." Copy in Weber papers.

178. Letter to Clara Mommsen of 16 March 1920, Weber papers.

179. Letter of 20 April 1920, in the possession of Professor Baumgarten.

180. Letter to Clara Mommsen, undated, mid-April 1920, Weber papers: He says further: "Only leave *this* association [the German National party]—it is a sorrow to me to see you in that society—and look at them. The local minister president [v. Kahr] has discussed 'separation from the Reich' (because the overfed middle class fears the Spartacists—the civil guard with rubber truncheons does not appear to be enough for them). In cowardly fashion he now denies this: 'German National'"; in *Lebensbild*, pp. 702 f. as usual recast in a much weaker way. Weber suspected at the time that v. Kahr had publicly discussed the possible secession of Bavaria from the Reich, and felt impelled to oppose this most strenuously. When it was denied, Weber planned to provoke a suit by the minister

would rob the progressive democratic forces of the possibility of effectiveness for some time.[181] He wrote pessimistically in March 1920 to Georg Lukács that now everything would be reactionary for decades. He decided to stay out of politics once and for all.[182]

Finally, we need to consider the question of whether Max Weber was really called in 1918 to be the "leader of the nation" in its most difficult hour, as was argued by his circle of friends in Heidelberg.[183] I believe he was not. It was not only significant personal reasons that prevented Max Weber from rising to a leading position in the new democratic order but,

---

president against the accusation with a sharp article so that he could later prove that these statements had been made. The article is reproduced in a *much weakened* form in *Lebensbild* (pp. 701 f.); the original reads as follows: "According to a published report, the Bavarian minister president is said to have made statements the gist of which would involve the advocacy of high treason. In the denial, the statements are so put right that there can be no doubts among honorable men about the circumstances, and the minister president would gladly seize the opportunity to affirm the situation under oath. I should also remark that those who falsely attributed these statements to him would have to be viewed as low curs by every respectable person. I trust that this coward would at least publicly step forward *in a court.* I make this declaration, because the French must have gained the false impression that this would help to further their plans. The French must be informed about what rabble they are dealing with exclusively." The matter was then dropped.

181. Cf. also Weber's passionate arousal about monarchistic agitation in Berlin in spring 1920: "Who *now* knows how the spring will develop? *First* politically (I *can*not read any newspapers: it is too terrible). Then: financially. There too, *everything* is dark and close to the precipice. The most annoying thing is this 'monarchism' for *this* Monarch! (in Berlin!) *These* gentlemen ought to be prevented from doing harm. But what is done? All of the disgraces that *they* are guilty of, end up helping them. That is the grotesque part." Letter to Mina Tobler, 10 February 1920, A.E. II, 120.

182. Cf. letter to Marianne Weber of 14 May 1919, in the possession of Professor Baumgarten: he wished to remain "apart" from the planned organization of the student left in Munich. He drew the same consequence for his students; he wrote to Georg Lukács at the time: "did you abandon it (Lukács's communistic activities)—or what? But you claim the right alone to decide, understandably. But when I consider *what* the current political troubles (since 1918) have cost us in doubt-free values, regardless of which political affiliation, e.g., Schumpeter, and now you, and what they will still cost us, without, I am convinced, achieving anything—since we are all living under foreign domination!—then I become somewhat embittered about this senseless destiny." At the time, Weber tried to make use of Lukács, who, having fled Hungary, was homeless and wandering aimlessly.

183. *Lebensbild*, pp. 633 f., 640 ff., 655: "The call . . . which he had awaited from the depths of his being." The thesis on Weber's political leadership role in Arthur Liebert, "Max Weber," *Preussische Jahrbücher* 110 (1927): 304 ff.; Gertrud Bäumer, "Nachruf auf Max Weber," *Die Hilfe*, 1920, p. 386; Ernst Troeltsch, "Nachruf auf Max Weber," *Deutscher Geist und Westeuropa*, p. 250; Schulze-Gävernitz, "Max Weber als Nationalökonom und Politiker," *Hauptprobleme der Soziologie: Erinnerungsgabe für Max Weber*, vol. 1, p. xxii. The obituaries by Bäumer, Troeltsch, and Schulze-Gävernitz are now handily available in "Max Weber zum Gedächtnis," *loc. cit.*, pp. 43 ff. A contrary view from the beginning, Jaspers, *Heidelberger Gedenkrede* (Tübingen, 1921), p. 18 and *Max Weber: Deutsches Wesen im politischen Denken, Forschen und Philosophieren*, pp. 25 f.

above all, the fact that his basic political ideals were rooted in an era that was forever in the past.[184] Domestically, he pressed for a democratic and social constitutional order; but democratization was only a *means* for him to produce qualified political leaders who would bring the legacy of the great "Caesarist" statesman, Bismarck, to new glory. He had no concrete plans for the form that the social reorganization of Germany would take, although he had spent so much time playing with socialist notions without, however, believing in them. Even now the international power status of the German nation remained very much more important to him than domestic issues. He totally rejected the efforts of the early twenties to break the diabolical cycle of European power politics of the imperialistic era and to seek new forms for political relations between nations. He despised the idea of hastily adjusting his basic political ideals to the changed situation and the demands of the moment, a path taken by Stresemann and many others without any great scruples and conscience. This was not the course that Weber envisioned for himself. On the contrary, honor demanded that he remain unwaveringly loyal to his own political convictions in the hour of defeat and collapse, rather than bow in cowardly fashion to the pressure of circumstances. If necessary, he had to wait and to keep silent and not to try to chase after destiny with a quick conversion.[185] It was precisely at this time that Weber reaffirmed the values that had determined his political activity in the past: the *power* of the *national* state in the world, supported by a strong army, protected by a bold and decisive foreign policy. These ideals, however, had lost their persuasive power in the climate of the years of 1918 and 1919. Therefore, Weber's position toward the concrete political questions of the revolutionary period wavered repeatedly between a "realpolitische" tactical orientation and one determined by his political convictions only. For this reason he was denied any major political role in the political arena in 1919. Modest chances for the implementation of his political ideas arose only in the area of constitutional policy. He succeeded in a significant way in influencing the structure of the Weimar constitution. But otherwise his ultimate political ideals were not in tune with the trend of the immediate postwar years. He was fully aware of this, and therefore withdrew to "scholarly endeavors" since he believed that he could achieve more fruitful things there than in the politics of the day. The failure of his attempt to play a leading role in the construction of a democratic Ger-

184. Cf. also Wilbrandt, *Max Weber,* p. 450: "As a politician, Max Weber never freed himself of "Germany in its old majesty," which he would have liked to reconstruct after the collapse.

185. In any case in the essential question of the nation's future. See Weber's letter to Crusius of 24 November 1918, *Pol. Schr.* 1, p. 484: "What we now *publicly* say is of course 'rebus sic stantibus,' *never* pour jamais! 'Toujours y penser . . .'"

many was a symbol of the end of the era of the power state and imperialism in German history, built proudly upon Bismarck's legacy but finally doomed to failure because a clear view of the possible had been lost and the signs of the new era were not correctly recognized. In the past, Max Weber's plea for internal reform, for a foreign policy free of a quest for prestige, had fallen on deaf ears. The nation had not then known how to make use of one of its greatest personalities and had been incapable of following his advice. In 1919, it was too late.

9

Weber and the Making of the Weimar Constitution

1. Weber's November 1919 Articles on Germany's Future Governmental System

The downfall of the Bismarckian Reich and the destruction of its constitutional system by the revolution took the democratic forces by surprise. They were totally unprepared for the task of immediately setting up a new constitutional order from the ground up. Otherwise the Reich might well disintegrate again into its separate components or sink into the whirlpool of communist Soviet rule. The creators of the Weimar constitution were not able to build upon a broad democratic tradition that had been working in a determined way for a constitutional reform of imperial Germany. Even in the last years of the imperial Reich, only a few outstanding personalities had pleaded for parliamentarization of the Reich constitution. The parliamentary system that was established in response to Ludendorff's demand at the moment of defeat had to a certain extent to be "improvised," for the intellectual and internal preconditions for it were present only to some degree.[1] Hugo Preuss himself repeatedly expressed his concern that the German people were not politically mature enough for the democratic government that fell almost without a struggle into their laps at the moment of defeat.[2]

1. Cf. Theodor Eschenburg's splendid study, "Die improvisierte Demokratie der Weimarer Republik," *Geschichte und Politik*, Heft 10 (Laupheim, 1951); the concept "improvising" stems from Preuss. Cf. his article: "Die Improvisierung des Parlamentarismus," *Staat, Recht und Freiheit*, October 1918, pp. 361 ff.

2. Cf. Preuss's speech in the constitutional committee of the National Assembly, "Protokolle des 8. Ausschusses der Nationalversammlung," *Verhandlungen der verfassungsgebenden deutschen Nationalversammlung*, vol. 336, Anlagen zu den stenographischen Berichten, no. 391 (Berlin, 1920), pp. 275 f. Hereafter cited as "Protokolle des Verfassungsausschusses."

The constitutional concepts that Weber had presented to the public in his article series "Deutschlands Parlamentarismus in Vergangenheit und Zunkunft" now suddenly gained enormous practical importance. In 1917 his proposals had aroused great interest and much political activity, but there had been no direct impact on constitutional affairs.[3] The Reich did not interfere in the Prussian suffrage question, nor was the right of inquiry granted to the Reichstag. Even the hasty parliamentarization at the end of the war had not come about via an opening of the Bundesrat to party leaders, as Weber had proposed in line with the basic principles of the Bismarckian constitutional system. In November 1918, the fundamental premise for Weber's parliamentary reform proposals had come to nought since Prussian hegemony had collapsed. Nonetheless, when the old system collapsed, arguments put forward in these articles met with considerable attention and found support. Carl Schmitt said, with some exaggeration but not without truth, that Weber's notion of the parliamentary system as a means of bringing political leaders to governmental power had been the "only strong ideology" that existed in 1918 in favor of parliamentarization.[4] The thesis that a powerful parliament would offer the ideal place for leadership selection was now taken up by the liberal proponents of a new democratic order, especially Hugo Preuss.

It was therefore quite logical that, in the first days of November 1918 following the proclamation of the German Republic, Friedrich Ebert should have considered Max Weber for the position of secretary of state for the interior, along with Hugo Preuss, who had developed a draft for a reorganization of the Reich and the Prussian constitution in 1917. But this great opportunity for Max Weber to participate in responsible political activity did not materialize. Ebert himself decided almost at once for Hugo Preuss, perhaps because of the rumor that he already had a draft for a democratic constitution in his drawer, and in retrospect we have to admit that this was a sensible and logical decision.[5] Preuss's views corresponded to that middle ground that alone could unite the diverse constitutional opinions of all parties, from the Independent Social Democrats, who were represented in the government, to the Center party.

To be sure, there is something attractive retrospectively about the idea of Max Weber as Reich interior minister in a cabinet of the Rat der Beauftragten, entrusted with the preparation of the new Reich constitution. Perhaps Weber might have achieved a stronger constitution, containing fewer compromises between different constitutional ideas. Certainly he would not have encountered the same degree of opposition from

3. Only Robert von Piloty took this up directly in his study *Das parlamentarische System: Eine Untersuchung seines Wesens und Wertes* (Berlin, 1917). Of course, he remained only half way to parliamentarization. Cf. above, p. 192, n. 146.

4. *Verfassungslehre* (Munich and Leipzig, 1928), p. 341.

5. Cf. above, chap. 8, text at notes 68-73.

the federal states to the original drafts that arose in response to Preuss's dogmatic, somewhat academic unitarianism. But there can be no doubt that Weber's volcanic temperament would have made it far more difficult to resolve partisan quarrels and conflicts within the government camp than the calm objectivity and the dogged tenacity of Hugo Preuss, who was able to win the loyal cooperation of otherwise widely diverging groupings. Surely Weber would not have carried on the negotiations with the coolness and sobriety that Preuss displayed and for which he was criticized at the time.[6] He would have given the constitutional effort more of an image of a great new national beginning than Hugo Preuss's cool and sober manner was able to do.

As early as November 1918, Max Weber attempted to sketch the basic lines of Germany's future state form in a significant series of articles in the *Frankfurter Zeitung*, "Die Staatsform Deutschlands," at a time when it was by no means certain that a democratic constituent assembly would actually be convened.[6a] Although Weber in no way presented a firm program but merely discussed the conceivable possibilities in light of the situation, these articles were a milestone along the way to the Weimar constitution. Through them, Weber achieved considerable influence on the enactment of the Weimar constitution, although he was ultimately excluded from an official position in which he could actively have participated in this process.[7]

Weber took off immediately from the issue that had been a key problem in his constitutional reform proposals of 1917. He saw the primary problem of democratic reorganization in the question of how a strictly democratic and at the same time *federalist* constitution could be achieved. Although the disappearance of the dynasties in principle erased the necessity of a federal system, Weber continued to support a federal solution; so the question of which way the states should participate in the Reich government had a central position in his constitutional plan of 1918–19. If he—who would definitely have preferred a unitary republic—repeatedly called himself a federalist against his inclination, for tactical reasons, this should not lead us to see him as a representative of the idea of a unitary Reich who supported federalist conceptions *merely* on the grounds of Realpolitik.[8] In spite of his frequent unitarian

6. Cf. Ziegler, *Die deutsche Nationalversammlung*, pp. 108 f.

6a. Cf. *Frankfurter Zeitung*, 22 November, 24 November, 28 November, 30 November, and 5 December 1918. These essays were later published in a revised edition under the title "Deutschlands künftige Staatsform," now in *Pol. Schr.*, pp. 436–71.

7. On this, in many ways in agreement with the presentation here but in a broader context, see Gerhard Schulz, *Zwischen Demokratie und Diktatur: Verfassungspolitik und Reichsreform in der Weimarer Republik*, vol. 1 (Berlin, 1963), pp. 114 ff.

8. *Pol. Schr.*, p. 465.

statements, he still did not sever his links with south German federalist traditions.

To start with a radically unitarist constitution was in Weber's view inexpedient from the point of view of foreign policy. He feared that it would elicit mistrust with the Entente governments and therefore might well move them to impose even harsher peace conditions. Second, merger of German Austria to the Reich could only be realized within a federal system, for economic reasons, if for no other. In addition, Weber could not conceive of a unitary constitution because the federal states seemed to have survived the revolution with considerably less loss of power than the Reich, which, dependent upon the Vollzugsrat (executive council) of the *Berlin* workers and soldiers councils, had faced the putsch attempts of the radical left almost disarmed and in November and December still seemed completely powerless. In his view, it could not be expected that the federal states would voluntarily give up their restored power in favor of the central government.

The decisive issue in regard to the future constitution was whether Prussia should be maintained within its territorial boundaries and thereby retain, even after forfeiting its constitutionally guaranteed hegemony of the past, its immense territorial, numerical and economic predominance in the Reich. It is well known that Hugo Preuss at that time wanted to cut the Gordian knot of greater-Prussian hegemony by dismembering Prussia into ten new federal states. Max Weber was much more realistic than Preuss about the immense resistance that this radical suggestion was likely to raise. He considered Preuss's proposal impracticable and, moreover, by no means desirable.[9] There is no doubt that, in contrast to Preuss, Weber considered the total fragmentation of the powerful Prussian state and the Prussian administration, which was now proving itself once again, an unnecessary loss of strength on grounds of both domestic and foreign policy. He approved of the secession of individual provinces from the Prussian state, but did not believe that there was a serious chance that this would occur.

The underlying premise of Max Weber's constitutional considerations was the predicted survival of the Prussian state. He sought to construct the future constitutional system in such a way that continued Prussian predominance, even in the absence of constitutional privileges, would be compensated for by appropriate federative stipulations in the constitution. In arguing this case, Weber was still guided by the model of the Bismarckian Bundesrat. The smaller federal states should be granted a

9. Compare Weber's statement in Fürth on 14 January 1919, according to the report of the *Fürther Zeitung* of 15 January 1919: "The division of Prussia, which is demanded by a wide variety of people, is not advisable."

somewhat stronger political position in a revitalized Bundesrat through a moderate increase in the number of votes they commanded, thereby alleviating Prussian preponderance to a bearable level. Thus Weber supported the view that the absolutely necessary representative body of the federal states should take the form of a Staatenhaus consisting of delegates from the parliaments of the individual federal states, or else that the old Bundesrat system should be restored.[10] He saw little difference between delegates to a Bundesrat or to a Staatenhaus, assuming that the representatives delegated by parliamentary majorities of the federal states into a Staatenhaus would vote in accordance with the wishes of their governments, just as well as representatives instructed by the individual governments. This opinion had also been the basis of his previous scheme for the parliamentarization of the Bundesrat. Furthermore, a directly elected Staatenhaus would have had the drawback that it would not allow a distribution of the number of delegates by which the smaller federal states were given a numerically stronger representation.

Without doubt, Weber saw much more clearly than Preuss that the situation demanded giving proper attention to the demands of the federal states, whose power position had been restored almost to the full, but he tended to go too far in the opposite direction. One readily perceives the continued impact upon him of the Bismarckian Reich constitution. When he argued that "perhaps the simple acceptance of the present Bundesrat would be the cleanest solution"[11]—a view that he still maintained in February 1919—he came very close to Bavaria's extreme federalist demands, which called for no more and no less than the total retention of the old system.[12] Weber was prepared to permit the survival of the traditional rights of the federal states to an astonishingly broad degree. They would retain not only complete financial independence and administrative sovereignty but even the formal military sovereignty over their military contingents, according to the provisions of the old Reich constitution, with the sole exception of the technical troops and the navy, for whom organization on a Reich level was necessary. To be sure, Weber's

10. Weber argued similarly on 5 December 1918 in Wiesbaden: "We shall have to create a federal state in which Prussia's predominence is ended or, more correctly, in which Prussia has a counterweight. But the Reichstag will remain, if possible, without suffrage for twenty-year-olds. In place of the Bundesrat, a House of States with 50 to 60 members, who are representative of their governments, is to be created. A popular vote is less expedient." According to the report of the *Wiesbadener Zeitung* of 6 December 1918.

11. *Pol. Schr.*, p. 466.

12. How closely Weber's proposals of this nature suggested Bavarian efforts for autonomy is indicated perhaps by an article by a Herr Mühling that appeared just at this time in the *Münchener Allgemeine Zeitung* of 16 December 1918. Mühling proposed to save the Bundesrat by following the American example and dispensing with the parliamentary system altogether.

concern for the potential effect of the constitutional decisions on the allies played a considerable role here. But he was justly criticized at the time for pleading for the retention of too many elements of the Bismarckian Reich constitution.[13]

According to Weber, a federal constitutional system that abolished Prussia's hegemonic position and guaranteed the other federal states sufficient influence on Reich policy was not compatible with a pure parliamentary system on the Reich level, no matter what the form.[14] Weber believed that if decisive control over power was given to a unitary Reichstag dominated by Prussian votes, the result would be the mediatization of the federal states. If the executive were entrusted to a Reich government that emanated from the Reichstag and were responsible to it only, the federal states would scarcely be in a position to play any substantial role in the formulation of Reich policy. The mere participation of the federal states in the legislative process in the form of a second chamber composed either of directly elected deputies or of deputies delegated by the state legislatures would not suffice to prevent this from happening. Only a Staatenhaus of between fifty and sixty members who represented their governments, much as in the old Bundesrat, could, Weber tirelessly argued, guarantee real influence on Reich policy for the federal states.[15] Weber was sufficiently consistent to concede that under such conditions the Reichstag would fall back into a secondary position within the constitutional edifice provided that the Bundesrat would be resurrected in its old form, or even if the members of the Bundesrat were no less democratically legitimate than those of the Reichstag. The twofold responsibility of the chancellor to the Reichstag and to the Bundesrat resulting from such a constitutional order of things would force the Reichstag to share its constitutional prerogatives with the Bundesrat. The Reich government would then have to direct more attention to the position of the Bundesrat, which in turn would be responsible to the state parliaments, than to the majority in the Reichstag.[16]

Weber even played with the idea that the focal point of the political decision-making process might be placed in a Bundesrat possessing equal or even greater rights than the Reichstag, much as he had done in his 1907

13. See Kaufmann, *Grundfragen der künftigen Reichsverfassung* (Berlin, 1919), p. 37.

14. Cf. *Pol. Schr.*, pp. 481 f., 471. This view was expressed more clearly in Weber's electoral speeches than in the limited formulation in the article series in the *Frankfurter Zeitung*. Cf. the report of the *Wiesbadener Zeitung* and the *Wiesbadener Tagblatt* of 6 December 1918, also perhaps the report of the *Heidelberger Tagblatt* of 3 January 1919: "Weber rejected the parliamentary system for the Reich and announced his support for the plebiscitary system."

15. Cf. the report of the *Wiesbadener Zeitung* cited above, note 10.

16. *Pol. Schr.*, pp. 481 f.

proposal for the parliamentarization of the Bundesrat.[17] Only a popularly elected Reich president would then serve as a sufficient counterweight to the Bundesrat. The chancellor would then have to deal primarily with that body. The Reichstag would continue in its previous form, though restricted to "negative" politics. In this case, Weber argued, the effective responsibility of the chancellor to the Reichstag would be even less meaningful, since all weighty political decisions would be made in the Bundesrat, whose members were responsible to the parliaments of the *federal states*.[18] The power of the Reichstag would thus be substantially restricted, but it would still be capable of "controlling the administrative apparatus." We know that for Weber this was the most important task of the parliament next to the selection and education of political leaders.[19] This solution would have severely limited the Reichstag's power. It would then have played a far smaller role than Weber had intended in his constitutional proposals of 1917 (in which for very similar reasons the responsibility of the chancellor to the Reichstag was omitted), for the possibility no longer existed that the leader of the Reichstag majority might be sent into the Bundesrat as a Prussian representative.[20] In principle, this would have meant a new version of the Bismarckian constitution in democratic form, since a popularly elected president would have assumed Prussia's presiding vote.[21]

In the event that the Reich president was elected by a vote of the Reichstag rather than directly, Weber wished to strengthen the federal states' rights even more. The Bundesrat should then not only be authorized to issue "administrative ordinances" as in the past, but possibly also "legal ordinances," with the reservation of a ministerial veto. In a genuine parliamentary system, where political power was concentrated in the Reichstag, the federal states needed to retain extensive powers in their hands in order to offer a strong federative counterweight against the power of a unitary and Prussian-controlled parliament, and an executive dependent upon the Reichstag.

It is difficult to understand retrospectively why Weber claimed, in spite of this far-reaching federalist program, that basically he favored a highly unitary solution. The contradiction is partly explained by Weber's considerable respect for the formally strong federalist system of the old Reich constitution. Through the Bundesrat, the federal states had di-

17. Compare the report of the *Wiesbadener Zeitung*, which of course inaccurately reflected Weber's views: "The executive should rest in the hands of the Bundesrat, not in parliament." Not so distinctly in the *Wiesbadener Tagblatt's* report of the same day.

18. *Pol. Schr.*, p. 471.

19. Cf. above, chap. 6, text at note 125.

20. Cf. above, chap. 6, sec. 3.

21. Cf. below, note 106.

rectly participated in the *government* of the Reich, and this participation was not limited to legislation and administration. Weber believed that the federal states would never be content with participation in the legislative process alone. He argued that the entire constitutional effort would be condemned to weakness if it ignored the actual power position of the federal governments and challenged them by contrasting them with a Reich government on which they could not exercise any influence whatever. Then all the disadvantages of a many-headed system of domination would be called into play. The states would seek means to assert their influence outside of the constitution. Weber therefore rejected in advance a parliamentary system based upon a popularly elected Volkshaus (house of people's representatives) which would determine the chancellor and the president alike, while the authority of the representatives would be limited to participation in the legislative process only. Although Weber correctly pointed out that the real power of the states ought not to be ignored, it is clear that he was inclined to overestimate the power of the existing state apparatus. He tended to capitulate before the "normativity of what exists" and further reason to reject a far-reaching reorganization. His notion of the immortality of governmental bureaucracies endowed his constitutional proposals with much of their characteristic conservative coloration.

At the same time, these constitutional proposals represented a *move away from true parliamentarism*. The Reich parliament was discredited along with the old governmental powers, Weber argued, and he saw this opinion strengthened with the reassertion of the old party apparatuses and the reappearance, like jack-in-the-boxes of the old "career politicians without calling," as if nothing had happened.[22] Temporarily, he took the view that "today [it was] neither an honor nor a pleasure" to sit in parliament.[23] For this reason alone, he did not wish to see the Reichstag entrusted with decisive authority. When he championed the "strongest possible *unitary* solution," in spite of the strongly federalist character of his proposals and the recurrent emphasis on the old Bundesrat system, he did so above all in favor of a plebiscitary president and his cabinet, *not* of the Reichstag.[24] He assumed that the Bundesrat would return essentially in its old form and argued that the result would be that there would not be "the possibility of true Reich parliamentarism."[25] In these circumstances, Weber did not believe it possible for the Reichstag to be a sufficient

22. *Pol. Schr.*, pp. 450 f., 455; note especially the sharp polemic against the National Liberal party's attempt to revive itself. At the time, Stresemann attempted to further this after his rejection by the German Democratic party.

23. Letter to Petersen of 14 April 1920; cf. above, chap. 8, note 105.

24. *Pol. Schr.*, p. 476.

25. Ibid., p. 481; similarly in the article "Der Reichspräsident," ibid., p. 500.

unitarian counterweight to the federalist representative body. The plebiscitary Reich president would have to assume that function.[26]

Weber thereby reached two conclusions. On the one hand, he argued for giving real power to the federal states, on the other hand for a Reich president who was relatively independent of the Reich parliament. In a sense, this construction was similar to the situation under Bismarck, who had established himself as sovereign master of the Reichstag, although he was formally only the executive governing instrument of the collegial Bundesrat, whose decisions he was able to influence by means of control over the presidential votes. Now, however, this Bundesrat was to be a democratic representative body of the federal states and not merely of dynastic governments. Weber's idea of the parliamentarization of the Bundesrat was a consideration very much alive in his constitutional proposals of 1918–19. The difference was that now the Reich president and not the Reich chancellor was to be the pivotal figure of the entire constitutional system. Weber assigned to him the role of a great Caesarist leader, a role that he regarded as indispensable in a modern mass democracy.[27]

Weber thereby opted for the model of a plebiscitary führer democracy, which he had merely sketched as a possibility in 1917. At that time his chart for the future of the German constitution projected plebiscitary-charismatic rule by great democratic leaders, balanced by a powerful parliament, which would control the administration. Now the institution of the plebiscitary Reich presidency offered the chance to construct the constitutional basis for this model. In 1917, the implicit restriction of the power of parliament in favor of rule by a charismatic leader was not yet fully manifest; in 1918–19 it became central; the Reich president was expected to assume a leadership role vis-à-vis the Reichstag and the cabinet nominated by the Reichstag.

One consequence of such a constitutional solution would be that the Reich president's power would not derive from parliament but from the electorate. In 1917, Max Weber had pointed to "some sort of direct

26. Cf. also the report of the *Wiesbadener Zeitung* of 6 December 1918 on Weber's related statements in his Wiesbaden speech: "Parliamentarism and with it partisan quarrels are avoidable if the unified executive of the Reich is in the hands of a president elected by the entire nation." The author accepts Schulz's objection here against the formulation in the first edition of the present book, p. 121, note 44.

27. Compare also Weber's sharp opposition to the classical model of a parliamentary government with a collegial cabinet in a speech in Heidelberg on 17 January 1919: "We are supporters of a strong governmental power on a democratic basis and supporters of a president directly elected by the people. We would experience a sorry and stupid shopkeepers' convention or the like if we had a college of ministers without the power of a president above it. This might produce, for example, a minister of culture from the Center, a Socialist finance minister, etc." Report of the *Heidelberger Tageblatt*, 18 January 1919.

election of the supreme authority" in principle as the most suitable form of democratic "selection of leaders" in the conditions of a plebiscitary mass democracy.[28] Now he stressed that the Reich president ought to be elected directly by the people and not by the Reichstag or a combination of the Reichstag and the house of states: "A Reich president supported by the revolutionary legitimacy of a popular election, who thereby faces Reich institutions in his *own* independent right, would have incomparably stronger authority than one elected by parliament."[29]

Max Weber wished to give the Reich president a constitutional position that was in many ways similar to that of the American president. The Reich president, supported by plebiscitary legitimacy like the American president, ought to constitute the head of the executive, unlike the situation in the French republic, whose chief of state was limited to purely representative functions and where the executive authority was the exclusive province of a cabinet responsible to parliament. The Reich president ought to stand at the head of the civil service hierarchy and of the army and to be responsible for the appointment and dismissal not only of ministers but of all Reich civil servants and officers. He should have control of patronage for all Reich offices. It appears that Weber was not talking about mere formal responsibility, which in reality would be exercised by the Reich chancellor, as was to be the case in the Weimar Republic. Apparently the president was personally to exercise a part of patronage that was not more closely defined, that was independent of the formal responsibility of the chancellor or of the relevant Reich minister. Weber regarded this as one of the most important functions of the Reich president. Further, the president ought to be given the option of interfering directly with the "Reich machine" by appealing to the electorate through referenda.

Nevertheless, Weber rejected the idea of giving the president power freely to appoint his political aides, as was the case in the United States. On this point, he remained attached to the parliamentary system. The Reich president should be assisted in carrying out his responsibilities by a cabinet of parliamentary ministers who were responsible to the Reichstag and who required the Reichstag's confidence. At first Weber appears to have considered the possibility of establishing an executive independent of parliament similar to the American model, but quickly dismissed this idea. He did not regard such a system of strict division of powers to be opportune, above all because this would render the administrative bureaucracy independent of parliament. He feared the American method of changing all the leading officials with each new government

28. *Pol. Schr.*, p. 394; cf. above, chap. 6, text at notes 163 ff.
29. *Pol. Schr.*, p. 469.

because of the corruption that was attached; in any case he regarded that system as doomed.[30] In a modern state, career bureaucrats would become more and more indispensable. These could only be effectively controlled with the help of a powerful parliament. Weber had previously pointed out that even a constitutional monarch would be powerless against his own leading bureaucrats in the absence of parliamentary bodies that exercised administrative control.[31] Weber therefore wanted parliament to be involved in appointments to the highest Reich offices also. In contrast to the American system, where the representative bodies were denied any direct influence upon the administration, a parliament endowed with the right of inquiry could bring about the fall of one or another minister or even the entire cabinet. If this were not the case, then it could not achieve effective control of the administration and would have largely forfeited the capacity for selection of leaders that a powerful parliament needed to possess.[32]

In contrast to the American presidential system, the Reich president would hold a position similar to that of a constitutional monarch, a fact that Weber recognized.[33] Like a monarch in a constitutional system, the Reich president had to work through ministers in all his public functions. There was another area where Max Weber's Reich president had a pseudomonarchical nature: he replaced the monarchical head of state. In the place of the hereditary charismatic monarch would now be found an "elected monarch" supported not by dynastic legitimacy, but by the "revolutionary legitimacy" of the direct election of the people.[33a] Weber attached great importance to the legitimizing function of such a plebiscitary presidency. He doubted that belief in the legitimacy of legal rule through contracted rules (constitution) possessed sufficient power, under the conditions of modern mass society, to legitimize the new governmental and social order in the eyes of the people at large. The vacuum left by the fall of the Hohenzollerns was to be filled by the charismatic legitimacy of the Reich president, "proclaimed" as leader of the nation and representative of the masses in a direct popular election.[34]

30. Ibid.

31. Cf. ibid., pp. 337 f.

32. Cf., earlier, *Pol. Schr.*, pp. 397 f. (1917).

33. *Wirtschaft und Gesellschaft*, p. 173: "If the party government's appropriation of power is incomplete, and the prince (or a president elected by, e.g., plebiscite and corresponding to a prince) retains independent power, especially over patronage (including officers), then a *constitutional government* exists. It can exist in particular through a formal *division of powers*. A special case is the coexistence of a plebiscitary presidency and a representative parliament: a *plebiscitary-representative government*." The chief example of the last type would be the Weimar constitution.

33a. Cf. letter to Hartmann, above, chap. 8, note 65.

34. Cf. also *Wirtschaft und Gesellschaft*, p. 552.

The importance of continuity, apparent in the conception of a parliamentary electoral monarchy on a Caesarist basis, is also revealed by the fact that the Reich president was to partake of the Kaiser's rights in all areas, both positive and negative. In order to guarantee his supremacy over parliamentary power and thereby to put him into a position where he could exercise his leadership role, Weber wished to give him the classic rights of the constitutional monarch: participation in patronage, appointment and dismissal of ministers, a suspensive veto, and above all the authority to dissolve the Reichstag or as a substitute for this, the possibility of appealing over the Reichstag to the people through a referendum.[35] The Reich president would also have the weapon of the plebiscite to use against the representative body of the federal states in the event they could not agree with the Reichstag about a law passed by the latter.

Max Weber believed that the stipulation of this degree of constitutional powers to the president would be sufficient to give him an autonomous leadership role, based upon the expressed confidence by the electorate, although he would remain bound in his actions to a Reich cabinet dependent upon the confidence of the parliament. Weber counted upon the natural weight of the electorate's expression of their support of the Reich president. Even if "the popularly elected president were bound in his choice of ministers to the confidence of parliament, he would still, as the representative of the millions, have the upper hand over the representatives of the current party majority, and this predominance would increase in proportion to the length of the presidential term."[36] To achieve this predominence, Weber argued for the "longest possible" period of office for the Reich president, about seven years (as was later provided for in the Weimar constitution). To balance this, he wished to give the Reichstag the possibility to call a recall referendum through a suitable majority resolution if it came into conflict with the Reich president. This was of course a very weak weapon because of the conservative tendency of all referenda, which would preordain the outcome in favor of the president. Only in cases of the most striking misuse of power by the Reich president would such a recall referendum have a chance of success. During the life of the Weimar Republic, this right, guaranteed by article 43 of the Weimar constitution, was in fact never exercised.

Max Weber hoped, through the institution of the Reich presidency, to

35. *Pol. Schr.*, p. 469.

36. Ibid., p. 470; Weber suggested in this sentence, which in the German original is grammatically faulty, somewhat inadvertently that the legislators ought to stipulate a long term of office for the Reich president in the constitution. Cf. the report in the *Wiesbadener Zeitung*, 6 December 1918: "The president can be stronger than a minister president, who only has a parliamentary majority behind him."

enable capable statesmen to rise to power even outside of the party machines and to create sufficient room for maneuver for them to realize their most important political goals even if these differed from the intentions of the existing parliamentary majority. The constitutional position that Weber would have given the office of the presidency would have assured key authority over policy for a Reich president who was politically active, ambitious for power, and gifted—and Weber expected this. He anticipated a plebiscitary dictator of the masses. He would have considerable control over the Reichstag and—of course to a lesser extent—over the state representation. His weapons against a recalcitrant parliamentary majority would be an effective suspensive veto and then a popular referendum or the dissolution of the Reichstag, that is, an appeal to the people against a Reichstag majority. One need only recall, for example, what a finely honed weapon the right of dissolution had been in Bismarck's hands. He had forged all his majorities in this way, and those parties that challenged him were thrown into an electoral campaign at the worst possible moment. But the English example should also be recalled. The English prime minister was no less sovereign in his ability to have the crown dissolve Parliament at the most favorable moment and thereby to have an important advantage over the opposition.

This conception of the Reich president was a bold combination of heterogeneous constitutional ideas, full of unresolved contradictions. On the one hand, the Reich president was supposed to be a kind of monarch, limited by Parliament, who ruled through his ministers. On the other hand, he was intended to be a great Caesarist statesman who mediatized the position of a chancellor responsible to the Reichstag and might even work against him, on the basis of his presidential prerogatives. Such a "plebiscitary-representative" constitution was an attempt to avoid a true parliamentary system without giving up the advantages of parliamentarization (selection of leaders, control of the administration). The independence of a normally monarchical executive that had, in the tradition of German governmental theory, become dogma, was retained and a high degree of division of powers preserved.[37] Weber artfully associated the revolutionary idea of the Caesarist leader selected in a mass democracy with the classical liberal idea of the balance of powers, in this case within the executive (Reich president versus Reich chancellor) and between the executive and the legislative (Reich president versus Reichstag.) In view of the strong position of the Reich president, a high degree of federalism in the constitutional framework seemed harmless.

In 1917, Max Weber had expressed the view that a Caesaristic form of government would be most appropriate for Germany if great statesmen

37. Compare perhaps Laband, *Deutsches Reichsstaatsrecht*, 6th ed. (Tübingen, 1912), pp. 17, 56 ff.; also Carl Schmitt, *Verfassungslehre*, pp. 53 ff.

were always available.[38] The institution of the plebiscitarian Reich presidency now appeared to be the necessary means to construct the new Reich constitution so as to permit a great leader's plebiscitary-charismatic rule within the framework of a parliamentary system. At the same time, parliamentary institutions would be present to compensate for the leader's faults and vacillations and to bring about the resignation of the leading statesman if his charisma had failed. The model of Bismarck as a "Caesarist" statesman who had ruled sovereignly over the Reichstag and the Bundesrat certainly had inspired Weber to put forward these constitutional proposals. Weber wished, by including a plebiscitarian element in the constitution, to prepare the way to power for great democratic statesmen who, so to speak, combined the qualities of a Gladstone with those of a Bismarck.

In February 1919, Max Weber somewhat softened his proposal for a strong presidential position in his article "The Reich President" in the *Berliner Börsenzeitung*.[39] He did so primarily with an eye to public opinion, which then seemed opposed to the popular election of the president. For Weber, popular election was the most important element. He therefore tried wherever possible to allay the fears that a plebiscitary president might abuse his authority. Normally, the Reich president ought only to interfere in the course of Reich policy at times of crisis. He must, however, have the constitutional power of assuming leadership when a parliamentary majority is not otherwise possible, in order to create a purely bureaucratic ministry to maintain the continuity of Reich policy. In general, of course, his policy influence ought to be limited to the choice of a suitable chancellor, a certain degree of patronage, and possibly through the use of the suspensive veto and through the occasional call for a referendum and, only in the most extreme cases, for the dissolution of parliament.[40]

However, the basic principles of Weber's constitutional proposals remained unchanged. Once again he emphasized that "the much discussed 'dictatorship' of the masses . . . [called for] a 'dictator' . . . , an elected representative of the masses who would submit to him as long as he possessed their confidence."[41] The Reich president, not the Reich chancellor, who was powerless against the representative body of the federal states, should fulfill the task of guaranteeing a strong Reich policy with the authority of his office derived from the confidence of the masses and if necessary through directly appealing to the people against the sectional interests of the federal states. It was *he* who was called upon to

38. Cf. above, chap. 6, text at note 182.
39. *Pol. Schr.*, pp. 498 ff.
40. *Pol. Schr.*, pp. 498 ff.; cf. below, sec. 4.
41. *Pol. Schr.*, p. 499.

set the integrating power of his charisma against the divergent political forces and economic interests within and outside parliamentary institutions.

2. The Republican Constitution and German Public Opinion

The revolution unexpectedly presented German political science with the question of what a parliamentary-democratic constitution should look like, once the monarchical elements formerly assumed to be essential were dispensed with. Parliamentarization in October 1918 had been introduced in imitation of the English model under pressure from outside of Germany. Now, with the fall of the Hohenzollerns, the English example was no longer valid. But there were no theoretical weapons readily available for the new situation. Even the small number of decided proponents of a parliamentary system, among whom Hugo Preuss was in the first rank, had never even theoretically considered anything beyond the creation of a parliamentary monarchy and were at first completely helpless when it came to the question of how a *republican* constitution could be created on a democratic basis. For this reason, Max Weber's powerful conception of a plebiscitary Reich president as head of the executive and the guarantor of Reich unity, with a Reich parliament supporting him, aroused great respect and interest.

Even the politicians had no concrete notions as to the question of how Germany would be constituted as a parliamentary democratic *republic*. The Majority Social Democrats, who always and ever had favored a "Freier Volksstaat" (free people's state), had no design for how this Volkstaat ought to be arranged in detail and therefore now had to entrust the task of designing a new constitution to a bourgeois specialist in governmental law. This was, nevertheless, a decision that deserves respect. The Social Democrats were aware of their own limitations and were conscious enough of their responsibility to accept the consequences and to avoid false vanity. The Social Democrats were inclined to a purely parliamentary system with a collegial cabinet as the executive, which would be exclusively dependent upon the will of the representatives of the people. They were not united on the question of the chief of state. Many sympathized with the Swiss system, but did not exclude the possibility of a single president. The tactical interests of the moment demanded that the head of state's position should be as different as possible from the position of the monarch in order to forestall attempts at restoration of the monarchy. This view was associated with the dimly perceived but firmly held demand that the position of the head, if indeed it was to be separate from the cabinet, should be kept as weak as possible and be permitted only a purely representative function.

The Independent Social Democratic party, in contrast, consistently demanded the retention of the directorial system that they had bullied the Majority Social Democrats into accepting when they joined the revolutionary government of the Rat der Volksbeauftragten. Although not opponents of the parliamentary system in principle, they initially wanted the revolution to continue if only to assure the workers' and soldiers' councils a greater measure of participation in the new democratic system of the Reich. The Independent Social Democrats championed their standpoint clearly and consistently, however, without hope of success, while the Majority Social Democrats wavered until the last moment on the presidential question, so that their *positive* impact upon the form of the institution of the Reich presidency turned out to be limited.

The democratic forces among the middle classes were generally inclined to the idea of a plebiscitary head of state with strong powers, primarily for the same reasons that had motivated Weber, namely a deep mistrust of "parliamentary absolutism." It was not only the politicians of the right but the liberals as well, who had grown up with the realities of German constitutionalism, who feared true parliamentary rule. Had they not been repeatedly told that parliament exhausted itself with "parliamentary rowdiness, hairsplitting," and factional intrigue, and did they not have to concede that parliamentary debates had been conducted on a low intellectual level in the past?[42] During the imperial regime, the Reichstag had restricted its endeavors to cautiously extending its parliamentary influence, while the strong position of the monarchy had never been questioned in principle. They had possessed neither the courage nor the self-confidence ever to attempt a resolute leap into a true parliamentary system in a republican state.

The chief reservation that the liberals had regarding the idea of the exclusive and unlimited popular rule in a true parliamentary system was the old liberal idea that the citizen's freedom could only be protected by the balance of governmental powers—especially at a time when a socialist majority was likely in the forthcoming Reich parliament. For these reasons, the American presidential system had a great deal of appeal for some of the leading representatives of the German middle classes. Friedrich Meinecke, Walter Simons, Kurt Riezler, and initially even Friedrich Naumann favored a presidential constitution similar to the American model.[43] But many were also concerned about the spoils system consid-

42. Cf., inter alia, Bismarck's letter to Hobrecht of 25 May 1878, *Gesammelte Werke*, vol. 6c, p. 110, and his Reichstag speech of 5 May 1884, in Kohl, *Reden Bismarcks*, vol. 10, p. 130.

43. Cf. Gustav Schmidt, *Deutscher Historismus und der Übergang zur parlamentarischen Demokratie, Untersuchungen zu den politischen Gedanken von Meinecke, Troeltsch, Weber* (Lübeck, Hamburg, 1964), pp. 117 f. et passim.

ered essential for the functioning of the American presidential constitution—a system whose impact they tended to exaggerate. The American system was all too closely identified with a reputation of corruption and corruptibility, while in Germany the rectitude and high moral ethos of the Prussian-German civil service was much appreciated and not lightly dispensed with. The German party system, too, with its multiplicity of ideologically oriented parties, scarcely offered a basis for the application of the American presidential constitution to German conditions.

As a result, the liberals readily grasped the concept of a plebiscitary Reich president who at the same time would take on the position of a monarch in a constitutional system, in connection with a parliamentary government dependent on a liberal legislature. This solution appeared to offer the possibility of a genuine division of powers even under the conditions of a parliamentary republic. Erich Kaufmann, who at the time played a leading role in the preparation of a constitutional draft by the Verein "Recht und Wirtschaft" ("Law and Economics" Association), characteristically summed up this bourgeois-liberal tendency with the following words: "If we wish to create the basis for a healthy parliamentarism, we must take care that our Reich president can assume a role similar to that of the English king."[44]

It was symptomatic of German bourgeois constitutional thought in the latter part of 1918 and early in 1919 that much attention was given to Robert Redslob's theory of parliamentary system of government, even though it had been published before the revolution. Redslob's work to be sure still adhered closely to the conceptions of constitutional governmental theory and treated the republic as an anomoly among the varieties of parliamentary rule.[45] Since Redslob's thesis had a considerable impact upon the makers of the Weimar constitution, it must be examined in some detail. Redslob based his theory of parliamentary government on the liberal principle of a mechanical balance of power. At the same time, he emphasized the axiom that a *true* parliamentary system was present only when a full balance existed between the executive and the legislative. If all power was concentrated in the hands of parliament and the executive delegated from its midst, that was not a parliamentary system but, rather, parliamentary absolutism. The premise for the development of a *balance* between legislative and executive was for each power to have its own source. The head of state should not owe his position in any form to a parliamentary vote; his power therefore had to be based either on monarchical legitimacy or—in a republic—on the direct election of the people.

44. *Grundfragen der künftigen Reichsverfassung* (Berlin, 1919), p. 21.

45. *Die parlamentarische Regierung in ihrer wahren und in ihrer unechten Form* (Tübingen, 1918).

Redslob argued that parliament ought not to force its will on the government but should possess only "a right to criticism."[46] On the other hand, the government ought not to act against the expressed will of the parliament, therefore the ministers named by the head of state should be tied to the confidence of the parliament. A balance of powers that functioned in this way represented the essence of genuine parliamentarism. To maintain this system was the chief function of the head of state. The means of preventing parliament from transcending its legal position and controlling the executive was the authority to dissolve, combined with the option to dismiss a cabinet based on the parliamentary majority. The power of dissolution was the correlative of ministerial responsibility and signified in practice the appeal to the people as the sole bearer of sovereignty.[47] Only such a "dualistic system" was capable of "endowing the people with sovereignty. It thereby made the people the arbiter among powers of equal strength, which neutralized each other in the case of a division, and gave them the opportunity to support the side that represented their true will. When, in contrast, only a single or a predominant power was present, then the people had no recourse to a rival power and would therefore be unable to assert their will."[48] The head of state in this system had the role of "the creative force within the mechanism" of the balance of power.[49]

Redslob believed that the equal position of the executive and the legislative was ideally realized in the parliamentary monarchy. The monarch was free in principle from the grip of the parliamentary power as a result of his hereditary rights. The existence of a president in a republic was always more precarious, since ultimately it could be disturbed at any time by a change in the constitution.[50] Redslob viewed the English and especially the Belgian constitutional relationships to be, from this standpoint, the best models. He criticized the French constitutional system root and branch. Because, in the French case, the president was chosen not by the people but by both chambers, the legislative was clearly supreme: "The president cannot be compared with the chambers. He does not have the same authority. He is incapable of defying them. He is dependent upon them."[51] He did not have control over the use of the decisive weapon of the executive, the dissolution of parliament, because to do this he required the countersignature of the minister and, above all,

46. Ibid., p. 2.
47. Ibid., p. 6.
48. Ibid., p. 180.
49. Ibid., p. 4.
50. Ibid., pp. 116 f.
51. Ibid., p. 119.

the approval of the *Senate*. But even if this were not the case, the president would not be in a position to defend the balance between the two powers since his own power came from parliament and was therefore of an inferior nature. Therefore, France had an *impure* parliamentary regime—even less, only the "reminiscence of a parliamentary regime. . . . It does not live at all. Its soul is dead."[52]

Although, by his recognition of popular sovereignty, Redslob had taken a decisive step beyond traditional constitutionalist state theory, he remained in part characteristically imprisoned by this theory. This was clear in his affirmation of monarchy in principle because it had the advantage of assuring a genuine balance of power, while republics tended in the direction of establishing a one-sided regime. Of most importance was the thorough identification of the chief of state with the entire executive, that is, of the monarch with his ministers. It cannot immediately be seen why the power of dissolution cannot be effectively exercised by the actual head of the executive, the prime minister, as the responsible director of policy, but must be reserved in principle to the monarch, who is independent of the people's representatives or to the plebiscitary president. The conception that the head of state along with the leading minister, and in some circumstances over his head, must retain the possibility of an independent policy, arises from the praxis of the constitutionalist system. To be sure, Redslob argued that dissolution was "not an offensive weapon."[53] But was it not, for all that, the major weapon of the constitutional monarch in his struggle against a recalcitrant parliament? Redslob's inclination to reject any far-reaching limitation of monarchical prerogatives was very much in the tradition of Rudolf von Gneist. In Redslob's view, the decisive criterion necessary to establish whether a *true* parliamentary system existed or not was the *balance of power* of the executive and legislative powers, not the degree of powers of the representative body of the people. In his theory, the boundaries between a constitutional and a parliamentary system were therefore fluid.[54] Indeed, Redslob's theory evaded the full consequences of the parliamentary system, which in fact transcended the liberal conception of the balance of powers and crossed the border of the liberal "legislative state," in that it provided the representative body of the people the right of delegation of power to a government dependent upon it over and beyond the simple legislative authority.

52. Ibid., p. 179.

53. Ibid., p. 131. A suggestion that Preuss later seized upon by inserting the provision in the Weimar Reich constitution that the Reichstag could only be dissolved once about the same issue.

54. Redslob thus characterized the Swedish case as "a simple variation of the parliamentary system," although a cabinet responsible to the Reichstag did not even exist there.

Redslob's theory of the balance of powers, in spite of or perhaps because of the constitutionalist shell that still encapsulated it, greatly influenced the creators of the Weimar constitution and was the main reason why the French example was not followed and the Reich president was elected by the Reichstag or by the Reichstag and the Reichsrat.[55] This corresponded to the widespread desire to evade parliamentary omnipotence and to balance parliament with an "elected parliamentary monarch." Hugo Preuss, the father of the Weimar constitution, was influenced by Redslob especially in the creation of "two equally founded high governmental organs," between which a parliamentary government would serve as a dynamic "unifying body."[56] As early as the discussions in the Reich Office of the Interior between 9 and 12 December 1918, Preuss used Redslobian language to attack the French model. The latter was "an *impure* parliamentary system . . . ; it is not logical for the president to be elected by parliament."[57] In general, the balance-of-power idea as formulated by Redslob suited Preuss perfectly, although he did not copy it in every detail. To offset "parliamentary absolutism," he wished to establish a plebiscitary Reich president who possessed the powers of a monarch in a parliamentary monarchy.[58] This would prevent the "suppression of parliamentarism by democracy."[59] However, Preuss energetically rejected the granting of further responsibilities to the Reich president that he could exercise without the countersignature of the responsible minister.[60]

55. Cf. also Carl Schmitt, *Verfassungslehre*, p. 304; also Carl J. Friedrich, *Der Verfassungsstaat der Neuzeit* (Berlin, 1953), p. 433.

56. Draft of the future Reich constitution, edited on behalf of the Reich Office of the Interior, with an explanatory memorandum by Hugo Preuss (Berlin 1919), p. 24. This reflected Preuss's own principles completely. He also saw the essence of the liberal constitutional state in a balance of powers. As early as 1891, he had opposed the unitarist tendencies of the Social Democrats: "Only that decentralization which freely releases forces and thereby creates a *multiplicity of power centers* makes true *political freedom* possible. Political life exists in the manifestation of power, political freedom merely in the possibility of honorable struggle by various power factors; it therefore presumes a multiplicity of such factors." *Staat, Recht und Freiheit*, p. 168.

57. Notes about the discussions in the Reich Office of the Interior about the main features of the constitutional draft of 9–12 December 1918 to be laid before the constituent National Assembly, formerly Reichsarchiv, now DZA I, Potsdam, Reichsamt des Innern III, no. 40, vol. 1 (unfortunately a much abbreviated account of the negotiations).

58. *Staat, Recht und Freiheit*, p. 426.

59. Memo on the draft of the future Reich constitution, *loc. cit.*, p. 24.

60. Preuss repeatedly referred to Redslob without of course mentioning his name. Redslob's theses, inter alia, were also fundamental for the draft by the association "Recht und Wirtschaft." In the speech explaining the basis of the draft of the constitution before the National Assembly, Preuss began with the statement that he viewed it as necessary "to balance the parliament elected by direct, purely democratic suffrage, by a strong presidential power elected on the basis of the same democratic principles. I also believe that the parliamentary system . . . demands and presumes such a balance of powers. *French*

In view of this situation, we must in part dispute the commonly held opinion that Hugo Pruess was influenced primarily by Max Weber when he prescribed the plebiscitary election of the Reich president.[61] The

parliamentarism has been justly labeled impure parliamentarism from the point of view of constitutional law, because it actually is a monocracy of parliament." *Protokolle der Verhandlungen der verfassungsgebenden Nationalversammlung* (cited in future as *Verhandlungen*), vol. 326, p. 291; also *Staat, Recht und Freiheit*, p. 417; cf. ibid., p. 426; also "Denkschrift zum Entwurf . . . ," p. 24: "Our task cannot be the suppression of parliamentarism by democracy; rather, the development and strengthening of a parliamentary democracy. However, the election of the president by parliament as in France does not further this. On the contrary, we can fittingly designate this French system as impure parliamentarism. Pure parliamentarism presupposes two governmental organs that are essentially equal to each other. . . . In the parliamentary monarchy, the crown exists next to the parliament. In parliamentary democracy, in which all political power stems from the will of the people, the president is in a position equal to the representative body directly elected by the people only when he himself is elected directly by the people." The parallel here between "parliamentary monarchy" and "parliamentary democracy" is a characteristic borrowing from Redslob.

For Redslob's influence on the creators of the Weimar constitution, especially on Hugo Preuss, see also Ernst Fraenkel, "Die repräsentative und die plebiszitäre Komponente im demokratischen Verfassungsstaat," *Recht und Staat in Geschichte und Gegenwart*, nos. 219–220 (Tübingen, 1958), esp. pp. 48 ff. Nevertheless, Fraenkel has not sufficiently worked out the divergence between the standpoints of Redslob and Preuss. Preuss appears to be a stronger representative and path breaker for plebiscitary constitutional tendencies, as opposed to representative tendencies, than is justified. For Preuss, the concept of a balance of power was crucial for his constitutional construction of two independent governmental organs, the parliament and the presidency, rather than, as Fraenkel assumes, the necessity for the extensive harmony between the popular will and the will of parliament. He also did not go nearly as far as Redslob. In our view, one cannot speak about a "hypertrophy of the plebiscitary component in the governmental system of the first Republic" on the basis of the text of the Weimar constitution (Fraenkel, ibid., p. 55). The National Assembly, conforming to Hugo Preuss, stopped halfway on the question of the Reich presidency, in contrast to Redslob's radical proposals, and bound the president by the consent of the Reich chancellor in his conduct of office and especially on the dissolution of the Reichstag. If the plebiscitary factors in the Weimar constitutional framework later took on such predominence, this stemmed more from the interpretation that was given to the Weimar constitution than from any basis in the actual text. Aside from these limitations and modifications, my own treatment conforms with Fraenkel's critique of the mixture of plebiscitary and representative constitutional elements under the influence of "authoritarian concepts" (ibid., p. 53) and his judgment of Redslob's theories of constitutional law. This will be clear below. Compare also the most recent treatment by Schulz, *Zwischen Demokratie and Diktatur*, p. 126, which incomprehensibly mentions Redslob's role only in passing.

61. Willibald Apelt, *Geschichte der Weimarer Verfassung* (Munich, 1946), p. 57: *Weber* succeeded "in winning Preuss, who at first was inclined to relegate the election to the people's representative body, to the plebiscitary Reich presidency." Winckelmann accepts this in *Gesellschaft und Staat in der verstehenden Soziologie Max Webers* (Berlin, 1957), p. 43, as well as in Max Weber, *Soziologie, Weltgeschichtliche Analysen, Politik*, p. 488: "*carried through* . . . popular election of the Reich president." We cannot speak of carrying through! Also Baumgarten, ibid., p. xxv and Heuss in the introduction to the second edition of *Pol. Schr.*, p. xxv.

sweeping statement of the last imperial chancellor, Prince Max von Baden—that "we have Max Weber to thank for the greatest political deed after the revolution: in alliance with Simons, he prevailed against the admirers of the French system, and the Reich president was elected by the people and not by the Reichstag"—was not entirely justified.[62] On this point, Weber's concept of the charismatic leadership position of the Reich president happened to parallel the balance-of-power concept that originated from traditional constitutionalist state theory oriented to the model of the prerevolutionary constitutional state. Weber's concept was influential *only* insofar as it was in accord with the latter. Carl Schmitt later pointed out that one general characteristic of the bourgeois-constitutional state was its mixed foundations.[63] The Weimar constitution was definitely of this type. In practice, the creators of the Weimar liberal constitution were attracted by the idea of creating a "democratic *Rechtsstaat*" by incorporating a system of the balance of powers within a parliamentary-republican constitution.[64] They hoped thereby to replace the constitutional monarchy, which had essentially developed the liberal legislative state, by a "constitutional democracy."[65]

Max Weber's concept of a plebiscitary Reich president incorporated essential elements of the liberal concept of balance. The Reich president was to be at the same time an "elected monarch" and a counterweight to the Reichstag's omnipotence. But this did not exhaust his concept. The Reich president ought at the same time to be a Caesarist leader. The mechanist balance-of-power theory as Redslob developed it in contrast to the French constitutional model was altogether anachronistic compared to Max Weber's views about the essence of leadership by a statesman in a modern mass democracy. The charismatic statesman is expected to rule with Caesaristic tools and thereby to recruit a retinue in parliament and the acclamation of the masses. Both have to follow him unconditionally as long as he is successful. Parliament, in fact, has not to operate as a mechanistic counterbalance to the power of the executive. Its major purpose is to perpetually remind him of his responsibilities and to overthrow him if and *when* he fails. Max Weber was in no way concerned with the creation of constitutional guarantees when he wished to see the president in an independent position even in relation to the leading ministers. On the contrary, the presidential office should be a valve for the selection of genuine political leaders and should permit its occupant,

62. Prince Max von Baden, *Erinnerungen und Dokumente*, p. 128.

63. *Verfassungslehre*, p. 200.

64. The concept in Hugo Preuss, *Staat, Recht und Freiheit*, p. 428.

65. Carl Schmitt, loc. cit., p. 200; cf. also Leibholz, *Die Auflösung der liberalen Demokratie in Deutschland und das autoritäre Staatsbild* (Munich, 1933,) pp. 28 f.; also, but without a constitutional basis, Max Weber, *Wirtschaft und Gesellschaft*, p. 173, cited above, note 33.

if need be, to pursue his personal policies even against the will of the current party majority in parliament.

Max Weber thus went far beyond Hugo Preuss, who believed that the Reich president should generally exercise his "characteristics as a leader" *only* in the selection of an appropriate Reich chancellor.[66] His political actions in office should be undertaken in complete agreement with the chancellor. Practically, Preuss thereby weighted the balance of power distinctly in favor of parliament, and this tendency was to prevail.[67] He accepted Weber's enthusiastic appeals to strengthen the Reich president in relation to parliament in only a few areas. We shall look at these more closely later. Overall, we should note at least at this point that Weber was not able to convince Preuss to accept his concepts of presidential rule, in spite of the powerful impression they doubtless made.

If Preuss and Weber were considerably apart on the question of how independent a leadership position the president should have, they were in accord about the rejection of a pure plebiscitary presidential system according to the American model. Hugo Preuss accepted Weber's argument that parliament, if it lacked any direct influence upon the government and the administration, would be reduced to a very low intellectual niveau. It would then be incapable of accomplishing "the selection of political leaders."[68] Like Weber, Hugo Preuss opposed the American spoils system and emphatically defended the preservation of the career

66. "Denkschrift zum Entwurf der künftigen Reichsverfassung," p. 25.

67. Therefore Walter Simons could later accuse Preuss of incorporating "parliamentarism in its French-continental form in the constitutional structure" that had furthered the destructive consequences of the proportional representation system; Walter Simons, "Hugo Preuss," *Meister des Rechts*, vol. 6 (Berlin, 1930), p. 118.

68. *Verhandlungen der Nationalversammlung*, vol. 326, p. 292; or, *Staat, Recht und Freiheit*, p. 419. Cf. especially the statements in the "Denkschrift zum Entwurf der künftigen Reichsverfassung," p. 23, that refer directly to Max Weber's critique of the constitutional system in the empire: having come to know the dualistic system of pure division of powers through "long and fundamental experience in the Reich and in the individual states, namely in Prussia, we can scarcely harbor longings for its revival in an altered form. Since the executive, which was independent of parliament, did not change periodically here, the total dependence of the administrative offices on the executive made them the permanent spoils of one-sided political tendencies. And, on the other hand, parliament, in the light of dualism, was limited to abstract legislation, to criticism and negation, and was powerless in relation to the administration, which actually determined practical affairs. Parliament's external political powerlessness brought internal political impotence in its wake and the splintering into purely dogmatic parties as well as all of the other much discussed and deplored evils of our old situation. When, even before the revolution, we sought a remedy to this through parliamentarization, that was the correct approach. But under the rule of the old powers it was not possible to travel far enough or pursue the approach sufficiently. The revolution has finally freed the path; they would destroy this *important* success if they strayed into this area and sought to restore the old dualism, altered only by the difference at the top."

civil service.[69] As early as 1917, Preuss had demanded that the Reichstag have the right of inquiry in order to empower it with effective administrative control over the bureaucracy.[70] In these areas, Weber's proposals for a responsible Reich cabinet and a parliament endowed with important responsibilities and especially with control of the administration, alongside of a plebiscitary president, corresponded to a considerable degree with Preuss's own ideas. But Weber accentuated the Reich president's leadership position. His articles, not accidently, said little about the cabinet or its responsibility to the popularly elected house. For Hugo Preuss, however, in spite of the plebiscitary presidency, the parliamentary system was central. Preuss could well have drawn support from Weber's own 1917 arguments, which had centered upon the German constitutional problem and had culminated in the question, "How can we make parliament capable of power?"[71] He could not be persuaded, however, to agree to Max Weber's model of a "leadership democracy," which would logically have led to the reduction of the power of the people's representative body in favor of the power of the Reich president based upon the direct confidence of the people.

3. The Constitutional Deliberations in the Reichsamt des Innern, 9–12 December 1918, and Hugo Preuss's Original Draft of the Constitution

In spite of the considerable differences between Preuss and Weber, Weber's constitutional articles impressed Preuss, and he invited Weber to participate in the deliberations about the general outlines of the constitutional draft that was to be submitted to the National Assembly. These deliberations took place 9–12 December 1918 in the Reichsamt des Innern (Office of the Interior). Since Gerhard Anschütz, a Heidelberg constitutional law professor who was also invited to participate, could not attend, Weber was the only one of the thirteen participants who was there in an unofficial capacity. It was his greatest hour. Now he could finally exercise direct influence over the making of the Reich constitution, whereas so far he had only been able to influence the decisions through journalistic commentary. The Verfassungsausschuss (constitutional committee) was the delivery room of the Weimar constitution, although it had no official character, met with strict secrecy, and did not allow any decisions by vote. Its decisions established the fundamental framework of

69. Weber for the preservation of the career civil service, *Pol. Schr.*, pp. 478 f.; Preuss, *Staat, Recht und Freiheit*, p. 427.

70. Cf. Preuss, *Staat, Recht und Freiheit*, p. 320, art. 27a.

71. *Pol. Schr.*, p. 363, compare above, p. 186.

the Weimar constitution that remained essentially unchanged in the parliamentary and extraparliamentary deliberations that were to follow.[72]

The committee's composition was overwhelmingly unitarian in sentiment. No representatives of the federal states participated, while almost all the members were high Reich officials. The two socialist representatives in the Reich Office of the Interior, Max Quarck and Josef Herzfeld, pursued an extremely centralistic solution. Weber found himself from the start at the other end of the spectrum, seconded only by Kurt Riezler, the representative of the Foreign Office who pointed to the expected opposition of the south German states against too unitary a constitution, and Theodor Lewald, the undersecretary in the Reich Office of the Interior, and to a certain degree also Carl Petersen, a senator from Hamburg. When Preuss introduced the key issue—centralized state or federal state?—and in this connection declared the preservation of Prussia in its prior form to be out of the question, Weber immediately took this thesis by the horns. He opposed Preuss with the argument that the structure of the new constitution should arise "as little as possible from legal considerations and as much as possible from practical considerations," and thereby touched on the root problem of the somewhat doctrinaire pressure for a solution that was, in legal and constitutional respects, decidedly centralist. Weber is reported to have said that "a far-reaching degree of federalism will be demanded by the facts, however preferable unitarianism may be. The question is whether we should take our stand on the concept of the '49 or the '67 constitution. Prussia, with its forty million inhabitants, would become too powerful in the Reich if its authority were in proportion to its population." He did not believe in the dismemberment of Prussia.[73] Weber therefore, unlike Preuss, proceeded from the postulate that in the given situation only a truly federalist constitution was attainable, if only for reasons of foreign policy. In principle, he wished to retain the existing Bundesrat structure and to compensate for Prussian preponderance by a relative increase in the number of votes held by the non-Prussian states, since he did not expect Prussia to be dismembered or regard that as desirable. By now supporting the construction of a house of states, as specified in the Frankfurt Reich constitution, he came closer to Preuss's insistent rejection of the Bundesrat. The Frankfurt Reich constitution had stipulated that half the delegates would be delegated by the state parliaments and half by the state governments and had given proportionally more representation to the non-Prussian states than was justified by their population.[74] In Weber's eyes, as we have already

72. Cf. Schulz, *loc. cit.*, pp. 129 ff.

73. This and all of the following citations are taken from the "notes" about the discussions in the Reich Ministry of the Interior, 9–12 December, unless otherwise indicated.

74. Cf. Frankfurt Reich Constitution, section IV, article II, paragraph 87, appendix.

seen, the distinction between a Staatenhaus and one similar to the Bundesrat was not especially important since as a rule the delegates in the house of states would vote according to their governments' wishes even without instructions, since both would be elected by the same party majority.

Weber's proposals met with fairly general opposition. Max Quarck and Josef Herzfeld especially, but also Ludo Moritz Hartmann, who participated as the Austrian delegate in the negotiations, strongly argued for a unitary constitution. Quarck was only prepared to agree to delegations from the federal states, who from time to time should be given a hearing before the introduction of a proposal that affected them, or at most a Reichsrat with an advisory role. Hartmann held similar views. Privy Councillor A. Schulze, chief administrative advisor in the Reich Office of the Interior, proposed a Reichsrat with advisory functions only, which would have a voting rule requiring changing of the boundaries of those federal states that were either too large or too small. Preuss seized upon this idea. The south German states would then be represented in their present form while Prussia would be represented by its provinces.

Weber spoke up strongly against such dogmatic unitarianism. He regarded such a scheme as theoretical speculation that ignored the basic fact that the power of the Reich had collapsed while the federal states had regained their power and the old, highly trained bureaucracies were exercising that power effectively. To ignore the existing power of the federal states in the process of making the constitution would be a great mistake. Weber vigorously opposed the idea that they be put off with a "Staatsrat" (council of states). Councils of states were almost always powerless. "Such an institution can only be bureaucratic and technical and will not allow any effective participation of the federal states in the exercise of power by central government." Weber himself had proposed a Staatsrat in 1917 in which the representatives of the south German states would have come more to the fore than in the Bundesrat, in which Prussia had practically assumed a hegemonic position, but he had regarded this primarily as a makeshift solution, which would not lessen the necessity of parliamentarizing the Bundesrat. He also regarded commissions of representatives of the federal states in the individual ministries as desirable but as by no means an adequate substitute for a representative body of the federal states.[75] Nevertheless, Weber made a significant concession to the unitarian trend of the committee when he no longer insisted on the retention of the Bundesrat or on a mixed system similar to that in the Frankfurt constitution, but agreed to a genuine Staatenhaus.

75. This suggestion was met in paragraph 15 of Preuss's draft: "As occasion demands, *Reichsräte* consisting of representatives of the Freistaaten should be created in all the Reich ministries, whose opinion is to be sought before the introduction of bills in the Reichstag and before the decree of general administrative orders necessary to carry out Reich laws."

"This is the least that the states must be offered and a lesser evil than the Bundesrat. If we go too far, then the south German states, especially Bavaria, will turn completely to particularism." A federalist solution that would take account of the existing distribution of power was after all unavoidable. He did not believe that the notions *federal*, *state*, and *parliamentary* government "were irreconcilable."

Hugo Preuss did not dismiss this argument, which was presented with a great deal of force and conviction. An organ for the representation of the individual states was inevitable. To this end, Preuss returned to the idea of a Staatenhaus consisting of delegates from the parliaments of the federal states—an idea he had already voiced in a rather hedged manner in his constitutional draft of 1917.[76] He did not wish to go any further. He regarded the revival of the Bundesrat with group voting based on instructions—in contrast to Weber—as a very bad thing indeed. The first draft that Preuss prepared on the basis of the discussions from 9 through 12 December envisioned a Staatenhaus formed by delegates as a better solution for the governments of the federal states than one elected directly by the people.[77] Weber's call for a moderate overrepresentation in favor of the non-Prussian states was also taken into account, though only indirectly. In paragraph 33 of the draft, the provision that no German free state could be represented by more than a third of the delegates was included.[78] At this stage, Preuss was still counting on the division of Prussia into ten states.[79]

In the constitutional deliberations of 9–12 December, Weber pointed to the only path that under given conditions appeared open: "We must incorporate as much unitarianism as possible in a federalist constitution." In this sense, Weber emphatically supported Preuss's efforts to strengthen the Reich's influence over the administrative praxis of the states. This influence had been very limited in the Bismarckian Reich and had therefore been a source of constant friction. To this end, Weber wished to include "the acceptance of normative stipulations in the Reich constitution" concerning the basic principles of administrative procedure, and believed the Reichsverwaltungsgericht (administrative court) should be given the task of supervising their correct execution. In this instance, Weber fell into the error of attempting to solve political questions with legal tools. The Reichsverwaltungsgericht would doubtless

76. *Staat, Recht und Freiheit*, p. 305.

77. Preuss's original draft of 3 January, 1919 (draft I), in Heinrich Triepel, *Quellensammlung zum Deutschen Reichsstaatsrecht*, 4th ed. (Tübingen, 1926), p. 7, para. 26, which becomes para. 32 of the published draft of 20 January 1919 (draft II).

78. Draft I, paragraph 27, section 2 (=Draft II, parag. 33, section 2).

79. See draft I, para. 29. However, the Reich government immediately excised this article, which envisioned such a radical division of Prussia, from the draft.

have been overburdened with controlling the administrative activities of the federal states. These activities inevitably had a political character. For Weber, however, any means to fight bureaucratic arbitrariness was welcome. Moreover, as we have seen, he had a liking for solving political problems by judicial means if possible. Hugo Preuss took a more suitable approach by stipulating in the constitution that the Reich be given the right to instruct and control the federal state administrations.[80] Weber was not correct, however, in thinking that such a formula would not survive the resistance of the federal states.[81] In spite of a serious conflict over this issue, Preuss essentially succeeded in establishing the Reich's instruction and control powers in all administrative matters.[82]

Weber was also on Preuss's side in the effort to permit the creation of new federal states by the Reich, even though he did not wish the dismemberment of the Prussian state. Because he favored a federalist constitutional system on principle, he thought it desirable that a thorough revision of the territory of Germany should come about, whereby the dwarf states would be eliminated and some territories taken away from the Prussian colossus. Paradoxically, the famous reorganization paragraph of Preuss's draft that evoked the passionate resistance of the states was phrased largely in accordance with Weber's suggestions. Preuss was taken by surprise by the reactions of the federal state governments in the Staatenausschuss, and was almost helpless in the face of these protests.[83]

80. Drafts I and II, para. 8.

81. Letter to Preuss of 25 December 1918.

82. Para. 15, Weimar Reich Constitution (hereafter cited as WRC); cf. below, end of sec. 3.

83. H. Petzke, "Max Weber und sein Einfluss auf die Reichsverfassung" (diss., Leipzig, 1925, machine printed), reports that "according to a personal statement by Dr. Preuss . . . Max Weber personally formulated para. 11 in draft I, and Dr. Preuss adopted it verbatim in his draft" (p. 125). This is impossible; even stylistic reasons point against it. Weber did *not* wish plebiscites to be proposed by the relevant regional bodies but by popular initiative. Weber sent his *own draft* to the Reich Office of the Interior, "regarding: reception of newly created states ('division of Prussia'):

"Within any administrative region of one of the existing free states which, according to the last census, has at least three million inhabitants, 100,000 eligible votes can propose, through a written declaration, the institution of a plebiscite with the purpose of constituting a separate free state. If this occurs, the Reich should then reach provisional unity on the conditions after consulting the central power of the affected free state as well as the highest offices of the administrative region and seeking the advice of the professional associations. A Reich law determining the manner and conditions of the secession is to be drawn up then, independent of the results of these negotiations, and a plebiscite is to be called along with the publication of the preparatory negotiations and advisory statements. If the plebiscite supports secession and an organized representation is established, then, upon application, the Reich president admits the new state as a member of the Reich."

Paragraph 11 of the first draft differs significantly from the above. Not only had Preuss reduced the minimum population requirement to two million, expressing the general

Weber insisted that the creation of new states follow the principle of the democratic self-organization of the population, effected, however, with the indirect participation of the Reich. A significant proportion of the population of these regions should be entitled to petition a referendum about the question of the creation of new states or annexation to an already existing state.[84] Then the Reich should take up the issue, determine the conditions of an eventual secession by adequate legislation, and arrange for a plebiscite. Weber submitted a draft for paragraph 11 in connection with the discussions at the Reichsamt des Innern that expressed these basic principles.[85] Eventually, paragraph 11 was to receive a very different form. Instead of a popular initiative, the paragraph called for a vote by the local government bodies involved in the regions in question. In addition, Preuss reduced the minimum population required for a state to be created anew from Weber's figure of three million inhabitants to two million.[86] All this, however, came to nothing. The reorganization paragraph became by far the most controversial article of the Weimar constitution. Only the principle of indirect participation by the Reich survived from the original draft.[87]

Provision for the Reich to have power to influence the constitutional organization of the federal states, if needs be in a democratic sense, Weber considered far more important than the participation of the Reich in any possible territorial reorganization of federal states. He therefore called for normative provisions in the Reich constitution that would mandate a republican form of government for the federal states and

---

tendency of his draft (see the notorious reorganization paragraph 29 in draft I), but he had expressly taken up the question of the unification of several member states. Above all, he did not adopt the popular initiative, which he did not exactly treasure, although in fact this favored the *existing* states; and he also gave up the participation of the president. Could Preuss perhaps have been trying to escape the presumed odium of sole responsibility for this paragraph retrospectively at least in part by ascribing the verbatim authorship of paragraph 11 to Max Weber? The paragraph prompted stormy opposition from the individual states.

Petzke's study attempts to force Max Weber into the procrustean bed of the unitary terminology of Anschütz's commentary on the Reich constitution; this leads to unfortunate distortions and misunderstandings and misses the core of Max Weber's constitutional considerations. Petzke seeks to make Max Weber into a unitarian who wished for the "formal and complete elimination of state autonomy" (p. 2). Since this is in diametrical contradiction to Weber's actual position, Petzke is forced to the singular construct of a prerevolutionary and a postrevolutionary "manifestation of the postulate of the Reich state concept" in Weber's work. Multiple individual contradictions are therefore not surprising; they seem occasionally even to have disquieted Petzke.

84. According to *Pol. Schr.*, p. 462n.: one-fifth of the population, in the draft reproduced above of para. 11, 100,000 eligible votes from 3 million inhabitants.

85. See above, note 83.

86. See the version of para. 11 in draft I (=para. 11 in draft II).

87. Cf. para. 18 WRC.

guarantee that the state and local government constitutions conformed to democratic principles. The Reich constitution ought to prescribe that in all cases the responsible chief executives should have the confidence of a representative body elected according to general, equal, secret, and direct suffrage. This applied to the states as well as to local governments. This proposal won general support and was incorporated in article 12 of Preuss's constitutional draft. It was phrased in accordance with a draft proposal that Weber had forwarded to the Reichsamt des Innern soon after the discussions in Berlin.[88] Nevertheless, the deliberators rejected Weber's suggestion that an appeal to the Reich, when these normative provisions appeared to have been broken, ought to be possible on the demand of one-tenth of the voters or one-fifth of the members of the representative bodies in the states, as in local government. Weber sought to give the supreme court the power to adjudicate such matters while the Reich president would necessarily carry out the necessary corrective measures. Preuss justifiably refused to burden the supreme court with such questions. He was also no friend of the popular initiative, in contrast

88. "*Draft*—Regarding: guarantees of the constitutions of the free states and communities.

"1. The Reich guarantees a republican constitution to the states in which the responsible leader of the administration is bound to the confidence of a popular representative body elected on the basis of general, equal, secret, direct suffrage.

"2. It further guarantees every minority of at least one-fifth of the members of the popular representative body the right to demand the establishment of an investigatory commission in which it is represented proportionately, and the right to interrogate witnesses and experts if there are doubts about the legality or integrity of the administration. The investigatory minutes are to be published in their entirety.

"3. The Reich guarantees a constitution to the communities in which the head of the community, or if one exists, the collegial administration, either is directly elected according to general, equal, direct, secret suffrage, or is elected by a representative body which is elected through the aforesaid suffrage.

"4. The Reich also guarantees the communities independence of administration, reserving only control over legality and integrity as well as the soundness of the financial administration. It guarantees every minority of at least one-half of the town citizens or at least one-half of the community representative body the right to demand the establishment of an investigatory commission with the same rights as in the state.

"5. One-tenth of the eligible voters or one-fifth of the members of the elected representative body are empowered to appeal to the Reich on the basis of the assertion that the rights guaranteed to them have been violated. The decision about this appeal will be made by the Supreme Court. The execution is accomplished necessarily through an appeal by the same minority to the Reich president. If an equivalent minority raises questions about the legality of the execution of the relevant measures, the Supreme Court adjudicates."

Cf. above, note 83. If Max Weber chose the form of a constitutional guarantee here, he must have considered the idea of not injuring the states' self-assurance by a constitutional *superimposition*. It was, however, probably decisive for him that the populace of respective administrative areas would thereby be in a position to *force* the intervention of the Reich if necessary.

to Weber, who saw it as the correlate of the plebiscitary vote for the Reich president. It is noteworthy that, in this instance too, Weber wished to draw the president in.

Bitter experience in the Prussian suffrage question led to the demand for such normative stipulations. Similar occurrences ought to be forestalled by all means. Therefore in the future the Reich must have the constitutional right to interfere on issues affecting state constitutions. There was also the danger of attempts at monarchistic restoration in individual states, some of which would of necessity threaten Reich unity. However, these stipulations would soon gain significance in the opposite direction as they could also be invoked against Communist minority dictatorships in individual states. For Max Weber, one other factor was equally important. He hoped through such a constitutional stipulation to assure the right to set up commissions of inquiry to the representative bodies of the federal states and of local government. This was hardly surprising, considering how important the right of inquiry was for Weber. It was, in his view, not only the correlate of ministerial responsibility but almost more important than the latter. In Weber's aforementioned draft on the Reich guarantee of the constitutions of the federal states and of local government, the right of inquiry for the minority was put on the same footing as the principle of the political responsibility of the chief executive to the respective representative body. Weber even wanted the Reich to guarantee the representative bodies of local government the right, on the initiative of one-tenth of the voters, to appoint an investigatory committee.[89]

With the exception of this final suggestion, which really went too far, Preuss included Weber's proposals almost word for word in his draft.[90] But in the first meeting of the provisional Staatenausschuss, sharp resistance emerged against granting the Reich government such extensive competences. The Bavarian representative Conrad von Preger protested that the right of inquiry was a matter for the federal states. At the joint insistence of Bavaria and Prussia, the normative stipulations affecting the right of inquiry and the constitutional arrangements of local government were stricken.[91] The National Assembly subsequently restored the Reich guarantee of democratic constitutional procedure to the representative assemblies of local government, while the right of inquiry, understandably, was dropped.[92]

89. Cf. the draft, above, note 88.

90. Draft I, para. 12.

91. Minutes of the meeting of the state representatives in the Reich Office of the Interior, here followed in the papers of the Prussian Interior Ministry, Ehemaliges Geheimes Preussisches Staatsarchiv, now DZA II, Act. betr. die neue Verfassung des Reichs; compare draft III of the Reich Constitution of 17 February 1919, para. 16, in Triepel, loc. cit., pp. 17 ff.

92. Cf. *Verhandlungen im Verfassungsausschuss*, *Protokolle*, pp. 437 ff.

Max Weber was victorious, however, in his demand for a constitutional anchoring of the right of inquiry for the Reichstag. Yet it would be wrong to attribute this to his initiative alone. Preuss, too, had called for the right of inquiry as early as 1917. But Weber achieved a guarantee that even minorities would have the right to introduce an investigatory committee. Article 52 of the original draft by Preuss, the formulation of which can be traced directly to Weber's proposals, provided that, on the demand of one-fifth of the members of the Reichstag, a committee had to be appointed "to investigate the facts if doubt existed about the legality or integrity of governmental or administrative measures by the Reich."[93]

Weber wished to sharpen the right of inquiry still more by the provision that "investigatory proceedings were to be published in toto" according to the English model.[94] In addition, parliamentary immunity should not be so interpreted as to permit members of parliament to refuse to testify before investigative committees. This was "a crucial issue . . . for minority inquiries and would determine whether or not it was possible to attack parliamentary corruption. The latter would be the case if the members of the Volkshaus [popularly elected house] had an unconditional right to refuse to testify even in regard to the voting intrigues in which they were involved." This formulation makes clear the specific goals that Weber believed the investigatory committees should serve: (1) control of the administration, to which Weber attributed the utmost importance as he was fiercely opposed to bureaucratic infringements on policy matters; (2) fighting parliamentary cliques and manipulation of votes by career politicians without calling—i.e., the control of party bureaucracies as well as governmental bureaucracies, insofar as this was possible by parliamentary action.

The right of inquiry entered the constitution essentially in the form Max Weber had wished, though with some important changes and elaborations. In particular, the Staatenausschuss eliminated the limitation of paragraph 52 to administrative control, which Weber and Hugo Preuss had somewhat unintentionally permitted to creep in by striking the passages[95] "for the investigation of facts"[96] and "if the legality or the integrity of governmental or administrative measures is in doubt."[97] This

93. Draft I, para. 52; compare Weber's formulation of the right of inquiry in his draft of para. 12, above, note 88, especially the almost identical passage: "If there are doubts about the legality or the integrity of the administration." Cf. also Weber's proposal for a constitutional establishment of the right of inquiry from the year 1908, above, chap. 6, text at note 59.

94. Cf. Weber's draft of para. 12, sec. 2.

95. Cf. draft III, para. 55; also H.H. Lammers, "Parlamentarische Untersuchungsausschüsse," *Handbuch des deutschen Staatsrechts*, vol. 2, pp. 457 ff.

96. This passage stems from Preuss, compare *Staat, Recht und Freiheit*, p. 320; Preuss stood steadfast in the Verfassungsausschuss about this, *Protokolle*, p. 265.

97. This passage arose in association with Weber's formulation.

made it clear what narrow goals Max Weber had had for the right of inquiry. Furthermore, in the Verfassungsausschuss the possibility of secret committee hearings was accepted if a two-thirds majority so willed, which scarcely harmonized with Weber's intention of protecting the minority.[98] All in all, however, Weber's hope of creating at once a means of control of the administration and the protection of minorities received general support.[99] Of course, exaggerated hopes were associated with the right of inquiry, and Weber probably contributed to this overestimation. As it happened, parliamentary investigatory committees in no way stood the test of praxis and were only able to achieve a limited influence over practical administration.[100]

Max Weber's central desire remained of course the creation of a plebiscitary Reich president who, as chief executive and the immediate representative of the electorate, would be the real bearer of Reich policy in opposition to the secondary, derived authority of the government and of the parliament, which was comprised by party machines and career politicians without calling. He took this point of view in the constitutional discussions in the Reichsamt des Innern with the same passionate eloquence and prudent argumentation with which he had successfully won over his own followers. The weight of his arguments did not lack effect even on the representatives of the Left, perhaps because he knew how to approach their position tactically. Weber attacked a directorate, as the Independent Social Democratic party proposed, because every collegial decision would lead to a harmful division and therefore to the elimination of all responsibility. "A president is necessary so that a chief chosen by a popular vote can be at the head of the administration. The bureaucracy and the officers must have their ultimate superior in the president." Weber sought to persuade the Social Democrats to agree to the institution of a plebiscitary Reich president by pointing out that "the socialization of Germany would be impossible without the occasional personal intervention of the head of the Reich."

Walter Simons went further than Weber in his suggestions. He favored a presidency in the American image. "It is impossible for a cabinet of ministers to be at the head of the Reich government. We made this attempt under Chancellor Max von Baden and it failed completely[!] In Germany, party divisions are too great for such a form of government." Of course, Hugo Preuss still emphatically rejected the American system.

98. *Verhandlungen des Verfassungsausschusses, Protokolle*, pp. 264 f., p. 455. Cf. the final version: article 34 WRC.

99. Cf. also Preuss's statements in the constitutional committee (*Protokolle*, p. 265), in which he expressly supported the combination of the right of inquiry and minority protection and ascribed their great importance for the functioning of the parliamentary system.

100. Cf. Apelt, *Geschichte der Weimarer Verfassung* (Munich, 1946), p. 98.

He did not approve of the rigid separation between executive and legislative in the United States any more than their coincidence in the French system. The American system too was contradictory; "a middle line had to be chosen in Germany." In line with Redslob's theory of the balance of powers, he favored a plebiscitary Reich presidency along with a fully developed parliamentary system with a responsible cabinet constructed along the English model. The Majority Socialist Quarck disapproved of even this degree of power for the president. He proposed a president similar to the Swiss model, who comes to the fore organically from both parliament and ministry.

Max Weber pressed for more. He would not have been content with a mere representational role for the Reich president, which Preuss's proposal would have meant in spite of a popular election. In particular, however, he attacked Quarck's proposals. He did not want a president who had his roots in parliament and the parliamentary parties, but an independent leader who came to power outside of the party machines. He believed that if Quarck's route was followed, the result would probably be "the election of a compromise candidate with strong parliamentary experience" as a result of the negotiations among the four largest political parties, which were likely to dominate German politics in the future. "It would [therefore] be very doubtful whether this president would *rule* or rather his subordinates."[101] For Weber it was important that the Reich president really be the chief executive and not merely a formal head of state, even if he were to govern as a rule through a cabinet responsible to the Reichstag. He confirmed this position with a sharp turn against parliament: "He did not wish, either, that only the parliamentarians had a chance for leadership in Germany. Even if the division of powers was not completely realizable [to this extent Weber distanced himself from the presidential system of the American kind], he regarded it as useful to retain some aspects of it in the constitution. Parliaments today have come under serious criticism. To trust them with total power would be rather problematic. He wished for a counterweight against parliament, such as could be found in a president elected by the people." Weber's program was clear. It amounted to a real division of executive powers between the Reich cabinet, which remained responsible to the Reichstag, and a "plebiscitary dictator," who enjoyed the confidence of the masses.[102] Weber therefore demanded a plebiscitary equivalent for the demise of the Reich chancellor by a vote of no confidence in parliament. The responsibility of the Reich president had to be guaranteed by

101. Emphasis mine.

102. In any case, this formulation was used by Weber only later, in his article "Der Reichspräsident" of February 1919, *Pol. Schr.*, p. 499. Here we read: The "dictatorship" of the masses demands the "dictator."

the possibility of removing him by a referendum to be initiated by a popular initiative (about one-tenth of the voters) which would not require any announcement of reasons. This was, in his view, the essential correlate to the *plebiscitary* authority of the Reich president. Otherwise there would be no necessary counterweight to force him to "prove" his qualification for leadership. To repeat what we have stated earlier: the masses ought to follow the Caesarist leader as long as he was successful. If he fails: "Away with him."

Weber's proposal to give the Reich president such a powerful position, especially as it was in part directed against the power of parliament, provoked an expectedly sharp protest from the left. Herzfeld used an argument against Weber that was to recur throughout the constitutional debates—the danger that "the presidency would be too much like a monarchy." That objection, of course, was inadequate, since Weber wished for something quite different than a mere parliamentarily elected monarch. He called for something incomparably more modern, the plebiscitary leadership position of the "highest Reich functionary."[103] Preuss took on the Left's attack on the possibility of a powerful presidency: "There is nothing to fear from too much power in a Reich president if his position is made similar to that of a *limited parliamentary* monarch."[104] Here he effectively cut short Weber's implicit demands, which went much farther. In spite of the plebiscitary election, the Reich president would be limited to a representative function while the responsible leadership of policy would belong exclusively to the Reich chancellor. The majority of the committee took Preuss's line as to the Reich president's responsibilities: they decided "that his position ought to be designed in a form similar to that of a monarch in a parliamentarily governed state."

Apparently Weber approved this formulation as a compromise.[105] To be sure, he counted on the fact that the impact of a presidential authority based upon popular confidence would make itself felt even without explicit institutional authorization. But in fact this was tantamount to a death blow to his original concept. A parliamentary monarch, even if he were Edward VII, was not the necessary "counterweight" to the rule of career parliamentarians. A Reich president defined according to this model could not be an effective counterweight either.

Weber therefore put on a fight in order to secure the Reich president

103. For the phrase "highest Reich functionary," see ibid.

104. Emphasis mine.

105. The relevant place in the minutes reads: "Majority, which he sees as necessary, in agreement that his position should be constructed like that of a monarch in a parliamentary state." This permits the conclusion that the supporters of the plebiscitary Reich presidency all joined this compromise proposal by Preuss, in opposition to the Left's opposition.

some involvement in the legislative process.[106] "We should . . . not go so far as to deny the president any influence on legislation. This would be a false approach to democracy. A genuine democracy could not deny the president's right, as the elected representative of the people, to appeal over the parliament to the people, and the best means for this would be the referendum. His ability to do so must be *freed from the requirement of a ministerial countersignature*."[107] The Reich president, on the basis of a fully free decision for which he is responsible to the people alone, should be able through a referendum to put to the people for their decision a bill rejected by the Reichstag.

Weber gave precedence to the referendum over the dissolution of the Reichstag because he believed that an immediate appeal to the people on a disputed issue by means of a plebiscitary expression of confidence in the Reich president was a more direct means of determining popular opinion. At the same time, it was a good tactical move, since the presidential initiative for a referendum was attractive for both the supporters of a strong Reich president and also the representatives of the Left. The apparent radical-democratic nature of the referendum reconciled the Left to the fact that the Reich president would thereby gain additional power. An additional reason was that Weber, who was very apt at tactics, drew attention to the fact that the popular initiative for a referendum, important as it was to permit it, was much less practicable because a popular initiative had "to be made dependent on a declaration of intent by a large number of citizens," and therefore it was likely to be a very costly affair.

Everyone present *unanimously* supported the Reich president's power to initiate a popular referendum. But Weber's wish to free the president from the countersignature of the chancellor received no support. Preuss stuck to his line. In view of this situation, Weber apparently decided not to demand the right of dissolution for the Reich president without a countersignature, although it must have been his view. Since the Left would have denied the president the right of dissolution altogether, such a suggestion would have had no chance of acceptance. It appeared to

106. Here the minutes read: "Prussia has long, if not legally, nevertheless practically, been able to hinder any law that it did not like. This is no longer the case. But it is not necessary to go so far . . ." etc. This permits the conclusion that Weber, to a certain extent, regarded the Reich president as the successor to the presidium of the previous Bundesrat. Apparently he wished to give the president a similar leadership position to that which the Reich chancellor had had in his capacity as the bearer of the presidial votes in the Bundesrat, if now in a weakened form. This demonstrates how remarkably strong Max Weber's framework of continuity was, even when the new constitutional institutions had an entirely different form.

107. Emphasis mine.

Weber that the presidential initiative for a referendum was a sufficient substitute for the right to dissolve the parliament.[108]

Hugo Preuss's approach emerged victorious in the discussions, while Weber was defeated on points of principle. Nonetheless, he wrote to his wife expressing satisfaction with the committee proceedings: "So, the Reich constitution is complete in principle and *very* close to my proposals."[109] In fact, Hugo Preuss included several essential suggestions of Weber's in the draft that was subsequently prepared in the Reichsamt des Innern and then presented to the Reich cabinet at the beginning of January 1919. He made use of Weber's drafts for articles 11 and 12 written in connection with the deliberations. Article 12, paragraphs 1–4, were especially close to Weber's proposals. In addition, the regulations affecting the right of inquiry adhered to Weber's proposals. The phrasing of article 1, too, originated with Max Weber: "The German Reich is composed of its existing member states as well as those regions whose population desires to be accepted into the Reich on the basis of the right to self-determination and who are accepted by a law of the Reich."[110] On the other hand, Preuss deviated from Weber's wishes when he gave the draft a strongly unitary form. More important, he endowed the position of the Reich president with representative functions only by binding him in all civil and military orders to the countersignature of the responsible Reich minister. But he did accept some of Weber's key ideas. Originally, he permitted the Reich president a suspensive veto, a provision that the Reich cabinet struck from the draft.[111] Preuss apparently also initially wished to give the Reich president the right to initiate a referendum in accordance with the unanimous support for Weber's proposal in the committee. But at the last minute this proposal was dropped.[112] Instead,

108. Cf. *Pol. Schr.*, p. 469: "It could not be good to take the right of dissolution—or an equivalent of it, perhaps the calling of a referendum—from him [the Reich president], considering our party situation."

109. Letter of 13 December 1918. Weber was very much at home in the discussions: "The whole day involved heated discussions with *very* intelligent people, it was a pleasure." *Lebensbild*, p. 651; cf. the letter cited there of 10 December 1918: "Thus, yesterday, a meeting . . ."

110. Verhandlungen des Verfassungsausschusses, p. 46: "Professor Weber proposed stating: 'The territory of the Reich is constituted from the areas of the former German federal states together with those areas that declare their accession on the basis of the right of self-determination'"; Preuss accepted this formulation with minor modifications in his draft and only added the passage: "acceptance through a Reich law". The final version in article 2, WRC, approached Weber's formulation even more closely.

111. Draft I, para. 55, sec. 2: "He is empowered to return laws agreed to by the Reichstag to the Reichstag for a second discussion and decision within this time limit [one month]. If, after further discussion, the Reichstag sustains its decision, the president is required to proclaim tne Reich law." Cf. "Denkschrift zum Verfassungsentwurf," p. 26.

112. The memorandum on the constitutional draft of 3 January 1919 presupposes such an article; *loc. cit.*, p. 26.

Preuss accepted Weber's suggestion that the president might appeal to the people by a referendum in the event of a deadlock over a law between the house of the people and the house of states.[113] In addition, in accord with Weber's suggestion, he envisioned that a sufficient majority of the Reichstag could introduce a plebiscite for the recall of the president, a right that really hung somewhat in the air considering the strict limitation of the president's authority, which made the occasion and importance of such action of little significance. Because of the mistrust of the Left of any possible independence for a plebiscitary president, this provision was retained in the final constitution.[114] A little later, in a letter to Preuss, Max Weber praised the manner in which the negotiations had been conducted.

> Without "a father's joy"—as you put it—in your own ideas, open to the most diverse suggestions and—I may say this without the suspicion of making "compliments"—with admirable precision and objectivity. The result is overall —as with most "committees"—a *compromise product* between parliamentary and plebiscitary, Bundesrat-like and Staatenhauslike constructions. I am certain that it will *not* completely satisfy you. I am certain, too, after conversations with prominent south Germans, that the *Bundesrat* will somehow or other reappear. You yourself will become converted to it. The federal state governments will never permit themselves to be pushed out of their share in the decision making regarding the *administration*. They must therefore be neutralized in such a way as only a "Bundesrat" can do, even though this is not a happy solution. *If*, however, the Reich has the authority to *issue orders* to the state administrations, then, even with a plebiscitary president and a responsible Reich chancellor, the Bundesrat will be completely untroublesome. We cannot make a formally more "unitary" constitution because this will strongly arouse the mistrust of the Entente and would have cost us 20–30 billion more payments, pawns, and loss of territory. *That* is the central difficulty!

If Preuss's original draft of the constitution appeared to Max Weber as a compromise product between a parliamentary and plebiscitary, federalist and unitary framework, one of the clearly apparent reasons was his own wish to make the plebiscitary elements far stronger through the

113. Draft I, par. 55, sec. 3 (=draft II, par. 60, sec. 2); cf. above, p. 364.

114. Draft I, par. 67, sec. 2, in contents the same as art. 43, sec. 2, WRC. Preuss even favored a ten-year period of office for the Reich president, in agreement with Weber's proposal to make this as long as possible. See draft I, par. 67, sec. 1 (=art. 43, sec. 1, WRC).

115. Letter of 25 December 1918; moreover, Weber strongly advised Nuremberg as the meeting place of the National Assembly. The constitution could then turn out fully 100 percent more unitarian.

strengthening of the Reich president's position. Weber even now tried to persuade Preuss to return to the Bundesrat system. His pessimistic prediction that the individual states would never agree to Preuss's draft proved only too well justified. In the discussions of the provisional committee of states in January 1919, a storm arose against Preuss, which finally forced him to deny his original intentions: "I never favored the dismemberment of Prussia."[116] But in spite of the states' serious resistance, Preuss and the Reich government succeeded in achieving a far more centralized constitution than Weber ever thought possible. To be sure, a representative body for the states was created in the Reichsrat, which appeared similar to the Bundesrat in its composition, but its competence remained much more limited. Instead of an unlimited veto power, whose retention Weber had expected, the Reichsrat retained only the right to take a position on all government proposals before they were introduced in the Reichstag, and the possibility of objecting to Reichstag decisions that they did not approve of. But in this case the Reichsrat could be overriden by a two-thirds vote of the Reichstag. Weber's expectation that the Bundesrat system would return in its old form therefore was not borne out. Weber was not in accord with the dominant tendency in constitutional policy if in February 1919 he still believed that a dualistic system was likely in which the Bundesrat and the Reich president, the latter either as arbiter or as a unifying force vis-à-vis the parliamentary institutions, would have decisive power even in relation to the Reichstag and the cabinet elected by the Reichstag.[117]

In the weeks that followed, however, Weber to some extent modified his position on the relationship between the Reich government and the governments of the federal states. In two articles on "Unitarismus, Partikularismus und Föderalismus in der Reichsverfassung," published 28 and 29 March 1919, he observed that as a result of changes made to the original proposals during the debates in the National Assembly, the balance of power had shifted in favor of central government. But he pointed to the fact that the federal states had indeed retained a say in administrative matters, where these affected them directly. Inasmuch as the Reich government was to issue general instructions to the administrations of individual states, the prior approval of the Reichsrat was required. This, Weber maintained, was far more important than the Reichsrat's right to veto bills it objected to. But at the same time he energetically demanded that the right to give and, if necessary, to enforce

116. Note about the discussions of the State Committee in Weimar, from 5–8 February 1919, Preuss. Ministerium des Innern, Acta betr. die neue Verfassung des Reiches, now DZA II.

117. "Der Reichspräsident," *Pol. Schr.*, pp. 498 f.; also "Politik als Beruf," ibid., p. 544.

direct orders to the administrative bodies of the federal states in matters concerning Reich affairs be restored to the Reich government. This was so important that it might be better to concede a strengthening in the Reichsrat's power of veto than to give in on this point.[117a] Although he was arguing within a federalist framework, Weber had by now become more of a unitarian in constitutional affairs.

4. The Fate of Weber's Constitutional Proposals in the Ensuing Legislative Process

Weber hoped that after the conclusion of the constitutional deliberations in the Reichsamt des Innern, which had an unofficial character, he would be able to continue to participate in the development of the constitution. At the end of December 1918, he asked Hugo Preuss to entrust him, insofar as it might be useful, with the task of "preparing proposals for—in a good sense—a 'demogogic' *formulation* of the Reich constitution." To this end, he asked for "*the currently completed part of* the manuscript" by special delivery: "I know something about 'demogoguery' in the formulation of 'captions.'"[118] Probably Weber would have given the text of the constitution a much less abstract and formalist form than Hugo Preuss's sober, legal approach engendered. But some anxiety was also present in this idea: Did it make sense to formulate a constitution in such a way that its provisions were popular and "captionized" according to the principles of demagogic technique? This makes it clear that Max Weber regarded a constitution as a functional instrument. Preuss, in contrast, must have had little taste for the idea of couching the Reich constitution in demagogically effective language. He viewed the constitution as the visible expression of the long-sought democratic "Reichsstaat" (state based on law). There were other reasons, too, why Weber's suggestion could not be followed. Because of the mistrust of the federal states, who demanded their immediate inclusion in the internal discussions in the Reichsamt des Innern, Preuss restricted participation in the preparation of the constitution, under the strongest security, to a narrow circle of the Reichsamt and the Reich cabinet.[119]

For the time being, Weber sought to win public support for his constitutional program in his election speeches. He energetically championed a federalist framework for the Reich combined with a strong centralist power and argued that the latter could be established only through a

117a. Cf. *Heidelberger Zeitung*, no. 74 (28 March) and no. 75 (29 March), 1919.

118. Letter of 25 December 1918.

119. It is worth considering whether Weber prompted Naumann's well-known efforts to give the basic laws a "cultural" rather than a formally legal wording. In any case, his direct contacts with Naumann at the time were either very limited or nonexistent.

popularly elected Reich president "with the broadest possible powers."[120] The president had to have the right to call a general referendum even against the will of parliament.[121] He repeatedly emphasized that it was impossible to dispense with the Bundesrat, even if Prussian hegemony had to be eliminated and the Prussian vote considerably reduced from what it had been in the past.[122] Weber counted at the time on being elected in Frankfurt and hoped therefore to resume relations with Preuss and participate in the further preparation of the constitution.[123] He anticipated that the National Assembly would offer him the possibility of playing a leading role in the discussions and would draw greater attention to his constitutional ideas than had been possible hitherto.[124] To his deep disappointment, the failure of his candidacy destroyed all these plans with one blow. His constitutional efforts, which had for the first time presented him with the possibility of active political influence and in an area in which he felt very much at home, had an unexpectedly early end.

On 25 February 1919, on the occasion of the presentation of the draft of the Reich constitution to the National Assembly, Weber once again entered into the controversy over the form of the Reich constitution. In an article in the *Berliner Börsenzeitung*, he emphatically called for the popular election of the Reich president, combining his plea with a very sharp attack upon the "almost blind faith in the infallibility and omnipotence of the majority—not of the people, but of the parliamentarians." The tendency of his constitutional proposals to minimize the Reichstag's influence was now made clear in very blunt form. His own unhappy experience with the party bureaucracy of the Hessian German Democratic party may have contributed to this. *Only* the popular election of a Reich president could be a valve for the selection of distinguished political leaders, but instead the old career politicians, against the will of the people, had succeeded in spinning their traditional webs and excluding all really capable leaders. The proportional ballot promoted these tendencies catastrophically. In the future, as a result, the representatives of professional and interest associations would set the tone in parliament:

120. *Fürther Zeitung*, 15 January 1919; cf. *Nordbayrische Zeitung* of the same date, also *Vossische Zeitung*, 22 December 1918.

121. *Badische Landeszeitung*, 6 January 1919.

122. According to the Heidelberger Tagblatt of 3 January 1919. Compare *Fürther Zeitung*, 15 January 1919: "It may be advisable to retain the system of the Bundesrat, because a governmental form following the Swiss or the American model would exclude the individual state governments, which would scarcely be realizable in Germany."

123. Cf. above, chap. 8, text at notes 89–90.

124. Compare letter to Petersen, 14 April 1920, cited above, chap. 8, note 105: "The parliament . . . to which I did not feel impelled, to be a member of which today would be neither an honor or a joy, but where I probably would have belonged while the constitution was discussed."

"People for whom national policy is 'Hecuba,' who act pragmatically, under the imperative mandate of economic interests." As a result, the popular representative body would be reduced to a "parliament of philistines" and would be "incapable in any sense of being a site for the selection of political leaders."[125]

Weber appealed passionately to the parliamentarians who had themselves to recognize the necessity of a popularly elected president. Only such a president would be capable, in the event of parliamentary crises, which in the light of the structure of German partisan life were all too likely, to intervene effectively. Only one so elected could, supported by the confidence of the masses, guarantee the nation's unity. "Like those rulers who act in the best and wisest way by limiting their own power in favor of the parliamentary representatives at the correct time, parliament must freely recognize the Magna Charta of democracy: the right of the direct election of leadership."[126] This was Max Weber's last public statement on the constitutional question. Its arguments are comparable to those in his lecture "Politics as a Vocation."[127] He intervened only one more time in the discussions about the presidency, on the occasion of a visit with Friedrich Ebert during the deliberations of the National Assembly. Ebert wanted to hear at first hand Weber's opinions about the plebiscitary election of the Reich president. According to the report by Kurt Riezler, who was the sole reporter of this meeting, he had decided with Weber to support the *American* system in spite of Weber's reservations about it. But when Ebert posed the question whether the corruption of the spoils system did not militate against this solution, Max Weber is said to have described the sources of corruption in America in a one-hour lecture. The objective of the meeting, to win Ebert for a plebiscitary presidential system, was thereby lost. Weber is said to have replied to Riezler's accusation that he upset the tactical program by pointing out that in view of the Reich president's direct interrogation, he had only replied truthfully and without political tactics.[128] Whatever the course of this encounter, it is certain that it had no further consequences.

125. Now *Pol. Schr.*, pp. 498 ff.: Knoll's (*Führungsaslese*, p. 166) contrary assertion that Weber considered the proportional electoral system to be democratic and stable is a blatant misinterpretation. He discusses "inconsistency" in Weber, although the only place he brings in proportionality is in the *construction of governments*, not in the context of electoral procedure. Knoll's statement about an upper chamber, to which Weber ascribed a great importance as a corrective organ, is also not tenable; cf. ibid., pp. 165 f.

126. *Pol. Schr.*, p. 501.

127. Ibid., p. 544. Cf. above, chap. 8, note 151.

128. In René König, "Max Weber," *Die grossen Deutschen*, vol. 4, pp. 408 ff. The description is based, as Professor König kindly informed me, on a later report by Riezler in a circle of students in which he was present. There is no mention in the correspondence of this meeting with Ebert, so far as we can determine. Whether this occurred in the form described

Although Max Weber himself had no further influence upon the later constitutional deliberations, important elements of his conception were taken up by leading representatives of the German Democratic party—Bruno Ablass, Erich Koch-Weser, and Friedrich Naumann—and firmly introduced in the discussions in the National Assembly. This was true above all for the institution of the plebiscitary Reich presidency, which "in its main points" reached the debates in the National Assembly "unaltered from the first draft," in contrast to the question of the relationship between the Reich and the federal states, where the negotiations in the Staatenausschuss had led to the acceptance of major changes in Preuss's original draft.[129]

The representatives of the German Democratic party called for a strong presidency along the lines of Max Weber's proposals. Erich Koch-Weser revealed the goal of his party on this question with the assertion that a president who was not merely a "representational figure" must stand at the head of the Reich. He ought to be endowed with the necessary power to descend from his tower in the hour of danger and intervene in the struggle of opinions.[130] In the light of the widespread mistrust of a purely representative system, such a representative of the Reich's power, elected by the entire nation with far-reaching powers, was indispensable.[131] The goals of the German Democratic party were distinctly and repeatedly expressed. The president should have the role of counterweight to the parliamentary power in order to create a balance of powers within the parliamentary system.[132] The delegate Ablass declared

---

remains uncertain, since it is quite improbable that Weber would ever have been prepared to favor the *pure* American presidential system. For Riezler's role as the temporary head of the Bureau of the Reich President, see Karl Dietrich Erdmann, ed., *Kurt Riezler: Tagebücher, Aufsätze, Dokumente* (Göttingen, 1972), p. 127, which does not, however, report on the audience.

129. According to Preuss's testimony; "Protokolle des Verfassungsausschusses," p. 235.

130. *Verhandlungen der Nationalversammlung*, vol. 326, p. 393.

131. Ibid., vol. 327, pp. 1346 and 1356.

132. In the first reading in the Verfassungsausschuss (*Protokolle*, p. 232), Ablass said: "My standpoint vis-à-vis our constitution is that we should be steadfast about providing strong power for the Reich president in the framework of the parliamentary system." The omnipotence of the parliament in France is unsuccessful. "True parliamentarism exists when parliament may not be all-powerful, that it is subject to a countercontrol that also must be exercised by a democratic power, and that democratic power here is the Reich president." He referred (on p. 231) expressly to Redslob. He amplified this similarly in the second reading in the National Assembly (*Verhandlungen*, vol. 327, p. 1309). The parliamentary system must be checked by a "strong control power of another organ organized in parallel fashion." The organ of the Reich presidency serves in this way. "Democracy also cries for and demands men, strong men, who are active in the democratic sense in achieving the rights of freedom." Deputy Koch also emphasized this in the National Assembly. Ibid.,

on behalf of the party in the constitutional committee that "I am an enemy of an absolutely unlimited parliamentary majority."[133]

These efforts by the Democrats were supported by the parties of the Right since they viewed the construction of the president's power, in the sense of a more strongly authoritarian Reich constitution, to be desirable. These attributes of the Reich president did not in fact go far enough for them, and they would gladly have constructed the office to reflect that of a real constitutional monarch.

The Majority Social Democrats, on the other hand, wanted to reduce the power of the presidency as much as possible, while the Independents were opposed to the institution altogether. Because the popular election of the president appeared to be a democratic approach to the Majority Social Democrats, they supported it especially because they hoped that the first president would come from their ranks. But they emphatically rejected Preuss's and the representatives of the Democrats' view that the Reich president should be a counterweight to parliamentary power.[134] In spite of the popular election of the president, they championed a true parliamentary system, widened through the apparently democratic institution of the referendum. Their mistrust of a strong presidency continued to the last minute. Only this can explain their sudden attempt during the third reading to have the president elected jointly by the Reichstag and Reichsrat and not by the entire people, "so that the possibility of a Bonapartist plebiscitary politics" would not be created.[135] This proposal was subsequently withdrawn.

Weber had long since criticized the Social Democrats for their confused opposition to a strong Reich president, which was occasioned in part by their fear of a restoration of the monarchy and in part by the opposition of the radical Left, whose agitational pressure they faced, to the institution itself. In a letter to the Social Democrat Ludo Moritz Hartmann, which was earmarked for Otto Bauer, the Austrian secretary of state for foreign affairs, Weber accused the German Social Democrats at the beginning of January 1919 of recognizing the necessity of a "plebiscitary, unified" head of state for any policy of socialization, but of not having the courage to draw the consequences. They had therefore been guilty of "the oldest mistake of the old bourgeois philistine democracy" and "only out of resentment against an 'elected monarch.'" They would therefore bungle the question of the Reich presidency "completely, out

p. 1356, and passim. Cf. also Fraenkel, *Die repräsentative und die plebiszitäre Komponente im demokatischen Verfassungsstaat*, pp. 50 ff.

133. *Protokolle*, p. 460.

134. Cf. especially the speech of Deputy Fischer at the first reading in the Constitutional Committee. *Protokolle*, pp. 274 f.

135. *Verhandlungen der Nationalversammlung*, vol. 328, p. 2076.

of dogmatism, . . . and thereby," he believed it necessary to predict, "bungle the future of the Reich and the socialization of the economy."[136] Eventually, the Social Democrats proved more ready to compromise than Weber had expected. But in the end they prevented the provision of a powerful position for the Reich president, which would have conformed to Weber's wishes.

The prerogatives of the president—the right of dissolution, the referendum, and Reich executive power (along with emergency law)—were the subject of a tense parliamentary struggle. The German Democratic party, supported by the parties of the Right, demanded, along the line of Hugo Preuss's proposals, that the Reich president should be able to initiate the dissolution of the Reichstag, the appointment and dismissal of the Reich chancellor, and a popular referendum without the countersignature of a responsible chancellor. They touched here upon the decisive point because, without freedom from the countersignature, the Reich president would remain, in spite of his election by popular vote, a purely representative figure as the Reich chancellor consequently took on full responsibility for all governmental acts including those of the Reich president.[137] This was Max Weber's view. Moreover, Naumann acted as a spokesman for Max Weber in the debates, when he pointed to the "need for *a* personality who can see the broad view" in contrast to the rapid changes of coalition ministries. The Reich president must be able to form a government independently especially in crisis situations when a parliamentary majority did not exist.[138] Naumann was also the only one who supported Weber's stern criticism of the proportional suffrage in the discussions: proportional representation was "suited to limited situations—unsuited for the determination of political leadership in important situations." However, he received no support.[139]

The Left violently opposed any expansion of the presidential prerogatives beyond the boundaries of a true parliamentary system and therefore opposed freeing the president from the requirement of the countersignature of the Reich chancellor in special cases. Preuss agreed with them fully. He decisively answered no to the question: "Should the Reich president" in the matter of the dissolution of the Reichstag "to a certain extent govern through his civil cabinet?" Preuss argued that if a Reich

136. Letter of 3 January 1919; cf. above, chap. 8, note 65.

137. "Protokolle des Verfassungsausschusses," vol. 233, p. 290; this demand was also raised in numerous private drafts of the future Reich constitution, as by the "Recht und Wirtschaft" association; see Kaufmann, *Grundfragen der künftigen Reichsverfassung* (Berlin, 1919), pp. 21 f. Here Redslob's concepts are clearly involved; Weber's demands played only a secondary role. Cf. also Delbrück's committee report in the National Assembly, *Verhandlungen*, vol. 327, p. 1302.

138. "Protokolle des Verfassungsausschusses," p. 278.

139. Ibid., p. 243, in contrast to earlier characteristic observations.

president wished to dissolve the Reichstag against the will of the chancellor, or to present a law to a popular vote, then he must seek a ministry that was prepared to take over this responsibility and in the event try to create a majority for this minority ministry by dissolving the Reichstag.[140] The possibility of an independent leadership role for the Reich president was thereby extraordinarily restricted.

The Social Democrats, however, were won over to expanding the prerogatives of the Reich president on individual points. When they proposed the introduction of the plebiscite, the Right seized on the opportunity to use this for the strengthening of the president's position. At the instigation of the German Democratic party, the Assembly agreed with rare unanimity to give the Reich president the right to submit to referendum not only those laws on which the Reichstag and the Reichsrat were deadlocked but any national law.[141] This reflected Weber's prior proposal in the discussions at the Reich Office of the Interior, which Preuss had initially accepted in his draft but had then stricken.[142] In this instance, of course, the need for a countersignature remained, and Weber's desire to strengthen the president's power in fact and not merely formally was not achieved.

The referendum turned out not to possess any of the political significance that Max Weber and the fathers of the Weimar constitution expected. It proved to be difficult and unsuited for the correction and supplementation of parliamentary legislation. Neither Ebert nor Hindenberg exercised their right to bring laws before a referendum.

The power of the Reich to act on the basis of the emergency article, the only provision of the constitution that actually permitted the president to carry on a policy independent of parliament and which was, of course, later used as the basis for the illegitimate extension of his sphere of influence, was also hotly disputed. Preuss energetically defended the position that the Reich president in his use of the emergency power should not be bound by excessive restrictions, and he was supported on this issue by the Democrats and the entire Right. The Social Democrats, in contrast, pressed for greater assurances and succeeded against Preuss's will in achieving the provision of a Reich law to be passed in the future.[143] For our purposes, however, the developmental history of article 48 is of

140. Ibid., p. 236.

141. Article 73, sec. 1, of the WRC.

142. In the Constitutional Committee, Preuss stated in reaction to the Democrats' proposal to introduce the referendum at the initiative of the Reich president: "I originally had foreseen one point in Dr. Ablass's proposal, namely to give the *Reich president*, in general, *the right* to appeal through a referendum." "Protokolle des Verfassungsausschusses," p. 309; cf. above, text at note 106.

143. Cf. the "Protokolle des Verfassungsausschusses," pp. 288 f., *Verhandlungen der Nationalversammlung*, vol. 327, pp. 1303 ff., 1322 ff., vol. 328, pp. 2111 f.

limited importance because Max Weber had taken no interest in it.[144] Moreover, the praxis of the later governments on the basis of article 48 in no way corresponded to the intentions of the makers of the Weimar constitution, who saw in it only a substitute for article 68 of the old Reich constitution, concerning martial law.

The National Assembly generally gave the Reich president all the powers and authorities that Hugo Preuss had intended in his first draft. The president was to be responsible for representing the Reich abroad, for exercising supreme command over the army, and for naming of officials and officers. He appointed and discharged the Reich chancellor without being bound by a formal proposal by the Reichstag majority. His constitutional position as head of the executive was advanced through his authority for administration of justice and emergency measures, and his prerogative to call a referendum against a decision of the Reichstag or the Reichsrat. But did this create a position of independent power for the president? As in a constitutional system, the Reich chancellor assumed responsibility for all governmental acts of the Reich president with the exception of his own nomination to the chancellorship. According to the spirit of the Weimar constitution, therefore, the Reich chancellor and not the Reich president was formally and constitutionally the political leader.[145] The only really independent authority of the Reich president was the choice of a suitable chancellor who must, however, have the Reichstag's confidence. Leadership and political responsibility are interdependent. The Reich president was politically responsible only in a very limited sense. He could formally be recalled by a referendum following the initiative of a sufficient majority of the Reichstag, an almost meaningless provision as has already been pointed out. At the time, Weber had argued consistently that *recall* through a *popular* initiative be permitted as a correlate of the Reich president's independent leadership position, which was not subject to direct parliamentary control.[146]

In fact, as the Social Democrat Richard Fischer said in the committee discussions, the institution of the plebiscitary Reich president, insofar as it was to represent an independent counterweight to parliamentary power, "hovered politically in the air." Nonetheless, Preuss and the Democrats, to say nothing of the Right, remained loyal to this idea during the debates.[147] The despised Independent Social Democrats were basically correct when they wished to transfer the authority for introducing a plebiscite to the Reich cabinet. In retrospect, we cannot deny our agree-

144. In disagreement with Baumgarten, in Max Weber, *Soziologie, Weltgeschichtliche Analysen, Politik*, Intro., p. xxv, who also attributes article 48 to Weber's influence.

145. Carl Schmitt, also, in *Verfassungslehre*, p. 346.

146. Cf. above, text at note 102.

147. "Protokolle des Verfassungsausschusses," p. 274.

ment with Deputy Oskar Cohn when he pointed out to the Majority Social Democrats in the National Assembly: "It is precisely from your standpoint that the Reich Ministry is to be treated as the responsible committee of confidence of the parliament, that it is necessary to entrust this body with the task of initiating a *vote of the people*, in the event that this committee of confidence believes itself to be wiser and more farseeing than the parliament which has given the committee its confidence. For this, a Reich president is not needed."[148]

Weber's ideal of a genuine leadership position of the Reich president therefore fell through, at least in the formal constitutional sense. Only a facade, a pretension, remained of the conception of the Reich president as an independent political factor. In the period that followed, this ambiguity favored the widening of presidential authority. Because the Reich president was seen as a republican or, as Weber had expressed it, an "elected" monarch, all those prerogatives were in part ascribed to him that had previously been exercised by the Kaiser, as long as the constitution did not expressly rule this out.[149] The overwhelming majority of Weimar constitutional law scholars attributed, for example, the power of organization to the Reich president.[150] Although this can only be justified by the text of the constitution in a very limited way to say the least, the opinion was generally held that the Reich presidency was on a par with the Reichstag as a constitutional organ. Even Hugo Preuss, in his posthumously published fragment of a commentary on the Weimar constitution, refused to acknowledge the Reichstag as the sole representative of the constitutionally organized people, and emphasized that "nothing" originally speaks for "'the presumption of competence' for the Reichstag" and to the detriment of the Reich president, even if the central position among the highest secondary organs of the self-organization of the people belongs to the Reichstag.[151]

The compromise character of the Weimar constitution, the mixing of the presidential with the parliamentary system, in no way proved to have the special elasticity that had been envisioned by its creators. It led instead to a dangerous confusion about responsibilities. The position of the president impaired the leadership position and thereby the authority of the Reich chancellor in the eyes of the public and the parliament. This permitted the idea to surface that if necessary it was possible to fall back on presidential authority alone. The assumption that a safety valve existed in the form of the Reich presidency and its powers, especially in

148. *Verhandlungen der Nationalversammlung*, vol. 327, p. 1357.

149. Cf. above, text at note 136; also Carl Schmitt, *Verfassungslehre*, pp. 290 f.

150. Cf. Apelt, *Geschichte der Weimarer Verfassung*, pp. 205 f.

151. Hugo Preuss, *Reich und Länder: Bruchstücke eines Kommentars zur Verfassung des Deutschen Reiches*, ed. H. Anschütz (Berlin, 1928), p. 238.

article 48, put the sense of "consciousness of parliamentary responsibility" to sleep and created "a situation, completely opposed to a parliamentary regime, that there was a last resort of responsibility beyond the responsibility of the parliament to the nation."[152] To this degree, the theory of the institution of the Reich presidency as a presumed independent power contributed its part to the decline of parliamentarism in the Weimar Republic.

Of course it is possible (with reference to Max Weber) to take the opposite point of view. Had the chronic atrophy of the authority of the governments of the Weimar Republic and the astonishing lack of truly effective politicians not proved the necessity of the institution of a popularly elected Reich president as a "valve for the selection of leadership" outside of parliament and the parties? The latter feuded with each other bitterly and in the end were no longer capable of constructive politics. Much speaks for this view. The second candidacy of Hindenburg especially lends itself to this interpretation. It was an attempt to circumvent the partisan quarrels by falling back on a nonpartisan personality admired by wide sections of the population. At base, however, the election of a national hero from the years of the First World War as president demonstrated the bankruptcy of the forces of parliamentary democracy. Hindenburg, moreover, was by no means nonpartisan. In spite of his sincere affirmation of the constitution, he remained sympathetic at heart to a policy of conservative restoration, which probably played no small role in the critical months that preceded Hitler's seizure of power. It would be difficult to say that his election was really an act of leadership selection. In spite of his personal qualities, Hindenburg was certainly no statesman. To what extent Wilhelm Marx would have been one remains uncertain. In reality, a plebiscitary election proved less of a guarantee than the parliamentary election for bringing a genuinely statesmanlike personality to the head of the state.

Above all, it was necessary to have statesmen in the post of *chancellor* rather than in the presidential chair. In the existing constitutional situation, the parties of the conservative Right in the later years of the Weimar Republic supported Hindenburg, but did not want anything to do with his chancellors and the parliamentary system. This led to a weakening of the image of parliamentary government and of the chancellor's authority. The division between the Reich president and parliament that gave rise to the presidential cabinets of the 1930s was inherent in the Weimar constitutional framework and even more so in its interpretation. Only the failure of the Reichstag made a presidential cabinet possible that pre-

152. Richard Grau, "Die Diktaturgewalt des Reichspräsidenten," *Handbuch des deutschen Staatsrechts*, vol. 2, p. 292.

pared the way for the quasi-legal seizure of power by the National Socialists. There is no doubt about that. But would such a questionable way out of a situation of parliamentary crisis have been possible if not for the existence of the institution of the Reich president supposedly responsible only to the people? Would not the democratic parties have managed to unite and fight fiercely for the rescue of the republic, instead of sitting back, hoping to avoid the poison cup of National Socialist dictatorship by tolerating the authoritarian administrations that ruled by the grace of the president, though disapproving of their objective goals? Probably, we have to say, Hitler would have succeeded in coming to power anyway, but German parliamentarism and the German democratic parties would have had a somewhat more honorable end.

One further point must be made. Would Hitler have had as easy a time if he had owed his office to the decision of a president who, in turn, owed his own office to a parliamentary vote rather than to national mass emotions? An experienced parliamentary politician who had risen to the top of the German republic through parliament would not have succumbed quite as readily to the questionable manipulations of a Franz von Papen and would not so easily have retained the vague hope that Hitler would at least in general terms keep within the framework of the constitution.

The fate of the Weimar Republic made clear the problems involved in the constitutional provision of a plebiscitary presidency. The parliamentary council of 1948 was prompted therefore to take a different approach to the establishment of the position of chief of state.

5. The Aftereffects of Weber's Theory of the Reich President as Political Leader

The significance of Max Weber's theory of the Reich president as a political leader who, by virtue of his direct commission by the people, was called to exercise an independent policy beside and beyond the parliamentary power was not definitively limited to the shaping of the constitutional institution of the Reich presidency in the Weimar Republic. In this instance his proposals were only partially implemented. His wish to give the Reich president partial and independent responsibility for patronage was not seriously considered. The Reich presidency in the Weimar constitution was essentially a product of the liberal theory of the balance of powers, which fell far short of Weber's theory of a Caesarist-plebiscitary leadership position for the "highest Reich functionary." Weber's theory, however, had a great deal of impact. The efforts during the Weimar period to build up the power of the presidency at the cost of the rights and responsibilities of the Reichstag relied significantly upon

Weber's theory of plebiscitary-charismatic rule. During the 1920s it gained in influence and contributed significantly to the theoretical legitimization of the praxis of presidential government.[153]

Weber had not decisively stressed the individual constitutional responsibilities of the Reich president because he was convinced that the plebiscitary support of the masses would endow a powerful politician in the presidency with sufficient political weight to transcend the formal constitutional limits of his office and to make his influence felt outside of it. Nothing stood in the way of the rule of a plebiscitary "dictator of the election battlefield" even in a formally representative-plebiscitary constitution.[154] Carl Schmitt, a willing student of Max Weber's, seized upon the conception of a popularly elected Reich president as political leader.[155] He developed it to its ultimate conclusions by the thorough repression of all constitutional safeguards that Weber had included in order to force the president to permanently live up to his charismatic leadership endowments.[156] Schmitt's theory of the plebiscitary authority

153. It is not possible for us to pursue these efforts specifically within the present framework; we will give a general overview that certainly does not claim completeness. This will only bring the meaning of Max Weber's Reich presidency theory to the attention of the reader and make possible a historical-political judgment about it.

154. *Pol. Schr.*, p. 535.

155. Carl Schmitt was influenced by Weber from many reference points, e.g., his famous thesis that sovereignty resides with whoever decides about a state of emergency, already appears implicitly in Weber's work. Cf. *Wirtschaft und Gesellschaft*, p. 166: "Constitutional division of powers is an especially unstable construction. The *actual* structure of rule is determined by the answer to the question, What *would* occur if a constitutionally indispensable compromise (e.g., over the budget) were *not* arrived at? A budgetless governing king in England would in that case risk his crown (today), a budgetless Prussian king would not; in the prerevolutionary German Reich [sic!] the *dynastic* powers would have been decisive." Cf. also Carl Schmitt's review of the first edition of this book, which of course does not mention his own debt to Weber, in *Historisch-Politisches Buch* 8 (1960), no. 6.

156. No passage in this presentation has met such passionate opposition as the demonstration of continuity between Max Weber and Carl Schmitt in constitutional theory. Reference should be made to the entirely emotional protest by Karl Loewenstein that Max Weber was included in "the intellectual ancestry" of Carl Schmitt, "the Mephistopheles of the pre-Hitler period." ("Max Weber as 'ancestor' of the plebiscitarian leadership state," *Kölner Zeitschrift für Soziologie und Sozialpsychologie* 13 (1961): 287 f. See also Adolf Arndt's no less solemn statement on the occasion of his commentary on Raymond Aron's lecture "Max Weber und die Machtpolitik" at the Heidelberg sociologists' convention (*Max Weber und die Soziologie heute*, ed. Otto Stammer [Tübingen, 1965], p. 152). At the time, I merely pointed to the fact that Carl Schmitt's succession cannot be doubted as such, and that we can at most ask whether this development of Weber's ideas was objectively possible, and to what extent they stem from the framework of the conception of "plebiscitary leadership democracy." The first must in any event be affirmed, regardless of the eclectic character of Carl Schmitt's theories. Aside from his indignation, Loewenstein does not dispute the fact that meaningful relations exist between Max Weber and Carl Schmitt; he himself writes, without naming Carl Schmitt, of course, that he never would have been reconciled with "the

of the Reich president as the representative of the combined political will of the people, in contrast to partisan pluralism, is a one-sided but conceptually consistent extension of Weber's own program. In Weber's work too, the Reich president was essentially conceived as a counterweight to the petty activities of a leaderless parliament and as a valve for the emergence of leadership in a bureaucratic society that tended to leaderlessness. To be sure, Schmitt gave the form of the plebiscitary president a character that stressed its diametrical opposition to the principle of representation. In his theory, the plebiscitary authority of the Reich president as the representative of the people's common will was directed against party pluralism of any kind. The Reich president

> is essentially conceived of as a man who unites the confidence of the entire people beyond the limits and the framework of party organizations and party bureaucracies, not as a party man but as a man with the confidence of *all* the people. A Reich presidential election that genuinely takes account of this meaning of the constitutional provision would be more important than any of the frequent elections that take place in a democratic state. It would be a splendid proclamation by the German people and would have the irresistibility that is attached to such proclamations. What purpose and meaning could the position of the Reich presidency established in this way have, other than political leadership? If the entire people are really united in their confidence in such a man, this does not happen so that he can remain politically insignificant, deliver holiday speeches and sign his name to the decisions of others.[157]

---

conceptual-antithesis pair, legality and legitimacy, derived from Weber, which later performed such useful service as a battering ram against Western democracy in general and the Weimar system in particular" (ibid., p. 205). In fact, continuity exists, no matter how much we may dispute whether Carl Schmitt was a legitimate, an illegitimate, or, as Jürgen Habermas suggests, a "natural son" of Max Weber (cf. Habermas's commentary in Heidelberg, 1964, in Stammer, p. 80 f.) Personal polemics against me, which unfortunately Professor Loewenstein especially has lent himself to, do not alter the facts (cf. my statement in "Plebiszitäre Führerdemokratie," pp. 311 f. and notes 40, 62, 85, as well as in "Neue Max-Weber-Literature," *Historische Zeitschrift* 211 [1970]: 624 f.). At most, it raises the question of whether a judgment of Max Weber's political works can be based on an analysis of the future development of his political conceptions, over which he of course could in no way be responsible. It seems to me that the historian has the responsibility of such an analysis, perhaps in contrast to constitutional theoreticians, who deal with the theory's immanent importance. I also admit that the influence of Max Weber's theory of the "plebiscitary Reich president" ought to be pursued more broadly than it has been here, and that the interpretation given above is open to criticism. Critics should of course make such criticism concrete, rather than exhausting themselves in emotional indignation over the linking of Max Weber with the German "Mephistopheles" Carl Schmitt.

157. *Verfassungslehre*, p. 350.

Carl Schmitt thereby superimposed an antiparliamentary bias upon the idea of the leadership position of the Reich president in a system where parliament had lost its genuine meaning due to the pluralism of parties and the dominance of material interest groups. This approach was already implicit, in a sense, in Weber's theory of rule, although Weber certainly never intended to question the party system as such. He had justified the necessity of a plebiscitary Reich presidency precisely with the failure of the "politicians without calling" in the German postwar parliaments.[158] It was Carl Schmitt's view that the Reich president should be at once a political leader and a *pouvoir neutre* beyond a parliament dominated by particularist partisan interests. The task of the political integration of the people had shifted from parliament—which had changed "from a theater where independent representatives of the people reached consensus in free negotiations, from a transformer of partisan interests into a transparty will, into a theater for the pluralistic distribution of power by organized social forces"—to the presidency.[159] The president had become the "protector of the constitution" against the particularist egoism of the parties, that is, the Weimar constitution not in the sense of constitutional law but as the "constitutional unity and totality of the German people."[160]

After the Weimar state had entered into its final period of crisis following the collapse of the great coalition in 1930, these theories of Carl Schmitt aroused support from widening circles.[161] Notable politicians and public personalities demanded the vigorous expansion of the president's authority or, at the least, the use of all the authorities that were formally provided for in the Weimar constitution, for they hoped that this would heal Germany's political wounds. By emphasizing the president's independent leadership in relation to the Reichstag and limiting the necessity of a countersignature, these efforts were based upon the theory of the Reich presidency that Max Weber had represented with much force and conviction in 1918 and 1919, although the threat to the parliamentary system was now the impetus. As early as 1926, Prince Max von Baden praised Weber's support for a plebiscitary Reich presidency as a great political deed, especially because it offered a way out of the partisan splintering in the Weimar Republic. This theory offered the possibility that the chancellor could appeal to the people with the support of the Reich president. "Only in this way, clearly foreseen in the constitution, is

158. Cf. above, text at note 22.

159. *Der Hüter der Verfassung* (Tübingen, 1931), p. 89.

160. Ibid., p. 159.

161. Cf. Karl Dietrich Bracher, *Die Auflösung der Weimarer Republik* (Villingen, 1956), pp. 37 ff.

it possible at all for a leader to create a new party that supplants antiquated and lifeless factions."[162]

This same desire to shift the fulcrum of political decision from a Reichstag disabled by extremist parties to the Reich president was championed especially by the Bund zur Erneuerung des Reiches (Alliance for the Renewal of the Reich), consisting of numerous prominent personalities including members of the democratic Left.[163] This association championed an extension of the president's prerogatives without formally jeopardizing the framework of the existing constitution. With direct reference to Carl Schmitt, they sought to justify a government of the president with a cabinet that was not supported by the confidence of the Reichstag, at least until the Reichstag carried a formal vote of no confidence.[164] These theses led to the justification of presidential government on the basis of article 48, although this constitutional article was by no means the central justification. Like Schmitt, they saw the Reich president as the real "defender of the constitution" of the Reich, and by this they meant not the text of 11 August 1919 but the "real" constitution of the German people and of "its existence in the face of the forces of other nations that oppose it, even if in friendly competition; and its existence in and of itself as a self-contained body of people, with its own life, that ought not to fall apart through its own contradictions, but should, through the employment of all its people's strengths, be brought to its highest development. [It is] the Reich president's leadership task to dedicate all of his personal and political power to the goal of the unity of the German people and their preservation as a people among other peoples."[165]

Carl Schmitt, of course, here went one step farther in this direction, right up to the frontier that divided the Weimar Republic from an authoritarian Führer state and finally beyond it. Weber's principle of a "plebiscitary leadership democracy," whose concrete application had been his notion of the Reich president as a popularly elected monarch, was radicalized by Schmitt beyond recognition, in a way that Weber had never had in mind. Weber had wished to base the democratic Weimar

162. *Erinnerungen und Dokumente*, p. 128; cf. above, p. 377.

163. Bund zur Erneuerung des Reiches, *Die Rechte des deutschen Reichspräsidenten nach der Reichsverfassung* (Berlin, 1933). The signatories included, inter alia, Count von Bernstorff, former Reich War Minister Gessler, former Reich Chancellor Luther, Dr. Jarres, Count Roedern, many aristocrats and high civil servants, personalities from commercial circles, especially the banks.

164. Directly citing Carl Schmitt, "The Reich president should be the political leader," it states in ibid., p. 11: "by having the Reich president . . . elected directly by the people, they wished to endow him with a right to leadership at the frontiers of the constitution."

165. Ibid., p. 79.

state upon two complementary principles of legitimacy—the constitutional legality of the parliamentary legislative state and the "revolutionary legitimacy" of a popularly elected Reich president as charismatic leader. Carl Schmitt ignored the first form of legitimacy and accepted only plebiscitary-democratic legitimacy as a valid form of legitimacy. With the disappearance of the social preconditions of the classical parliamentary legislative state, the principle of legality as the characteristic form of legitimacy of rule became powerless. Any reference to the essential moral basis in which the principle of legality in a parliamentary constitutional state is rooted was abandoned. Legality was only understood tangentially in a formalistic sense. A law or any governmental action qualified as legal if it came into existence in a form that was formally constitutionally correct, and this was true even if the constitutional system was thereby attacked in its substance. The neutrality of Weimar democracy in regard to its own fundamental values was a typical result of a concept of legality that had deteriorated into pure formalism and functionalism and had thereby forfeited all its legitimizing power.[166] Moreover, the liberal-constitutional state system of legality was undermined by the use of emergency law and the degeneration of the concept of law as a result of the failure to distinguish between general laws that established norms and "Massnahmen" (measures) to implement such laws. This made it difficult to return to the classical form of the parliamentary legislative state.[167] Of the two diverse sources of legitimacy that competed in the Weimar constitution after the destruction of the basis of the liberal parliamentary legislative state, only plebiscitary legitimacy survived as the sole recognized "system of justification."[168]

The theory that both sources of legitimacy, formal constitutional legality and plebiscitary-democratic legitimacy, were "two manifestations of law" was a radical development of Max Weber's implicit dualism between rational legality and plebiscitary-charismatic legitimacy.[169] Carl Schmitt correctly pointed out that for Max Weber legality had sunk to the merely formal correctness of statutes in conformity with general norms, whose value was a matter of faith or custom (or both at the same time).[170] This is why Weber tried to give the Weimar state additional legitimacy through the preservation of the monarchy and, when that proved im-

166. *Legalität und Legitimität* (Berlin, 1932), pp. 14 f.

167. Ibid., p. 89.

168. Ibid., p. 93.

169. Ibid., p. 69: "The duality of the two modes of legislation and legislator is a duality of two different systems of justification, parliamentary legislation governmental legitimacy and plebiscitary-democratic legitimacy; between both possible competitors there is not only a competition of powers but also a struggle between two modes of law."

170. Ibid., p. 14; see also below, text at notes 40 ff., and the argument with Winckelmann, below in "Digression."

possible, through the plebiscitary-charismatic legitimacy of the Reich president. To that extent it was only a logical conclusion of Max Weber's plebiscitary leader concept, which was not in the least excluded by his conceptual phraseology, when Carl Schmitt took the position that the plebiscitary-democratic legitimacy of the Reich president—in contrast to the powerless, merely functionally developed legitimacy of the parliamentary legislative state—had to be made the crystallization point for a new "substantial order."[171] This would be supported by the provisions of the second part of the Weimar constitution. The pluralism of social and economic power groups that threatened the unity of the nation would be overcome.[172] In Schmitt's view, the means to do this lay in the "administrative state," which had already been employed by involving the emergency article 48 for ordinary legislation.[173] Schmitt of course avoided a more precise explanation of what this new order would look like. It is not difficult, however, to recognize the outlines of the authoritarian leader state that not long after was to sweep away the constitutional and democratic principles of the Weimar constitution.

Logically, Carl Schmitt discarded parliamentary institutions as such since they could no longer fulfill the task of the political integration of the people in the face of partisan and group pluralism. Max Weber had assigned the task of control of the administration and leadership selection to parliament, alongside of the Caesarist "dictator of the election battlefield." Carl Schmitt understood clearly that the concept of parliament as the first line of defense against the technical-rational bureaucracy of the administrative state had its origins in the situation of prewar Germany. With reason, he could not assign the same importance to these factors as Weber had done a generation ago.[174] He discarded in particular

171. *Legalität und Legitimität*, p. 98.

172. Cf. *Der Hüter der Verfassung*, p. 159: "By the fact that it makes the Reich president the center of a system of plebiscitary as well as neutral non-partisan structures and authorities, the current Reich constitution establishes a counterweight against the pluralism of social and economic power groups and guarantees the unity of the people, as a political whole, precisely on the basis of democratic principles." Cf. also ibid., p. 156.

173. Cf. *Legalität und Legitimität*, p. 17. Carl Schmitt's theory that the Reich president has the authority according to article 48, apart from the invalidation of the fundamental laws expressly mentioned in article 48, to take *measures* with unlimited power but not to issue legal ordinances with the power of law practically signifies a significant *limitation* of the emergency power, if in practice the distinction between the two is fluid. The so-called dominant theory in German legal discussions of the time, however, fully corresponded on this point with the tendencies that were already approved in the constitutional deliberations. Cf. the speech of Prussian Interior Minister Heine, who insisted on the words "and order," because economic directives, e.g., establishment of price controls, would otherwise not be possible. *Verhandlungen der Nationalversammlung*, vol. 327, p. 1336.

174. Cf. *Legalität und Legitimität*, p. 16: for Max Weber "the word 'bureaucracy' [has] . . . the central purpose of throwing into bold relief, in an ostensibly 'value-free' category, the technical-rationalistic-morally neutral machinery of an apparatus of officials that is

the function of parliament as a means for "leader selection," which even Max Weber had no longer been able to defend under the conditions of the proportional suffrage: "The idea of the selection of political leadership justifies no parliament consisting of several hundred party functionaries, but leads rather to the desire for political leadership based directly on the confidence of the masses. If such leadership is successfully found, then a new, powerful *representation* comes to the fore. But it is a representation *against* parliament, whose inherited presumption of being a representation is thereby terminated."[175] The contest between parliamentary and Caesaristic selection of leaders, to which Weber had drawn attention, was thus finally decided in favor of the latter form of selection. The logical conclusion of this theory was of course the authoritarian mass party of the authoritarian leadership state, successfully justifying its despotic rule on the plebiscitary acclamation of the masses, though actually achieved by demagogic and police state methods, which would now in reality unfold its "irresistible" power for evil.

To be sure, Weber himself never intended the notion of plebiscitary leadership to be employed against the party state, let alone as a means of justifying the totalitarian rule of the charismatic politician Hitler and the National Socialist party; nor did he anticipate any such occurrence in the foreseeable future.[176] Such perspectives lay beyond his horizon, and he never would have approved of what happened. He just wanted to bring the charismatic leadership concept to bear in the state and in the parties in order to check the rise of narrow-minded "politicians without calling" and thereby to enlist new energies in the German political arena that might help to restore Germany's power and reputation in the world. In particular, the institution of the Reich presidency was to serve this purpose. But political concepts have their own momentum. All too often they free themselves of their original framework and take on a form

---

primarily interested in functioning smoothly." Of course this view was utterly polemical in light of the German governmental situation before the war and created an incorrect contrast between the German career civil service, as something "unpolitical and technical," and parliament, which Max Weber held to be a means for the selection of political leaders and the instruction of the elite.

175. *Verfassungslehre*, pp. 314 f.

176. See Weber's theoretical remark in *Wirtschaft und Gesellschaft*, p. 168: "If a party becomes a closed association through the introduction of association regulation by the administrative staff—as, for example, the 'parte Guelfa' became finally in the thirteenth century Florentine statutes—then it is no longer a 'party' but a section of a political association." Parties like the NSDAP or the KPD or the SED in Communist states are no longer "parties" in the sense of Max Weber's concept of voluntary parties.

diametrically opposed to the motives of their creators.[177] The constitutional ideals that Weber had worked hard to get implemented in the Weimar constitution turned out to be not immune to distortion in an antidemocratic sense. This fact throws light on their controversial nature. The final task of this book will be to investigate the democratic substance of those ideals.

177. This very emphatic limitation apparently escaped those of my critics who disapproved of the demonstration of the continuation of the possibilities in Max Weber's theory of "plebiscitary führer democracy" by Carl Schmitt, because he did not do justice to the purity of Weber's views. Otherwise, the criticism would not have taken that emotional and even personally defamatory tone that was struck in particular by Loewenstein and Baumgarten at the time. It is not possible simply to close one's eyes to the objective problem that Weber's conception of a popularly elected president as a means of direct leadership selection outside of parliament could apparently be reinterpreted in an antiparliamentary, even totalitarian direction. We should ask, instead, how this was possible at all. Compare here my article "Plebiszitäre Führerdemokratie," pp. 311 ff.

10
From a Liberal Constitutional State to Plebiscitary Leadership Democracy

Our study of Max Weber and German politics has reached a point where it is necessary to look back at the totality of Weber's political thought.

When Max Weber took his first steps into politics, German liberalism, which he supported as a result of heritage and personal conviction, was in a period of decline. The rapid development of capitalism and the powerful economic upswing that began with the 1880s weakened the political activity of the German bourgeoisie. They began to favor the retention of the economic and social status quo over the goals of a progressive liberal policy. The struggle for the expansion of parliamentary rights and a responsible Reich government was postponed for the time being. The existing semiconstitutional system appeared not to limit either the citizen's pursuit of economic prosperity or his economic freedom of movement. Indeed, it appeared to provide protection against the revolutionary designs of the working classes and guaranteed a high degree of legal security and internal order, which permitted bourgeois capitalism to function without disturbance. The liberal bourgeoisie therefore contented themselves with the measure of political rights that they had won from Bismarck in 1867, and they directed their main efforts toward further developing and maintaining formal constitutionality in politics and administration. In addition, their political energies were directed against the allegedly autocratic leanings of Catholicism in the *Kulturkampf*. Rudolf von Gneist's political activities were paradigmatic for this position, especially that of the National Liberals of the age of Bismarck. Bismarck himself sought to promote the bourgeoisie's inclination to compromise with the existing order in the light of their own divisions as to their constitutional goals and the rising pressure from the Left. He knew how to employ the "red specter" to bully and to split the liberal movement. He repeatedly succeeded in creating conflict among the bourgeois forces between their liberal constitutional objectives and their desire to stabilize the social and economic position they believed to be seriously threatened.

The haute bourgeoisie especially had discarded the idea of the transformation of Germany according to those bourgeois liberal constitutional ideals that had prompted them to favor the 1848 revolution against the dynastic governments. They were increasingly inclined to accommodate themselves to the existing social system and to seek acceptance into the dominant feudal classes. An outward and internal process of feudalization gripped the German haute bourgeoisie and the educated and intellectual classes as well. They hoped to participate, at least in a modest way, in the luster and reputation of the crown and the officers' corps.

In this situation, Max Weber had passionately appealed to the German bourgeoisie to recall their own cultural and political ideals and, instead of devoting themselves to the most contemptible renegadism, to come home to their own class consciousness. Weber's famous study *The Protestant Ethic and the Spirit of Capitalism* can also be seen as an attempt to revitalize bourgeois-puritanical class consciousness. Weber exhorted the bourgeoisie not to accommodate themselves to the privileged class of the Prussian nobility, as was the case in Prussia under Miquel's aegis. With class-conscious resolve they should enter the struggle against the aristocracy, whose pretensions to leadership had been outstripped by economic developments. With a liberal social policy, not in the Manchesterian sense but in the manner of Brentanoist social liberalism, Weber hoped to be able to win the support of the working class in the struggle against conservatism, guided by the firm and accurate conviction that the bourgeoisie and the proletariat would be able to make common cause for many decades to come.

Weber sought to overcome the inferiority complex and the security mentality of the bourgeoisie by offering them, as a new positive goal, a German liberal world power policy. In the face of the Conservatives' pretensions that they were the real defenders of the Bismarckian inheritance, Weber asserted that only a national imperialist policy, supported by the economically dominant strata of German society, would genuinely follow the path of Bismarck's great national accomplishment, the establishment of the German Reich as a great power. With Bismarck, he wished to lead the struggle against his false paladins who had opportunistically and in cowardly fashion transferred their allegiance to the "new sun" in 1890. For Weber, Prussian conservatism was not only the refuge of domestic reaction but also the chief brake on Germany's rise to economic and political power in the world.

In 1895, Weber therefore believed that the most decisive and fateful issue for Germany was whether or not the German bourgeoisie would finally have the maturity and the will to assume the political leadership of the nation that its economic development seemed to dictate, now that the control of governmental affairs had been transferred from Bismarck's hands to those of conservative bureaucrats. National Liberalism's stagnation, which Weber had observed at first hand in his parents' home, aroused his contempt. He called for energetic politics with the goal of bringing about the parliamentarization of the German constitution and, especially, the removal of the Prussian three-class suffrage, the constitutional bastion that alone permitted the Prussian nobility to retain their privileged position and their indirect influence on Reich policy. Weber attempted to inoculate liberalism with a positive relationship to power, and to great political leaders; the liberals ought once and for all to forsake their negative attitude toward the state.

Weber championed the parliamentarization and democratization of imperial Germany in order to remove the conservative, feudal classes from power. The specific democratic ideals that gave the parliamentary constitutional state its legitimacy and higher dignity over and against other forms of government played a lesser roll for him. He called, to be sure, for a liberal constitution, in which the citizens would be given a fair say in the determination of political affairs, if only for cultural reasons. The lack of full civil liberties in Germany impaired the image of German culture abroad, where a much higher degree of personal liberty had long ago been achieved. Weber could say emphatically that only "master peoples" (*Herrenvölker*), that is, peoples who had established their domestic affairs on the basis of liberty, had a legitimate claim to a great world policy. At the same time, he increasingly deemphasized the specific ideal values that justify the principle of the free self-determination of a sovereign people. The universal process of "demagification of the world" did not stop at liberal and democratic theories.

Max Weber considered the natural-law justification of democracy and the liberal constitutional state to be outmoded and an insufficient basis for a modern theory of government. The "rights of mankind" were a product of religious sectarianism and were in essence "extremely rationalized fanaticisms."[1] But who today is capable of being "a 'sect' man *himself*?" he asked.[2] Certainly he emphasized that no one would be capable of living "today" without the achievements "of the age of 'human rights,'" without the degree of "'individualist' freedom of movement" that the sects' "*radical* idealism" had created.[3] But he believed that the

1. *Wirtschaft und Gesellschaft*, p. 2.
2. Letter to Harnack of 5 February 1906.
3. *Pol. Schr.*, p. 333, similarly the letter to Harnack of January 12, 1905: "We must never forget that we owe things to the sects that *none* of us could today do without: freedom

axioms of natural law were no longer providing clear directions for a just social order under the conditions of higher capitalism.[4] He also felt that "the old individualist principles of 'inalienable' human rights" had lost much of their power of persuasion under the conditions of modern industrial society.[5] He did not hesitate, on occasion, to set them aside.[6]

Max Weber criticized the liberal theory of the "constitutional state" mercilessly and without illusions. He rejected its natural law foundations. "The axioms of natural law [had] . . . lost their capacity to act as a foundation for law."[7] He considered the development of pure legal positivism to be irresistible. "The growing estimation is that currently valid law is merely rational law, which can therefore be reconstructed freely according to purpose-rational calculations, as it lacks any intrinsic sanctity." This was an inevitable course.[8] The legitimacy of a legal order was no longer supported by a positive belief in fundamental, "pre-eminently valid" norms on the order of natural law. Moreover, the sharp contrast that existed between formal and material natural law norms had shaken the validity of natural law theory.[9] Weber pointed to the classical liberal theory of the constitutional state as a system of generally valid formal norms, as the specific legal form that best suited bourgeois capitalism. "Freedom of contract," thus "the principle of free competition," was among the basic axioms of natural law. Formal rationality of the legal system was a general precondition of bourgeois capitalist calculation and therefore in the interest of the bourgeois classes. These axioms generally worked in favor of anyone economically powerful who was interested in the free exploitation of that power in his own self-interest, while at the same time they frequently offended the "substantive ideals of justice" on account of their abstract and formal character.[10] A proletarian society would have no direct interest in such a formal rational legal order and would, given the opportunity, give preference to the principles of material rationality, for example the "right to work" and the "right to full employment." Such a society would, if possible, also replace formalistic

---

of conscience and the most elementary 'human rights', which today are self-evident possessions. *Only radical* idealism could create this." Also *Wirtschaft und Gesellschaft*, pp. 732 ff.

4. "Zur Lage," p. 118: "These 'natural law' axioms offer few distinct directions for a social and economic program; just as they too were not at all distinctly engendered by any economic conditions alone—least of all the 'modern ones."

5. Ibid.

6. Cf. above, chap. 2, note 25.

7. *Wirtschaft und Gesellschaft*, p. 502. The "latent influence of implicit natural law axioms upon legal practice" here appear to be something to root out!

8. Ibid., p. 513.

9. Ibid., pp. 501 f.

10. Ibid., p. 470; still sharper, p. 455.

justice with a Qadi justice that decided according to substantive legal principles.[11]

It is therefore no accident that Max Weber—as has been justly pointed out—never employed the classical concept of the "constitutional state" (Rechtsstaat), which had been one of the chief weapons in the political arsenal of nineteenth-century bourgeois liberalism in a positive sense. This concept had not accidentally attracted Bismarck's sarcastic mockery about this "artificial expression discovered by Robert von Mohl." Weber indeed had substituted the concept of legality.[12] For Weber, the concept of the constitutional state had forfeited its validity and dignity for two reasons: its class character and the invalidation of the belief in natural law on which it was based.

The classical democratic theory of popular sovereignty suffered the same fate. In Weber's view, this theory ignored the fundamental fact that any kind of rule, whatever specific form it took, was exercised by an oligarchy of leaders. The various types of rulership differed only in the manner in which leaders were selected. Weber believed that popular self-government was only possible in the form of direct democracy and that could occur only in small political units.[13] He did not share the specific ideals associated with popular sovereignty, namely, the "minimization of rule" and the rejection of "rule by men over men" in favor of the administration of things. In his view, this neither could be realized nor was desirable. His democratic concept of the state hinged upon his wish to see the external power of the state increased as much as possible, and accordingly he also welcomed a strengthening of state power internally. He emphasized that the policy of major states can never exhaust itself with the mere administration of things; it has to "rule." National power politics and mere administration were irreconcilable contradictions.[14] With the utmost intellectual rationalism, Weber departed from the principle of the democratic idea of the free self-organization of the people. "Any thought . . . of removing the rule of men over men through even the most sophisticated forms of 'democracy'" is "utopian."[15] Democratization could only have a precise meaning, if any, as the "minimization of the ruling power of the 'professional administrators'"—the ruling staff—"in favor of the most 'direct rule of the demos,' which means, in

11. Cf. ibid., pp. 470, 500. A very penetrating demonstration of this conflict between "bourgeois" formal law and "proletarian" "just" law is present in Brecht's *Caucasian Chalk Circle*, flying in the face of the "legal"-praxis of the DDR.

12. Winckelmann, *Gesellschaft und Staat in der verstehenden Soziologie Max Webers* (Berlin: Duncker und Humblot, 1957,) pp. 35 f., in any event without exhausting the significance of this fact.

13. *Wirtschaft und Gesellschaft*, pp. 169 f.

14. *Pol. Schr.*, p. 289.

15. Letter to Michels of 4 August 1908, after a copy in the Weber papers.

practice, their current party leaders."[16] The demos, as an undifferentiated mass, never rules by itself; it is ruled. Only the leader at the head of the administrative staff changes, and then only through the action of rival individual party leaders. Max Weber wrote with sober cynicism to Robert Michels who passionately struggled with the question of how the ethical-political postulate of popular sovereignty could be reconciled with the reality of the inexorable rise of ever new oligarchies: "But oh, how much resignation you will still have to face! Such notions as the 'will of the people,' the true will of the people, ceased to exist for me years ago; they are *fictions*. It is as if we were to speak of the will of the shoe buyer who has to decide what skills the shoemaker should employ. The shoe buyer knows, to be sure, *where* the shoe *pinches*, but he never knows how it could be made to fit."[17] Weber made no attempt to save even the ideal core of the classical democratic theory under the conditions of modern mass democracy. He replaced the postulate of the free self-determination of the people, which, since Rousseau, had bestowed a special dignity on the democratic idea, with the principle of a *formally* free choice of leaders. The ordinary citizens were no longer supposed to actively participate as responsible individuals in the creation of political community life. They acclaim their leaders thanks to their confidence in their leadership qualities. Hence, democracy is conceived as a functionalist system that gives the people no more and no less than the guarantee that the direction of governmental affairs is always in the hands of leaders who, at least formally, are optimally qualified for this task. There will no longer be any question of active participation by the people, in any form, in the material formulation of the political objectives to be pursued by the community. This will be the sole responsibility of the political leaders, who create the necessary following for the realization of their goals through their demagogic qualities. The democratic constitutional state was peceived essentially as a technical organization for the purpose of training political leaders and enabling them to rise to power and to rule.[18]

Max Weber therefore favored a parliamentary constitutional system for Germany, not so much because he expected it to secure a maximum degree of free self-determination for the citizens or a *Rechtsstaat*-like constitutional order, but above all for reasons of *national* policy. He wished for a powerful national state that was supported internally by the rising classes of the German nation and was therefore capable of great *foreign policy* achievements. Lukács's pointed judgment that for Weber

16. *Wirtschaft und Gesellschaft*, p. 576.

17. Letter to Michels of 4 August 1908.

18. Compare here Wilhelm Hennis's sharp critique of Weber's technical concept of the state: "Zum Problem der deutschen Staatsanschauung," *Vierteljahreshefte für Zeitgeschichte* 7 (1959): no. 1, pp. 19 ff.

democratization was only a "technical measure to help achieve a better functioning imperialism" is very difficult to quarrel with.[19] Weber himself repeatedly emphasized that parliamentarization and democratization were for him principally a *means* to create the domestic political preconditions of a German world policy. "As far as I'm concerned, forms of government are techniques like any other machinery," he admitted.[20] It was very characteristic of Weber, in his statement on the question of value judgments for the Verein für Sozialpolitik in the year 1913, to comment: "He who would have 'national' power interests as an 'ultimate' goal ought to consider an absolutist as much as a radical democratic constitution, depending on the situation, as the (relatively) best suited 'means,' and it would be quite ridiculous to regard a change in the viewpoint about these purely functional governmental mechanisms(!) as a change in the 'ultimate' viewpoint of a person."[21] This was Weber's own view: he consistently subordinated the democratic constitutional ideal to the interests of national power. He confessed with no pangs of conscience that, as far as he was concerned, Germany's power interests towered over all questions of governmental form. To this extent, Weber's staunch belief in national power was accompanied by a dismissal of the internal value content of the democratic idea and prepared the way for a purely functional concept of democratic rule. Democracy ceased to be a form of government with special dignity. Its chief advantage lay in its greater "efficiency" in the field of foreign policy. It guaranteed, at its best, that minimum of support by the citizens without which a powerful policy would be impossible under the conditions of modern mass society, especially in times of crisis.

In Weber's view, the task and purpose of parliamentary democracy could essentially be reduced to two functions: the selection of political leaders and the control of the purely technical administrative bureaucracy, which was not to take a leadership role. Weber thereby hypostatized the concrete conclusion that his analysis contemporary German policy had reached. He viewed the failure of German world policy to have resulted primarily from the fact that, after Bismarck's fall, the leadership of German affairs had fallen to pure bureaucrats. Moreover, as a result of Bismarck's antiparliamentary demogoguery and the chronic powerlessness of the Reichstag, a complete vacuum in political lead-

19. *Die Zerstörung der Vernunft* (Berlin, 1954), p. 488.

20. Letter to Ehrenberg of 16 July 1917, *Pol. Schr.* 1, pp. 469 f.: "The governmental form is all the same to me, *if* only politicians govern the country and not dilettantish fops like Wilhelm II and his kind."

21. Now in *Werk und Person*, p. 122. Cf. *Wissenschaftslehre*, p. 512, where the word "national" is replaced by the neutral formulation "governmental" power interests and the words "as means" are inserted after "functional governmental mechanisms."

ership existed. The situation in parliament-governed England seemed very different to him. Had the English parliament not produced those politicians that had led a third of the world, often voluntarily, to accept the suzerainty of the British crown? Politicians, not officials, ought to be at the head of the state, and this could be achieved through parliamentarization. Only tough parliamentary work, through constant struggle for recognition and a share in decision making and the perpetual soliciting of support and votes could train political leaders. Only powerful parliaments were in a position to select capable leaders. However, Weber by no means shared the view that parliament, as a free decision-making body, should prescribe policy for the government, being in principle an executive committee delegated from its ranks. Weber's notion of political leadership was, as we have seen, diametrically opposed to this notion. In his view the leading politician ought not to be the executive organ of the will of the parliamentary majority but something qualitatively different: a leader; that is, he must not be limited by a confining structure. He must create and articulate parliament's will through his influence and his demagogic powers to convince. He must win support in parliament for his personal goals. If he cannot achieve this, then he should resign. Hence, in principle parliament has a largely passive role. The great politician must prove his leadership qualities to the parliament. Parliament, in turn, has to remind him of his specific responsibilities. Parliament has only one genuine function to fulfill by itself: the control of the administration. Weber put unusual emphasis on this function, as we have seen. His exaggerated support of the right of inquiry was characteristic of this emphasis.

The dialectical antithesis of Weber's theory—that with the growth of bureaucratization and the reduction to uniformity of all social relations the social structures would increasingly petrify—was the limitation of the tasks of parliamentary democracy to leadership selection and administrative control. Democratic rule was a natural enemy of bureaucracy and therefore a means to keep at bay the development of an "iron cage of serfdom in the future." Weber sought a point of departure here for a new ideal foundation for democracy that broke completely with classical natural law theory and proclaimed the plebiscitary-charismatic leadership position of the leading politician.

Weber accepted it as a given that the universal process of bureaucratization had led to fundamental changes in the way decisions are brought about in parliamentary democracy. Above all, Ostrogorsky and Bryce had described the rise of the modern bureaucratic party machines and had drawn wide-ranging conclusions about the essence of modern party-government mass democracy. Max Weber accepted these findings and tried to apply them to German constitutional reality.

He was one of the first to see that the idealistic basis of the liberal constitutional state had been shaken both by the creation of rigidly organized party machines and by the rise to primacy of purely material interests. The parliament ceased to be a place for free rational debates and deliberations; it became the locus of struggles between the parties for public power. The members of parliament lost their character as independent, freely elected personalities; parliament was populated by party functionaries and representatives of various interests. The mass of the citizens, who according to liberal-democratic theory should in principle have participated equally in the formulation of the political will of the nation, were divided into a few politically active and an overwhelming number of passive elements.[22] The individual citizen was incapable of any real influence outside of mass organizations, without significant financial means, or without personal contacts. His participation in the political process was limited to periodically casting a vote for one or another party on the basis of its election promises.[23] This was in fact a *plebiscitary* decision, all the more so as proportional suffrage replaced majority suffrage; now the choice was merely among various party machines. Political decisions were no longer made in parliament but inside the parties. The leaders of the party machines determined, with attention to the reaction of the masses, the direction of policy. The party apparatus concerned itself with assuring the necessary "yes" of the people.[24]

Weber drew radical conclusions from this diagnosis of modern mass democracy. These conclusions departed far more than Ostrogorsky's theses from classical democratic theory. He insisted that under these conditions only genuinely qualified, independent personalities that were capable of establishing goals for the bureaucratic apparatus of rule were called to political leadership. He thereby gave his theory of democratic rule a distinct personal-plebiscitary emphasis. The charismatically qualified leader should win support and acclamation from the masses with the use of the tools of mass demagoguery and in this way put himself at the head of a party machine. The party machine was not a goal in itself, but a tool in the hands of the great politician to gain the support of the people for his political goals. Weber recognized the danger of the "castration of the charisma" of the born politician by bureaucratic party machines.[25] He nevertheless believed that the more a party was organized like a machine,

22. *Pol. Schr.*, p. 401.

23. Ibid., p. 529.

24. Cf. Gerhard Leibholz, "Die Auflösung der liberalen Demokratie," *Deutschland und das autoritäre Staatsbild* (Munich, 1933), pp. 51 ff.; and *Der Strukturwandel der modernen Demokratie* (Karlsruhe, 1952). Leibholz especially stressed the plebiscitary character of modern democracy.

25. Cf. *Wirtschaft und Gesellschaft*, p. 677; *Pol. Schr.*, pp. 401 f.

the more it would require a great leader and the more it would be inclined to support one. Only a strong leader could win the support of the masses in an election by virtue of his personal charisma. Rule by a charismatic leader with a bureaucratic machine appeared to Max Weber to be the ultimate conclusion of the development of modern mass democracy. He regarded Gladstone's great personal victory in the *home rule* election of 1886 as the first major example of a plebiscitary leader election in the history of modern mass democracy.[26] The future seemed to belong to the "rule of the dictator of the election battlefield."[27] He therefore quite consciously called for a plebiscitary leadership democracy.

One other important consideration led Weber to such radical conclusions. Weber recognized the advance of material interest groups in the field of politics. But he significantly retained his ideal that only economically independent, "interestless" individuals, who lived for and not by politics, should be called to political leadership.[28] He repeatedly emphasized that politics was an "undertaking of *vested* interests," but added that he did not thereby mean "those material interests that in different degrees influenced every form of governmental order" but "those political interests that strive for political power and responsibility with the goal of realizing specific political ideas."[29] Through his demagogic attributes, in the positive sense, the genuine politician could win support and acclamation, as Weber hoped, and thus bypass the interplay of mere material interests. A parliament made up of representatives of interests, in contrast, tended to "leaderlessness"; for representatives of interests, "national policy" would be "Hecuba."

In Weber's view, politics had a basically voluntarist nature, unlike administration, which operated according to strict rules and competencies. For him, uninhibited competition, in principle, of political leaders for power and responsibility was a precondition of any genuinely responsible policy. To be a leader meant to act out of free, independent personal responsibility. Functionaries or delegates of political or social associations were by definition not political leaders. Actions tied to directives, no matter what their substantive content, were basically not reconcilable with a politician's responsibility, according to Weber's rigoristic theory. It was not accidental that he insisted on the principle of voluntarism even in his definition of the concept of parties. Although he himself demonstrated that the modern mass parties with their almost indestructible apparatuses had shattered the old ways that political

26. Cf. *Pol. Schr.*, pp. 534 ff.; *Wirtschaft und Gesellschaft*, pp. 677 f.
27. The term was applied to Gladstone in *Pol. Schr.*, p. 535.
28. Cf. ibid., p. 389.
29. Ibid., pp. 401, 528 f.; also *Wirtschaft und Gesellschaft*, pp. 167, 175.

opinion was shaped, he pointed to the parties as "social organizations based on (formally) free recruitment."[30]

But he saw very well and with great concern that increasing bureaucratization and "apparatusization" of all political and social associations could gradually stifle the voluntarism of politics and that the dealings of rigid interest associations and professional representatives threatened to replace the free competition of parties for support among the public. In the misty future, he envisaged a socially petrified social order emerging that would finally stifle all free initiative and individual freedom of movement in the field of politics also. Weber feared what Hans Freyer since has described as the emergence of "secondary systems" that functionalize and segment modern man.[31] Weber was even gloomier about the future, which seemed to promise a return to the ritualistic government of late antiquity. In spite of the truth contained in this prognosis from the standpoint of universal history, Weber still grossly overestimated the tendency toward bureaucratization in his own day. He anticipated a far stronger solidification in social relationships in the near term than actually occurred.

In the light of the bureaucratization of all political associations and the increasing rise of organized material interests in the field of policy, it appeared to Weber that only the personal-plebiscitary choice of leaders and the use of methods of demagogic mass influence could any longer provide for free and responsible political leadership. "We have the choice of leadership democracy with 'machine' or leaderless democracy, which means the leadership of 'career politicians' without calling and without the internal charismatic qualities that makes a leader," Weber declared in February 1919 in his now famous lecture "Politics as a Vocation."[32] He wished for a solution that would permit the rise of free and gifted leaders in a society dominated by party machines, corporate bureaucracies, and interest groups. His solution was the rule of great demagogues on the strength of their personal qualities. He regarded the extent of democracy as restricted by the conditions of modern industrial mass society. This was the only means through which the universal process of bureaucratization could be effectively braked and a minimum of individual freedom of movement, in the common rather than the political meaning of the word, could be protected.

Weber did not hesitate to carry the plebiscitary leadership concept to its extreme conclusions. He did not stop at the thesis that the masses were "politically passive" and that politicians set goals and then created sup-

30. *Wirtschaft und Gesellschaft*, p. 167.

31. Hans Freyer, *Theorie des gegenwärtigen Zeitalters* (Stuttgart, 1955,) especially pp. 103 f.

32. *Pol. Schr.*, p. 544.

port for their realization through the employment of demagogic methods. He was prepared to reduce the participation of the masses in the political process to a minimum—to the acclamation of the leader thanks only to their confidence in his *formal* leadership qualities. The people followed the leader because of his charismatic qualities and only secondarily because he pursued certain objective goals that corresponded to their wishes or, to be more precise, of whose desirability he had convinced them. Max Weber did not consider "plebiscitary leader democracy" to belong to the legitimacy type of "legal rule" but viewed it as an anti-authoritarian reinterpretation of "charismatic rule."[33] An essential characteristic of charismatic rule, in Weber's theory, was the necessity of constant "review." If the charismatic leader failed, then his charisma had the "chance to disappear."[34] As a result, he would lose his following. Conversely, the people owed recognition and support to those who were charismatically qualified.[35] Weber concluded that the supporters of the democratic statesman, who ruled, in his view, through the charisma of his "great demagoguery" in the ancient sense of the word, had to obey him "blindly, . . . as long" as he was "success[ful]."[36] As long as he ruled, the people ought not to interfere. Only after he had resigned, could they "judge." "The leader has made mistakes—to the gallows with him!"[37] This was especially true of the party machines: "The leadership of parties by plebiscitary rulers means the 'depersonalization' of the followers, their spiritual proletarianization, one could say. In order to be useful as an apparatus for the leader they must be blindly obedient machines in the American sense and not beholden to the vanities and pretensions of party functionaries. . . . That is the price that must be paid for the leadership of leaders."[38]

We, who have experienced the rule of authoritarian parties that perfectly fulfilled these conditions favored by Weber in a technical sense, and believe in the possibility of a genuine party democracy, must have reservations about such opinions. They seem to offer the real danger of the transformation of plebiscitary-democratic rule into charismatic authoritarian rule. But they also show quite clearly what Weber was aiming at. Plebiscitary leadership democracy appeared to be the best possible

33. Compare *Wirtschaft und Gesellschaft*, pp. 155 f. For a systematic discussion of the question of the place of plebiscitary democracy in Weber's typology of the "three pure types of legitimate rule," cf. my book *The Age of Bureaucracy*, pp. 72 ff.

34. *Wirtschaft und Gesellschaft*, p. 140.

35. Ibid., pp. 140, 156.

36. *Pol. Schr.*, p. 348, cited above, chap. 6, text at note 180. In the original sense, the formulation is related to the English whip technique, but in Weber's theory it takes on a far more general meaning than a mere parliamentary technique.

37. From Weber's famous talk with Ludendorff in May 1919, *Lebensbild*, p. 665.

38. *Pol. Schr.*, p. 544.

way to bring a new elite gifted for leadership to power under the conditions of a society now dominated by powerful bureaucratic organizations. This new elite would take over the role once held by the conservative nobility, which by now had forfeited its leadership qualifications through the loss of its "unassailable position." This was the class of the "professional politicians" with an inner calling, who through their charismatic qualities thrust themselves above the mass of the passive citizens.[39] With this theory of democratic elites, Weber came remarkably close to Pareto's theory of the permanent rotation of leadership elites.

Max Weber was himself fully aware that plebiscitary democracy would transcend the bases of the traditional parliamentary legislative system, even if it formally made use of its organs and institutions. The principle of *legal* democratic rule, according to the legislative decisions of a body representative of the will of the people, within the limits of a constitutional order supported by normative ideals, would be replaced by the plebiscitary-charismatic leader idea: "'Plebiscitary democracy,' the most important type of leadership democracy, is in its genuine sense a kind of charismatic rule that hides behind the *form* of rule through the will of the ruled and shelters the legitimacy derived from it. The leader (demagogue) rules in fact on the basis of the support and confidence of his political following to his *person* as such."[40] Plebiscitary charismatic legitimacy displaces the rational legitimacy of the parliamentary-constitutional state. The latter becomes a technical means to assure the rule of charismatic elites permanently.

We have already discussed the question of the sources of legitimacy of the parliamentary-democratic constitutional state in connection with Weber's call for a plebiscitary Reich president. It appears that Weber wished to introduce the charismatic form of legitimacy into the constitutional system of the Weimar state because he did not have a high estimation of the legitimizing power of mere rational legality under the conditions of modern mass democracy. If we recall that for Weber the democratic form of government represented above all a technique for producing leaders and that the original natural law foundation no longer possessed any supportive norm-setting power for him, then it is not surprising that legitimacy supported by legality based on faith, the typical form of legitimacy of the pure parliamentary constitutional state, took on a purely formal, positivistic character. "The most familiar form of legitimacy today is the faith in *legality*: submission to *formally* correct statutes

39. Cf. also Carlo Antoni, *Vom Historismus zur Soziologie* (Stuttgart, 1950), pp. 178 f.

40. *Wirtschaft und Gesellschaft*, p. 156. It is not evident what *other* types of leadership democracy Weber had in mind. Compare also my discussion in "Plebiszitäre Führerdemokratie," pp. 308 ff.

that have been enacted in the usual form."[41] This purely formal respect for governmental and administrative acts, not oriented to a material order of values, was the major characteristic of the modern "legal rule through statutes: . . . The basic notion is: that any legal system whatever can be created or changed through discretionary statutes, provided they are enacted in a formally correct way."[42] The modern constitutional state thereby lost its specific dignity founded on a system of inalienable and unalterable constitutional and democratic norms. The constitution was reduced to a system of practical "rules of the game" of merely de facto value.[43] All "intrinsic sanctity" was lost.[44] Weber emphasized that this opportunistic orientation to a system of norms of formal character was not a sufficient basis for genuine agreement on legitimacy; in addition, there also had to be a belief that it either had been enacted by a corporate body viewed as legitimate[45] or that it had been decreed by rulers deemed legitimate.[46] But all intrinsic values thereby retreat into the background. The constitution becomes an expedient system of rules of a formal character within which the politicians by profession carry on their struggle among themselves for popularity and power with the use of demagogic methods.

Alongside of this type of a purely expedient rational basis for legal rule by statutes was the type that was founded upon a system of norms of a value-rational nature. The old democracy based on natural law was the chief example of this type.[47] But Weber personally did not believe any more in the realizability of this type of democratic rule of law. With the advance of the universal process of rationalization, all supposedly objective values that would have served as the basis of such a system seemed to melt away. Max Weber honestly believed it impossible to replace the old postulates of natural law with new ones. The distinction in principle between the empirical sphere and the sphere of values, and the personal

41. *Wirtschaft und Gesellschaft*, p. 19.

42. "Die drei reinen Typen der Legitimität," now in *Wirtschaft und Gesellschaft*, p. 551.

43. The concept "rules of the game" from *Wissenschaftslehre*, pp. 337 ff. Compare here Carl Schmitt, *Verfassungslehre*, p. 307: In Weber's view, parliamentarism was a "practical 'rules of the game.'" Freyer then (*Theorie des gegenwärtigen Zeitalters*, pp. 93 ff.) made the term "rules of the game" a fundamental concept in his description of the essence of "secondary systems."

44. "Inner sacredness," see *Wirtschaft und Gesellschaft*, p. 513.

45. Ibid., p. 19, para. 7 d alpha.

46. Ibid., p. 19, para. 7 d beta.

47. Cf. ibid.: "The purest type of the ethical-rational value is described by 'natural law.' However limited it always is in relationship to its ideal claims, we cannot deny that its logically derived propositions may significantly influence action; and these propositions should be distinguished as much from revealed law as from statuted law as well as traditional law." One can observe the relatively low estimation here that Weber had for natural law.

nature of the latter sphere, excluded the empirical-normative establishment of distinct constitutional principles in a form that would hold the support of all citizens. Weber believed that the victory of "formalistic juristic rationalism" in the occident was irreversible.[48] The "legitimacy of rule" had been replaced by the "legality of general, formally correct legislated and proclaimed rules" that were viewed as expedient. In his view, the constitutional structure of modern rule was only conceivable on the grounds of rational *expediency*. A constitution had a normative character, not because of the values that were expressly included in its text, but as a result of positive legal statutes by an organ considered to be legitimate. Weber's explicit comparison between the legal forms of rule in the state, in local government, and in private capitalist business is demonstration enough.[49] In this instance, where were the imminent rational values that legitimatized the rule of the businessman over the workers?

It was only because Weber was concerned with *formal* recognition of statutes and *formal* correctness of governance on the basis of such statutes that he could point to bureaucratic rule as the "purest type of legal rule."[50] Only here in the formally correct carrying out of administrative tasks according to prescribed formal rules was bureaucratic rule superior to any other form of rule. In contrast, a rule of law based upon rational values must assure that the bureaucracy materially and not merely formally administers and governs according to the norms and values upon which it is based. A less technically advanced administration can be more satisfactory when ethical norms are recognized materially than a highly specialized one.[51] The conflict between democracy and bureaucracy rests essentially upon this dualism between formal legalism and material realization of values. Weber himself repeatedly emphasized that bureaucracy always had to be a bitter enemy of democracy. For him, however, the problem of leadership dominated the foreground. His chief concern was for bureaucracy to carry out the goals set by the leader and not detract from the effectiveness of his value-setting charisma.

For this reason it was possible for Carl Schmitt to use Weber as a chief witness for his thesis that faith in legality of the parliamentary legislative state had to a great extent hardened into mere formalism.[52] In a constitu-

48. *Gesammelte Aufsätze zur Religionssoziologie*, vol. 1 (Tübingen, 1920), pp. 273 f.

49. *Wirtschaft und Gesellschaft*, p. 552.

50. "Die drei reinen Typen der legitimen Herrschaft," ibid., p. 551.

51. Weber even referred to this fact incidentally, when he described the American citizens who preferred a corrupt *spoils system* to an expert bureaucracy because they did not wish to be ruled by the latter.

52. Winckelmann's attempt (in his study *Legitimität und Legalität in Max Webers Herrschaftssoziologie* [Tübingen, 1952]) to prove the contrary, seems to us to have failed. In our view, it is impossible to say that Weber only attributed legitimizing power to *ethical-*

tional system that had taken on the character of merely formal rules of the game, "internal limitations of legitimacy" of an *ethical* character could not exist.[53] For Weber, certainly, democracy was a technically expedient apparatus whose meaning lay in the fact that it assured the optimal contemporary form of leadership selection and that it set effective limits on bureaucracy.[54] There were, in any event, no immanent ethical norms standing in the way of a changeover to other forms of typical leadership selection, as long as these were in a position to produce *formally* qualified leaders. For this reason, Weber had no reservations about the replacement of parliamentary forms of selection by Caesarist ones.

Weber not only believed in what he viewed as the unavoidable pure formal legalism of modern rational government. At the same time, he described its weak legitimizing powers in contrast to other sources of legitimacy. He pointed to the fact that every *legal* government required enhancement through elements of traditional *and* charismatic legitimacy. "The existence of *legal* governmental relations rests, insofar as belief in legitimacy plays a role in its stability, on mixed intrinsic principles. Traditional habits and 'prestige' (charisma) join with the—also habitual—belief in the significance of formal legality. Disturbance of one of these principles through untraditional demands on the governed, an extraordinary misfortune that undermines prestige, or injury to the usual correct forms, undermines the belief in legitimacy to the same degree."[55] The charisma of the rulers, the "normativity of what exists," and tradition join together and to a considerable degree support the acceptance of legitimacy on the basis of a formal belief in legality. The idea of a substantive order of values, in the sense of eternal principles and fundamental rights based on fundamental rational values that are capable through their own force of legitimizing government in the framework of a democratic constitutional state, lay, in contrast, outside the circle that Weber deemed realizable under the conditions of modern demystified

---

rational-based legality. Cf. in this connection "Digression," below. Weber argued that "*arbitrary law* [could] be *statuted* through agreement or rational imposition, either ethical-rational, expedient (or both)." *Wirtschaft und Gesellschaft*, p. 125. Schmitt correctly argued that *arbitrary* law could not be statuted in a formally correct manner on the basis of ethical-rational principles, but only such law that did not materially contradict fundamental ethical norms. Ethical neutrality in relation to inherent basic values, which is expressed in such positivistic and formalistic legalism, signifies no more and no less than the collapse of the legitimizing system of the parliamentary legislative state. See *Legalität und Legitimität*, pp. 14 ff.

53. Winckelmann postulates such "internal limitations of legitimacy," without sufficient basis, as Weber's third type of legitimacy. See below, p. 452.

54. Compare also Wilhelm Hennis's critique, "Zum Problem der deutschen Staatsanschauung, pp. 20 f.

55. *Wirtschaft und Gesellschaft*, p. 556.

mass society. He therefore sought to combine the value-free functionalism of the parliamentary constitutional state in its democratic form with the value-setting charisma of plebiscitary leadership democracy. A leader's plebiscitary-charismatic legitimacy, supported "formally and fictitiously" by the free confidence of the masses in him, would expand a legitimacy based upon belief in legality.[56] If, however, the leader consciously employed irrational methods of popular appeal, the rational legality of the parliamentary constitutional state would be further undermined. The legitimizing force of the essentially emotional belief in the leadership qualities of any ruler basically contradicted the essence of rational government according to the law.

Here we encounter the ambiguity in Max Weber's democratic ideology. It sought to combine, with a grand gesture, the opposing extremes of rational legal rule employing the tools of a fully developed bureaucratic governing staff, and rule exercised by great charismatic leadership personalities who governed by virtue of their personal qualities on a Caesarist-plebiscitary basis. Weber's theory was rooted in his bitter experience with the lack of genuine political leaders in the Germany of his day, together with his recognition that the bureaucratization of political and social activities increasingly blocked the rise to power of independent leaders. This experience led him to favor a "leadership democracy." Democracy was reduced to the rule of leaders who, in theory, were freely elected but in fact were elected by virtue of their personal demagogic qualities. Weber did not question the constitutional system of parliamentary democracy. In contradiction to its original sense, however, he conceived of it as a technical apparatus that brought leaders to power and then served them as an apparatus of rule, as long as these leaders were successful. He discarded the rationalistic idea of equality of all citizens within an egalitarian democracy in favor of a theory of leadership that arose from charisma. He rejected the idea of free self-determination and self-organization of the sovereign people. In practice, he favored the rule of an oligarchy of charismatically qualified leaders within a formally democratic constitutional system.

Max Weber's views notably influenced Schumpeter's well-known theory of democracy as a "competition for political leadership."[57] Although Schumpeter never credited Weber, there is no doubt that he adopted essential arguments from Weber's work.[58] Schumpeter also saw the real

56. Ibid., p. 156.

57. Joseph A. Schumpeter, *Kapitalismus, Sozialismus und Demokratie* (Bern, 1946), p. 427.

58. Compare also Heuss, "Max Weber in seiner Gegenwart," *Pol. Schr.*, p. xxxi. Schumpeter said under the impact of Max Weber's sudden death: "Whoever has passed into his sphere of influence, became clearer and healthier ever after."

function of the electorate as the "recognition of leaders."[59] Like Weber, he viewed Gladstone as the classic example of the great demagogue who achieved power through his personal appeal to the electorate outside of the party apparatus and parliament.[60] Schumpeter, too, championed the professional politician as the classical figure in the competitive battle for the political favor of the people. Max Weber might have used the same words that Schumpeter employed when he defined the essence of democracy in terms of leadership: "Democracy is the rule of the politician."[61] In Schumpeter's view, the single unconditional requirement of this system was the free competition of leaders with each other: in other words, the fair observation of democratic "rules of the game."

Nevertheless, there remained an essential difference between the two theories. In Schumpeter's view, politicians were above all technicians of government who carried out distinct political projects because, under existing conditions, they promised to be successful with the electorate. To this extent they modulated and formulated the amorphous will of the electorate when they propagandized for their plans with all of the publicistic means at their disposal. Weber's leaders were qualitatively quite different. They formulated their programs on the basis of their inner convictions and then won support and agreement from the masses through the appeal of their merely formal leadership qualities. Shumpeter's theory gives rise to the question of whether or not this degree of respect for the "rules of the game," for fairness and tolerance, can be maintained indefinitely if an internal respect for values based in natural law is not used to support the democratic system and democratic conduct. It is difficult to imagine how a democracy can continue to function if the regulative principle of the free self-determination of the citizens, no matter how little this might actually be realized, is replaced by the proposition that the only real object is to bring *formally* qualified leaders to the head of government who seek to win the people's support for their policies with demagogic means. This would open the way for the leader with the greatest formal demagogic gifts, who then could conduct his favorite policies, even if they were objectively antidemocratic, with the necessary degree of emotional mass propaganda. Such a democracy would tend rapidly to oligarchy and would always be in danger of transformation into authoritarian rule. This argument also applies with special force to Weber's democratic elite theory.

We can be grateful to Weber for restoring the honor of the figure of the great democratic demagogue in the face of the hierarchical tradition in

59. Schumpeter, *Kapitalismus, Sozialismus und Demokratie*, p. 433.
60. Ibid., pp. 440 f.
61. Ibid., p. 452.

Germany and for his attempt to restore the concept of demagoguery in its ancient positive sense. But he neglected the question of the limits in principle of the use of mass demagogic means. His (at least in intention) value-free sociology bestowed the concept of charisma upon good and bad demagogues alike. With his theory that the masses should acclaim their leaders solely on the basis of their formal leadership qualities, Weber opened the door in principle to the subjectification of politics, however contrary that was to his own views. Leadership democracy was, he argued, "generally characterized by the instinctive emotional quality of submission to and trust in a leader, the desire to follow a leader who was extraordinary, who promised the most, who knew how to win a following."[62] It is thus astounding that he never more closely investigated the question of whether the plebiscitary-charismatic leadership of a great demagogue, as he proposed it, could lead to subjectification and emotionalization of political life and end in a charismatic autocracy.[63]

In this regard, the insistence on the role of the charismatically qualified leader in a system of plebiscitary leadership democracy as an absolute, with the concomitant degradation of the popular will to the act of acclamation and the reduction of the legitimizing system of a democratic constitutional state to merely formal legality, contained the seeds of a transformation into such a charismatic dictatorship. As long as charisma remained successful, support was a *duty*. On the basis of this principle, there were no limits that could prevent plebiscitary-democratic rule by the "dictator of the electoral battlefield" from becoming in practice the plebiscitary rule of a totalitarian dictator. Weber's conceptual system, since it prescribed radical agnosticism regarding values and therefore only considered political phenomena in a formal framework, did not permit a distinction between genuine democratic charisma, dedicated to the positive realization of values in the service of the people, and that false charisma that made use of an appeal to the lower instincts and the emotional drives of the masses, corrupting the popular will in order to create dictatorship.[64]

Of course, Weber did not fear the transformation of a leadership democracy into a charismatic dictatorship although he held this to be

62. *Wirtschaft und Gesellschaft*, p. 157: "Here are also the limits of the rationality of such stewardship in modern times." Cf. ibid., p. 676.

63. Occasionally this seems to have occurred to him; thus *Pol. Schr.*, pp. 403 f.: "The governmental policy *danger* in mass democracy lies above all in the possibility that *emotional* elements in politics may be strongly predominant."

64. Compare Arnold Bergstraesser, "Max Webers Antrittsvorlesung," pp. 217 f. For an overview of the recent discussion on the concept of "charisma," see my study *The Age of Bureaucracy*, pp. 91 ff.

theoretically possible.[65] He expected the opposite to happen: increasing bureaucratic rigidification of voluntary political action that would make it less and less possible for charismatic leaders to arise.[66] He believed that the rationally and bureaucratically organized mass parties could offer an effective corrective to emotional excesses in the political struggle.[67] Charisma was a typically "extraordinary" power for him, steadily devolving into routinization and institutionalization. The inescapable and overpowering tendencies of bureaucratization and rationalization appeared always to subdue it and increasingly to limit the room for maneuver of charismatic forces: "With the rationalization of political and economic fulfillment of needs," "discipline will everywhere make headway as a universal phenomenon and increasingly" limit the "significance of charisma and of all individually differentiated activity."[68] Weber therefore neglected the question of the limits and misuse of charisma. We who have lived under the totalitarian rule of fascism, which must be considered a charismatic phenomenon in Weber's own terminology, regard this as a burning issue.[69] Weber viewed bureaucratic rigidification as so much a universal threat that he unhesitatingly favored plebiscitary-charismatic government by a great demagogue as the one available means of escaping "the iron cage of future serfdom."

A malignant inflammation of the lung brought Weber's life to a sudden end in June 1920 during a period of great creativity. He never lived to see that the plebiscitary-charismatic rule by a leader would take the form not of a powerful democracy but of a totalitarian, fascist dictatorship. There can be no doubt about his own attitude to this form of charismatic rule. A

65. Cf. *Wirtschaft und Gesellschaft*, p. 154: "Stubborn, striking failures" must "lead any government to destruction, destroy its prestige and permit the time for charismatic revolutions to ripen."

66. A systematic treatment of this aspect can be found in the author's article "Universalgeschichtliches und politisches Denken bei Max Weber," *Historische Zeitschrift* 201 (1965): 557–612. Now also in Dirk Käsler, ed., *Max Weber, sein Werk und seine Wirkung* (Munich, 1972), pp. 246 ff.

67. *Pol. Schr.*, p. 404.

68. *Wirtschaft und Gesellschaft*, p. 695. Cf. also pp. 669 f., 677, 688, 690.

69. Winckelmann's contrary thesis finds no support in Weber's statements. Winckelmann sees it clear to write: "No one—since Jacob Burckhardt—except [Weber] heard the muffled underground thunder of history roaring, which seemed to announce to him the passing of a bourgeois-rational age and the arrival of an irrational demagogic-Caesaristic epoch with the predominant empirical importance of charismatic forms of rule." *Legitimität und Legalität in Max Webers Herrschaftssoziologie*, p. 64. Weber had in reality expected a still more rationalistic age and saw in charisma only a retarding factor, a way out of the total rule of bureaucratic life ideals. He did not consider the possibility that the balance might move in favor of charisma, let alone in the form which we have experienced. If Winckelmann's view were relevant, Weber would have to be counted among the direct precursors of fascism.

policy that served the lowest instincts of the masses and nationalist emotions would have been anathema to him. His theory of the ethic of responsibility, which demanded of politicians that they account rationally for their ultimate motives and all possible consequences of their actions, was diametrically opposed to the brutal intolerance of fascist rule.

Nevertheless, his theory of plebiscitary leadership democracy was susceptible to reinterpretation in an authoritarian sense. When Otto Koellreutter put Max Weber in the same political camp as Oswald Spengler, he was certainly mistaken.[70] But it is instructive that such an attempt at comparison could be made. Pure plebiscitarianism was not that far from Max Weber's reduction of parliament to a "training school for politicians" and a mere control organ for the administration,[71] while the responsibility for government was to be in the hands of a great demagogue ruling on the strength of his charismatic gifts. It was quite possible for Carl Schmitt to take plebiscitarianism to its logical conclusions by building upon Weber's theories. Schmitt's undertaking was all the easier because Max Weber had subordinated basic democratic values to the interests of national power. Weber's elitist democratic theory was altogether adaptable to a position that advised the "retreat from a state of parties" and the refinement of "egalitarian democracy by its transformation into a leadership oligarchy" as a way out of the mass-democratic reality of the Weimar state, as little as this may have concurred with Weber's own intentions.[72] The charismatic-plebiscitary leadership "with machine" materialized in 1933 in a completely different form from that which Weber had in mind. Nonetheless, we have to concede that Weber's theory of charismatic leadership combined with the radical formalization of the meaning of democratic institutions helped, if only marginally, to make the German people receptive to support of a leader, and to that extent to Adolf Hitler.[73]

70. Otto Koellreutter, "Die staatspolitischen Anschauungen Max Webers und Oswald Spenglers," pp. 481 ff.

71. *Pol. Schr.*, p. 537; cf. Carlo Antoni, *Vom Historismus zur Soziologie*, pp. 177 ff.

72. An assessment to that end in Heinrich Triepel, *Die Staatsverfassung und die politischen Parteien* (Berlin, 1928). The quotation, ibid., pp. 28 f.

73. I gladly accept Ernst Nolte's suggested modification of the formulation in the first edition of this book—" . . . to make the German people inwardly willing to acclaim Adolf Hitler's leadership position"—in the manner chosen above in order to permit less room for misunderstandings (cf. Ernst Nolte, "Max Weber vor dem Faschismus," *Der Staat* 2 [1963]: 11, note 33). But at the same time it should be pointed out that this formulation is close to a statement by Karl Löwith, to whom it would be difficult to ascribe a malicious interpretation of Max Weber. Löwith wrote as early as 1939: "He prepared the way to an authoritarian and dictatorial leadership state positively by advocating, generally, irrational 'charismatic' leadership and 'rule of a leader with machine' and negatively through his intentional nihilism, through the formula of his ethos, the ultimate source of which was only the decisive choice of one arbitrary set of values; which one did not matter!" (*Mass und Wert*, III, 1 (1939), p. 171.) In addition, it had already been clearly pointed out in the first edition that

Today, we again face the task of creating a democratic order that does not lead to leaderlessness and the lack of genuine authority and at the same time preserves the basic values of free self-determination in the midst of a society dominated by all kinds of bureaucratically organized corporations and interest groups. The significance of this task is all the clearer now because of modern industrial mass society's tendency to gravitate to authoritarian forms of rule in more or less democratic guise, has recently come to the fore again. Mixed forms of authoritarian-charismatic and constitutional government have not only become common among the new nations but have even appeared in the place of parliamentary democracies with long traditions. The fate of the Fourth French Republic demonstrates this clearly. The rise of Gaullism confirms Max Weber's thesis that parliamentary democracy requires qualified leaders and strong authorities if it is not to freeze into a rigid party system and a system of mutual status protection by diverse economic and social interest groups. The parliamentary structure of the Fifth Republic, which combines the parliamentary and presidential principles, is very similar to Max Weber's proposals for the structure of the Weimar constitution.[74] At

---

one cannot speak of a direct or even an indirect identification of Max Weber with National Socialist or fascist tendencies. Weber himself viewed the dangers to the free order that threatened from the opposite direction, i.e., from the side of overwhelming bureaucracies. This does not free us of the responsibility of dealing candidly, and in conformity with Weber's own intellectual principles, with the question of the value of Max Weber's constitutional conceptions in the light of the experiences with National Socialism and other fascist systems. I have said here and elsewhere that Max Weber himself would have fought National Socialism with all his might.

74. Karl Loewenstein sharply criticized the comparison between Max Weber's constitutional conceptions from the year 1918–19 with the Fifth Gaullist Republic, which I had proposed in spring 1959 on the basis of still quite inadequate information at the time the Gaullist system was still in formation. He accused me of a great deficiency in the knowledge of constitutional history. "Max Weber als 'Ahnherr' des plebiszitären Führerstaates," pp. 279, 286 f. Nevertheless, the parallels between the system of the Fifth Republic—unquestionably the most significant modern case of a combination of the parliamentary and the presidential system—and Weber's conceptions of that time cannot be denied. Loewenstein protested at the time that "the presidential vote by a one-sidedly composed conservative-agrarian electoral college" could have no other result, and that therefore there was no question of a pure plebiscitary election of de Gaulle in the sense of Weber's terminology. Historical development alone at times even proves the "information" of "knowledgeable constitutional lawyers" to be mistaken. It is well known that the law of 6 November 1962 altered article 6 of the French constitution of 28 September 1958, that established the complicatedly composed electoral college which originally had to elect the president. The change introduced direct popular election of the president and thereby retrospectively eliminated the single essential point of difference between Weber's conception of a plebiscitary leadership democracy with a presidential apex and the Gaullist constitutional system (to which I specifically referred at the time.) Cf. also the treatment in my "Plebiszitäre Führerdemokratie," p. 318, note 40). Accordingly, Weber's constitutional constructs ought to be tested critically in the light of the experiences which have since been at hand in the Fifth French Republic instead of indulging in blind anti-Gaullism.

the least, dc Gaulle was a statesman who has to be categorized among the Caesarist mass leaders who on the strength of charismatic prestige was able to secure support for the masses outside of the parties and the parliament. The plebiscitary leadership position of the French president, within the constitutional system of the Fifth Republic, is similar in many ways to the position that Max Weber had sought for the Reich president in 1918–19. As in Weber's plan, the French president governs with a cabinet of ministers who themselves require the confidence of parliament in order to remain in office. In practice they are equally dependent upon the president. The French president also has the authority to deal with political questions of central importance either by dissolving parliament and calling new elections or calling a popular referendum to permit the people to decide directly. Not only de Gaulle, but his successor Pompidou, repeatedly made use of these possibilities. Proportional suffrage has been replaced by an electoral system which, unlike the British system, permits a runoff election and therefore does not strengthen majorities to the same degree. This is similar to Weber's proposal to establish a system of majority voting in place of the proportional representation that brought about an unbearable increase in the power of party bureaucracies at the expense of the individual deputies. There are also more general analogies between Weber's conception of a plebiscitary leadership democracy with a president at its head and de Gaulle's bold attempt to stabilize French democracy with the help of the techniques of plebiscitary rule. De Gaulle made conscious use of France's great national past in order to come to power. As we have seen, Max Weber was also very receptive to this strategy. In Weber's view, the office of the Reich presidency ought to give great charismatic statesmen the chance to restore the glory of Bismarck's national achievement, which his Lilliputian successors had destroyed.

But it would be incorrect to overplay the comparison between Max Weber's constitutional plans and the constitution of the Fifth Republic. There are many areas in which they were different. The power of parliamentary institutions in the constitution of the Fifth Republic, because of a whole series of limitations on their activities and influence, is in a way far smaller than Weber would have deemed advisable.[75] This is especially true of the prohibition on simultaneous government office and membership in the legislature, which de Gaulle had introduced in order to limit parliamentary influence. As we know, Max Weber passionately opposed an analogous restriction in the Bismarckian Reich constitution. He wished to permit party leaders to rise to the highest positions in the

75. Compare Dorothy Pickles, *The Fifth French Republic* (New York, 1960), pp. 126 ff.; Maurice Duverger, *Institutions Politiques et droit constitutionnel*, 11th ed. (Paris, 1970), pp. 683 ff.

government without forfeiting their following in their parties or party groups. The experience of the Fifth Republic appears to indicate that the principle of the incompatibility of governmental and parliamentary offices in fact sharply limits the possibilities for advancement of parliamentary politicians and therefore opens the path for members of the upper ranks of the bureaucracy, a group that Weber seriously mistrusted. Beyond this, it can be said that under Pompidou, who lacked the plebiscitary-charismatic image that his predecessor had, the Fifth Republic returned to a calmer course and the legislature regained some of its power.

This is not the place to attempt a systematic comparison of Weber's constitutional plans from the year 1918–19 with the constitutional system of the Fifth Republic, or to evaluate his plans in this light. The comparison demonstrates that Weber's conception of a "plebiscitary leadership democracy" with a president at the head was not a mere theoretical construct. Even the relative success of the Gaullist system in France does not dispel the underlying question of whether such a plebiscitary system can provide a supportable way out of the problems that have befallen democracy in modern industrial society. It appears that much depends upon the presence of suitable leaders who are able to exploit the plebiscitary possibilities of such a system. The Gaullist example also does not clearly dispel the basic objection that such a structure may be more easily transformed into an authoritarian or even a totalitarian form of government.

It is possible to take the view that a Weimar constitution similar to that of the present French one would have spared the German people the events of 1933. In the context of our analysis of Max Weber's plans for the Reich presidency, we have taken the opposite view. In spite of their basically democratic character, Weber's constitutional projects had an undeniably authoritarian tinge and were not immune to a totalitarian reformulation. Political charisma in itself, in the absence of intrinsic moral principles, cannot furnish the firm ground necessary to create a stable democratic order.

We need therefore to diverge from Weber on essential points. An appeal to charisma and the great demagoguery of a political leader can no longer be viewed as an effective way out of the dilemma the democratic ideal faces today in light of the growing weight of party apparatuses and the predominance of material interests in politics. We must seek new forms of moral justification for a free political order that effectively checks the bureaucratic and interest-group influences in the politics of our day. The constitutionally guaranteed rights of the citizen and constitutional principles must be restored to a more central position in our democratic governmental theory than seemed possible or necessary to

Max Weber. The national state can no longer be the exclusive and undisputed norm of our political activities. We must overcome, once and for all, the impulse to view the power of our own national state as an ultimate ideal. But Max Weber's intellectual attitude, his passionate search for "intellectual honesty," his lack of contentedness with middle-of-the-road ideological models, must be an obligatory maxim for us as well.

Afterword

Toward a New Interpretation of Max Weber

This monograph about Max Weber's political efforts and thought, which is being offered once again to the scholarly public, was sharply attacked when it first appeared, though it was generally greeted with acceptance.[1] A rather passionate and heated debate about Max Weber's political

1. The following overview of the reviews of this book at the time of its first appearance in no way claims to be complete:

Boesch-Jung, in *Schweizersche Zeitschrift für Geschichte* 10 (1960): 488; Bernhard Knauss, "Max Webers Hinterlassenschaft," *Süddeutsche Zeitung*, 15/16/17 June 1960; Wolfgang Schwarz, *Politische Studien* 11, no. 121 (1960); Carl Schmitt, *Das Historisch-Politische Buch* 8 (1960); Ernst Johann, "Entzauberung der Welt," *Frankfurter Allgemeine Zeitung*, 6 August 1960; Helmut Seifert, *Bücherei und Bildung* 148 (June 1960); also in *Bücherei und Bildung*, 12 (1960): 451; E.M., "Max Weber und die deutsche Politik," *Das Parlament* 14 (6 April 1960); Ernst Forsthoff, "Ein politischer Mensch—kein Politiker," *Christ und Welt* 40 (29 September 1960); N.N., "Begegnung mit Max Weber, ein Nationalliberaler mit einem Schuss ins Romantische," *Schwäbische Zeitung* 231 (6 October 1960); Klaus Epstein, *American Historical Review* 66 (1960): 155 f.; Kurt Sontheimer, "Weber als Politiker," *Neue Politische Literatur* 5 (1960): 278 ff.; L., *De Standaard* 214 (1960); Rudolf von Albertini, "Max Weber und die deutsche Politik 1890–1920," *Neue Zürcher Zeitung* 64, no. 2279 (3 July 1960); N.N., *Der Pfälzer* 10, no. 24 (1960); Carl Rainer, "Max Weber:Ein Wegbereiter Hitlers?" *Berliner Tagesspiegel*, 22 November 1961; Wolfram Fischer, *Blätter für deutsche Landesgeschichte* 97 (1961): 285; Norman Birnbaum, "Demon of the Concrete: A Note on Max Weber and Contemporary Sociology," *New Left Review* 8 (March–April 1961): 35 ff.; Reinhard Bendix, "Einige Bemerkungen zu einem Buch von Wolfgang Mommsen," *Kölner Zeitschrift für Soziologie und Sozialpsychologie* 13 (1961): 258 ff.: Paul Honigsheim, "Max Weber und die deutsche Politik," ibid., pp. 263 ff.; Karl Loewenstein, "Max Weber als 'Ahnherr' des plebiszitären Führerstaats," ibid., pp. 275 ff.; N.N., *Revue Française de Science Politique* 11 (1961); Victor Leemans, in *Tijdschrift voor Filosofie* 24 (1962): 740; Eberhard Kessel, "Zur inneren Entwicklung Deutschlands unter Wilhelm II, und in der Weimarer Republik. Ein Literaturbericht," *Archiv für Kulturgeschichte* 40 (1962): 262 ff.; Heinrich Muth, "Innenpolitik 1918–1945 (Literaturbericht)," *Geschichte in*

position and its consequences for his sociological work developed at the time. The debate arose in part from the special historical situation in which this book appeared. The political and intellectual climate of the fifties in the German Federal Republic was perceptibly influenced by the renaissance of the Weimar period intellectual and political traditions. It was therefore natural that Max Weber, who was widely recognized as a bitter critic of the weaknesses of the Wilhelminian system, was viewed as one of those few authorities who could be used to justify the newly restored German democracy and to help it grow in political self-consciousness. In this situation, many were inclined to overlook critical evaluations of Max Weber's political position in previous research or to view such work as immaterial. The prudent, discriminating introduction that Theodor Heuss wrote for the new edition of Max Weber's *Politische Schriften* (Political Writings) in 1958 was a creditable exception in this regard.[2] In such a situation, an extensive analysis of Max Weber's political works that described his basic political position as one of consistent, if also realistic, nationalism and imperialism had to have an irritating effect. The evidence that Max Weber's support of a parliamentary democratic order was designed to serve the power of the German national state above all provoked even more discomfort because, as Raymond Aron formulated it, this robbed "the New German democracy of a 'founding father,' a glorious ancestor, and a spokesman of genius."[3]

For these reasons alone, a heated controversy became unavoidable. It happened that a group of former members of the Max Weber circle in Heidelberg, who at one time had been very much under Weber's influence and during the twenties upheld the myth that Weber had been a natural but cruelly unappreciated leader, found this picture of the great man to be entirely improper. In reality, only the cliché that had emerged during the three decades since Weber's death was exposed as a falsehood. At the time it was widely overlooked that my interpretation differed substantially from older interpretations, specifically that of Christoph

---

Wissenschaft und Unterricht 5 (1962): 312 f.; Joachim H. Knoll, *Zeitschrift für Religions- und Geistesgeschichte* 14 (1962): 303 ff.: Rudolf Vierhaus, *Vierteljahrsschrift für Sozial- und Wirtschaftsgeschichte* 50 (1963): 273 ff.; Annette Kuhn, *Zeitschrift für Politik* 10, no. 2 (July 1963); Ernst Fraenkel, *Historische Zeitschrift*, 196 (1963): 418 ff.; Eric C. Kollman, *Journal of Central European Affairs* 23 (1963): 231 f.; Georges Castellan, "Histoire de l'Allemagne depuis 1914," *Revue Historique*, June 1964, p. 431 f.: Eugene Fleischmann, "Métamorphoses Wébériennes," *Archives européennes de sociologie* 5 (1964): 126 ff.; N. N., "Tradični koncepce?" *Host do dumu* 14 (1967): 50 ff. (*A Guest in the House*. Monthly for Art, Literature and Criticism, edited by the Czechoslovakian Union of Writers, Prague); Wolfram Fischer, *Zeitschrift für die gesamte Staatswissenschaft* 121 (1965): 368 f.

2. "Max Weber in seiner Gegenwart," *Pol. Schr.*, pp. vii ff., especially pp. x, xvii.

3. *Main Currents in Sociological Thought*, vol. 2 (New York, 1967), p. 248.

Steding, who had depicted Weber from the obtuse viewpoint of fascism as the contradictory representative of a bourgeoisie condemned to decline,[4] or of Jacob Peter Mayer, who had sweepingly labeled Weber a "Machiavellian of the age of steel" and had identified Weber with the destructive tradition of German Realpolitik after Bismarck. My goal was to depict Weber's political personality on the basis of careful analysis of the sources. It was not a one-sided ideological interpretation, but an attempt to portray Weber in all his complexity, including his internal contradictions and ambiguities. Eric Kollmann wrote at the time in his review: "This is not a debunking book." I gladly accept this formulation since a denigrating criticism of Max Weber was never my intention.[5]

Today, the conclusions of this republished investigation are hardly still the subject of debate in their basic lines, although the discussion of some of the interpretations as well as the significance of Max Weber's political works in general will never cease. At the Heidelberg sociology convention in 1964, which was dedicated to the memory of Max Weber, Raymond Aron, in a great lecture on "Max Weber and power politics," renewed the theme, if with a different accent. Aron emphasized the close relationship between power and culture in Weber's thought and argued that to an extent this can be seen as a justification of his will to national power. "Power is surely a goal, but it is also a precondition for the strength of culture."[6] At the same time, Aron emphasized that Weber had stood for the "power interests of the German people as an ultimate goal," a thesis that actually goes beyond the views represented in this book.[7] It is noteworthy that Aron's description was not disputed in substance by anyone in Heidelberg. My attempt at the time, in association with Aron, to point out the universal principles that prompted Weber to support a great, unsentimental politics of power—among those especially notable were his concern about the future of a dynamic economic and social order—found very little understanding; backward-looking arguments were not absent. Already in the controversial lecture by Herbert Marcuse on "industrialization and capitalism" in Max Weber's work, a new level of interpretation of Max Weber's political works appeared that is far more radical than mine. This view ought to be evaluated objectively. Marcuse demonstrated also that it is no longer

4. Christoph Steding, *Politik und Wissenschaft bei Max Weber* (Breslau, 1932). Compare also Steding's later work *Das Reich und die Krankheit der europäischen Kulture*, Schriften des Reichsinstituts für die Geschichte des neuen Deutschland, vol. 19 (Hamburg, 1938).

5. *Journal of Central European Affairs* 23 (1963): 231 f.

6. *Max Weber und die Soziologie heute*, p. 107.

7. Ibid., p. 119.

possible to escape the sober analysis of Max Weber as a man, who, although he towered over his contemporaries, still belonged to the Wilhelmine era.

At the time that this book was first published, there were several major criticisms relating to the premises. First of all, the presentation was said to concentrate too much on the person. Some critics argued that the context of intellectual history and contemporary history in which he lived should have been emphasized more. A second criticism was that Weber's theoretical and practical policy positions were frequently treated as one. This was seen as inappropriate methodologically. Third, the exact opposite accusation appeared: the depiction of Max Weber, the politician, was said to have been treated without sufficient reference to his scholarly and theoretical work.

I cannot deny the first objection a measure of justification. But it must be pointed out that my first responsibility had to be to describe Max Weber's role precisely in the politics of his day, before it was possible to interpret that role in a larger context. At the time, the necessary parallel studies were not available, nor do they exist today. The monographs that have since appeared by James Sheehan on Lujo Brentano, by Dieter Düding on Friedrich Naumann, and by Dieter Lindenlaub on the Verein für Sozialpolitik have filled important lacunae, but they do not really provide a sufficient basis for a definitive description of Max Weber's political position against the background of the group history of the German intellectuals. The attempts by Stuart Hughes and Fritz K. Ringer are too general for this purpose;[8] and of course the somewhat summarized description of the political position of the German professoriat during the First World War by Klaus Schwabe is not very helpful in this regard. One should of course mention Gustav Schmidt's detailed study of Meinecke, Troeltsch, and Max Weber.[9] This study, however, is based upon highly constructivist interpretive methods that are not completely satisfactory. Schmidt's attempt to trace Max Weber's basic political position to the intellectual tradition of later German historicism, and at the same time to the English model, is contradictory in itself and therefore not convincing. The significance of the English model for Weber's political thinking is greatly overemphasized.

The second objection, which has been raised in particular by Karl

8. H. Stuart Hughes, *Consciousness and Society: The Reorientation of European Social Thought, 1890–1930* (New York, 1961); Fritz K. Ringer, *The Decline of the German Mandarins: The German Academic Community, 1890–1933* (Cambridge, 1969).

9. *Deutscher Historismus und der Übergang zur parlamentarischen Demokratie: Untersuchungen zu den politischen Gedanken von Meinecke—Troeltsch—Max Weber* (Lübeck 1964), esp. pp. 47 ff., 226 ff.

Loewenstein and Guenther Roth, is unfounded.[10] This objection proves under closer analysis to be an attempt to shield Max Weber's sociological works against any possible criticism based on political aspects. They are treated almost as something providential. An appeal to Max Weber's principle of abstention from value judgments ought not to lead to the digging of a trench between Weber's political views and his theoretical sociological works. They both spring from a common root, the postulate of the self-assertion and self-realization of the personality in an administered world, according to the principles of a rational ethic of responsibility. Beyond this, it has to be permissible to make use of the conceptual instruments of Max Weber's sociology to interpret his own political views. Moreover, it would be a great misunderstanding if we were to agree that Weber's sociology can be cleanly divided from his political and social opinions. On the contrary, every detailed analysis demonstrates that his sociological work rests upon specific intellectual and social positions that also have a political side. Weber himself repeatedly declared that the personal ethical position of the researcher had the function of guiding the understanding and setting the direction of all scientific research. Fruitful research requires this.

H. H. Bruun recently demonstrated that Max Weber's insistence on value-free judgments had two aspects. One aspect is the postulate of shielding science from values that are apparently objective but are in fact imposed upon the subjects. The second is the shielding of the ethical sphere against the false pretensions of an apparently pseudo-objective science.[11] Values and science, in Weber's thought, were interdependent. A pure separation of Max Weber the social scientist from Max Weber the politician may perhaps be expedient from the point of view of scholarly politics, but is an impossible task. If it were attempted consistently, it would lead to sterile interpretations of his sociological works as well as his political theories. Its significance in universal history would be distorted as much as its human objectives. Social science was always an escape from daily politics for Max Weber. At the same time, he was conscious that science was certainly in a position to affect long-term changes in the

10. Karl Loewenstein, "Max Weber als 'Ahnherr' des pleszitären Führerstaats," p. 277: "The biographer appears to me to keep Weber the scholar and Weber the political thinker or politician appropriately in opposition." The "scholarly evidence, for example from *Wirtschaft und Gesellschaft*," does not, according to Loewenstein, have "the same real value" as evidence from *Pol. Schr.* Similarly, Guenther Roth, who naively presumes the separability of science and politics in Max Weber's work. Compare Guenther Roth, "Political Critiques of Max Weber," in Reinhard Bendix and Guenther Roth, *Scholarship and Partnership: Essays on Max Weber*, pp. 55 f.

11. H. H. Brunn, *Science, Values and Politics in Max Weber's Methodology* (Copenhagen, 1972), pp. 16 ff.

social consciousness, since it studied and clarified social reality with reference to significant processes that affect men.

The thesis that science and politics can be cleanly separated in Max Weber's works must thus be rejected. This author must also take exception to the objection that insufficient connections have been drawn in this monograph to Weber's theoretical ideas. I admit freely that the possibilities of drawing associations between Weber's scholarly work and his political opinions were not exhausted in the 1974 (German) edition. His scientific positions have been thoroughly taken into consideration in the interpretation of individual problems. It has been repeatedly pointed out that the central concepts of Weber's political journalism, like the dichotomy between politicians and officials, or the accentuation of the problem of the selection of political leaders, appear also in his political sociology. It can, however, be said in addition that Max Weber's entire sociological corpus rests on a conception of universal history that is only partially explicit. This conception is closely linked to his political convictions. I have attempted to remedy this deficiency of my monograph elsewhere and have specifically discussed the relationship between Weber's political views and his concern that the liberal social order of the west was mortally threatened by the inexorable growth of all-powerful bureaucracies.[12]

The description of Max Weber's constitutional position, presented here once again, has been the subject of especially heated controversy. To be sure, there is scarcely any more dispute about some of the central points; no one quarrels with the fact that the problem of leadership selection is at the center of Weber's concept of democracy and that Weber based his concept of democracy far more on pragmatic categories than on natural law. But beyond this point, consensus does not exist. In my view, Weber's conception of a democratic mass leader who wins the masses for his policies with the help of his charismatic capacities can be traced to aristocratic individualism in which liberal assumptions are combined with the Nietzschean idea of the value-setting personality. Charismatic leaders, who win the necessary support from the masses with personal plebiscitary techniques, ought to give the bureaucratic governmental apparatus goals and directions. For Weber, parliament served above all as a counterweight against leaders legitimized by mass plebiscites. Its chief responsibility was to assure the leaders' orderly removal if they failed.

Weber's democratic model, of course, can be accentuated in different ways and evaluated differently. Even Weber's contemporaries were in no way unanimous in their judgment of whether his constitutional proposals

12. Cf. my "Universalgeschichtliches und politisches Denken," pp. 557 ff.; also *The Age of Bureaucracy*, pp. 95 ff.

were sensible in all respects. In the light of our experience with fascist systems, which established "leadership domination with machine" in precisely the opposite direction from that which Weber had intended, I believe it necessary to examine his constitutional structures critically and of course completely independently of their original intention. In this procedure, I feel I am in agreement with Weber himself, who once wrote to Friedrich von Gottl-Ottlilienfeld: "Argue with my views as sharply as possible on those points where we differ," a statement that once served as the motto of this book. I have no brief for synthetic descriptions that slide over the characteristics as well as the tensions and contradictions of Max Weber's position instead of portraying them in all their keenness. This divides me especially from Reinhard Bendix, who in his book *Max Weber: An Intellectual Portrait* presents the social scientist and politician Max Weber in a harmonized and tailor-made form to suit the contemporary requirements of social science, but ignores that volcanic personality with the Nietzschean requirements who never was content with comfortable compromises but always carried things to their extremes.[13]

I believe we cannot avoid paying special attention to Max Weber's turn to extraparliamentary leadership selection after 1918 and testing his conception of "plebiscitary leadership democracy" as to its democratic substance. I believe that interpretations like that of Günter Abramowski, which view the 1917 stage of the conception of plebiscitary democracy as the whole idea instead of carefully distinguishing among the individual phases of the concept, are essentially in error.[14] I have never quarreled with the position that Weber *intended* "plebiscitary leadership democracy" to be democratic; the question of the extent to which, as an antiauthoritarian version of democratic government, it crossed the boundaries of the traditional understanding of democracy and was amenable to reinterpretation in an antidemocratic sense, is something quite different. Furthermore, reference should be made to the fact that Abramowski absolutizes an earlier stage of Weber's theory of charismatic rule when he argues that charisma was "of decreasing importance" for Weber and therefore should not be assessed too highly as an element of his governmental sociology.[15] Certainly, Weber observed a universal trend to

13. Cf. *Max Weber: An Intellectual Portrait* (Garden City, N.Y., 1960). See also the German edition, *Max Weber—Das Werk: Darstellung, Analyse, Ergebnisse* (Munich, 1964), corresponding to the second English edition. Cf. also my review, "Neue Max-Weber-Literatur," *Vierteljahrsschrift für Sozial- und Wirtschaftsgeschichte* 53 (1966): 94 f.

14. *Das Geschichtsbild Max Webers: Universalgeschichte am Leitfaden des okzidentalen Rationalisierungsprozesses* (Stuttgart, 1966). Cf. also my "Neue Max-Weber-Literatur," *Historische Zeitschrift* 211 (1970): 618 ff.

15. Abramowski, *Das Geschichtsbild Max Webers*, p. 158.

the rationalization of all life relationships, but he was not prepared to accept this resignedly. On the contrary, it was because of these premises that he viewed the only way out to be a return to the revolutionary power of charisma. In the later writings, charisma is no longer something that was limited to antiquity but is valued as the source of all individually responsible creative action. Especially in the area of politics, charisma is viewed as the root of genuine political leadership in dichotomous contrast to the leaderless bureaucratic apparatus of an administered world, which, if it were not to make itself absolute, would have to have goals set for it either from above or from outside.

In this connection we cannot overlook the significance this conception of the political leader has in the framework of Weber's model of parliamentary democracy. It would be intellectually dishonest to sidestep the problems that arise here by pointing to the obvious fact that Weber never intended the parliamentary system to be undermined in favor of plebiscitary leadership rule. I have made it very clear that Weber never anticipated the development of new forms of charismatic rule of a totalitarian kind. He was far more concerned about the dangers arising from the process of bureaucratization. According to all that we know about him, he would have been a bitter foe of fascism. His passionate invective against the criminal activities of the reactionary right after 1919 permit no doubts about this. (He lived long enough to see the high point of this in the Kapp Putsch.) But this does not permit us to sidestep the question of the historical significance of his leader-biased conception of democracy. In this regard, Loewenstein's emotional polemic at the time this book was published missed the key issue. He formulated the problem falsely when he attempted to attach to my thesis the phrase that "Max Weber [was] the 'sire' of the plebiscitarian leadership state."[16]

Gustav Schmidt's interpretation also seems to us to have ended up without a plausible solution to the problem. It is highly questionable to try to seek the intellectual roots of Weber's conception of "plebiscitary leadership democracy" in the Anglo-Saxon tradition. The function that Weber ascribed to the "plebiscitary-charismatic leader" within the parliamentary system can be associated only in form, not in substance, with

16. *Kölner Zeitschrift für Soziologie und Sozialpsychologie* 13 (1961): 275 ff. (Cf. my answer at the time, "Zum Begriff der 'plebiszitären Führerdemokratie' bei Max Weber," in the same journal, vol. 15 (1963). Also Karl Loewenstein, "Max Webers Beitrag zur Staatslehre in der Sicht unserer Zeit," in Karl Engisch, Bernhard Pfister, Johannes Winckelmann, eds., *Max Weber*: *Gedächtnisschrift der Ludwig-Maximilians-Universität München zur 100jährigen Wiederkehr seines Geburtstages 1964* (Berlin, 1966), pp. 142 ff.; by the same author, *Max Webers staatspolitische Auffassungen in der Sicht unserer Zeit* (Bonn, 1965), pp. 70 f., esp. note 16. Cf. also my "Neue Max-Weber-Literatur" (1970), pp. 625 f.

the pragmatic concept of democracy of the Anglo-Saxon tradition and not at all with the English prime minister cabinet as such.[17] The radical reduction of the institutions of parliamentary democracy to a mere instrument in the hand of government can, to be sure, be traced in its roots to the Puritan tradition, but Weber gave it a more radical form that has no parallel in Anglo-Saxon political thought. As to the idea of the opposition to the misuse of power through the division of power into a multiplicity of political institutions that we know in the Anglo-Saxon tradition, Weber opposed this with his dichotomy between political leadership and parliamentary and other political institutions. As long as the leader retained the trust of the masses, he could demand absolute discipline from his supporters and exclusively direct the bureaucratic apparatus of power for the achievement of his goals. This approach is completely alien to Anglo-Saxon political thought. Even in those places where Weber referred specifically to English models, he tended to overemphasize certain aspects, for example, in his description of Gladstone as a "dictator of the electoral battlefield"—an interpretation that did not do justice to Gladstone's actual role and exaggerated its plebiscitary dimension.[18]

It is difficult to escape the core of Weber's political concept of leadership, namely, the fact that the leader, once elected in a formally free election, was exclusively responsible in his own right and not according to the declared or suspected will of his electors. He was expected to act solely in agreement with his own personal convictions. This emphasis on the personal-plebiscitary aspect of leadership does not originate in western European constitutional thought and is difficult to reconcile with the basic principles of parliamentary government. There is an elitist-aristocratic element hidden here that reminds us of Nietzsche's theory about great individuals who, motivated by a strongest sense of personal responsibility, set new goals for mankind and thereby prevent it from sinking into the mediocrity of a leaderless "herd" of "equals." Nor do I consider the concepts of leader and demagogue so widely separated, as Schmidt maintained, in view of the undisputed fact that Weber counted demagogic gifts among the elementary qualities of political leadership.[19] If we put the problem this way, then attempts at synthesizing fall apart. It then becomes impossible to avoid discussion of where the formal distinction between charismatic leadership in a democracy and fascist leadership lies, all the more so as Weber himself deliberately excluded a substantive approach to the problem. In this regard, it should be pointed out that not only Carl Joachim Friedrich, but also Karl Loewenstein, ignoring his

17. Schmidt, *Deutscher Historismus*, pp. 291 f.
18. Cf. also Karl Loewenstein, *Max Webers staatspolitische Auffassungen*, p. 71, n. 17.
19. Cf. Schmidt, *Deutscher Historismus*, p. 291 and also *Pol. Schr.*, p. 525.

already cited polemics against the "'retroactive projections' of a generation of scholars that had lived through the Hitler period,"[20] had pointed to the concept of charisma as unfortunate and unsuited for the description of the role of leadership in modern democracy.[21] The lack of content in charisma in the Weberian sense, which makes it possible to apply it to plebiscitary leaders of Lloyd George's type as well as to Karl Liebknecht, Benito Mussolini, or Adolf Hitler, in practice raises difficult questions of differentiation.

Since the removal of a charismatic mass leader elected under caesaristic conditions is formally regulated through the continually existing parliamentary institutions, it appears that the ambivalence of this structure has not been eliminated. To this extent, I agree with Loewenstein. If a situation were to arise in which parliament and parties had sunk to mere followers of such a mass leader, they would not be in a position, in the event of a conflict, to effectively defy the manipulations of a mass leader who was still in power but had lost the confidence of the masses. In principle, as well as in a technical-constitutional sense, does not the radical accentuation of the function of the leader by Weber have the effect of reducing the democratic process almost entirely to the problem of the selection of leaders? Under Weber's influence, in 1920, Theodor Heuss argued that it was necessary to see the future of German democracy in the light of two alternatives. "The problem that would decide the future of the people" was "leadership in democracy. Are the people waiting to submit their future to the personal will to power of a usurper, or will they purify their instincts and recognize greatness in selflessness, granting her their spontaneous support in determining their own destiny?"[22] Weber's emphasis on the personally responsible position of the great politician, who was to act as a counterbalance to the anonymous rule of the bureaucratic apparatus and the mediocrity of the career politician without calling, points to the structural weakness of late bourgeois liberalism, namely, the tendency to compensate for the undermining of the autonomy of the individual in industrial mass society by falling back on a plebiscitary appeal of the individual to the masses.

Reference should also be made at this point to Ernst Nolte's "Max Weber vor dem Faschismus" ("Max Weber as a Precursor of Fascism"). This study departs from mainstream scholarship insofar as it deals squarely with the issue at stake here rather than sidestepping it with the

20. Carl Joachim Friedrich, "Political Leadership and the Problem of Charismatic Power," *Journal of Politics* 23 (1961): 16 f.

21. Cf. Karl Loewenstein, *Max Webers staatspolitische Auffassungen*, pp. 74 ff. The quotation is from "Max Weber als Ahnherr des plebiszitären Führerstaats," p. 280.

22. *Pol. Schr.*, p. xxxi.

soothing words of most of the authors so far discussed.[23] Nolte does not hesitate to identify those elements of Max Weber's political thought that in a certain way include prefascist components. On the other hand, he offers precise criteria showing why Max Weber, though in a sense his thought belongs in the context of "pre-fascism," nonetheless was a decisive opponent of National Socialism. He correctly points out that one element totally characteristic of fascism was entirely absent from Weber's political thought—namely, militant anti-Marxism. Rather, Weber always pleaded for a united front of the bourgeoisie against the traditionally privileged aristocratic leadership classes. The social constellation that enabled National Socialism to come to power, namely the alliance of the petite bourgeoisie with the traditional feudal elite, was in marked contrast to his thesis of the necessity of political cooperation between the Social Democrats and democratic liberalism. On the other hand, we cannot overlook the fact that Max Weber's ambivalent attitude toward the universal process of rationalization and bureaucratization of all life relationships, combined with his theory of the growing "alienation" of the individual and the antimodern ideologies that were so characteristic of fascist movements, in principle have some common ground. Weber's tireless plea for rationality made him fully immune to such trends of thought. It is well known that he refused to follow the path of Stefan George or Oswald Spengler, and to look out for new prophets or Caesars.

Essentially, the conclusion is plain. Yet, without further comment, we cannot count Weber as belonging to what Nolte designated as a European alternative coalition to fascism, namely a coalition ranging from the "reform-friendly wing of the Conservatives to the Social Democrats."[24] In truth, it is impossible to assign Weber precisely to any political position. Nolte, too, points out that Weber's position, irrespective of his opposition in principle to fascist solutions, demonstrated a series of weak points in relation to the appeal of fascist ideologies.[25] These include, in addition to a certain approval of the Social Darwinist doctrine of struggle as the basic element of politics, and the temporary recommendation of irredentist fighting tactics against the Treaty of Versailles, the tendential devaluation of parliamentary institutions to technical arrangements for the purpose of protecting an optimum of political leadership, with the

23. *Der Staat*, 2 (1963): 1 ff.

24. Ibid., p. 10.

25. Nevertheless, we can in no way agree with Nolte when he points to Max Weber's Nietzscheesque critique of religions of salvation, and his acceptance of the rationalization process as an unavoidable fate, as factors that would have weakened Weber's position toward fascism. The reference point here is Nolte's own concept of fascism, which views fascism as a revolt against transcendence. This view in our opinion mistakes the social nature of fascism.

provision only that such leadership rest upon formally free elections. This construction must be understood in the context of Weber's governmental sociology as an attempt to find a way out of the dilemma of how, under the conditions of industrial mass society, the personal rule of great, gifted leaders could still be assured. Weber thereby indirectly illuminated a central problem of liberalism in the postbourgeois world. The suspicion is inescapable that the bourgeois classes' lack of immunity to the siren call of fascism was at least in part associated with such notions. Hitler, in his speeches to west German industrialists, tried to point out, with special warmth, that the free, creative activity of the personality in economy and society needed an open path once again. The supposed or real lack of qualified leaders formed one of the chief arguments of those groups of the bourgeoisie who were cool toward the Weimar Republic. In fact, Max Weber could be quoted in defense of this argument, even though, in most instances, those who did so were rarely aware of the subtlety and complex nature of his arguments.

Nevertheless, there can certainly be a number of opinions as to whether it is possible or advisable today to criticize Weber's understanding of democracy from a standpoint that involves commitment to certain fundamental political principles. But even if a conclusive ethical-rational justification of modern "constitutional democracy" is no longer possible, it still remains the legitimate task of social science to analyze the multiple possibilities of political systems from the point of view of whether, and how much, under current social conditions, an optimum of freedom for the individual can be combined with a maximum of self-determination for all. In this respect, Weber's position as described in this book, regardless of his subjective intentions, seems to me not beyond reproach. Situations could perhaps arise in which it is necessary to take refuge in plebiscitary charismatic forms of political leadership, for example, if the rigidification of industrial society of the western type that Weber feared should actually reach a critical stage. But taking recourse to such political techniques does not seem to fit the contemporary situation. We need, far more than great leaders who attract the masses and provide them with goals, statesmen who are capable of integration and compromise between different political persuasions and who have the will to formulate the interests and objectives of the social groups whom they represent and to transform them into political action. To this extent, Weber's conception of "plebiscitary leadership democracy" is also subject to criticism from a pragmatic vantage point.

The final word also does not appear to have been spoken about the problem of legitimacy in modern society. In the 1950s, the question of legitimacy of political rule appeared to be reducible in a technical sense to effective provision for human existence and constant improvement in the welfare of the masses. Today the question has returned in full force. Once again we face the problem of whether "formal legality" or "technical rationality" are sufficient to provide a stable basis for modern societies of the western type in the long run and can form the foundation for a political and social consensus.[26] It is possible that "technical rationality" may be exposed as a form of pseudolegitimacy that is of value only as long as it is assumed that the political process in modern industrial society is almost exclusively determined by the technological and material conditions of economic progress.

Considerations of this nature owe much to Max Weber, although his solutions cannot simply be accepted under changed political and social conditions. Whatever we may think of their material realizability, it is unsatisfying when they are countered by an apparently objective, neopositivist position that sees a way out in the reduction of value ambiguity—a strategy that in any case is diametrically opposed to Max Weber's basic position, namely, that all questions ultimately relate to one's own fundamental point of view. It seems of little use to throw my own interpretation of Max Weber's political thought, an interpretation that arises from a consistent liberal position, into the same pot as many completely different interpretations. The author admits that nothing annoyed him more than to see his interpretation of Max Weber as a politician lumped together, by a series of authors close to neopositive social science, with the fascist description of Christoph Steding and the Catholic-fundamentalist critiques of Leo Strauss and Erich Vögelin, while at the same time they insist on their own objectivity.[27] It is remarkable that these authors cite Max Weber in their defense, although Weber repeatedly and distinctly said that an interpretation that takes the middle position is not a hair truer than one that takes an extreme position.[28] His whole life long, Weber himself staked all on thinking through his own positions to their radical conclusions with an almost self-destructive rigorism, rather than resting content with comfortable compromises of middle-of-the-road solutions, even when he ended up in contradictions and unsolvable aporias. He once said: "Any meaningful *evaluation* of an alien will can only involve a critique from the vantage point of one's own 'Weltanschauung.' A struggle against an *alien* ideal [must arise from] the

26. Cf. esp. Jürgen Habermas, *Technik und Wissenschaft als "Ideologie"* (Frankfurt, 1968), pp. 78 ff.; and the same author's *Legitimitätsprobleme im Spätkapitalismus* (Frankfurt, 1973).

27. Thus, for example, Gerhard Hufnagel, *Kritik als Beruf: Der kritische Gehalt im Werk Max Webers* (Frankfurt, 1971), pp. 191 f.; and Guenther Roth, *Political Critics of Max Weber*, in Bendix and Roth, *Scholarship and Partisanship*, pp. 55 ff.

28. Cf. *Wissenschaftslehre*, p. 499.

base of one's own ideals."[29] Nothing could therefore be more misguided than the attempt to lay a claim to Max Weber with a form of empirical social science that does not reflect upon the metascientific premises of its own approach and is unconscious—or insufficiently aware—of the links between its own hypotheses and methods and their roots in a contemporary social situation. The method of critical analysis of Max Weber's political works from a definite point of view, which has been followed here, is closer to his own epistemological position than that of those authors who abstract Weber's scientific and intellectual achievements out of the context of his political wishes and his social position and attempt to interpret them as more or less value-free in substance.

From this standpoint, Gerhard Hufnagel's study of Max Weber appears quite inadequate.[30] Hufnagel attempts to solve the problem of a synthetic interpretation of Weber's political and sociological works by reducing Weber to the role of a totally uncommitted critic who analyzed everything on the basis of his current assumptions. Weber the "critic," according to Hufnagel, proclaimed no new values but saw his task merely as a continuous dissection of the existing situation. Hufnagel's thought has a positivist foundation that rejects all ethical-rational positions equally and dogmatically, no matter what their nature, and seems thereby to be committed to the "critical rationalism" of Hans Albert and an anti-ideologism similar to that of Ernst Topitsch. This is combined, in a remarkable way, with a romantic, antiauthoritarian neo-Marxism that seems to see good in the systematic criticism of all existing governmental systems, ethical positions, and opinions. To be sure, Hufnagel admits that—in the words of René König—"criticism always [requires] a point of view from which to criticize."[31] But he does not succeed, in spite of vigorous attempts to break through his closed description of Max Weber's position, in escaping the technical-empirical hypothesis that Max Weber was a "rebel without a cause" without any ultimate point of view. Rather, he is stuck in the statement that Weber "was nowhere reliably at home"—an interpretation that comes remarkably close to the bitterly disputed position of Leo Strauss, who accused Weber of nihilism.[32] Finally, the reader is dispatched with the equally relevant if not exactly new observation that the core of Weber's thought and his aims was the "will to truth," a formalist statement that he ought to have elaborated upon.[33]

29. Ibid., p. 157.
30. Cf. above, note 27.
31. Hufnagel, *Kritik als Beruf*, p. 264.
32. Ibid., p. 355.
33. Ibid., p. 341.

Specifically, Hufnagel's presentation exhausts the political aspects of Weber's works in the negative sense, more precisely in the description of Max Weber's opposition to the most diverse political phenomena and tendencies, for example, his protesting any "accommodation to 'Realpolitik,'" his critique of "nonobjective motivations," his rejection of Marxism as a special case of objectivist belief in laws, etc. He does not ask why Weber chose these and not other phenomena of the social reality of his time, as subjects for criticism. The goal of his interpretation is not to determine the social background or core of Weber's political work. Rather, he himself says: "An ordered sketch of a theory of political action or a philosophy of politics will be found not in a description of the destructiveness of the political critic [Max Weber—(author)], but, rather, in a mosaic of critical and criticized views, arguments, and attitudes."[34] In fact, Hufnagel does not even achieve this. He only gives us broken pieces of a mosaic. The individual stones in no way come together in a convincing total picture.

In my view, this description does not do justice to Weber, who himself repeatedly emphasized that all political action and, ultimately, all scientific research is fruitful only if it is oriented to final, personally responsible ethical convictions. For Max Weber, personality rested on the constancy of its insistence on ultimate ideal values and the readiness to rationalize one's own conduct fully in the light of these ideals and, as it were, to test it constantly. Hufnagel, from his fundamentalist viewpoint, neglects that side of Weber that was an aristocratic, somewhat Nietzschean individualist and "rational" nationalist who did not shrink from the final consequences of his nationalism. Hufnagel's view abstracts Weber and distorts him into an extreme example of a rootless intellectual. It scarcely does justice to his constant attempt at "intellectual honesty." Both as a social scientist and as a politically engaged citizen and political thinker, Max Weber towered above the common opinions of his time. Regardless of the severe inner tensions it contains, his life work reveals an inner unity and force that still has power today for those who consider it seriously. For this reason, Hufnagel's attack on workers who refuse to forsake their own positions when confronting Weber and seek to illuminate and interpret his work both in *his* context and in their own, is neither appropriate nor convincing, no matter how self-confidently it is presented.

Arthur Mitzman took another tack, which was in many ways opposite to Hufnagel's.[35] His was the first attempt to analyze Max Weber's works as well as his political convictions with the use of Freudian psychoanalytic categories. Like the historical school that derives from Erikson's psycho-

34. Ibid., p. 109.
35. *The Iron Cage: An Historical Interpretation of Max Weber* (New York, 1970).

analytical historiography, Mitzman studies conflicts and problems in Max Weber's personal development and seeks on this basis to interpret his political position and his scientific works. The point of departure is Max Weber's conflict with his father. The ground was prepared by his emotional preference for his mother and expanded several weeks before his father's death to an open break. The resulting guilt complex was the real cause of Weber's nervous breakdown and at the same time the ultimate source of his decisive partisanship against the authoritarian political order of Wilhelminism and its self-satisfied nationalism. In addition, Mitzman attempts to relate Max Weber's intellectual development by broadly associating it with the bourgeois society of his time and its widespread repression of sexual and emotional needs in such a manner as to make assertions of general significance. This analysis is ingenious and provocative, but to a large degree it seems to rest upon interpretive arbitrariness. It is, for example, not clear why Max Weber associated the Prussian Junkers with the person of his father and therefore bitterly opposed them. The elder Max Weber was a typical representative of the traditionalist, innerly rigid National Liberalism of the Bismarckian era, but even in his later years he was in no way as reactionary as Mitzman's analysis assumes. The younger Weber's criticism of the Prussian Junkers corresponded to his conscious preference for a progressive bourgeois liberalism that saw in a dynamic economy and society of a capitalist sort the essential conditions of both personal freedom and the greatness of the nation. This does have some indirect association with individual psychological factors. It is possible, too, to support Mitzman's view that Weber's radical support of a puritanical individual and social ethic had individual psychological origins and was closely related to his own personal experience. Overall, however, the bridge between the psychic dimensions of Weber's personality and his political views seems to me to have been insufficiently based.

This applies less, perhaps, to Mitzman's depiction of Weber's intellectual development. Mitzman describes that development as a constantly renewed attempt to break out of the "iron cage" of a rational asceticism in which Weber found himself imprisoned around the turn of the century, or, as he puts it in another place, a revolt proceeding step by step against his own ascetic-puritanical background. Mitzman associated the decisive change in the years 1911–14 with the discovery of charisma, which he called, with reference to Nietzsche, a "Dionysian category." Parallel to this, Weber came to a new appreciation of the aristocratic life ideal, although not in the narrow political sense. Mitzman saw this development as conditioned by the gradual resolution of the unsolvable sexual problems that entangled Weber as a result of his unsuccessful marriage to Marianne.

Overall, it is possible to agree with this analysis, though not to accept its preconceptions uncritically. However, we question whether Weber's intellectual development can really be so cleanly divided into a "puritanical" and a "Dionysian" period. Even outwardly, this appears incorrect. In his letters to Mina Tobler, a Swiss pianist with whom Max Weber carried on a very personal, if platonic, relationship during the war years, he confessed that he had to struggle with inward despair against the domination of anonymous powers. Even in 1919, Weber said that a rope was around his throat and someone had been twisting it, "slowly, slowly, for many years, ever more tightly, ever more tightly."[36] Weber never overcame his lifelong fear of sustaining a teaching career. Invitations to Vienna, Bonn, Munich, and the later unrealized prospect of going to the newly founded Johann-Wolfgang-Goethe University in Frankfurt, something that appeared very exciting to Max Weber, as well as his acceptance into the Bavarian Academy of Sciences (whose meetings he found very boring), proved that even after 1918 he was generally recognized as a teaching professor. But he was never free of the inner fears about his academic existence.

The same is true of the development of his personal Weltanschauung. In later life, Max Weber did not break nearly as radically from the rigorism of his puritanical opinions as Mitzman would have it. The concept of charisma, as a form of revolutionary power that gripped people from within, can be more easily interpreted as an expansion of Weber's conception of the importance of otherworldly values for social change. This had been the basis of *The Protestant Ethic*. Now the emphasis was more strongly placed upon the great personality.[37] The revolutionary inner-worldly power of charisma is therefore not an alternative to the older idealistic model of social change as it was developed in *The Protestant Ethic* and elsewhere. It involved a modification of this model that was suited to the conditions of a world dominated by bureaucratic bodies, in which all forms of individual activity had a chance only when they could be transformed to reality with the help of a "following" that did not fear the use of the instruments of bureaucratic techniques of rule. The conflict between charisma and the powers of rationalization and bureaucratization is a constant motif in Max Weber's sociology, though it was not until his later works that he made it a direct central theme. For this reason, the category of charisma is more than the later product of a development that was characterized by the breakthrough to "Dionysian

36. Letter to Mina Tobler, undated, probably spring 1919, A.E. II, 86. He wrote similarly once in 1917: political things pull "on the iron ring that one feels pressing upon one's breast, head, and neck." Letter to Mina Tobler, 23 November 1917, A.E. II, 45.

37. For a detailed justification of this thesis, see my study, *Universalgeschichtliches und politisches Denken*, pp. 578 ff.

life forms." This is true too of his political opinions in a narrow sense. In his later years, Weber had felt himself to be a partisan of the liberal bourgeoisie and identified with its political values. But in these later years the aristocratic side of his thought grew in importance, especially in his stress on his own model of democracy as a form of government by a plebiscitary mass leader.

Mitzman succeeds in opening up a new approach to the political thought of Max Weber. Doubtless, the problems of an entire generation are mirrored in an extreme form in Weber's personal life. His generation did not feel at home in the rigid and authoritarian structure of Wilhelmine society, yet saw no possibility of escaping it. Nevertheless, can the key to this problem really be sought in the personal life history of the individual? Is such an attempt at explanation, which flies in the face of a social reality that the historian by virtue of his profession must research in its historical dimensions, immunized against a radical critique? This author sees his scholarly task to be the study of social relationships in another sense. I recognize that historiography always has and should have a critical function.[38] For this reason I have attempted to study Max Weber's political positions, not only from the point of view of their inner freedom from contradiction, but in terms of their historical significance in the light of later discoveries. I have concluded that Max Weber should in many ways be viewed as a representative of a late variety of classical liberal thought and that he reflected the crisis of liberalism in exemplary form in his political thought.

This analysis of Max Weber also differs from recent Marxist interpretations. Joachim Streisand's *Max Weber: Soziologie, Politik und Geschichtsschreibung* (*Max Weber: Sociology, Politics and the Writing of History*), published in 1965, appears comparatively less probing. He contents himself with describing Max Weber as an exponent of German bourgeois imperialism, as Georg Lukács had already done, without, however, seriously considering Weber's overall arguments, especially those involving bureaucratic governmental systems, good examples of which can be found in contemporary socialist states.[39] He is somewhat hasty in dismissing Weber's epistemological position as a theoretical justification of the anarchy of production in the bourgeois capitalist system, and in calling it irrational, without recognizing the foundations of his own view and his dogmatic assertion of the Marxist-Leninist position as the only completely rational one.[40]

38. Cf. my study *Die Geschichtswissenschaft jenseits des Historismus*, 2nd ed. (Düsseldorf, 1972), pp. 33 f.

39. Joachim Streisand, ed., *Studien über die deutsche Geschichtswissenschaft*, vol. 2: *Die bürgerliche deutsche Geschichtsschreibung von der Reichseinigung bis zur Befreiung Deutschlands vom Faschismus* (Berlin, 1965), pp. 179 ff.

40. Ibid., p. 188.

In contrast, Herbert Marcuse's lecture at the Heidelberg sociologists' convention of 1964 on "industrialization and capitalism in the work of Max Weber," which at the time was dismissed as the presentation of an abstruse outsider, has since had a considerable impact upon research, especially in the neo-Marxist camp. Marcuse's interpretation, contrary to the appraisals of some authors, touches on the real problems of Max Weber's sociological theory even more than Marcuse himself realized.[41] In a sense, he radicalizes our own objection to Max Weber's model of democracy, namely that parliamentary institutions as such became mere technical instruments of a system in which charismatic leaders fought for power with personal-plebiscitary weapons, and extends it to the area of a capitalistically structured economic order. Marcuse argues that the concept of "formal rationality" is "inconspicuously" transformed into "reason."[42] This permits Weber to justify capitalism materially and support a system of government necessary for its preservation. The principle of "formal rationality" is also applied to the system of government. But since the bureaucratic apparatus has its limits in rationality, it is subjected to super- and extrabureaucratic forces, and these, in contrast to the former, are irrational. Marcuse summarizes his thesis in the statement that the "Weberian concept of reason" terminates in "irrational charisma."[43] By the "equation of technical and bourgeois capitalist reason,"[44] Weber obstructs the recognition of the irrationality of capitalism that consists in the fact that in it the technologically conditioned control by things is made absolute.[45]

This thesis is correct insofar as it points out that Max Weber in fact described capitalist "market economy" as the formally most rational

41. Cf., e.g., Benjamin Nelson's commentary at the Heidelberg sociologists convention 1964 in *Max Weber und die Soziologie heute*, pp. 192 ff. Nelson believes he has ascertained that "rarely, almost never, do the critics of Weber meet him on his own ground" (p. 197). My interpretation shows that the contrary is true in the case of Marcuse, insofar as he has moved far less beyond Weber's "ground" than he himself tends to assume. See also Hans Albert, *Plädoyer für kritischen Rationalismus* (Munich, 1971), pp. 104 f., who goes a little beyond his goal when he depicts Marcuse as "a natural enemy of Max Weber's theories."

42. "Industrialisierung und Kapitalismus (im Werk Max Webers)," in *Max Weber und die Soziologie heute*, pp. 161 ff, as well as in Herbert Marcuse, *Kultur und Gesellschaft*, vol. 2 (Frankfurt, 1965), pp. 107 ff. We quote below from the latter, pp. 118 f.

43. Ibid., pp. 121, 125.

44. Ibid., p. 127.

45. Cf. here Wolfgang Schluchter's brilliant analysis, *Aspekte bürokratischer Herrschaft. Studien zur Interpretation der fortschreitenden Industriegesellschaft* (Munich, 1972,) pp. 256 ff. with which the following statements agree on many points. Schluchter takes the view that Marcuse "rather than unmasking Weber, had for the first time correctly portrayed him." (p. 267). This agrees with our interpretation in so far has we demonstrate that the decisive takeoff point for Marcuse's critique of the thesis of the "formal rationality" of capitalism, had basically already been formulated by Weber.

form of modern economy and in this regard viewed it as the economic form most capable of maximum production. Even when Weber painstakingly avoided speaking about maximum efficiency in this connection, his logic came close to this conclusion. His conviction that free competition in the market combined with complete freedom of contract permitted a high degree of formal rationality (and therefore technological capacity) of the economic system was in fact of central importance for his position. Weber was convinced that every economic form that differed from the type of pure market economy based upon absolutely free competition of economic forces in the market and full contractual freedom would pay for that difference in the form of formal irrationalities that would necessarily restrict the system's technological and economic capacity. This applied especially—but in no way exclusively—to the various conceivable socialist economic systems as Weber systematically developed them in his ideal typical analysis in *Economy and Society*.[46] Moreover, Weber preferred the system of "market economy" of a capitalist type in the prevailing social circumstances because it was capable of releasing the greatest dynamism in the economic as well as in the political realm.

Weber always expressly defended the capitalist system in political praxis against the criticism of the socialists from various camps as well as intellectuals, in spite of his occasional verbal concessions to socialism. He never intended to canonize capitalism, certainly not in its formally most rational form. The ideal typical picture that Weber sketched of a formally rational market economy in *Economy and Society* is an example of ice-cold reasoning and has a somewhat frightening effect. It can in no way be interpreted as an apology for capitalism. Rather, Weber was—as Marcuse also correctly points out—convinced that the "formal rationality" of the capitalist system was necessarily linked to "material irrationality."[47] Viewed from the standpoint of ethical rationalism, it necessarily had to be judged "irrational." Weber pointed out expressly, for example, that the "subjugation of the worker under the rule of the businessmen" was one of the "specific *material* irrationalities" of the modern capitalist system.[48]

We must therefore maintain that Max Weber in no way set the capitalist system up as an absolute, as the neo-Marxist critics maintain. He never abandoned the possibility of modifying the capitalist system from the standpoint of material ethical ideals. Weber even favored this in praxis, as when he called for the restoration of the balance of power between employers and workers, which had been destroyed by the rise of "giant

46. *Wirtschaft und Gesellschaft*, pp. 59 f. Cf. *The Age of Bureaucracy*, pp. 64 ff.
47. Industrialisierung und Kapitalismus, pp. 116 f.
48. *Wirtschaft und Gesellschaft*, p. 78.

concerns," with the tools of governmental social policy. If Weber so strongly emphasized "formal rationality" as a condition of modern industrial economies, it was his aim to make it clear that the implementation of material ideals of value, no matter what their nature, could not proceed without social "costs." For him, this had less to do with a defense of the capitalist system as such than with the clarification of the alternative ethical positions that lay behind the quarrel about capitalism. For this reason, Marcuse's criticism of Weber's conception of capitalism had already been anticipated by Weber as a possible alternative position, even if we have to admit that the relevant passages in *Economy and Society* are susceptible to various misunderstandings.

Marcuse's alternative proposal, beyond the "technical rationality" of the capitalist system, or more precisely to return behind it, reveals itself as a form of utopianism that thinks little of the technological assumptions of modern industrial civilization (no matter how it is politically and socially organized) and believes that "technical rationality," no matter how a society is constructed, would always be sufficiently at hand. In contrast, Weber had already pointed out that the realization of a socialism without government—if it were at all possible—could only happen with a substantial loss in technology and civilization (which does not necessarily rule out the desirability of such a system.) It would be possible on the other hand to raise doubts about Max Weber's thesis that the competitive character of the market forces has a more or less rationalizing effect of itself, without calling into question the postulate of "formal rationality" as to the organization of the economy. Such a criticism would then have to present the arguments that speak against the regulation of the economic processes through bureaucratic bodies of officials.

How much such a critique of Max Weber's analysis of capitalism is in danger of ending in utopianism, if the weaknesses he pointed out in the socialist alternative are not taken into account, is demonstrated by Wolfgang Lefèvre's study *Zum historischen Character und zur historischen Funktion der Methode bürgerlicher Soziologie* (*On the Historical Character and the Historical Function of the Methods of Bourgeois Sociology*).[49] Lefèvre attempts, taking Weber as his example, to show that the formalist epistemological method of bourgeois social science has the actual goal of immunizing the capitalist system against every criticism. This is a radical elaboration of Herbert Marcuse's thesis that, through his conceptual method, Weber had shielded "what should be [*das Seinsollen*] from scientific criticism." Lefèvre is anxious to prove Weber's "methodological insufficiency": "It recognizes what the dominant conditions accord

49. *Zum historischen Character und zur historischen Funktion der Methode bürgerlicher Soziologie. Untersuchung am Werk Max Webers* (Frankfurt, 1971).

with; it does not recognize what contradicts those conditions."[50] Of course it is tempting to speak about Lefèvre's "insufficiency of method," if in a somewhat limited sense, since his own thesis is illustrated exclusively by *The Protestant Ethic*, while the later works, especially *Economy and Society*, are treated summarily at best (let alone his apparently consciously sloppy style of citation, which certainly demonstrates a contempt for bourgeois social science—something that Marx and Lenin would never have permitted). Lefèvre's critique is justified as to *The Protestant Ethic*, in which only one significant developmental thread among the incomparable multiplicity of historical reality is singled out. In this work, the phenomenon of capitalism was not in fact examined as such; the working class remained completely in the background although it was formally included in the thesis. We can accept Lefèvre's view to a certain degree when he maintains, with respect to *The Protestant Ethic*, that "the class character of production" is covered "with an indulgent cloud."[51] But this can hardly be said of Max Weber's writings as a whole. Rather, in *Economy and Society*, to take just one example, the class situation of the workers is described with sober and occasionally icy words that are not far from those of Karl Marx.

We have criticized Max Weber's radical formalist interpretation of the modern capitalist system, and especially of "constitutional democracy," from the point of view that in principle it is "serviceable," or can be used in a functionalist way for the most diverse positions. This is also true to a certain extent of the ideal typical model that Weber sketched of a capitalist market economy with maximal rationality. This model can be brought in to defend unlimited rule by employers as much as it can be used as the justification for governmental planning in the interests of specific substantive ideals, e.g., a progressive social policy, especially when this serves the preservation of the system. Marcuse and, to an even greater extent, Lefèvre maintain that the material rationality of bourgeois class rule is hidden behind capitalism's "formal rationality" without being clearly recognized as such. In contrast, it is must be pointed out that Weber took a fundamentally pluralistic position—or, it can be said, a liberal one—which is open to alternatives and rests upon formally preferable prior decisions based on rational values. In no way did Weber dispute the possibility of various socialist alternatives to capitalism, assuming that the supporters of these alternatives did not shrink from the accompanying consequences.

With this consideration, the accusation of dogmatism, veiled by formalist language, returns like a boomerang to Lefèvre himself. For what is

50. Ibid., p. 29.
51. Ibid., p. 72 f.

Lefèvre's concept of truth but a substitution, a Marxist approach, of those social ideals he would like to achieve for historical reality. This can also be clearly recognized as naive Hegelianism that seeks "rationality in the contents of reality," although he himself is incapable of stating it.[52] It is quite possible to exaggerate Lefèvre's research startegy a little by saying: "It recognizes what contradicts the dominant circumstances; it does not recognize what coresonds to these circumstances." How else is it possible to understand when Lefèvre takes on the criticism of the functionalist character of Weber's concept of government, only to logically conclude that it did not go far enough; that it was even more necessary, in tandem with the removal of the capitalist system of production, to free the "political essence" of society "from the power that is separate from it," that is, "to do away with the state."[53] Only extreme blindness to reality could lead him to hold fast to the view, in the knowledge of Weber's analysis in this regard, that a change in the form of the appropriation of the means of production in modern industrial societies characterized by high technological development and an extensive division of labor could make political rule obsolete, instead of asking how such rule under contemporary circumstances can be democratically controlled in an optimal way in the interests at least of those who are immediately affected. From this utopian perspective, those of us who remain attached to a pluralistic liberal society, and who are open to varied forms of social organization, can be dismissed as "salesmen in the goods of 'positive values'" and as "representatives of the Middle Ages."[54] The free communist society offered as an alternative, if it is at all realizable, lies in a very distant future. We are in agreement with Max Weber that society itself cannot govern.[55] Therefore, the problem is to find forms of political organization that with attention to the existing real social conditions combine a high degree of self-determination for the body politic with an optimum of freedom for the individual.

As our analysis of Herbert Marcuse has shown, Max Weber's thesis that the capitalist system, because it is capable of achieving a high degree of formal rationalization in all its operations, is superior to all existing or conceivable alternative economic systems cannot be seen as an ideological justification of late capitalism. Weber also established the point of departure for a criticism of capitalism from the preferred theoretical standpoint of rational values. Weber himself described the tendency of capitalism to produce ever larger bureaucratic apparatuses and to draw a

52. Ibid., p. 56.
53. Ibid., p. 87 f.
54. This no doubt the author's coinage; ibid., p. 92.
55. Cf. ibid., p. 65.

tighter and tighter net of expedient regulations over society from the points of view of universal history and cultural sociology. Weber saw this as a mortal threat to a mankind oriented to free individual values. This is an interpretation that Wolfgang Schluchter has recently pointed to.[56] Weber's position is even less adaptable to utopian plans for the future of a neo-Marxist kind like Lefèvre's.

Jürgen Habermas offers a much more fruitful development of the problem that Marcuse introduced.[57] Habermas concentrates on Weber's concept of rationalization and his conception of legitimacy on the basis of formal legality, and seeks to develop this further in the framework of an altered system of relationships, at the same time excluding the antimodernist, utopian elements of Marcuse's interpretation. Habermas adopts the pluralistic tendency of Weber's theory insofar as he designates the so-called "institutional framework" (which next to the system of government as such also includes the whole complex of traditional value positions, norms, and cultural artifacts) as the bearer of the process of rationalization. The capitalist economic system must of course be considered such a subsystem. Habermas further takes the view that the subsystem of capitalism, at least for the time being, namely in the characteristic phase of late capitalism, has had the function of a secondary legitimation for the political system: "The superiority of the capitalist manner of production over those that preceded it is rooted: (1) in the construction of an economic mechanism that permanently widens the subsystem of purpose-oriented action, and (2) in the creation of an economic justification through which the governmental system can be adapted to the new demands for rationality of these advancing subsystems."[58]

As a result of this process, according to Habermas, the traditional justifications of government are replaced by new ones that appeal to modern social science and are reinforced by a critique of ideology, although they themselves are ideologies.

Habermas views the essential points here of what Max Weber designated as "rationalization." But this does not entirely accord with the diagnosis that Weber applied to his own situation. Weber assigned the political sphere (what Habermas refers to with the more restrictive phrase "institutional framework") an independent position, even under the conditions of rationalization, vis-à-vis the expediently organized subsystems. Recently, Christian von Ferber expressed these circumstances suggestively: "Political action represents the stage in societal leadership that still remains uncontrolled by purpose-oriented action. It is an exten-

56. *Aspekte bürokratischer Herrschaft*, pp. 266 f.

57. "Technik und Wissenschaft als 'Ideologie,'" in *Technik und Wissenschaft als "Ideologie,"* 2d ed. (Frankfurt, 1970), pp. 48 ff.

58. Ibid., p. 70.

sion of mechanized routine actions but at the same time possesses a totally different character."[59] At least in the conditions of his own time, Weber insisted on the fundamental opposition between the political order and the capitalist subsystem although it must be admitted that the relationship between the two was never clearly worked out in his sociology.[60] Weber was therefore not of the view that the capitalist order unequivocally determined the political structure. As early as 1905, he warned against the assumption that the capitalist system was in any way necessarily linked to a liberal or even a democratic order. In his view, the signs pointed largely in the other direction.[61] Within the system of relationships that Weber traced, the problem of legitimacy occurs primarily in the realm of political rule. As we have shown, there is a certain vacuum here in which Weber inserted charismatic legitimacy on the basis of personal authority. Habermas's interpretation goes beyond that of Weber—in our view with good reason—insofar as the possibility for an independent basis of the political system, or as he himself says of the "institutional framework," is doubtful under the conditions of late capitalism.

On the other hand, Habermas starts with a description of conditions that he views as the existing situation, and that Max Weber had viewed as a great danger of the future, namely, the undermining of the autonomy of the political system by the expedient subsystem. From a universal-historical vantage point, Weber saw the greatest threat to the western liberal order in the possibility that the purpose-rational structures of bureaucracy might gradually reduce the voluntarism of the political system and, in the end, do away with it. This would be equivalent to the eventual establishment of the "iron cage of future serfdom." Weber's efforts as a political thinker and sociologist were directed at building protective walls against this trend, which he viewed, at least in tendency, as the dominant feature of the late capitalistic epoch. As a result, it was in no way his view to ascribe legitimizing powers to the capitalist system in relation to the system of government, even if his construction of a formally legal type of legitimacy and his constant mention of "formal rationality" of the capitalist system seemed to point in that direction. On the contrary, he wished to strengthen the internal dynamism of the political system by whatever means available. He saw his conception of "plebiscitary leader democracy" as a suitable tool for counteracting the rigid tendencies of modern bureaucratic societies.

For the same reasons, Max Weber was far from believing that social science as such ought to have the legitimizing function in the societal

59. *Die Gewalt in der Politik* (Stuttgart, 1970), p. 70.
60. Cf. also Ferber, ibid., pp. 68 f.
61. Cf. *Pol. Schr.*, pp. 63 f.

sphere that Habermas designates as a characteristic of late capitalist society. Weber's entire work in sociological theory can be far better understood as an effort to combat the misuse of social science as an instrument for the pseudolegitimation either of ideal values or of governmental systems. He took this position as early as the Freiburg inaugural address, and his bitter struggle for objectivity in the social sciences served the same goals. Weber always insisted that science cannot establish any normative statements. Science can provide information about the means that can be used to achieve distinct goals. It can teach us whether, in the light of our basic moral convictions, these or perhaps other goals should be striven for. It can help us in the end to justify "the ultimate basis of our actions." But it cannot tell us what we ought to do; or, to use Weber's neo-Kantian language, it cannot establish any values. The belief that social science, as a purely positive theory of social techniques or as a critique of ideologies in the service of counterideologies, can itself play a role in justifying governmental systems of a formal legal type, as Habermas has developed it, will be looked for in vain in Weber's work.

For this reason, it is surprising that an attempt has been made to circumscribe by reference to the "examinability of practical positions" the fundamentally voluntarist character of Max Weber's political views with the help of rational science.[62] As we have shown, this affects the very core of Weber's political thought. Hans Albert has asserted that Weber, with his thesis about the noncriticizability of final positions, had conceded far too much to a fundamentalist plane that in no way accorded with his own concept of science.[63] Rather, it is possible to proceed from the postulate of ethics of responsibility—that the politician always has to rationally justify the consequences of his actions—to the conclusion that "convictions relevant to decisions of both objective or value-bearing character" are "rectifiable" on the basis of scientific understanding and "therefore the choice of goals and means in the end are subject to a critical investigation and the evaluation of the consequences."[64] Such an interpretation is, however, not easily reconcilable with Weber's views. Relevant convictions, in his view—at least those of "value-bearing character"—are not fundamentally "rectifiable" through scientific criticism

62. See Maurice Weyembergh's study "Le volontarisme rationnel de Max Weber," Académie Royale de Belgique, *Mémoires de la classe des lettres*, Collection in -8—2e série, T.LXI—Fascicule 1 (Brussels, 1972).

63. Hans Albert, *Traktat über kritische Vernunft*, 2d ed. (Tübingen, 1969), pp. 62 ff.; by the same author, *Plädoyer für kritischen Rationalismus*, pp. 98 ff., and, going into Weber's position in more detail, "Theorie und Praxis: Max Weber und das Problem der Wertfreiheit und der Rationalität," in Hans Albert, *Konstruktion und Kritik: Aufsätze zur Philosophie des kritischen Rationalismus* (Hamburg, 1972), pp. 41 ff.

64. *Plädoyer für kritischen Rationalismus*, p. 100.

but are entirely a matter of personal decision. Science can only make conscious the value priorities that come into play when a decision is being made and thereby facilitate a choice that is, in relation to the goal, the most rational one. Science is even less in a position to narrow down the choice of "goals" as such; it can only provide instrumental knowledge and thereby facilitate responsible action. If it were in the position to have a substantive effect upon the choice of final goals, then it would achieve a legitimizing function of a direct or indirect nature. But Weber's scientific theory does not permit such a possibility.

It was a function of these fundamental convictions that Weber permitted no independent role as such in the sphere of political decision making to the social scientist but was, rather, of the view that both spheres must be strictly kept aloof. "The politician *has to* make compromises, the scholar must not justify them," he once said, characteristically.[65] In the same way, Weber supported the strict separation of science and politics in the institutional sphere. If Weber conceded science a role in politics, it was distinctly a serving one; science was, as Ferber has said, more or less restricted to being "a handmaiden of politics."[66] The political arena is determined by the politicians who set the goals and bring along a mass following or create one, and the bureaucrats who possess the necessary expertise and who thereby furnish the bureaucratic instrumentation of rule. In this connection, Habermas pointed pertinently to the circumstance that the "confrontation of government by [bureaucratic] officials with the political leadership" that is found in pronounced form in Weber's work is tantamount to a strict separation "between the functions of the experts and the politicians."[67]

Such a position, from today's viewpoint which tends to see science as an autonomous productive power, is in a sense unsatisfying. For this reason, Wolfgang Schluchter has recently attempted to determine the role of science within the political decision-making process in Max Weber's work through an extensive investigation of the two speeches "Science as a Vocation" and "Politics as a Vocation." Going beyond Weber, he seeks to determine more precisely the place of science within the political sphere. However, it is difficult to get away from the fact that Weber had fundamentally insisted on a decisionist model of political action. The leading politician had an exclusive "self-responsibility," as Wolfgang Schluchter also emphasizes, to set goals for the body politic and through the application of his charisma to invoke adequate political

65. See above, pp. 309–10 and note 105. "The politician should and must make compromises. But I am a *scholar*."

66. Ferber, *Die Gewalt in der Politik*, pp. 45 f.

67. "Verwissenschaftlichte Politik und Öffentliche Meinung," *Technik und Wissenschaft als "Ideologie*," p. 121.

support. In this regard, the social scientists' skills, whether manifested by officials or expert committees or through the medium of public opinion, cannot take an iota of his responsibility away. That is to say, all attempts by rational science partially to limit the sphere of possible choices of goods by the politician cannot be accommodated within Weber's sociological theory of government.

This does not mean that science has no role whatever to play in the realm of decision making. On the contrary, the politician who acts in accord with the principles of ethics of responsibility has to reflect in advance, and in the best possible way, about the possible consequences of his actions. To this extent, he must inevitably turn to science, which can help reduce the complexity of specific social situations. But it is not automatically possible to set limits on the sphere of decision with the help of scientific criticism, as Schluchter and Albert have recently attempted. In this respect, it is relevant that for Weber personally it was the ethics of responsibility and not the ethics of conviction, which does not offer an analogous point of departure, that was the specific ethic of the politician.[68] Nevertheless, he himself repeatedly made it clear that no material conclusions could be drawn from this fact. The ethics of responsibility were not necessarily superior to the ethics of conscience. Rather, he constantly pointed out that he who acts according to the principles of the ethics of conviction need not take into account the likely consequences of his action and thereby can do without a rationalization of his decision and of the values guiding it with the help of scientific knowledge. This notwithstanding, he must be accorded in principle the same justification for his deeds as he who acts in accordance with the standards of the ethics of conviction, as long as he is prepared to answer for his ideals with his whole person—if necessary with his body and life.[69] Weber's sympathy for the anarchists and his support for Ernst Toller in 1920 confirm this interpretation. In critical situations, Weber's own conduct in political matters also corresponded with the norms of the ethics of conviction rather than those of the ethics of responsibility. It may be said, however, that the notion of the ethics of responsibility could well have served as the point of departure for the development of a normative ethics, but this was never, apparently, worked out.[70]

68. Cf. also the cautious, limited treatment by H. H. Bruun, *Science, Values, and Politics in Max Weber's Methodology*, pp. 269 ff.

69. Cf., e.g., *Pol. Schr.*, p. 546.

70. To that extent, Wolfgang Schluchter's attempt (in his treatise *Wertfreiheit und Verantwortungsethik: Zum Verhältnis von Wissenschaft und Politik bei Max Weber*) to prove that the ethic of responsibility in Weber's work is in principle given a higher value than the ethic of conviction is not completely convincing. Cf. my review in *Historische Zeitschrift* 215 (1972): 434 ff.

Moreover, the model of an ethic of responsibility permitted the choice of extreme positions that would customarily be referred to as irrational, and this accords completely with the requirement of rationally taking into account the likely consequences of extreme positions. Weber saw the rigorous rationalization of one's life conduct by a man or a group of men in the service of "ultimate positions" or "otherworldly" ideals as the most significant means of social change: it is tantamount to a projection of the inner life outward, as for example in Puritanism or Jewish prophecy. In no case, however, can the criterion of "realizability" proposed by Albert and Schluchter bridge the distance between responsible decisions, which involve the rational control of the goals and ultimate values guiding them by scientific means, and decisions arrived at on the basis of ultimate value convictions.[71] Certainly, politics is bound to be successful; but Weber fought nothing so much as the maxim that political goals should be adjusted toward what is currently realizable. Grand politics is precisely the opposite of adjustment to the given circumstances. It aims beyond the ordinary. Only then can the crust of political structures be pierced and new ground broken.[72] Unrealistic political positions ought to be eliminated as a result of political competition, not as the result of scientific criticism. A "scientific filter" would lead to a dangerous weakening of the free dynamic strugge between Weltanschauungen and different political persuasions.[73]

What remains is this: science ought not to trace the boundaries of the possible. It ought rather to help the politician choose consistently from various alternatives in the light of his own ultimate ideals. As H. H. Bruun has convincingly pointed out, Weber's call for abstention from value judgments had a dual purpose: on the one hand to prevent the mediatization of the political by transferring "final" decisions to science; on the other hand to shield science from the direct influence of the politicians and thereby to prevent scientists from producing pseudo-normative assumptions by confusing values and facts.[74] Rather, science ought to offer only the information, criteria, and techniques that make possible the rational choice between various goals, taking into account

71. Cf. Schluchter, *Wertfreiheit und Verantwortungsethik*, pp. 51 ff.; Albert, *Plädoyer*, pp. 98 ff.

72. Cf. *Wissenschaftslehre*, p. 514: "It is—rightly understood—relevent that a successful policy is always the 'art of the possible.' But it is no less correct that the possible can often be achieved only by grasping for what lies beyond what appears impossible."

73. Cf. also Ferber, *Die Gewalt in der Politik*, p. 74: "Politics represents for him [i.e., Max Weber] the sphere of primary freedom in society, that will be won and maintained in struggle, in constant argument. A freedom that lives from the rivalry of equal, necessarily irreconcilable positions. The law of the strongest decides who prevails in the struggle."

74. Bruun, *Science, Values, and Politics* in *Max Weber's Methodology*, pp. 17 ff.

the current social context, and that help increase the efficiency of goal implementation.

This can be summed up as follows: In Weber's view, science and politics had complementary functions. Without being directly linked, they were related to one another. They received their impulse from the same root, namely, the will to create a rational world in accord with the final values and ideals that individuals believed themselves bound by. Only asceticism, only abstinence from immediate partisanship, as well as independence from the political pressures of the day, would permit science to be in a position to fulfill its social function satisfactorily. Max Weber emphatically defended the relative freedom that the bourgeois liberal system permitted science. He was among those who never had illusions about the limits of scholarly freedom in Wilhelminian Germany. All his life he combatted the exclusion of Social Democrats from the academic community and the occasional discrimination against Jews by not admitting them to the *Habilitation* (the qualification for lecturing at universities). He argued against confessionally restricted professorial chairs as well as against the manipulation of university appointments by the cultural ministries. At the same time, he was a stern defender of the principle of unrestricted competition within the academic system. In this regard, the American university system seemed to have considerable advantages over the German.[75] Weber's concern that the bureaucratization of advancement in the universities would have unfortunate consequences prompted him to reject material security for younger university instructors as well: "It must be written in the soul of every *Privatdozent* that under no circumstances does he have any tangible right to any support. Away with all points of view that remind us of the bureaucracy and of the career schemes of petty officers, sergeants, etc., or about equal rights, etc., in short, of any kind of bureaucratic frame of reference."[76] The model of inexorable competition that we encounter in the economic-societal field, and even more in the political sphere, Weber applied to the academic community as well. In this instance the struggle focused on the power over minds, while the proof of accomplishment was assured by scholarly associations and academic publicity.

Substantial similarities between politics and science may be observed

75. Cf. Max Weber's speech at the Vierten Deutschen Hochschullehrertag in 1911, which referred directly to Professor Fullerton's (New York) paper "Die von den deutschen abweichenden Einrichtungen an den amerikanischen Hochschulen," in *Verhandlungen des 4. Deutschen Hochschullehrertags zu Dresden am 12. und 13. Oktober 1911*. Bericht erstattet vom engeren geschäftsführenden Ausschuss (Leipzig, 1910,) p. 47.

76. Proceedings of the Third Convention of German High School Teachers, Leipzig, 12–13 October 1909. Report of steering committee, Leipzig, 1910, p. 47.

here. As Schluchter has also correctly shown,[77] the politician and the scientist are related to the extent that both act from "self-responsibility" for their "subject."[78] Both types of conduct are rooted in strict personal moral convictions, which give their action goals and direction, however different their objects are. If the politician lacks "belief" in his cause, "then even apparently great political successes are burdened . . . by the curse of mundane nothingness."[79] Similarly, all creative scientific activity rests in the end on the "*belief* in the meta-empirical importance of final and ultimate value ideas, on which we base the meaning of our existence."[80] Both the politician and the scientist work, each in his way, to achieve the reification of social reality, to transform the alienated products of human action and to do so in a manner that will constantly remake those products for the world of man—of creative, responsible man.

The basic structure of Max Weber's thought can be seen in the common condition that prompts the politician's and the scientists's creative power: the fact that each stands with one foot in the "axiological" sphere of absolute, unbridgeable conflicts of values,[81] which scientific methods cannot circumvent. As Bruun has pointed out, this has its parallel in the political sphere in the ideal of the permanent struggle between different political parties, camps, nations, and comparable groups.[82] The politician's central task therefore lies in setting social goals.[83] To be sure, we can scarcely go along with Bruun when he also attributes the definition of politics as the "carrying out of transindividual goals" to Max Weber himself. This does not accord with the special function in Weber's work of the political leader, who we have shown acts out of "personal responsibility" and does not represent the average opinion of a group. It is not fortuitous that the ideal-typical model of "domination" in Weber's work is reducible to the *individual* relationship between "command" and "submission." This command model, however, as Niklas Luhmann has explained, places the basis of the rationalization of governmental relations in "the standpoint of an individual participant: of the founder, the entrepreneur, the ruler."[84]

The highly personal individual goals that the great, charismatically

77. *Wertfreiheit und Verantwortungsethik*, pp. 43 f.

78. The formulation is modeled on Weber's treatment in *Pol. Schr.*, p. 335.

79. *Pol. Schr.*, p. 548.

80. *Wissenschaftslehre*, p. 213.

81. Cf. Weyembergh, *Le volontarisme rationnel de Max Weber*, pp. 378 ff.

82. Cf. Bruun, *Science, Values, and Politics*, p. 241, whose treatment is close to mine on this matter.

83. Ibid., pp. 242 f.

84. "Zweck, Herrschaft, System," in Niklas Luhmann, *Politische Planung: Aufsätze zur Soziologie von Politik und Vervaltung* (Opladen, 1971), p. 97.

qualified politician establishes from his personal conviction of course require implementation in the social sphere. For this reason, the normal requirement is the creation of a "following," in other words, the establishment of a relationship of authority over a narrow circle of supporters, which in Weber's sense is described throughout as the exercise of power, namely "power over minds." The specific tool of the politician, however, is power, so that he can assert his will also over those who do not immediately follow his opinions. Power is, as a rule, already reified by the institutionalized opportunity in a system of government to find obedience to orders. Only in extreme instances is it manifested in the application of "physical force." But it is such extreme cases that demonstrate reality in its true dimension. It is impossible to sidestep the fact that Weber identified the political with the readiness to exercise "physical force."[85] Bruun's thesis that the recourse to "physical force" is almost exclusively relegated to foreign policy, and that Weber withdrew from force in domestic policy, does not in the least detract from the characteristic emphasis on power that is the dominant feature of Max Weber's political theory.[86] To be sure, the application of "physical power" is found above all in foreign policy, since it is not to the same degree contained by institutional regulations of various sorts. Weber himself said that in domestic politics the application of "physical force" had become an exceptional case—e.g., the carrying out of death sentences, or indirectly in the form of the obligation to stake one's life in case of war for the state. But it is well known that the exception proves the rule. Moreover, it is incorrect to stipulate a strict separation between foreign and domestic policy in Weber's notion of politics. Few have ever recognized as clearly as did Weber, or stressed so repeatedly, the dependence of a strong foreign policy on domestic affairs.

Weber's political work forms an impressively unified conception that cannot be disproved by reference to internal inconsistencies. If one accepts Weber's premises, it is easy to be imprisoned by them.[87] I have attempted to avoid this dilemma without being willfully unjust to Weber's thinking. The basis of my presentation is the careful compilation and evaluation of all accessible materials against the background of the

85. Cf. Ferber, *Die Gewalt in der Politik*, pp. 54 ff.

86. Bruun's objections to my interpretation (*Science, Values, and Politics*, p. 251, note 15, and p. 253, note 23) overshoot their goal, for I have never maintained that Max Weber favored power politics as a goal in itself, i.e., as an end of power purely in itself. The passages from *Wirtschaft und Gesellschaft* that Bruun employs against my "'radical' interpretation" have been taken into account in detail in my work.

87. I make use here of a formulation of Luhmann's (loc. cit., p. 52) in somewhat altered circumstances.

contemporary situation of his day. From the point of view of method, I started with an internal interpretation of Max Weber's works and sought to clarify the inconsistencies and contradictions in his position, while at the same time recognizing its fundamental consistency, notwithstanding the changes in his attitude toward numerous individual questions occasioned by the dramatic political events of his lifetime. Moreover, it was my intention to explore Weber's political position and political thought from a radical-liberal position to which he, in many regards, was quite close. I thereby essentially limited myself to Max Weber the "politician" in the narrow sense. If I had to write this book again, I would choose a more comprehensive framework, giving equal balance to the theoretical work, like the approach taken by H. H. Bruun and Maurice Weyembergh.[88] Yet I hope that my approach will be of value along with these works, even if its chief importance is as a definitive portrayal of the political role and thought of Max Weber against the background of the German politics of his time.

88. Unfortunately I cannot go further into the study by David Beetham, *Max Weber and the Theory of Modern Politics* (London, 1974), which appeared after the completion of this manuscript.

Digression

On the Question of the Relationship between the Formal Legality and the Rational Legitimacy of Rule in Max Weber's Works

Carl Schmitt was probably the first to criticize Max Weber's third type of legitimacy of rule because of its purely formalistic, functional character. Formal legality alone in the sense of Max Weber's definition—"the most common form of legitimacy today is the belief in *legality*, the submission to *formally* correct laws that are enacted in the usual form"[1]—could never engender sincere belief in the internal justification of contemporary ruling powers and could therefore never form an effective basis for legitimacy. Only a moral basis for statutes could create the necessary legitimizing power. The appearance of a purely functionalist constitutional theory, which ignored the moral foundations of the constitutional democratic state and instead found a criterion for the validity of statutes only in the formal correctness of the legislative procedure, was a sign that these moral foundations had lost their legitimizing power.[2]

Johannes F. Winckelmann has attempted to show that Max Weber had not sought to base his third pure type of legitimacy of rule upon a purely formal conception of legality.[3] But the opposite is true; Max Weber's view of legitimacy and legality as a legitimizing principle implicitly encompassed Carl Schmitt's critique of the concept of legality and in fact assumed it. Schmitt failed to recognize this because of his legal-normative

1. *Wirtschaft und Gesellschaft*, p. 19.
2. *Legalität und Legitimität*, p. 140.
3. *Legitimität und Legalität in Max Webers herrschaftssoziologie* (Tübingen, 1952), p. 140 (hereafter cited as *Legitimität und Legalität*); cf. also "Die Herrschaftskategorien der politischen Soziologie und die Legitimität der Demokratie," *Archiv für Rechts- und Sozialphilosophie* 40 (1946): 383 ff.

approach as opposed to an empirical-sociological one. At the time, Winckelmann agreed with Carl Schmitt's arguments against the purely formal basis of the concept of legality in the Weimar state, which had ultimately facilitated the quasi-legal seizure of power by National Socialism, but he attempted to demonstrate that this did not contradict Weber's views.[4]

We have already discussed Weber's influence on Carl Schmitt's theory of the conflict between parliamentary legality and plebiscitary legitimacy. In fact, to a certain degree, Carl Schmitt merely drew radical conclusions from the premises that were already outlined in Weber's theory of legitimacy. Of course, he went beyond Weber when he interpreted the relationship between rational legality and plebiscitary legitimacy as an absolute contradiction. But I think he could have drawn upon Weber here too, since Weber had also recognized the conflict between plebiscitary leadership and the nomination of political leaders according to formal democratic procedures.[5] If this conflict does not surface directly in Weber's work, it is because he believed that legitimacy based upon accepted legality had taken on a formalist character in the modern constitutional state. For this reason, we can only accept half of Winckelmann's thesis.

Winckelmann, like Weber, distinguishes between legitimacy based upon value-rational belief in legality and the purpose-rational belief in legality. He assumes it to be possible to conclude that Max Weber had not thought to ascribe the latter line of legality, in any genuine sense, with a legitimizing effect. He argues: "In principle, Max Weber draws upon rational, and certainly value-rationally oriented, rule of law in his concept of 'legal domination.' Only when it is debased and appears in its degenerative form does it become a debased, ethically neutral, purely purpose-rational and formal authority of legality."[6] In other words, Weber, in principle, in no way defended a purely formal, functionalist view of the modern democratic constitutional state, a view that dispensed with all morally rational justifications for constitutions and law. Nevertheless, in the framework of his empirical, value-free sociology, Weber had to accept the possibility of the impure form of legitimacy based on customary belief in the legality of laws passed in a formally correct manner, since in an empirical sense these laws could have a legitimizing effect. From the point of view of value-free empirical sociology, he had to treat the correct and the "false" consciousness equally.

4. Cf. Alfred Karsten, *Das Problem der Legitimität in Max Webers Idealtypus der rationalen Herrschaft* (Hamburg, 1960).

5. Cf. *Wirtschaft und Gesellschaft*, pp. 562 f.

6. *Legitimität und Legalität*, pp. 72 f.

We cannot agree with this description in its central points. It is admittedly correct that, from the reference point of empirical sociology, Weber had to treat merely formal legality as a form of legitimacy, even if no legitimizing effect could be attributed to it from a normative point of view. Yet, in the sense of Winckelmann's terminology, Weber had "false" consciousness. He could no longer believe in the possibility of an ethical-rational democratic order in a pure sense. For him, the characteristic of all modern constitutional rule was *formal* legalism; the democratic constitutional state was no different from others in this respect.

Winckelmann himself has to admit that Weber, "in his discussion of the 'three pure types,' frequently stressed the type of rational rule (hence not traditional or charismatic) that appeared most frequently at the time and was the most problematic for him: the type of purely *formal* legal rule, instead of the third type of legitimacy that he envisioned *in principle*: 'rational rule.'"[7] In fact, the passages that support Winckelmann's thesis shrink to *two* in which Weber expressly distinguishes between value-rational and purpose-rational legitimacy: *Economy and Society*, pp. 36 and 217.[8] Here as well, the value-rationally oriented belief in legality takes a back seat to the form of purpose-rational legality (this can be seen especially in *Economy and Society*, p. 36, par. 7). Here, the value-rational type is treated separately and *not* subsumed under rationally enacted law, with which we have to deal in the case of modern legal rule. Statuted law appears here for Weber to be purely purpose-rational. Weber presents natural law as the purest type of value-rational validity. The special treatment of the value-rational type of legitimacy belief in this reference is tailored to this, but clearly with the reservation that it has only a small significance today. The second reference reads: "Arbitrary law" could "be *statuted* through agreement or rational imposition, either value-rational or purpose-rational (or both)."[9] This contradicts the previously cited reference insofar as "statuted" law is seen here under some circumstances to have a value-rational character. This absolutely excludes the interpretation that Max Weber, in principle, ascribed legitimizing force only to value-rationally oriented legality. It is precisely in regard to this reference that Carl Schmitt's objection—that *arbitrary* law cannot be proclaimed in a value-rational framework—has validity.

In further defense of his thesis Winckelmann adds that "(objectively

7. Ibid., p. 64.

8. The reference cited by Winckelmann (ibid., note 16) from *Religionssoziologie*, vol. 1 (I), also excludes any basis for his thesis. The formulation on p. 273 clearly validates pragmatically based legality; the formulation on pp. 267 f. is not relevent, because the constitution, which is what is under discussion here, could be statuted, in Weber's view, either ethically-rationally or pragmatically.

9. *Wirtschaft und Gesellschaft*, p. 125.

speaking) a merely expedient order as such cannot claim such legitimate validity, nor does a merely pragmatically motivated orientation express an agreement about legitimacy in an actually existing order. Otherwise it would not be possible to distinguish a *legitimate* order from an expediently statuted illegitimate order."[10] This point can be affirmed, but not the consequence that Winckelmann attempts to draw, namely that true legitimacy can only be based on value-rational principles, at least insofar as this point is also attributed to Weber. For Weber a purely expediently statuted order is conceivable if it is accepted as legitimate in the eyes of the subjects. Weber always envisioned *this* case, while the type of rule based upon "substantial value order" possessed no significance for him whatever and thus played a purely secondary role in the sociological casuistic of *Economy and Society*. His expressed parallel between the legal rule situation in the state and in the private capitalist enterprise does not permit any other interpretation.[11] The relationship between employer and employee rests frankly on a purely purpose-rational order, which is formally legitimized by a contract between them or their representatives. In Weber's view, the statuted order received its dignity and its normative character formally, through positive statutes passed by an organ accepted as legitimate and not because of any ethical norms, whether immanent or expressed, nor on the basis of "internal sacredness." It passed these statutes either in the form of the agreement of "interests" in this existing order, or—far more frequently in practice—through imposition by a legitimately valid ruler.[12] Winckelmann's attribution to Weber of the belief that the democratic order belongs, "as a form of rule, in the category of legitimately rational rule" only when it is "oriented to material principles of legitimacy on a value-rational basis" and supported by a belief in legitimacy, is therefore untenable.[13] Weber believed that any modern legal rule was possible only on the basis of pragmatic principles. In the evolution of occidental modes of rationalization, as he himself described it, "the legitimacy of rule" evolved into "the legality of general *rules* that were pragmatically devised, statuted in correct form, and proclaimed."[14] In connection with Weber, Winckelmann describes this universal process of demagification,[15] but forgets to draw Weber's consequences for himself. In total contrast to the conclusions that arise from Winckelmann's views, Weber never perceived value-rationally based

10. *Legitimität und Legalität*, pp. 95 f.
11. Cf. *Wirtschaft und Gesellschaft*, p. 551.
12. Cf. ibid., p. 19.
13. Ibid., p. 48.
14. *Religionssoziologie*, Vol. 1, p. 273.
15. *Legitimität und Legalität*, pp. 66 ff.

legitimacy of domination to be a genuine source of legitimacy. For Weber, parliamentary democracy was a pragmatic institution for the selection of leadership personalities, and nothing more. He therefore did not take into account the standard of any "substantive principles of legitimacy." Rather, he laid the accent on purely formal legality. Only in the background do we have the idea that democracy was *rebus sic stantibus* the most appropriate means of keeping bureaucratization in check. But Weber *never* consciously took the path of establishing a *value*-rational basis for democracy. Winckelmann's interpretation is blatently incorrect when he points to so-called "immanent limits of legitimacy" of an ethical kind in Weber's theory of democratic rule. The quasi-natural-law material ethical norms that Winckelmann is evidently thinking of (e.g., freedom of conscience) no longer play a role in Weber's functionalist theory of democratic rule.[16]

Winckelmann's efforts to free the type of rational legitimacy from its formalist character and thus make it applicable to modern political theory strike me as meaningful and applaudable. He should not, however, attribute his own neo-natural-law views, which I consider fully justified within certain limits, to Weber retrospectively. It is totally misleading to try to attribute such a neo-natural-law interpretation to Weber, even tangentially. Weber's "leadership democracy" does not represent the affirmation of a fundamental ethical order, or even the "minimization of rule," but the opposite—an increase in the power of the nation state and the selection of leaders who are charismatically gifted within a society hardened into bare legalism. For Weber, democracy in an institutional sense was just what Winckelmann justifiably rejects, a "*purely* expedient" system.[17] When Winckelmann points out that the questions of a "technical form of state" were subordinate to realizable ethical values for Max Weber,[18] we should certainly not seek these values in a value-rational order based upon ultimate values or anything similar. In Weber's view, values could be realized only by individuals; in modern mass democracy, this task fell to charismatic leaders. The government organization, along with the legal order on which it is based, was merely a functionalist system of "rules of the game" and could be rationally restructured at any time. Immanent "limits on legitimacy" did not exist in

16. Winckelmann's (p. 41, n. 43) specific references to *Wirtschaft und Gesellschaft* relate entirely to the mechanical limits on the exercise of power, which are determined by the division of power but as a general rule do *not* rest upon ethical conceptions in principle but are themselves entirely positively statuted. Beyond this, no stress whatsoever is laid on them.

17. Winckelmann, *Staat und Gesellschaft*, p. 37.

18. *Legitimität und Legalität*, p. 45, note 58a.

it. In the context of Carl Schmitt's ideas, Winckelmann has attempted to point out the dualistic character of modern legal consciousness and the parallel existence of purely formal "legality of statutory law" and the "legitimacy of a higher law in the sense of ideal and generally held legal convictions in the legally constituted society." He should not try to defend this view by invoking Max Weber, who considered the trend to pure legal positivism to be irreversible.[19]

19. Compare Winckelmann, "Die verfassungsrechtliche Unterscheidung von Legitimität and Legalität," *Zeitschrift für die gesamte Staatswissenschaft* 112 (1956): 173.

Bibliography

I. A Selection of Works by Max Weber Available in English

This section was prepared especially for the English edition. The order is by date of publication of the German originals.

"Developmental Tendencies in the Situation of East Elban Rural Labourers." Translated by Keith Tribe. *Economy and Society* 8 (1979): 172–205.

"The National State and Economic Policy" (Freiburg address). Translated by Keith Tribe. *Economy and Society* 9 (1980): 420–49.

"The Social Causes of the Decay of Ancient Civilization." Translated by Christian Mackauer. *Journal of General Education* 5 (1950–51): 75–88. Reprinted in *The Interpretation of Social Reality*, ed. J. E. T. Eldridge (New York: Scribner, 1971). Also translated by R. I. Frank in *The Agrarian Sociology of Ancient Civilizations* (see below).

The Protestant Ethic and the Spirit of Capitalism. Translated by Talcott Parsons. 2d ed., with Introduction by Anthony Giddens. London: Allen & Unwin, 1976; New York: Scribner, 1977.

"Anticritical Last Word on *The Spirit of Capitalism*." Translated by Wallace M. Davis. *American Journal of Sociology* 83 (1977–78): 1105–31.

Roscher and Knies: The Logical Problems of Historical Economics. Translated by Guy Oakes. New York: Free Press, 1975.

"R. Stammler's 'Surmounting' of the Materialist Conception of History." Translated by Martin Albrow. *British Journal of Law and Society* 2, no. 2 (Winter 1975): 129–52; and 3, no. 1 (Summer 1976): 17–43.

Critique of Stammer. Translated by Guy Oakes. New York: Free Press, 1977.

The Methodology of the Social Sciences. Translated by Edward A. Shils and Henry A. Finch. Glencoe, Ill.: Free Press, 1949.

"Max Weber on Bureaucratization in 1909." Translated by J. P. Mayer. Appendix I, pp. 125–31, to J. P. Mayer, *Max Weber and German Politics: A Study in Political Sociology*, 2d ed. London: Faber & Faber.

On Universities: The Power of the State and the Dignity of the Academic Calling in Imperial Germany. Translated by Edward Shils. Chicago: University of Chicago Press, 1974.

The Agrarian Sociology of Ancient Civilizations. Translated by R. I. Frank. London: NLB; Atlantic Highlands, N.J.: Humanities Press; 1976.

The Religion of China: Confucianism and Taoism. Translated by Hans H. Gerth. Glencoe, Ill.: Free Press, 1951.

The Religion of India: The Sociology of Hinduism and Buddhism. Translated by Hans H. Gerth and Don Martindale. New York: Free Press, 1958.

Ancient Judaism. Translated by Hans H. Gerth and Don Martindale. New York: Free Press, 1952.

Socialism. Occasional Paper no. 11. Durban, Natal: Institute for Social Research, University of Natal, 1967.

Basic Concepts in Sociology. New York: Philosophical Library; London: Peter Owen; 1962.

The Theory of Social and Economic Organization. A translation by A. M. Henderson and Talcott Parsons of part 1 of *Wirtschaft und Gesellschaft*. London and Edinburgh: William Hodge; New York: Oxford University Press; 1947. Reprinted New York: Free Press, 1968. Also reprinted as part 1 of *Economy and Society: An Outline of Interpretative Sociology* (see below).

"The Three Types of Legitimate Rule." Translated by Hans H. Gerth. *Berkeley Publications in Society and Institutions* 4 (1958): 1–11.

"Some Categories of Interpretive Sociology." Translated by Edith Graber. *Sociological Quarterly* 22 (1981): 145–80.

The Sociology of Religion. Boston, Mass.: Beacon Press, 1963; London: Methuen, 1965.

Economy and Society: An Outline of Interpretive Sociology. Translated by Ephraim Fischoff, Hans H. Gerth, A. M. Henderson, Ferdinand Kolegar, C. Wright Mills, Talcott Parsons, Max Rheinstein, Guenther Roth, Edward Shils, and Claus Wittich. Edited by Guenther Roth and Claus Wittich. 3 vols. New York: Bedminster Press, 1968. Reprinted, in 2 vols., Berkeley and Los Angeles: University of California Press, 1978. Includes, as Appendix I, "Types of Social Action and Groups" (short excerpts from the 1913 *Logos* paper on categories of *verstehende* sociology); and, as Appendix II, "Parliament and Government in a Reconstructed Germany" (1917–18).

The Rational and Social Foundations of Music. Translated by Don Martindale, Johannes Riedel, and Gertrude Neuwirth. Carbondale: Southern Illinois University Press, 1958.

General Economic History. Translated by Frank H. Knight. New Brunswick and London: Transaction Books, 1982.

From Max Weber: Essays in Sociology. Translated by Hans H. Gerth and C. Wright Mills. Includes "Politics as a Vocation."

Selections in Translation. Translated by E. Matthews. Edited by W. G. Runciman. Cambridge: Cambridge University Press, 1976. New translations of 24 papers or excerpts, 19 of which had, and 5 had not, previously appeared in English.

Max Weber on Capitalism, Bureaucracy, and Religion. Edited and, in part, newly translated by Stanislav Andreski. London: Allen & Unwin, 1983.

II. Literaturverzeichnis

Reproduced from the German edition of 1974

1. Benutzte Nachlaß- und Aktenmaterialien

Nachlaß Max Weber:
Teil I: Ehem. Preußisches Geheimes Staatsarchiv, jetzt Deutsches Zentralarchiv II, Merseburg, Rep. 92.
Teil II: Im Besitz von Prof. Dr. Baumgarten, Mannheim = Archiv Ebnet (A. E.)
Einzelne Materialien: Max Weber Archiv, München

Nachlaß Eduard Bernstein
Institut für Sozialgeschichte, Amsterdam

Nachlaß Lujo Brentano; Korrespondenz:
Bundesarchiv Koblenz

Nachlaß Hans Delbrück:
Teil I: Deutsche Staatsbibliothek Berlin
Teil II: Bundesarchiv Koblenz
Deutsche Staatsbibliothek Berlin

Nachlaß Adolf v. Harnack: Korrespondenz:
Deutsche Staatsbibliothek Berlin

Nachlaß Conrad Haußmann:
Hauptstaatsarchiv Stuttgart (HStA Stgt.)

Nachlaß Wolfgang Heine:
Archiv für die Soziale Demokratie, Bonn-Bad Godesberg

Nachlaß Georg Gothein: Korrespondenz 1913–1916, Fasz. 14:
Bundesarchiv Koblenz

Nachlaß Georg Jellinek:
Bundesarchiv Koblenz

Nachlaß Friedrich Naumann:
Deutsches Zentral-Archiv I Potsdam

Nachlaß Schiffer:
Hauptstaatsarchiv Berlin-Dahlem

Nachlaß Gustav v. Schmoller:
Ehem. Preußisches Geheimes Staatsarchiv, jetzt Deutsches Zentralarchiv II, Merseburg

Nachlaß Gustav Stresemann:
Bundesarchiv Koblenz

Akten des Reichsamts des Innern
Deutsches Zentral-Archiv I, 19487, 19523
Akten des Reichsamts des Innern III, Verfassung und Verwaltung, Nr. 40 betr. die Verfassung des Deutschen Reiches Bd. 1–9 (16807–815)
Akten des Reichskanzleramts
I Gr. 34, Reichsbehörden, 2[2]a:
Staatssekretäre im Reichsamt des Innern
II Kriegsakten
1, Bd. 11 und 12 vom 2. 1. 1917 bis 28. 7. 1918 (2398/10 u. 11)
5[1], U-Boot-Krieg (2410)
15, Vorschläge zu Friedensverhandlungen, 17 Bde., umfassend den Zeitraum vom 14. 9. 1914 bis 5. 11. 1918 (2442/10–2447/2)
15 geh., Deutscher National-Ausschuß, Bd. 1, 2 (2248)
IV Revolutionsakten
3[1], Geschäftsgang: 12. 5. 1918 bis 6. 2. 1919
38, Reichsverfassung, 13. 12. 1918 bis 6. 2. 1919
Akten der Sozialisierungskommission:
Bd. III (3107).
Alle angeführten Reichsakten befinden sich im ehem. Reichsarchiv, jetzt Deutsches Zentralarchiv I, Potsdam
Preußisches Ministerium des Innern:
Akta betr. die neue Verfassung des Reiches 1918/19
Befindlich im ehem. Preußischen Geheimen Staatsarchiv, jetzt Deutsches Zentralarchiv II, Merseburg
Protokolle der ersten beiden Sitzungen des Arbeitsausschusses Mitteleuropa, vom 22. 2. und 28. 2. 1916. Nachlaß Baernreither. Österreichisches Haus-, Hof- und Staatsarchiv Wien. (Ich danke die Beschaffung dieser Materialien Herrn cand. phil. Dieter Flamm)

2. Schriften Max Webers

Gesammelte Politische Schriften, 1. Aufl., München 1921
Gesammelte Politische Schriften, 2. Aufl., herausgegeben von J. F. Winckelmann, Tübingen 1958
Gesammelte Politische Schriften, 3., erneut vermehrte Auflage, herausgegeben von J. F. Winckelmann, Tübingen 1971
Gesammelte Aufsätze zur Religionssoziologie, 3 Bde., Tübingen 1920/21
Gesammelte Aufsätze zur Soziologie und Sozialpolitik, Tübingen 1924
Gesammelte Aufsätze zur Sozial- und Wirtschaftsgeschichte, Tübingen 1924
Gesammelte Aufsätze zur Wissenschaftslehre, 1. Aufl., Tübingen 1922, 3. Auflage, hg. von Johannes Winckelmann, Tübingen 1968
Grundriß der Sozialökonomik, Bd. 1, Wirtschaft und Gesellschaft, 1. Aufl., Tübingen 1920

Wirtschaft und Gesellschaft. Grundriß der verstehenden Soziologie, 4. Aufl., hg. von Johannes Winckelmann, 2 Halbbde., Tübingen 1956
Die protestantische Ethik I. Eine Aufsatzsammlung. Hg. von Johannes Winckelmann, 3. Aufl., München, Hamburg 1973
Die protestantische Ethik II. Kritiken und Antikritiken. Hg. von Johannes Winckelmann, 2. Aufl., München, Hamburg 1972
Rechtssoziologie. Aus dem Manuskript herausgegeben und eingeleitet von Johannes Winckelmann, 2. Auflage, Neuwied 1967
Economy and Society. An Outline of Interpretive Sociology, ed. by Guenther Roth and Claus Wittich, New York 1968
From Max Weber: Essays in Sociology, tranls., edited and with an introduction by Hans H. Gerth and C. Wright Mills, Oxford 1946
Die drei reinen Typen der legitimen Herrschaft, Preußische Jahrbücher Bd. 187, 1921, S. 1–12
Wirtschaftsgeschichte. Aus den nachgelassenen Vorlesungen herausgegeben von S. Hellmann und Dr. M. Palyi, München, Leipzig 1923
Max Weber: Soziologie, Weltgeschichtliche Analysen, Politik, herausgegeben von J. F. Winckelmann (Auswahlausgabe mit nahezu erschöpfender Bibliographie der Schriften Max Webers) Stuttgart 1956
Jugendbriefe, Tübingen o. J. (1936)
Die Verhältnisse der Landarbeiter im ostelbischen Deutschland. Auf Grund der Erhebungen des Vereins für Sozialpolitik, Schriften des Vereins für Sozialpolitik Bd. 55, Teil 3, Leipzig 1892
Entwicklungstendenzen in der Lage der ostelbischen Landarbeiter, Archiv für soziale Gesetzgebung und Statistik Bd. 7, 1894
Entwicklungstendenzen in der Lage der ostelbischen Landarbeiter, Preußische Jahrbücher Bd. 77, 1894 (jetzt in den Gesammelten Aufsätzen zur Soziologie und Sozialpolitik)
Privatenquêten über die Lage der Landarbeiter, Mitteilungen des evangelisch-sozialen Kongresses, April, Juni, Juli 1892
Zur Rechtfertigung Göhres, Christliche Welt, 6. Jahrg., 1892, Sp. 1104–1109
Die Erhebung des evangelisch-sozialen Kongresses über die Verhältnisse der Landarbeiter Deutschlands, Christliche Welt, 7. Jahrg. 1893, Sp. 535–40
Die Erhebung des Vereins für Sozialpolitik über die Lage der Landarbeiter. In 6 Teilen. Das Land, 1. Jahrg., 1893, S. 8 f., 24 ff., 43 ff., 58 f., 129 f., 147 f.
Besprechung von Theodor Frh. v. d. Goltz, Die ländliche Arbeiterklasse und der preußische Staat, und Max Sering, Die innere Kolonisation im östlichen Deutschland. Das Land, 1. Jahrg., 1893, S. 231 f.
Was heißt Christlich-Sozial? Christliche Welt, 8. Jahrg., 1894, Sp. 472–77
Die Verhandlungen auf der preußischen Agrarkonferenz, Sozialpolitisches Zentralblatt Bd. 3, 1894, S. 573 ff.

Die Kampfesweise des Freiherrn v. Stumm, Neue Preußische Zeitung (Kreuzzeitung) vom 26. 2. 1895; nebst einem Eingesandt vom 12. 3. 1895

Der preußische Gesetzentwurf über das Anerbenrecht bei Rentengütern, Soziale Praxis, 4. Jahrg., 1895, S. 956–960

Besprechung von Vallentin, Westpreußen in den ersten Jahrzehnten dieses Jahrhunderts, Historische Zeitschrift Bd. 76, 1896, S. 308 f.

Berichte der Frankfurter Zeitung, Nr. 48 vom 17. 2. 1896 und Nr. 75 vom 15. 3. 1896, 3. Morgenblatt über Max Webers Vorlesungen über Agrarpolitik am Freien Deutschen Hochstift

Bericht des Frankfurter Volksboten vom 14. 3. 1896 über Max Webers Vortrag am Freien Deutschen Hochstift über «Agrarschutz und positive Agrarpolitik» vom 13. 3. 1896

Bericht der Frankfurter Zeitung vom 8. 3. 1896 über eine Rede Max Webers im Frankfurter Christlich-Sozialen Verein über «die zukünftige Bodenverteilung in Deutschland»

Die Ergebnisse der deutschen Börsenenquête, Zeitschrift für das gesamte Handelsrecht, Bde. 43, 44, 45, 1895/96

Die technische Funktion des Terminhandels, Deutsche Juristenzeitung Jahrg. 1, Nr. 11 vom 1. Juni 1896, S. 207 ff., und Nr. 13 vom 1. Juli 1896, S. 248 ff.

Artikel Börsenwesen im Handwörterbuch der Staatswissenschaften, 1. Aufl. 1. Supplementband, Jena 1895

Artikel Börsengesetz im Handwörterbuch der Staatswissenschaften, 1. Aufl. 2. Supplementband, Jena 1897

Diskussionsrede auf der Gründungsversammlung des National-Sozialen-Vereins vom 23. bis 25. November 1896, Protokoll über die Vertreterversammlung aller National-Sozialen in Erfuhrt vom 23. bis 25. Nov. 1896, Berlin 1896

Bericht der Badischen Landeszeitung Nr. 294, 2. Blatt vom 16. 12. 1897 über einen Vortrag Max Webers in Mannheim über die geschichtliche Stellung des modernen Kapitalismus

Stellungnahme zur Flottenumfrage der Münchener Allgemeinen Zeitung. Außerordentliche Beilage, Nr. 3 zu Nr. 46 vom 13. Januar 1898, S. 4 f.

Die Landarbeiter in den evangelischen Gebieten Norddeutschlands. In Einzeldarstellungen nach den Erhebungen des evangelisch-sozialen Kongresses. Herausgegeben von Max Weber, Tübingen 1899. Mit einer Vorbemerkung Max Webers

Herr v. Miquel und die Landarbeiterenquête des Vereins für Sozialpolitik, Soziale Praxis, 8. Jahrg., 1899, Sp. 640–42

The Relations of the Rural Community to other Branches of Social Science (Translated by Professor Charles W. Seidenadel, Ph. D., University of Chicago), in: Congress of Arts and Science, Universal Exposition, St. Louis, 1904, hg. von Howard J. Rogers, Bd. 7, Boston 1906

Kapitalismus und Agrarverfassung. Vortrag in St. Louis 1904. Rückübersetzung von Prof. H. Gerth. Zeitschrift für die gesamte Staatswissenschaft Bd. 108, 1952

Zur Beurteilung der gegenwärtigen politischen Entwicklung Rußlands. Zusammen mit S. J. Giwago. Archiv für Sozialwissenschaft und Sozialpolitik Bd. 22, 1906, Beilage

Rußlands Übergang zum Scheinkonstitutionalismus. Archiv für Sozialwissenschaft und Sozialpolitik Bd. 23, 1906, Beilage

Zuschrift betr. die badische Fabrikinspektion. Frankfurter Zeitung Nr. 24 vom 24. 1. 1907, 1. Morgenblatt

Der Fall Bernhard. Zuschrift an die Frankfurter Zeitung. Nr. 168, 1. Morgenblatt vom 18. 6. 1908

Die Kredit- und Agrarpolitik der preußischen Landschaften. Bankarchiv Bd. 8, 1908, S. 87–91

Der «Fall Bernhard» und Professor Delbrück. Frankfurter Zeitung vom 10. 7. 1908, Nr. 190, 4. Morgenblatt

Die sogenannte «Lehrfreiheit» an den deutschen Universitäten. Frankfurter Zeitung vom 20. September 1908, 3. Morgenblatt

Bericht des Heidelberger Tagblatts über einen Vortrag Georg Jellineks über «Kaiser und Reichsverfassung» nebst der sich daran anschließenden Diskussion. Nr. 282 vom 2. 12. 1908, S. 4

Die Lehrfreiheit der Universitäten 1909. Wiederabgedruckt in: Süddeutsche Zeitung. 3. 11. 1973

Rede auf dem 3. Deutschen Hochschullehrertag. Verhandlungen des 3. Hochschullehrertages zu Leipzig am 12. und 13. 10. 1909. Bericht erstattet vom engeren geschäftsführenden Ausschuß, Leipzig 1910

Stellungnahme zum Fall Althoff. Tägliche Rundschau Nr. 497 vom 22. Oktober 1911, 2. Beilage

Die Handelshochschulen. Eine Entgegnung. Berliner Tageblatt Nr. 548 vom 27. 10. 1911

Denkschrift an die Handelshochschulen vom 7. 11. 1911, in: Werk und Person

Rede auf dem 4. Deutschen Hochschullehrertag. Verhandlungen des 4. Deutschen Hochschullehrertages. Bericht, erstattet vom engeren geschäftsführenden Ausschuß, Leipzig 1912, S. 66 ff.

Gutachten über die Werturteilsfrage. In: Äußerungen zur Werturteilsdiskussion im Ausschuß des Vereins für Sozialpolitik. Als Manuskript gedruckt 1913

An der Schwelle des dritten Kriegsjahres, Rede für den «Deutschen National-Ausschuß» am 1. 8. 1916; Bericht des Fränkischen Kuriers, 84. Jg., Abendausgabe vom 2. 8. 1916 (Abgedruckt in Anhang I)

Bericht der Fränkischen Tagespost vom 2. 8. 1916 über dieselbe Rede

Bericht der Nürnberger Zeitung vom 2. 8. 1916 über dieselbe Rede

Bericht über Max Webers Vortrag in München vom 22. Oktober 1916 über «Deutschlands weltpolitische Lage». Münchener Neueste Nachrichten Nr. 551 vom 28. 10. 1916, Abendausgabe

Ein Wahlrechtsnotgesetz des Reichs. Das Recht der heimkehrenden Krieger. Frankfurter Zeitung vom 28. 3. 1917, 1. Morgenblatt. Jetzt Pol. Schr., 3. Auflage, S. 192 ff.

Parlamentarisierung und Föderalismus. Frankfurter Zeitung vom 26. 4. 1917. (Etwas verändert in den Pol. Schr., 3. Auflage, S. 406 ff. abgedruckt)

Eine katholische Universität in Salzburg. Frankfurter Zeitung vom 10. 5. 1917, 1. Morgenblatt

Die Abänderung des Artikels 9 der Reichsverfassung. Erschienen als Leitartikel der Frankfurter Zeitung vom 8. 9. 1917. (Nachdruck in der 1. Auflage dieses Buches. Jetzt Pol. Schr. S. 192 ff.)

Die siebente deutsche Kriegsanleihe, Frankfurter Zeitung, 1. Morgenblatt, vom 18. 9. 1917 (mit Kürzungen abgedruckt in Pol. Schr. S. 226 ff.)

Für den Verständigungsfrieden gegen die alldeutsche Gefahr, Rede auf einer Massenkundgebung in München am 5. 11. 1917, Bericht der Münchener Neuesten Nachrichten, Jg. 70, Nr. 662, vom 6. 11. 1917. Abgedruckt in Anhang IV

Schwert und Parteienkampf, Frankfurter Zeitung, 1. Morgenblatt, vom 13. 12. 1917

Aristokratie und Demokratisierung in Deutschland, Berliner Tageblatt, 47. Jg., Nr. 30, vom 17. 1. 1918, Morgenausgabe, abgedruckt in Anhang V.

Bericht der Münchener Allgemeinen Zeitung über eine Rede Max Webers auf einer Versammlung der Fortschrittlichen Volkspartei in München vom 4. 11. 1918 über Deutschlands politische Neuordnung. Nr. 559 vom 5. 11. 1918

Bericht der Wiesbadener Zeitung über eine Rede Max Webers für die Deutsche Demokratische Partei in Wiesbaden vom 5. 12. 1918. Nr. 621, Abendausgabe vom 6. 12. 1918

Bericht des Wiesbadener Tagblatts über dieselbe Rede. Nr. 570, Abendausgabe vom 6. 12. 1918

Bericht der Vossischen Zeitung über eine Rede Max Webers für die Deutsche Demokratische Partei im ersten Berliner Reichstagswahlkreis vom 20. 12. 1918, Nr. 653 vom 22. 12. 1918, S. 2

Bericht des Berliner Tageblatts über dieselbe Rede. Nr. 651 vom 21. 12.

Bericht der Heidelberger Neuesten Nachrichten über Max Webers Wahlrede für die Deutsche Demokratische Partei am 2. Januar 1919 in Heidelberg

Bericht des Heidelberger Tagblatts über dieselbe Rede, «Deutschlands Wiederaufrichtung», Nr. 2 vom 3. 1. 1919

Bericht der Badischen Presse über Webers Wahlrede für die Deutsche Demokratische Partei in Karlsruhe am 4. Januar 1919 über «Deutschlands Vergangenheit und Zukunft». Nr. 7, Mittagsblatt vom 6. 1. 1919, S. 2

Bericht der Badischen Landeszeitung Nr. 7, Mittagsblatt, vom 6. 1. 1919 über dieselbe Rede
Bericht des Karlsruher Tagblatts, 1. Blatt vom 5. 1. 1919 über dieselbe Rede
Bericht der Fürther Zeitung über Webers Wahlrede für die Deutsche Demokratische Partei am 14. Januar in Fürth vom 15. 1. 1919
Bericht der Nordbayrischen Zeitung vom 15. 1. 1919 über dieselbe Rede
Bericht des Heidelberger Tageblatts vom 18. 1. 1919 über Webers Rede vom 17. 1. 1919: «Der Volksstaat und die Parteien»
Gegen Frankreichs Anspruch auf Pfalz und Rheinbecken. Protestkundgebung von Lehrkörper und Studentenschaft der Ruprecht-Karls-Universität Heidelberg vom 1. März 1919. Ansprachen von Rektor Prof. Dr. Chr. Bartholomae, Oncken, Wolfgang Windelband, stud. phil. et nat. Thiel, Max Weber. Heidelberg 1919
Bemerkungen zum Bericht der Kommission der alliierten und assoziierten Regierungen über die Verantwortlichkeit der Urheber des Krieges. Nebst einer Vorbemerkung zu den Anlagen der Denkschrift. Vom 27. Mai 1919 (sogenannte Viererdenkschrift). In: Das deutsche Weißbuch über die Schuld am Kriege. Mit der Denkschrift der deutschen Viererkommission zum Schuldbericht der Alliierten und Assoziierten Mächte. 1. Aufl., Berlin 1919

3. Periodica

Frankfurter Zeitung, Jahrg. 1896–1919
Die Hilfe, Selbsthilfe, Bruderhilfe, Staatshilfe. Eine Wochenschrift. Herausgegeben von Friedrich Naumann, Jahrg. 1, 1894/95 bis Jahrg. 26, 1920
Die Verhandlungen des evangelisch-sozialen Kongresses. Nach den stenographischen Protokollen. 1.–8. Kongreß, 1890–1897
Verhandlungen der Generalversammlung des Vereins für Sozialpolitik zu Berlin, 1893. Auf Grund der stenographischen Niederschrift herausgegeben vom ständigen Ausschuß. Schriften des Vereins für Sozialpolitik Bd. 58, 1893
Verhandlungen der Generalversammlung des Vereins für Sozialpolitik zu Mannheim 1905. Auf Grund der stenographischen Niederschrift herausgegeben vom ständigen Ausschuß. Schriften des Vereins für Sozialpolitik Bd. 116, 1905
Verhandlungen der verfassungsgebenden Deutschen Nationalversammlung zu Weimar. Stenographische Berichte Bd. 326, 327, 328, 1919
Verhandlungen der verfassungsgebenden Deutschen Nationalversammlung Bd. 336. Anlagen zu den stenographischen Berichten Nr. 391: Bericht und Protokolle des 8. Ausschusses der deutschen Nationalversammlung über den Entwurf einer Verfassung des Deutschen Reiches. Berlin 1920

Heidelberger Neueste Nachrichten, Jahrg. 1917–1919
Statistisches Jahrbuch der Stadt Berlin, Jg. 1 (1889/90)

4. Allgemeine Literatur

Abramowski, Günter:
Das Geschichtsbild Max Webers. Universalgeschichte am Leitfaden des okzidentalen Rationalisierungsprozesses, Stuttgart 1966
Agulla, Juan Carlos:
Max Weber und die Theorie des sozialen Handelns, phil. Diss. München, Cordoba 1964
Albert, Hans:
Plädoyer für kritischen Rationalismus, München 1971
– Traktat über kritische Vernunft, Tübingen [2]1969
– Konstruktion und Kritik. Aufsätze zur Philosophie des kritischen Rationalismus, Hamburg 1972
Albertin, Lothar:
Liberalismus und Demokratie am Anfang der Weimarer Republik, Düsseldorf 1972
Andrewski, Stanislav:
Method and Substantive Theory in Max Weber. The British Journal of Sociology, Bd. 15, 1964
Annäherung:
Die wirtschaftliche Annäherung zwischen dem Deutschen Reiche und seinen Verbündeten. Hrsg. im Auftrage des Vereins für Sozialpolitik von Heinrich Herkner. Schriften des Vereins für Sozialpolitik Bd. 155. Teil 1 und 3. Berlin 1916
Anschütz, Gerhard:
Die Verfassung des Deutschen Reichs. Ein Kommentar für Wissenschaft und Praxis, 5. Aufl., Berlin 1926
Antoni, Carlo:
Vom Historismus zur Soziologie. Übersetzt von Walter Goetz, Stuttgart 1950
Apelt, Willibald:
Geschichte der Weimarer Verfassung, München 1946
Aron, Raymond:
Max Weber und die Machtpolitik. Zeitschrift für Politik, Bd. 11, 1964
– Main Currents in Sociological Thought, Bd. 2, New York 1967
Baden, Prinz Max v.:
Erinnerungen und Dokumente, Berlin 1927
Barkin, Kenneth D.:
The Controversy over German Industrialization 1890–1902, Chicago 1970

Barth, Theodor, und Naumann, Friedrich:
Die Erneuerung des Liberalismus, Berlin 1906
Basler, Werner:
Deutschlands Politik in Polen und im Baltikum 1914–1918, Berlin 1962
Baumgart, Winfried:
Deutsche Ostpolitik 1918, München 1968
Baumgarten, Eduard:
Die Bedeutung Max Webers für die Gegenwart. Die Sammlung, 5. Jahrg., 1950, S. 385–401
– Max Weber. Werk und Person, Tübingen 1964
Baumgarten, Hermann:
Der deutsche Liberalismus. Eine Selbstkritik. Preußische Jahrbücher Bd. 18, 1866, S. 455 ff., 575 ff.
– Historische und politische Aufsätze und Reden. Mit einer biographischen Einleitung von Erich Marcks. Straßburg 1894
– Treitschkes Deutsche Geschichte, 3. Aufl., Straßburg 1883
Baumgarten, Otto:
Meine Lebensgeschichte, Tübingen 1929
Beetham, David:
Max Weber and the Theory of Modern Politics, London 1974
Bendix, Reinhard:
Max Weber. Das Werk Darstellung, Ergebnisse, Analyse München 1964
– Max Weber. An Intellectual Portrait, New York 1960
– Einige Bemerkungen zu einem Buch von Wolfgang Mommsen. Kölner Zeitschrift für Soziologie und Sozialpsychologie 13, 1961
Bendix, Reinhard/Roth, Guenther:
Scholarship and Partisanship. Essays on Max Weber, London 1971
Bergstraesser, Arnold:
Max Webers Antrittsvorlesung in zeitgeschichtlicher Perspektive. Vierteljahrshefte für Zeitgeschichte, 5. Jahrg., 1957, S. 209 ff.
Bergstraesser, Ludwig:
Geschichte der politischen Parteien in Deutschland, 7. Aufl., München 1952
Bierstedt, Robert:
The Problem of Authority, in: M. Berger, Th. Abel, Ch. H. Page, Freedom in Modern Society, New York 1954
Birnbaum, Norman:
Conflicting Interpretations of the Rise of Capitalism. The British Journal of Sociology, Bd. 4, 1953
Bismarck, Otto v.:
Gesammelte Werke, Friedrichsruher Ausgabe, Berlin 1926–1935
– Gedanken und Erinnerungen. Bd. 1 und 2, Stuttgart 1898, Bd. 3, Stuttgart und Berlin 1919

Bonhard, Otto:
Geschichte des Alldeutschen Verbandes, Berlin 1920
Born, Karl Erich:
Staat und Sozialpolitik seit Bismarcks Sturz, Wiesbaden 1958
Boese, Franz:
Geschichte des Vereins für Sozialpolitik 1872–1932, Berlin 1939
Bracher, Karl Dietrich:
Die Auflösung der Weimarer Republik, 1. Aufl., Stuttgart 1956, 2. Aufl., Stuttgart 1957, mit umfassendem Literaturverzeichnis
Brecht, Arnold:
Politische Theorie, Tübingen 1961
Bruun, H. H.:
Science, Values, and Politics in Max Weber's Methodology, Copenhagen 1972
Bund zur Erneuerung des Reiches:
Die Rechte des Reichspräsidenten nach der Reichsverfassung, Berlin 1933
Burckhardt, Jakob:
Weltgeschichtliche Betrachtungen, Krönerausgabe, 7. Aufl., Stuttgart 1949
Burián, Stefan Graf:
Drei Jahre, Berlin 1923
Burin, Frederic S.:
Bureaucracy and National Socialism: A Reconsideration of Weberian Theory, in: Robert K. Merton u. a., Reader in Bureaucracy, Glencoe/Ill. 1952, S. 33 ff.
Bussmann, Walter:
Treitschke als Politiker. Historische Zeitschrift Bd. 174, 1954, S. 249 ff.
Cerny, H.:
Storm over Max Weber, The Encounter, Bd. 23.2, 1964
Chickering, Roger:
A Voice of Moderation in Imperial Germany. Journal of Contemporary History, Bd. 8, 1973
Conrad, Else:
Der Verein für Sozialpolitik und seine Wirksamkeit auf dem Gebiet der gewerblichen Arbeiterfrage, Jena 1906
Conze, Werner:
Friedrich Naumann. Grundlagen und Ansatz seiner Politik in der national-sozialen Zeit (1895–1903) in: Schicksalswege deutscher Vergangenheit (Festschrift Kaehler), Düsseldorf 1952
– Die Wirkungen der liberalen Agrarreform auf die Volksordnung in Mitteleuropa im 19. Jahrhundert. Vierteljahrshefte für Sozial- und Wirtschaftsgeschichte Bd. 38, 1949
– Polnische Nation und deutsche Politik im ersten Weltkrieg, Heidelberg 1953

– Nationalstaat oder Mitteleuropa? Die Deutschen des Reichs und die Nationalitätenfragen Ostmitteleuropas im ersten Weltkrieg. In: Deutschland und Europa, Festschrift für Hans Rothfels, 1951
Dehio, Ludwig:
Ranke und der deutsche Imperialismus. Historische Zeitschrift, Bd. 170, 1950
– Gedanken über die deutsche Sendung 1900–1918. Historische Zeitschrift, Bd. 174, 1952
Dibble, Vernon:
Social Science and Politcal Committments in the Young Max Weber, Archives Européennes de Sociologie, Bd. 9, 1968
Dieckmann, Johann:
Max Webers Begriff des modernen okzidentalen Rationalismus, Köln (phil. Diss.) 1961
Drahomanov, Mykhaylo:
A Symposium and Selected Writings. The Annals of the Ukrainian Academy of Arts and Sciences in the U. S., vol. II, Nr. 1, New York 1952
Dronberger, Ilse:
The Political Thought of Max Weber. In Quest of Statesmanship, New York 1971
Düding, Dieter:
Der National-Soziale Verein 1896–1903. Der gescheiterte Versuch einer parteipolitischen Synthese von Nationalismus, Sozialismus und Liberalismus, München 1972
Duverger, Maurice:
Institutions Politiques et droit constitutionnel, Paris ^{11}1970
– Die politischen Parteien, Tübingen 1959
– La IVème République et le Régime présidentiel, Paris 1961
Eisenstadt, S. N.:
The Protestant Ethic and Modernization, New York 1968
Eisermann, Gotfried:
Max Weber und Amerika. Cahiers Wilfrido Pareto, Bd. 4, Genève 1964
Emmet, Dorothy:
Function, Purpose, and Power, London 1958
Engisch, Karl, Pfister, Bernhard und Winckelmann, Johannes: Max Weber. Gedächtnisschrift der Ludwig-Maximilian-Universität München zur 100. Wiederkehr seines Geburtstages, Berlin 1966
Ensor, R. C. K.:
England 1890–1914. Oxford Modern History of England, vol. 4, Oxford 1936
Entwurf, Reichsverfassung:
Entwurf der künftigen Reichsverfassung (allgemeiner Teil). Herausgege-

ben im Auftrage des Reichsamts des Innern, Berlin 1919 (enthält die Denkschrift zum 1. Entwurf von Hugo Preuß)
Eschenburg, Theodor:
Die improvisierte Demokratie der Weimarer Republik. In: Geschichte und Politik, Heft 10, Laupheim 1954
– Das Kaiserreich am Scheidewege, Berlin 1929
Eyck, Erich:
Das persönliche Regiment Wilhelms II., Zürich 1948
Falk, Werner:
Democracy and Capitalism in Max Weber's Sociology. Sociological Review, Vol. XXVII, London 1935
Ferber, Christian von:
Die Gewalt in der Politik, Stuttgart 1970
Fischer, Fritz:
Griff nach der Weltmacht. Die Kriegszielpolitik des kaiserlichen Deutschland 1914–1918, 3. Aufl., Düsseldorf 1964
Fleischmann, Eugène:
De Weber à Nietzsche, Archives Européennes de Sociologie, Vol. 5, 1964
Frank, Walter:
Hofprediger Adolf Stoecker und die christlich-soziale Bewegung, 2. Aufl., Hamburg 1935
Fraenkel, Ernst:
Die repräsentative und die plebiszitäre Komponente im demokratischen Verfassungsstaat. In: Recht und Staat in Geschichte und Gegenwart, Heft 219/220, Tübingen 1958
Frantz, Constantin:
Bismarckismus und Fridericianismus. O. O., 1873
Freund, Julien:
The Sociology of Max Weber, New York 1968
Freyer, Hans:
Soziologie als Wirklichkeitswissenschaft, Leipzig, Berlin, 1930
– Theorie des gegenwärtigen Zeitalters, Stuttgart 1955
Friedensburg, Ferdinand:
Die Weimarer Republik, Berlin 1946
Friedrich, Carl J.:
Der Verfassungsstaat der Neuzeit, Berlin, Göttingen, Heidelberg, 1953
– Political Leadership and the Problem of the Charismatic Power, in: Journal of Politics, Febr. 1961
– Die Legitimität in politischer Perspektive, in: Politische Vierteljahresschrift, Jg. 1 (1960), S. 119 ff.
– Politische Autorität und Demokratie, in: Zeitschrift für Politik, N. F. Jg. 7 (1960), S. 1 ff.
– Authority, Reason and Discretion, in: Nomos, Bd. 1 (hg. v. C. J. Fried-

rich für The American Society of Political and Legal Philosophy), Harvard University Press 1958, S. 28 ff.
– Some Observations on Weber's Analysis of Bureaucracy, in: Robert K. Merton u. a., Reader in Bureaucracy, Glencoe/Ill., 1962, S. 27 ff.
Frye, Bruce B.:
A Letter from Max Weber. Journal of Modern History, Vol. 39, 1967
Gatzke, Hans W.:
Germany's Drive to the West. A Study of Germany's Western War Aims during the First World War, Baltimore 1950
Gegenadresse gegen die Seebergadresse:
mitgeteilt von Delbrück in den Preußischen Jahrbüchern Bd. 169, S. 306 f. (1917). Die Liste der Unterzeichner abgedruckt in den Preußischen Jahrbüchern Bd. 162, 1915, S. 169 f.
Genarotti, Franco:
Max Weber e il destino della ragione, Bari 1965
Gerth, Hans:
in: Gerth/Mills, From Max Weber, Essays in Sociology, New York 1958
Giddens, Anthony:
Capitalism and Modern Social Theory. An analysis of the writings of Marx, Durkheim and Max Weber, Cambridge 1971
– Politics and Sociology in the Thought of Max Weber, London 1972
Gneist, Rudolf v.:
Zur Verwaltungsreform und Verwaltungsrechtspflege in Preußen, Leipzig 1880
Grab, H. J.:
Der Begriff des Rationalen in der Soziologie Max Webers, Karlsruhe 1927
Grau, Richard:
Die Diktaturgewalt des Reichspräsidenten. In: Handbuch des deutschen Staatsrechts, Bd. 2, 1930–32, S. 274 ff.
Green, Robert W.:
Protestantism and Capitalism. The Weber Thesis and its critics, New York 1959
Grell, H.:
Der Alldeutsche Verband. Seine Geschichte, seine Bestrebungen und Erfolge, München 1898
Grosser, Dieter:
Vom monarchischen Konstitutionalismus zur parlamentarischen Demokratie, Den Haag 1970
Habermas, Jürgen:
Technik und Wissenschaft als Ideologie, Neuwied 1968
– Legalitätsprobleme im Spätkapitalismus, Frankfurt 1973
Habermas, Jürgen/Luhmann, Nicklas:
Theorie der Gesellschaft oder Sozialtechnologie, Neuwied 1971

Hallgarten, George F. W.:
Imperialismus vor 1914. 2 Bde., München 1951
Hättich, Manfred:
Der Begriff des Politischen bei Max Weber, Politische Vierteljahresschrift, Bd. 8, 1967
Hauptprobleme:
Hauptprobleme der Soziologie. Erinnerungsgabe für Max Weber. 2 Bde., München 1923
Haußmann, Conrad:
Schlaglichter, Reichstagsbriefe und Aufzeichnungen, Frankfurt 1924
Haußner, Arthur:
Die Polenpolitik der Mittelmächte und die österreichisch-ungarische Militärverwaltung in Polen während des Weltkrieges, Wien 1935
Heffter, Heinrich:
Die deutsche Selbstverwaltung im 19. Jahrhundert, Stuttgart 1950
Heieck, Ludwig (Hg.):
Staat, Gesellschaft, Wirtschaft. Quellentexte zur politischen Bildung aus Max Webers gesammelten Werken, Heidelberg 1967
Helfferich, Karl:
Der Weltkrieg. 3 Bde., Berlin 1919
Hellmann, G.:
Max Weber. Deutsche Akademische Rundschau, 6. u. 7. Jahrg. 12. Semesterfolge, 1925
Hennis, Wilhelm:
Zum Problem der deutschen Staatsanschauung. Vierteljahrshefte für Zeitgeschichte, 7. Jahrg., 1959, Heft 1
Henrich, Dieter:
Die Einheit der Wissenschaftslehre Max Webers. Heidelberger phil. Diss. 1949, Tübingen 1952
Herzfeld, Hans:
Die moderne Welt 1789–1945. Teil II, Braunschweig 1957
Heuß, Alfred:
Theodor Mommsen und das 19. Jahrhundert, Kiel 1956
– Max Weber und das Problem der Universalgeschichte, in: Zur Theorie der Weltgeschichte, Berlin 1968
– Max Webers Bedeutung für die Geschichte des griechisch-römischen Altertums. Historische Zeitschrift, Bd. 201, 1965
Heuß, Theodor:
Friedrich Naumann. Der Mann, das Werk, die Zeit, 1. Aufl., Berlin 1937, 2. Aufl., Stuttgart, Tübingen 1949
– Deutsche Gestalten, Stuttgart 1947
– Max Weber in seiner Gegenwart. In: Max Weber, Gesammelte Politische Schriften, 2. Aufl., Tübingen 1958

Hintze, Otto:
Wirtschaft und Politik im Zeitalter des modernen Kapitalismus. Zeitschrift für die gesamte Staatswissenschaft Bd. 87, 1929

Honigsheim, Paul:
Max Weber als Soziologe. Kölner Vierteljahreshefte für Sozialwissenschaft, Jahrg. 1/2, 1921/22
– Max Webers geistesgeschichtliche Stellung. Die Volkswirte, 29. Jahrg. Heft 13/16, 1930
– Der Max-Weber-Kreis in Heidelberg. Kölner Vierteljahreshefte für Soziologie, Jahrg. 5, Heft 3, 1926
– On Max Weber. Collected Essays, New York 1968

Hufnagel, Gerd:
Kritik als Beruf. Der kritische Gehalt im Werk Max Webers, Frankfurt 1971

Hughes, Stuart H.:
Consciousness and Society. The Reorientation of European Thought 1890–1930, London 1959

Huizinga, Johan:
Geschichte und Kultur, Stuttgart 1954

Janoska-Bendl, Judith:
Methodologische Aspekte des Idealtypus. Max Weber und die Soziologie der Geschichte, Berlin 1965

Janssen, Karl-Heinz:
Die Kriegsziele der deutschen Bundesstaaten 1914–1918, Göttingen 1973

Jaspers, Karl:
Three Essays: Leonardo, Descartes, Max Weber, New York 1964
– Bemerkungen zu Max Webers politischem Denken, in: Antidoron, Festschrift für Edgar Salin, Tübingen 1962
– Max Weber. Eine Gedenkrede, Tübingen 1920
– Max Weber. Deutsches Wesen im politischen Denken, im Forschen und Philosophieren, Oldenburg 1932
2. Aufl., Bremen, 1946 unter dem Titel: Max Weber. Politiker, Forscher, Philosoph

Karsten, Alfred:
Das Problem der Legitimität in Max Webers Idealtypus der rationalen Herrschaft, Hamburg 1960

Käser, Dirk (Hg.):
Max Weber. Sein Werk und seine Wirkung, München 1972

Kaufmann, Erich:
Grundfragen der künftigen Reichsverfassung, Berlin 1919
– Bismarcks Erbe in der Reichsverfassung, Berlin 1917

Kehr, Eckart:
Schlachtflottenbau und Parteipolitik 1894–1901, Historische Studien 197, Berlin 1930
Kelsen, Hans:
Der juristische und der soziologische Staatsbegriff, Tübingen 1928
Knoll, Joachim H.:
Führungsauslese in Liberalismus und Demokratie, Stuttgart 1957
Kocka, Jürgen:
Karl Marx und Max Weber. Ein methodologischer Vergleich. Zeitschrift für die gesamte Staatswissenschaft, Bd. 122, 1966. Neudruck in: Hans-Ulrich Wehler (Hg.), Geschichte und Ökonomie, Neue wissenschaftliche Bibliothek 58, Köln 1973
Köhler, Walter:
Ernst Troeltsch, Tübingen 1941
Kolko, Gabriel:
A Critique of Max Weber's Philosophy of History, in: Ethics, Vol. 70, 1959
– Max Weber on America. Theory and Evidence, in: History and Theory, Vol. 1, 1961
Kollmann, Eric C.:
Eine Diagnose der Weimarer Republik. Ernst Troeltschs politische Anschauungen. Historische Zeitschrift Bd. 182, 1956, S. 291 ff.
Koellreutter, Otto:
Die staatspolitischen Anschauungen Max Webers und Oswald Spenglers. Zeitschrift für Politik, Jahrgang XIV, 1925
König, René:
Max Weber. In: Die Großen Deutschen, Bd. 4, 1957, S. 408 ff.
– Einige Überlegungen zur Frage der 'Werturteilsfreiheit' bei Max Weber, in: Kölner Zeitschrift für Soziologie und Sozialpsychologie, Jg. 16 (1964)
– Zur Soziologie der zwanziger Jahre, in: Die Zeit ohne Eigenschaften. Eine Bilanz der zwanziger Jahre, Stuttgart 1961
Kruck, Alfred:
Geschichte des Alldeutschen Verbandes 1890–1939, Wiesbaden 1954
Kühlmann, Richard v.:
Erinnerungen, Heidelberg 1948
Laband, Paul:
Deutsches Reichsstaatsrecht, 6. Aufl., Tübingen 1912
Lachmann, Ludwig M.:
The Legacy of Max Weber: Three Essays, London 1970
Lammers, H. H.:
Parlamentarische Untersuchungsausschüsse. Handbuch des deutschen Staatsrechts, Bd. 2, Tübingen 1930–32

Landshut, Siegfried:
Max Webers geistesgeschichtliche Bedeutung. Jahrbuch für Wissenschaft und Jugendbildung, Heft 6, 1931

Langer, William J.:
The Diplomacy of Imperialism 1890–1902, 2. Aufl., New York 1951

Laubert, Martin:
Die preußische Polenpolitik von 1772–1914, 3. Aufl., Berlin 1944

Lazarsfeld, Paul/Oberschall, Anthony:
Max Weber and Empirical Social Research. The American Sociological Review, Vol. 30,2, 1965

Lefèvre, Wolfgang:
Zum historischen Charakter und zur historischen Funktion der Methode bürgerlicher Soziologie. Untersuchung am Werk Max Webers. Neuwied 1972

Leibholz, Gerhard:
Die Auflösung der liberalen Demokratie in Deutschland und das autoritäre Staatsbild, München 1933
– Der Strukturwandel der modernen Demokratie, Karlsruhe 1952

Lenk, Kurt:
Ideologie, 2. Aufl. Neuwied 1964

Lenk, Kurt, unter Mitwirkung von Hočevar, Rolf K.:
Max Weber. In: Hans Maier, Heinz Rausch, Horst Denzer, Klassiker des politischen Denkens, Bd. 2, München 1968

Lewinskij, Vladimir:
Volk, Nation und Nationalität. Abhandlungen des Ukrainischen Wissenschaftlichen Institutes in Berlin, Bd. 2, 1929

Liebert, Arthur:
Max Weber, Preußische Jahrbücher, Bd. 210, 1927

Lindenlaub, Dieter:
Richtungskämpfe im Verein für Sozialpolitik. Wissenschaft und Sozialpolitik im Kaiserreich, vornehmlich vom Beginn des 'Neuen Kurses' bis zum Ausbruch des Ersten Weltkrieges, 1890–1914. Vierteljahresschrift für Sozial- und Wirtschaftsgeschichte, Beiheft 52/3, Wiesbaden 1967

Loewenstein, Karl:
Max Webers staatspolitische Auffassungen in der Sicht unserer Zeit, Frankfurt 1965
– Max Weber als 'Ahnherr' des plebiszitären Führerstaats. Kölner Zeitschrift für Soziologie und Sozialpsychologie, Bd. 13, 1961

Löwith, Karl:
Max Weber und Karl Marx, Archiv für Sozialwissenschaft und Sozialpolitik, Bd. 67, 1927; Neudruck in: Gesammelte Abhandlungen. Zur Kritik der geschichtlichen Existenz, Stuttgart 1969

– Max Weber und seine Nachfolger. Maß und Wert, 3. Jahrg., Heft 1, 1939, S. 166–176
– Die Entzauberung der Welt durch Wissenschaft. Merkur, Bd. 18, 1964
Luckemeyer, Ludwig:
Die Deutsche Demokratische Partei bis zur Nationalversammlung 1918 bis 1919, Gießen (phil. Diss., MS.) 1972
Luhmann, Niklas:
Zweck – Herrschaft – System. Grundbegriffe und Prämissen Max Webers, Der Staat, Bd. 3, 1964
– Politische Planung. Aufsätze zur Soziologie von Politik und Verwaltung, Opladen 1971
Lukács, Georg:
Die Zerstörung der Vernunft, Berlin 1954
Lukes, Steven:
Methodological Individualism Reconsidered. The British Journal of Sociology, Vol. 19, 1968
– Emile Durkheim. His Life and Work. A historical and critical study, New York 1972
Lüthy, Herbert:
Once Again: Calvinism and Capitalism. The Encounter, Vol. 22,1, 1964
Maier, Hans:
Max Weber und die deutsche Politische Wissenschaft, in: H. Maier, Politische Wissenschaft in Deutschland, München 1969
Marcuse, Herbert:
Der Kampf gegen den Liberalismus in der totalitären Staatsauffassung, in: Kultur und Gesellschaft 1, Neuwied 1965. Erstdruck in Zeitschrift für Sozialforschung, Bd. 3, Paris 1934
– Industrialisierung und Kapitalismus, in: Max Weber und die Soziologie heute. Verhandlungen des 15. Deutschen Soziologentages, Tübingen 1965. Abgedruckt unter dem Titel «Industrialisierung und Kapitalismus im Werk Max Webers» auch in: Herbert Marcuse, Kultur und Gesellschaft 2, Neuwied 1965
Mayer, Jacob P.:
Max Weber in German Politics, 1. Aufl., London 1944
2. Aufl., London 1956
McCormack, Th.:
The Protestant Ethic and the Spirit of Capitalism, British Journal of Sociology, Vol. 20, 1969
Meinecke, Friedrich:
Staat und Persönlichkeit, Berlin 1933
– Drei Generationen deutscher Gelehrtenpolitik. Historische Zeitschrift, Bd. 125, 1922, S. 248 ff.

Meyer, Henry Cord:
Mitteleuropa in German Thought and Action, Den Haag 1955
Meynell, Hilde:
The Stockholm-Conference of 1917, International Review of Social History, Bd. 5, 1960
Michels, Robert:
Zur Soziologie des Parteiwesens in der modernen Demokratie. Untersuchungen über die oligarchischen Tendenzen des Gruppenlebens. Neudruck der 2. Auflage. Herausgegeben und mit einem Nachwort versehen von Werner Conze, Stuttgart 1957
– Bedeutende Männer, Charakterologische Studien, Leipzig 1927
Mill, John Stuart:
Principles of Political Economy, ed. Ashley, London 1909
Miller, S. M.:
Max Weber. New York 1968
Miller, Susanne/Potthoff, Heinrich (Hgg.):
Die Regierung der Volksbeauftragten 1918/1919, Teil I, Düsseldorf 1969
Mitzman, Arthur:
The Iron Cage. An Historical Interpretation of Max Weber, New York 1970
Mommsen, Wolfgang J.:
Zum Begriff der 'plebiszitären Führerdemokratie' bei Max Weber. Kölner Zeitschrift für Soziologie und Sozialpsychologie, Vol. 15, 1963
– Max Weber's Political Sociology and his Philosophy of World History, International Social Science Journal, Vol. 17, 1965
– Universalgeschichtliches und politisches Denken bei Max Weber. Historische Zeitschrift, Vol. 201, 1965
– Die Vereinigten Staaten von Amerika im politischen Denken Max Webers. Historische Zeitschrift, Vol. 213, 1971
– Neue Max Weber-Literatur. Vierteljahrsschrift für Sozial- und Wirtschaftsgeschichte, Bd. 53, 1966
– Neue Max Weber-Literatur, Historische Zeitschrift, Bd. 211, 1970
– Die deutsche öffentliche Meinung und der Zusammenbruch des Regierungssystems Bethmann Hollweg im Juli 1917. Geschichte in Wissenschaft und Unterricht, Jg. 19, 1968
– Die Regierung Bethmann Hollweg und die öffentliche Meinung, Vierteljahreshefte für Zeitgeschichte, Bd. 17, 1969
– The Age of Bureaucracy. Perspectives on the Political Sociology of Max Weber, Oxford 1974
– Einleitung zu Friedrich Naumann, Verfassungspolitische Schriften, Werke, Bd. 2, Opladen 1964
– Max Weber [als Historiker], in: Deutsche Historiker, hg. v. Hans-Ulrich Wehler, III Göttingen 1972

Muncy, Lisbeth W.:
The Junker in the Prussian Administration under William II, 1888–1914. Brown University Studies, Vol. IX, Providence, Rhode Island 1944

Naumann, Friedrich:
Werke. Politische Schriften (Hg. Theodor Schieder). Zweiter bis Vierter Band, Opladen 1964
– Demokratie und Kaisertum, 1. Aufl., Berlin 1900, 4. Aufl., Berlin 1905
– Klassenpolitik des Liberalismus. Die Hilfe, 10. Jahrg., 1904, Nr. 2
– Freiheitskämpfe, Berlin 1911
– Kann man Liberale organisieren? Die Hilfe, 19. Jahrg., 1913, Nr. 8
– Mitteleuropa, Berlin 1915
– Was wird aus Polen? Berlin 1917

Nawiaski, Hans:
Staatstypen der Gegenwart, St. Gallen 1934

Nipperdey, Thomas:
Die Organisation der deutschen Parteien vor 1918, Düsseldorf 1961

Nisbet, Robert A.:
The Sociological Tradition, New York 1966

Nolte, Ernst:
Max Weber vor dem Faschismus, Der Staat, Bd. 2, 1963

Oberschall, Anthony:
Empirical Social Research in Germany 1848–1914, Paris, Den Haag 1965

Oncken, Dirk:
Das Problem des Lebensraums in der deutschen Politik vor 1914. Freiburg (phil. Diss. Maschinenschrift) 1948

Oncken, Hermann:
Das Deutsche Reich und die Vorgeschichte des Weltkrieges, Bd. 2, Leipzig 1933

Ostrogorski, M.:
La Démocratie et l'organisation des parties politiques. 2 vols., Paris 1903

Parisius, Ludolf:
Deutschlands politische Parteien und das Ministerium Bismarck, Berlin 1878

Parsons, Talcot:
The Structure of Social Action, Vol. 2, Reprint d. 2. Auflage, New York 1968

Petzke, Hans:
Max Weber und sein Einfluß auf die Reichsverfassung. Leipzig (jur. Diss., Maschinenschrift) Leipzig 1925

Pickles, Dorothy:
The Fifth French Republic, New York 1960

Piloty, Robert v.:
Das parlamentarische System, eine Untersuchung seines Wesens und Wertes, 2. Aufl., Berlin 1917
Pipes, Richard:
Max Weber und Rußland. Außenpolitik, 6. Jahrg., Heft 10, 1955
Prades, J. A.:
La Sociologie de la religion chez Max Weber, Essai d'analyse et de critique de la méthode, Louvain-Paris 1966
Preuß, Hugo:
Staat, Recht und Freiheit, Tübingen 1926
– Reich und Länder. Bruchstücke eines Kommentars zur Verfassung des Deutschen Reiches. Herausgegeben von H. Anschütz, Berlin 1928
Ranke, Leopold v.:
Die großen Mächte. Das politische Gespräch. Neu herausgegeben von Theodor Schieder, Göttingen 1955
Rassow, Peter:
Schlieffen und Holstein. Historische Zeitschrift, Bd. 173, 1952, S. 257 ff.
Rauch, Georg v.:
Rußland. Staatliche Einheit und nationale Vielfalt, München 1953
Recke, Walter:
Die polnische Frage als Problem der europäischen Politik, Berlin 1927
Redlich, Joseph:
Das Politische Tagebuch, Bd. 2, 1915–1918, herausgegeben von Fritz Fellner, Köln, Graz 1954
Redslob, Erwin:
Die parlamentarische Regierung in ihrer wahren und in ihrer unechten Form, Tübingen 1918
Rex, John:
Key Problems of Sociological Theory. London 1961
– Max Weber, in: Timothy Raison (Hrsg.), The Founding Fathers of Social Science, Harmondsworth 1969
– Typology and Objectivity: a Comment on Weber's four Sociological Methods in: Arun Sahay, Max Weber and Modern Sociology, London 1971
Ringer, Fritz K.:
The Decline of the German Mandarins: The German Academic Community 1890–1933, Cambridge 1969
Ritter, Gerhard:
Staatskunst und Kriegshandwerk. Das Problem des «Militarismus» in Deutschland, Bd. 2, 3 und 4, München 1960/1964/1968
Robertson, H. M.:
Aspects of the Rise of Economic Individualism. A Criticism of Max Weber and his School, Cambridge 1933

Rogers, Rolf E.:
Max Weber's Ideal Type Theory, New York 1969
Rosenberg, Arthur:
Die Entstehung der deutschen Republik, Berlin 1928
– Entstehung und Geschichte der Weimarer Republik. Neu herausgegeben von Kurt Kersten, Frankfurt 1955
Roth, Guenther:
s. Bendix, Reinhard u. G. Roth
Rothfels, Hans:
Bismarck und der Osten, Leipzig 1934
– Zeitgeschichtliche Betrachtungen. Vorträge und Aufsätze, Göttingen 1959
Runciman, Walter G.:
A Critique of Max Weber's Philosophy of Science, Cambridge 1972
– Social Science and Political Theory, Cambridge 1965
Sachse, Arnold:
Althoff und sein Werk, Berlin 1928
Salomon, Albert:
Max Weber. Die Gesellschaft Bd. 3, 1, 1926, S. 131 ff.
Salz, Arthur:
Das Wesen des Imperialismus, Leipzig, Berlin 1931
Samuelson, Kurt:
Religion und Economic Action, hg. v. D. C. Coleman, Stockholm 1961
Schaaf, Adam:
Geschichte und Begriff, Tübingen 1946
Schäfers, Bernhard (Hg.):
Ein Rundschreiben Max Webers zur Sozialpolitik, in: Soziale Welt, Jg. 18, 1967
Scheidemann, Phillip:
Memoiren eines Sozialdemokraten. 2 Bde., Dresden 1928
Schelting, Alexander von:
Max Weber's Wissenschaftslehre. Das logische Problem der Kulturerkenntnis. Tübingen 1934
Schérer, André und Grunwald, Jacques (Hg.):
L'Allemagne et les problèmes de la paix pendant la première guerre mondiale, 2. Bde., Paris 1962, 1966
Schieder, Theodor:
Die Theorie der Parteien im älteren deutschen Liberalismus. In: Aus Geschichte und Politik. Festschrift für Ludwig Bergstraesser, Düsseldorf 1951
– Das Reich unter der Führung Bismarcks. In: Deutsche Geschichte im Überblick. Herausgegeben von Peter Rassow, Stuttgart 1953
– Staat und Gesellschaft im Wandel unserer Zeit, München 1958 (enthält die meisten der von uns separat zitierten Aufsätze)
– Das Verhältnis von politischer und gesellschaftlicher Verfassung und die

Krise des bürgerlichen Liberalismus. Historische Zeitschrift, Bd. 177, 1954
– Der Liberalismus und die Strukturwandlungen der modernen Gesellschaft vom 19. zum 20. Jahrhundert. Relazioni del X Congresso Internazionale di Scienze Storiche, Vol. 5, Storia Contemporanea, Rom 1955
– Idee und Gestalt des übernationalen Staates seit dem 19. Jahrhundert. Historische Zeitschrift, Bd. 184, S. 336 ff.
Schieder, Wolfgang (Hg.):
Erster Weltkrieg. Ursachen, Entstehung und Kriegsziele, Köln 1969 (Neue Wissenschaftliche Bibliothek)
Schlesinger, Arthur jr.:
Demokratie und heldisches Führertum, Referat auf dem Kongreß für kulturelle Freiheit, Berlin 1960, in: Die Bewährung der Demokratie im zwanzigsten Jahrhundert, Zürich 1961
Schluchter, Wolfgang:
Wertfreiheit und Verantwortungsethik. Zum Verhältnis von Wissenschaft und Politik bei Max Weber, Tübingen 1971
– Aspekte bürokratischer Herrschaft. Studien zur Interpretation der fortschreitenden Industriegesellschaft, München 1972
Schmidt, Gustav:
Deutscher Historismus und der Übergang zur parlamentarischen Demokratie. Untersuchungen zu den politischen Gedanken von Meinecke, Troeltsch, Max Weber, Hamburg 1964
Schmitt, Carl:
Die geistesgeschichtliche Lage des heutigen Parlamentarismus, München, Leipzig 1923
– Verfassungslehre, München, Leipzig 1928
– Die Diktatur, 2. Aufl., München 1928
– Hugo Preuß. Sein Staatsbegriff und seine Stellung in der deutschen Staatslehre, Tübingen 1930
– Der Hüter der Verfassung, Tübingen 1931
– Der Begriff des Politischen, München 1932
– Legalität und Legitimität, München, Leipzig 1932
– Staat, Bewegung, Volk, Hamburg 1933
– Staatsgefüge und Zusammenbruch des zweiten Reiches, Hamburg 1934
– Positionen und Begriffe im Kampf mit Weimar, Genf, Versailles 1923 bis 1939, Hamburg 1940
Schmölz, M.:
Webers politische Ethik, in: Festschrift Voegelin, München 1962
Schuhmacher, Hermann:
Artikel Max Weber in: Deutsches Biographisches Jahrbuch, Jena 1920
Schulz, Gerhard:
Zwischen Demokratie und Diktatur. Verfassungspolitik und Reichsreform in der Weimarer Republik, Bd. 1, Berlin 1963

– Geschichtliche Theorie und politisches Denken bei Max Weber, Vierteljahreshefte für Zeitgeschichte, Bd. 12, 1964

Schulze-Gävernitz, G. v.:
Britischer Imperialismus und englischer Freihandel, Leipzig 1906
– Max Weber als Nationalökonom und Politiker. In: Hauptprobleme der Soziologie. Erinnerungsgabe für Max Weber. 2 Bde., München 1923

Schumpeter, Joseph A.:
Soziologie der Imperialismen. Archiv für Sozialwissenschaft und Sozialpolitik Bd. 46, 1918/19
– Kapitalismus, Sozialismus und Demokratie, Bern 1946

Schwabe, Klaus:
Wissenschaft und Kriegsmoral. Die deutschen Hochschullehrer und die politischen Grundfragen des ersten Weltkrieges, Göttingen u. a. 1969
– Zur politischen Haltung der deutschen Professoren im Ersten Weltkrieg, in: Historische Zeitschrift, Bd. 193, 1961

Schweitzer, Artur:
Typological Method in Economics. Max Weber's Contribution, in: History of Political Economy, April 1970
– The Method of Social Economics. A Study of Max Weber. Bloomington 1961

Sell, Friedrich:
Die Tragödie des deutschen Liberalismus, Stuttgart 1953

Sering, Max:
Westrußland in seiner Bedeutung für die Entwicklung Mitteleuropas, Leipzig 1917

Seyfarth, Constans und Sprondel, Walter M.:
Seminar: Religion und gesellschaftliche Entwicklung, Studien zur Protestantismus-Kapitalismus-These Max Webers, Frankfurt 1973

Sheehan, James J.:
The Career of Lujo Brentano. A Study of Liberalism and Social Reform in Imperial Germany, Chicago 1966

Simey, T. S.:
Max Weber: Man of Affairs or Theoretical Sociologist? Sociological Review, Vol. 14, 1966
– Weber's Sociological Theory of Value: An Appraisal in Mid-Century, Sociological Review, Vol. 13, 1965

Simons, Walter:
Hugo Preuß. Meister des Rechts, Bd. 6, Berlin 1930

Slarosolskij:
Bogdan Kistiakowskij und das russische soziologische Denken. Abhandlungen des Ukrainischen Wissenschaftlichen Institutes in Berlin Bd. 2, 1929, S. 117 ff.

Smend, Rudolf:
Verfassung und Verfassungsrecht, München, Leipzig 1928; neuerdings in: Staatsrechtliche Abhandlungen, 2. Aufl., Berlin 1968
Sombart, Werner:
Die deutsche Volkswirtschaft im 19. Jahrhundert und im Anfang des 20. Jahrhunderts, 4. Aufl., Berlin 1919
Spencer, Martin E.:
Weber on Legitimate Norms and Authority, British Journal of Sociology, Vol. 21, 1970
Spindler, Arno:
Der Handelskrieg mit U-Booten, Bd. 3, In: Der Krieg zur See 1914–18, herausgegeben vom Reichsmarinearchiv, Berlin 1934
Stadelmann, Rudolf:
Friedensversuche im ersten Jahre des Weltkriegs. Historische Zeitschrift, Bd. 156, 1937, S. 485 ff.
Steding, Christoph:
Politik und Wissenschaft bei Max Weber. Marburg (phil. Diss.) 1932. Breslau 1932
Das Reich und die Krankheit der europäischen Kultur (=Schriften des Reichsinstituts für die Geschichte des neuen Deutschland, Bd. 19), Hamburg 1938
Steger, H. A.:
Deutsche Weltpolitik bei Hans Delbrück, Marburg (phil. Diss.) 1955, Maschinenschrift
Steglich, Wolfgang:
Die Friedenspolitik der Mittelmächte 1917–1918, Bd. I, Wiesbaden 1964
Stegmann, Dirk:
Die Erben Bismarcks, Köln 1970
Stier-Somlo, Fritz:
Die Verfassungsurkunde der Vereinigten Staaten von Deutschland. Ein Entwurf mit Begründung, Tübingen 1919
– Die Verfassung des Deutschen Reiches vom 11. August 1919, Bonn 1925
Stolper, Gustav:
This Age of Fable, New York 1942
Strauß, Leo:
Natural Right and History, Chicago 1953
Streisand, Joachim:
Max Weber: Soziologie, Politik und Geschichtsschreibung von der Reichseinigung von oben bis zur Befreiung Deutschlands vom Faschismus, Berlin 1965
– (Hg.), Studien über die deutsche Geschichtswissenschaft, Bd. II: Die bürgerliche deutsche Geschichtsschreibung von der Reichseinigung bis zur Befreiung Deutschlands vom Faschismus, Berlin 1965

Tawney, Richard H.:
Religion and the Rise of Capitalism, Harmondsworth 1964
Tenbruck, Friedrich H.:
Die Genesis der Methodologie Max Webers. Kölner Zeitschrift für Soziologie und Sozialpsychologie, Bd. 11, 1959
– «Science as a Vocation» – Revisited, in: Festschrift für Arnold Gehlen, 1974
Thimme, Annelise:
Hans Delbrück als Kritiker der Wilhelminischen Epoche, Düsseldorf 1955
Tirpitz, Alfred v.:
Erinnerungen, Leipzig 1919
– Politische Dokumente. 2 Bde., Stuttgart 1924/26
Topitsch, Ernst:
Max Webers Geschichtsauffassung, Wissenschaft und Weltbild, Bd. 3, 1950
Treitschke, Heinrich v.:
Politik, Vorlesungen. Herausgegeben von Max Cornicelius, 2 Bde., Leipzig 1897
Triepel, Heinrich:
Die Staatsverfassung und die politischen Parteien, Berlin 1928
– Quellensammlung zum Deutschen Reichsstaatsrecht, 4. Aufl., Tübingen 1926
Troeltsch, Ernst:
Deutscher Geist und Westeuropa, Berlin 1925
– Imperialismus. Die neue Rundschau, Januar 1915, S. 1–14
Truman, David B.:
The Governmental Process, New York 1955
Tucker, R. C.:
The Theory of Charismatic Leadership, in: Daedalus 97, 1968, S. 731 ff.
Voegelin, Erich:
Max Weber. Deutsche Vierteljahrsschrift für Literatur und Geistesgeschichte, Jahrg. III, 2, 1925
– Max Weber. Eine Rede. Kölner Vierteljahreshefte für Soziologie, Jahrg. 9, Heft 1/2, 1930
– The New Science of Politics, Chicago 1952
Weber, Marianne:
Max Weber. Ein Lebensbild, 1. Aufl., Tübingen 1926
2. Aufl., Heidelberg 1950[1]
– Lebenserinnerungen, Bremen 1948

---

[1] Da es sich bei der 2. Auflage nur um einen Nachdruck handelt, ist durchweg nach der 1. Auflage zitiert.

Max Weber zum Gedächtnis:
Hg. von René König und Johannes Winckelmann, Sonderheft 7 der Kölner Zeitschrift für Soziologie und Sozialpsychologie, Köln 1963
Max Weber and Modern Sociology
hg. von Arun Sahay, London 1971
Max Weber und die Soziologie heute
Verhandlungen des 15. Deutschen Soziologentages, hg. von Otto Stammer, Tübingen 1965
Wegener, Walther:
Die Quellen der Wissenschaftsauffassung Max Webers und die Problematik der Werturteilsfreiheit in der Sozialökonomie. Ein wissenssoziologischer Beitrag, Berlin 1962
Wehler, Hans-Ulrich:
Bismarck und der Imperialismus, Köln 1969
– Die Polenpolitik im Deutschen Kaiserreich 1871–1918, in: Politische Ideologien und nationalstaatliche Ordnung. Festschrift für Theodor Schieder, hg. von Kurt Kluxen und Wolfgang J. Mommsen, München 1968
Wenck, Martin:
Die Geschichte der Nationalsozialen 1895–1903, Berlin 1905
Werner, Lothar:
Der Alldeutsche Verband 1890–1918. Historische Studien Bd. 278, Berlin 1935
Wertheimer, Mildred S.:
The Pan-German League 1890–1914, New York 1924
Weyembergh, Maurice:
Le volontarisme rationnel de Max Weber, Brüssel 1972
Wheeler-Bennet, John W.:
Brest Litovsk. The Forgotten Peace, London 1938
Wiegand, G.:
Artikel Hermann Baumgarten in der Allgemeinen Deutschen Biographie, Nachträge, Bd. 55
Wilbrandt, Robert:
Max Weber. Ein deutsches Vermächtnis. Die neue Rundschau, Jahrg. 39, Mai 1928
Winckelmann, Johannes F.:
Legitimität und Legalität in Max Webers Herrschaftssoziologie, Tübingen 1952
– Max Webers opus posthumum. Zeitschrift für die gesamte Staatswissenschaft, Bd. 105, 1948/49, S. 368 ff.
– Max Webers große Soziologie. Archiv für Rechts- und Sozialphilosophie, Bd. 43, 1957, S. 117–124
– Die Herrschaftskategorien der politischen Soziologie und die Legitimität

der Demokratie. Archiv für Rechts- und Sozialphilosophie, Bd. 42, 1956, S. 383 ff.
- Die verfassungsrechtliche Unterscheidung von Legitimität und Legalität. Zeitschrift für die gesamte Staatswissenschaft, Bd. 112, 1956, S. 164 ff.
- Gesellschaft und Staat in der verstehenden Soziologie Max Webers, Berlin 1957

Wrong, Dennis (Hg.):
Makers of Modern Social Science: Max Weber, Englewood Cliffs, New Jersey 1970

Ziegler, Wilhelm:
Die deutsche Nationalversammlung 1919–20 und ihr Verfassungswerk, Berlin 1932

Index